T0326281

Computational Finance
Using C and C#

Quantitative Finance Series

Aims and Objectives

- Books based on the work of financial market practitioners and academics
- Presenting cutting-edge research to the professional/practitioner market
- Combining intellectual rigour and practical application
- Covering the interaction between mathematical theory and financial practice
- To improve portfolio performance, risk management and trading book performance
- Covering quantitative techniques

Market

Brokers/Traders; Actuaries; Consultants; Asset Managers; Fund Managers; Regulators; Central Bankers; Treasury Officials; Technical Analysis; and Academics for Masters in Finance and MBA market.

Series Titles

Computational Finance Using C and C#
The Analytics of Risk Model Validation
Forecasting Expected Returns in the Financial Markets
Corporate Governance and Regulatory Impact on Mergers and Acquisitions
International Mergers and Acquisitions Activity Since 1990
Forecasting Volatility in the Financial Markets, Third Edition
Venture Capital in Europe
Funds of Hedge Funds
Initial Public Offerings
Linear Factor Models in Finance
Computational Finance
Advances in Portfolio Construction and Implementation
Advanced Trading Rules, Second Edition
Real R&D Options
Performance Measurement in Finance
Economics for Financial Markets
Managing Downside Risk in Financial Markets
Derivative Instruments: Theory, Valuation, Analysis
Return Distributions in Finance

Series Editor: Dr. Stephen Satchell

Dr. Satchell is Reader in Financial Econometrics at Trinity College, Cambridge; Visiting Professor at Birkbeck College, City University Business School and University of Technology, Sydney. He also works in a consultative capacity to many firms, and edits the journal *Derivatives: use, trading and regulations and the Journal of Asset Management*.

Computational Finance Using C and C#

Derivatives and Valuation
SECOND EDITION

George Levy

AMSTERDAM • BOSTON • HEIDELBERG • LONDON
NEW YORK • OXFORD • PARIS • SAN DIEGO
SAN FRANCISCO • SINGAPORE • SYDNEY • TOKYO

Academic Press is an Imprint of Elsevier

Academic Press is an imprint of Elsevier
125 London Wall, London EC2Y 5AS, UK
525 B Street, Suite 1800, San Diego, CA 92101-4495, USA
50 Hampshire Street, 5th Floor, Cambridge, MA 02139, USA
The Boulevard, Langford Lane, Kidlington, Oxford OX5 1GB, UK

Notices

Knowledge and best practice in this field are constantly changing. As new research and experience
broaden our understanding, changes in research methods, professional practices, or medical
treatment may become necessary.

Practitioners and researchers must always rely on their own experience and knowledge in
evaluating and using any information, methods, compounds, or experiments described herein. In
using such information or methods they should be mindful of their own safety and the safety of
others, including parties for whom they have a professional responsibility.

To the fullest extent of the law, neither the Publisher nor the authors, contributors, or editors,
assume any liability for any injury and/or damage to persons or property as a matter of products
liability, negligence or otherwise, or from any use or operation of any methods, products,
instructions, or ideas contained in the material herein.

Library of Congress Cataloging-in-Publication Data
A catalog record for this book is available from the Library of Congress

British Library Cataloguing-in-Publication Data
A catalogue record for this book is available from the British Library

ISBN: 978-0-12-803579-5

For information on all Academic Press publications
visit our website at https://www.elsevier.com/

Working together
to grow libraries in
developing countries

www.elsevier.com • www.bookaid.org

Publisher: Nikki Levy
Acquisition Editor: J. Scott Bentley
Editorial Project Manager: Susan Ikeda
Production Project Manager: Julie-Ann Stansfield
Designer: Mark Rogers

Typeset by Focal Image (India) Pvt Ltd.

Dedication

To my parents Paul and Paula and also my grandparents Friedrich and Barbara.

Contents

List of Figures

List of Tables

Preface

It has been seven years since the initial publication of *Computational Finance Using C and C#*, and in that time the *Global Credit Crisis* has come and gone. The author therefore thought that it would be opportune to both correct various errors and update the contents of the first edition. Numerous problems/exercises and C# software have been included, and both the solutions to these exercises and the software can be downloaded from the book's companion website.

http://booksite.elsevier.com/9780128035795/

There is also now a short chapter on the History of Finance, from the Babylonians to the 2008 Credit Crisis. It was inspired by my friend Ian Brown who wanted me to write something on the Credit Crisis that he could understand - I hope this helps.

As always I would like to take this opportunity of thanking my wife Kathy for putting up with the amount of time I spend on my computer.

Thanks are also due to my friend Vince Fernando, who many years ago now, suggested that I should write a book - until then the thought hadn't occurred to me.

I am grateful to Dr. J. Scott Bentley, Susan Ikeda and Julie-Ann Stansfield of Elsevier for all their hard work and patience, and also the series editor Dr. Steven Satchell for allowing me to create this second edition.

George Levy
Benson
November 2015

Chapter 1

Overview of Financial Derivatives

A financial derivative is a contract between two counterparties (here referred to as *A* and *B*), which *derives* its value from the *state* of underlying financial quantities. We can further divide derivatives into those which carry a future *obligation* and those which do not. In the financial world, a derivative which gives the owner the *right* but not the *obligation* to participate in a given financial contract is called an *option*. We will now illustrate this using both a Foreign Exchange Forward contract and a Foreign Exchange option.

Foreign Exchange Forward – A Contract with an Obligation

In a Foreign Exchange Forward contract, a certain amount of foreign currency will be bought (or sold) at a future date using a prearranged foreign exchange rate.

For instance, counterparty *A* may own a Foreign Exchange forward which, in 1-year time, contractually obliges *A* to purchase from *B*, the sum of $200 for £100. At the end of one year, several things may have happened.

(i) The value of the pound may have decreased with respect to the dollar.
(ii) The value of the pound may have increased with respect to the dollar.
(iii) Counterparty *B* may refuse to honour the contract – *B* may have gone bust, etc.
(iv) Counterparty *A* may refuse to honour the contract – *A* may have gone bust, etc.

We will now consider events (i)–(iv) from *A*'s perspective.

First, if (i) occurs then *A* will be able to obtain $200 for less than the current market rate, say £120. In this case, the $200 can be bought for £100 and then immediately sold for £120, giving a profit of £20. However, this profit can only be realised if *B* honours the contract, that is, event (iii) does not happen.

Second, when (ii) occurs then *A* *is obliged to* purchase $200 for *more* than the current market rate, say £90. In this case, the $200 are be bought for £100 but could have been bought for only £90, giving a loss of £10.

The probability of events (iii) and (iv) occurring are related to the *Credit Risk* associated with counterparty *B*. The value of the contract to *A* is not affected by (iv), although *A* may be sued if both (ii) and (iv) occur. Counterparty *A* should only be concerned with the possibility of events (i) and (iii) occurring, that is the probability that the contract is worth a positive amount in one year and probability that *B* will honour the contract (which is one minus the probability that event (iii) will happen).

From *B*'s point of view, the important Credit Risk is when both (ii) and (iv) occur, that is, when the contract has positive value but counterparty *A* defaults.

Foreign Exchange Option – A Contract without an Obligation

A Foreign Exchange option is similar to the Foreign Exchange Forward, the difference is that if event (ii) occurs then *A* is not *obliged* to buy dollars at an unfavourable exchange rate. To have this flexibility, *A* needs to *buy* a Foreign Exchange *option* from *B*, which here we can be regarded as insurance against unexpected exchange rate fluctuations.

For instance, counterparty *A* may own a Foreign Exchange option which, in one year, contractually *allows* *A* to purchase from *B*, the sum of \$200 for £100. As before, at the end of one year the following may have happened.

 (i) The value of the pound may have decreased with respect to the dollar.
 (ii) The value of the pound may have increased with respect to the dollar.
(iii) Counterparty *B* may refuse to honour the contract – *B* may have gone bust, etc.
(iv) Counterparty *A* may have gone bust, etc.

We will now consider events (i)–(iv) from *A*'s perspective.

First, if (i) occurs then *A* will be able to obtain \$200 for less than the current market rate, say £120. In this case, the \$200 can be bought for £100 and then immediately sold for £120, giving a profit of £20. However, this profit can only be realised if *B* honours the contract, that is, event (iii) does not happen.

Second, when (ii) occurs then *A* will decide not to purchase \$200 for *more* than the current market rate – in this case, the option is worthless.

We can thus see that *A* is still concerned with the *Credit Risk* when events (i) and (iii) occur simultaneously.

The Credit Risk from counterparty *B*'s point of view is different. *B* has sold to *A* a Foreign Exchange option, which matures in one year and has already received the money – the current fair price for the option. Counterparty *B* has no Credit Risk associated with *A*. This is because if event (iv) occurs, and *A* goes bust, it does not matter to *B* since the money for the option has already been received. On the other hand, if event (iii) occurs *B* may be sued by *A* but *B* still has no Credit Risk associated with *A*.

This book considers the valuation of financial derivatives which carry obligations and also financial options.

Chapters 1–7 deal with both the theory of stochastic processes and the pricing of financial instruments. In Chapter 8, this information is then applied to a C# portfolio valuer. The application is easy to use (the portfolios and current market rates are defined in text files) and can also be extended to include new trade types.

The book has been written so that (as far possible) financial mathematics results are derived from first principles.

Finally, the appendices contain various information which it is hoped the reader will find useful.

Chapter 2

Introduction to Stochastic Processes

2.1 BROWNIAN MOTION

Brownian motion is named after the botanist Robert Brown who used a microscope to study the fertilization mechanism of flowering plants. He first observed the random motion of pollen particles (obtained from the American species *Clarkia pulchella*) suspended in water and wrote the following:

> *The fovilla or granules fill the whole orbicular disk but do not extend to the projecting angles. They are not spherical but oblong or nearly cylindrical, and the particles have manifest motion. This motion is only visible to my lens which magnifies 370 times. The motion is obscure yet certain ..*

Robert Brown, 12th June 1827; see Ramsbottom (1932)

It appears that Brown considered this motion no more than a curiosity (he believed that the particles were *alive*) and continued *undistracted* with his botanical research. The full significance of his observations only became apparent about eighty years later when it was shown (Einstein, 1905) that the motion is caused by the collisions that occur between the pollen grains and the water molecules. In 1908 Perrin, see Perrin (1910), was finally able to confirm Einstein's predictions experimentally. His work was made possible by the development of the ultramicroscope by Richard Zsigmondy and Henry Siedentopf in 1903. He was able to work out from his experimental results and Einstein's formula the size of the water molecule and a precise value for Avogadro's number. His work established the physical theory of Brownian motion and ended the skepticism about the existence of atoms and molecules as actual physical entities. Many of the fundamental properties of Brownian motion were discovered by Paul Levy, see Levy (1939), and Levy (1948), and the first mathematically rigorous treatment was provided by Norbert Wiener, see Wiener (1923) and Wiener (1924). In addition, see Karatzas and Shreve (2000), is an excellent text book on the theoretical properties of Brownian motion, while Shreve *et. al.*, see Shreve et al. (1997), provides much useful information concerning the use of Brownian processes within finance.

Computational Finance Using C and C#: Derivatives and Valuation.

Brownian motion is also called a *random walk*, a Wiener process, or sometimes (more poetically) the *drunkards walk*. We will now present the three fundamental properties of Brownian motion.

The Properties of Brownian Motion

In formal terms, a process is $W = (W_t : t \geq 0)$ is (one-dimensional) Brownian motion if

(i) W_t *is continuous, and $W_0 = 0$,*
(ii) $W_t \sim N(0,t)$,
(iii) *the increment $dW_t = W_{t+dt} - W_t$ is normally distributed as $dW_t \sim N(0,dt)$, so $E[dW_t] = 0$ and $Var[dW_t] = dt$. The increment dW_{dt} is also independent of the history of the process up to time t.*

From (iii), we can further state that, since the increments dW_t are independent of past values W_t, a Brownian process is also a *Markov* process. In addition, we shall now show that Brownian process is also a martingale process.

In a martingale process P_t, $t \geq 0$, the conditional expectation $E[P_{t+dt}|\mathcal{F}_t] = P_t$, where $\mathcal{F}_t$ is called the *filtration* generated by the process and contains the information learned by observing the process up to time t. Since for Brownian motion, we have

$$E[W_{t+dt}|\mathcal{F}_t] = E[(W_{t+dt} - W_t) + W_t|\mathcal{F}_t] = E[W_{t+dt} - W_t] + W_t$$
$$= E[dW_t] + W_t = W_t,$$

where we have used the fact that $E[dW_t] = 0$. Since $E[W_{t+dt}|\mathcal{F}_t] = W_t$, the Brownian motion Z is a martingale process.

Using property (iii) we can also derive an expression for the covariance of Brownian motion. The independent increment requirement means that for the n times $0 \leq t_0 < t_1 < t_2 \ldots, t_n < \infty$ the random variables $W_{t_1} - W_{t_0}, W_{t_2} - W_{t_1}, \ldots, W_{t_n} - W_{t_{n-1}}$ are independent. So

$$Cov\left[W_{t_i} - W_{t_{i-1}}, W_{t_j} - W_{t_{j-1}}\right] = 0, \quad i \neq j. \tag{2.1.1}$$

We will show that $Cov[W_s, W_t] = s \wedge t$.

Proof. Using $W_{t_0} = 0$ and assuming $t \geq t$, we have

$$Cov\left[W_s - W_{t_0}, W_t - W_{t_0}\right] = Cov[W_s, W_t] = Cov[W_s, W_s + (W_t - W_s)].$$

From Appendix C.3.2, we have

$$Cov[W_s, W_s + (W_t - W_s)] = Cov[W_s, W_s] + Cov[W_s, W_t - W_s]$$

$$= Var[W_s] + Cov[W_s, W_t]$$

$$= s + Cov[W_s, W_t - W_s].$$

Now since
$$Cov\left[W_s, W_t\right] = Cov\left[W_s - W_{t_0}, W_t - W_s\right] = 0,$$
where we have used equation (2.1.1) with $n = 2$, $t_1 = t_s$, and $t_2 = t$.
We thus obtain
$$Cov\left[W_s, W_t\right] = s.$$
So
$$Cov\left[W_s, W_t\right] = s \wedge t. \tag{2.1.2}$$

We will now consider the Brownian increments over the time interval dt in more detail. Let us first define the process X such that

$$dX_t = dW_t, \tag{2.1.3}$$

where dW_t is a random variable drawn from a normal distribution with mean zero and variance dt, which we denote as $dW_t \sim N(0, dt)$. Equation (2.1.3) can also be written in the equivalent form

$$dX_t = \sqrt{dt}\, dZ, \tag{2.1.4}$$

where dZ is a random variable drawn from a *standard* normal distribution (that is a normal distribution with zero mean and unit variance).

Equations (2.1.3) and (2.1.4) give the incremental change in the value of X over the time interval dt for *standard* Brownian motion.

We shall now generalize these equations slightly by introducing the extra (*volatility*) parameter σ which controls the variance of the process. We now have
$$dX_t = \sigma dW_t, \tag{2.1.5}$$
where $dW_t \sim N(0, dt)$ and $dX_t \sim N(0, \sigma^2\, dt)$. Equation (2.1.5) can also be written in the equivalent form as

$$dX_t = \sigma\,\sqrt{dt}\, dZ, \quad dZ \sim N(0,1), \tag{2.1.6}$$

or equivalently
$$dX_t = \sqrt{dt}\, d\hat{Z}, \quad d\hat{Z} \sim N(0, \sigma^2). \tag{2.1.7}$$

We are now in a position to provide a mathematical description of the movement of the pollen grains observed by Robert Brown in 1827. We will start by assuming that the container of water is perfectly level. This will ensure that there is no drift of the pollen grains in any particular direction. Let us denote the position of a particular pollen grain at time t by X_t, and set the position at $t = 0$, X_{t_0}, to zero. The statistical distribution of the grain's position, X_T, at some later time $t = T$, can be found as follows.

Let us divide the time T into n equal intervals $dt = T/n$. Since the position of the particle changes by the amount $dX_i = \sigma\,\sqrt{dt}\, dZ_i$ over the ith time interval dt, the final position X_T is given by

$$X_T = \sum_{i=1}^{n}\left(\sigma\,\sqrt{dt}\, dZ_i\right) = \sigma\,\sqrt{dt}\,\sum_{i=1}^{n} dZ_i.$$

Since $dZ_i \sim N(0,1)$, by the law of large numbers (see Appendix C.1), we have that the expected value of position X_T is

$$E[X_T] = \sigma \sqrt{dt}\, E\left[\sum_{i=1}^{n} dZ_i\right] = 0.$$

The variance of the position X_T is

$$Var[X_T] = Var\left[\sigma \sqrt{dt} \sum_{i=1}^{n} dZ_i\right] = \sigma^2\, dt\, Var\left[\sum_{i=1}^{n} dZ_i\right]. \qquad (2.1.8)$$

Since all the dZ_i variates are IID $N(0,1)$, we have $Var[dZ_i] = 1$ and $Var\left[\sum_{i=1}^{n} X_i\right] = \sum_{i=1}^{n} Var[X_i]$, see Appendix C.3.1. Thus,

$$Var[X_T] = \sigma^2\, dt \sum_{i=1}^{n} Var[dZ_i] = \sigma^2\, dt \sum_{i=1}^{n} 1, \qquad (2.1.9)$$

which gives

$$Var[X_T] = \sigma^2 n\, dt = T\, \sigma^2. \qquad (2.1.10)$$

So, at time T, the position of the pollen grain, X_T is distributed as $X_T \sim N(0, T\, \sigma^2)$.

If the water container is not perfectly level then the pollen grains will exhibit drift in a particular direction. We can modify equation (2.1.5) to take this into account as follows:

$$dX_t = \mu dt + \sigma \sqrt{dt}\, dZ_i, \quad dZ_i \sim N(0,1), \qquad (2.1.11)$$

or equivalently

$$dX_t = \mu dt + \sigma dW_t, \quad dW_t \sim N(0, dt), \qquad (2.1.12)$$

where we have included the *constant* drift μ. Proceeding in a similar manner to that for the case of *zero drift* Brownian motion, we have

$$X_T = \sum_{i=1}^{n}\left(\mu dt + \sigma \sqrt{dt}\, dZ_i\right) = \mu \sum_{i=1}^{n} dt + \sigma \sqrt{dt} \sum_{i=1}^{n} dZ_i = \mu T + \sigma \sqrt{dt} \sum_{i=1}^{n} dZ_i,$$

which gives

$$E[X_T] = E\left[\mu T + \sigma \sqrt{dt} \sum_{i=1}^{n} dZ_i\right],$$

$$E[X_T] = \mu T + \sigma \sqrt{dt}\, E\left[\sum_{i=1}^{n} dZ_i\right] = \mu T.$$

The variance of the position X_T is

$$Var[X_T] = Var\left[\mu T + \sigma \sqrt{dt} \sum_{i=1}^{n} dZ_i\right] = Var\left[\sigma \sqrt{dt} \sum_{i=1}^{n} dZ_i\right].$$

Here, we have used the fact (see Appendix C.3.1) that $Var[a+bX] = b^2 Var[X]$, where $a = \mu T$ and $b = 1$. From equation (2.1.9) and equation (2.1.10), we have

$$Var[X_T] = Var\left[\sigma \sqrt{dt} \sum_{i=1}^{n} dZ_i\right] = T \sigma^2.$$

So, at time T, the position of the pollen grain, X_T is distributed as $X_T \sim N(\mu T, T \sigma^2)$.

We have just shown that when we vary the drift of a Brownian motion, its volatility remains unchanged. This is a very important property and (as we will see later) is used extensively in the theory of derivative pricing.

2.2 A BROWNIAN MODEL OF ASSET PRICE MOVEMENTS

In the previous section, we showed how Brownian motion can be used to describe the random motion of small particles suspended in a liquid. The first attempt at using Brownian motion to describe financial asset price movements was provided by Bachelier (1900). This however only had limited success because the *significance* of a given *absolute* change in asset price depends on the original asset price. For example, a £1 increase in the value of a share originally worth £1.10 is much more *significant* than a £1 increase in the value of a share originally worth £100. It is for this reason that asset price movements are generally described in terms of *relative* or percentage changes. For example, if the £1.10 share increases in value by 11 pence and the £100 share increases in value by £10, then both of these price changes have the same significance and correspond to a 10% increase in value. The idea of relative price changes in the value of a share can be formalized by defining a quantity called the *return*, R_t, of a share at time t. The return R_t is defined as follows:

$$R_t = \frac{S_{t+dt} - S_t}{S_t} = \frac{dS_t}{S_t}, \tag{2.2.1}$$

where S_{t+dt} is the value of the share at time $t + dt$, S_t is the value of the share at time t, and dS_t is the change in value of the share over the time interval dt. The percentage return R^*, over the time interval dt is simply defined as $R^* = 100 \times R_t$.

We are now in a position to construct a simple Brownian model of asset price movements, further information on Brownian motion within finance can be found in Shreve et al. (1997).

The asset *return* at time t is now given by

$$R_t = \frac{dS_t}{S_t} = \mu dt + \sigma dW_t, \quad dW_t \sim N(0, dt), \tag{2.2.2}$$

or equivalently

$$dS_t = S_t \mu dt + S_t \sigma dW_t. \tag{2.2.3}$$

The process given in equation (2.2.2) and equation (2.2.3) is termed *geometric Brownian motion*, which we will abbreviate as GBM. This is because the relative (rather than absolute) price changes follow Brownian motion.

2.3 ITO'S FORMULA (OR LEMMA)

In this section, we will derive Ito's formula, a more rigorous treatment can be found in Karatzas and Shreve (2000).

Let us consider the stochastic process X,

$$dX = adt + bdW = adt + b\sqrt{dt}\, dZ, \quad dZ \sim N(0,1), \; dW \sim N(0,dt), \qquad (2.3.1)$$

where a and b are constants. We want to find the process followed by a function of the stochastic variable X, that is, $\phi(X,t)$. This can be done by applying a Taylor expansion, up to second order, in the two variables X and t as follows:

$$\phi^* = \phi + \frac{\partial\phi}{\partial t}dt + \frac{\partial\phi}{\partial X}dX + \frac{1}{2}\frac{\partial^2\phi}{\partial X^2}dX^2 + \frac{1}{2}\frac{\partial^2\phi}{\partial t^2}dt^2 + \frac{\partial\phi}{\partial X\partial t}dXdt, \qquad (2.3.2)$$

where ϕ^* is used to denote the value $\phi(X + dX, t + dt)$, and ϕ denotes the value $\phi(X,t)$. We will now consider the magnitude of the terms dX^2, $dXdt$, and dt^2 as $dt \to 0$. First,

$$dX^2 = (adt + b\sqrt{dt}\,dZ)(adt + b\sqrt{dt}\,dZ) = a^2dt^2 + 2ab\,dt^{3/2}\,dZ + b^2\,dt\,dZ^2,$$

then

$$dXdt = adt^2 + b\,dt^{3/2}\,dZ.$$

So as $dt \to 0$, and ignoring all terms in dt of order greater than 1, we have

$$dX^2 \sim b^2dt\,dZ^2, \quad dt^2 \sim 0, \text{ and } dXdt \sim 0.$$

Therefore, equation (2.3.2) can be rewritten as

$$d\phi = \frac{\partial\phi}{\partial t}dt + \frac{\partial\phi}{\partial X}dX + \frac{1}{2}\frac{\partial^2\phi}{\partial X^2}E\left[dX^2\right], \qquad (2.3.3)$$

where $d\phi = \phi^* - \phi$, and we have replaced dX^2 by its expected value $E\left[dX^2\right]$. Now

$$E[dX^2] = E[b^2dt\,dZ^2] = b^2dt E[dZ^2] = b^2dt,$$

where we have used the fact that, since $dZ \sim N(0,1)$, the variance of dZ, $E[dZ^2]$, is by definition equal to 1. Using these values in equation (2.3.3) and substituting for dX from equation (2.3.1), we obtain

$$d\phi = \frac{\partial\phi}{\partial t}dt + \frac{\partial\phi}{\partial X}(adt + bdw) + \frac{b^2}{2}\frac{\partial^2\phi}{\partial X^2}dt. \qquad (2.3.4)$$

This gives Ito's formula

$$d\phi = \left(\frac{\partial\phi}{\partial t} + a\frac{\partial\phi}{\partial X} + \frac{b^2}{2}\frac{\partial^2\phi}{\partial X^2}\right)dt + \frac{\partial\phi}{\partial X}b\,dW. \qquad (2.3.5)$$

In particular, if we consider the geometric Brownian process

$$dS = \mu S dt + \sigma S dW,$$

where μ and σ are constants then substituting $X = S$, $a = \mu S$, and $b = \sigma S$ into equation (2.3.5) yields

$$d\phi = \left(\frac{\partial \phi}{\partial t} + \mu S \frac{\partial \phi}{\partial S} + \frac{\sigma^2 S^2}{2} \frac{\partial^2 \phi}{\partial S^2} \right) dt + \frac{\partial \phi}{\partial S} \sigma S dW. \tag{2.3.6}$$

Equation (2.3.6) describes the change in value of a function $\phi(S,t)$ over the time interval dt, when the stochastic variable S follows GBM. This result has very important applications in the pricing of financial derivatives. Here, the function $\phi(S,t)$ is taken as the price of a financial derivative, $f(S,t)$, that depends on the value of an underlying asset S, which is assumed to follow GBM. In Chapter 4, we will use equation (2.3.6) to derive the (Black–Scholes) partial differential equation that is satisfied by the price of a financial derivative.

We can also use equation (2.3.3) to derive the process followed by $\phi = \log(S_t)$. We have

$$\frac{\partial \phi}{\partial S_t} = \frac{\partial \log(S_t)}{\partial S} = \frac{1}{S}, \quad \frac{\partial^2 \phi}{\partial S_t^2} = \frac{\partial}{\partial S_t} \left(\frac{\partial \log(S_t)}{\partial S_t} \right) = \frac{\partial}{\partial S_t} \left(\frac{1}{S_t} \right) = -\frac{1}{S_t^2},$$

$$\frac{\partial \phi}{\partial t} = \frac{\partial \log(S_t)}{\partial t} = 0.$$

So,

$$d\left(\log(S_t) \right) = \nu dt + \sigma \, dW_t, \quad \text{where } \nu = \mu - \frac{\sigma^2}{2}. \tag{2.3.7}$$

Integrating equation (2.3.7) yields

$$\int_{t=t_0}^{T} d\left(\log(S_t) \right) = \int_{t=t_0}^{T} \nu dt + \int_{t=t_0}^{T} \sigma \, dW_t,$$

so

$$\log\left(S_T \right) - \log\left(S_{t_0} \right) = \nu T + \sigma \, W_T, \tag{2.3.8}$$

where we have used $t_0 = 0$ and $W_{t_0} = 0$.

We obtain

$$\log\left(\frac{S_T}{S_{t_0}} \right) \sim N\left(\nu T, \sigma^2 T \right), \tag{2.3.9}$$

and so

$$\log\left(\frac{S_T}{S_{t_0}} \right) = \nu T + \sigma \, W_T. \tag{2.3.10}$$

The solution to the GBM in equation (2.2.3) is

$$S_T = S_{t_0} \exp\left(\nu T + \sigma \, W_T \right), \quad \nu = \mu - \frac{\sigma^2}{2}. \tag{2.3.11}$$

The asset value at time $t + dt$ can therefore be generated from its value at time t by using

$$S_{t+dt} = S_t \exp\left\{ \nu dt + \sigma \, dW_t \right\}.$$

We have shown that if the asset price follows GBM, then the logarithm of the asset price follows standard Brownian motion. Another way of stating this is that, over the time interval dt, the change in the logarithm of the asset price is a Gaussian distribution with mean $[\mu - (\sigma^2/2)]\, dt$ and variance $\sigma^2 dt$.

These results can easily be generalized to include time varying drift and volatility. Now instead of equation (2.2.3) we have

$$dS_t = S_t \mu_t t dt + S_t \sigma_t dW_t, \qquad (2.3.12)$$

which results in

$$d\left(\log(S_t)\right) = v_t dt + \sigma_t\, dW_t, \qquad (2.3.13)$$

so

$$\int_{t=t_0}^{T} d\left(\log(S_t)\right) = \int_{t=t_0}^{T} v_t dt + \int_{t=t_0}^{T} \sigma_t\, dW_t,$$

which results in the following solution for S_T:

$$S_T = S_{t_0} \exp\left(\int_{t=t_0}^{T} v_t dt + \int_{t=t_0}^{T} \sigma_t\, dW_t\right), \quad \text{where } v_t = \mu_t - \frac{\sigma_t^2}{2}. \qquad (2.3.14)$$

The results presented in equation (2.3.11) and equation (2.3.14) are very important and will be referred to in later sections of the book.

2.4 GIRSANOV'S THEOREM

This theorem states that for any stochastic process $k(t)$ such that $\int_0^t k(s)^2 ds < \infty$ then the Radon Nikodym derivative $d\mathbb{Q}/d\mathbb{P} = \rho(t)$ is given by

$$\rho(t) = \exp\left\{\int_0^t k(s)dW_s^P - \frac{1}{2}\int_0^t k(s)^2 ds\right\}, \qquad (2.4.1)$$

where W_t^P is Brownian motion (possibly with drift) under probability measure $\mathbb{P}$, see Baxter and Rennie (1996). Under probability measure $\mathbb{Q}$, we have

$$W_t^Q = W_t^P - \int_0^t k(s)ds, \qquad (2.4.2)$$

where W_t^Q is also Brownian motion (possibly with drift).

We can also write

$$dW^P = dW^Q + k(t)dt. \qquad (2.4.3)$$

Girsanov's theorem thus provides a mechanism for changing the drift of a Brownian motion.

2.5 ITO'S LEMMA FOR MULTI-ASSET GBM

We will now consider the n-dimensional stochastic process

$$dX_i = a_i dt + b_i \sqrt{dt}\, dZ_i = a_i dt + b_i dW_i, \quad i = 1, \ldots, n, \qquad (2.5.1)$$

or in vector form

$$dX = A dt + \sqrt{dt}\, B\, dZ = A dt + B\, dW, \tag{2.5.2}$$

where A and B are n element vectors respectively containing the constants, $a_i, i = 1,\ldots,n$ and $b_i, i = 1,\ldots,n$. The stochastic vector dX contains the n stochastic variables $X_i, i = 1,\ldots,n$.

We will assume that the n element random vector dZ is drawn from a multivariate normal distribution with zero mean and covariance matrix $\hat{C}$. That is we can write

$$dZ \sim N(0, \hat{C}).$$

Since $\hat{C}_{ii} = Var[dZ_i] = 1$, $i = 1,\ldots,n$, the diagonal elements of $\hat{C}$ are all unity and the matrix $\hat{C}$ is in fact a *correlation matrix* with off-diagonal elements given by

$$\hat{C}_{ij} = E[dZ_i\, dZ_j] = \rho_{i,j}, \quad i = 1,\ldots,n, \ j = 1,\ldots,n, \ i \neq j,$$

where ρ_{ij} is the correlation coefficient between the ith and jth elements of the vector dZ.

Similarly, the n element random vector dW is drawn from a multivariate normal distribution with zero mean and covariance matrix C. We can thus write

$$dW \sim N(0, C).$$

The diagonal elements of C are $C_{ii} = Var[dW_i] = dt$, $i = 1,\ldots,n$ and off-diagonal elements are

$$C_{ij} = E[dW_i\, dW_j] = \rho_{i,j}\, dt, \quad i = 1,\ldots,n, \ j = 1,\ldots,n, \ i \neq j.$$

As in Section 2.3, we want to find the process followed by a function of the stochastic vector X, that is, the process followed by $\phi(X,t)$. This can be done by applying a n-dimensional Taylor expansion, up to second order, in the variables X and t as follows:

$$\phi^* = \phi + \frac{\partial \phi}{\partial t} dt + \sum_{i=1}^{n} \frac{\partial \phi}{\partial X_i} dX_i + \frac{1}{2} E\left[\sum_{i=1}^{n} \sum_{j=1}^{n} \frac{\partial^2 \phi}{\partial X_i \partial X_j} dX_i dX_j \right] + \frac{1}{2} \frac{\partial^2 \phi}{\partial t^2} dt^2$$

$$+ \sum_{i=1}^{n} \frac{\partial \phi}{\partial X_i \partial t} dX_i dt, \tag{2.5.3}$$

where ϕ^* is used to denote the value $\phi(X + dX, t + dt)$, and ϕ denotes the value $\phi(X,t)$. We will now consider the magnitude of the terms $dX_i dX_j, dX_i dt$, and dt^2 as $dt \to 0$. Expanding the terms $dX_i dX_j$ and $dX_i dt$, we have

$$dX_i dX_j = (a_i dt + b_i \sqrt{dt}\, dZ_i)(a_j dt + b_j \sqrt{dt}\, dZ_j),$$

$$\therefore dX_i dX_j = a_i a_j dt^2 + a_i b_j\, dt^{3/2}\, dZ_j + a_j b_i\, dt^{3/2}\, dZ_i + b_i b_j\, dt\, dZ_i dZ_j,$$

$$dX_i dt = a_i dt^2 + b_i dt^{3/2}\, dZ_i. \tag{2.5.4}$$

So as $dt \to 0$, and ignoring all terms in dt of order greater than 1, we have

$$dX_i dt \sim 0$$

and
$$dX_i \, dX_j \sim b_i b_j \, dt \, dZ_i \, dZ_j.$$

Therefore, equation (2.5.3) can be rewritten as

$$d\phi = \frac{\partial \phi}{\partial t} dt + \sum_{i=1}^{n} \frac{\partial \phi}{\partial X_i} dX_i + \frac{1}{2} E \left[\sum_{i=1}^{n} \sum_{j=1}^{n} \frac{\partial^2 \phi}{\partial X_i \partial X_j} dX_i \, dX_j \right], \qquad (2.5.5)$$

where $d\phi = \phi^* - \phi$.

Now

$$E[dX_i \, dX_j] = E[b_i b_j \, dt \, dZ_i \, dZ_j] = b_i b_j \, dt \, E[dZ_i \, dZ_j] = b_i b_j \rho_{ij} \, dt,$$

where ρ_{ij} is the correlation coefficient between the ith and jth assets.

Using these values in equation (2.5.5), and substituting for dX_i from equation (2.5.1), we obtain

$$d\phi = \sum_{i=1}^{n} \frac{\partial \phi}{\partial X_i} (a_i \, dt + b_i \, dW_i) + \frac{\partial \phi}{\partial t} dt + \frac{1}{2} \sum_{i=1}^{n} \sum_{j=1}^{n} b_i b_j \rho_{ij} \, dt \frac{\partial^2 \phi}{\partial X_i \partial X_j}. \qquad (2.5.6)$$

This gives Ito's n-dimensional formula

$$d\phi = \left\{ \frac{\partial \phi}{\partial t} + \sum_{i=1}^{n} a_i \frac{\partial \phi}{\partial X_i} + \frac{1}{2} \sum_{i=1}^{n} \sum_{j=1}^{n} b_i b_j \rho_{ij} \frac{\partial^2 \phi}{\partial X_i \partial X_j} \right\} dt + \sum_{i=1}^{n} \frac{\partial \phi}{\partial X_i} b_i \, dW_i. \qquad (2.5.7)$$

In particular, if we consider the GBM

$$dS_i = \mu_i S_i \, dt + \sigma_i S_i \, dW_i, \quad i = 1, \ldots, n,$$

where μ_i is the constant drift of the ith asset and σ_i is the constant volatility of the ith asset, then substituting $X_i = S_i$, $a_i = \mu_i S_i$, and $b_i = \sigma_i S_i$ into equation (2.5.7) yields

$$d\phi = \left\{ \frac{\partial \phi}{\partial t} + \sum_{i=1}^{n} \mu_i S_i \frac{\partial \phi}{\partial S_i} + \frac{1}{2} \sum_{i=1}^{n} \sum_{j=1}^{n} \sigma_i \sigma_j S_i S_j \rho_{ij} \frac{\partial^2 \phi}{\partial S_i \partial S_j} \right\} dt + \sum_{i=1}^{n} \frac{\partial \phi}{\partial S_i} \sigma_i S_i \, dW_i.$$
$$(2.5.8)$$

2.6 ITO PRODUCT AND QUOTIENT RULES IN TWO DIMENSIONS

We will now derive expressions for the product and quotient of two stochastic processes. In this case, $\phi \to \phi(X_1, X_2)$, with

$$dX_1 = a_1 \, dt + b_1 \, dW_1 \quad \text{and} \quad dX_2 = a_2 \, dt + b_2 \, dW_2.$$

The following two-dimensional version of Ito's lemma will be used:

$$d\phi = \frac{\partial \phi}{\partial X_1} dX_1 + \frac{\partial \phi}{\partial X_2} dX_2 + \frac{1}{2} E \left[\sum_{i=1}^{2} \sum_{j=1}^{2} \frac{\partial^2 \phi}{\partial X_i \partial X_j} dX_i \, dX_j \right], \qquad (2.6.1)$$

where we have used the fact that $\frac{\partial \phi}{\partial t} = 0$.

2.6.1 Ito Product Rule

Here, $\phi = \phi(X_1 X_2)$ and the partial derivatives are as follows:

$$\frac{\partial \phi}{\partial X_1} = X_2, \qquad \frac{\partial \phi}{\partial X_2} = X_1 \quad \frac{\partial^2 \phi}{\partial X_1^2} = \frac{\partial^2 \phi}{\partial X_2^2} = 0, \qquad \frac{\partial^2 \phi}{\partial X_1 \partial X_2} = \frac{\partial^2 \phi}{\partial X_2 \partial X_1} = 1.$$

Therefore, using (2.6.1),

$$d\phi = X_2 dX_1 + X_1 dX_2 + \frac{2E[dX_1 dX_2]}{2},$$

and the product rule is

$$d(X_1 X_2) = X_2 dX_1 + X_1 dX_2 + E[dX_1 dX_2]. \tag{2.6.2}$$

Brownian Motion with One Source of Randomness

For the special case where X_1 is Brownian motion and X_2 has no random term, we have

$$dX_1 = X_1 \mu_1 dt + X_1 \sigma_1 dW_1 \quad \text{and} \quad dX_2 = X_2 \mu_2 dt.$$

Now

$$\begin{aligned} E[dX_1 dX_2] &= E[(X_1 \mu_1 dt + X_1 \sigma_1 dW_1) X_2 \mu_2 dt] \\ &= X_1 X_2 \mu_1 \mu_2 dt^2 + X_1 X_2 \sigma_1 \mu_2 dt X_2 \mu_2 dt\, E[dW_1] \\ &= 0, \end{aligned}$$

where we have ignored terms in dt with order higher than 1 and used $E[dW_1] = 0$.

Therefore, equation (2.6.2) becomes

$$d(X_1 X_2) = X_2 dX_1 + X_1 dX_2,$$
$$d(X_1 X_2) = X_2 (X_1 \mu_1 dt + X_1 \sigma_1 dW_1) + X_1 X_2 \mu_2 dt.$$

So, we finally obtain

$$d(X_1 X_2) = (X_1 X_2)\{\mu_1 + \mu_2\} dt + (X_1 X_2)\sigma dW_1. \tag{2.6.3}$$

2.6.2 Ito Quotient Rule

Here, $\phi = \phi(X_1/X_2)$ and the partial derivatives are as follows:

$$\frac{\partial \phi}{\partial X_1} = \frac{1}{X_2}, \quad \frac{\partial \phi}{\partial X_1} = -\frac{X_1}{X_2^2}, \quad \frac{\partial^2 \phi}{\partial X_1^2} = 0, \quad \frac{\partial^2 \phi}{\partial X_2^2} = 2\frac{X_1}{X_2^3}, \quad \frac{\partial^2 \phi}{\partial X_1 \partial X_2} = \frac{\partial^2 \phi}{\partial X_2 \partial X_1} = -\frac{1}{X_2^2}.$$

Therefore, using equation (2.6.1),

$$d\phi = \frac{dX_1}{X_2} - X_1 \frac{dX_2}{X_2^2} + \frac{1}{2}E\left[\left\{\frac{2X_1}{X_2^3}dX_2^2 - 2\frac{dX_1 dX_2}{X_2^2}\right\}\right].$$

We obtain the following expression for the quotient rule:

$$d\left(\frac{X_1}{X_2}\right) = \left(\frac{X_1}{X_2}\right)\left\{\frac{dX_1}{X_1} - \frac{dX_2}{X_2} + E\left[\left(\frac{dX_2}{X_2}\right)\left(\frac{dX_2}{X_2}\right)\right] - E\left[\left(\frac{dX_1}{X_1}\right)\left(\frac{dX_2}{X_2}\right)\right]\right\}. \quad (2.6.4)$$

(i) *Brownian motion*

Here, we have

$$dX_1 = X_1\mu_1 dt + X_1\sigma_1 dW_1 \quad \text{and} \quad dX_2 = X_2\mu_2 dt + X_2\sigma_2 dW_2,$$

or equivalently

$$\frac{dX_1}{X_1} = \mu_1 dt + \sigma_1 dW_1 \quad \text{and} \quad \frac{dX_2}{X_2} = \mu_2 dt + \sigma_2 dW_2.$$

Therefore,

$$\begin{aligned}
E\left[\left(\frac{dX_2}{X_2}\right)\left(\frac{dX_2}{X_2}\right)\right] &= E\left[(\mu_2 dt + \sigma_2 dW_2)(\mu_2 dt + \sigma_2 dW_2)\right] \\
&= E\left[\mu_2^2 dt^2\right] + E\left[\sigma_2^2(dW_2)^2\right] + 2E\left[\sigma_2 dt dW_2\right] \\
&= \mu_2^2 dt^2 + \sigma_2^2 dt + 2\sigma_2 dt E\left[dW_2\right],
\end{aligned}$$

which results in

$$E\left[\left(\frac{dX_2}{X_2}\right)\left(\frac{dX_2}{X_2}\right)\right] = \sigma_2^2 dt, \quad (2.6.5)$$

where we have ignored all terms in dt with order higher than 1 and used the fact that $E\left[dW_2\right] = 0$.

In a similar manner,

$$\begin{aligned}
E\left[\left(\frac{dX_1}{X_1}\right)\left(\frac{dX_2}{X_2}\right)\right] &= E\left[(\mu_1 dt + \sigma_1 dW_1)(\mu_2 dt + \sigma_2 dW_2)\right] \\
&= E\left[\mu_1\mu_2 dt^2\right] + E\left[\sigma_1\mu_2 dt dW_1\right] + E\left[\sigma_2\mu_1 dt dW_2\right] \\
&\quad + E\left[\sigma_1\sigma_2 dt dW_1 dW_2\right] \\
&= \mu_1\mu_2 dt^2 + \sigma_1\mu_2 dt E\left[dW_1\right] + \sigma_2\mu_1 dt E\left[dW_2\right] \\
&\quad + \sigma_1\sigma_2 dt E\left[dW_1 dW_2\right],
\end{aligned}$$

which gives

$$E\left[\left(\frac{dX_1}{X_1}\right)\left(\frac{dX_2}{X_2}\right)\right] = \sigma_1\sigma_2 dt \rho_{12}, \quad (2.6.6)$$

where we have proceeded as before but also used the fact that $E\left[dW_1 dW_2\right] = \rho_{12} dt$.

Substituting these into equation (2.6.4), we have

$$\begin{aligned}
d\left(\frac{X_1}{X_2}\right) &= \left(\frac{X_1}{X_2}\right)\left\{\frac{dX_1}{X_1} - \frac{dX_2}{X_2} + \sigma_2^2 dt - \sigma_1\sigma_2\rho_{12} dt\right\} \\
&= \left(\frac{X_1}{X_2}\right)\left\{\mu_1 dt + \sigma_1 dt - \mu_2 dt - \sigma_2 dt + \sigma_2^2 dt - \sigma_1\sigma_2\rho_{12} dt\right\} \\
&= \left(\frac{X_1}{X_2}\right)\left\{\mu_1 dt + \sigma_1 dW_1 - \mu_2 dt - \sigma_2 dW_2 + \sigma_2^2 dt - \sigma_1\sigma_2\rho_{12} dt\right\}.
\end{aligned}$$

This yields

$$d\left(\frac{X_1}{X_2}\right) = \left(\frac{X_1}{X_2}\right)\left\{\mu_1 - \mu_2 + \sigma_2^2 - \sigma_1\sigma_2\rho_{12}\right\}dt + \left(\frac{X_1}{X_2}\right)\left\{\sigma_1 dW_1 - \sigma_2 dW_2\right\}. \quad (2.6.7)$$

(ii) *Brownian motion with one source of randomness*

We have

$$dX_1 = X_1\mu_1 dt + X_1\sigma_1 dW_1 \quad \text{and} \quad dX_2 = X_2\mu_2 dt.$$

As before

$$E\left[\left(\frac{dX_2}{X_2}\right)\left(\frac{dX_2}{X_2}\right)\right] = E\left[\mu_2^2 dt^2\right] = \mu_2^2 dt^2 \to 0,$$

$$E\left[\left(\frac{dX_1}{X_1}\right)\left(\frac{dX_2}{X_2}\right)\right] = E\left[(\mu_1 dt + \sigma_1 dW_1)\mu_2 dt\right]$$

$$= E\left[\mu_1\mu_2 dt^2 + \sigma_1\sigma_2 dt dW_1\right]$$

$$= \mu_1\mu_2 dt^2 + \sigma_1\sigma_2 dt E\left[dW_1\right] \to 0.$$

Therefore,

$$d\left(\frac{X_1}{X_2}\right) = \left(\frac{X_1}{X_2}\right)\left\{\frac{dX_1}{X_1} - \frac{dX_2}{X_2}\right\}$$

$$= \left(\frac{X_1}{X_2}\right)\left\{\mu_1 dt + \sigma_1 dW_1 - \mu_2 dt\right\}.$$

So, the final expression is

$$d\left(\frac{X_1}{X_2}\right) = \left(\frac{X_1}{X_2}\right)\left\{\mu_1 - \mu_2\right\}dt + \left(\frac{X_1}{X_2}\right)\sigma_1 dW_1. \quad (2.6.8)$$

2.7 ITO PRODUCT IN *n* DIMENSIONS

Using equation (2.5.7) we will now derive an expression for the product of *n* stochastic processes. In this case, $\phi \to \prod_{i=1}^n X_i$, and the partial derivatives are as follows:

$$\frac{\partial\phi}{\partial X_i} = \phi\frac{dX_i}{X_i}, \quad \text{for } i = 1,\dots,n,$$

$$\frac{\partial^2\phi}{\partial X_i^2} = 0, \quad \text{for } i = 1,\dots,n,$$

$$\frac{\partial^2\phi}{\partial X_i X_j} = \frac{\partial^2\phi}{\partial X_j X_i} = \left(\frac{dX_i}{X_i}\right)\left(\frac{dX_j}{X_j}\right)\phi, \quad \text{for } i \neq j, i = 1,\dots,n, j = 1,\dots,n,$$

$$\frac{\partial\phi}{\partial t} = 0.$$

So substituting into (2.5.7), we have

$$d\phi = \phi\sum_{i=1}^n\left(\frac{dX_i}{X_i}\right) + \phi E\left[\sum_{i=1}^n\sum_{j=1(i\neq j)}^n\left(\frac{dX_i}{X_i}\right)\left(\frac{dX_j}{X_j}\right)\right], \quad (2.7.1)$$

which in full is

$$d\left(\prod_{i=1}^{n} X_i\right) = \left(\prod_{i=1}^{n} X_i\right) \sum_{i=1}^{n}\left(\frac{dX_i}{X_i}\right) + \left(\prod_{i=1}^{n} X_i\right) E\left[\sum_{i=1}^{n}\sum_{j=1(i\neq j)}^{n}\left(\frac{dX_i}{X_i}\right)\left(\frac{dX_j}{X_j}\right)\right]. \quad (2.7.2)$$

2.8 THE BROWNIAN BRIDGE

Let a Brownian process have values W_{t_0} at time t_0 and W_{t_1} at time t_1. We want to find the conditional distribution of W_t, where $t_0 < t < t_1$. This distribution will be denoted by $P\left(W_t | \{W_{t_0}, W_{t_1}\}\right)$ to indicate that W_t is conditional on the end values W_{t_0} and W_{t_1}. We now write W_{t_0} and W_{t_1} as

$$W_t = W_{t_0} + \sqrt{(t - t_0)}\, X_t, \quad X_t \sim N(0,1), \quad (2.8.1)$$

$$W_{t_1} = W_t + \sqrt{(t_1 - t)}\, Y_t, \quad Y_t \sim N(0,1), \quad (2.8.2)$$

where X_t and Y_t are independent normal variates.

Combining equation (2.8.1) and equation (2.8.2), we have

$$W_{t_1} = W_{t_0} + \sqrt{(t - t_0)}\, X_t + \sqrt{(t_1 - t)}\, Y_t,$$

which can be re-expressed as

$$W_{t_1} - W_{t_0} = \sqrt{(t - t_0)}\, X_t + \sqrt{(t_1 - t)}\, Y_t.$$

Using the Brownian motion property (iii) in Section 2.1,

$$W_{t_1} - W_{t_0} = \sqrt{(t_1 - t_0)}\, Z_t, \quad Z_t \sim N(0,1).$$

So

$$\sqrt{(t_1 - t_0)}Z_t = \sqrt{(t - t_0)}\, X_t + \sqrt{(t_1 - t)}\, Y_t$$

and

$$Y(X_t, Z_t) = \frac{\sqrt{(t_1 - t_0)}\, Z_t - \sqrt{(t - t_0)}\, X_t}{\sqrt{(t_1 - t)}}. \quad (2.8.3)$$

Now $P\left(W_t | \{W_{t_0}, W_{t_1}\}\right) = P(X_t | Z_t)$, the probability distribution of X_t conditional on Z_t. From Bayes law,

$$P(X_t | Z_t) = \frac{P(X_t)P(Y(X_t, Z_t))}{P(Z_t)} = \frac{1}{\sqrt{2\pi}} \exp\left\{-\frac{\left(X_t^2 + Y_t^2 - Z_t^2\right)}{2}\right\}. \quad (2.8.4)$$

Since X_t, Y_t, and Z_t are Gaussians, we can write

$$P(X_t | Z_t) = \frac{1}{\sqrt{2\pi}} \exp\left\{-\frac{\left(X_t^2 + Y_t^2 - Z_t^2\right)}{2}\right\}. \quad (2.8.5)$$

First let us compute Y_t^2,

$$Y_t^2 = \left(\frac{\sqrt{(t_1 - t_0)}Z_t - \sqrt{(t - t_0)}X_t}{\sqrt{(t_1 - t)}}\right)^2,$$

so

$$Y_t^2 = \frac{(t_1 - t_0)Z_t^2 + (t - t_0)X_t^2 - 2\sqrt{(t_1 - t_0)}\sqrt{(t - t_0)}\, X_t\, Z_t}{(t_1 - t)}. \tag{2.8.6}$$

Next we compute $X_t^2 + Y_t^2 - Z_t^2$ as follows:

$$X_t^2 + Y_t^2 - Z_t^2 = \frac{(t_1 - t_0)X_t^2 + (t - t_0)Z_t^2 - 2\sqrt{(t_1 - t_0)}\sqrt{(t - t_0)}\, X_t\, Z_t}{(t_1 - t)}. \tag{2.8.7}$$

Dividing top and bottom of equation (2.8.7) by $t_1 - t_0$, we obtain

$$X_t^2 + Y_t^2 - Z_t^2 = \frac{X_t^2 + \left(\frac{t-t_0}{t_1-t_0}\right)Z_t^2 - 2\frac{\sqrt{(t_1-t_0)}\sqrt{(t-t_0)}}{(t_1-t_0)}X_t\, Z_t}{\left(\frac{t_1-t}{t_1-t_0}\right)}$$

$$= \frac{X_t^2 + \frac{(t-t_0)}{(t_1-t_0)}Z_t^2 - 2\sqrt{\left(\frac{t-t_0}{t_1-t_0}\right)}X_t\, Z_t}{\frac{(t_1-t)}{(t_1-t_0)}},$$

which gives

$$X_t^2 + Y_t^2 - Z_t^2 = \frac{\left(X_t - \sqrt{\left(\frac{t-t_0}{t_1-t_0}\right)}Z_t\right)^2}{\left(\frac{t_1-t}{t_1-t_0}\right)}, \tag{2.8.8}$$

where we have used

$$\left(X_t - \sqrt{\frac{(t-t_0)}{(t_1-t_0)}}Z_t\right)^2 = X_t^2 + \frac{(t-t_0)}{(t_1-t_0)}Z_t^2 - 2\sqrt{\left(\frac{t-t_0}{t_1-t_0}\right)}X_t\, Z_t.$$

Substituting equation (2.8.8) into (2.8.5) yields

$$P(X_t|Z_t) = \frac{1}{\sqrt{2\pi}}\exp\left\{-\frac{\left(X_t - \sqrt{\left(\frac{t-t_0}{t_1-t_0}\right)}Z_t\right)^2}{2\left(\frac{t_1-t}{t_1-t_0}\right)}\right\}.$$

Therefore, $P(X_t|Z_t)$ is a Gaussian distribution with

$$E[X_t] = \sqrt{\frac{t-t_0}{t_1-t_0}}Z_t \quad \text{and} \quad Var[X_t] = \left(\frac{t_1-t}{t_1-t_0}\right).$$

Substituting for Z_t, we have

$$E[X_t] = \sqrt{\frac{t-t_0}{t_1-t_0}} = \sqrt{\frac{t-t_0}{t_1-t_0}}\left(\frac{W_{t_1} - W_{t_0}}{\sqrt{t_1-t_0}}\right),$$

which gives

$$E[X_t] = \frac{\sqrt{t-t_0}}{t_1-t_0}(W_{t_1} - W_{t_0}). \tag{2.8.9}$$

The variate $\hat{X}_t = E[X_t] + \sqrt{Var[X_t]}\, Z_t$ has the same distribution as $P(X_t|Z_t)$.

So we can substitute $\hat{X}_t$ for X_t in equation (2.8.1) to obtain

$$W_t = W_{t_0} + \sqrt{t - t_0}\left\{E[X_t] + \sqrt{Var[X_t]}\, Z_t\right\},$$

which gives

$$W_t = W_{t_0} + \sqrt{t - t_0}\left\{\frac{\sqrt{t - t_0}}{t_1 - t_0}(W_{t_1} - W_{t_0}) + \sqrt{\frac{(t_1 - t)}{t_1 - t_0}}\, Z_t\right\},$$

and simplifying we obtain

$$W_t = W_{t_0}\frac{(t_1 - t_0)}{(t_1 - t_0)} + \frac{(t - t_0)}{(t_1 - t_0)}(W_{t_1} - W_{t_0}) + \sqrt{\frac{(t_1 - t)(t - t_0)}{t_1 - t_0}}\, Z_t. \tag{2.8.10}$$

Variates, W_t, from the distribution of $P\left(W_t | \{W_{t_0}, W_{t_1}\}\right)$ can therefore be generated by using

$$W_t = W_{t_0}\frac{(t_1 - t)}{(t_1 - t_0)} + W_{t_1}\frac{(t - t_0)}{(t_1 - t_0)} + \sqrt{\frac{(t_1 - t)(t - t_0)}{t_1 - t_0}}\, Z_t. \tag{2.8.11}$$

An alternative derivation of the Brownian bridge is given in Appendix G.

2.9 TIME TRANSFORMED BROWNIAN MOTION

Let us consider the Brownian motion

$$dW_t = \sigma \sqrt{dt}\, dZ_t, \tag{2.9.1}$$

and also the scaled and time transformed Brownian motion

$$Y_{W,t} = a_t W_{f_t}, \tag{2.9.2}$$

where the scale factor, a_t, is a real function and the time transformation, f_t, is a continuous increasing function satisfying $f_t \geq 0$, see Cox and Miller (1965). Using Ito's lemma,

$$dY_{W,t} = \frac{\partial Y_t}{\partial t} dt + \frac{\partial Y_t}{\partial W_t} dW_t, \tag{2.9.3}$$

where we have used the fact that $\dfrac{\partial^2 Y_t}{\partial W_t^2} = 0$.

From equation (2.9.3),

$$dY_{W,t} = \left(\frac{\partial a_t}{\partial t}\right) W_{f_t} dt + a_t dW_{f_t}. \tag{2.9.4}$$

Now

$$dW_{f_t} = \sqrt{df_t}\, dZ_t = \sqrt{\frac{\partial f_t}{\partial t} dt}\, dZ_t, \tag{2.9.5}$$

so we can write

$$dY_{W,t} = a_t' W_{f_t} dt + a_t \sqrt{f_t' dt}\, dZ_t, \tag{2.9.6}$$

where

$$a_t' = \frac{\partial a_t}{\partial t} \quad \text{and} \quad f_t' = \frac{\partial f_t}{\partial t}.$$

2.9.1 Scaled Brownian Motion

We will prove that $\hat{W}_t$ defined by

$$\hat{W}_t = \frac{1}{c} W_{c^2 t}, \quad c > 0$$

is Brownian motion.

Let us consider the process

$$Y_t = W_{c^2 t}.$$

From equation (2.9.2), we have $a_t = 1$, $f_t = c^2 t$, $a'_t = 0$, and $f'_t = c^2$. Substituting these values into equation (2.9.6) yields

$$dY_t = \sqrt{c^2 dt} \, dZ_t,$$

which gives

$$dY_t = c \sqrt{dt} \, dZ_t = c \, dW_t.$$

Therefore, $\hat{W}_t = \dfrac{dY_t}{c}$ is Brownian motion.

2.9.2 Mean Reverting Process

We will now show that the mean reverting Ornstein–Uhlenbeck process (see Section 2.10) can be represented as follows:

$$Y_{W,t} = \exp(-\alpha t) \, W_{\psi_t}, \quad \text{where} \quad \psi_t = \frac{\sigma^2 \exp(2\alpha t)}{2\alpha} \quad \alpha > 0. \tag{2.9.7}$$

Proof. From equation (2.9.2) and equation (2.9.7), we have

$$f_t = \frac{\sigma^2 \exp\left(\sigma^2 \exp(2\alpha t)\right)}{2\alpha} \quad \text{and} \quad a_t = \exp(-2\alpha t). \tag{2.9.8}$$

Therefore,

$$\frac{a'_t}{a_t} = -\frac{\alpha \exp(-\alpha t)}{\exp(-\alpha t)} = -\alpha \tag{2.9.9}$$

and

$$f'_t = \frac{\sigma^2}{2\alpha} 2\alpha \exp(2\alpha t) = \sigma^2 \exp(2\alpha t). \tag{2.9.10}$$

So,

$$\sqrt{f'_t dt} = \sqrt{\sigma^2 \exp(2\alpha t)} = \sigma \exp(\alpha t) \sqrt{dt}. \tag{2.9.11}$$

Thus,

$$dY_{W,t} = -\alpha Y_{W,t} dt + \exp(-\alpha t) \sigma \exp(\alpha t) \sqrt{dt} \, dZ, \tag{2.9.12}$$

which means that

$$dY_{W,t} = -\alpha Y_{W,t} dt + \sigma dW_t. \tag{2.9.13}$$

From equation (2.9.13), it can be seen that conditional mean and variance are

$$E\left[dY_{W,t} | F_t\right] = \alpha Y_{W,t} dt, \tag{2.9.14}$$

$$Var\left[dY_{W,t} | F_t\right] = \sigma^2 dt. \tag{2.9.15}$$

Unconditional Mean

The unconditional mean is

$$E\left[Y_{W,t}\right] = E\left[\exp\left(-\alpha t\right) W\left(\frac{\sigma^2 \exp\left(2\alpha t\right)}{2\alpha}\right)\right], \quad \text{where } \alpha > 0 \text{ and } t \to \infty. \quad (2.9.16)$$

So,

$$E\left[Y_{W,t}\right] = 0. \quad (2.9.17)$$

Unconditional Variance and Covariance

Let

$$Y_{W,t} = \exp\left(-\alpha t\right) W_{\psi_t}, \quad \text{where } \psi_t = \left(\frac{\sigma^2 \exp\left(2\alpha t\right)}{2\alpha}\right) \quad (2.9.18)$$

and

$$Y_{W,s} = \exp\left(-\alpha s\right) W_{\psi_s}, \quad \text{where } \psi_s = \left(\frac{\sigma^2 \exp\left(2\alpha s\right)}{2\alpha}\right). \quad (2.9.19)$$

The covariance is

$$Cov\left[Y_{W,s}, Y_{W,t}\right] = E\left[Y_{W,t} Y_{W,s}\right] - E\left[Y_{W,t}\right] E\left[Y_{W,s}\right]$$
$$= E\left[Y_{W,t} Y_{W,s}\right], \quad (2.9.20)$$

since $E\left[Y_{W,s}\right] = E\left[Y_{W,t}\right] = 0$.

Shortening the notation of $Y_{W,t}$ to Y_t, we obtain

$$Cov\left[Y_s, Y_t\right] = E\left[\exp\left(-\alpha t\right) W_{\psi_t} \exp\left(-\alpha t\right) W_{\psi_s}\right]$$
$$= \exp\left(-\alpha(t + s)\right) E\left[\{W_{\psi_t} W_{\psi_s}\}\right].$$

From equation (2.1.2),

$$E\left[W_s, W_t\right] = s \wedge t. \quad (2.9.21)$$

Therefore, if $s \leq t$,

$$E\left[W_{\psi_t} W_{\psi_s}\right] = W_{\psi_s} \quad (2.9.22)$$

and

$$Cov\left[Y_s, Y_t\right] = \frac{\exp\left(-\alpha(t + s)\right) \sigma^2 \exp\left(2\alpha s\right)}{2\alpha} = \frac{\sigma^2}{2\alpha} \exp\left(-\alpha(t - s)\right). \quad (2.9.23)$$

The unconditional variance (obtained by setting $s = t$) is

$$Var\left[Y_t\right] = \frac{\sigma^2}{2\alpha}. \quad (2.9.24)$$

2.10 ORNSTEIN UHLENBECK PROCESS

The Ornstein Uhlenbeck process is often used to model interest rates because of its mean reverting property. It is defined by the equation

$$dX_t = -\alpha X_t dt + \sigma dW_t. \quad (2.10.1)$$

Using the integrating factor $\exp(\alpha t)$, we have

$$\exp(\alpha t)\, dX_t = -\alpha X_t \exp(\alpha t)\, dt + \sigma \exp(\alpha t)\, dW_t,$$

so

$$\exp(\alpha t)\, dX_t + \alpha X_t \exp(\alpha t)\, dt = \sigma \exp(\alpha t)\, dW_t. \tag{2.10.2}$$

Using the Ito product rule, we have

$$d\left(X_t \exp(\alpha t)\right) = \exp(\alpha t)\, dX_t + \alpha X_t \exp(\alpha t)\, dt. \tag{2.10.3}$$

So from equation (2.10.2) and equation (2.10.3), we obtain

$$d\left(X_t \exp(\alpha t)\right) = \sigma \exp(\alpha t)\, dW_t. \tag{2.10.4}$$

Integrating equation (2.10.4) gives

$$\int_{s=0}^{s=t} d\left(X_s \exp(\alpha s)\right) = \sigma \int_{s=0}^{s=t} \exp(\alpha s),$$

which yields

$$X_t \exp(\alpha t) - X_{t_0} = \sigma \int_{s=0}^{s=t} \exp(\alpha s),$$

and thus, the solution of equation (2.10.1) is

$$X_t = X_{t_0} \exp(-\alpha t) + \sigma \exp(-\alpha t) \int_{s=0}^{s=t} \exp(\alpha s)\, dW_s. \tag{2.10.5}$$

We will now derive expressions for both the unconditional mean and the unconditional variance of X_t.

The mean

Taking expectations of both sides of equation (2.10.5) yields

$$E[X_t] = E\left[X_{t_0} \exp(-\alpha t)\right] + E\left[\sigma \exp(-\alpha t) \int_{s=0}^{s=t} \exp(\alpha s)\, dW_s\right]. \tag{2.10.6}$$

Since

$$E\left[\sigma \exp(-\alpha t) \int_{s=0}^{s=t} \exp(\alpha s)\, dW_s\right] = \sigma \exp(-\alpha t)\, E\left[\int_{s=0}^{s=t} \exp(\alpha s)\, dW_s\right] = 0,$$

the unconditional mean is

$$E[X_t] = X_{t_0} \exp(-\alpha t). \tag{2.10.7}$$

The variance

To derive the expression for unconditional variance requires a bit more effort. We have

$$Var[X_t] = E\left[\{X_t - E[X_t]\}^2\right] \tag{2.10.8}$$

$$= E\left[\{X_t - X_{t_0} \exp(-\alpha t)\}^2\right].$$

However from equation (2.10.5),

$$X_t - X_{t_0} \exp(-\alpha t) = \sigma \exp(-\alpha t) \int_{s=0}^{s=t} \exp(\alpha s) \, dW_s.$$

So substituting the above expression into equation (2.10.8),

$$Var\,[X_t] = E\left[\left\{\exp(-\alpha t)\sigma \int_{s=0}^{s=t} \exp(\alpha s)\,dW_s\right\}^2\right], \qquad (2.10.9)$$

$$Var\,[X_t] = \sigma^2 \exp(-2\alpha t) E\left[\left\{\int_{s=0}^{s=t} \exp(\alpha s)\,dW_s\right\}^2\right]. \qquad (2.10.10)$$

Using Ito's isometry (see Section 2.12.2),

$$E\left[\left\{\int_{s=0}^{s=t} \exp(\alpha s)\,dW_s\right\}^2\right] = E\left[\int_{s=0}^{s=t} \{\exp(\alpha s)\}^2\,ds\right].$$

Then using Fubini's theorem (see Section 2.12.1),

$$\begin{aligned} E\left[\int_{s=0}^{s=t} \{\exp(\alpha s)\}^2\,ds\right] &= \int_{s=0}^{s=t} E\left[\{\exp(\alpha s)\}^2\right]ds \\ &= \int_{s=0}^{s=t} \exp(2\alpha s)\,ds \\ &= \left[\frac{\exp(2\alpha s)}{2\alpha}\right]_{s=0}^{s=t} \\ &= \left(\frac{\exp(2\alpha t) - 1}{2\alpha}\right). \end{aligned}$$

Substituting the above result into equation (2.10.10),

$$Var\,[X_t] = \sigma^2 \exp(-2\alpha t)\left\{\frac{\exp(2\alpha t) - 1}{2\alpha}\right\},$$

which yields the following expression for the variance:

$$Var\,[X_t] = \sigma^2\left\{\frac{1 - \exp(-2\alpha t)}{2\alpha}\right\}. \qquad (2.10.11)$$

The expressions for the mean and variance derived in equations (2.10.7) and (2.10.11) allow us to write the distribution of X_t as

$$X_t \sim N\left(X_{t_0}\exp(-\alpha t), \sigma^2\left\{\frac{1 - \exp(-2\alpha t)}{2\alpha}\right\}\right), \qquad (2.10.12)$$

which if $X_{t_0} = 0$ reduces to

$$X_t \sim N\left(0, \sigma^2\left\{\frac{1 - \exp(-2\alpha t)}{2\alpha}\right\}\right). \qquad (2.10.13)$$

The transition density from X_{t_0} to X_t is

$$P(X_t|X_{t_0}) = \sqrt{\frac{K}{2\pi(1-\gamma^2)}} \exp\left\{-\frac{K\left(X_t - X_{t_0}\exp(-\alpha(t-t_0))\right)^2}{(1-\gamma^2)}\right\}, \qquad (2.10.14)$$

where $K = 2\alpha/\sigma^2$ and $\gamma = \exp(-\alpha(t-t_0))$.

Ornstein Uhlenbeck stochastic paths can thus be simulated using

$$X_{t+dt} = X_t \exp(-\alpha dt) + \sigma \sqrt{\left\{\frac{1 - \exp(-2\alpha dt)}{2\alpha}\right\}} dZ. \qquad (2.10.15)$$

From equation (2.10.14), we can write

$$E[X_{t+dt}|X_t] = X_t \exp(-\alpha dt),$$

$$Var[X_{t+dt}|X_t] = \sigma^2 \left\{\frac{1 - \exp(-2\alpha dt)}{2\alpha}\right\}.$$

We will now show that in the limit $dt \to 0$ equation (2.10.15) reduces to GBM.

For small dt, we can take a first order expansion of the exponentials in (2.10.15) to obtain

$$X_{t+dt} = X_t \{(1 - \alpha dt)\} + \sigma \sqrt{\frac{(1 - (1 - 2\alpha dt))}{2\alpha}} dZ,$$

so

$$X_{t+dt} = X_t - X_t \alpha dt + \sigma \sqrt{\frac{(2\alpha dt)}{2\alpha}} dZ.$$

Therefore,

$$X_{t+dt} - X_t = -\alpha X_t dt + \sigma \sqrt{dt} dZ.$$

This can be expressed as

$$dX_t = -\alpha X_t dt + \sigma dW_t,$$

which is GBM with drift $-\alpha$ and volatility σ.

2.11 THE ORNSTEIN UHLENBECK BRIDGE

Let an Ornstein Uhlenbeck process have value X_{t_0} at time t_0 and X_{t_1} at time t_1. We are interested in the distribution of X_t at an intermediate point, that is, $P(X_t|\{X_{t_0}, X_{t_1}\})$, where $t_0 < t < t_1$.

We will show that X_t is a Gaussian with conditional mean

$$\mu_t = X_{t_0}\exp(-\alpha(t-t_0))\left\{\frac{1 - \exp(-2\alpha(t_1 - t))}{(1-\gamma^2)}\right\}$$
$$+ X_{t_1}\exp(-\alpha(t_1 - t))\left\{\frac{1 - \exp(-2\alpha(t - t_0))}{(1-\gamma^2)}\right\} \qquad (2.11.1)$$

and conditional variance

$$V_t = \frac{(1 - \exp(-2\alpha(t - t_0)))(1 - \exp(-2\alpha(t_1 - t)))}{2\alpha(1 - \exp(-2\alpha(t_1 - t_0)))}, \tag{2.11.2}$$

where $\gamma = \exp(-\alpha(t_1 - t_0))$.

Proof. The standard Ornstein Uhlenbeck process ($\sigma = 1$) is defined by the process

$$dX_t = -\alpha X_t dt + \sqrt{dt}\, dZ_t. \tag{2.11.3}$$

From Section 2.10, we have that

$$X_t = X_{t_0} \exp(-\alpha(t - t_0)) + \left\{ \frac{1 - \exp(-2\alpha(t - t_0))}{2\alpha} \right\} dZ_t, \tag{2.11.4}$$

and that the transition density from X_{t_0} to X_t is

$$P(X_t|X_{t_0}) = \frac{\sqrt{2\alpha}}{\sqrt{2\pi(1 - \exp(-2\alpha(t - t_0)))}} \exp\left\{ -\frac{\alpha(X_t - X_{t_0}\exp(-\alpha(t - t_0)))^2}{(1 - \exp(-2\alpha(t - t_0)))} \right\}. \tag{2.11.5}$$

The joint density of X_t and X_{t_1} given X_{t_0} is

$$P(\{X_t, X_{t_1}\}|X_{t_0}) = P(X_{t_1}|X_t)\, P(X_t|X_{t_0}). \tag{2.11.6}$$

We thus have

$$P(\{X_t, X_{t_1}\}|X_{t_0}) = \kappa \exp\left\{ -\frac{\alpha(X_t - X_{t_0}\exp(-\alpha(t - t_0)))^2}{(1 - \exp(-2\alpha(t - t_0)))} \right\}$$

$$\times \exp\left\{ -\frac{\alpha(X_{t_1} - X_t\exp(-\alpha(t_1 - t)))^2}{(1 - \exp(-2\alpha(t_1 - t)))} \right\},$$

where $\kappa = (1/2\pi) \times 2\alpha/[\sqrt{(1 - \exp(-2\alpha(t - t_0)))(1 - \exp(-2\alpha(t_1 - t)))}]$.

The distribution of X_t given X_{t_0} and X_{t_1}, $P(X_t|X_{t_0}, X_{t_1})$ is

$$P(X|\{X_{t_0}, X_{t_1}\}) = \frac{P(\{X_{t_1}, X\}|X_{t_0})}{P(X_{t_1}|X_{t_0})}, \tag{2.11.7}$$

where

$$P(X_{t_1}|X_{t_0}) = \frac{\sqrt{2\alpha}}{\sqrt{2\pi(1 - \exp(-2\alpha(t_1 - t_0)))}} \exp\left\{ -\frac{\alpha(X_{t_1} - X_{t_0}\exp(-\alpha(t_1 - t_0)))^2}{(1 - \exp(-2\alpha(t_1 - t_0)))} \right\}. \tag{2.11.8}$$

After some algebra, we can re-express equation (2.11.7) as

$$P(X_t|\{X_{t_0}, X_{t_1}\}) = \sqrt{\frac{\alpha}{\pi\phi_t}} \exp\{A\}, \tag{2.11.9}$$

where

$$A = -\frac{\alpha}{\phi}(B_1 + B_2 - B_3),$$

$$B_1 = \left\{ X_t^2 + X_{t_0}^2 \exp\left(-2\alpha(t - t_0)\right) - 2X_t X_{t_0} \exp\left(-\alpha(t - t_0)\right) \right\}$$
$$\times \left\{ \frac{1 - \exp\left(-2\alpha(t_1 - t)\right)}{1 - \gamma^2} \right\}, \tag{2.11.10}$$

$$B_2 = \left\{ X_{t_1}^2 + X_t^2 \exp\left(-2\alpha(t_1 - t)\right) - 2X_t X_{t_1} \exp\left(-\alpha(t_1 - t)\right) \right\}$$
$$\times \left\{ \frac{1 - \exp\left(-2\alpha(t - t_0)\right)}{1 - \gamma^2} \right\}, \tag{2.11.11}$$

$$B_3 = \left\{ X_{t_1}^2 + X_{t_0}^2 \exp\left(-2\alpha(t_1 - t_0)\right) - 2X_{t_1} X_{t_0} \exp\left(-\alpha(t_1 - t_0)\right) \right\}$$
$$\times \left\{ 1 - \exp\left(-2\alpha(t - t_0)\right) \right\} \left\{ \frac{1 - \exp\left(-2\alpha(t_1 - t)\right)}{(1 - \gamma^2)^2} \right\}, \tag{2.11.12}$$

$$\phi_t = \frac{(1 - \exp\left(-2\alpha(t - t_0)\right))(1 - \exp\left(-2\alpha(t_1 - t)\right))}{(1 - \exp\left(-2\alpha(t_1 - t_0)\right))}, \quad \text{and} \quad \gamma = \exp\left(-\alpha(t_1 - t_0)\right).$$

Let us now assume that $P(X_t | \{X_{t_0}, X_{t_1}\})$ is a normal distribution with conditional mean μ_t and conditional variance V_t. We thus have

$$P(X_t | \{X_{t_0}, X_{t_1}\}) = \frac{1}{\sqrt{2\pi V_t}} \exp\left\{ -\frac{(X_t - \mu_t)^2}{2V_t} \right\}. \tag{2.11.13}$$

Equating equations (2.11.7) and (2.11.13) yields

$$-\frac{1}{2V_t} \left\{ (X_t - \mu_t)^2 \right\} = -\frac{1}{2V_t} \left\{ X_t^2 - \mu_t^2 - 2X_t \mu_t \right\} = -\frac{\alpha}{\phi} (B_1 + B_2 - B_3). \tag{2.11.14}$$

The conditional variance V_t can be obtained by noting that

$$\frac{1}{2V_t} = \frac{\alpha}{\phi_t},$$

and hence,

$$V_t = \frac{\phi}{2\alpha}, \tag{2.11.15}$$

so substituting for ϕ in equation (2.11.15), we obtain the following expression for the conditional variance:

$$V_t = \frac{(1 - \exp\left(-2\alpha(t - t_0)\right))(1 - \exp\left(-2\alpha(t_1 - t)\right))}{(1 - \exp\left(-2\alpha(t_1 - t_0)\right))} = \frac{\phi_t}{2\alpha}.$$

The conditional mean can be obtained by noting that X_{t_0} and X_{t_1} are constants and the coefficients of X_t and X_t^2 in equation (2.11.14) must be the same. Comparing coefficients of X_t, we thus have

$$-2\mu_t = -2X_{t_0} \exp\left(-\alpha(t - t_0)\right) \left\{ \frac{1 - \exp\left(-2\alpha(t_1 - t)\right)}{1 - \gamma^2} \right\}$$
$$- 2X_{t_1} \exp\left(-\alpha(t_1 - t)\right) \left\{ \frac{1 - \exp\left(-2\alpha(t - t_0)\right)}{1 - \gamma^2} \right\}.$$

So the conditional mean μ_t is

$$\mu_t = X_{t_0} \exp\left(-\alpha(t - t_0)\right) \left\{ \frac{1 - \exp\left(-2\alpha(t_1 - t)\right)}{(1 - \gamma^2)} \right\}$$
$$+ X_{t_1} \exp\left(-\alpha(t_1 - t)\right) \left\{ \frac{1 - \exp\left(-2\alpha(t - t_0)\right)}{(1 - \gamma^2)} \right\}.$$

This completes the proof.

Relation to the Brownian Bridge

We will now prove that in the limit $(t_1 - t_0) \to 0$ the Brownian bridge result is obtained.

For the conditional mean, we have

$$\mu = X_{t_0} \exp\left(-\alpha(t - t_0)\right) \left\{ \frac{1 - \exp\left(-2\alpha(t_1 - t)\right)}{(1 - \gamma^2)} \right\}$$
$$+ X_{t_1} \exp\left(-\alpha(t_1 - t)\right) \left\{ \frac{1 - \exp\left(-2\alpha(t - t_0)\right)}{(1 - \gamma^2)} \right\},$$

where

$$\gamma = \exp\left(-\alpha(t_1 - t_0)\right),$$

which is

$$\mu = X_{t_0} \left\{ \frac{\exp\left(-\alpha(t - t_0)\right) - \exp\left(-2\alpha(t_1 - t)\right)}{(1 - \exp\left(-2\alpha(t_1 - t_0) - \alpha(t - t_0)\right))} \right\}$$
$$+ X_{t_1} \left\{ \frac{\exp\left(-\alpha(t_1 - t)\right) - \exp\left(-2\alpha(t - t_0) - \alpha(t_1 - t)\right)}{(1 - \exp\left(-2\alpha(t_1 - t_0)\right))} \right\}.$$

For small $(t_1 - t_0)$, both $(t_1 - t)$ and $(t - t_0)$ are small, so

$$\mu \to X_{t_0} \left\{ \frac{1 - \alpha(t - t_0) - \{1 - 2\alpha(t_1 - t) - \alpha(t - t_0)\}}{1 - \{1 - 2\alpha(t_1 - t_0)\}} \right\}$$
$$+ X_{t_1} \left\{ \frac{1 - \alpha(t_1 - t) - \{1 - 2\alpha(t - t_0) - \alpha(t_1 - t)\}}{1 - \{1 - 2\alpha(t_1 - t_0)\}} \right\},$$

which yields the Brownian bridge result for the conditional mean

$$\mu \to X_{t_0} \frac{(t_1 - t_0)}{(t_1 - t_0)} + X_{t_1} \frac{(t - t_0)}{(t_1 - t_0)}.$$

For the conditional variance,

$$V_t = \frac{(1 - \exp\left(-2\alpha(t - t_0)\right))(1 - \exp\left(-2\alpha(t_1 - t)\right))}{2\alpha(1 - \exp\left(-2\alpha(t_1 - t_0)\right))}.$$

For small $(t_1 - t_0)$, both $(t_1 - t)$ and $(t - t_0)$ are small, so we can write

$$V \to \frac{(1 - \{1 - 2\alpha(t - t_0)\})(1 - \{1 - 2\alpha(t_1 - t)\})}{2\alpha(1 - \{1 - 2\alpha(t_1 - t_0)\})},$$

which yields the Brownian bridge result for the conditional variance

$$V_t \to \frac{(t - t_0)(t_1 - t)}{(t_1 - t_0)}.$$

2.12 OTHER USEFUL RESULTS

2.12.1 Fubini's Theorem

Fubini's theorem states that (for well-behaved functions) the value of a multidimensional integral is independent of the order in which the integral is evaluated.

For example, the two-dimensional integral of the function $f(X,Y)$ can be evaluated as

$$\int_{X=a}^{b} \int_{Y=c}^{d} f(X,Y) dX dY = \int_{Y=c}^{d} \left\{ \int_{X=a}^{b} f(X,Y) dX \right\} dY$$
$$= \int_{X=a}^{b} \left\{ \int_{Y=c}^{d} f(X,Y) dY \right\} dX.$$

We will mainly use this result in the form

$$E\left[\int_{s=0}^{t} f(W,s) ds \right] = \int_{s=0}^{t} E\left[f(W,s) \right] ds. \tag{2.12.1}$$

Since

$$E\left[f(W,s) \right] = \int_{-\infty}^{\infty} P(W,s) f(W,s) dW,$$

where $P(W,s)$ is the probability density function of $f(W,s)$. We can thus write equation (2.12.1) in full as

$$\int_{W=-\infty}^{\infty} \left\{ \int_{s=0}^{t} P(W,s) f(W,s) ds \right\} dW = \int_{s=0}^{t} \left\{ \int_{W=-\infty}^{\infty} P(W,s) f(W,s) dW \right\} ds.$$

2.12.2 Ito's Isometry

The expected value of the integral of the well-behaved function $f(W_t,t)$ satisfies

$$E\left[\left(\int_{s=t_a}^{t_b} f(W_s,s) dW_s \right)^2 \right] = E\left[\int_{s=t_a}^{t_b} \{ f(W_s,s) \}^2 ds \right]. \tag{2.12.2}$$

Proof. We first use the following approximation:

$$\int_{s=t_a}^{s=t_b} f(W,s) dW_s = \sum_{i=0}^{n-1} f(W_{t_i},t_i) \{ W_{t_{i+1}} - W_{t_i} \},$$

where $t_a < t_0 < t_1 < \ldots < t_n < t_b$, $t_{i+1} - t_i = (t_b - t_a)/n = dt$, and $t_i = t_a + i dt, i = 0, \ldots, n - 1$. Thus, the integral on the left-hand side (LHS) of equation (2.12.2) is

$$\left(\int_{s=t_a}^{t_b} f(W_s,s)\,dW_s\right)^2 = \sum_{i=0}^{n-1}\sum_{j=0}^{n-1} f(W_{t_i},t_i)\,f\left(W_{t_j},t_j\right)\left\{W_{t_{i+1}} - W_{t_i}\right\}\left\{W_{t_{j+1}} - W_{t_j}\right\}.$$

(2.12.3)

Taking expectations of equation (2.12.3), we obtain

$$E\left[\left(\int_{s=t_a}^{t_b} f(W_s,s)\,dW_s\right)\right]^2$$
$$= E\left[\sum_{i=0}^{n-1}\sum_{j=0}^{n-1} f(W_{t_i},t_i)\,f\left(W_{t_j},t_j\right)\left\{W_{t_{i+1}} - W_{t_i}\right\}\left\{W_{t_{j+1}} - W_{t_j}\right\}\right],\qquad (2.12.4)$$

which means that

$$E\left[\left(\int_{s=t_a}^{t_b} f(W_s,s)\,dW_s\right)\right]^2$$
$$= \sum_{i=0}^{n-1}\sum_{j=0}^{n-1} f(W_{t_i},t_i)\,f\left(W_{t_j},t_j\right) E\left[\left\{W_{t_{i+1}} - W_{t_i}\right\}\left\{W_{t_{j+1}} - W_{t_j}\right\}\right].\qquad (2.12.5)$$

However from the Brownian motion property (iii) in Section 2.1, we have

$$E\left[\left\{W_{t_{i+1}} - W_{t_i}\right\}\left\{W_{t_{j+1}} - W_{t_j}\right\}\right] = 0 \quad \text{when } i \neq j \text{ and } dt \text{ when } i = j.$$

Therefore, equation (2.12.5) can be rewritten as

$$E\left[\left(\int_{s=t_a}^{t_b} f(W_s,s)\,dW_s\right)\right]^2 = \sum_{i=0}^{n-1}\left\{f(W_{t_i},t_i)\right\}^2 dt,$$

which means

$$E\left[\left(\int_{s=t_a}^{t_b} f(W_s,s)\,dW_s\right)\right]^2 = E\left[\int_{s=t_a}^{t_b}\left\{f(W_s,s)\right\}^2 ds\right].$$

2.12.3 Expectation of a Stochastic Integral

If $f(t)$ is a deterministic function of time, then

$$E\left[\int_{s=a}^{s=b} f(s)\,dW_s\right] = 0.\qquad (2.12.6)$$

Proof. We first express the integral (2.12.6) by the following summation:

$$\int_{s=t_a}^{s=t_b} f(s)\,dW_s = \sum_{i=0}^{n-1} f(t_i)\left\{W_{t_{i+1}} - W_{t_i}\right\}, \quad \text{where } a < t_0 < t_1 < \ldots < t_n < t_b.$$

Taking expectations of the above equation yields

$$E\left[\int_{s=a}^{s=b} f(s)\, dW_s\right] = E\left[\sum_{i=0}^{n-1} f(t_i)\{W_{t_{i+1}} - W_{t_i}\}\right]$$

$$= \sum_{i=0}^{n-1} f(t_i) E\left[W_{t_{i+1}} - W_{t_i}\right]$$

$$= 0,$$

where we have used $E\left[W_{t_{i+1}} - W_{t_i}\right] = 0$, which is Brownian motion property (iii) in Section 2.1.

2.13 SELECTED EXERCISES

In this section, we provide various problems which test the readers understanding of stochastic calculus.

Problem 1 (Problem 4.5, Øksendal (2003)). Let $\beta_t^k = E\left[W_t^k\right], k = 0, 1, 2, \ldots, \ t \geq 0$, where $W_{t_0} = 0$.

(a) Show using Ito's formula for $k = 2, 3, 4, \ldots$, that

$$\beta_t^k = \frac{1}{2}(k-1)\int_{s=0}^{t} \beta_s^{k-2}\, ds.$$

(b) Deduce that $E\left[W_t^4\right] = 3t^2$.
(c) What is $E\left[W_t^6\right]$.

Problem 2 (Problem 5.4 (ii), Øksendal (2003)). Solve the stochastic differential equation

$$dX_t = X_t dt + dW_t.$$

Problem 3 (Problem 5.4 (iii), Øksendal (2003)). Solve the stochastic differential equation

$$dX_t = -X_t dt + \exp(-t)\, dW_t.$$

Problem 4 (Problem 4.2, Øksendal (2003)). Use Ito's formula to prove that

$$\int_{s=0}^{t} W_s^2 dW_s = \frac{1}{3}W_t^3 - \int_{s=0}^{t} W_s ds,$$

where $W_{t_0} = 0$.

Problem 5 (Problem 5.6, Øksendal (2003)). Solve

$$dY_t = r dt + \alpha Y_t dW_t,$$

where r and α are real constants. Use the integrating factor $F_t = \exp\left[-\alpha W_t + (\alpha^2/2)t\right]$.

Problem 6 (Problem 5.7, Øksendal (2003)). The mean reverting Ornstein Uhlenbeck process is the solution X_t of the stochastic differential equation

$$dX_t = (m - X_t)\, dt + \sigma dW_t,$$

where m and σ are constants.

(a) Solve this equation.

(b) Find $E[X_t]$ and $Var[X_t] = E\left[\{X_t - E[X_t]\}^2\right]$.

Problem 7. Consider the equation $dS_t = \mu_t S_t dt + \sigma_t S_t dW_t$, where the value of S_t at time $t = 0$ is denoted by S_0.

(a) Show that the mean is

$$E[\log(S_t)] = \log(S_0) + \int_{\tau=0}^{t} \left\{\mu_\tau - \frac{\sigma_t^2}{2}\right\} d\tau.$$

(b) Show that the variance is

$$Var[\log(S_t)] = \int_{\tau=0}^{t} \sigma_\tau^2 d\tau.$$

Problem 8. Prove that if $\phi = \exp(tW_t)$, then

$$d\phi = \phi\left(W_t + \frac{t^2}{2}\right) dt + t\phi dW_t.$$

Problem 9 (Problem 4.4, Øksendal (2003)). Define

$$Z_t = \exp\left(\int_{s=0}^{t} \theta_s dW_s - \frac{1}{2}\int_{s=0}^{t} \theta_s^2 ds\right).$$

(a) Use Ito's formula to prove that

$$dZ_t = Z_t \theta_t dW_t.$$

Problem 10. Let $S_t = S_0 \exp(\mu t + \sigma W_t)$, where μ and σ are constants.

(a) Show by Ito's lemma that

$$dS_t = \left(\mu + \frac{\sigma^2}{2}\right) S_t dt + \sigma S_t dW_t.$$

(b) Show that

$$E[S_t] - E[S_0] = \left(\mu + \frac{\sigma^2}{2}\right) \int_{\tau=0}^{t} E[S(\tau)]\, d\tau.$$

(c) Show that

$$E[S_t] = S_0 \exp\left(\mu t + \frac{\sigma^2}{2}t\right).$$

Problem 11 (Problem 4.3, Øksendal (2003)). Let X_t, Y_t be stochastic processes. Prove that

$$d(X_t Y_t) = X_t dY_t + Y_t dX_t + E[dX_t dY_t].$$

Deduce the following general integration by parts formula:

$$\int_{s=0}^{t} X_s dY_s = X_t Y_t - X_{t_0} Y_{t_0} - \int_{s=0}^{t} Y_s dX_s - \int_{s=0}^{t} E[dX_s dY_s].$$

Chapter 3

Generation of Random Variates

3.1 INTRODUCTION

Monte Carlo simulation and random number generation are techniques that are widely used in financial engineering as a means of assessing the level of exposure to risk. Typical applications include the pricing of financial derivatives and scenario generation in portfolio management. In fact many of the financial applications that use Monte Carlo simulation involve the evaluation of various stochastic integrals which are related to the probabilities of particular events occurring.

In many cases however, the assumptions of constant volatility and a lognormal distribution for S_T are quite restrictive. Real financial applications may require a variety of extensions to the standard Black–Scholes model. Common requirements are for non-lognormal distributions, time varying volatilities, caps, floors, barriers, etc. In these circumstances, it is often the case that there is no closed form solution to the problem. Monte Carlo simulation can then provide a very useful means of evaluating the required integrals.

When we evaluate the integral of a function, $f(x)$, in the s-dimensional unit cube, I^S, by the Monte Carlo method, we are in fact calculating the average of the function at a set of randomly sampled points. This means that each point adds linearly to the accumulated sum that will become the integral and also linearly to the accumulated sum of squares that will become the variance of the integral.

When there are N sample points, the integral is

$$v = \frac{1}{N} \sum_{i=1}^{N} f(x^i),$$

where v is used to denote the approximation to the integral and $x^1, x^2, \ldots, x^N$ are the N, s-dimensional, sample points. If a pseudo-random number generator is used the points x^i will be (*should be*) independently and identically distributed. From standard statistical results, we can then estimate the expected error of the integral as follows.

If we set $\chi^i = f(x^i)$, then since x^i is independently and identically distributed, χ^i is also independently and identical distributed. The mean of χ^i is v and we will denote the variance as $Var[\chi^i] = \Delta^2$. It is a well-known statistical property that the variance of v is given by $Var[v] = N^{-1}\Delta^2$, see Appendix E.1

for further details. We can therefore conclude that the estimated integral v has a standard error of $N^{-1/2}\Delta$. This means that the estimated error of the integral will decrease at the rate of $N^{-1/2}$.

It is possible to achieve faster convergence than this if the sample points are chosen to lie on a Cartesian grid. If we sample each grid point exactly once, then the Monte Carlo method effectively becomes a deterministic quadrature scheme, whose fractional error decreases at the rate of N^{-1} or faster. The trouble with the grid approach is that it is necessary to decide in advance how fine it should be, and all the grid points need to be used. It is therefore not possible to sample until some convergence criterion has been met.

Quasi-random number sequences seek to bridge the gap between the flexibility of pseudo-random number generators and the advantages of a regular grid. They are designed to have a high level of uniformity in multidimensional space, but unlike pseudo-random numbers, they are not statistically independent.

3.2 PSEUDO-RANDOM AND QUASI-RANDOM SEQUENCES

Here, we consider the generation of multidimensional pseudo-random and quasi-random sequences to approximate the multidimensional uniform distribution over the interval $[0,1]$, that is, the distribution $U(0,1)$.

Quasi-random numbers are also called low-discrepancy sequences. The discrepancy of a sequence is a measure of its uniformity and is defined as follows.

Given a set of points $x^1, x^2, \ldots, x^N \in I^S$ and a subset $G \subset I^S$, define the counting function $S_N(G)$ as the number of points $x^i \in G$. For each $x = (x_1, x_2, \ldots, x_s) \in I^S$, let G_x be the rectangular s-dimensional region $G_x = [0, x_1) \times [0, x_2) \times \ldots \times [0, x_s)$, with volume $x_1, x_2, \ldots, x_n$. Then the discrepancy of the points $x^1, x^2, \ldots, x^N$ is given by

$$D_N^*(x^1, x^2, \ldots, x^N) = \sup_{x \in I^S} |S_N(G_x) - N x_1 x_2, \ldots, x_s|.$$

The discrepancy is therefore computed by comparing the actual number of sample points in a given volume of multidimensional space with the number of sample points that should be there assuming a uniform distribution.

It can be shown that the discrepancy of the first terms of quasi-random sequence has the form

$$D_N^*(x^1, x^2, \ldots, x^N) \leq C_S (\log N)^S + O((\log N)^{S-1}),$$

for all $N \geq 2$.

The principal aim in the construction of low-discrepancy sequences is thus to find sequences in which the constant is as small as possible. Various sequences have been constructed to achieve this goal. Here, we consider the following quasi-random sequences: Niederreiter, Sobol, and Faure.

Pseudo-random sequences

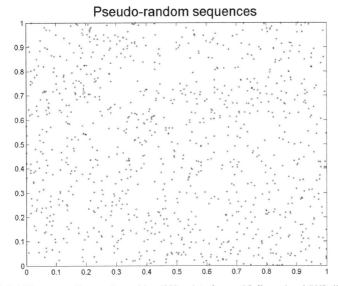

FIGURE 3.1 The scatter diagram formed by 1000 points from a 16-dimensional $U(0, 1)$ pseudo-random sequence. For each point, the 4th-dimension component is plotted against the 5th-dimension component.

The results of using various random number generators are shown below. Figures 3.1–3.3 illustrate the visual uniformity of the sequences. They were created by generating one thousand, 16-dimensional $U(0, 1)$ sample points, and then plotting the 4th-dimension component of each point against its 5th-dimension component.

In Fig. 3.1, it can be seen that the pseudo-random sequence exhibits clustering of points, and there are regions with no points at all.

Visual inspection of Fig. 3.2 and Fig. 3.3 shows that both the Sobol and Niederreiter quasi-random sequences appear to cover the area more uniformly.

It is interesting to note that the Sobol sequence appears to be a structured lattice which still has some gaps. The Niederreiter sequence on the other hand appears to be more irregular and covers the area better. However, we cannot automatically conclude from this that the Niederreiter sequence is the best. This is because we have not considered all the other possible pairs of dimensions.

Perhaps, the easiest way to evaluate the random number sequences is to use them to calculate an integral.

In Fig. 3.4, Monte Carlo results are presented for the calculation of the six-dimensional integral

$$I = \int_0^1 \int_0^1 \int_0^1 \int_0^1 \int_0^1 \int_0^1 \prod_{i=1}^6 \cos(ix_i)dx_1dx_2dx_3dx_4dx_5dx_6.$$

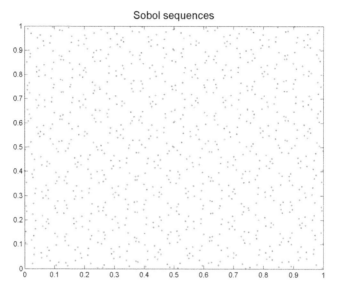

FIGURE 3.2 The scatter diagram formed by 1000 points from a 16-dimensional $U(0, 1)$ Sobol sequence. For each point, the 4th-dimension component is plotted against the 5th-dimension component.

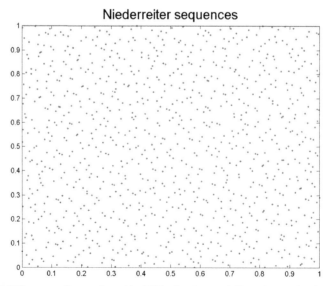

FIGURE 3.3 The scatter diagram formed by 1000 points from a 16-dimensional $U(0, 1)$ Niederreiter sequence. For each point, the 4th-dimension component is plotted against the 5th-dimension component.

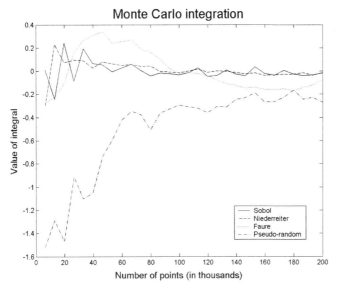

FIGURE 3.4 Monte Carlo integration using random numbers.

The exact value of this integral is

$$I = \prod_{i=1}^{6} \sin(i),$$

which for $i = 6$, gives $I = -0.0219$.

It can be seen that the pseudo-random sequence gives the worst performance. But as the number of points increases, its approximation to the integral improves. Of the quasi-random sequences, it can be seen that the Faure sequence has the worst performance, whilst both the Sobol and Niederreiter sequences give rapid convergence to the solution.

Finance literature contains many references to the benefits of using quasi-random numbers for computing important financial integrals. For instance, Brotherton-Ratcliffe (1994) discusses the use of Sobol sequences for the valuation of geometric mean stock options and provides results which show that the root mean squared pricing error obtained using quasi-random numbers is considerably less than that computed with pseudo-random numbers. Another financial application of quasi-random numbers is the efficient pricing mortgage backed securities (Caflisch et al., 1997). Here, Brownian bridge techniques are employed to reduce the effective dimension of the problem and thus provide greater pricing accuracy than if pseudo-random numbers were used.

3.3 GENERATION OF MULTIVARIATE DISTRIBUTIONS: INDEPENDENT VARIATES

In this section, we show how to generate multivariate distributions which contain independent variates, that is, the variates have zero correlation.

3.3.1 Normal Distribution

The most fundamental distribution is the univariate standard normal distribution, $N(0, 1)$, with zero mean and unit variance. In the case of p independent variates, this takes the form of a p variate independent normal distribution $N(0, I_p)$ with zero mean and $p \times p$ unit covariance matrix I_p.

First, we will quote a result concerning multivariate probability density functions, see Press et al. (1992). If $x_1, x_2, \ldots$ are random variates with a joint probability density function $p(x_1, x_2, \ldots)$, and if there are an equal number of y variates $y_1, y_2, \ldots$ that are functions of the x's, then the joint probability density function of the y variates, $p(y_1, y_2, \ldots)$, is given by the following expression:

$$p(y_1, y_2, \ldots) dy_1 dy_2, \ldots = p(x_1, x_2, \ldots) \mathcal{J}_{x,y} dy_1 dy_1, \tag{3.3.1}$$

where $\mathcal{J}_{x,y}$ is the Jacobian determinant of the x's with respect to the y's.

An important application of this result is the Box Muller transformation, see Box and Muller (1958), in which a p variate independent normal distribution $N(0, I_p)$ is generated from a p variate uniform distribution $U(0, 1)$.

The method works are follows.

Consider two independently distributed $N(0, 1)$ variables x and y, and use the polar transformation to obtain

$$x = r \cos \theta, \quad y = r \sin \theta, \quad \text{and} \quad r^2 = x^2 + y^2. \tag{3.3.2}$$

From equation (3.3.1), the joint probability density functions $f(r, \theta)$ and $f(x, y)$ obey the equation

$$f(r, \theta)\, dr\, d\theta = f(x, y) \mathcal{J}_{xy, r\theta}\, dr\, d\theta,$$

where the Jacobian is

$$\mathcal{J}_{xy, r\theta} = \begin{vmatrix} \cos \theta & \sin \theta \\ -r \sin \theta & r \cos \theta \end{vmatrix} = r.$$

We therefore have

$$f(r, \theta) = r f(x, y). \tag{3.3.3}$$

Furthermore, since x and y are independent $N(0, 1)$,

$$f(x, y) = f(x) f(y),$$

where

$$f(x) = \frac{e^{-x^2/2}}{\sqrt{2\pi}} \quad \text{and} \quad f(y) = \frac{e^{-y^2/2}}{\sqrt{2\pi}}.$$

Therefore,

$$f(r,\theta) = r f(x) f(y) = r \frac{e^{-x^2/2}}{\sqrt{2\pi}} \frac{e^{-y^2/2}}{\sqrt{2\pi}},$$

which gives

$$f(r,\theta) = \frac{r}{2\pi} e^{(-x^2+y^2)/2} = \frac{1}{2\pi} r e^{-r^2/2} = f(\theta) f(r), \tag{3.3.4}$$

where $f(\theta) = \dfrac{1}{2\pi}$, $f(r) = r e^{-r^2/2}$ are independent probability density functions.

The corresponding cumulative probability distribution functions $F(\theta)$ and $F(r)$ can be found by evaluating the following integrals:

$$F(\theta) = \frac{1}{2\pi} \int_0^\theta d\theta = \frac{\theta}{2\pi}$$

and

$$F(r) = \int_0^r r e^{-r^2/2} dr = \left[-e^{-r^2/2} \right]_0^r = 1 - e^{-r^2/2}.$$

We can now use the result, see, for example, Evans et al. (2000), that any variate x with a probability density function $f(x)$ has a cumulative distribution function $F(x) = \int_{-\infty}^x f(x) dx$, which is $F(x) \sim U(0,1)$, where $U(0,1)$ is the uniform distribution between 0 and 1.

The variables $V_1' = F(r) = 1 - e^{-r^2/2}$ and $V_2' = F(\theta) = \dfrac{\theta}{2\pi}$ are therefore uniformly distributed on the interval $(0,1)$.

For convenience, we will define the, $U(0,1)$, variables

$$V_1 = 1 - V_1' = e^{-r^2/2} \quad \text{and} \quad V_2 = V_2'.$$

So we have

$$V_1 = e^{-r^2/2}, \quad V_2 = \frac{\theta}{2\pi}.$$

Therefore,

$$\log V_1 = -r^2/2, \quad r = (-2 \log V_1)^{1/2}, \quad \text{and} \quad \theta = 2\pi V_2.$$

Substituting these results into equation (3.3.2) gives

$$x = (-2 \log V_1)^{1/2} \cos 2\pi V_2, \quad y = (-2 \log V_1)^{1/2} \sin 2\pi V_2, \tag{3.3.5}$$

where x and y are $N(0,1)$.

The Box Muller method is contained in equation (3.3.5), which shows that the $N(0,1)$ variates are generated in pairs from the uniform $U(0,1)$ variates V_1 and V_2.

Since the $N(0,1)$ variates are created two at a time, if we want to generate a normal distribution with an odd number of dimensions, n_{odd}, it is necessary to generate $n_{odd} + 1$ dimensions and discard one of the dimensions.

It is easy to modify equation (3.3.5) so that we can specify the means and variances of the variates x and y; this is accomplished as follows:

$$x = \sigma_1 (-2 \log V_1)^{1/2} \cos 2\pi V_2 + \mu_1, \quad y = \sigma_2 (-2 \log V_1)^{1/2} \sin 2\pi V_2 + \mu_2, \tag{3.3.6}$$

where the distributions of x and y are now

$$x \sim N(\mu_1, \sigma_1^2) \quad \text{and} \quad y \sim N(\mu_2, \sigma_2^2).$$

Code excerpt 3.1 illustrates how to generate quasi-random normal variates with given means and standard deviations.

```
long Quasi_Normal_Independent(long fcall, long seq, double xmean[], double std[], long idim, double quasi[])
{
/* Input parameters:
   ==================
   fcall   -  if fcall == 1 then it is an initialisation call, if fcall == 0 then a continuation call
   seq     -  if seq == 0 then a Faure sequence, if seq == 1 then a Niederreiter sequence,
              if seq == 2 then a Sobol sequence
   xmean[] -  the means of the independent Normal variates
   std[]   -  the standard deviations of the independent Normal variates
   idim    -  the number of independent Normal variates, idim must be less than 40
   Output parameters:
   ==================
   quasi[] -  the elements quasi[0], .. quasi[idim-1] contain the independent Normal variates
*/

long ierr, i, j;
double twopi, v1, v2, pi;
long ind1, ind2;
#define QUASI(I) quasi[(I)-1]
#define STD(I) std[(I)-1]
#define XMEAN(I) xmean[(I)-1]

    if ((idim / 2) * 2 != idim) {
        printf("Error on entry, idim is not an even number: idim = %ld\n" ,idim);
        return 1;
    } else if (idim > 40) {
        printf("On entry, idim > 40: idim = %ld\n" ,idim);
        return 1;
    }
    for (i = 1; i <= idim; ++i) {
        if (STD(i) <= 0.0) {
            printf("On entry, the standard deviation is not greater than zero: STD(%ld) = %12.4f\n" ,i,STD(i));
            return 1;
        }
    }
    pi = 4.0*atan(1.0);
    if (fcall) { /* first call for initialisation */
        if (seq == 0) {
          Generate_Faure_Sequence(fcall, idim, &QUASI(1));
        }
        else if (seq == 1) {
            Generate_Niederreiter_Sequence(fcall, idim, &QUASI(1));
        }
        else if (seq == 2) {
            Generate_Sobol_Sequence(fcall, idim, &QUASI(1));
        }
    } else { /* a continuation call */
        if (seq == 0) {
            Generate_Faure_Sequence(fcall, idim, &QUASI(1));
        }
        else if (seq == 1) {
            Generate_ Niederreiter_Sequence(fcall, idim, &QUASI(1));
        }
        else if (seq == 2) {
            Generate_Sobol_Sequence(fcall, idim, &QUASI(1));
        }
        for (i = 1; i <= idim/2; ++i) { /* generate the normal variates */
            ind1 = i * 2 - 1;
            ind2 = i * 2;
            twopi = pi * 2.0;
            v1 = sqrt(log(QUASI(ind1)) * -2.0);
            v2 = twopi * QUASI(ind2);
            QUASI(ind1) = XMEAN(ind1) + STD(ind1) * v1 * cos(v2);
            QUASI(ind2) = XMEAN(ind2) + STD(ind2) * v1 * sin(v2);
        }
    }
    return 0 ;
}
```

Code excerpt 3.1 Generating quasi-random normal variates using the Box Muller transformation.

3.3.2 Lognormal Distribution

The lognormal distribution can be generated from the normal distribution discussed in the previous section by means of a simple transformation. If $y \sim N(\mu, \sigma^2)$ and $y = \log(x)$ then $x = \exp(y)$, and we say that the variable x has the lognormal distribution $\Lambda(\mu, \sigma^2)$.

The lognormal density function is

$$f(x) = \frac{1}{x\sigma(2\pi)^{1/2}} \times \exp\left(\frac{-(\log x - \mu)^2}{2\sigma^2}\right). \tag{3.3.7}$$

If $z_i, i = 1, \ldots, p$ are independent normal variates $N(\mu_i, \sigma_i^2), i = 1, \ldots, p$, then lognormal variates $\ell_i, i = 1, \ldots, p$ can be generated using the transformation

$$\ell_i = \exp(z_i), \quad i = 1, \ldots, p, \tag{3.3.8}$$

where the mean of the ith lognormal variate is

$$E[x_i] = \bar{m}_i = \exp\left(\mu_i + \frac{\sigma_i^2}{2}\right), \tag{3.3.9}$$

and the variance is

$$Var[x_i] = s_i^2 = \exp(2\mu_i + \sigma_i^2)\left(\exp(\sigma_i^2) - 1\right). \tag{3.3.10}$$

The ratio of variance to the mean squared is therefore

$$\frac{s_i^2}{\bar{m}_i^2} = \exp(\sigma_i^2) - 1 \tag{3.3.11}$$

or equivalently

$$\sigma_i^2 = \log\left(1 + \frac{s_i^2}{\bar{m}_i^2}\right). \tag{3.3.12}$$

A lognormal distribution consisting of p independent variates with means $\bar{m}_i, i = 1, \ldots, p$ and variances $s_i^2, i = 1, \ldots, p$ can thus be generated using the following procedure.

First, generate the p independent normal variates

$$z_i \sim N(\mu_i, \sigma_i^2), \quad i = 1, \ldots, p,$$

where

$$\mu_i = \log(\bar{m}_i) - \frac{\sigma_i^2}{2} \tag{3.3.13}$$

and

$$\sigma_i^2 = \log\left(1 + \frac{s_i^2}{\bar{m}_i^2}\right). \tag{3.3.14}$$

Then create the independent lognormal variates using

$$\ell_i = \exp(z_i), \quad i = 1, \ldots, p.$$

3.3.3 Student's *t*-Distribution

If $S_t(\mu, \nu)$ represents the Student's *t*-distribution with mean μ and number of degrees of freedom ν, then variates $X \sim S_t(0, \nu)$ can be generated as follows:

$$X \sim \frac{Z}{\sqrt{Y/\nu}}, \tag{3.3.15}$$

where $Z \sim N(0, 1)$ and $Y \sim \chi_\nu^2$. The variance of X is

$$E[X^2] = \frac{\nu}{\nu - 2}.$$

Variates X' from a Student's *t*-distribution having ν degrees of freedom with mean μ and variance s can be generated by modifying equation (3.3.15) as follows:

$$X' \sim \mu + \frac{s^{1/2}}{\sqrt{\nu/(\nu - 2)}} \frac{Z}{\sqrt{Y/\nu}}. \tag{3.3.16}$$

The probability density function, $f(x)$, for X' is

$$f(x) = \frac{\Gamma((\nu + 1)/2)(\nu - 2)^{-1/2}s^{-1/2}}{\pi^{1/2}\Gamma(\nu/2)} \left[1 + \frac{(x - \mu)^2}{s(\nu - 2)}\right]^{-(\nu+1)/2}, \tag{3.3.17}$$

where $\nu > 2$.

3.4 GENERATION OF MULTIVARIATE DISTRIBUTIONS: CORRELATED VARIATES

In this section, we will show how to generate variates from a multivariate distribution with a known mean and a given covariance or correlation matrix. The methods described for covariance matrices are also applicable to correlation matrices, although in this case the generated variates are normalized to have unit variance.

3.4.1 Estimation of Correlation and Covariance

Here, we show how to obtain a valid correlation matrix C_r or covariance matrix C from historic market data.

Let $\hat{X}$ be an n by p data matrix, with the entries in the ith row corresponding to the ith observation, and the jth column containing the values of the jth variable. If we create a new matrix X such that the entries of the jth column of X are $X_{i,j} = \hat{X}_{i,j} - \mu_j, i = 1, \ldots, n$, where μ_j is the mean of the jth column of $\hat{X}$, then the p by p matrix $C = X^T X$ is the covariance matrix of $\hat{X}$.

Further, if another matrix $\bar{X}$ is defined such that $\bar{X}_{i,j} = \frac{\hat{X}_{i,j} - \mu_j}{\sigma_j}, i = 1, \ldots, n$, where μ_j is the mean of the jth column of $\hat{X}$, and σ_j is the standard deviation of the jth column, then the p by p matrix $C_r = \bar{X}^T \bar{X}$ is the correlation matrix of $\hat{X}$.

Correlation matrix

Let us first consider the properties of a valid correlation matrix. They are the following:

- The matrix is symmetric with unit diagonal.
- The matrix has to be positive definite, that is, all the eigenvalues need to be positive.

We will now show that the p by p matrix C_r is a valid correlation matrix if it can be factored as $C_r = X^T X$, where X is a non-singular n by m data matrix.

The proof is as follows:

Since X is non-singular, we can perform the singular value decomposition

$$X = UKV^T,$$

where U is a n by n unitary matrix, K is a n by p matrix containing the (nonzero) singular values $\sigma_i, i = 1, \ldots, p$, as the *diagonal* elements and zero elsewhere, and V is a p by p unitary matrix.

We thus have

$$
\begin{aligned}
X^T X &= (U\,K\,V^T)^T\,U\,K\,V^T \\
&= V\,K^T\,U^T\,U\,K\,V^T \\
&= V^T\,K^T K V^T \qquad \text{since } U^T U = UU^T = I_n \\
&= V\,\Sigma V^T.
\end{aligned}
$$

Therefore,

$$C_r = X^T X = V\,\Sigma V^T,$$

where Σ is the p by p diagonal matrix containing the eigenvalues of C_r, and V is the corresponding matrix of eigenvectors. Since the ith eigenvalue satisfies $\lambda_i = \sigma_i^2$, it can be seen that all the eigenvalues are positive, and thus, C_r must be positive definite. *QED*

If C_r is positive definite, then we can perform the Cholesky decomposition $C_r = L\,L^T$ where L is a lower triangular matrix.

3.4.2 Repairing Correlation and Covariance Matrices

There are situations when a supplied *correlation* matrix is not positive definite. Some of the reasons for this are the following:

- There may be missing data, or asynchronous data feeds. As a consequence, the elements in the correlation matrix may have then been computed using pairwise correlations, with a variety of sequence lengths. Under these circumstances, the equation $C_r = X^T X$ is no longer true, and so C_r cannot be guaranteed to be positive definite.

- Manual adjustment of a correlation matrix may have occurred to reflect expected market conditions. This especially occurs when the market crashes and certain stock prices become highly correlated.
- There may be rounding error in computing $C_r = X^T X$.

Under these circumstances, the best that can be done is to try and repair the correlation matrix C_r into a valid correlation matrix $\hat{C}_r$.

We proceed as follows.

When C_r is not positive definite (the Cholesky decomposition fails), then we use the eigen decomposition

$$C_r = V \Sigma V^T,$$

where

$$\Sigma = \begin{pmatrix} \lambda_1 & & & \\ & \lambda_2 & & \\ & & \cdot & \\ & & & \cdot \\ & & & & \lambda_p \end{pmatrix};$$

we then form the matrix

$$C_r^+ = V K K^T V^T = V K (V K)^T,$$

where the matrix K is formed by taking the square root of the maximum of each eigenvalue and a very small number ϵ (say $\sim 10^{-16}$). Thus,

$$K = \begin{pmatrix} \sqrt{\max(\lambda_1, \epsilon)} & & & \\ & \sqrt{\max(\lambda_2, \epsilon)} & & \\ & & \cdot & \\ & & & \cdot \\ & & & & \sqrt{\max(\lambda_p, \epsilon)} \end{pmatrix}.$$

The matrix C_r^+ is not acceptable as a correlation matrix because, although real, symmetric, and positive definite, its diagonal elements are not unity. It is possible to remedy this by pre- and post-multiplying C^+ by the diagonal matrix F,

$$\hat{C}_r = F C_r^+ F = F C_r^+ F^T,$$

where $\hat{C}$ is the new *repaired* correlation matrix, i.e., it is positive definite, symmetric and has unit diagonal elements. To achieve this, the diagonal elements of F must be given by

$$F_{ii} = \frac{1}{\sqrt{C_{r_{ii}}^+}}.$$

We thus have

$$
\begin{aligned}
\hat{C}_r &= F \, C_r^+ \, F^T \\
&= F \, V \, K \, (V \, K)^T \, F^T \\
&= (F \, V \, K)(K^T \, V^T \, F^T) \\
&= (F \, V \, K)(F \, V \, K)^T.
\end{aligned}
\tag{3.4.1}
$$

An *optimally repaired* correlation matrix C_r^*, which minimizes the distance $\|C_r - C_r^*\|$, can be obtained via numerical optimization on the n-dimensional unit hypersphere; this is described below.

However, it has been found that $\hat{C}_r$ is a very good approximation for the optimal estimate C_r^*.

Optimally repaired correlation matrix

Here, we provide details of how to obtain an optimally repaired correlation matrix by using hyperspherical coordinates, see Rebonato and Jäckel (1999) – for a different approach see Higham (2002) or Qi and Sun (2006).

The Cartesian coordinates of the ith point on an n-dimensional hypersphere with radius r can be shown to be

$$
\begin{aligned}
x_{i,1} &= r \cos(\theta_{i,1}), \\
x_{i,2} &= r \sin(\theta_{i,1}) \cos(\theta_{i,2}), \\
x_{i,3} &= r \sin(\theta_{i,1}) \sin(\theta_{i,2}) \cos(\theta_{i,3}), \\
x_{i,4} &= r \sin(\theta_{i,1}) \sin(\theta_{i,2}) \sin(\theta_{i,3}) \cos(\theta_{i,4}),
\end{aligned}
$$

$$
\begin{aligned}
. \quad . \quad . \\
x_{i,n-1} &= r \sin(\theta_{i,1}) \sin(\theta_{i,2}). \; . \; . \; \sin(\theta_{i,n-3}) \sin(\theta_{i,n-2}) \cos(\theta_{i,n-1}), \\
x_{i,n} &= r \sin(\theta_{i,1}) \sin(\theta_{i,2}). \; . \; . \; \sin(\theta_{i,n-2}) \sin(\theta_{i,n-1}),
\end{aligned}
$$

where $\theta_{i,1}$ are spherical coordinates and have the following constraints: $0 \le \theta_{i,k} \le \pi$, $k = 1,\ldots,n-2$, and $0 \le \theta_{i,n-1} \le 2\pi$.

By construction, the radius of the sphere satisfies

$$
r^2 = \sum_{k=1}^{n} (x_{i,k})^2.
$$

This can be seen as follows:

$$
\begin{aligned}
\left(B^T B\right)_{i,i} &= r^2 \left\{ \cos^2(\theta_{i,1}) + \sin^2(\theta_{i,1}) \left(\cos^2(\theta_{i,2}) + \sin^2(\theta_{i,2})\right) \left(\cos^2(\theta_{i,3}) + \sin^2(\theta_{i,3})\right) \right. \\
&\quad \times \left. \left(\cos^4(\theta_{i,1}) \; + \; + \; + \; \sin^2(\theta_{i,n-2}) \left(\cos^2(\theta_{i,n-1}) + \sin^2(\theta_{i,n-1})\right) \, . \, . \, \right) \right\} \\
&= r^2,
\end{aligned}
$$

where we have used

$$
\cos^2(\theta_{i,k}) + \sin^2(\theta_{i,k}) = 1, \quad k = 1,\ldots,n-1.
$$

If, when $r = 1$, the coordinates of n-hyperspherical points are stored in the n rows of the n by n matrix B^T, then

$$B_{i,1}^T = \cos\left(\theta_{i,1}\right),$$

$$B_{i,j}^T = \cos(\theta_{i,j}) \prod_{k=1}^{j-1} \sin(\theta_{i,k}) \quad j = 2,\ldots,n-1,$$

$$B_{i,n}^T = \prod_{k=1}^{n-1} \sin(\theta_{i,k}), \quad n > 1,$$

$$B^T = \begin{pmatrix} \cos(\theta_{1,1}) & \sin(\theta_{1,1})\cos(\theta_{1,2}) & \sin(\theta_{1,1})\sin(\theta_{1,2})\cos(\theta_{1,3}) & \cdots \\ \cos(\theta_{2,1}) & \sin(\theta_{2,1})\cos(\theta_{2,2}) & \sin(\theta_{2,1})\sin(\theta_{2,2})\cos(\theta_{2,3}) & \cdots \\ \cos(\theta_{3,1}) & \sin(\theta_{3,1})\cos(\theta_{3,2}) & \sin(\theta_{3,1})\sin(\theta_{3,2})\cos(\theta_{3,3}) & \cdots \\ \cdot & \cdot & \cdot & \cdot \\ \cdot & \cdot & \cdot & \cdot \\ \cdot & \cdot & \cdot & \cdot \end{pmatrix}.$$

It can thus be seen that the diagonal elements of $B^T B$ are

$$\left(B^T B\right)_{i,i} = \sum_{k=1}^{n} \left(x_{i,k}\right)^2 = 1.$$

The Cholesky decomposition can be formed by setting the angles of the upper triangular elements of B^T to zero, and this results in

$$L^T = \begin{pmatrix} 1 & 0 & 0 & \cdots \\ \cos(\theta_{2,1}) & \sin(\theta_{2,1}) & 0 & \cdots \\ \cos(\theta_{3,1}) & \sin(\theta_{3,1})\cos(\theta_{3,2}) & \sin(\theta_{3,1})\sin(\theta_{3,2}) & \cdots \\ \cdot & \cdot & \cdot & \cdot \\ \cdot & \cdot & \cdot & \cdot \end{pmatrix},$$

$$L_{1,1}^T = 1,$$

$$L_{i,1}^T = \cos(\theta_{i,1}),$$

$$L_{i,j}^T = \cos(\theta_{i,j}) \prod_{k=1}^{j-1} \sin(\theta_{i,k}), \quad j = 2,\ldots,i-1,$$

$$L_{i,i}^T = \prod_{k=1}^{i-1} \sin(\theta_{i,k}), \quad i > 1,$$

$$L_{i,j}^T = 0, \quad j = i+1,\ldots,n.$$

We want to find the positive definite matrix C_r^* which minimizes $\|C_r - C_r^*\|$. This can be found by writing

$$C_r^* = L^T L$$

and using numerical optimization to determine the appropriate $n(n-1)/2$ angles. An initial approximation can be obtained by computing the Cholesky factorization $\hat{C}_r = \hat{L}^T\hat{L}$ and then calculating the angles corresponding to each nonzero element of $\hat{L}^T$.

Covariance matrix

We will now consider the case when a covariance matrix C is supplied which is not positive definite – that is there is no Cholesky decomposition $C = L^T L$, where L is lower triangular.

In these circumstances, since a covariance matrix does not require unit diagonal elements, it is possible to repair C using

$$C^+ = VK(VK)^T,$$

where V and K have the same meanings as before. A better approximation could be obtained via numerical optimization of the elements of the Cholesky decomposition; however, these optimal points are no longer constrained to lie on the n-dimensional unit hypersphere.

3.4.3 Normal Distribution

Here, we show how to generate a p variate normal distribution with a given mean and covariance matrix.

We will denote the vector containing the variates of the ith observation from a p variate zero mean normal distribution by Z_i, that is, we write a sample of n observations as

$$Z_i \sim N(0,C), \quad i = 1,\ldots,n, \tag{3.4.2}$$

where C is the $p \times p$ covariance matrix.

Further $Z_{i,k}$ is used to denote the kth element of Z_i, which contains the value of the kth variate for the ith observation.

From a computational point of view, we can then consider a sample of n observations to be represented by the $n \times p$ matrix Z. The ith row of Z contains the values for ith observation, and the kth column of the ith row, $Z_{i,k}$, contains the value of the kth variate for the ith observation.

Also, since the distribution has zero mean, the sample covariance matrix is given by $C = Z^T Z$

To generate variates with covariance matrix C, we can use the fact that if the matrix C is positive definite, a Cholesky factorization exists in which

$$C = AA^T, \tag{3.4.3}$$

where A is lower triangular.

We can therefore generate p variates which have a covariance matrix C as follows.

First, generate, by (for example) using the Box Muller method described in Section 3.3.1, the independent normal variates

$$X \sim N(0,I_p),$$

where the vector X contains the p variates, I_p is the unit matrix, and XX^T $= I_p$.

Then, using the Cholesky factorization of equation (3.4.4), form

$$Y = AX, \qquad (3.4.4)$$

where Y is a p element vector.

Now since $YY^T = AX(AX)^T = A(XX^T)A^T = AA^T = C$, we have that

$$Y \sim N(0, C).$$

Variates that have nonzero means $\mu_k, k = 1, \ldots, p$ can be obtained by simply modifying equation (3.4.4) to

$$Y' = AX + \mu, \qquad (3.4.5)$$

where Y' is a p variate vector that is distributed as $N(\mu, C)$, and the p elements of vector μ contain the means of the variates $Y'_k, k = 1, \ldots, p$.

If the matrix C is not positive definite, then we can create a repaired matrix, $\hat{C}$, by using the approach outlined in Section 3.4.2.

We now use the decomposition

$$\hat{C} = VK(VK)^T.$$

Under these circumstances, the p element vectors Y and Y' are generated using the following modified versions of equation (3.4.4) and equation (3.4.5):

$$Y = VKX \quad \text{and} \quad Y' = VKX + \mu. \qquad (3.4.6)$$

The method for generating variates Y from a given correlation matrix C_r is identical. However, in this case, non-positive definite matrices are repaired as $\hat{C}_r = FVK(FVK)^T$, see Section 3.4.2.

A function to generate correlated normal and lognormal variates is given in Code excerpt 3.2.

```
long Quasirandom_Normal_LogNormal_Correlated(long fcall, long seq, long lnorm, double means[], long n,
                double c[], long tdc, double tol, long *irank, double x[], double work[], long lwk) {

/* Input parameters:
   =================
   fcall    -  if fcall == 1 then it is an initialisation call, if fcall == 0 then a continuation call
   seq      -  if seq == 0 then a Faure sequence, if seq == 1 then a Niederreiter sequence,
               if seq == 2 then a Sobol sequence
   lnorm    -  if lnorm == 1 then it is a lognormal distribution, if lnorm == 0 then a normal distribution
   n        -  the number of variates, n must be less than 40
   c[]      -  a matrix which contains the required covariance matrix, C
   tdc      -  the second dimension of the matrix C
   tol      -  the tolerance used for calculating the rank of the covariance matrix C
   means[]  -  the means of the independent Normal variates
   std[]    -  the standard deviations of the independent Normal variates
   lwk      -  the size of the work array, work

   Output parameters:
   =================
   rank     -  the computed rank of the covariance matrix C
   x[]      -  the elements x[0], .. x[n-1] contain the variates
```

Code excerpt 3.2 The functions `Quasirandom_Normal_LogNormal_Correlated` which generate correlated quasi-random normal variates and correlated quasi-random lognormal variates.

```
   Input/Output parameters:
   =========================
   work     -   a work array
*/

   double zero = 0.0, one = 1.0, two = 2.0;
   long n1, i, j, k, kk;
   double mtol, alpha;
   long ptrc, ptre, ptrv, ptrw, ptrw0, ptrw1;

#define C(I,J) c[((I)-1) * tdc + ((J)-1)]
#define MEANS(I) means[(I)-1]
#define X(I) x[(I)-1]
#define WORK(I) work[((I)-1]

       if (lwk < (2 + 3*n + 2*n*n + 3)) {
          printf ("Error lwk is too small \n");
          return 1;
       }
       ptre = 2;
       ptrv = n+2;
       ptrw = n*n + n + 2;
/* add extra 1 to allow for odd values of n */
       ptrw0 = ptrw + 1 + n;
       ptrw1 = ptrw0 + 1 + n;
       ptrc  = ptrw1 + n + 1;
       n1 = n;
       if (((n/2)*2) != n) { /*  test for odd n */
          n1 = n + 1;
       }
       if (fcall) {  /* first call for initialisation */
          if (lnorm) { /* lognormal distribution */
             for (i = 1; i <=n; ++i) { /* Load the modified covariance matrix into WORK */
                for (j = 1; j <= n; ++j) {
                   WORK(ptrc+(i-1)*n+j-1) = log(one + C(i,j)/(MEANS(i)*MEANS(j)));
                }
             }
          }
          else { /* normal distribution */
             for (i = 1; i <=n; ++i) { /* Load the covariance matrix into WORK */
                for (j = 1; j <= n; ++j) {
                   WORK(ptrc+(i-1)*n+j-1) = C(i,j);
                }
             }
          }
          /* calculate the eigenvalues and eigenvector of the matrix that has been loaded into WORK */
          calc_eigvals_eigvecs (n,&WORK(ptrc),n,&WORK(ptre),&WORK(ptrv),n);
          *irank = 0;
/*        printf ("The eigenvalues are \n");
          for (j=n; j >= 1; --j) {
             printf ("%12.5f \n", WORK(ptre+j-1));
          }
*/
          for (j=n; j >= 1; --j) { /* use the eigenvalues to calculate the rank of the matrix */
             if (WORK(ptre+j-1) < tol) goto L24;
             *irank = *irank + 1;
          }
          printf ("*irank = %ld \n",*irank);
          L24:
          mtol = -tol;
          if (WORK(ptre) < mtol) {
             printf ("Warning there is an eigenvalue less than %12.4f \n",mtol);
          }
          for (j=1; j <= *irank; ++j) {
             kk = 1;
             for (k=1; k <=n; ++k) {
                if(WORK(ptrv+(k-1)*n+(j-1)) != zero) goto L28;
                kk = kk + 1;
             }
             L28:
             /* ensure that all eigenvectors have the same sign on different machines */
             alpha = sqrt(WORK(ptre+j-1));
             if  (WORK(ptrv+(kk-1)*n+(j-1)) < zero)  alpha = -sqrt(WORK(ptre+j-1));
             for (i = 1; i <= n; ++i) {
                WORK(ptrv+(j-1)+(i-1)*n)=WORK(ptrv+(j-1)+(i-1)*n)*alpha;
             }
          }
/*        printf ("The eigenvectors are \n");
          for (j=1; j <= *irank; ++j) {
             for (i = 1; i <= n; ++i) {
                printf ("%10.5f ", WORK(ptrv+(j-1)+(i-1)*n));
             }
             printf ("\n");
          }
```

Code excerpt 3.2 (*Continued*).

```
*/
      for (i = 1; i <=n; ++i) { /* store a vector of ones and zeros for generating the quasi-random numbers */
         WORK(ptrw0+i-1) = zero;
         WORK(ptrw1+i-1) = one;
      }
      for (i = n; i <= n1; ++ i) {
         WORK(ptrw0+i-1) = zero;
         WORK(ptrw1+i-1) = one;
      }
   } /* end of first  call section */

 /* generate a vector of n1 random variables from a standard normal distribution, zero mean and unit variance */
      Quasi_Normal_Independent(&call, seq, &WORK(ptrw0), &WORK(ptrw1),  n1, &WORK(ptrw));

/*    printf ("The quasi random numbers are:\n");
      for (i = 1; i <= n; ++i) {
         printf ("%12.4f \n", WORK(ptrw+(i-1)));
      }
*/
   /* Now generate variates with the specified mean and variance */
      if (lnorm) { /* a lognormal distribution */
         for (i = 1; i <= n; ++i) {
            X(i) =  log(MEANS(i)) - WORK(ptrc+(i-1)*n+i-1)/two;
            for (k = 1; k <= *irank; ++k) {
               X(i)=X(i)+WORK(ptrv+(k-1)+(i-1)*n)*WORK(ptrw+k-1);
            }
         }
         for (i = 1; i <= n; ++i) {
            X(i) = exp(X(i));
         }
      }
      else { /* a normal distribution */
         for (i = 1; i <= n; ++i) {
            X(i) =  MEANS(i);
            for (k = 1; k <= *irank; ++k) {
               X(i)=X(i)+WORK(ptrv+(k-1)+(i-1)*n)*WORK(ptrw+k-1);
            }
         }
      }
/*    printf ("The generated variates are:\n");
      for (i = 1; i <= n; ++i) {
         printf (" %12.4f \n", X(i));
      }
*/
      return 0;
   }
```

Code excerpt 3.2 (*Continued*).

In order to visualize the effect of the covariance matrix, we will display the results of using function `Quasirandom_Normal_LogNormal_Correlated` to generate the following variates:

- A vector of three normal independent variates with covariance matrix

$$C_1 = \begin{pmatrix} 1.0 & 0.0 & 0.0 \\ 0.0 & 1.0 & 0.0 \\ 0.0 & 0.0 & 1.0 \end{pmatrix}.$$

- A vector of three normal variates in which the elements of the covariance matrix are all positive; the covariance matrix is

$$C_2 = \begin{pmatrix} 1.0 & 0.8 & 0.8 \\ 0.8 & 1.0 & 0.8 \\ 0.8 & 0.8 & 1.0 \end{pmatrix}.$$

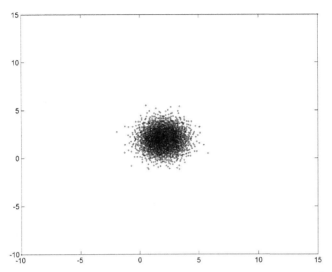

FIGURE 3.5 Scatter diagram for a sample of 3000 observations (Z_i, $i = 1, \ldots, 3000$) generated from a multivariate normal distribution consisting of three variates with covariance matrix C_1 and mean μ. Here, we plot the values of the first variate against the values of the second variate. If we use the notation of equation (3.4.2), then the (x, y) co-ordinates for the points are $x_i = Z_{i,1}$, $i = 1, \ldots, 3000$, and $y_i = Z_{i,2}$, $i = 1, \ldots, 3000$.

- A vector of three normal variates in which two elements of the covariance matrix are negative; the covariance matrix is

$$C_3 = \begin{pmatrix} 1.0 & -0.7 & 0.2 \\ -0.7 & 1.0 & 0.2 \\ 0.2 & 0.2 & 1.0 \end{pmatrix}.$$

In all case the mean vector is given by

$$\mu = \begin{pmatrix} 2.0 \\ 2.0 \\ 2.0 \end{pmatrix}.$$

The results are displayed in Figs 3.5–3.7.

3.4.4 Lognormal Distribution

The multivariate lognormal distribution is important because it is the asset returns distribution assumed by the Black–Scholes equation.

Let the p element vectors Y and X be related by $Y = \log(X)$ where $Y \sim N(\mu, \Sigma)$, μ is a p element vector, and Σ is a $p \times p$ matrix. Then $X =$

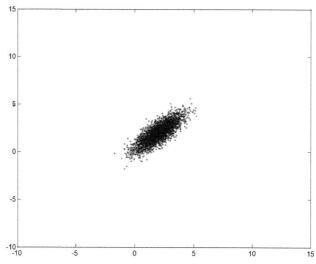

FIGURE 3.6 Scatter diagram for a sample of 3000 observations ($Z_i, i = 1, \ldots, 3000$) generated from a multivariate normal distribution consisting of three variates with covariance matrix C_2 and mean μ. Here, we plot the values of the first variate against the values of the second variate. If we use the notation of equation (3.4.2), then the (x, y) co-ordinates for the points are $x_i = Z_{i,1}, i = 1, \ldots, 3000$, and $y_i = Z_{i,2}, i = 1, \ldots, 3000$.

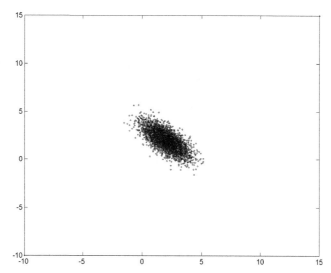

FIGURE 3.7 Scatter diagram for a sample of 3000 observations ($Z_i, i = 1, \ldots, 3000$) generated from a multivariate normal distribution consisting of three variates with covariance matrix C_3 and mean μ. Here, we plot the values of the first variate against the values of the second variate. If we use the notation of equation (3.4.2), then the (x, y) co-ordinates for the points are $x_i = Z_{i,1}, i = 1, \ldots, 3000$, and $y_i = Z_{i,2}, i = 1, \ldots, 3000$.

$\exp(Y)$ and X has multivariate lognormal distribution which we denote by $X \sim \Lambda(\mu, \Sigma)$.

We will represent the p element mean vector of X by $\bar{m}$ and the $p \times p$ covariance matrix of X by S.

It can be shown that

$$\Sigma_{i,j} = \log\left(1 + \frac{S_{i,j}}{\bar{m}_i \bar{m}_j}\right) \tag{3.4.7}$$

and

$$\mu_i = \log(\bar{m}_i) - \frac{\Sigma_{i,i}}{2}, \quad i = 1, \ldots, p, \text{ and } j = 1, \ldots, p. \tag{3.4.8}$$

For the case of independent variates, we then have

$$\mu_i = \log(\bar{m}_i) - \frac{\sigma_i^2}{2}, \quad i = 1, \ldots, p$$

and

$$\Sigma_{i,i} = \sigma_i^2 = \log\left(1 + \frac{s_i^2}{\bar{m}_i^2}\right), \quad i = 1, \ldots, p \text{ and for } i \neq j, \Sigma_{i,j} = 0,$$

which are just equation (3.3.13) and equation (3.3.14) given in Section 3.3.2.

Code excerpt 3.3 shows how to generate a multivariate lognormal distribution with a given mean $\bar{m}$ and covariance matrix S. More complete information can be found in the function `Quasirandom_Normal_LogNormal_Correlated` which is provided in Code excerpt 3.2.

```
double sig[40][40], s[40][40]; /* limit of 40 */
double means[40], x[40], lx[40], tmp;

#define S(I,J) s[(I)-1][(J)-1]
#define SIG(I,J) sig[(I)-1][(J)-1]
#define MEANS(i) means[(I)-1]   /* the means of the lognormal distribution */
#define X(I) x[(I)-1] /* normal variates */
#define LX(I) lx[(I)-1] /* lognormal variates */

        .   .   .
/* obtain the Gaussian covariance matrix SIG, that corresponds to the
   lognormal covariance matrix S. */

    for (i=1; i <= m; ++i) {
      for (j=1; j <= m; ++j) {
        tmp = MEANS(i) * MEANS(j);
        SIG(i,j) = log( 1 + (S(i,j)/tmp));
      }
    }
        .   .   .
/* Generate multivariate Gaussian variates X(i),i = 1,..,m, with zero mean and
   covariance matrix SIG, using section ..   */
        .   .   .
/* Using equation () generate normal variates with the correct mean */
    for (i=1; i <= m; ++i) {
      X(i) = X(i) + log(MEANS(i)) - SIG(i,i)/2;
    }
/* Now exponentiate to create lognormal lognormal variates with mean
   XMEAN, and covariance matrix S */
    for (i=1; i <= m; ++i) {
      LX(i) = exp(X(i));
    }
```

Code excerpt 3.3 Illustrating how to generate variates from a lognormal distribution with a given mean and covariance matrix.

3.5 SELECTED EXERCISES

1. Write a program to generate normal variates using the method outlined in Section 3.3.1.
2. Perform a logarithmic transformation on the variates generated in question 1 and verify that the mean and variance are in agreement with the expressions given in Section 3.3.2.
3. Show from first principals that the mean and variance of uniform random variates U(a, b) are $1/2(a + b)$ and $(a - b)/12$ respectively.
4. Prove that normal variates x_i, y_i, $i = 1, \ldots, n$ with correlation ρ rho can be generated by using $x_i = Z_i$ and $y_i = \rho.x_i + \sqrt{1 - \rho^2}.Y_i$, where $Z_i \sim N(0, 1)$ and $Y_i \sim N(0, 1)$.
5. Calculate the elements of the lower triangular matrix L for the Cholesky factorization $C = LL^T$, where C is a 3×3 correlation matrix.
6. Write a computer program to simulate multivariate random numbers using the result from question 5 and verify that the correlations are in agreement with matrix C.
7. The binomial distribution $B(n, p, k)$ is defined by

$$B(n, p, k) = \frac{n!}{k!(n - k)!} p^k (1 - p)^{n-k},$$

where n is the number of trials, p is the probability of success, and k is the number of successes. The mean is np and the variance is $np(1 - p)$. Prove that as $n \to \infty$ and $k \sim np$, the distribution tends to the normal distribution

$$\frac{1}{\sqrt{2\pi np(1 - p)}} \exp \left\{ -\frac{(k - np)^2}{2np(1 - p)} \right\}.$$

Hint: Use Stirling's formula $n! \sim n^n \exp(-n) \sqrt{2\pi n}$ and $\log(1 + x) \sim x - (1/2)x^2$.

8. Prove that as $n \to \infty$ and $p \to 0$, the binomial distribution in exercise 7 tends to the Poisson distribution

$$\exp(-np) \frac{(np)^k}{k!}.$$

Hint: As $n \to \infty$, we have $[1 - (x/n)]^n \to \exp(-x)$.

Chapter 4

European Options

4.1 INTRODUCTION

A European option taken out at current time t gives the owner the right (but not the obligation) to do *something* when the option *matures* at time T. This could, for example, be the right to buy or sell stocks at a particular *strike* price. The option would of course only be exercised if it was in the owner's interest to do so. For example, a single asset European *vanilla put* option, with strike price E and *expiry* time T, gives the owner the right at time T to sell a particular asset for E. If the asset is worth S_T at maturity, then the value of the put option at maturity, known as the *payoff*, is thus $\max(E - S_T, 0)$. By contrast, a single asset European vanilla *call* option, with strike price E and expiry time T, gives the owner the right at time T to buy an asset for E; the payoff at maturity for a call option is $\max(S_T - E, 0)$.

The owner of an American option has the right (but not the obligation) to exercise the option *at any time* from current time t to option maturity. These options are more difficult to value than European options because of this extra flexibility. Even the *simple* single asset American vanilla put has no analytic solution and requires finite-difference and lattice methods to estimate its value. Many European options on the other hand take the form of a *relatively easy* definite integral from which it is possible to compute a closed form solution. The valuation of multi-asset European options, dependent on a large number of underlying assets, is more complicated but can conveniently be achieved by using Monte Carlo simulation to compute the required multidimensional definite integral.

The expected *current value* of a single asset European vanilla option will depend on the current asset price at time t, S, the duration of the option, $\tau = T - t$, the strike price, E, the riskless interest rate, r, and the probability density function of the underlying asset at maturity, $p(S_T)$.

4.2 PRICING DERIVATIVES USING A MARTINGALE MEASURE

In this section, we will briefly summarize the results of Harrison and Kreps (1979), and Harrison and Pliska (1981). Let us consider an economy over the time interval $[0,T]$ which consists of n assets $S^i, i = 1, \ldots, n$, which can take the values $S_t^i, i = 1, \ldots, n, \ 0 \le t \le T$. Any asset S^i which only takes values that are greater than zero is called a *numeraire*. Numeraires can be used to denominate all the asset prices in the economy. So (for example) if S^1 is a numeraire, then the prices of the other assets denominated in units of S_1 are the relative prices $Z_t^i = \left(S_t^i / S_t^1 \right), i = 2, \ldots, n$.

One can find a unique probability measure $\mathbb{Q}$ such that the relative prices $Z_t^i, i = 2, \ldots, n$ are martingales. If the economy is free of arbitrage opportunities, then every payoff pattern H_T can be represented as a linear combination of the asset values $S_t^i, i = 1, \ldots, n$, and in addition, the relative price process $\left(H_T / S_T^1 \right)$ is a martingale.

This means that we can write

$$ E^{\mathbb{Q}} \left[\frac{H_t}{S_t^1} \right] = E^{\mathbb{Q}} \left[\frac{H_T}{S_T^1} \right], \quad \text{where } 0 \le t \le T. $$

The current (time t) value V_t of the payoff H_T is thus

$$ V_t = S_t^1 E^{\mathbb{Q}} \left[\frac{H_T}{S_T^1} \right]. $$

In general for a numeraire N which takes the values $N_t, 0 \le t \le T$, we can write

$$ V_t = N_t E^{\mathbb{Q}} \left[\frac{H_T}{N_T} \right]. \tag{4.2.1} $$

Equation (4.2.1) is very important because V_t is the current (time t) price of a financial derivative with maturity T and payoff H_T.

It should be mentioned that the price of a financial derivative is independent of the martingale measure under which it is valued, and thus, the same price V_t will be obtained for different numeraires N.

4.3 PUT CALL PARITY

4.3.1 Discrete Dividends

Here, we consider single asset European put and call options, and derive the following relationship between their values in the presence of cash dividends:

$$ c(S, E, \tau) + E \exp(-r\tau) + D = p(S, E, \tau) + S, \tag{4.3.1} $$

where D is the *present value* of the dividends that are paid during the life of the option. That is,

$$ D = \sum_{k=1}^{n} D_k \exp(-r(t_k - t)), $$

with D_k the kth cash dividend paid at time t_k; the other symbols have already been defined in the Introduction.

This result can be proved by considering the following two investments:

Portfolio A:

One European call, $c(S, E, \tau)$, and cash of value $E \exp(-r\tau) + D$.

Portfolio B:

One European put, $p(S, E, \tau)$, and one share of value S.

At option maturity, the value of the call and put are $c(S_T, E, 0)$ and $p(S_T, E, 0)$ respectively; also at time T, the value of the dividends paid during the life of the option is $D \exp(r\tau)$.

We now consider the value of both portfolios at time T under all possible conditions.

If $S_T \geq E$

Portfolio A is worth,

$$\max(S_T - E, 0) + \exp(r\tau) \{E \exp(-t\tau) + D\} = S_T - E + E + D \exp(r\tau) = S_T + D \exp(r\tau).$$

Portfolio B is worth,

$$\max(E - S_T, 0) + S_T + D \exp(r\tau) = 0 + S_T + D \exp(r\tau) = S_T + D \exp(r\tau).$$

If $S_T < E$

Portfolio A is worth,

$$\max(S_T - E, 0) + \exp(r\tau) \{E \exp(-t\tau) + D\} = 0 + E + D \exp(r\tau) = E + D \exp(r\tau).$$

Portfolio B is worth,

$$\max(E - S_T, 0) + S_T + D \exp(r\tau) = E - S_T + S_T + D \exp(r\tau) = E + D \exp(r\tau).$$

We have therefore shown that under all conditions the value of portfolio A is the same as that of portfolio B.

4.3.2 Continuous Dividends

Here, we consider single asset European put and call options, and derive the following relationship:

$$c(S, E, \tau) + E \exp(-r\tau) = p(S, E, \tau) + S \exp(-q\tau), \qquad (4.3.2)$$

where q is the asset's continuous dividend yield that is paid during the life of the option. The result can be proved by considering the following two investments:

Portfolio A:

One European call, $c(S, E, \tau)$, and cash of value $E \exp(-r\tau)$.

Portfolio B:

One European put, $p(S, E, \tau)$, and one share of value $S \exp(-q\tau)$.

At option expiry, the value of the call and put are $c(S_T, E, 0)$ and $p(S_T, E, 0)$ respectively. Also, if the value of the share at time t is denoted by S, the combined value of shares and dividends at time T is $S \exp(q\tau)$: Note that q is treated in a similar manner to the continuously compounded riskless interest rate r.

If $S_T \geq E$

Portfolio A is worth,

$$\max(S_T - E, 0) + \exp(r\tau)E\exp(-r\tau) = S_T - E + E = S_T.$$

Portfolio B is worth,

$$\max(E - S_T, 0) + S_T \exp(-q\tau)\exp(q\tau) = 0 + S_T = S_T,$$

where $S_T \exp(-q\tau)\exp(q\tau)$ is the combined value of the shares and dividends at option maturity.

If $S_T < E$

Portfolio A is worth,

$$\max(S_T - E, 0) + \exp(r\tau)E\exp(-r\tau) = 0 + E = E.$$

Portfolio B is worth,

$$\max(E - S_T, 0) + S_T \exp(-q\tau)\exp(q\tau) = E - S_T + S_T = E.$$

We have therefore shown that under all conditions the value of portfolio A is the same as that of portfolio B.

4.4 VANILLA OPTIONS AND THE BLACK–SCHOLES MODEL

4.4.1 The Option Pricing Partial Differential Equation

In this section, we will derive the (Black–Scholes) partial differential equation that is obeyed by options written on a single asset.

Previously, in Sections 2.3 and 2.5, we derived Ito's lemma, which provides an expression for the change in value of the function $\phi(X, t)$, where X is a stochastic variable. When the stochastic variable, X, follows GBM, the change in the value of ϕ was shown to be given by equation (2.3.6). Here, we will assume that the function $\phi(S, t)$ is the value of a financial option and that the price of the underlying asset, S, follows GBM.

If we denote the value of the financial derivative by f, then its change, df, over the time interval dt is given by

$$df = \left(\mu S \frac{\partial f}{\partial S} + \frac{\partial f}{\partial t} + \frac{\sigma^2 S^2}{2} \frac{\partial^2 f}{\partial S^2} \right) dt + \frac{\partial f}{\partial S} \sigma S dW, \quad dW \sim N(0, dt).$$

The discretized version of this equation is

$$\Delta f = \Delta t \left(\mu S \frac{\partial f}{\partial S} + \frac{\partial f}{\partial t} + \frac{\sigma^2 S^2}{2} \frac{\partial^2 f}{\partial S^2} \right) + \frac{\partial f}{\partial S} \sigma S \Delta W, \quad \Delta W \sim N(0, \Delta t), \quad (4.4.1)$$

where the time interval is now Δt and the change in derivative value is Δf.

If we assume that the asset price, S, follows GBM, we also have

$$\Delta S = \mu S \Delta t + \sigma S \Delta W, \quad \Delta W \sim N(0, \Delta t), \quad (4.4.2)$$

where μ is the constant drift and the definition of the other symbols is as before. Let us now consider a portfolio consisting of -1 derivative and $\partial f/\partial S$ units of the underlying stock. In other words, we have gone *short* (that is sold) a derivative on an asset and have $\partial f/\partial S$ stocks of the (same) underlying asset. The value of the portfolio, Π, is therefore

$$\Pi = -f + \frac{\partial f}{\partial S}S, \qquad (4.4.3)$$

and the change, $\Delta\Pi$, in the value of the portfolio over time Δt is

$$\Delta\Pi = -\Delta f + \frac{\partial f}{\partial S}\Delta S. \qquad (4.4.4)$$

Substituting equation (4.4.1) and equation (4.4.2) into equation (4.4.4), we obtain

$$\Delta\Pi = -\left(\mu S\frac{\partial f}{\partial S} + \frac{\partial f}{\partial t} + \frac{1}{2}\sigma^2 S^2 \frac{\partial^2 f}{\partial S^2}\right)\Delta t - \sigma S\Delta W\frac{\partial f}{\partial S} + \frac{\partial f}{\partial S}\{\mu S\Delta t + \sigma S\Delta W\},$$

$$\therefore \Delta\Pi = -\mu S\Delta t\frac{\partial f}{\partial S} - \Delta t\frac{\partial f}{\partial t} - \frac{1}{2}\Delta t\sigma^2 S^2 \frac{\partial^2 f}{\partial S^2} - \sigma S\Delta W\frac{\partial f}{\partial S} + \mu S\Delta t\frac{\partial f}{\partial S} + \sigma S\Delta W\frac{\partial f}{\partial S}.$$

$$\qquad (4.4.5)$$

Cancelling the terms, we obtain

$$\Delta\Pi = -\Delta t\left\{\frac{\partial f}{\partial t} + \frac{1}{2}\sigma^2 S^2 \frac{\partial^2 f}{\partial S^2}\right\}. \qquad (4.4.6)$$

If this portfolio is to grow at the riskless interest rate, r, we have

$$r\Pi\Delta t = \Delta\Pi.$$

So we have that

$$r\Pi\Delta t = -\Delta t\left\{\frac{\partial f}{\partial t} + \frac{1}{2}\sigma^2 S^2 \frac{\partial^2 f}{\partial S^2}\right\}. \qquad (4.4.7)$$

Substituting for Π and we obtain

$$r\Delta t\left(f - S\frac{\partial f}{\partial S}\right) = -\Delta t\left\{\frac{\partial f}{\partial t} + \frac{1}{2}\sigma^2 S^2 \frac{\partial^2 f}{\partial S^2}\right\}. \qquad (4.4.8)$$

On rearranging, we have

$$\frac{\partial f}{\partial t} + S\frac{\partial f}{\partial S} + \frac{1}{2}\sigma^2 S^2 \frac{\partial^2 f}{\partial S^2} = rf, \qquad (4.4.9)$$

which is the Black–Scholes partial differential equation.

Let us now consider put and call options on the same underlying asset. If we let c be the value of a European call option and p that of a European put option, then we have the following equations:

$$\frac{\partial p}{\partial t} + S\frac{\partial p}{\partial S} + \frac{1}{2}\sigma^2 S^2 \frac{\partial^2 p}{\partial S^2} = rp \qquad (4.4.10)$$

and

$$\frac{\partial c}{\partial t} + S\frac{\partial c}{\partial S} + \frac{1}{2}\sigma^2 S^2 \frac{\partial^2 c}{\partial S^2} = rc. \qquad (4.4.11)$$

If we now form a linear combination of put and call options, $\Psi = a_1 c + a_2 p$, where both a_1 and a_2 are constants, then Ψ also obeys the Black–Scholes equation

$$\frac{\partial \Psi}{\partial t} + S\frac{\partial \Psi}{\partial S} + \frac{1}{2}\sigma^2 S^2 \frac{\partial^2 \Psi}{\partial S^2} = r\Psi. \qquad (4.4.12)$$

We will now prove that Ψ satisfies equation (4.4.12).

First we rewrite equation (4.4.12) as

$$\frac{\partial(a_1 c + a_2 p)}{\partial t} + S\frac{\partial(a_1 c + a_2 p)}{\partial S} + \frac{1}{2}\sigma^2 S^2 \frac{\partial^2(a_1 c + a_2 p)}{\partial S^2} = r(a_1 c + a_2 p) \qquad (4.4.13)$$

and use the following results from elementary calculus:

$$\frac{\partial(a_1 c + a_2 p)}{\partial t} = a_1\frac{\partial c}{\partial t} + a_2\frac{\partial p}{\partial t},$$

$$\frac{\partial(a_1 c + a_2 p)}{\partial S} = a_1\frac{\partial c}{\partial S} + a_2\frac{\partial p}{\partial S},$$

and

$$\frac{\partial^2(a_1 c + a_2 p)}{\partial S^2} = a_1\frac{\partial^2 c}{\partial S^2} + a_2\frac{\partial^2 p}{\partial S^2}.$$

If we denote the left-hand side of equation (4.4.12) by LHS, then we have

$$\text{LHS} = a_1\left\{\frac{\partial c}{\partial t} + S\frac{\partial c}{\partial S} + \frac{1}{2}\sigma^2 S^2 \frac{\partial^2 c}{\partial S^2}\right\} + a_2\left\{\frac{\partial p}{\partial t} + S\frac{\partial p}{\partial S} + \frac{1}{2}\sigma^2 S^2 \frac{\partial^2 p}{\partial S^2}\right\}. \qquad (4.4.14)$$

We now use equation (4.4.10) and equation (4.4.11) to substitute for the values in the curly brackets in equation (4.4.14), and we obtain

$$\text{LHS} = a_1 rc + a_2 rp, \qquad (4.4.15)$$

which is just the right-hand side of equation (4.4.12); so we have proved the result. It should be noted that this result is also true for American options, since they also obey the Black–Scholes equation.

The above result can be generalized to include a portfolio consisting of n single asset options. Here, we have

$$\Psi = \sum_{j=1}^{n} a_j f_j, \quad j = 1, \ldots, n,$$

where f_j represents the value of the jth derivative and a_j is the number of units of the jth derivative. To prove that Ψ follows the Black–Scholes equation, we simply partition the portfolio into sectors whose options depend on the same underlying asset. We then proceed as before by showing that the value of each individual sector obeys the Black–Scholes equation, and thus, the value of the complete portfolio (the sum of the values of all the sectors) obeys the Black–Scholes equation. It should be mentioned that this result applies for both American and European options and it does not matter whether we have bought or sold the options.

In Chapter 5, we will use the fact that the difference between the value of a European option and the equivalent American option obeys the Black–Scholes equation. We can see this immediately by considering the following portfolios that are long in an American option and short (i.e., have sold) in a European option

$$\Psi^P = P - p, \qquad \Psi^c = C - c,$$

where P and C are the values of American put and call options. Ψ^P and Ψ^c both obey the Black–Scholes equations and are the respective differences in value of American/European put options and American/European call options.

4.4.2 The Multi-asset Option Pricing Partial Differential Equation

In this section, we will derive the multi-asset (Black–Scholes) partial differential equation that is obeyed by options written on n assets. Proceeding as in Section 4.4.1 we will use the n-dimensional version of Ito's lemma to find the process followed by the value of a multi-asset financial derivative. We will denote the value of this derivative by $f(S, t)$, where S is a n-element stochastic vector containing the prices of the underlying assets, $S_i, i = 1, \ldots, n$. If we assume that S follows n-dimensional GBM, then the change in the value of the derivative, df, is (see equation (2.5.8)) given by

$$df = \left\{ \frac{\partial f}{\partial t} + \sum_{i=1}^{n} \mu_i S_i \frac{\partial f}{\partial S_i} + \frac{1}{2} \sum_{i=1}^{n} \sum_{j=1}^{n} \sigma_i \sigma_j S_i S_j \rho_{ij} \frac{\partial^2 f}{\partial S_i \partial S_j} \right\} dt + \sum_{i=1}^{n} \frac{\partial f}{\partial S_i} \sigma_i S_i dW_i.$$

(4.4.16)

The discretized version of this equation is

$$\Delta f = \left\{ \frac{\partial f}{\partial t} + \sum_{i=1}^{n} \mu_i S_i \frac{\partial f}{\partial S_i} + \frac{1}{2} \sum_{i=1}^{n} \sum_{j=1}^{n} \sigma_i \sigma_j S_i S_j \rho_{ij} \frac{\partial^2 f}{\partial S_i \partial S_j} \right\} \Delta t + \sum_{i=1}^{n} \frac{\partial f}{\partial S_i} \sigma_i S_i \Delta W_i,$$

(4.4.17)

where the time interval is now Δt and the change in derivative value is Δf.

Let us now consider a portfolio consisting of -1 derivative and $\partial f / \partial S_i$ units of the ith underlying stock. In other words, we have gone *short* (that is sold) a derivative that depends on the price, $S_i, i = 1, \ldots, n$, of n underlying assets and have $\partial f / \partial S_i$ units of the ith asset. The value of the portfolio, Π, is therefore

$$\Pi = -f + \sum_{i=1}^{n} \frac{\partial f}{\partial S_i} S_i,$$

(4.4.18)

and the change, $\Delta \Pi$, in the value of the portfolio over the time interval Δt is

$$\Delta \Pi = -\Delta f + \sum_{i=1}^{n} \frac{\partial f}{\partial S_i} \Delta S_i.$$

(4.4.19)

Since the stochastic variables $S_i, i = 1,\ldots,n$ follow n-dimensional GBM, the change in the ith asset price, ΔS_i, over the time interval Δt is given by

$$\Delta S_i = \mu_i S_i \Delta t + \sigma_i S_i \Delta W_i, \quad i = 1,\ldots,n, \tag{4.4.20}$$

where $\Delta W_i = dZ_i \sqrt{\Delta t}$,

$$E[dZ_i^2] = 1, \quad i = 1,\ldots,n,$$

and

$$E[dZ_i \, dZ_j] = \rho_{i,j}, \quad i = 1,\ldots,n, \quad j = 1,\ldots,n, \quad i \neq j.$$

Substituting equation (4.4.17) and equation (4.4.20) into equation (4.4.19), we obtain

$$\Delta \Pi = -\left\{ \frac{\partial f}{\partial t} + \sum_{i=1}^{n} \mu_i S_i \frac{\partial f}{\partial S_i} + \frac{1}{2} \sum_{i=1}^{n} \sum_{j=1}^{n} \sigma_i \sigma_j \rho_{ij} S_i S_j \frac{\partial^2 f}{\partial S_i \partial S_j} \right\} \Delta t$$

$$- \sum_{i=1}^{n} \sigma_i S_i \Delta W_i \frac{\partial f}{\partial S_i} + \sum_{i=1}^{n} \frac{\partial f}{\partial S_i} \{ \mu_i S_i \Delta t + \sigma S_i \Delta W_i \},$$

$$\therefore \Delta \Pi = - \sum_{i=1}^{n} \mu_i S_i \Delta t \frac{\partial f}{\partial S_i} - \Delta t \frac{\partial f}{\partial t} - \frac{1}{2} \Delta t \sum_{i=1}^{n} \sum_{j=1}^{n} \sigma_i \sigma_j \rho_{ij} S_i S_j \frac{\partial^2 f}{\partial S_i \partial S_j}$$

$$- \sum_{i=1}^{n} \sigma_i S_i \Delta W_i \frac{\partial f}{\partial S_i} + \sum_{i=1}^{n} \mu_i S_i \Delta t \frac{\partial f}{\partial S_i} + \sum_{i=1}^{n} \sigma_i S_i \Delta W_i \frac{\partial f}{\partial S_i}. \tag{4.4.21}$$

Cancelling the terms, we obtain

$$\Delta \Pi = -\Delta t \left\{ \frac{\partial f}{\partial t} + \frac{1}{2} \sum_{i=1}^{n} \sum_{j=1}^{n} \sigma_i \sigma_j \rho_{ij} S_i S_j \frac{\partial^2 f}{\partial S_i \partial S_j} \right\}. \tag{4.4.22}$$

If this portfolio is to grow at the riskless interest rate, r, we have

$$r \Pi \Delta t = \Delta \Pi.$$

So from equation (4.4.22), we have that

$$r \Pi \Delta t = -\Delta t \left\{ \frac{\partial f}{\partial t} + \frac{1}{2} \sum_{i=1}^{n} \sum_{j=1}^{n} \sigma_i \sigma_j \rho_{ij} S_i S_j \frac{\partial^2 f}{\partial S_i \partial S_j} \right\}. \tag{4.4.23}$$

Substituting for Π and we obtain

$$r \Delta t \left\{ f - \sum_{i=1}^{n} S_i \frac{\partial f}{\partial S_i} \right\} = -\Delta t \left\{ \frac{\partial f}{\partial t} + \frac{1}{2} \sum_{i=1}^{n} \sum_{j=1}^{n} \sigma_i \sigma_j \rho_{ij} S_i S_j \frac{\partial^2 f}{\partial S_i \partial S_j} \right\}. \tag{4.4.24}$$

Rearranging equation (4.4.24) gives

$$\frac{\partial f}{\partial t} + \sum_{i=1}^{n} S_i \frac{\partial f}{\partial S_i} + \frac{1}{2} \sum_{i=1}^{n} \sum_{j=1}^{n} \sigma_i \sigma_j \rho_{ij} S_i S_j \frac{\partial^2 f}{\partial S_i \partial S_j} = rf, \tag{4.4.25}$$

which is the n-dimensional Black–Scholes partial differential equation.

4.4.3 The Black–Scholes Formula

The Black–Scholes model consists of two assets, the riskless money account and an equity it can be cast as the following two-dimensional Ito equation:

$$dS_t = \mu S_t dt + \sigma S_t dW^P,$$
$$dB_t = r B_t dt, \tag{4.4.26}$$

where W^P is Brownian motion (without drift) under measure $\mathbb{P}$, so $dW^P \sim N(0, dt)$.

Current time will be denoted by t_0, and the option maturity time by T. The money market account has value $B_{t_0} = 1$ at time t_0 and $B_T = \exp(r(T - t_0))$ at time T.

We will now consider the process followed by the relative value $\phi(S_t, B_t) = S_t / B_t$.

Using the Ito quotient rule with described in Section 2.6.2 and substituting $X_1 = S_t$ and $X_2 = B_t$ in equation (2.6.8), we have

$$d\left(\frac{S_t}{B_t}\right) = \left(\frac{S_t}{B_t}\right)(\mu - r) dt + \left(\frac{S_t}{B_t}\right)\sigma dW^P.$$

So finally we can write

$$dS_t^* = S_t^*(\mu - r) dt + S_t^* \sigma dW^P, \tag{4.4.27}$$

where $S_t^* = S_t / B_t$.

Referring to Girsanov's theorem in Section 2.4, we can choose a probability measure $\mathbb{Q}$ such that

$$dW^P = dW^Q - \left(\frac{\mu - r}{\sigma}\right) dt. \tag{4.4.28}$$

In equation (2.4.3), we thus have $k(t) = -\left(\frac{\mu - r}{\sigma}\right)$ and

$$\frac{d\mathbb{Q}}{d\mathbb{P}} = \exp\left\{-\left(\frac{\mu - r}{\sigma}\right)W^P - \frac{1}{2}\left(\frac{\mu - r}{\sigma}\right)^2 t\right\}, \tag{4.4.29}$$

see page 114 Musiela and Rutkowski (1998). Substituting for dW^P in equation (4.4.27) yields

$$dS_t^* = S_t^* \{\mu - r\} dt - S_t^* \sigma \left(\frac{\mu - r}{\sigma}\right) dt + S^* \sigma dW^Q,$$

which simplifies to

$$dS_t^* = S_t^* \sigma dW^Q. \tag{4.4.30}$$

Equation (4.4.30) means that the process for S_t^* is a martingale under probability measure $\mathbb{Q}$.

Replacing dW^P in equation (4.4.26) with the value in equation (4.4.28) yields

$$dS_t = \mu S_t dt + S_t \sigma dW^P$$
$$= \mu S_t dt + S_t \sigma \left\{dW^Q - \left(\frac{\mu - r}{\sigma}\right) dt\right\}$$
$$= \left\{S_t \mu dt - S_t \sigma \left(\frac{\mu - r}{\sigma}\right)\right\} dt + S_t \sigma dW^Q.$$

So in the risk-neutral measure $\mathbb{Q}$, the dynamics of dS are

$$dS_t = S_t r dt + S_t \sigma dW^Q. \tag{4.4.31}$$

Comparing equation (4.4.31) with the original equation in (4.4.26), we see that changing from the real world measure to the risk-neutral measure simply involves substituting dW^Q for dW^P and r for μ.

We can now solve equation (4.4.31) by using the result given in equation (2.3.11). We have

$$S_T = S \exp\left(v\left(T - t_0\right) + \sigma W^Q_{T-t_0}\right),$$

where S is the asset price at current time t_0, and $v = r - \sigma^2/2$.

The forward price with maturity T, denoted by $S(t_0, T)$ is $E[S_T]$. From Appendix D.2, we have

$$S(t_0, T) = E[S_T] = S \exp\left(r\left(T - t_0\right)\right). \tag{4.4.32}$$

Using equation (2.3.9), the distribution of the asset price at time T is

$$\log\left(\frac{S_T}{S}\right) \sim N\left(v\left(T - t_0\right), \sigma^2\left(T - t_0\right)\right). \tag{4.4.33}$$

We want to obtain the current price of a vanilla European option with strike price E which matures at future time T and thus has a duration of $\tau = T - t_0$. The approach we will adopt here is to first derive an expression for the value of a European call option and then use the put/call parity relationships of Section 2.2 to obtain the value of the corresponding European put option.

Referring to (4.2.1), we have

$$V_{t_0} = B_{t_0} E^Q\left[\frac{H_T}{B_T}\right] = \frac{B_{t_0}}{B_T} E^Q[H_T]. \tag{4.4.34}$$

Substituting $B_{t_0} = 1$, $B_T = \exp\left(r\left(T - t_0\right)\right) = \exp\left(r\tau\right)$, and $H_T = \max\left(S_T - E, 0\right)$, we have

$$V_{t_0} = \frac{1}{\exp\left(r\tau\right)} E^Q\left[\max\left(S_T - E, 0\right)\right], \tag{4.4.35}$$

and so denoting the value of the call option by $c(S, E, \tau)$, we obtain

$$c(S, E, \tau) = \exp\left(-r\tau\right) E^Q\left[\max\left(S_T - E, 0\right)\right]. \tag{4.4.36}$$

It can be seen from equation (4.4.36) that the value of the European call option is the expected value of the option's payoff at maturity, discounted to current time t by the riskless interest rate r.

This means that the value of the call option can be written as

$$c(S, E, \tau) = \exp(-r\tau) \int_{S_T=E}^{\infty} f(S_T)(S_T - E) dS_T, \tag{4.4.37}$$

where $f(S_T)$ is the probability density function of S_T.

Instead of integrating over S_T we will evaluate (4.4.37) by using the variable $X = \log(S_T/S)$. From equation (4.4.33), we know that the probability density function of X is

$$f(X) = \frac{1}{\sigma\sqrt{\tau}\sqrt{2\pi}} \exp\left(-\frac{(X - (r - \sigma^2/2)\tau)^2}{2\sigma^2\tau}\right), \tag{4.4.38}$$

and therefore, the value of option is

$$c(S,E,\tau) = \exp(-r\tau) \int_{X=\log(E/S)}^{\infty} \{S\exp(X) - E\}\, f(X)\, dX, \tag{4.4.39}$$

where we have used $S_T = S\exp(X)$. The lower limit in equation (4.4.39) corresponding to $S_T = E$ in equation (4.4.37) is found by setting $E = \exp(X)$; this yields the lower limit $X = \log(E/S)$.

The integral in equation (4.4.39) is evaluated by splitting it into the two parts

$$c(S,E,\tau) = I_A - I_B, \tag{4.4.40}$$

where

$$I_A = \frac{S\exp(-r\tau)}{\sigma\sqrt{\tau}\sqrt{2\pi}} \int_{X=\log(E/S)}^{\infty} \exp(X)\exp\left(-\frac{\{X - (r - \sigma^2/2)\tau\}^2}{2\sigma^2\tau}\right) dX \tag{4.4.41}$$

and

$$I_B = \frac{E\exp(-r\tau)}{\sigma\sqrt{\tau}\sqrt{2\pi}} \int_{X=\log(E/S)}^{\infty} \exp\left(-\frac{\{X - (r - \sigma^2/2)\tau\}^2}{2\sigma^2\tau}\right) E\, dX. \tag{4.4.42}$$

To evaluate these integrals, we will make use of the fact that the univariate cumulative normal function $N_1(x)$ is

$$N_1(x) = \frac{1}{\sqrt{2\pi}} \int_{u=-\infty}^{x} \exp\left(-\frac{u^2}{2}\right) du;$$

by symmetry, we have $N_1(-x) = 1 - N_1(x)$ and

$$\frac{1}{\sqrt{2\pi}} \int_{x}^{\infty} \exp\left(-\frac{u^2}{2}\right) du = \frac{1}{\sqrt{2\pi}} \int_{-\infty}^{-x} \exp\left(-\frac{u^2}{2}\right) du = N_1(-x).$$

We will first consider I_B, which is the easier of the two integrals,

$$I_B = \frac{E\exp(-r\tau)}{\sigma\sqrt{\tau}\sqrt{2\pi}} \int_{X=\log(E/S)}^{\infty} \exp\left(-\frac{\{X - (r - \sigma^2/2)\tau\}^2}{2\sigma^2\tau}\right) dX.$$

If we let $u = \dfrac{X - (r - \sigma^2/2)\tau}{\sigma\sqrt{\tau}}$, then $dX = \sigma\sqrt{\tau}\,du$. So

$$I_B = \frac{E\exp(-r\tau)\sigma\sqrt{\tau}}{\sigma\sqrt{2\pi}\sqrt{\tau}} \int_{u=k_2}^{\infty} \exp\left(-\frac{u^2}{2}\right) du,$$

where the lower integration limit is $k_2 = [\log(E/S) - (r - \sigma^2/2)\tau]/\sigma\sqrt{\tau}$.

We therefore have

$$I_B = E \exp(-r\tau)N_1(-k_2).$$ (4.4.43)

We will now consider the integral I_A,

$$I_A = \frac{S\exp(-r\tau)}{\sigma\sqrt{\tau}\sqrt{2\pi}} \int_{X=\log(E/S)}^{\infty} \exp(X)\exp\left(-\frac{\{X - (r - \sigma^2/2)\tau\}^2}{2\sigma^2\tau}\right) dX.$$

Rearranging the integrand,

$$I_A = \frac{\exp(-r\tau)}{\sigma\sqrt{\tau}\sqrt{2\pi}} \int_{X=\log(E/S)}^{\infty} \exp\left(-\frac{\{X - (r - \sigma^2/2)\tau\}^2 - 2\sigma^2\tau X}{2\sigma^2\tau}\right) dX.$$ (4.4.44)

Expanding the terms in the exponential,

$$\{X - (r - \sigma^2/2)\tau\}^2 - 2\sigma^2\tau X = X^2 - 2\{(r - \sigma^2/2)\tau\} X + \{(r - \sigma^2/2)\tau\}^2 - 2\sigma^2\tau X$$

$$= X^2 - 2\{(r + \sigma^2/2)\tau\} X + \{(r - \sigma^2/2)\tau\}^2$$

$$= \{X - (r + \sigma^2/2)\tau\}^2 + \{(r - \sigma^2/2)\tau\}^2 - \{(r + \sigma^2/2)\tau\}^2,$$

which results in

$$\{X - (r - \sigma^2/2)\tau\}^2 - 2\sigma^2\tau X = \{X - (r + \sigma^2/2)\tau\}^2 - 2\sigma^2 r\tau^2.$$ (4.4.45)

Substituting equation (4.4.45) into the integrand of equation (4.4.44), we have

$$\exp(X)\exp\left(-\frac{\{X - (r - \sigma^2/2)\tau\}^2}{2\sigma^2\tau}\right) = \exp(r\tau)\exp\left(-\frac{\{X - (r + \sigma^2/2)\tau\}^2}{2\sigma^2\tau}\right).$$

The integral I_A can therefore be expressed as

$$I_A = \frac{S\exp(r\tau)\exp(-r\tau)}{\sigma\tau\sqrt{2\pi}} \int_{X=\log(E/S)}^{\infty} \exp\left(-\frac{\{X - (r + \sigma^2/2)\tau\}^2}{2\sigma^2\tau}\right) dX.$$

If we let $u = \dfrac{X - (r + \sigma^2/2)\tau}{\sigma\sqrt{\tau}}$, then $dX = \sigma\sqrt{\tau}du$.

So

$$I_A = \frac{S\sigma\sqrt{\tau}}{\sigma\sqrt{2\pi}\sqrt{\tau}} \int_{u=k_1}^{\infty} \exp\left(-\frac{u^2}{2}\right) du,$$

where the lower limit of integration is $k_1 = [\log(E/S) - (r + \sigma^2/2)\tau]/\sigma\sqrt{\tau}$. We therefore have

$$I_A = SN_1(-k_1).$$ (4.4.46)

Therefore, the value of a European call is

$$c(S, E, \tau) = SN_1(-k_1) - E\exp(-r\tau)N_1(-k_2),$$

which gives the usual form of the Black–Scholes formula for a European call as

$$c(S,E,\tau) = SN_1(d_1) - E\exp(-r\tau)N_1(d_2), \qquad (4.4.47)$$

where

$$d_1 = \frac{\log(S/E) + (r + \sigma^2/2)\tau}{\sigma\sqrt{\tau}} \quad \text{and} \quad d_2 = \frac{\log(S/E) + (r - \sigma^2/2)\tau}{\sigma\sqrt{\tau}} = d_1 - \sigma\sqrt{\tau}. \tag{4.4.48}$$

To gain some insight into the meaning the above equation, we will rewrite it in the following form:

$$c(S,E,\tau) = \exp(-r\tau)\left\{SN_1(d_1)\exp(r\tau) - EN_1(d_2)\right\}. \qquad (4.4.49)$$

The term $N_1(d_2)$ is the probability that the option will be exercised in a risk-neutral world, so that $EN_1(d_2)$ is the strike price multiplied by the probability that the strike price will be paid. The term $SN_1(d_1)\exp(r\tau)$ is the expected value of a variable, in a risk-neutral world, that equals S_T if $S_T > E$ and is otherwise zero.

The corresponding formula for a put can be shown using put call parity, see Section 4.3, to be

$$p(S,E,\tau) = E\exp(-r\tau)N_1(-d_2) - SN_1(-d_1), \qquad (4.4.50)$$

or equivalently, using $N_1(-x) = 1 - N_1(x)$ we have

$$p(S,E,\tau) = E\exp(-r\tau)\left\{1 - N_1(d_2)\right\} - S\left\{1 - N_1(d_1)\right\}. \qquad (4.4.51)$$

The Inclusion of Continuous Dividends

The effect of dividends on the value of a European option can be dealt with by assuming that the asset price is the sum of a riskless component involving known dividends that will be paid during the life of the option and a risky (stochastic) component, see Hull (2003).

As continuous dividends q are paid, the stock price is reduced by the same amount, and by the time the European option matures, all the dividends will have been paid leaving only the risky component of the asset price.

From equation (4.4.26), we thus have

$$dS = \mu Sdt - Sqdt + \sigma SdW^P,$$
$$dB = rBdt, \qquad (4.4.52)$$

where under probability measure $\mathbb{P}$, we know that $dW^P \sim N(0,dt)$.

As before (using Girsanov's theorem), we choose probability measure $\mathbb{Q}$ so that

$$dW^P = dW^Q - \left(\frac{\mu - r}{\sigma}\right)dt,$$

and thus under this measure, the process for S is

$$dS = S\mu dt - Sqdt - \left(\frac{\mu - r}{\sigma}\right)dt + S\sigma dW^Q, \quad \text{where} \quad dW^Q \sim N(0,dt),$$

which results in

$$dS = S(r - q)\, dt + \sigma S dW^Q, \quad \text{where } dW^Q \sim N(0, dt). \tag{4.4.53}$$

Proceeding as before, we obtain

$$X \sim N\left(\left\{r - q - \frac{\sigma^2}{2}\right\}\tau, \sigma^2\tau\right),$$

where $X = S_T/S$. The probability density function of X is now

$$f(X) = \frac{1}{\sigma\sqrt{\tau}\sqrt{2\pi}}\exp\left(-\frac{(X - (r - q - \sigma^2/2)\tau)^2}{2\sigma^2\tau}\right).$$

The value of a call option is thus

$$c(S, E, \tau) = \frac{\exp(-r\tau)}{\sigma\sqrt{\tau}\sqrt{2\pi}}\int_{X=\log(E/S)}^{\infty}\{S\exp(X) - E\}$$
$$\times \exp\left(-\frac{(X - (r - q - \sigma^2/2)\tau)^2}{2\sigma^2\tau}\right)dX, \tag{4.4.54}$$

with

$$I_A = \frac{S\exp(-r\tau)}{\sigma\sqrt{\tau}\sqrt{2\pi}}\int_{X=\log(E/S)}^{\infty}\exp(X)\exp\left(-\frac{\left\{X - (r - q - \sigma^2/2)\tau\right\}^2}{2\sigma^2\tau}\right)dX$$

and

$$I_B = \frac{E\exp(-r\tau)}{\sigma\sqrt{\tau}\sqrt{2\pi}}\int_{X=\log(E/S)}^{\infty}\exp\left(-\frac{\left\{X - (r - q - \sigma^2/2)\tau\right\}^2}{2\sigma^2\tau}\right)E dX.$$

So $I_B = E\exp(-r\tau)N_1(-k_2)$, where $k_2 = [\log(E/S) - (r - q - \sigma^2/2)\tau]/\sigma\sqrt{\tau}$. We will now consider the integral I_A,

$$I_A = \frac{S\exp(-r\tau)}{\sigma\sqrt{\tau}\sqrt{2\pi}}\int_{X=\log(E/S)}^{\infty}\exp(X)\exp\left(-\frac{\left\{X - (r - q - \sigma^2/2)\tau\right\}^2}{2\sigma^2\tau}\right)dX.$$

Rearranging the integrand,

$$I_A = \frac{\exp(-r\tau)}{\sigma\sqrt{\tau}\sqrt{2\pi}}\int_{X=\log(E/S)}^{\infty}\exp\left(-\frac{\left\{X - (r - q - \sigma^2/2)\tau\right\}^2 - 2\sigma^2\tau X}{2\sigma^2\tau}\right)dX.$$

Expanding the exponential, we obtain

$$\left\{X - (r - q - \sigma^2/2)\tau\right\}^2 - 2\sigma^2\tau X = \left\{X - (r - q + \sigma^2/2)\tau\right\}^2 - 2\sigma^2(r - q)\tau^2.$$

The integral I_A can therefore be expressed as

$$I_A = \frac{S\exp((r - q)\tau)\exp(-r\tau)}{\sigma\tau\sqrt{2\pi}}\int_{X=\log(E/S)}^{\infty}\exp\left(-\frac{\left\{X - (r - q + \sigma^2/2)\tau\right\}^2}{2\sigma^2\tau}\right)dX,$$

which gives $I_A = S\exp(-q\tau)N_1(-k_1)$, where $k_1 = \dfrac{\log(E/S) - (r - q + \sigma^2/2)\tau}{\sigma\sqrt{\tau}}$.

The Black–Scholes formula for the value of a European call including continuous dividends is thus

$$c(S,E,\tau) = S\exp(-q\tau)N_1(d_1) - E\exp(-r\tau)N_1(d_2), \qquad (4.4.55)$$

and the corresponding formula for a put can be shown (using put call parity) to be

$$p(S,E,\tau) = -S\exp(-q\tau)N_1(-d_1) + E\exp(-r\tau)N_1(-d_2), \qquad (4.4.56)$$

or equivalently, using $N_1(-x) = 1 - N_1(x)$, we have

$$p(S,E,\tau) = E\exp(-r\tau)\{1 - N_1(d_2)\} - S\exp(-q\tau)\{1 - N_1(d_1)\}, \qquad (4.4.57)$$

where

$$d_1 = \frac{\log(S/E) + (r - q + \sigma^2/2)\tau}{\sigma\sqrt{\tau}}, \quad d_2 = \frac{\log(S/E) + (r - q - \sigma^2/2)\tau}{\sigma\sqrt{\tau}}.$$

Thus, European put/call options with continuous dividends can be priced using equations (4.4.47) and (4.4.50) but with S replaced by $S\exp(-q\tau)$.

These formulae can also be re-expressed in terms of the current equity forward price with maturity T, $S(t,T)$, as follows:

$$c_t = \exp(-r(T - t))\{S(t,T)N_1(d_1) - EN_1(d_2)\}, \qquad (4.4.58)$$

$$p_t = \exp(-r(T - t))\{-S(t,T)N_1(-d_1) + EN_1(-d_2)\}, \qquad (4.4.59)$$

where we have used the shortened notation p_t and c_t to denote the current (time t) value of put and call options, and the current equity forward price with maturity T is

$$S(t,T) = S\exp((r - q)(T - t)), \quad t \le T$$

and

$$d_1 = \frac{\log(S(t,T)/E) + (\sigma^2/2)(T - t)}{\sigma\sqrt{(T - t)}}, \quad d_2 = \frac{\log(S(t,T)/E) - (\sigma^2/2)(T - t)}{\sigma\sqrt{(T - t)}}.$$

The Inclusion of Discrete Dividends

Here, we consider n discrete cash dividends $D_i, i = 1,\ldots,n$, paid at times $t_i, i = 1,\ldots,n$ during the life of the option. In these circumstances, the Black–Scholes formula can be used to price European options, but the with current asset value S reduced by the present value of the cash dividends.

This means that instead of S we use the quantity S_D which is computed as

$$S_D = S - \sum_{i=1}^{n} D_i\exp(-rt_i),$$

where r is the (in this case constant) riskless interest rate. The formulae for European puts and calls are then

$$c(S,E,\tau) = S_D N_1(d_1) - E\exp(-r\tau)N_1(d_2), \qquad (4.4.60)$$

$$p(S,E,\tau) = E\exp(-r\tau)\{1 - N_1(d_2)\} - S_D\{1 - N_1(d_1)\}, \qquad (4.4.61)$$

where

$$d_1 = \frac{\log(S_D/E) + (r + \sigma^2/2)\tau}{\sigma\sqrt{\tau}} \quad \text{and} \quad d_2 = \frac{\log(S_D/E) + (r - \sigma^2/2)\tau}{\sigma\sqrt{\tau}} = d_1 - \sigma\sqrt{\tau}.$$

(4.4.62)

The Greeks

Now that we have derived formulae to price European vanilla puts and calls, and it is possible to work out their partial derivatives (hedge statistics). We will now merely quote expressions for the Greeks (hedge statistics) for European options. Here, the subscript c refers to a European call, and the subscript p refers to a European put. Complete derivations of these results can be found in Appendix A.

Gamma:

$$\Gamma_c = \frac{\partial^2 c}{\partial S^2} = \Gamma_p = \frac{\partial^2 p}{\partial S^2} = \exp(-q\tau)\frac{n(d_1)}{S\sigma\sqrt{\tau}}.$$

(4.4.63)

Delta:

$$\Delta_c = \frac{\partial c}{\partial S} = \exp(-q\tau)N_1(d_1), \quad \Delta_p = \frac{\partial p}{\partial S} = \exp(-q\tau)\{N_1(d_1) - 1\}.$$

(4.4.64)

Theta:

$$\Theta_c = \frac{\partial c}{\partial t} = q\exp(-q\tau)SN_1(d_1) - rE\exp(-r\tau)N_1(d_2) - \frac{Sn(d_1)\sigma\exp(-q\tau)}{2\sqrt{\tau}},$$

$$\Theta_p = \frac{\partial p}{\partial t} = -q\exp(-q\tau)SN_1(-d_1) + rE\exp(-r\tau)N_1(-d_2) - \frac{Sn(d_1)\sigma\exp(-q\tau)}{2\sqrt{\tau}}.$$

(4.4.65)

Rho:

$$\rho_c = \frac{\partial c}{\partial r} = E\tau N_1(d_2), \quad \rho_p = \frac{\partial p}{\partial r} = -E\tau N_1(-d_2).$$

(4.4.66)

Vega:

$$\mathcal{V}_c = \frac{\partial c}{\partial \sigma} = \mathcal{V}_p = \frac{\partial p}{\partial \sigma} = S\exp(-q\tau)n(d_1)\sqrt{\tau},$$

(4.4.67)

where $n(x) = (1/\sqrt{2\pi})\exp(-x^2/2)$.

We now present, in Code excerpt 4.1, a computer program to calculate the Black–Scholes option value and Greeks given in equations (4.4.63) to (4.4.67). The routine uses EPS = 1.0e-16 to identify whether the arguments are too small, PI = 3.14159, and also the function cum_norm to compute the cumulative normal distribution function.

```
void black_scholes(double *value, double greeks[], double s0, double x,
                   double sigma, double t, double r, double q, long put, long *iflag)
{
/* Input parameters:
   =================
   s0        - the current price of the underlying asset
```

Code excerpt 4.1 Function to compute the Black–Scholes value for European options.

```
x          - the strike price
sigma      - the volatility
t          - the time to maturity
r          - the interest rate
q          - the continuous dividend yield
put        - if put is 0 then a call option, otherwise a put option
Output parameters:
==================
value      - the value of the option
greeks[]   - the hedge statistics output as follows: greeks[0] is gamma, greeks[1] is delta
             greeks[2] is theta, greeks[3] is rho, and greeks[4] is vega
iflag      - an error indicator
*/
    double one=1.0,two=2.0,zero=0.0;
    double eps,d1,d2,temp,temp1,temp2,pi,np;

    if( (x < EPS) || (sigma < EPS) || (t < EPS) ) { /* Check if any of the the input arguments are too small */
        *iflag = 2;
        return;
    }
    temp = log(s0/x);
    d1 = temp+(r-q+(sigma*sigma/two))*t;
    d1 = d1/(sigma*sqrt(t));
    d2 = d1-sigma*sqrt(t);
    /* evaluate the option price */
    if (put==0)
        *value = (s0*exp(-q*t)*cum_norm(d1)- x*exp(-r*t)*cum_norm(d2));
    else
        *value = (-s0*exp(-q*t)*cum_norm(-d1) + x*exp(-r*t)*cum_norm(-d2));
    if (greeks) { /* then calculate the greeks */
        temp1 = -d1*d1/two;
        d2 = d1-sigma*sqrt(t);
        np = (one/sqrt(two*PI)) * exp(temp1);
        if (put==0) { /*  a call option */
            greeks[1] = (cum_norm(d1))*exp(-q*t); /* delta */
            greeks[2] = -s0*exp(-q*t)*np*sigma/(two*sqrt(t))
                + q*s0*cum_norm(d1)*exp(-q*t)- r*x*exp(-r*t)*cum_norm(d2); /* theta */
            greeks[3] = x*t*exp(-r*t)*cum_norm(d2); /* rho */
        }
        else { /* a put option */
            greeks[1] = (cum_norm(d1) - one)*exp(-q*t);  /* delta */
            greeks[2] = -s0*exp(-q*t)*np*sigma/(two*sqrt(t)) -
                q*s0*cum_norm(-d1)*exp(-q*t) + r*x*exp(-r*t)*cum_norm(-d2); /* theta */
            greeks[3] = -x*t*exp(-r*t)*cum_norm(-d2); /* rho */
        }
        greeks[0] = np*exp(-q*t)/(s0*sigma*sqrt(t)); /* gamma */
        greeks[4] = s0*sqrt(t)*np*exp(-q*t); /* vega */
    }
    return;
}
```

Code excerpt 4.1 (*Continued*).

It can be seen in Table 4.1 and Table 4.2 that the values for gamma andvega are the same for both puts and calls. We can also demonstrate that the option values are consistent by using put call parity.

$$c(S,E,\tau) + E\exp(-r\tau) = p(S,E,\tau) + S\exp(-q\tau).$$

For example, when $\tau = 1.0$ we have $c(S,E,\tau) = 12.952$ and $P(S,E,T) = 9.260$. So $c(S,E,\tau) + E\exp(-r\tau) = 12.952 + 100 \times \exp(-0.1) = 103.436$ and $p(S,E,\tau) + S\exp(-q\tau) = 9.260 + 100 \times \exp(-0.06) = 103.436$.

4.4.4 Historical and Implied Volatility

Obtaining the best estimate of the volatility parameter, σ, in the Black–Scholes formula is of crucial importance. There are many different approaches to volatility estimation. These include the following:

- Historical estimation.
- Implied volatility.

We will now consider both historical and implied volatility estimations.

TABLE 4.1 European Put: Option Values and Greeks. The Parameters are $S = 100.0, E = 100.0, r = 0.10, \sigma = 0.30$, and $q = 0.06$

τ	Value	Delta	Gamma	Theta	Vega	Rho
0.100	3.558	-0.462	0.042	-16.533	12.490	-4.971
0.200	4.879	-0.444	0.029	-10.851	17.487	-9.860
0.300	5.824	-0.431	0.024	-8.298	21.204	-14.663
0.400	6.571	-0.419	0.020	-6.758	24.241	-19.377
0.500	7.191	-0.408	0.018	-5.698	26.832	-24.004
0.600	7.720	-0.399	0.016	-4.909	29.100	-28.544
0.700	8.179	-0.390	0.015	-4.292	31.118	-32.997
0.800	8.582	-0.381	0.014	-3.792	32.935	-37.364
0.900	8.940	-0.373	0.013	-3.377	34.585	-41.646
1.000	9.260	-0.366	0.012	-3.025	36.093	-45.843

TABLE 4.2 European Call: Option Values and Greeks. The Parameters are $S = 100.0, E = 100.0, r = 0.10, \sigma = 0.30$, and $q = 0.06$

τ	Value	Delta	Gamma	Theta	Vega	Rho
0.100	3.955	0.532	0.042	-20.469	12.490	4.929
0.200	5.667	0.544	0.029	-14.724	17.487	9.744
0.300	6.996	0.552	0.024	-12.109	21.204	14.451
0.400	8.121	0.558	0.020	-10.508	24.241	19.054
0.500	9.113	0.562	0.018	-9.387	26.832	23.557
0.600	10.007	0.566	0.016	-8.539	29.100	27.962
0.700	10.826	0.569	0.015	-7.863	31.118	32.271
0.800	11.584	0.572	0.014	-7.305	32.935	36.485
0.900	12.290	0.574	0.013	-6.832	34.585	40.608
1.000	12.952	0.576	0.012	-6.422	36.093	44.640

Historical Volatility

In this method, we calculate the volatility using $n + 1$ historical asset prices, $S_i, i = 0, \ldots, n$, and we assume that the asset prices are observed at the regular time interval, $d\tau$. Since the asset prices are assumed to follow GBM, the volatility is computed as the standard deviation of the n continuously compounded returns, $u_i, i = 1, \ldots, n$, where

$$S_i = S_{i-1} \exp(u_i)$$

or

$$u_i = \log\left(\frac{S_i}{S_{i-1}}\right).$$

We already know (see equation (2.1.10)) that the expected standard deviation of the asset returns over the time interval is $\sigma \sqrt{d\tau}$. This means that we obtain the following expression for $\hat{\sigma}$, the estimated volatility:

$$\hat{\sigma} \ \sqrt{d\tau} = \sqrt{\frac{1}{n-1} \sum_{i=1}^{n} (u_i - \bar{u})^2} \tag{4.4.68}$$

or

$$\hat{\sigma} = \sqrt{\frac{1}{(n-1) \ d\tau} \sum_{i=1}^{n} (u_i - \bar{u})^2}. \tag{4.4.69}$$

It is accepted practice to express all times in years, and so the volatility is the *annualized* standard deviation of the returns. There is also the issue of how to account for non-trading days such as weekend and holidays. For example, let us suppose that the history of assets prices $S_i, i = 0, \ldots, n$ was obtained by recording the price on each *trading* day. One approach is to use $d\tau = 1/N_{td}$, where N_{td} is the number of trading days in a year. If we take $N_{td} = 250$, then equation (4.4.69) becomes

$$\hat{\sigma} = \sqrt{\frac{250}{(n-1)} \sum_{i=1}^{n} (u_i - \bar{u})^2}. \tag{4.4.70}$$

The estimated standard error in $\hat{\sigma}$ is, see, for example, Hull (2003), given by

$$\hat{\sigma}_{std} = \hat{\sigma} \sqrt{\frac{1}{2(n-1)}}. \tag{4.4.71}$$

A computer program to perform these calculations is given below in Code excerpt 4.2.

```
void hist_vol(double *sigma, double *err, double data[], long n, double dt, long *ifail)
{
/* Input parameters:
   ==================
   data[]      - the data, which consists of n asset prices
   n           - the number of data points
   dt          - the (constant) time spacing between the data points (in years)
   Output parameters:
   ==================
   sigma       - the computed historical volatility
   err         - the standard error in the volatility estimate sigma
   iflag       - an error indicator
*/

#define DATA(I) data[(I)-1]
```

Code excerpt 4.2 Function to compute the historical volatility from asset data.

```
double mean=0.0,sum=0.0;
double temp,tn;
long i;

for(i = 2; i <= n; ++i)
    mean = mean + log(DATA(i))-log(DATA(i-1));
mean = mean/(double)(n-1);

for(i = 2; i <= n; ++i) {
    temp = log(DATA(i))-log(DATA(i-1));
    sum = sum + (temp-mean)*(temp-mean);
}
sum = sum/(double)(n-2);
*sigma = sqrt(sum/dt);
tn = (double)(2*(n-1));
*err = *sigma/sqrt(tn);
return;
}
```

Code excerpt 4.2 (*Continued*).

Implied Volatility

The implied volatility of a European option is the volatility, which when substituted into the Black–Scholes equation yields the market value quoted for the same option. In general, the implied volatility will depend on both the time to expiry of the option and also the ratio of the current asset price to the strike – this is known as the volatility smile. These values are usually stored in a multidimensional implied volatility surface, and the volatility for pricing a given option obtained via multidimensional interpolation.

The routine provided in Code excerpt 4.3 uses Newton's method to calculate the implied volatility for a European option from its market price. We will now illustrate this technique for a European call option with market value opt_value. The implied volatility, σ, is then that value which satisfies

$$K(\sigma) = c(S, E, \tau, \sigma) - \texttt{opt\_value} = 0,$$

where $c(S, E, \tau, \sigma)$ represents the value of the European call and the other symbols have their usual meaning.

From Newton's method, we have

$$\sigma_{i+1} = \sigma_i - \frac{F(\sigma_i)}{F'(\sigma_i)},$$

where

$$F'(\sigma_i) = \frac{\partial F}{\partial \sigma} = \frac{\partial c(S, E, \tau, \sigma)}{\partial \sigma} = \mathcal{V}_c.$$

Therefore, the iterative procedure is

$$\sigma_{i+1} = \sigma_i - \frac{c(S, E, \tau, \sigma) - \texttt{opt\_value}}{\mathcal{V}_c},$$

where σ_0 is the initial estimate, and σ_{i+1} is the improved estimate of the implied volatility based on the ith estimate σ_i. Termination of this iteration occurs when $ABS(\sigma_{i+1} - \sigma_i) < \texttt{tol}$, for a specified tolerance, $\texttt{tol}$.

It can be seen that as $\sigma \to 0$, $d_1 \to \infty$, $d_2 \to \infty$, and, from equation (4.4.67), we have $\mathcal{V}_c \to 0$. Under these circumstances, Newton's method fails.

The same procedure can be used to compute the implied volatility for a European put; in this, can we just replace $c(S, E, \tau, \sigma)$ by $p(S, E, \tau, \sigma)$, the value of a European put, and from equation (4.4.67), $\mathcal{V}_c = \mathcal{V}_p$.

```
void implied_volatility(double value, double s0, double x, double sigma[],
                        double t, double r, double q, long put, long *iflag)
{
/* Input parameters:
   =================
   value     - the current value of the option
   s0        - the current price of the underlying asset
   x         - the strike price
   sigma[]   - the input bounds on the volatility: sigma[0], the lower bound and, sigma[1], the upper bound
   t         - the time to maturity
   r         - the interest rate
   q         - the continuous dividend yield
   put       - if put is 0 then a call option, otherwise a put option
   Output parameters:
   =================
   sigma[]   - the element sigma[0] contains the estimated implied volatility
   iflag     - an error indicator
*/
  double zero=0.0;
  double fx, sig1, sig2;
  double val,tolx;
  double temp,eps,epsqrt,temp1,v1;
  long max_iters, i, ind, ir;
  double greeks[5],c[20],sig,vega;
  long done;

  tolx = eps;
  epsqrt = sqrt(EPS);
  if(put == 0)                                 /* a call option */
    temp1 = MAX(s0*exp(-q*t)-x*exp(-r*t),zero);
  else                                         /* a put option */
    temp1 = MAX(x*exp(-r*t)-s0*exp(-q*t),zero);
  v1 = fabs(value-temp1);
  if (v1 <= epsqrt) {                          /* the volatility is too small */
    *iflag = 3;
    return;
  }
  *iflag = 0;
  i = 0;
  max_iters = 50;
  done = 0;
  sig = sigma[0];                              /* initial estimate */
  val = value;
  while ((i < max_iters) && (!done)) {         /* Newton iteration */
    black_scholes(&val,greeks,s0,x,sig,t,r,q,put,iflag); /* compute the Black Scholes option value, val   */
    vega = greeks[4];                          /* and vega. */
    sig1 = sig - ((val - value)/vega);         /* compute the new estimate of sigma using Newton's method */

    if (tolx > fabs((sig1 - sig)/sig1)) {      /* check whether the specified accuracy has been reached */
      done = 1;
    }
    sig = sig1;                                /* up date sigma */
    ++i;
  }
  sigma[0] = sig1;                             /* return the estimate for sigma */
  return;
}
```

Code excerpt 4.3 Function to compute the implied volatility of European options.

If the implied volatility of American options is required, the procedure is exactly the same. However, instead of using the Black–Scholes formula to compute both the option value and vega, we use a binomial lattice to do this. The use of binomial lattices to obtain the option prices and the Greeks is described in Chapter 5.

Below, in Code excerpt 4.4, provides the simple test program which illustrates the use of the function `implied_volatility`; the results are presented in Table 4.3.

TABLE 4.3 Calculated Option Values and Implied Volatilities from Code excerpt 4.4

Time (in years)	Option value	True σ	Error in estimated σ
0.5	0.1959	0.1	2.7756×10^{-16}
1.0	0.8158	0.2	2.2204×10^{-16}
1.5	1.5435	0.3	3.8858×10^{-16}
2.0	2.3177	0.4	5.5511×10^{-17}
2.5	3.1033	0.5	1.1102×10^{-16}

```
double X,  value,  S,  sigma[2], sigmat, T, r, q;
long i, ifail, put;

ifail = 0;
S     = 10.0;
X     = 10.5;
r     = 0.1;
sigmat = 0.1;
q     = 0.04;
put   = 0;
printf (" Time        option value      implied  volatility  (Error)\n");
for(i = 1;i < 6; ++i) {
    T = (double)i*0.5;
    black_scholes(&value,NULL,S,X,sigmat,T,r,q,put,&flag);
    sigma[0] = 0.05;
    sigma[1] = 1.0;
    implied_volatility(value,S,X,sigma,T,r,q,put,&flag);
    printf("%8.4f         %15.4f             %15.4f (%8.4e) \n",T,value,sigma[0], fabs(sigmat-sigma[0]));
    sigmat = sigmat + 0.1;
}
```

Code excerpt 4.4 Simple test program for function `implied_volatility`.

4.4.5 Pricing Options with Microsoft Excel

In this section, we show how the Visual Basic within Excel can be used to create powerful derivative pricing applications based on the Black–Scholes formula. We will explain how Excel's Visual Basic can be used to create an application that prices a selection of simple European put and call options at the press of a button.

In Section 4.4.3, we derived the Black–Scholes formula

$$c(S,E,\tau) = SN_1(d_1) - e^{-r\tau}EN_1(d_2) \text{ and}$$
$$p(S,E,\tau) = -SN_1(-d_1) + e^{-r\tau}EN_1(-d_2),$$

where

$$d_2 = \frac{\log(S/E) + (r - \sigma^2/2)\tau}{\sigma\sqrt{\tau}} = d_1 - \sigma\sqrt{\tau},$$

where S is the current value of the asset and σ is the volatility of the asset, and $N_1(x) = (1/\sqrt{2\pi}) \int_{-\infty}^{x} e^{-x^2/2}dx$.

The univariate cumulative standard normal distribution, $N_1(x)$, can be evaluated in Excel by using its built-in function NORMDIST. The definition of this function is as follows:

```
NORMDIST(x,mean,standard_dev,cumulative)
```

This function returns the normal cumulative distribution for the specified mean and standard deviation.

Function parameters:

`x`: the value for which you want the distribution.

`mean`: the arithmetic mean of the distribution.

`standard_dev`: the standard deviation of the distribution.

cumulative: a logical value that determines the form of the function. If cumulative is `TRUE`, `NORMDIST` returns the cumulative distribution function; if `FALSE`, it returns the probability density function.

If `mean` = 0 and `standard_dev` = 1, `NORMDIST` returns the standard normal distribution.

This function can be used to create a Visual Basic function to calculate European option values within Excel, see Code excerpt 4.5.

```
Function bs_opt(S0 As Double, _
  ByVal X As Double, sigma As Double, T As Double, _
  r As Double, q As Double, ByVal putcall As Long) As Double

' Visual Basic Routine to calculate the value of
' either a European Put or European Call option.
' Author: George Levy

  Dim temp As Double
  Dim d1 As Double
  Dim d2 As Double
  Dim SQT As Double
  Dim value As Double

  temp = Log(S0 / X)
  d1 = temp + (r - q + (sigma * sigma / 2#)) * T
  SQT = Sqr(T)
  d1 = d1 / (sigma * SQT)
  d2 = d1 - sigma * SQT

  If (putcall = 0) Then ' a call option
    value = S0 * Exp(-q * T) * WorksheetFunction.NormDist(d1, 0#, 1#, True) _
           - WorksheetFunction.NormDist(d2, 0#, 1#, True) * X * Exp(-r * T)

  Else ' a put option
    value = -S0 * Exp(-q * T) * WorksheetFunction.NormDist(-d1, 0#, 1#, True) + _
         X * WorksheetFunction.NormDist(-d2, 0#, 1#, True) * Exp(-r * T)

  End If

  bs_opt = value

End Function
```

Code excerpt 4.5 Visual basic code to price European options using the Black–Scholes formula.

Once the function has been defined, it can be accessed interactively using the Paste Function facility within Excel as shown in Fig. 4.1.

The function `bs_opt` can also be incorporated into other Visual Basic code within Excel. To illustrate, if the following Visual Basic subroutine is defined in Code excerpt 4.6.

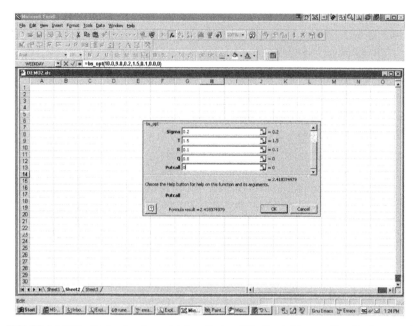

FIGURE 4.1 Using the function `bs_opt` interactively within Excel. Here, a call option is proceed with the following parameters: $S = 10.0$, $X = 9.0$, $q = 0.0$, $T = 1.5$, $r = 0.1$, and $\sigma = 0.2$.

```
Private Sub MANY_EUROPEANS_Click()

Dim i As Long
Dim putcall As Long
Dim S0 As Double
Dim q As Double
Dim sigma As Double
Dim T As Double
Dim r As Double

q = 0#
T = 1.5
r = 0.1
sigma = 0.2

For i = 1 To 22

  S0 = Sheet1.Cells(i + 1, 1).value
  X = Sheet1.Cells(i + 1, 2).value
  putcall = Sheet1.Cells(i + 1, 3).value
  Sheet1.Cells(i + 1, 4).value = bs_opt(S0, X, sigma, T, r, q, putcall)

Next i

End Sub
```

Code excerpt 4.6 Visual basic code that uses the function `bs_opt`.

When the button labelled "CALCULATE OPTIONS" is clicked, the values of 22 European options will be calculated using the data in columns 1–3 on worksheet 1, see Figs 4.2 and 4.3.

The cumulative standard normal distribution can also be used to provide analytic solutions for a range of other *exotic* options such as Barrier options, Exchange options, Lookback options, Binary options, etc.

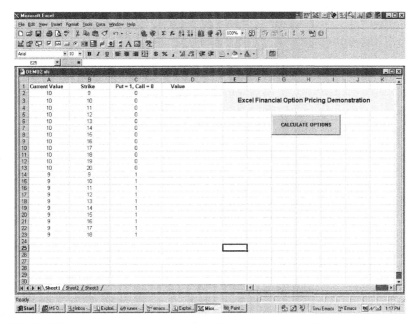

FIGURE 4.2 Excel worksheet before calculation of the European option values.

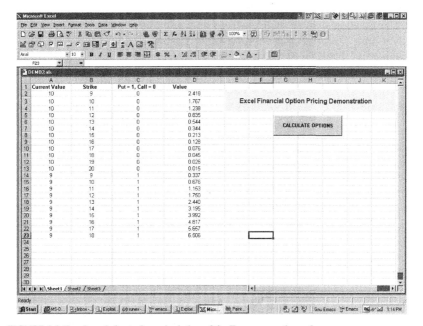

FIGURE 4.3 Excel worksheet after calculation of the European option values.

4.5 BARRIER OPTIONS

4.5.1 Introduction

Barrier options are derivatives where the payoff depends on whether the asset price reaches a given barrier level, B. *Knockout options* become worthless (cease to exist) if the asset price reaches the barrier, whereas *knockin options* come into existence when the asset price *hits* the barrier. We will consider the following single asset European barrier options:

- *Down and out call*: A knockout vanilla call option, value c_{do}, which ceases to exist when the asset price reaches or goes below the barrier level.
- *Up and out call*: A knockout vanilla call option, value c_{uo}, which ceases to exist when the asset price reaches or goes above the barrier level.
- *Down and in call*: A knockin vanilla call option, value c_{di}, which comes into existence when the asset prices reaches or goes below the barrier level.
- *Up and in call*: A knockin vanilla call option, value c_{ui}, which comes into existence when the asset price reaches or goes above the barrier level.

The following expressions must be true:

$$c = c_{uo} + c_{ui}, \tag{4.5.1}$$

$$c = c_{do} + c_{di}, \tag{4.5.2}$$

where c is the value of a vanilla call option. We thus need only derive expressions for both the knockout options and then use the above equations to calculate the value of the corresponding knockin options.

The notation that we will use is as follows: The symbol t represents the current time, T represents the time at which the option matures, and $\tau = T - t$, the duration of the option. The symbol s, with constraint $t \le s \le T$, is any intermediate time during which the option is alive.

4.5.2 Analytic Pricing of Down and Out Call Options

If we consider Brownian motion (with zero drift) $X_s \sim N(0, (s-t)\sigma^2), t \le s \le T$ which starts at $X_t = 0$ and, after time $\tau = T - t$, ends at the point $X_T = X$, then (e.g., Freedman (1983)) the probability density function for this motion not to exceed the value $X = b$ (where $b > 0$) during time τ is given by

$$f(b \ge X_s^{\max}, X) = \Omega \sqrt{\frac{2}{\pi}} \exp\left(\frac{2b(X-b)}{\sigma^2 \tau}\right) \exp\left(-\frac{X^2}{2\sigma^2 \tau}\right), \tag{4.5.3}$$

where for convenience we have used $\Omega = (2b - X)/\sigma^3 \tau^{3/2}$, and $X_s^{\max} = \max(X_s, t \le s \le T)$. Since X_s is Brownian motion without drift and volatility σ, then $-X_s$ is identical Brownian motion. Therefore by substituting $X \to -X$ and $b \to -b$ in the above equation, we obtain

$$f(b \le X_s^{\min}, X) = \Omega \sqrt{\frac{2}{\pi}} \exp\left(\frac{2b(X-b)}{\sigma^2 \tau}\right) \exp\left(-\frac{X^2}{2\sigma^2 \tau}\right), \tag{4.5.4}$$

where we have used $X_s^{\min} = \min(X_s, t \leq s \leq T)$. Equation (4.5.4) is the probability density function of $-X_s$ staying above the value $X = b$, where $b < 0$. These results can be generalized to include drift (e.g., Musiela and Rutkowski (1998), p. 212), so that $X_s \sim N((r - q - \sigma^2/2)(s - t), \sigma(s - t))$, for $t \leq s \leq T$. We now have the following results:

$$f(b \geq X_s^{\max}, X) = \Omega \sqrt{\frac{2}{\pi}} \exp\left(\frac{2b(X - b)}{\sigma^2 \tau}\right) \exp\left(-\frac{(X - (r - q - \sigma^2/2)\tau)^2}{2\sigma^2 \tau}\right), \quad (4.5.5)$$

$$f(b \leq X_s^{\min}, X) = -\Omega \sqrt{\frac{2}{\pi}} \exp\left(\frac{2b(X - b)}{\sigma^2 \tau}\right) \exp\left(-\frac{(X - (r - q - \sigma^2/2)\tau)^2}{2\sigma^2 \tau}\right),$$
$$(4.5.6)$$

where r is the risk free rate and q is the continuous dividend yield. A European down and out barrier option with maturity τ and a barrier at $X = B$ will cease to exist (become worthless) if at any time $X_s \leq B$, for $t \leq s \leq T$. The probability density function that the barrier option will continue to exist at time T if the end point is X is therefore

$$f(X > B) = -\sqrt{\frac{2}{\pi}} \int_{B = S \exp(b)}^{b = X} \Omega \exp\left(\frac{2b(X - b)}{\sigma^2 \tau}\right) \exp\left(-\frac{\left\{X - (r - q - \sigma^2/2)\tau\right\}^2}{2\sigma^2 \tau}\right) db$$
$$(4.5.7)$$

or

$$f(X > B) = -\sqrt{\frac{2}{\pi}} \exp\left(-\frac{\left\{X - (r - q - \sigma^2/2)\tau\right\}^2}{2\sigma^2 \tau}\right) \int_{b = \log(B/S)}^{b = X} \Omega \exp\left(\frac{2b(X - b)}{\sigma^2 \tau}\right) db,$$
$$(4.5.8)$$

where we have integrated over all possible values of b (i.e., $B < b < X$) that keep the option alive. Recalling that

$$-\int_{b = \log(B/S)}^{b = X} \Omega \exp\left(\frac{2b(X - b)}{\sigma^2 \tau}\right) db = \int_{b = \log(B/S)}^{b = X} \frac{(X - 2b)}{\sigma^3 \tau^{3/2}} \exp\left(\frac{2b(X - b)}{\sigma^2 \tau}\right) db$$

and noting that

$$\frac{\partial}{\partial b} \exp\left(\frac{2b(X - b)}{\sigma^2 \tau}\right) = \frac{2(X - 2b)}{\sigma^2 \tau} \exp\left(\frac{2b(X - b)}{\sigma^2 \tau}\right),$$

we have

$$\int_{b = \log(B/S)}^{b = X} \frac{2(X - 2b)}{\sigma^2 \tau} \exp\left(\frac{2b(X - b)}{\sigma^2 \tau}\right) db = \left[\exp\left(\frac{2b(X - b)}{\sigma^2 \tau}\right)\right]_{b = \log(B/S)}^{b = X}$$
$$= \left\{1 - \exp\left(\frac{2 \log(B/S)(X - \log(B/S))}{\sigma^2 \tau}\right)\right\}.$$

So we have

$$f(X > B) = \frac{1}{\sigma \sqrt{\tau} \sqrt{2\pi}} \exp\left(-\frac{\left\{X - (r - q - \sigma^2/2)\tau\right\}^2}{2\sigma^2 \tau}\right)$$
$$\times \left\{1 - \exp\left(\frac{2 \log(B/S)(X - \log(B/S))}{\sigma^2 \tau}\right)\right\}.$$

The value, c_{do} of a European down and out call option with strike E, satisfying $E > B$, is given by

$$c_{do} = \frac{\exp(-r\tau)}{\sigma\sqrt{\tau}\sqrt{2\pi}} \int_{X=\log(E/S)}^{\infty} \{S\exp(X) - E\}\, f(X > B)dX. \qquad (4.5.9)$$

This integral is evaluated in Appendix B.1, and the value of the down and out call option c_{do} is

$$c_{do} = c - c_{di}, \qquad (4.5.10)$$

where

$$c = S\exp(-q\tau)N_1(d_1) - E\exp(-r\tau)N_1(d_2),$$

$$c_{di} = S\exp(-q\tau)N_1(d_4)\left(\frac{B}{S}\right)^{\frac{2(r-q)}{\sigma^2}+1} - E\exp(-r\tau)N_1(d_3)\left(\frac{B}{S}\right)^{\frac{2(r-q)}{\sigma^2}-1},$$

$$d_1 = \frac{\log(S/E) + (r - q + \sigma^2/2)\tau}{\sigma\sqrt{\tau}}, \quad d_2 = \frac{\log(S/E) + (r - q - \sigma^2/2)\tau}{\sigma\sqrt{\tau}},$$

$$d_3 = \frac{\log(B^2/SE) + (r - q - \sigma^2/2)\tau)}{\sigma\sqrt{\tau}}, \quad \text{and} \quad d_4 = \frac{\log(B^2/ES) + (r - q + \sigma^2/2)\tau}{\sigma\sqrt{\tau}}.$$

In Code excerpt 4.7 below, we provide the function `bs_opt_barrier_downout_call` which uses equation (4.5.10) to price a down and out European call option. This routine will be used in Chapter 5 to measure the accuracy achieved by using various finite-difference grid techniques to solve the Black–Scholes equation.

```
void bs_opt_barrier_downout_call(double *value, double barrier_level,
            double s0, double x, double sigma, double t, double r,
            double q, long *iflag)
{
/* Input parameters:
   =================
   barrier_level       - the level of the barrier
   s0                  - the current price of the underlying asset
   x                   - the strike price
   sigma               - the volatility
   t                   - the time to maturity
   r                   - the risk free interest rate
   q                   - the dividend yield
   Output parameters:
   ==================
   value               - the value of the option
   iflag               - an error indicator
*/
   double one=1.0,two=2.0,zero=0.0;
   double temp,temp1,temp2,a,b,d1,d2,d3,d4,d5,d6,d7,d8;
   double fac;

   if(x < EPS) { /* then strike price (X) is too small */
       *iflag = 2;
       return;
   }
   if (sigma < EPS) { /* then volatility (sigma) is too small */
       *iflag = 3;
       return;
   }
   if (t < EPS) { /* then time to expiry (t) is too small */
       *ifail = 3;
       return;
   }
   if (barrier_level <= 0) { /* barrier level must be greater than zero */
       *iflag = 4;
   }

   if (s0 <= barrier_level) { /* option has already been knocked out */
```

Code excerpt 4.7 Function to compute the value for European down and out call options.

```
    *value = 0.0;
    return;
}

fac = sigma*sqrt(t);
temp1 = -one+(two*(r-q)/(sigma*sigma));
temp2 = barrier_level/s0;
a = pow(temp2,temp1);
temp1 = one+(two*(r-q)/(sigma*sigma));
b = pow(temp2,temp1);
if (x > barrier_level) {    /* strike > barrier_level */
    d1 = (log(s0/x)+(r-q+0.5*sigma*sigma)*t)/fac;
    d2 = (log(s0/x)+(r-q-0.5*sigma*sigma)*t)/fac;
    temp = (s0*x)/(barrier_level*barrier_level);
    d7 = (log(temp)-(r-q-0.5*sigma*sigma)*t)/fac;
    d8 = (log(temp)-(r-q+0.5*sigma*sigma)*t)/fac;

    temp1 = s0*exp(-q*t)*(cum_norm(d1)-b*(one-cum_norm(d8)));
    temp2 = x*exp(-r*t)*(cum_norm(d2)-a*(one-cum_norm(d7)));
    *value = temp1-temp2;
}
else { /* strike <= barrier_level */
    d3 = (log(s0/barrier_level)+(r-q-0.5*sigma*sigma)*t)/fac;
    d6 = (log(s0/barrier_level)-(r-q-0.5*sigma*sigma)*t)/fac;
    d4 = (log(s0/barrier_level)+(r-q+0.5*sigma*sigma)*t)/fac;
    d5 = (log(s0/barrier_level)-(r-q+0.5*sigma*sigma)*t)/fac;

    temp1 = s0*exp(-q*t)*(cum_norm(d3)-b*(one-cum_norm(d6)));
    temp2 = x*exp(-r*t)*(cum_norm(d4)-a*(one-cum_norm(d5)));
    *value = temp1-temp2;
}
return;
}
```

Code excerpt 4.7 (*Continued*).

4.5.3 Analytic Pricing of Up and Out Call Options

Here, we will obtain an expression for an *up and out* European call option with continuous dividend yield q, in a similar manner to that used in Section 4.5.2 for the down and out European call option. A European up and out barrier option with maturity τ and a barrier at $X = B$ will cease to exist (become worthless) if at any time $X_s \geq B$, for $t \leq s \leq T$. The probability density function that the barrier option will continue to exist at time T if the end point is X is therefore

$$f(X < B) = \sqrt{\frac{2}{\pi}} \int_{b=X}^{B=S\exp(b)} \Omega \exp\left(\frac{2b(X-b)}{\sigma^2 t}\right) \exp\left(-\frac{\left\{X-(r-q-\sigma^2/2)\tau\right\}^2}{2\sigma^2\tau}\right) db \tag{4.5.11}$$

or

$$f(X < B) = \sqrt{\frac{2}{\pi}} \exp\left(-\frac{\left\{X-(r-q-\sigma^2/2)\tau\right\}^2}{2\sigma^2\tau}\right) \int_{b=X}^{b=\log(B/S)} \Omega \exp\left(\frac{2b(X-b)}{\sigma^2\tau}\right) db, \tag{4.5.12}$$

where as in Section 4.5.2 we have used $\Omega = (2b-X)/\sigma^3\tau^{3/2}$ and have integrated over all possible values of b (i.e., $B > b > X$) that keep the option alive. Recalling that

$$\int_{b=X}^{b=\log(B/S)} \Omega \exp\left(\frac{2b(X-b)}{\sigma^2\tau}\right) db$$

$$= \int_{b=X}^{b=\log(B/S)} \frac{(2b-X)}{\sigma^3\tau^{3/2}} \exp\left(\frac{2b(X-b)}{\sigma^2\tau}\right) db$$

and noting

$$-\frac{\partial}{\partial b} \exp\left(\frac{2b(X-b)}{\sigma^2\tau}\right) = \frac{2(X-2b)}{\sigma^2\tau} \exp\left(\frac{2b(X-b)}{\sigma^2\tau}\right), \tag{4.5.13}$$

we have

$$\int_{b=X}^{b=\log(B/S)} \frac{2(2b-X)}{\sigma^2\tau} \exp\left(\frac{2b(X-b)}{\sigma^2\tau}\right) db - \left[-\exp\left(\frac{2b(X-b)}{\sigma^2\tau}\right)\right]_{b=X}^{b=\log(B/S)}$$

$$= \left\{1 - \exp\left(\frac{2\log(B/S)(X-\log(B/S))}{\sigma^2\tau}\right)\right\}.$$

Therefore,

$$f(X < B) = \frac{1}{\sigma\sqrt{\tau}\sqrt{2\pi}} \sqrt{\frac{2}{\pi}} \exp\left(-\frac{\left\{X - (r - q - \sigma^2/2)\tau\right\}^2}{2\sigma^2\tau}\right)$$

$$\times \left\{1 - \exp\left(\frac{2\log(B/S)(X-\log(B/S))}{\sigma^2\tau}\right)\right\}. \tag{4.5.14}$$

We will now derive the formula for an up and out call option when $E < B$. In fact if $E > B$, then the option is worthless, since at the current time t the call option's payout, $\max(S_t - E, 0) = 0$, and if $S_t > E$ then the option will be knocked out,

$$c_{uo} = \frac{\exp(-r\tau)}{\sigma\sqrt{\tau}\sqrt{2\pi}} \int_{X=\log(E/S)}^{\infty} \{S\exp(X) - E\} f(X < B) dX. \tag{4.5.15}$$

Taking into account the fact the option becomes worthless when $S\exp(X) > B$ (i.e., $X > \log(B/S)$), we have

$$c_{uo} = \frac{\exp(-r\tau)}{\sigma\sqrt{\tau}\sqrt{2\pi}} \int_{X=\log(E/S)}^{\log(B/S)} \{S\exp(X) - E\} f(X < B) dX. \tag{4.5.16}$$

This integral is evaluated in Appendix B.2, and the value of the down and out call option c_{uo} is

$$c_{uo} = c - c_{ui},$$

where c is the value of a vanilla call and c_{ui}, the value of an up and in call is given by

$$c_{ui} = S\exp(-q\tau)N_1(d_2) - E\exp(-r\tau)N_1(d_4)$$

$$- E\exp(-r\tau)\{N_1(d_5) - N_1(d_6)\}\left(\frac{B}{S}\right)^{\frac{2(r-q)}{\sigma^2}-1}$$

$$+ S\exp(-r\tau)\{N_1(d_7) - N_1(d_8)\}\left(\frac{B}{S}\right)^{\frac{2(r-q)}{\sigma^2}+1} \tag{4.5.17}$$

and

$$d_1 = \frac{\log(S/E) + (r - q + \sigma^2/2)\tau)}{\sigma\sqrt{\tau}}, \qquad d_2 = \frac{\log(S/B) + (r - q + \sigma^2/2)\tau}{\sqrt{\tau}},$$

$$d_3 = \frac{\log(S/E) + (r - q - \sigma^2/2)\tau}{\sigma\sqrt{\tau}}, \qquad d_4 = \frac{\log(S/B) + (r - q - \sigma^2/2)\tau}{\sigma\sqrt{\tau}},$$

$$d_5 = \frac{\log(B^2/ES) - (r - q - \sigma^2/2)\tau)}{\sigma\sqrt{\tau}}, \qquad d_6 = \frac{\log(B/S) + (r - q - \sigma^2/2)\tau)}{\sigma\sqrt{\tau}},$$

$$d_7 = \frac{\log(B^2/ES) + (r - q + \sigma^2/2)\tau}{\sigma\sqrt{\tau}}, \qquad d_8 = \frac{\log(B/S) + (r - q + \sigma^2/2)\tau}{\sigma\sqrt{\tau}}.$$

4.5.4 Monte Carlo Pricing of Down and Out Options

In this section, we show how Monte Carlo simulation can be used to price down and out barrier options. We will describe both a *basic* Monte Carlo approach and also a Brownian bridge method which gives more accurate results, see Chapter 8.

The asset price, S, will be assumed to be GBM, so the logarithm of the asset price Z follows the Brownian process

$$\Delta Z = v\Delta t + \sigma\Delta W_t, \tag{4.5.18}$$

where v is the drift and σ is the volatility.

If the barrier level is B, then the option will be *knocked out* when $S \le B$, or equivalently $\log(S) \le \log(B)$. This will be expressed as $Z \le b$, where $b = \log(B)$.

The basic approach to simulating the down and out option is to first decide how many Scenarios to use and also how many TimeSteps there are to be in each scenario. The size of each time step is then time_step = TimeToExpiry/TimeSteps. For each scenario, the path of Z_t is advanced in time from t to $t + \Delta t$ using equation (4.5.18), with $dt =$ time_step and a value for ΔW_t output from a Gaussian random number generator. Path construction is stopped if either the option expiry time is reached or if the option is knocked out, i.e., $Z \le b$. When the option is knocked out before expiry, the payoff for that scenario is zero. We will denote the option value obtained from the ith scenario by DO_i where $i = 1, \ldots,$ Scenarios. The option value is the average value of DO_i over all scenarios – for more details see Code excerpt 4.8.

One problem with this approach to simulation is that it does not take into account the possibility that $Z_\tau \le b$, $t < \tau < t + \Delta t$, even though $Z_t > b$ and $Z_{t+\Delta t} > b$. In these circumstances, the option should be treated as knocked out, since Z hit (or crossed) the barrier b at time τ, but then increased to the value $Z_{t+\Delta t} > b$ at time $t + \Delta t$.

We will now discuss how the Brownian bridge method deals with this situation.

Let us take two consecutive time points t_1 and $t_2 = t_1 + \Delta t$, and assume that the both Z_{t_1} and Z_{t_2} are above the (logarithmic) barrier level b. We want to find the probability that in the time interval $[t_1, t_2]$, the asset price went lower than B and use this to get more accurate values for down and out options. The required barrier crossing probability is thus

$$P\left(m^Z \le b|\{Z_{t_2}, Z_{t_1}\}\right),$$

where m^Z denotes the minimum of Z over the time interval $[t_1, t_2]$. The probability of Z_{t_2} conditional on Z_{t_1} is

$$P(Z_{t_2}|Z_{t_1}) = \frac{1}{\sigma \sqrt{2\pi\Delta t}} \exp\left\{-\frac{(Z_{t_2} - Z_{t_1} - v\Delta t)^2}{2\sigma^2 \Delta t}\right\},$$

where $\Delta t = t_2 - t_1$.

From Bayes law, we know that

$$P\left(m^Z \le b \ |\{Z_{t_2}, Z_{t_1}\}\right) = \frac{P(\{m^Z \le b, Z_{t_2}\}|Z_{t_1})}{P(Z_{t_2}|Z_{t_1})}.$$

We show in Appendix H.1 that

$$P\left(\{m^Z \le b, Z_{t_2}\}|Z_{t_1}\right)$$
$$= \frac{1}{\sigma \sqrt{2\pi\Delta t}} \exp\left\{\frac{2v(b - Z_{t_1})}{\sigma^2}\right\} \exp\left\{-\frac{(Z_{t_2} + Z_{t_1} - 2b - v\Delta t)^2}{2\sigma^2 \Delta t}\right\},$$

so

$$P\left(m^Z \le b|\{Z_{t_2}, Z_{t_1}\}\right)$$
$$= \exp\left\{\frac{2v(b - Z_{t_1})}{\sigma^2}\right\} \exp\left\{\frac{-(Z_{t_2} + Z_{t_1} - 2b - v\Delta t)^2 + (Z_{t_2} - Z_{t_1} - v\Delta t)^2}{2\sigma^2 \Delta t}\right\}.$$

We will now use some algebra to simplify this expression,

$$P\left(m^Z \le b|\{Z_{t_2}, Z_{t_1}\}\right)$$
$$= \exp\left\{\frac{4v\Delta t(b - Z_{t_1}) - (Z_{t_2} + Z_{t_1} - 2b - v\Delta t)^2 + (Z_{t_2} - Z_{t_1} - v\Delta t)^2}{2\sigma^2 \Delta t}\right\}$$
$$= \exp\left\{\frac{4v\Delta t(b - Z_{t_1}) - ((Z_{t_2} - Z_{t_1} - v\Delta t) - 2(b - Z_{t_1}))^2 + (Z_{t_2} - Z_{t_1} - v\Delta t)^2}{2\sigma^2 \Delta t}\right\}$$
$$= \exp\left\{\frac{4v\Delta t(b - Z_{t_1}) + 4(b - Z_{t_1})(Z_{t_2} - Z_{t_1} - v\Delta t) + 4(b - Z_{t_1})^2}{2\sigma^2 \Delta t}\right\}$$
$$= \exp\left\{-\frac{2(b - Z_{t_1})(b - Z_{t_2})}{\sigma^2 \Delta t}\right\},$$

which finally yields

$$P\left(m^Z \le b|\{Z_{t_2}, Z_{t_1}\}\right) = \exp\left\{-\frac{2\left(\log(B) - \log(S_{t_1})\right)\left(\log(B) - \log(S_{t_2})\right)}{\sigma^2 \Delta t}\right\}. \quad (4.5.19)$$

Equation (4.5.19) gives the probability of the option having been knocked out between times t_1 and t_2 even though the asset prices S_{t_1} and S_{t_2} are greater than B. The probability that the option has not been knocked out between times t_1 and t_2 is therefore

$$P\left(m^Z > b|\{Z_{t_2}, Z_{t_1}\}\right) = 1 - \exp\left\{-\frac{2\left(\log(B) - \log(S_{t_1})\right)\left(\log(B) - \log(S_{t_2})\right)}{\sigma^2 \Delta t}\right\}.$$

(4.5.20)

This means that for the (complete) ith scenario path, of n time steps, the probability that $m^Z > b$ is

$$BB_c^i = \prod_{j=0}^{n-1}\left\{1 - \exp\left\{-\frac{2\left(\log(B) - \log(S_{t_j}^i)\right)\left(\log(B) - \log(S_{t_{j+1}}^i)\right)}{\sigma^2 \Delta t}\right\}\right\},$$

where $S_{t_j}^i$ is the ith scenario asset price at time t_j.

The basic Monte Carlo ith scenario option value DO_i can therefore be adjusted as follows

$$DO_i^* = DO_i \ BB_c^i,$$

and the new Monte Carlo estimate DO^* is

$$DO^* = \frac{\sum_{i=1}^{\text{Scenarios}} DO_i^*}{\text{Scenarios}},$$

where more details can be found in Code excerpt 4.8.

```
private double MonteCarloSim(bool is_put)
{
    int seed = 111;
    double[] asset_path = new double[fTimeSteps];
    double time_step = fTimeToExpiry / fTimeSteps;
    double sqrt_time_step = System.Math.Sqrt(time_step);
    double disc = System.Math.Exp(-fRiskFreeRate * fTimeToExpiry);

    set_seed(seed);

    double opt_val = 0.0;
    bool not_out = true;
    int k = 0;
    double STN = 0.0;
    double mean = (fRiskFreeRate - fDividendYield - fSigma1 * fSigma1 * 0.5) * time_step;
    double std = System.Math.Sqrt(fSigma1 * fSigma1 * time_step);
    double z;
    double sum_opt_vals = 0.0;

    for (int i = 0; i < fNumberScenarios; ++i)
    {
        // generate the asset path
        double ST1 = fS1;
        not_out = true;
        k = 0;

        while (not_out && k < fTimeSteps)
        {
            z = RndNorm(mean, std);
            STN = ST1 * System.Math.Exp(z);
            if (STN < fBarrierLevel) not_out = false;
            ST1 = STN;
            asset_path[k] = STN;
            ++k;
        }
        if (is_put)
        {
            opt_val = System.Math.Max(fStrike - STN, 0.0);
```

Code excerpt 4.8 An example of using the Brownian bridge barrier crossing probability to enhance the pricing of a European down and out call option.

```
        }
        else
        {
            opt_val = System.Math.Max(STN - fStrike, 0.0);
        }

        if (not_out)
        { // only has value if asset value is above the barrier_level
            // compute the probability that the asset remained above the barrier
            if (UseBrownianBridge)
            {
                double total_probability_above = 1.0, pr;
                double sigma_2 = fSigma1 * fSigma1;
                double log_barrier_level = System.Math.Log(fBarrierLevel);
                double fac;
                for (int jj = 0; jj < fTimeSteps - 1; ++jj)
                {
                    double log_S_i = System.Math.Log(asset_path[jj]);
                    double log_S_i1 = System.Math.Log(asset_path[jj + 1]);

                    fac = 2.0 * (log_barrier_level - log_S_i) * (log_barrier_level - log_S_i1) / (sigma_2 * time_step);
                    pr = (1.0 - System.Math.Exp(-fac)); // probability of staying above the barrier between i and i+1
                    total_probability_above *= pr;
                }
                sum_opt_vals += total_probability_above * opt_val * disc;              }
            else
            { // don't use the Brownian Bridge
                sum_opt_vals += opt_val * disc;
            }
        }
    }
    double temp = sum_opt_vals / (double)fNumberScenarios;

    return temp;
}
```

Code excerpt 4.8 (*Continued*).

4.6 SELECTED EXERCISES

1. Write a program using Excel's functions NORMSINV and RAND to compute the value of European put and call options. Verify that the values agree with the expressions given in Section 4.4.5.

2. Write a program which finds the strike, E_p, required to make the value of a European put option the same as a European call option, that is, $C(S, E_c, \tau) = P(S, E_p, \tau)$.

3. Consider the mean reverting stochastic process

$$dS_t = \alpha(\mu - \log(S_t)) S_t dt + \sigma S_t dW_t,$$

where S_t is the asset value at time t, $\alpha > 0$ is the speed of mean reversion, μ is the long-term mean, σ is the volatility, and dW_t is the standard Brownian motion.

Let $X_t = \log(S_t)$ and show using the results of Section 2.10 that the mean and variance at time $T > 0$ are given by

$$E[X_T] = \exp(-\alpha T) X_0 + \left(\mu - \frac{\sigma^2}{2\alpha}\right)(1 - \exp(-\alpha T))$$

and

$$Var[X_T] = \left(\frac{\sigma^2}{2\alpha}\right)(1 - \exp(-2\alpha T))$$

respectively.

Hence, show that the value of a call European option is

$$c(S, E, \tau) = SN_1(d_1) - e^{-r\tau} EN_1(d_2),$$

where

$$d_2 = \frac{\log(S/E) + \left(r - \frac{1}{2}\hat{\sigma}^2\right)\tau}{\hat{\sigma}\sqrt{\tau}} = d_1 - \hat{\sigma}\sqrt{\tau}$$

and

$$\hat{\sigma}^2 = \left(\frac{\sigma^2}{2\alpha}\right)(1 - \exp(-2\alpha T)).$$

4. Let the price of an asset, S_t, follow GBM, and also let the interest rate be $r = 0$. Show that the conditional variance, $Var(S_t | S_t \geq K)$, when S_t is greater or equal to K is given by

$$Var(S_t | S_t \geq K) = S_o^2 \exp\left(\sigma^2 \tau\right) N(d_3) - 2SKN(d_1)$$
$$+ K^2 N(d_2) - C(S, K, \tau)^2,$$

where $C(S, K, \tau)$ is the value of a European call option and

$$d_1 = \frac{\log(S/K) + \frac{1}{2}\sigma^2\tau}{\sigma\sqrt{\tau}}, \quad d_2 = \frac{\log(S/K) - \frac{1}{2}\sigma^2\tau}{\sigma\sqrt{\tau}},$$

$$d_3 = \frac{\log(S/K) + \frac{3}{2}\sigma^2\tau}{\sigma\sqrt{\tau}}.$$

5. Let the variable X follow a Weibull distribution with density function

$$f(X) = \alpha\beta X^{\beta-1} \exp\left(-\alpha X^\beta\right).$$

The value of a European call option $C(X, K)$ is obtained by evaluating the integral $\int_{-\infty}^{\infty} (X - K)^+ \alpha\beta X^{\beta-1} \exp\left(-\alpha X^\beta\right) dX$.
Show that

$$C(X, K) = \frac{1}{\alpha^{\frac{1}{\beta}}} \Gamma\left(1 + \frac{1}{\beta}\right) \left\{1 - P\left(1 + \frac{1}{\beta}, \alpha K^\beta\right)\right\} - K \exp\left(-\alpha K^\beta\right),$$

where $P(a, b)$ is the incomplete gamma function given by

$$P(a, b) = \frac{1}{\Gamma(a)} \int_0^b \omega^{a-1} \exp(-\omega) d\omega,$$

and $\Gamma(a)$ is the gamma function.

Chapter 5

Single Asset American Options

5.1 INTRODUCTION

In Chapter 4, we discussed single asset European options and the analytic formulae which can be used to price them. Here, we will consider the valuation of single asset American style options using both numeric methods and analytic formulae; in addition, we will discuss the use of numerical techniques to value certain European options. The coverage in this section is as follows:

- Analytic approximation techniques for the valuation of American options.
- Binomial lattice techniques used for the valuation of American and European options.
- The valuation of American and European vanilla and barrier options using finite-difference grids.
- The valuation of American options via Monte Carlo simulation.

It should be mentioned that although much of the discussion here concerns the valuation of vanilla European and American puts and calls, the techniques used can be modified without much difficulty to include more exotic options with customized payoffs and early exercise features.

5.2 APPROXIMATIONS FOR VANILLA AMERICAN OPTIONS

5.2.1 American Call Options with Cash Dividends

In this section, we will consider the valuation of vanilla American call options with cash dividends and discuss the methods of both the Roll and Geske, and Whaley and Black. We will first consider the Roll, Geske, and Whaley method.

The Roll, Geske, and Whaley Approximation

This method uses the work of Roll (1977), Geske (1979), and Whaley (1981). Let S be the current (time t) price of an asset which pays a single cash dividend D_1 at time t_1. At the *ex-dividend* date, t_1, there will be a decrease in the asset's value from S_{t_1} to $S_{t_1} - D_1$. Also the current asset price net of *escrowed* dividends is

$$S_D = S - D_1 \exp(-r(t_1 - t)), \qquad (5.2.1)$$

where r is the riskless interest rate.

Now consider an American call option, with strike price E and expiry time T, which is taken out on this asset. At t_1, there will be a given ex-dividend asset price, S^*, above which the option will be exercised early. This value can be found by solving the following equation:

$$c(S^*, E, \tau_1) = S^* + D_1 - E, \tag{5.2.2}$$

where $c(S^*, E, \tau_1)$ is the Black–Scholes value of a European call option with strike price E and maturity $\tau_1 = T - t_1$, on an asset with current value S^* at time t_1. If just prior to the ex-dividend date $S_{t_1} > S^*$, then the American option will be exercised and realize a cash payoff of $S_{t_1} + D_1 - E$. On the other hand, if $S_{t_1} \leq S^*$, then the option is worth more unexercised and it will be held until option maturity at time T.

We can rewrite equation (5.2.2) so that S^* is the root of the following equation:

$$K(S^*) = c(S^*, E, \tau_1) - S^* - D_1 + E = 0, \tag{5.2.3}$$

where $K(S^*)$ denotes the function in the single variable S^*.

A well-known technique for solving equation (5.2.3) is Newton's method, which in this case takes the form

$$S^*_{i+1} = S^*_i - \frac{K(S^*_i)}{K'(S_i)^*}, \tag{5.2.4}$$

where S^*_i is the ith approximation to S^* and S^*_{i+1} is the improved $(i + 1)$th approximation.

If we now consider the terms in equation (5.2.4), we have from equation (5.2.2) and equation (5.2.3) that

$$K(S^*_i) = c(S^*_i, E, \tau_1) - S^*_i - D_1 + E$$

and

$$K'(S^*_i) = \frac{\partial K(S^*_i)}{\partial S^*_i} = \frac{\partial c(S^*_i, E, \tau_1)}{\partial S^*_i} - 1.$$

Also from equation (A.1.4) in Appendix A.3

$$\frac{\partial c(S^*_i, E, \tau_1)}{\partial S^*_i} = N_1(d_1(S^*_i)),$$

we note that here the *continuous* dividend yield, $q = 0$.
So

$$K'(S^*_i) = \frac{\partial K(S^*_i)}{\partial S^*_i} = N_1(d_1(S^*_i)) - 1, \quad \text{where } d_1 = \frac{\log(S^*_i/E) + (r + \sigma^2/2)\tau_1}{\sigma \sqrt{T - t_1}}.$$

Substituting these results into equation (5.2.4) gives

$$S^*_{i+1} = S^*_i - \frac{\left\{c(S^*_i, E, \tau_1) - (S^*_i + D_1 - E)\right\}}{N_1(d_1(S^*_i)) - 1}.$$

On rearrangement, this yields

$$S^*_{i+1} = \frac{S^*_i N_1(d_1(S^*_i)) - c(S^*_i, E, \tau_1) + D_1 - E}{N_1(d_1(S^*_i)) - 1}, \qquad \text{for } i = 0, \ldots, \texttt{max\_iter}, \quad (5.2.5)$$

where a convenient initial approximation is to choose $S^*_0 = E$, and $\texttt{max\_iter}$ is the maximum number of iterations that are to be used.

We will now quote the Roll, Geske, and Whaley (1981) formula for the current value of an American call which pays a *single* cash dividend D_1 at time t_1, it is

$$C(S, E, \tau) = S_D \left\{ N_1(b_1) + N_2(a_1, -b_1, \sqrt{(t_1 - t)/\tau}) \right\} + D_1 \exp(-r(t_1 - t)) N_1(b_2)$$
$$- E \exp(-r\tau) \left\{ N_1(b_2) \exp(r(\tau_1)) + N_2(a_2, -b_2, - \sqrt{(t_1 - t)/\tau})) \right\},$$
$$(5.2.6)$$

where S_D is given by equation (5.2.1), E is the exercise price, T is the option expiry date, t represents the current time, τ is the option maturity, $N_1(a)$ is the univariate cumulative normal density function with upper integral limit a, and $N_2(a, b, \rho)$ is the bivariate cumulative normal density function with upper integral limits a and b and correlation coefficient ρ. The other symbols used in equation (5.2.6) are defined as

$$a_1 = \frac{\log(S/E) + (r + \sigma^2/2)\tau}{\sigma \sqrt{\tau}}, \qquad a_2 = a_1 - \sigma \sqrt{\tau},$$

$$b_2 = \frac{\log(S/S^*) + (r + \sigma^2/2)(t_1 - t)}{\sigma \sqrt{(t_1 - t)}}, \qquad b_2 = b_1 - \sigma \sqrt{(t_1 - t)},$$

and S is the current (time t) asset price, S^* is found using equation (5.2.5), r is the riskless interest rate, σ is the asset's volatility, $\tau = T - t$, and $\tau_1 = T - t_1$.

To compute the value of an American call option which pays n cash dividends $D_i, i = 1, \ldots, n$ at times $t_i, i = 1, \ldots, n$, we can use the fact that optimal exercise normally only ever occurs at the final ex-dividend date t_n, see, for example, Hull (2003). Under these circumstances, equation (5.2.6) can still be shown to value the American call but now t_1 should be set to t_n, D_1 should be set to D_n, and S_D is given by

$$S_D = S - \sum_{i=1}^{n} D_i \exp(-r(t_i - t)). \qquad (5.2.7)$$

A program to compute the Roll, Geske, and Whaley approximation for an American call option with multiple cash dividends is given in Code excerpt 5.1 below. Here, the functions $\texttt{cum\_norm}$ and $\texttt{cum\_norm2}$ are used to calculate the values of $N_1(a)$ and $N_2(a, b, \rho)$ respectively. Code excerpt 5.3 was used to compute the values presented in Table 5.1. These compare the Roll, Geske, and Whaley approximation with the Black approximation, which we will now briefly discuss.

```
void RGW_approx(double *opt_value, double *critical_value, long n_divs, double dividends[], double Divs_T[],
                double S0, double X, double sigma, double T, double r, long *iflag)
{
/* Input parameters:
   ==================
   n_divs        - the number of dividends
   dividends[]   - the dividends: dividends[0] contains the first dividend, dividend[1] the second etc.
   Divs_T[]      - the times at which the dividends are paid: Divs_T[0] is the time at which the first dividend is paid
                   Divs_T[1] is the time at which the second dividend is paid, etc.
   S0            - the current value of the underlying asset
   X             - the strike price
   sigma         - the volatility
   T             - the time to maturity
   r             - the interest rate
   Output parameters:
   ==================
   opt_value     - the value of the option
   critical_value - the critical value
   iflag         - an error indicator
*/
    double A_1,A_2,S_star,a1,a2,nt1,t1,S;
    double b1,b2,d1,alpha,h,div,beta,temp,temp1,temp2,temp3;
    double pdf,b,eur_val,fac,tol,loc_q,err,zero=0.0;
    long iterate;
    long i,iflagx,putx;

    loc_q = 0.0;
    temp = 0.0;
    for (i=0; i < n_divs; ++i) { /Check the Divs_T array */
        if ((Divs_T[i] <= temp) || (Divs_T[i] > T) || (Divs_T[i] <= zero)) {
            *flag = 2;
            return;
        }
        temp = Divs_T[i];
    }
    /* calculate the present value of the dividends (excluding the final one) */
    temp = 0.0;
    for (i=0; i < n_divs-1; ++i) {
        temp = fac + dividends[i] * exp(-r*Divs_T[i]);
    }
    t1 = Divs_T[n_divs-1];
    /* decrease the stock price by the present value of all dividends */
    div = dividends[n_divs-1];
    S = S0-temp-div*exp(-r*t1);
    iterate = 1;
    tol = 0.000001;
    S_star = X;
    while (iterate) {   /* calculate S_star, iteratively */
        /* calculate the Black-Scholes value of a European call */
        d1 = (log(S_star/X) + (r+(sigma*sigma/2.0))*(T-t1))/(sigma*sqrt(T-t1));
        putx = 0;
        loc_q = 0.0;
        black_scholes(&eur_val,NULL,S_star,X,sigma,T-t1,r,loc_q,putx,&iflag);
        S_star = (S_star*cum_norm(d1)-eur_val+div-X)/(cum_norm(d1)-1.0);
        err = fabs(eur_val - (S_star + div- X))/X;
        if (err < tol) iterate = 0;
    }
    a1 = (log(S/X) + (r+(sigma*sigma/2.0))*T)/(sigma*sqrt(T));
    a2 = a1 - sigma*sqrt(T);
    b1 = (log(S/S_star)+(r+(sigma*sigma/2.0))*t1)/(sigma*sqrt(t1));
    b2 = b1 - sigma*sqrt(t1);
    nt1 = sqrt(t1/T);
    temp1 = S*(cum_norm(b1)+cum_norm2(a1,-b1,-nt1,&iflagx));
    temp2 = -X*exp(-r*T)*cum_norm2(a2,-b2,-nt1,&iflagx)-(X-div)*exp(-r*t1)*cum_norm(b2);
    *opt_value = temp1+temp2;
    *critical_value = S_star;
}
```

Code excerpt 5.1 Function to compute the Roll, Geske, and Whaley approximation for the value of an American call option with discrete dividends.

We will now consider the Black approximation.

Black's Approximation

The Black (1973) approximation for an American call with cash dividends is simpler than the Roll, Geske, and Whaley method we have just described. For an American call option which expires at time T, with n discrete cash dividends

TABLE 5.1 A Comparison of the Computed Values for American Call Options with Dividends, using the Roll, Geske, and Whaley Approximation, and the Black Approximation. The Parameters used were $E = 100.0$, $r = 0.04$, $\sigma = 0.2$, $\tau = 2.0$, and there is One Cash Dividend of Value 5.0 at Time $t = 1.0$. The Current Stock Price, S, is Varied from 80.0 to 120.0. The Results are in Agreement with those Given in Table 1 of Whaley (1981)

Stock price	Critical price, S^*	RGW approximation	Black approximation
80.0	123.582	3.212	3.208
85.0	123.582	4.818	4.808
90.0	123.582	6.839	6.820
95.0	123.582	9.276	9.239
100.0	123.582	12.111	12.048
105.0	123.582	15.316	15.215
110.0	123.582	18.851	18.703
115.0	123.582	22.676	22.470
120.0	123.582	26.748	26.476

$D_i, i = 1, \ldots, n$, at times $t_i, i = 1, \ldots, n$, it involves calculating the prices of European options that mature at times T, and t_n, and then setting the option price to the greater of these two values, see, for example, Hull (2003).

The Black approximation, C_{BL}, can be expressed more concisely in terms of our previously defined notation as

$$C_{BL}(S, E, \tau) = \max(v_1, v_2),$$

where v_1 and v_2 are the following European calls:

$$v_1 = c(S_D, E, \tau) \quad \text{and} \quad v_2 = c(S_D^+, E, \tau_1), \quad \tau = T - t, \ \tau_1 = T - t_n,$$

and

$$S_D = S - \sum_{i=1}^{n} D_i \quad \text{and} \quad S_D^+ = S - \sum_{i=1}^{n-1} D_i.$$

Code excerpt 5.2 below computes the Black approximation.

```
void black_approx(double *value, long n_divs, double dividends[], double Divs_T[],
        double S0, double X, double sigma, double T, double r, long put, long *ifail)
{
/* Input parameters:
    ===================
    n_divs      - the number of dividends
```

Code excerpt 5.2 Function to compute the value of the Black approximation for the value of an American call option with discrete dividends.

```
    dividends[] - the dividends, dividends[0] contains the first dividend, dividend[1] the second etc.
    Divs_T[]    - the times at which the dividends are paid, Divs_T[0] is the time at which the first dividend is paid
                  Divs_T[1] is the time at which the second dividend is paid, etc.
    S0          - the current value of the underlying asset
    X           - the strike price
    sigma       - the volatility
    T           - the time to maturity
    r           - the interest rate
    put         - if put is 0 then a call option, otherwise a put option
    Output parameters:
    ==================
    value       - the value of the option, iflag - an error indicator
*/
    double zero = 0.0;
    double beta,temp,temp1,temp2,temp3;
    double tn,val_T,val_tn,tol,loc_q,err,fac;
    long i,ifailx;

    loc_q = 0.0;
    temp = 0.0;
    for (i=0; i < n_divs; ++i) {
        if (Divs_T[i] <= temp ) printf ("Error in Divs_T array, elements not increasing \n");
        if (Divs_T[i] > T) printf ("Error in Divs_T array element has a value greater than T \n");
        if (Divs_T[i] <= zero) printf ("Error in Divs_T array element <= zero \n");
        temp = Divs_T[i];
    }
    /* calculate the present value of the dividends */
    fac = 0.0;
    for (i=0; i < n_divs; ++i) {
        fac = fac + dividends[i] * exp(-r*Divs_T[i]);
    }
    temp = S0 - fac;
    /* calculate the value of the option on expiry */
    black_scholes(&val_T,NULL,temp,X,sigma,T,r,loc_q,put,&ifailx);

    /* calculate the value of the option on last dividend date */
    tn = Divs_T[n_divs-1];
    temp = temp + dividends[n_divs-1]*exp(-r*tn);
    black_scholes_bs(&val_tn,NULL,temp,X,sigma,tn,r,loc_q,putx,&ifailx);
    *value = MAX(val_tn,val_T);
}
```

Code excerpt 5.2 (*Continued*).

Code excerpt 5.3 below uses the same values as in Whaley (1981) and compares the Roll, Geske, and Whaley approximation with that of Black; the results are presented in Table 5.1.

```
    double q,r,temp,loc_r;
    long i,m,m2,m_acc;
    double S0,E,T,sigma,t1,delta,value,ad_value,put_value;
    long is_american,ifail,put;
    double bin_greeks[5],greeks[5],bin_value,bs_value;
    double opt_value, critical_value, E1, E2, crit1, crit2;
    double black_value;
    double Divs_T[3],dividends[3];
    long n_divs, put;

    E = 100.0;
    r = 0.04;
    sigma = 0.2;
    T = 2.0;
    t1 = 1.0;
    put = 0;

/* check using the same parameters as in Whaley (1981) */
    Divs_T[0] = 1.0;
    dividends[0] = 5.0;
    n_divs = 1;
    printf ("\nPrice S   RGW Approximation        Black Approximation \n\n");
    for (i=0; i < 9; ++i) {
        put = 0;
        S0 = 80.0+(double)i*5.0;
        opt_RGW_approx(&opt_value,&critical_value,n_divs,dividends,Divs_T,S0,E,sigma,T,r,&ifail);
        printf("%8.4f ",S0);
        printf("%12.3f %12.3f ",opt_value,critical_value);
        opt_black_approx(&black_value,n_divs,dividends,Divs_T,S0,E,sigma,T,r,put,&ifail);
        printf("%12.3f (%8.4e) ",black_value);
    }
```

Code excerpt 5.3 Simple test program to compare the results of function opt_RGW_approx with function opt_black_approx, and the parameters used are the same as in Whaley (1981).

We will now consider a more general technique for pricing both American puts and calls.

5.2.2 The Macmillan, Barone-Adesi, and Whaley Method

Here, we consider a method of pricing American options which relies on an approximation that reduces a transformed Black–Scholes equation into a second order ordinary differential equation, see Barone-Adesi and Whaley (1987), and MacMillan (1986). It thus provides an alternative way of evaluating American options that can be used instead of computationally intensive techniques such as finite-difference methods. Although the method prices American options, it is really based on the value of an American option *relative* to the corresponding European option value (which can readily be computed using the Black–Scholes pricing formula).

Since an American option gives more choice, its value is always at least that of its European counterpart. This early exercise premium ($v(S, E, \tau) \geq 0$) is now defined more precisely for American puts and calls. If at current time t the asset price is S, then the early exercise premium for an American call which expires at time T, and therefore has maturity $\tau = T - t$, is

$$v_c(S, E, \tau) = C(S, E, \tau) - c(S, E, \tau) \geq 0, \tag{5.2.8}$$

where $C(S, E, \tau)$ denotes the value of the American call and $c(S, E, \tau)$ denotes the value of the corresponding European call. The early exercise premium of an American put option, $v_p(S, E, \tau)$, is similarly defined as

$$v_p(S, E, \tau) = P(S, E, \tau) - p(S, E, \tau) \geq 0, \tag{5.2.9}$$

where $P(S, E, \tau)$ is the value of the American put, and $p(S, E, \tau)$ is the value of the corresponding European put. The key insight provided by the Macmillan, Barone-Adesi, and Whaley method is that since both the American and European option values satisfy the Black–Scholes partial differential equation so does the early exercise premium, $v(S, E, \tau)$, see Section 4.4.1. This means that we can write

$$\frac{\partial v}{\partial t} + (r - q)S\frac{\partial v}{\partial S} + \frac{\sigma^2 S^2}{2}\frac{\partial^2 v}{\partial S^2} = rv, \tag{5.2.10}$$

where as usual S is the asset price, r the continuously compounded interest rate, q the continuously compounded dividend, σ the volatility, and time t increases from the current time to the expiry time T.

We will now introduce the variable $h(\tau) = 1 - \exp(-r\tau)$ and use the factorization $v(S, E, \tau) = h(\tau)g(S, E, h)$. From the standard calculus, we obtain

$$\frac{\partial v}{\partial t} = g\frac{\partial h}{\partial t} + h\frac{\partial g}{\partial t} = rg(h-1) + h\frac{\partial g}{\partial h}\frac{\partial h}{\partial t} = rg(h-1) + hr(h-1)\frac{\partial g}{\partial h}$$

and also $\dfrac{\partial v}{\partial S} = h\dfrac{\partial g}{\partial S}$ and $\dfrac{\partial^2 v}{\partial S^2} = h\dfrac{\partial^2 g}{\partial S^2}$.

Substituting these results into equation (5.2.10) yields the following transformed Black–Scholes equation:

$$\frac{S^2\sigma^2 h}{2}\frac{\partial^2 g}{\partial S^2} + (r-q)Sh\frac{\partial g}{\partial S} + rg(h-1) + rh(h-1)\frac{\partial g}{\partial h} = rgh, \qquad (5.2.11)$$

which can be further simplified to give

$$S^2\sigma^2\frac{\partial^2 g}{\partial S^2} + \frac{2(r-q)S}{\sigma^2}\frac{\partial g}{\partial S} - \frac{2rg}{h\sigma^2} - \frac{2r(1-h)}{\sigma^2}\frac{\partial g}{\partial h} = rgh \qquad (5.2.12)$$

or

$$S^2\frac{\partial^2 g}{\partial S^2} + \beta S\frac{\partial g}{\partial S} - \frac{\alpha}{h}g - (1-h)\alpha\frac{\partial g}{\partial h} = 0, \qquad (5.2.13)$$

where $\alpha = \dfrac{2r}{\sigma^2}$ and $\beta = \dfrac{2(r-q)}{\sigma^2}$.

We now consider the last term of equation (5.2.13) and note that when τ is large, $1 - h(\tau) \sim 0$. Also when $\tau \to 0$, the option is close to maturity, and the value both the European and American options converge, which means that $v(S, E, \tau) \sim 0$ and $\dfrac{\partial g}{\partial h} \sim 0$. It can thus be seen that the last term is generally quite small, and the Macmillan, Barone-Adesi, and Whaley approximation assumes that it can be ignored. This results in the following equation:

$$S^2\frac{\partial^2 g}{\partial S^2} + \beta S\frac{\partial g}{\partial S} - \frac{\alpha}{h}g = 0, \qquad (5.2.14)$$

which is a second order differential equation with two linearly independent solutions of the form aS^γ. They can be found by substituting $g(S, E, h) = aS^\gamma$ into equation (5.2.14) as follows:

$$\frac{\partial g}{\partial S} = \gamma S^{\gamma-1}, \qquad \frac{\partial^2 g}{\partial S^2} = a\gamma(\gamma-1)S^{\gamma-2} = a\gamma^2 S^{\gamma-2} - a\gamma S^{\gamma-2},$$

so

$$S^2\frac{\partial^2 g}{\partial S^2} = a\gamma^2 S^\gamma - a\gamma S^\gamma = \gamma^2 g - \gamma g$$

and

$$\beta S\frac{\partial g}{\partial S} = \beta S a\gamma S^{\gamma-1} = \beta\gamma S^\gamma = \beta\gamma g.$$

When the above results are substituted in equation (5.2.14), we obtain the quadratic equation

$$\gamma^2 g - \gamma g + \beta\gamma g - \alpha/h = g(\gamma^2 - \gamma + (\beta-1)\gamma - \alpha/h) = 0$$

or

$$\gamma^2 - \gamma + (\beta-1)\gamma - \alpha/h = 0, \qquad (5.2.15)$$

which has the two solutions

$$\gamma_1 = \frac{1}{2}\left\{-(\beta - 1) - \sqrt{(\beta - 1)^2 + 4(\alpha/h)}\right\} \tag{5.2.16}$$

and

$$\gamma_2 = \frac{1}{2}\left\{-(\beta - 1) + \sqrt{(\beta - 1)^2 + 4(\alpha/h)}\right\}, \tag{5.2.17}$$

where we note that since $\alpha/h > 0$, we have $\gamma_1 < 0$ and $\gamma_2 > 0$.

The general solution to equation (5.2.14) is thus

$$g(S, E, h) = a_1 S^{\gamma_1} + a_2 S^{\gamma_2}. \tag{5.2.18}$$

We will now derive the appropriate solutions pertaining to American call options and American put options.

American Call Options

Here, we use the fact that both the value and the early exercise premium $(v_c(S, E, \tau) = hg_c(S, E, h))$ of an American call tend to zero as the asset price $S \to 0$. This means that as $S \to 0$, $g_c(S, E, h) \to 0$.

However, since $\gamma_1 < 0$, the only way this can be achieved in equation (5.2.18) is if $a_1 = 0$. So $g_c(S, E, h) = a_2 S^{\gamma_2}$, and the value of an American call is

$$C(S, E, \tau) = c(S, E, \tau) + ha_2 S^{\gamma_2}. \tag{5.2.19}$$

An expression for a_2 can be found by considering the critical asset price (point on the early exercise boundary), S^*, above which the American option will be exercised. For $S < S^*$, the value of the American call is governed by equation (5.2.19), and when $S > S^*$, we have $C(S, E, \tau) = S - E$.

Now, since the value of the American option is continuous, at the critical asset value S^* the following equation applies

$$S^* - E = c(S^*, E, \tau) + ha_2 S^{*\gamma_2}. \tag{5.2.20}$$

Furthermore, since the gradient of the American option value is also continuous, at S^* we have

$$\frac{\partial(S^* - E)}{\partial S^*} = \frac{\partial}{\partial S^*}\left\{c(S^*, E, \tau) + ha_2 S^{*\gamma_2}\right\}, \tag{5.2.21}$$

which gives

$$1 = \exp(-q\tau)N_1(d_1(S^*)) + \gamma_2 ha_2 S^{*(\gamma_2 - 1)}, \tag{5.2.22}$$

where we have used the value of the hedge parameter Δ_c for a European call (see section on the Greeks)

$$\Delta_c = \frac{\partial c(S^*, E, \tau)}{\partial S^*} = \exp(-q\tau)N_1(d_1(S^*)).$$

Equation (5.2.22) can therefore be written as

$$ha_2 S^{*\gamma_2} = \frac{S^*}{\gamma_2}\left\{1 - \exp(-q\tau)N_1(d_1(S^*))\right\}. \tag{5.2.23}$$

When the LHS of the above equation is substituted into equation (5.2.20), we obtain the following equation for S^*:

$$S^* - E = c(S^*, E, \tau) + \frac{S^*}{\gamma_2}\{1 - \exp(-q\tau)N_1(d_1(S^*))\}. \tag{5.2.24}$$

This equation can be solved for S^* using standard iterative methods (see the section on the numerical solution of critical asset values). Once S^* has been found, equation (5.2.23) gives

$$ha_2 = A_2 S^{*-\gamma_2},$$

where

$$A_2 = \frac{S^*}{\gamma_2}\{1 - \exp(-q\tau)N_1(d_1(S^*))\}.$$

From equation (5.2.19), the value of an American call is thus of the form

$$C(S, E, \tau) = c(S, E, \tau) + A_2 \left(\frac{S}{S^*}\right)^{\gamma_2} \quad \text{when} \quad S < S^*, \tag{5.2.25}$$

$$C(S, E, \tau) = S - E \quad \text{when} \quad S \geq S^*. \tag{5.2.26}$$

American Put Options

For an American put option, we proceed in a similar manner to that for the American call. We now use fact that both the value and early exercise premium $(v_p(S, E, \tau) = hg_p(S, E, h))$ of an American put tend to zero as the asset price $S \to \infty$. So $g_p(S, E, h) \to 0$ as $S \to \infty$. Since $\gamma_2 > 0$, the only way this can be achieved by equation (5.2.18) is if $a_2 = 0$. This gives $g_p(S, E, h) = a_1 S^{\gamma_1}$ and the value of an American put is

$$P(S, E, \tau) = p(S, E, \tau) + ha_1 S^{\gamma_1}. \tag{5.2.27}$$

An expression for a_1 can be found by considering the critical asset price, S^{**}, below which the American option will be exercised. For $S > S^{**}$, the value of the American put is given by equation (5.2.27), and for $S < S^{**}$, we have $P(S, E, \tau) = E - S$.

Continuity of the American option value at the critical asset price gives

$$E - S^{**} = p(S^{**}, E, \tau) + ha_1 S^{**\gamma_1}, \tag{5.2.28}$$

and continuity of the option value's gradient at the critical asset price yields

$$\frac{\partial(E - S^{**})}{\partial S^{**}} = \frac{\partial}{\partial S^{**}}\{p(S^{**}, E, \tau) + ha_1 S^{**\gamma_1}\}, \tag{5.2.29}$$

which can be simplified to

$$-1 = -N_1(-d_1(S^{**}))\exp(-q\tau) + \gamma_1 a_1 S^{**(\gamma_1 - 1)}, \tag{5.2.30}$$

where we have used the value of hedge parameter Δ_p for a European put (see Appendix A.3),

$$\Delta_p = \frac{\partial p(S^{**}, E, \tau)}{\partial S^{**}} = \{N_1(d_1(S^{**})) - 1\}\exp(-q\tau) = -N_1(-d_1(S^{**}))\exp(-q\tau).$$

Equation (5.2.30) can therefore be written as

$$ha_1 S^{**\gamma_1} = -\frac{S^{**}}{\gamma_1} \left\{1 - N_1(-d_1(S^{**})) \exp(-q\tau)\right\}. \tag{5.2.31}$$

When the LHS of the above equation is substituted into equation (5.2.28), we obtain the following equation for S^{**}:

$$E - S^{**} = p(S^{**}, E, \tau) + \left\{1 - \exp(-q\tau)N[-d_1(S^{**})]\right\} \frac{S^{**}}{\gamma_1}, \tag{5.2.32}$$

which can be solved iteratively to yield S^{**} (see the section on the numerical solution of critical asset values). Once S^{**} has been found, equation (5.2.31) gives

$$ha_1 = A_1 S^{**-\gamma_1},$$

where

$$A_1 = -\left(\frac{S^{**}}{\gamma_1}\right) \left\{1 - \exp(-q\tau)N_1(-d_1(S^{**}))\right\}.$$

We note here that $A_1 > 0$ since, $\gamma_1 < 0$, $S^{**} > 0$, and $N_1(-d_1(S^{**})) \exp(-q\tau) < 1$.

From equation (5.2.27), the value of an American put is thus

$$P(S, E, \tau) = p(S, E, \tau) + A_1 \left(\frac{S}{S^{**}}\right)^{\gamma_2} \quad \text{when} \quad S > S^{**},$$

$$P(S, E, \tau) = E - S \quad \text{when} \quad S \le S^{**}.$$

Numerical Solution of Critical Asset Values

We now provide details on how to iteratively solve for the critical asset price in equation (5.2.24) and equation (5.2.32).

American Call Options

For American call options, we need to solve equation (5.2.24), which is

$$S^* - E = c(S^*, E, \tau) + \frac{S^*}{\gamma_2} \left\{1 - \exp(-q\tau)N_1(d_1(S^*))\right\}.$$

We denote the ith approximation to the critical asset value S^* by S_i^* and represent the LHS of the equation by

$$LHS(S_i^*, E, \tau) = S_i^* - E,$$

and the right-hand side of the equation by

$$RHS(S_i^*, E, \tau) = c(S_i^*, E, \tau) + \frac{S_i^*}{\gamma_2} \left\{1 - \exp(-q\tau)N_1(d_1(S_i^*))\right\}.$$

If we let $K(S_i^*, E, \tau) = RHS(S_i^*, E, \tau) - LHS(S_i^*, E, \tau)$, then we want to find the value of S_i^* which (to a specified tolerance) gives $K(S_i^*, E, \tau) \sim 0$. This can be achieved with Newton's root finding method, in which a better approximation, S^*_{i+1}, can be found using

$$S^*_{i+1} = S^*_i - \frac{K(S^*_i, E, \tau)}{K'(S^*_i, E, \tau)}, \tag{5.2.33}$$

where

$$K'(S^*_i, E, \tau) = \frac{\partial}{\partial S^*_i} \{RHS(S^*_i, E, \tau) - LHS(S^*_i, E, \tau)\}$$

$$= \frac{\partial}{\partial S^*_i} \{RHS(S^*_i, E, \tau)\} - \frac{\partial}{\partial S^*_i} \{LHS(S^*_i, E, \tau)\}$$

$$= b_i - 1.$$

Here, we have used $b_i = \dfrac{\partial}{\partial S^*_i} \{RHS(S^*_i, E, \tau)\}$, and the expression for b_i is given by equation (5.2.35), which is derived at the end of this section.

Substituting for $K(S^*_i, E, \tau)$ and $K'(S^*_i, E, \tau)$ into equation (5.2.32), we therefore obtain

$$S^*_{i+1} = S^*_i - \frac{(RHS(S^*_i, E, \tau) - LHS(S^*_i, E, \tau))}{(b_i - 1)}$$

$$= S^*_i - \frac{(RHS(S^*_i, E, \tau) - (S^*_i - E))}{(b_i - 1)}$$

$$= \frac{b_i S^*_i - RHS(S^*_i, E, \tau) - E}{(b_i - 1)}.$$

The final iterative algorithm for the American call is therefore

$$S^*_{i+1} = \frac{E + RHS(S^*_i, E, \tau) - b_i S^*_i}{(1 - b_i)}, \tag{5.2.34}$$

where we can use $S^*_0 = E$ for the initial estimate of the critical value (see the computer code excerpt below).

The Expression for b_i

Here, we derive an expression for the term b_i which is used in equation (5.2.34),

$$b_i = \frac{\partial c(S^*_i, E, \tau)}{\partial S^*_i} + \frac{1}{\gamma_2} \{1 - \exp(-q\tau)N_1(d_1(S^*_i))\} - \frac{S^*_i}{\gamma_2} \frac{\partial N_1(d_1(S^*_i))}{\partial d_1(S^*_i)} \frac{\partial d_1(S^*_i)}{\partial S^*_i}.$$

We will now quote the following results which are derived in Appendix A:

Appendix A, equation (A.1.3): $\dfrac{\partial N_1(d_1(S^*_i))}{\partial d_1(S^*_i)} = n(d_1(S^*_i)),$

Appendix A, equation (A.1.6): $\dfrac{\partial d_1(S^*_i)}{\partial S^*_i} = \dfrac{1}{S^*_i \sigma \sqrt{\tau}},$

Appendix A, equation (A.3.2): $\Delta_c = \dfrac{\partial c(S^*_i, E, \tau)}{\partial S^*_i} = \exp(-q\tau)N_1(d_1(S^*_i)).$

Substituting these results into the above expression, we therefore obtain

$$b_i = \exp(-q\tau)N_1(d_1(S_i^*)) + \frac{1}{\gamma_2} - \frac{\exp(-q\tau)N_1(d_1(S_i^*))}{\gamma_2} - \frac{\exp(-q\tau)n(d_1(S_i^*))}{\gamma_2 \sigma \sqrt{\tau}},$$

which can be rearranged to yield

$$b_i = \exp(-q\tau)N_1(d_1(S_i^*))\left\{1 - \frac{1}{\gamma_2}\right\} + \frac{1}{\gamma_2}\left\{1 - \frac{\exp(-q\tau)n(d_1(S_i^*))}{\sigma \sqrt{\tau}}\right\}. \qquad (5.2.35)$$

American Put Options

For American put options, we need to solve equation (5.2.32) which is

$$E - S_i^{**} = p(S_i^{**}, E, \tau) - \frac{S_i^{**}}{\gamma_1}\left\{1 - N_1(-d_1(S_i^{**}))\exp(-q\tau)\right\}.$$

If we let S_i^{**} denote the ith approximation to the critical asset value S^{**}, then we can represent the LHS of the equation by

$$LHS(S_i^{**}, E, \tau) = E - S_i^{**}$$

and the right-hand side of the equation by

$$RHS(S_i^{**}, E, \tau) = p(S_i^{**}, \tau) - \frac{S_i^{**}}{\gamma_1}\left\{1 - N_1(-d_1(S_i^{**}))\exp(-q\tau)\right\}$$

$$= p(S_i^{**}, E, \tau) - \frac{S_i^{**}}{\gamma_1}\left\{1 - [1 - N_1(d_1(S_i^{**}))]\exp(-q\tau)\right\}$$

$$= p(S_i^{**}, E, \tau) - \frac{S_i^{**}}{\gamma_1}\left\{1 - \exp(-q\tau) + N_1(d_1(S_i^{**}))\exp(-q\tau)\right\}.$$

We then denote $K(S_i^{**}, E, \tau) = RHS(S_i^{**}, E, \tau) - LHS(S_i^{**}, E, \tau)$ and using Newton's method, we obtain

$$S_{i+1}^{**} = S_i^{**} - \frac{K(S_i^{**}, E, \tau)}{K'(S_i^{**}, E, \tau)}, \qquad (5.2.36)$$

where as before

$$K'(S_i^{**}, E, \tau) = \frac{\partial}{\partial S_i^{**}}\left\{RHS(S_i^{**}, E, \tau) - LHS(S_i^{**}, E, \tau)\right\}.$$

So $K'(S_i^{**}, E, \tau) = 1 + b_i$, where $b_i = [\partial(RHS(S_i^{**}, E, \tau))]/\partial S_i^{**}$, and the expression for b_i is given by equation (5.2.38), which is derived at the end of this section.

Equation (5.2.36) can therefore be written as

$$S_{i+1}^{**} = S_i^{**} - \frac{(RHS(S_i^{**}, E, \tau) - LHS(S_i^{**}, E, \tau))}{1 + b_i}$$

$$= \frac{S_i^{**}(1 + b_i) - RHS(S_i^{**}, E, \tau) + E - S_i^{**}}{1 + b_i}.$$

The final iterative algorithm for the American put is therefore

$$S_i^{**} = \frac{E - RHS(S_i^{**}, E, \tau) + b_i S_i^{**}}{1 + b_i},$$ (5.2.37)

where we can use $S_0^{**} = E$ for the initial estimate of the critical asset value (see the computer code excerpt below).

The Expression for b_i

Here, we derive an expression for the term b_i which is used in equation (5.2.37). Since

$$b_i = \frac{\partial}{\partial S_i^{**}} \left\{ p(S_i^{**}, E, \tau) - \frac{S_i^{**}}{\gamma_1} \left(1 - \exp(-q\tau) + N_1(d_1(S_i^{**})) \exp(-q\tau) \right) \right\},$$

we have

$$b_i = \frac{\partial p(S_i^{**}, E, \tau)}{\partial S_i^{**}} - \frac{1}{\gamma_1} \{1 - \exp(-q\tau)\} - \frac{1}{\gamma_1} \exp(-q\tau) N_1(d_1(S_i^{**}))$$
$$- \frac{S_i^{**} \exp(-q\tau)}{\gamma_1} \frac{\partial N_1(d_1(S_i^{**}))}{\partial d_1(S_i^{**})} \frac{\partial d_1(S_i^{**})}{\partial S_i^{**}}.$$

We will now quote the following results which are derived in Appendix A:

Appendix A, equation (A.1.3): $\dfrac{\partial N_1(d_1(S_i^{**}))}{\partial d_1(S_i^{**})} = n(d_1(S_i^{**})),$

Appendix A, equation (A.1.6): $\dfrac{\partial d_1(S_i^{**})}{\partial S_i^{**}} = \dfrac{1}{S_i^{**} \sigma \sqrt{\tau}},$

Appendix A, equation (A.3.4):

$$\Delta_p = \frac{\partial p(S_i^{**}, E, \tau)}{\partial S_i^{**}} = \exp(-q\tau) \left\{ N_1(d_1(S_i^{**})) - 1 \right\}.$$

Substituting these results into the above expression, we therefore obtain

$$b_i = \exp(-q\tau) \left\{ N_1(d_1(S_i^{**})) - 1 \right\} - \frac{1}{\gamma_1} \left\{ 1 - \exp(-q\tau) + N_1(d_1(S_i^{**})) \exp(-q\tau) \right\}$$
$$- \frac{S_i^{**} \exp(-q\tau)}{\gamma_1} \frac{\partial N_1(d_1(S_i^{**}))}{\partial d_1(S_i^{**})} \frac{\partial d_1(S_i^{**})}{\partial S_i^{**}}$$
$$= \exp(-q\tau) \left\{ N_1(d_1(S_i^{**})) - 1 \right\} - \frac{1}{\gamma_1} \left\{ 1 - \exp(-q\tau) + N_1(d_1(S_i^{**})) \exp(-q\tau) \right\}$$
$$- \frac{S_i^{**} \exp(-q\tau) n(d_1(S_i^{**}))}{\gamma_1 \sigma \sqrt{\tau}},$$

which can be rearranged to yield

$$b_i = \exp(-q\tau) N_1(d_1(S_i^{**})) \left\{ 1 - \frac{1}{\gamma_1} \right\}$$
$$+ \frac{1}{\gamma_1} \left\{ \exp(-q\tau) - 1 - \frac{\exp(-q\tau) n(d_1(S_i^{**}))}{\sigma \sqrt{\tau}} \right\} - \exp(-q\tau).$$ (5.2.38)

In Code excerpt 5.4, we provide computer code to implement the Macmillan, Barone-Adesi, and Whaley method.

```
void MBW_approx(double *opt_value, double *critical_value, double S0, double X,
                double sigma, double T, double r, double q, long put, long *iflag)
{
/* Input parameters:
   ==================
   S0               - the current value of the underlying asset
   X                - the strike price
   sigma            - the volatility
   T                - the time to maturity
   r                - the interest rate
   q                - the continuous dividend yield
   put              - if put is 0 then a call option, otherwise a put option
   Output parameters:
   ==================
   opt_value        - the value of the option
   critical_value   - the critical value
   iflag            - an error indicator
*/
   double A_1,A_2,S_star,gamma_2,gamma_1;
   double d1,alpha,h,beta,temp,temp1;
   double pdf,pi,b,rhs,eur_val,tol,err;
   long iterate;
   long iflagx,putx;

   pi = PI;
   beta = 2.0 * (r - q) / (sigma * sigma);
   alpha = 2.0 * r / (sigma * sigma);
   h = 1.0 - exp(-r*T);
   temp = beta - 1.0;
   iterate = 1;
   tol = 0.000001;
   if (!put) {  /* An American call */
      gamma_2 = (-temp + sqrt((temp*temp) + (4.0*alpha/h)));
      gamma_2 = gamma_2 / 2.0;
      S_star = X;
      while (iterate) {  /* calculate S_star, iteratively */
         d1 = log(S_star/X) + (r-q+(sigma*sigma/2.0))*T;
         d1 = d1/(sigma*sqrt(T));
         pdf = (1.0/sqrt(2.0*pi))*exp(-d1*d1/2.0);
         temp = exp (-q*T)*cum_norm(d1)*(1.0 - (1.0/gamma_2));
         temp1 = (1.0 - ((exp(-q*T)*pdf)/(sigma*sqrt(T))))/gamma_2;
         b = temp + temp1;
         /* calculate the Black-Scholes value of a European call */
         putx = 0;
         black_scholes(&eur_val,NULL,S_star,X,sigma,T,r,q,putx,&iflagx);
         rhs = eur_val+(1.0-exp(-q*T)*cum_norm(d1))*S_star/gamma_2;
         S_star = (X + rhs - b*S_star)/(1.0-b);
         err = fabs((S_star - X) - rhs)/X;
         if (err < tol) iterate = 0;
      }
      A_2 = (S_star/gamma_2)*(1.0 - exp(-q*T)*cum_norm(d1));
      if (S0 < S_star) {
         temp1 = S0/S_star;
         black_scholes(&temp,NULL,S0,X,sigma,T,r,q,putx,&iflagx);
         *opt_value = temp + A_2 * pow(temp1,gamma_2);
      }
      else {
         *opt_value = S0 - X;
      }
   }
   else { /* An American put */
      gamma_1 = (-temp - sqrt((temp*temp) + (4.0*alpha/h)));
      gamma_1 = gamma_1 / 2.0;
      S_star = X;
      while (iterate) {  /* calculate S_star, iteratively */
         d1 = log(S_star/X) + (r-q+(sigma*sigma/2.0))*T;
         d1 = d1/(sigma*sqrt(T));
         pdf = (1.0/sqrt(2.0*pi))*exp(-d1*d1/2.0);
         temp = exp(-q*T)*(cum_norm(d1)*(1.0-(1.0/gamma_1))-1.0);
         temp1 = (exp(-q*T)-1.0-((exp(-q*T)*pdf)/(sigma*sqrt(T))))/gamma_1;
         b = temp + temp1;
         /* calculate the Black-Scholes value of a European put */
         putx = 1;
         black_scholes(&eur_val,NULL,S_star,X,sigma,T,r,q,putx,&iflagx);
         rhs = eur_val-(1.0-exp(-q*T)+exp(-q*T)*cum_norm(d1))*S_star/gamma_1;
         S_star = (X - rhs + b*S_star)/(1.0+b);
         err = fabs((X - S_star) - rhs)/X;
         if (err < tol) iterate = FALSE;
```

Code excerpt 5.4 Function to compute the Macmillan, Barone-Adesi, and Whaley approximation for American options.

```
}
A_1 = -(S_star/gamma_1)*(1.0 - exp(-q*T)*cum_norm(-d1));
if (S0 > S_star) {
    temp1 = S0/S_star;
    black_scholes(&temp,NULL,S0,X,sigma,T,r,q,putx,&iflagx);
    *opt_value = temp + A_1 * pow(temp1,gamma_1);
}
else {
    *opt_value = X - S0;
}
}
*critical_value = S_star;
}
```

Code excerpt 5.4 (*Continued*).

Mention that Tables 5.2 and 5.3 are results obtained by using the computer code given above.

5.3 LATTICE METHODS FOR VANILLA OPTIONS

5.3.1 Binomial Lattice

In this section, we will derive equations for a binomial lattice that describes the GBM movement of asset price changes. The approach that we will adopt is

TABLE 5.2 The Macmillan, Barone-Adesi, and Whaley Method for American Option Values Computed by the Routine MBW_approx. The Parameters used were $\tau = 0.5$, $X = 100.0$, $r = 0.1$, $q = 0.06$, and $\sigma = 0.2$ The Accurate Value was Calculated using a Standard Lattice with 2000 Time Steps, and the Error was the Macmillan, Barone-Adesi, and Whaley Estimate Minus the Accurate Value

	Call		Put	
Stock price	Accurate value	Error	Accurate value	Error
86.0	1.2064	5.54×10^{-4}	14.0987	-3.69×10^{-2}
89.0	1.8838	1.95×10^{-4}	11.5120	-4.85×10^{-2}
92.0	2.7890	7.03×10^{-4}	9.2478	-3.58×10^{-2}
95.0	3.9427	1.16×10^{-3}	7.3031	-1.66×10^{-2}
98.0	5.3522	1.15×10^{-3}	5.6674	7.19×10^{-4}
101.0	7.0119	1.10×10^{-3}	4.3209	1.35×10^{-2}
104.0	8.9043	2.21×10^{-3}	3.2362	2.22×10^{-2}
107.0	11.0072	2.63×10^{-3}	2.3823	2.63×10^{-2}
110.0	13.2905	4.20×10^{-3}	1.7235	2.80×10^{-2}
113.0	15.7264	4.77×10^{-3}	1.2272	2.66×10^{-2}

TABLE 5.3 The Macmillan, Barone-Adesi, and Whaley Critical Asset Values for the Early Exercise Boundary of an American Put Computed by the Routine MBW_approx. The Parameters used were $S = 101.0$, $X = 101.0$, $r = 0.1$, $q = 0.06$, and $\sigma = 0.20$

Time to expiry, τ	Critical asset value, S^{**}	Time to expiry, τ	Critical asset value, S^{**}
1.0	82.1510	0.50	85.1701
0.95	82.3751	0.45	85.6199
0.90	82.6115	0.40	86.1176
0.85	82.8618	0.35	86.6740
0.80	83.1273	0.30	87.3049
0.75	83.4098	0.25	88.0333
0.70	83.7115	0.20	88.8959
0.65	84.0349	0.15	89.9568
0.60	84.3830	0.10	91.3469
0.55	84.7598	0.05	93.4260

based on the work of Cox, Ross, and Rubinstein (1979) and will be referred to as the CRR lattice.

From Chapter 2 equation (2.3.9), we know that if the price of an asset, S_t, follows GBM, then the change in value of its price over time interval, Δt, has the following distribution:

$$\log\left(\frac{S_{t+\Delta t}}{S_t}\right) \sim N\left(\left(r - \frac{\sigma^2}{2}\right)\Delta t, \sigma^2 \Delta t\right).$$

If we use the notation

$$X = \frac{S_{t+\Delta t}}{S_t},$$

and

$$\eta = (r - \sigma^2/2)\Delta t, \qquad v^2 = \sigma^2 \Delta t,$$

the above equation becomes

$$\log(X) \sim N(\eta, v^2)$$

or equivalently

$$X \sim \Lambda(\eta, v^2),$$

where $\Lambda(\eta, v^2)$ is the lognormal distribution *derived* from a Gaussian distribution with mean η and variance v^2. It is well-known, see, for example,

Evans et al. (2000), that the first two moments of a variable X drawn from a lognormal distribution are the following.

Lognormal Mean

$$E[X] = \exp(\eta + v^2/2), \qquad (5.3.1)$$

substituting for η and v^2 gives

$$E[X] = \exp\left\{\left(r - \frac{\sigma^2}{2}\right)\Delta t + \frac{\sigma^2}{2}\Delta t\right\}. \qquad (5.3.2)$$

Lognormal Variance

$$Var[X] = E[(X - E[X])^2] = E[X^2] - (E[X])^2 = \exp(2\eta + v^2)\left\{\exp(v^2) - 1\right\}, \qquad (5.3.3)$$

substituting for η and v^2 gives

$$Var[X] = \exp\left\{2r\left(r - \frac{\sigma^2}{2}\right)\Delta t + \sigma^2\Delta t\right\},$$

which can be simplified to yield

$$Var[X] = \exp\left\{2r\Delta t\right\}\left\{\exp(\sigma^2\Delta t) - 1\right\}. \qquad (5.3.4)$$

Since we can assume that the expected value of X grows at the riskless interest rate, r, we can also write

$$E[X] = \exp(r\Delta t). \qquad (5.3.5)$$

The above results can be used to find the first two moments of the asset price distribution $S_{t+\Delta t}$, given that we know the asset price, S_t, at time instant t. To do this we will use (see Appendix C.3 for a proof) the fact that for a random variable G, we have

$$E[a + bG] = E[a] + bE[G], \quad \text{and} \quad Var[a + bG] = b^2 Var[G],$$

where a and b are constants. Applying this to the variable X gives

$$E[X] = E\left[\frac{S_{t+\Delta t}}{S_t}\right] = \frac{1}{S_t}E\left[S_{t+\Delta t}\right] \qquad (5.3.6)$$

and

$$Var[X] = Var\left[\frac{S_{t+\Delta t}}{S_t}\right] = \frac{1}{S_t^2}Var\left[S_{t+\Delta t}\right], \qquad (5.3.7)$$

where we have used $a = 0$ and $b = \frac{1}{S_t}$. Note: It is also easy to show that

$$Var[S_{t+\Delta t}] = Var[\Delta S], \qquad (5.3.8)$$

where the change in asset price over the time interval Δt is denoted by $\Delta S = S_{t+\Delta t} - S_t$. This elementary result sometimes is used without proof, see, for example, Hull (1997) page 344. The proof is simple,

$$Var[S_{t+\Delta t}] = Var[S_t + \Delta S] = Var[\Delta S],$$

where again we have used

$$Var[a + bG] = b^2 Var[G], \text{ this time with } a = 0 \text{ and } b = 1.$$

To find expressions for the mean and variance of $S_{t+\Delta t}$, we simply substitute equation (5.3.5) into equation (5.3.6) and obtain

$$E[S_{t+\Delta t}] = S_t \exp(r\Delta t), \tag{5.3.9}$$

and substituting equation (5.3.4) into equation (5.3.7) gives

$$Var[S_{t+\Delta t}] = S_t^2 \exp(2r\Delta t) \left\{\exp(\sigma^2 \Delta t) - 1\right\}. \tag{5.3.10}$$

Since we are modelling asset price movements with a binomial lattice, the asset price, S_t, at any given node is only permitted to either *jump-up* or *jump-down* in value over the next time step Δt. Here, we will assume that the new asset price, $S_{t+\Delta t}$, is $S_t u$ for an up-jump and $S_t d$ for a down-jump; where u and d are constants that apply to all lattice nodes. If we further denote the probability of an up-jump by p, then the probability of a down-jump must (by definition) be $1 - p$.

Now that we have specified the lattice parameters we will use these to match the first two moments of the lognormal distribution. This results in the following equation for the mean:

$$E[S_{t+\Delta t}] = pS_t u + (1 - p)S_t d = S_t \exp(r\Delta t). \tag{5.3.11}$$

The corresponding equation for the variance requires a little more work

$$Var[S_{t+\Delta t}] = E[(S_{t+\Delta t})^2] - (E[S_{t+\Delta t}]^2). \tag{5.3.12}$$

Since

$$E[(S_{t+\Delta t})^2] = p(S_t u)^2 + (1 - p)(S_t d)^2 = S_t^2 \left\{pu^2 + (1 - p)d^2\right\} \tag{5.3.13}$$

and, from equation (5.3.9), we have

$$(E[S_{t+\Delta t}])^2 = \{S_t \exp(r\Delta t)\}^2 = S_t^2 \exp(2r\Delta t), \tag{5.3.14}$$

we can substitute equation (5.3.13) and equation (5.3.14) into equation (5.3.12) to obtain

$$Var[S_{t+\Delta t}] = S_t^2 \left\{pu^2 + (1 - p)d^2\right\} - S_t^2 \exp(2r\Delta t). \tag{5.3.15}$$

So from equation (5.3.10) and equation (5.3.15),

$$\exp(2r\Delta t)\left\{\exp(\sigma^2\Delta t) - 1\right\} = pu^2 + (1-p)d^2 - \exp(2r\Delta t). \qquad (5.3.16)$$

So, restating equation (5.3.11) and simplifying equation (5.3.16), we obtain the following two equations:

$$pu + (1-p)d = \exp(r\Delta t), \qquad (5.3.17)$$

$$\exp(2r\Delta t + \sigma^2\Delta t) = pu^2 + (1-p)d^2, \qquad (5.3.18)$$

which we will use to solve for the three parameters u, d, and p. Since there are three unknowns and only two equations, we can impose an additional constraint to obtain a unique solution. The constraint used in the CRR binomial model is

$$u = \frac{1}{d}.$$

We now use the following notation:

$$a = \exp(r\Delta t)$$

and

$$b^2 = \exp(2r\Delta t)\left\{\exp(\sigma^2\Delta t) - 1\right\} = a^2\left\{\exp(\sigma^2\Delta t) - 1\right\}.$$

This means that equation (5.3.17) can be written as

$$a = pu + (1-p)d,$$

which gives

$$p = \frac{a-d}{u-d}. \qquad (5.3.19)$$

From equation (5.3.18), we have

$$\exp(2r\Delta t + \sigma^2\Delta t) = a^2\exp(\sigma^2\Delta t) = a^2 + b^2$$

and so

$$a^2 + b^2 = pu^2 + (1-p)d^2.$$

Rearranging we have

$$pu^2 + (1-p)d^2 - a^2 = b^2,$$

$$pu^3 + (1-p)d^2u - a^2u - b^2u = 0,$$

but

$$(1-p)d^2u = (1-p)d = a - pu$$

so

$$pu^3 = (a - pu) - a^2u - b^2u = 0$$

or

$$p(u^3 - u) + a - a^2 - b^2u = 0.$$

Now

$$p(u^3 - u) = u^2p(u - d) = u^2(a - d) = u^2a - u,$$

which gives

$$au^2 - u + a - a^2u - b^2u = 0.$$

So we obtain the following quadratic equation in u:

$$au^2 - u(1 + a^2 + b^2) + a = 0.$$

The solution is

$$u = \frac{(1 + a^2 + b^2) + \sqrt{(1 + a^2 + b^2)^2 - 4a^2}}{2a}.$$

If Δt is small, we can obtain a *reasonable approximation* to the solution by neglecting terms of order higher than Δt.

In these circumstances, we have

$$a^2 + b^2 + 1 = \exp(2r\Delta t) + \exp(2r\Delta t)\left\{\exp(\sigma^2\Delta t) - 1\right\} + 1$$

$$\sim 1 + 2r\Delta t + (1 + 2r\Delta t)\sigma^2\Delta t + 1 \sim 2 + 2r\Delta t + \sigma^2\Delta t.$$

Therefore,

$$\sqrt{(a^2 + b^2 + 1)^2 - 4a^2} \sim \sqrt{(2 + 2r\Delta t + \sigma^2\Delta t)^2 - 4(1 + 2r\Delta t)}$$

$$\sim \sqrt{4 + 8r\Delta t + 4\sigma^2 - 4 - 8r\Delta t} = \sqrt{4\sigma^2\Delta t} = 2\sigma\sqrt{\Delta t}$$

and so

$$u \sim \frac{2 + 2r\Delta t + \sigma^2\Delta t + 2\sigma\sqrt{\Delta t}}{2\exp(r\Delta t)},$$

$$u \sim \left(1 + r\Delta t + \frac{\sigma^2\Delta t}{2} + \sigma\sqrt{\Delta t}\right)(1 - r\Delta t),$$

$$u \sim 1 + r\Delta t + \frac{\sigma^2\Delta t}{2} + \sigma\sqrt{\Delta t} - r\Delta t = 1 + \sigma\sqrt{\Delta t} + \frac{\sigma^2\Delta t}{2},$$

which to order Δt gives

$$u = \exp(\sigma\sqrt{\Delta t}) \qquad (5.3.20)$$

since

$$\exp(\sigma\sqrt{\Delta t}) = 1 + \sigma\sqrt{\Delta t} + \frac{\sigma^2\Delta t}{2} + \frac{\sigma^3(\Delta t)^{3/2}}{6} + \ldots,$$

which also gives

$$d = \frac{1}{u} = \exp(-\sigma\sqrt{\Delta t}). \qquad (5.3.21)$$

It is interesting to note that when $r = 0$ we have $p \to \frac{1}{2}$.

Now that we know the values of the lattice parameters u, d, and p we can use these to build a lattice with a specified number of time steps. Once this has been

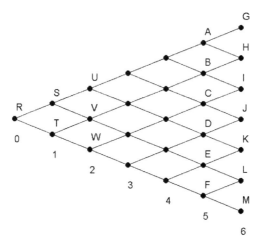

FIGURE 5.1 A standard binomial lattice consisting of six time steps. The root lattice node R corresponds to the current time t, the terminal nodes G to M are those at option maturity, that is, time $t + \tau$, where τ is the duration of the option. The asset value at node R is S, where S is the current asset value. Asset values at other nodes are, for example, node S: Su, node T: Sd, node V: S, and node A: Su^5. Option values are computed using a backward iterative process: the option values at nodes A to F on the penultimate time step are computed from the payouts of the terminal nodes G to M, and this process continues until the root node is reached, which yields the current value of the option. Here, we compute the Greeks using the following nodes: Delta uses nodes S and T, Gamma uses nodes U, V, and W, and Theta uses nodes R and V.

constructed it can be used to compute the values and Greeks for various types of financial options. These could simply be American/European vanilla options or more exotic options that may incorporate features such as *lockout periods*, *barriers*, and nonstandard payoff functions.

We will now discuss how to create a lattice which can be used to value American and European vanilla options.

If the current value of the underlying asset is S, and the duration of the option is τ and we use a lattice with n equally spaced time intervals Δt, then we have

$$\Delta t = \frac{\tau}{n}.$$

The values of the asset price at various nodes in the lattice can easily be computed. This is illustrated, in Fig. 5.1, for a lattice with six time steps (that is seven lattice levels).

The asset values at the labelled nodes are the following:
Lattice level 1: Time t

$$S_R = S.$$

Lattice level 2: Time t + Δt

$$S_S = Su, \qquad S_T = Sd.$$

Lattice level 6: Time t + 5Δt

$$S_A = Su^5, \qquad S_B = Su^3, \qquad S_C = Su, \qquad S_D = Sd,$$
$$S_E = S, \qquad S_F = Sd^5.$$

Lattice level 7: Time t + 6Δt

$$S_G = Su^6, \qquad S_H = Su^4, \qquad S_I = Su^2, \qquad S_J = S,$$
$$S_K = Sd^2, \qquad S_L = Sd^4, \qquad S_M = Sd^6.$$

In general, at time $t + i\Delta t$, there are $i + 1$, stock prices; these are

$$S_{i,j} = Su^j d^{i-j}, \quad j = 0, 1, \ldots, i.$$

We note, that since $u = 1/d$, an up movement followed by a down movement gives the same stock price as a down movement followed by an up movement, for instance $Su^2 d = Su$. This means that the tree recombines, and the number of nodes required to represent all the different asset prices is significantly reduced.

5.3.2 Constructing and using the Binomial Lattice

In this section, we are concerned with the practical details of how to construct, and then use, a *standard* one-dimensional binomial lattice to value American and European options. Since this lattice forms the basis for other one-dimensional and multidimensional lattice techniques we will discuss its construction in some detail. A complete computer program for a standard binomial lattice is given in Code excerpt 5.11, and we will use this as a basis for our discussions. The results of using this code are presented in Fig. 5.2. For easy reference we will now list the input parameters used by this computer program:

S0	the current price of the underlying asset, S
X	the strike price
sigma	the volatility of the asset
T	the maturity of the option in years
r	the risk free interest rate
q	the continuous dividend yield
put	if put equals 1 then the option is a put option, if put equals 0 then it is a call option
is_american	if is_american equals 1 then it is an American option, if is_american equals 0 then it is a European option
M	the number of time steps in the lattice

We will now discuss in more detail the computational issues involved in each stage of the calculation.

Compute the Values of the Constants Used by the Lattice

First calculate the values of various constants that will be used, see Code excerpt 5.5.

```
dt = T/(double)M;
t1 = sigma*sqrt(dt);
u = exp(t1);
d = exp(-t1);
a = exp((r-q)*dt);
p = (a - d)/(u - d);
if ((p < zero) || (p > 1.0)) printf ("Error p out of range\n");
discount = exp(-r*dt);
p_u = discount*p;
p_d = discount*(1.0-p);
```

Code excerpt 5.5 A code fragment which computes the values of various lattice constants.

For convenience, we have used the variables p_u and p_d to store respectively the up- and down-jump probabilities discounted by the interest rate r over one time step; these values will be used later on when we work backwards through the lattice to calculate the current option value.

Assign the Asset Values to the Lattice Nodes

We will now show that the number of different asset prices, $\mathcal{LS}_n$, for an n step recombining lattice is $2n + 1$.

The nodes in a recombining lattice can be considered as being composed of two kinds: those corresponding to an *even* time step and those corresponding to an *odd* time step.

This is because the set of node asset values, $\mathcal{ET}$, for an even time step is distinct from the set of node asset values, $\mathcal{OT}$, for an odd time step. Although $\mathcal{ET} \cap \mathcal{OT} = \emptyset$, the elements of $\mathcal{ET}$ and $\mathcal{OT}$ for any consecutive pair of time steps are related by the simple constant multiplicative factor d. Also for an even time step there is a central node corresponding to the current asset price S0, and the remaining nodes are symmetrically arranged about this, see Code excerpt 5.6. These features are illustrated in Fig. 5.1, for a standard lattice with six time steps.

The number of distinct asset prices in a lattice is therefore the sum of the number of nodes in the last two time steps. Since the number of nodes in the ith time step, S_i, is $i + 1$ (see Fig. 5.1), for an n time step lattice, we have

$$S_n = n + 1 \quad \text{and} \quad S_{n-1} = n.$$

This means that the number of different asset values in an n time step lattice is

$$\mathcal{LS}_n = S_n + S_{n-1} = 2n + 1.$$

The number of nodes in an n time step lattice, $\mathcal{LN}_n$, is

$$\mathcal{LN}_n = \sum_{i=0}^{n}(i + 1) = \frac{(n + 1)(n + 2)}{2},$$

where we have used the fact that $\mathcal{LN}_n$ is the sum of an arithmetic progression with first term 1, increment 1, and last term $n + 1$.

One might initially think that, in order to price options, it is necessary to store the asset value of each lattice node, which would entail storing $\mathcal{LN}_n$ values.

However, this is not the case. We only need to store the number of *different* asset values in the lattice, that is, $\mathcal{L}S_n$ values.

Storing $\mathcal{L}S_n$ values instead of $\mathcal{L}N_n$ can result in dramatic economies of storage. For example, an accurate, 1000-step lattice has $\mathcal{L}N_n = 2001 \times 2002 \times 1/2 = 2003001$, while the corresponding value of $\mathcal{L}S_n$ is only $2 \times 1000 + 1 = 2001$.

```
s[M] = S0;
for (i = 1; i <= M; ++i) {
    s[M+i] = u*s[M+i-1];
    s[M-i] = d*s[M-i+1];
}
```

Code excerpt 5.6 A code fragment which assigns the different binomial lattice asset values to the storage array s by using the up- and down-jump ratios u and d defined in Section 3.4.1. The current asset value S is assigned to the central array element s[M], where M is the number of time steps in the lattice. The array elements above centre are $S[M+i] = Su^i, i = 1, \ldots, M$, and the array elements below centre are $S[M-i] = Sd^i i = 1, \ldots, M$.

Compute the Option Payoff at the Terminal Nodes

The current value of an option is evaluated by starting at option maturity, the end of the tree, and working backwards. The option values for the *terminal nodes* of the tree are just given by the payoff (at maturity) of the option; this is independent of whether the option is an American or European. For a lattice with n time steps, there are $n+1$ terminal nodes, with option values, $f_{n,j}, j = 0, \ldots, n$.

To compute the values of vanilla American and European options, with exercise price E, then we will start with the following terminal node values: for put options,

$$f_{n,j} = \max(E - Su^j d^{n-j}, 0), \quad j = 0, \ldots, n$$

and for call options,

$$f_{n,j} = \max(Su^j d^{n-j} - E, 0), \quad j = 0, \ldots, n.$$

The computer code used to achieve this is Code excerpt 5.7.

```
if (((M+1)/2) == (M/2)) { /* then M is even */
    if (put)
        v[M/2] = MAX(X - s[M],zero);
    else
        v[M/2] = MAX(s[M]-X,zero);
}
P1 = 2*M;
P2 = 0;
for (i = 0; i < (M+1)/2; ++i) {
    if (put) {
        v[M-i] = MAX(X - s[P1],zero);
        v[i]   = MAX(X - s[P2],zero);
    }
    else {
        v[M-i] = MAX(s[P1]-X,zero);
        v[i]   = MAX(s[P2]-X,zero);
    }
    P1 = P1 - 2;
    P2 = P2 + 2;
}
```

Code excerpt 5.7 A code fragment that computes the payouts for puts and calls at the lattice terminal nodes. The payouts are assigned to elements of the array v and are computed using the strike price, X, and the previously computed asset values stored in array s, as before M is the number of time steps in the lattice, y.

Iterate Backwards through the Lattice

The probability of moving from node (i, j) at time $i\Delta t$ to node $(i + 1, j + 1)$ at time $(i + 1)\Delta t$ is p, and the probability of moving from node (i, j) at time $i\Delta t$ to the node $(i + 1, j)$ at time $(i + 1)\Delta t$ is $1 - p$. If we assume that there is no early exercise, then

$$f_{i,j}^E = \exp(-r\Delta t)\left\{pf_{i+1,j+1} + (1 - p)f_{i+1,j}\right\}, \quad j \leq i \leq n - 1, \ 0 \leq j \leq i. \quad (5.3.22)$$

When early exercise, for an American option, is taken into account, we have

$$f_{i,j}^A = \max\left\{E - S_{i,j}, f_{i,j}^E\right\}, \quad\quad\quad (5.3.23)$$

or for an American call option,

$$f_{i,j}^A = \max\left\{S_{i,j} - E, f_{i,j}^E\right\}, \quad j \leq i \leq N - 1, \ 0 \leq j \leq i, \quad (5.3.24)$$

where $f_{i,j}^E$ is given by equation (5.3.22).

The following Code excerpt 5.8 works backward through the lattice and uses the array **v** to store the option values.

```
P2 = 0;
for (m1 = M-1; m1 >= 2; --m1) {
  P2 = P2 + 1;
  P1 = P2;
  for (n =0; n <= m1; ++n) {
    if ((v[n] == zero) && (v[n+1] == zero)) {
      hold = zero;
    }
    else
      hold = p_d*v[n] + p_u*v[n+1];
    if (is_american) {
      if (put)
        v[n] = MAX(hold,X-s[P1]);
      else
        v[n] = MAX(hold,s[P1]-X);
    }
    else
      v[n] = hold;
    P1 = P1 + 2;
  }
}
```

Code excerpt 5.8 Computer code that works iteratively backward through the lattice computing the option values at each time step. The array v contains the option values computed from the previous time step, and these are overwritten with option values computed for the current time step. The iteration stops at the second time step, since we do not want to overwrite values in the array v which are required for calculating the Greeks in the neighbourhood of the root node.

At each time step, the newly calculated option values overwrite those computed by the previous time step. This process is continued until the second time step (m1 = 2) is reached. A different technique is then used, which does not overwrite the option values and thus allows the Greeks to be computed in the vicinity of the root lattice node R. If the Greeks are not required, continue working backward through the lattice until the root node R (m1 = 0) is reached, and the current value of the option is then given by v[0] (or its multidimensional equivalent).

The option values at all lattice nodes in time steps $0, 1$, and 2 are made accessible by the following Code excerpt 5.9:

```
jj = 2;
for (m1 = 2; m1 >= 1; --m1) {
    ind = M-m1+1;
    for (n =0; n < m1; ++n) {
        hold =  p_d*v[5-jj-m1-1] + p_u*v[5-jj-m1];
        if (is_american) {
            if (put)
                v[5-jj] = MAX(hold,X-s[ind]);
            else
                v[5-jj] = MAX(hold,s[ind]-X);
        }
        else
            v[5-jj] = hold;
        --jj;
        ind = ind + 2;
    }
}
*value = v[5];
```

Code excerpt 5.9 Code fragment illustrating how the option values are stored for the first two time steps so that the Greeks can be computed in the vicinity of the root node R.

Computing the Greeks: Δ, Γ, and Θ

We will now describe how to calculate the option's hedge statistics (Greeks).

Let the option value and asset value at lattice node k be denoted by f_k and S_k respectively. So, for instance, S_T represents the asset price at node T and f_T is the corresponding option value at node T. Table 5.4 supplies details of the lattice node values in the vicinity of the root node R.

The computation of each Greek is now considered.

Delta

The definition of Δ is the rate of change of the option value with asset price; all other parameters remaining fixed. Thus,

$$\Delta = \frac{\partial f}{\partial S} = \frac{\Delta f}{\Delta S},$$

where Δf is the change option value corresponding to the change in the asset price ΔS. Ideally, we would like to evaluate this partial derivative at the root node R (m1=0); however, we cannot because we need at least two lattice nodes

TABLE 5.4 Lattice Node Values in the Vicinity of the Root Node R

Node	Time step	Asset array element	Asset value	Option array element
R	0	s[M]	S	v[5]
S	1	s[M+1]	Su	v[4]
T	1	s[M-1]	Sd	v[3]
U	2	s[M+2]	Su^2	v[2]
V	2	s[M]	S	v[1]
W	2	s[M-2]	Sd^2	v[0]

to compute a value. The best we can do is to evaluate the derivative at the first time step (m1=1) as follows:

$$\Delta = \frac{f_S - f_T}{S_S - S_T} = \frac{v[4] - v[3]}{s[M+1] - s[M-1]}.$$

Gamma

The definition of Γ is the rate of change of Δ with asset price; all other parameters remaining fixed. Thus,

$$\Gamma = \frac{\partial^2 f}{\partial S^2} = \frac{\partial \Delta}{\partial S}.$$

In order to evaluate Γ, we require at least two values of Δ. The nearest this can be achieved to the root node R is at time step 2, where we have

$$\Gamma = \frac{\Delta^*_{UV} - \Delta^*_{VW}}{S^*_{UV} - S^*_{VW}},$$

with the midpoints

$$S^*_{UV} = \frac{1}{2}\{S_U + S_V\}$$

and the values of Δ at the midpoints S^*_{UV} and S^*_{VW} denoted by Δ^*_{UV} and Δ^*_{VW} respectively. Since

$$\Delta^*_{UV} = \frac{f_U - f_V}{S_U - S_V},$$

$$\Delta^*_{VW} = \frac{f_V - f_W}{S_V - S_W},$$

and

$$S^*_{UV} - S^*_{VW} = \frac{1}{2}\{S_U - S_W\},$$

we have

$$\Delta^*_{UV} = \frac{v[2] - v[1]}{s[M+2] - s[M]},$$

$$\Delta^*_{VW} = \frac{v[1] - v[0]}{s[M] - s[M-2]}.$$

The value of Γ can therefore be approximated as

$$\Gamma = \frac{2\{\Delta^*_{UV} - \Delta^*_{VW}\}}{s[M+2] - s[M-2]}.$$

Theta

The definition of Θ is the rate of change of option value with time; all other parameters remaining fixed. Thus,

$$\Theta = \frac{\partial f}{\partial t} = \frac{\Delta f}{\Delta t}.$$

The nearest to the root node R, this can be computed is over the time interval from time step 0 to time step 2. We then obtain the following approximation:

$$\Theta = \frac{f_V - f_R}{2\Delta t} = \frac{v[1] - v[5]}{2\Delta t}.$$

Code excerpt 5.10 below computes the Δ, Γ, and Θ by using the approximations we have just discussed.

Vega

The definition of $\mathcal{V}$ is the rate of change of the option value with volatility,

$$\mathcal{V} = \frac{\partial f}{\partial \sigma}.$$

In a standard binomial lattice, $\mathcal{V}$ cannot be computed directly. A simple approach is to use two binomial lattices as follows:

$$\mathcal{V} = \frac{f_{\sigma + \Delta\sigma} - f_\sigma}{\Delta\sigma},$$

where $f_{\sigma + \Delta\sigma}$ is the option value computed using a binomial lattice with volatility $\sigma + \Delta\sigma$, and f_σ is the option value computed using another binomial lattice with a volatility of σ; all other lattice parameters remain constant.

```
if(greeks) {
/* assign the value of delta (obtained from m1 = 1) */
  greeks[1] = (v[4]-v[3])/(s[M+1]-s[M-1]);
 /* assign the value of gamma (use the values at time step m1 = 2) */
  dv1 = v[2] - v[1];
  ds1 = s[M+2] - s[M];
  dv2 = v[1] - v[0];
  ds2 = s[M] - s[M-2];
  h = 0.5*(s[M+2] - s[M-2]);
  greeks[0] = ((dv1/ds1) - (dv2/ds2))/h;
 /* assign the value of theta */
  greeks[2] = (v[1]-*value)/(2.0*dt); /* can also write: greeks[2] = (v[1]-v[5])/(2.0*dt); */
}
```

Code excerpt 5.10 A code fragment that computes the values of the Greeks, Delta, Gamma, and Theta in the vicinity of the root lattice node R.

```
void standard_lattice(double *value, double greeks[], double S0, double X, double sigma, double T, double r,
                      double q, long put, long is_american, long M, long *iflag)

{
/* Input parameters:
   ==================
   S0          - the current price of the underlying asset
   X           - the strike price
   sigma       - the volatility
   T           - the time to maturity
   r           - the interest rate
   q           - the continuous dividend yield
   put         - if put is 0 then a call option, otherwise a put option
   is_american - if is_american is 0 then a European option, otherwise an American option
   M           - the number of time steps
   Output parameters:
   ==================
   value       - the value of the option,
   greeks[]    - the hedge statistics output as follows: greeks[0] is gamma, greeks[1] is delta, greeks[2] is theta,
   iflag       - an error indicator.
*/
       . . .

   /* Allocate the arrays s[2*M+1], and v[M+1] */
```

Code excerpt 5.11 Function to compute the value of an option using a standard binomial lattice.

```
dt = T/(double)M;
t1 = sigma*sqrt(dt);
u = exp(t1);
d = exp(-t1);
a = exp((r-q)*dt);
p = (a - d)/(u - d);
if ((p < zero) || (p > 1.0)) printf ("Error p out of range\n");
discount = exp(-r*dt);
p_u = discount*p;
p_d = discount*(1.0-p);

/* assign the 2*M+1 asset values */
s[M] = S0;
for (i = 1; i <= M; ++i) {
    s[M+i] = u*s[M+i-1];
    s[M-i] = d*s[M-i+1];
}
/* Find out if the number of time steps, M, is odd or even */
if (((M+1)/2) == (M/2)) { /* then M is even */
    if (put)
        v[M/2] = MAX(X - s[M],zero);
    else
        v[M/2] = MAX(s[M]-X,zero);
}
/* Calculate the option values at maturity */
P1 = 2*M;
P2 = 0;
for (i = 0; i < (M+1)/2; ++i) {
  if (put) {
      v[M-i] = MAX(X - s[P1],zero);
      v[i]   = MAX(X - s[P2],zero);
  }
  else {
      v[M-i] = MAX(s[P1]-X,zero);
      v[i]   = MAX(s[P2]-X,zero);
  }
  P1 = P1 - 2;
  P2 = P2 + 2;
}
/* now work backwards through the lattice to calculate the current option value */
  P2 = 0;
  for (m1 = M-1; m1 >= 2; --m1) {
    P2 = P2 + 1;
    P1 = P2;
    for (n =0; n <= m1; ++n) {
        if ((v[n] == zero) && (v[n+1] == zero))  {
            hold = zero;
        }
        else
            hold = p_d*v[n] + p_u*v[n+1];
        if (is_american) {
            if (put)
                v[n] = MAX(hold,X-s[P1]);
            else
                v[n] = MAX(hold,s[P1]-X);
        }
        else
            v[n] = hold;
        P1 = P1 + 2;
    }
  }
/* The values v[0], v[1] & v[2] correspond to the nodes for m1 = 2, v[3] & v[4] correspond
    to the nodes for m1 = 1 and the
    option value (*value) is the node for m1 = 0, v[5]. For a given time step v[0] corresponds
    to the lowest asset price,
    v[1] to the next lowest etc.. */

  jj = 2;
  for (m1 = 2; m1 >= 1; --m1) {
    ind = M-m1+1;
    for (n =0; n < m1; ++n) {
        hold =  p_d*v[5-jj-m1-1] + p_u*v[5-jj-m1];
        if (is_american) {
            if (put)
                v[5-jj] = MAX(hold,X-s[ind]);
            else
                v[5-jj] = MAX(hold,s[ind]-X);
        }
        else
            v[5-jj] = hold;
        --jj;
        ind = ind + 2;
    }
  }
```

Code excerpt 5.11 (*Continued*).

```
*value = v[5];
if(greeks) {
    /* assign the value of delta (obtained from m1 = 1) */
    greeks[1] = (v[4]-v[3])/(s[M+1]-s[M-1]);
    /* assign the value of gamma (use the values at time step m1 = 2)  */
    dv1 = v[2] - v[1];
    ds1 = s[M+2] - s[M];
    dv2 = v[1] - v[0];
    ds2 = s[M] - s[M-2];
    h   = 0.5*(s[M+2] - s[M-2]);
    greeks[0] = ((dv1/ds1) - (dv2/ds2))/h;
    /* assign the value of theta */
    greeks[2] = (v[1]-*value)/(2.0*dt);   /* can also write: greeks[2] = (v[1]-v[5])/(2.0*dt); */
}
```

Code excerpt 5.11 (*Continued*).

The implied volatility of American options can be computed using the method outlined for European options in Section 5.4.4; however in this case, the option value and Greeks are computed using a binomial lattice.

5.3.3 Binomial Lattice with a Control Variate

The control variate technique can be used to enhance the accuracy that a standard binomial lattice gives for the value of an American vanilla option. It involves using the same standard binomial lattice to value of both an American option and also the equivalent European option. The Black–Scholes formula is then used to compute the accurate value of the European option. If we assume that the error in pricing the European option is the same as that for the American

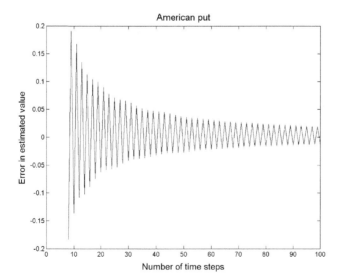

FIGURE 5.2 The error in the estimated value, est_val, of an American put using a standard binomial lattice. The parameters used were $T = 1.0$, $S = 105.0$, $X = 105.0$, $r = 0.1$, $q = 0.02$, and $\sigma = 0.3$. The very accurate value (acc_val) was 9.2508 and was computed using a 6000-step standard binomial lattice. The error in the estimated value was obtained as $est\_val - acc\_val$.

option, we can achieve an improved estimate for the value of the American option.

When applied to the valuation of an American put option, this can be expressed as follows:

European pricing error, $\Delta_E = p^{BS}(S, E, \tau) - p^L(S, E, \tau)$,

American pricing error, $\Delta_A = P^*(S, E, \tau) - P^L(S, E, \tau)$,

where as usual S is the current value of the asset, E is the strike price, and τ is the maturity of the option. Also $p^{BS}(S, E, \tau)$ is the Black–Scholes value of the European put option, $p^L(S, E, \tau)$ is the binomial lattice estimate of the European put option, $P^*(S, E, \tau)$ is the (*unknown*) accurate value of the American put option, and $P^L(S, E, \tau)$ is the binomial lattice estimate of the American put option.

Letting $\Delta_E = \Delta_A$, we then have

$$p^{BS}(S, E, \tau) - p^L(S, E, \tau) = P^*(S, E, \tau) - P^L(S, E, \tau),$$

which on rearrangement yields

$$P^*(S, E, \tau) = p^{BS}(S, E, \tau) - p^L(S, E, \tau) + P^L(S, E, \tau).$$

We thus use $P^*(S, E, \tau)$ as the improved, control variate estimate for the value of American put option. Of course exactly the same approach can be use to obtained an improved estimate for the value of an American call.

Code excerpt 5.12 shows the use of the control variate technique in a standard binomial lattice to provide improved estimates for both the value and the hedge statistics of an American option.

```
/* Set up the arrays as in the standard lattice */
        .   .   .
for (i = 0; i < (M+1)/2; ++i) { /* Calculate the option values at maturity */
    if (put) {
        a_v[M-i] = MAX(X - s[P1],zero);
        a_v[i]   = MAX(X - s[P2],zero);
    }
    else {
        a_v[M-i] = MAX(s[P1]-X,zero);
        a_v[i]   = MAX(s[P2]-X,zero);
    }
    e_v[i]   = a_v[i];
    e_v[M-i] = a_v[M-i];
    P1 = P1 - 2;
    P2 = P2 + 2;
}
/* now work backwards through the lattice to calculate the current option value */
    P2 = 0;
    for (m1 = M-1; m1 >= 2; --m1) {
        P2 = P2 + 1;
        P1 = P2;
        for (n =0; n <= m1; ++n) {
            if ((a_v[n] == zero) && (a_v[n+1] == zero))
                hold = zero;
            else
                hold = p_d*a_v[n] + p_u*a_v[n+1];
            if (put)
                a_v[n] = MAX(hold,X-s[P1]);
            else
                a_v[n] = MAX(hold,s[P1]-X);
            if ((e_v[n] == zero) && (e_v[n+1] == zero))
                e_v[n] = zero;
            else
                e_v[n] = p_d*e_v[n] + p_u*e_v[n+1];
```

Code excerpt 5.12 Function to compute the value and hedge statistics of an American option using a binomial lattice with a control variate.

```
        P1 = P1 + 2;
    }
  }
/* The American values are stored in the array a_v, and the European values in the array e_v. The array
   indexing is the same as for the standard lattice */

jj = 2;
for (m1 = 2; m1 >= 1; --m1) {
    ind = M-m1+1;
    for (n =0; n < m1; ++n) {
        hold = p_d*a_v[5-jj-m1-1] + p_u*a_v[5-jj-m1];
        if (put)
            a_v[5-jj] = MAX(hold,X-s[ind]);
        else
            a_v[5-jj] = MAX(hold,s[ind]-X);
        e_v[5-jj] = p_d*e_v[5-jj-m1-1] + p_u*e_v[5-jj-m1];
        --jj;
        ind = ind + 2;
    }
}
/* v1 = American binomial approximation, v2 = European Binomial approximation, temp = exact (European)
Black Scholes value */
black_scholes(&temp,bs_greeks,S0,X,sigma,T,r,q,put,&iflagx);
*value = (a_v[5] - e_v[5]) + temp; /* return the control variate approximation */
if(greeks) {
    /* assign the value of delta (obtained from m1 = 1) */
    a_delta = (a_v[4]-a_v[3])/(s[M+1]-s[M-1]);
    e_delta = (e_v[4]-e_v[3])/(s[M+1]-s[M-1]);
    greeks[1] = a_delta - e_delta + bs_greeks[1];
    /* assign the value of gamma (use the values at time step m1 = 2)  */
    dv1 = a_v[2] - a_v[1];
    ds1 = s[M+2] - s[M];
    dv2 = a_v[1] - a_v[0];
    ds2 = s[M] - s[M-2];
    h   = 0.5*(s[M+2] - s[M-2]);
    a_gamma = ((dv1/ds1) - (dv2/ds2))/h;
    dv1 = e_v[2] - e_v[1];
    dv2 = e_v[1] - e_v[0];
    e_gamma = ((dv1/ds1) - (dv2/ds2))/h;
    greeks[0] = (a_gamma - e_gamma) + bs_greeks[0];
    /* assign the value of theta */
    a_theta = (a_v[1]-a_v[5])/(2.0*dt);
    e_theta = (e_v[1]-e_v[5])/(2.0*dt);
    greeks[2] = (a_theta - e_theta) + bs_greeks[2];
}
```

Code excerpt 5.12 (*Continued*).

Finally, we should mention that the control variate technique does not just apply to American vanilla options. The method is quite general and can be used to obtain improved estimates for any integral (or exotic option) so long as an accurate (closed form) solution of a *similar* integral is known. One common use of the control variate method is to improve the accuracy of Monte Carlo estimates.

5.3.4 The Binomial Lattice with BBS and BBSR

Here, we consider the binomial Black–Scholes (BBS) method and also the binomial Black–Scholes method with Richardson extrapolation (BBSR), see Broadie and DeTemple (1996). As with the control variate method discussed in the previous section, both of these techniques can be used in conjunction with a standard binomial lattice to improve the computed results.

We will first discuss the BBS method.

The BBS Method

The BBS method is identical to the standard binomial lattice except that in the last time step (that is just before option maturity) the Black–Scholes formula is used to calculate the option values at maturity. For an n-time step binomial lattice, this involves evaluating the Black–Scholes formula at each of the n nodes in the penultimate time step, see Fig. 5.1. In Code excerpt 5.13, we define the function bs_lattice which incorporates the BBS method into a standard binomial lattice. The reader will have noticed that bbs_lattice is *rather lax* concerning the amount of storage that is required, see Section 5.3.2. It uses an array of size $\mathcal{L}N_n$ rather than $\mathcal{L}S_n$ to store the lattice asset prices; the modification to use an array of size $\mathcal{L}S_n$ is left as an exercise.

```
void bbs_lattice(double *value, double greeks[], double S0, double X, double sigma, double T, double r,
          double q, long put, long M, long *iflag)
{
/* Input parameters:
   ==================
   S0            - the current price of the underlying asset
   X             - the strike price
   sigma         - the volatility
   T             - the time to maturity
   r             - the interest rate
   q             - the continuous dividend yield
   put           - if put is 0 then a call option, otherwise a put option
   M             - the number of time steps
   Output parameters:
   ==================
   value         - the value of the option, greeks[] - the hedge statistics output as follows: greeks[0] is gamma,
                   greeks[1] is delta, greeks[2] is theta,
   iflag         - an error indicator.
*/
          . . .

   /* allocate the arrays s[((M+2)*(M+1))/2], and v[M+1] */

   dt = T/(double)M;
   t1 = sigma*sqrt(dt);
   u = exp(t1);
   d = exp(-t1);
   a = exp((r-q)*dt);
   p = (a - d)/(u - d);
   if ((p < zero) || (p > 1.0)) return; /* Invalid probability */
   discount = exp(-r*dt);
   p_u = p*discount;
   p_d = (1.0-p)*discount;
   jj = 0;
   s[0] = S0;
   /* The "higher" the value of jj, at a given time instant, the lower the  value of the asset price */
   for (ml = 1; ml <= M-1; ++ml) { /* Calculate asset values up to (M-1)th time step */
      for (n = ml; n >= 1; --n) {
         ++jj;
         s[jj] = u*s[jj-ml];
      }
      ++jj;
      s[jj] = d*s[jj-ml-1];
   }
   for (n = 0; n <= M-1; ++n) { /* Use Black Scholes for the final step */
      black_scholes(&temp,NULL,s[jj],X,sigma,dt,r,q,put,&iflagx);
      v[n] = temp;
      --jj;
   }
    for (ml = M-1; ml >= 3; --ml) { /* work backwards through the lattice */
      for (n =0; n < ml; ++n) {
         if ((v[n] == zero) && (v[n+1] == zero))  {
            hold = zero;
         }
         else
            hold = p_d*v[n] + p_u*v[n+1];
         if (is_american) {
            if (put)
               v[n] = MAX(hold,X-s[jj]);
            else
               v[n] = MAX(hold,s[jj]-X);
         }
         else
            v[n] = hold;
         --jj;
```

Code excerpt 5.13 The function bbs_lattice which incorporates the BBS method into a standard binomial lattice. The Black–Scholes formula is evaluated by using the function black_scholes, given in Code excerpt 4.1.

```
        }
    }
/* The values v[0], v[1] & v[2] correspond to the nodes for m1 = 2, v1 & v2 correspond to the nodes for m1 = 1 and the
   option value (*value) is the node for m1 = 0. For a given time step v[0] corresponds to the lowest asset price,
   v[1] to the next lowest etc.. */

    hold = p_d*v[0] + p_u*v[1];
    if (is_american) {
        if (put)
            v1 = MAX(hold,X-s[jj]);
        else
            v1 = MAX(hold,s[jj]-X);
    }
    else
        v1 = hold;
    --jj;
    hold = p_d*v[1] + p_u*v[2];
    if (is_american) {
        if (put)
            v2 = MAX(hold,X-s[jj]);
        else
            v2 = MAX(hold,s[jj]-X);
    }
    else
        v2 = hold;
    --jj;
    hold = p_d*v1 + p_u*v2;
    if (is_american) {
        if (put)
            *value = MAX(hold,X-s[0]);
        else
            *value = MAX(hold,s[0]-X);
    }
    else
        *value = hold;
    if(greeks) {
        /* assign the value of delta (obtained from m1 = 1) */
        greeks[1] = (v2-v1)/(s[1]-s[2]);
        /* assign the value of gamma (use the values at time step m1 = 2)  */
        dv1 = v[2] - v[1];
        ds1 = s[3] - s[4];
        dv2 = v[1] - v[0];
        ds2 = s[4] - s[5];
        h   = 0.5*(s[3] - s[5]);
        greeks[0] = ((dv1/ds1) - (dv2/ds2))/h;
        /* assign the value of theta */
        greeks[2] = (v[1]-*value)/(2.0*dt);
    }
}
```

Code excerpt 5.13 (*Continued*).

The benefits of using the BBS approach to price an American call are illustrated in Fig. 5.3. Here, we compare the results obtained using the function bbs_lattice with those computed by the function standard_lattice, the standard binomial lattice of Code excerpt 5.11. It can be clearly seen that BBS method is significantly more accurate than the standard binomial lattice approach, in which option pricing error exhibits pronounced oscillations.

The BBSR Method

The BBSR method applies two-point Richardson extrapolation to the computed BBS values, for more information concerning Richardson extrapolation see Marchuk and Shaidurov (1983). In this method, the option price estimates from two BBS lattices, with differing number of time steps, are combined to form an improved estimate.

Here, we use the following BBSR scheme to compute the value of an American call option:

$$C_{BBSR}(S,E,\tau,2n) = \frac{4}{3}C_{BBS}(S,E,\tau,2n) - \frac{1}{3}C_{BBS}(S,E,\tau,n), \qquad (5.3.25)$$

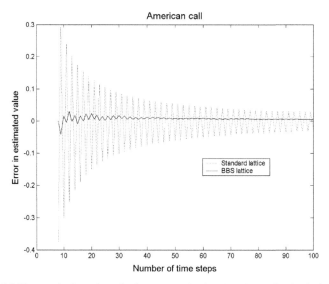

FIGURE 5.3 The error in the estimated value, est_val, of an American call using both a standard binomial lattice and a BBS binomial lattice. The parameters used were $T = 1.0$, $S = 105.0$, $E = 105.0$, $r = 0.1$, $q = 0.02$, and $\sigma = 0.3$. The very accurate value (acc_val) was 16.1697 and was computed using a 6000-step standard binomial lattice. The error in the estimated value was obtained as $est\_val - acc\_val$.

where S is the current asset value, E is the strike price, τ is the option maturity, $C_{BBS}(S, E, \tau, n)$ is the value of the call option computed using a BBS lattice with n time steps, $C_{BBS}(S, E, \tau, 2n)$ is the value of the call option computed using a BBS lattice with $2n$ time steps, and $C_{BBSR}(S, E, \tau, 2n)$ is the BBSR estimate. We compute the value of an American put using

$$P_{BBSR}(S, E, \tau, 2n) = \frac{4}{3} P_{BBS}(S, E, \tau, 2n) - \frac{1}{3} P_{BBS}(S, E, \tau, n). \qquad (5.3.26)$$

Figure 5.4 displays the computed BBSR results for an American call option with $S = 105.0$, $\tau = 1.0$, $E = 105.0$, $q = 0.02$, and $\sigma = 0.3$.

In Tables 5.5 and 5.6, the errors in computing both an American put and an American call option are presented; the methods used are the standard binomial lattice, the BBS lattice and the BBSR lattice. It can be seen that the BBSR lattice gives the most accurate results. This is not surprising since from equation 3.91 and equation 3.92 we see that when we use either an n-time step standard binomial lattice or an n-time step BBS lattice, the corresponding BBSR estimate is obtained using both an n-time step BBS lattice and also a $2n$-time step BBS lattice. One way of checking whether Richardson extrapolation is providing increased accuracy is to compare the results for a $2n$-time step BBS lattice with those for an n-time step BBSR lattice. Inspection of the results shows that Richardson extrapolation has in fact lead to an improvement. For example, in

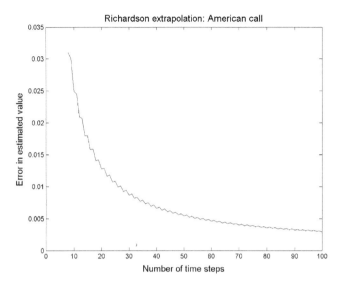

FIGURE 5.4 The error in the estimated value, est_val, of an American call, using a BBSR binomial lattice. The parameters used were $T = 1.0, S = 105.0, E = 105.0, r = 0.1, q = 0.02$, and $\sigma = 0.3$. The very accurate value (acc_val) was 16.1697 and was computed using a 6000-step standard binomial lattice. The error in the estimated value was obtained as $est\_val - acc\_val$.

Table 5.5, the error for a 160-time step BBS lattice is 5.0869e-003, while that for an 80-time step BBSR lattice is 3.5725e-003; in Table 5.6, the error for an 80-time step BBS lattice is 6.3858e-003 and that for a 40-time step BBSR lattice is 3.5725e-003.

5.4 GRID METHODS FOR VANILLA OPTIONS

5.4.1 Introduction

In Section 5.3, we discussed the use of binomial lattice methods for valuing both European and American options. The lattice methods we described have the advantage that they are fairly easy to implement and can value simple options, such as vanilla puts and calls, *reasonably* accurately. The use of up- and down-jump probabilities at the lattice nodes is also an appealing feature, since they are directly related to the stochastic process which is being modelled. However, lattice techniques have the following drawbacks:

- They require small time steps to ensure numerical stability.
- There is little control over where the lattice nodes are located. This can lead to very poor accuracy when valuing certain types of options, for example, those with barriers at particular asset prices.

TABLE 5.5 The Pricing Errors for an American Call Option Computed by a Standard Binomial Lattice, a BBS Lattice, and also a BBSR Lattice. The Pricing Error is Defined as *Estimated Value − Accurate Value*, where the Accurate Value, 16.1697, was Obtained by using a 6000-step Standard Binomial Lattice. The Option Parameters used were $T = 1.0$, $S = 105.0$, $E = 105.0$, $r = 0.1$, $q = 0.02$, and $\sigma = 0.3$

nsteps	Standard lattice	BBS lattice	BBSR lattice
20	-1.5075e-001	3.6187e-002	1.2754e-002
30	-1.0057e-001	2.4526e-002	8.6771e-003
40	-7.5382e-002	1.8612e-002	6.6361e-003
50	-6.0244e-002	1.5036e-002	5.4109e-003
60	-5.0141e-002	1.2639e-002	4.5939e-003
70	-4.2919e-002	1.0922e-002	4.0103e-003
80	-3.7499e-002	9.6302e-003	3.5725e-003
90	-3.3282e-002	8.6236e-003	3.2320e-003
100	-2.9908e-002	7.8171e-003	2.9596e-003
110	-2.7146e-002	7.1565e-003	2.7367e-003
120	-2.4844e-002	6.6053e-003	2.5509e-003
130	-2.2896e-002	6.1385e-003	2.3938e-003
140	-2.1226e-002	5.7382e-003	2.2590e-003
150	-1.9778e-002	5.3909e-003	2.1423e-003
160	-1.8511e-002	5.0869e-003	2.0401e-003
170	-1.7393e-002	4.8186e-003	1.9500e-003
180	-1.6399e-002	4.5799e-003	1.8698e-003
190	-1.5510e-002	4.3663e-003	1.7981e-003
200	-1.4710e-002	4.1740e-003	1.7336e-003

One method of avoiding these limitations is through the use of finite-difference grids. Although this approach no longer has the probabilistic interpretation of the binomial lattice, it has the following advantages:

- Fewer time steps are required to ensure numerical stability.
- There is complete control over the placement of grid lines and their associated grid nodes.

TABLE 5.6 The Pricing Errors for an American Put Option Computed by a Standard Binomial Lattice, a BBS Lattice, and also a BBSR Lattice. The Pricing Error is Defined as *Estimated Value − Accurate Value*, where the Accurate Value, 9.2508, was Obtained by using a 6000-step Standard Binomial Lattice. The Option Parameters used were $T = 1.0$, $S = 105.0$, $E = 105.0$, $r = 0.1$, $q = 0.02$, and $\sigma = 0.3$

nsteps	Standard lattice	BBS lattice	BBSR lattice
20	-6.1971e-002	2.3917e-002	7.6191e-003
30	-4.1648e-002	1.6800e-002	6.0465e-003
40	-3.2264e-002	1.1694e-002	4.6165e-003
50	-2.6538e-002	8.4790e-003	4.2654e-003
60	-2.1069e-002	8.7348e-003	3.2946e-003
70	-1.8298e-002	7.2743e-003	2.9633e-003
80	-1.5885e-002	6.3858e-003	2.6088e-003
90	-1.3977e-002	5.9417e-003	2.2099e-003
100	-1.2612e-002	5.3188e-003	2.1793e-003
110	-1.1338e-002	4.9652e-003	2.0992e-003
120	-1.0239e-002	4.6547e-003	1.8723e-003
130	-9.5208e-003	4.1505e-003	1.8808e-003
140	-8.6142e-003	4.0411e-003	1.7505e-003
150	-8.2382e-003	3.6020e-003	1.7341e-003
160	-7.5811e-003	3.5531e-003	1.6411e-003
170	-7.1097e-003	3.3726e-003	1.5507e-003
180	-6.7887e-003	3.1428e-003	1.5478e-003
190	-6.3033e-003	3.1345e-003	1.4134e-003
200	-6.0276e-003	2.9642e-003	1.3973e-003

5.4.2 Uniform Grids

The Black–Scholes equation for the value of an option, f, is given by

$$\frac{\partial f}{\partial t} + (r - q)S\frac{\partial f}{\partial S} + \frac{1}{2}\sigma^2 S^2 \frac{\partial^2 f}{\partial S^2} = rf. \tag{5.4.1}$$

We want to solve this equation over the duration of the option, that is from the current time t to the maturity of the option at time $t + \tau$. To do this we will use a grid in which the asset price S takes n_s uniformly spaced values,

$S_j = j\Delta S, j = 0, \ldots, n_{s-1}$, where ΔS is the spacing between grid points. If $S_{\max}$ is the maximum asset value we want to represent, then the grid spacing, ΔS^*, can be simply calculated as

$$\Delta S^* = \frac{S_{\max}}{(n_s - 1)}. \quad (5.4.2)$$

However, since we would like to solve the option values and Greeks at the current asset price S_0, we would also like an asset grid line to coincide with the current asset price. This avoids the use of interpolation which is necessary when the asset value does not correspond to a grid line. The method by which we achieve this is outlined in Code excerpt 5.12. Here, the user supplies the function opt_gfd with values for $S_{\max}$ and $n_s - 1$ from which ΔS^* is computed using equation (5.4.2). We then find the integer, n_1, that is just below (or equal to) the value $\frac{S_o}{\Delta S^*}$ and use this to obtain a new grid spacing $\Delta S = \frac{S_o}{n_1}$. This leads to the new asset price discretization $S_j = j\Delta S, j = 0, \ldots, n_{s-1}$, where we have now ensured that $S_{n_1} = S_o$.

The user also supplies the function opt_gfd with the number of time intervals for the grid. When there are n_t time intervals, the grid has $n_t + 1$ uniformly spaced time instants, $t_i = i\Delta t, i = 0, \ldots, n_t$, and the time step is simply

$$\Delta t = \frac{\tau}{n_t}. \quad (5.4.3)$$

As with the binomial lattice methods, we will solve the equation backwards in time from maturity (at time $t + \tau$) to the present (time t). So as we solve the equation, the time index will start at $i = n_t$ (time $t + \tau$) and decrease to $i = 0$ (current time t).

Here, we discuss the grid method of solving the Black–Scholes equation in terms of the following:

- The finite-difference approximation.
- The boundary conditions.
- Computation of the option values at a given time instant.
- Backwards iteration and early exercise.

Each of these aspects will now be considered in turn.

The Finite-Difference Approximation

The option value corresponding to the grid node at which $t_i = i\Delta t$ and $S_j = j\Delta S$ will be denoted by $f_{i,j}$. We will approximate the partial derivative of $f_{i,j}$ with respect to time simply as

$$\frac{\partial f}{\partial t} = \frac{f_{i+1,j} - f_{i,j}}{\Delta t}. \quad (5.4.4)$$

For the other terms in equation (5.4.1), we will use the weighted, Θ_m, method. This technique involves selecting an appropriate choice for Θ_m in the range $0 \le \Theta_m \le 1$ so that the *contribution* from node (i, j) is a weighted sum involving the values at nodes (i, j) and $(i + 1, j)$. For instance, the term $rf|_{i,j}$ in equation

(5.4.1) is approximated as

$$rf|_{i,j} = r\left\{\Theta_m f_{i+1,j} + (1 - \Theta_m)f_{i,j}\right\} \tag{5.4.5}$$

and the term $\left.\dfrac{\partial f}{\partial S}\right|_{i,j}$ in equation (5.4.1) is approximated as

$$\left.\frac{\partial f}{\partial S}\right|_{i,j} = \left\{\Theta_m \left.\frac{\partial f}{\partial S}\right|_{i+1,j} + (1 - \Theta_m) \left.\frac{\partial f}{\partial S}\right|_{i,j}\right\}. \tag{5.4.6}$$

Using this method, we thus obtain, at node (i, j), the following discretized version of equation (5.4.1):

$$\frac{f_{i+1,j} - f_{i,j}}{\Delta t} + (r - q)S_j \left\{\Theta_m f'_{i+1,j} + \Theta_m^* f'_{i,j}\right\}$$

$$+ \frac{1}{2}\sigma^2 S_j^2 \left\{\Theta_m f''_{i+1,j} + \Theta_m^* f''_{i,j}\right\} = r\left\{\Theta_m f_{i+1,j} + \Theta_m^* f_{i,j}\right\}, \tag{5.4.7}$$

where for compactness we have written $\Theta_m^* = 1 - \Theta_m$ and denote the partial derivatives with respect to S at node (i, j) as $f'_{i,j} = \left.\dfrac{\partial f}{\partial S}\right|_{i,j}$ and $f''_{i,j} = \left.\dfrac{\partial^2 f}{\partial S^2}\right|_{i,j}$.

Finite-difference approximations for these derivatives can be obtained by considering a Taylor expansion about the point $f_{i,j}$. We proceed as follows:

$$f_{i,j+1} = f_{i,j} + f'_{i,j}\Delta S + \frac{1}{2}f''_{i,j}(\Delta S)^2, \tag{5.4.8}$$

$$f_{i,j-1} = f_{i,j} - f'_{i,j}\Delta S + \frac{1}{2}f''_{i,j}(\Delta S)^2. \tag{5.4.9}$$

Subtracting equation (5.4.9) from equation (5.4.8), we obtain

$$f_{i,j+1} - f_{i,j-1} = 2f'_{i,j}\Delta S$$

and so

$$f'_{i,j} = \frac{f_{i,j+1} - f_{i,j-1}}{2\Delta S}. \tag{5.4.10}$$

Adding equation (5.4.9) and equation (5.4.8), we obtain

$$f_{i,j+1} + f_{i,j-1} = 2f_{i,j} + f''_{i,j}\Delta S^2,$$

which gives

$$f''_{i,j} = \frac{f_{i,j+1} - 2f_{i,j} + f_{i,j-1}}{\Delta S^2}. \tag{5.4.11}$$

The complete finite-difference approximation to the Black–Scholes equation can then be found by substituting the approximations for the first and second partial derivatives, given in equation (5.4.10) and equation (5.4.11), into equation (5.4.7). We thus obtain

$$r\Delta t\left\{\Theta_m f_{i+1,j} + \Theta_m^* f_{i,j}\right\} = f_{i+1,j} - f_{i,j} + \frac{(r - q)j\Delta t \mathcal{A}_1}{2} + \frac{\sigma^2 j^2 \Delta t \mathcal{A}_2}{2}, \tag{5.4.12}$$

where we have used the fact that $S_j = j\Delta S$, and for compactness have defined the terms

$$\mathcal{A}_1 = \Theta_m f_{i+1,j+1} - \Theta_m f_{i+1,j-1} + \Theta_m^* f_{i,j+1} - \Theta_m^* f_{i,j-1}$$

and

$$\mathcal{A}_2 = \Theta_m f_{i+1,j+1} + \Theta_m f_{i+1,j-1} - 2\Theta_m f_{i+1,j} + \Theta_m^* f_{i,j+1} + \Theta_m^* f_{i,j-1} - 2\Theta_m^* f_{i,j}.$$

Collecting like terms in $f_{i,j}$, $f_{i+1,j}$, etc., results in

$$\mathcal{B}_1 f_{i,j-1} + \mathcal{B}_2 f_{i,j} + \mathcal{B}_3 f_{i,j+1} + C_1 f_{i+1,j-1} + C_2 f_{i+1,j} + C_3 f_{i+1,j+1} = 0, \quad (5.4.13)$$

where

$$\mathcal{B}_1 = \frac{-\Theta_m^*(r-q)j\Delta t}{2} + \frac{\Theta_m^* \sigma^2 j^2 \Delta t}{2},$$

$$\mathcal{B}_2 = -1 - r\Delta t \Theta_m^* - \Theta_m^* \sigma^2 j^2 \Delta t$$

$$\mathcal{B}_3 = \frac{\Theta_m^*(r-q)j\Delta t}{2} + \frac{\Theta_m^* \sigma^2 j^2 \Delta t}{2},$$

$$C_1 = \frac{\Theta_m \sigma^2 j^2 \Delta t}{2} - \frac{\Theta_m(r-q)j\Delta t}{2},$$

$$C_2 = 1 - r\Delta t \Theta_m - \Theta_m \sigma^2 j^2 \Delta t,$$

$$C_3 = \frac{\Theta_m(r-q)j\Delta t}{2} + \frac{\Theta_m \sigma^2 j^2 \Delta t}{2}.$$

Since we are solving the equation backwards in time and we want to determine the option values at time index i from the known option values $(f_{i+1,j+1}, f_{i+1,j},$ and $f_{i+1,j-1})$ at time index $i + 1$. This can be achieved by rearranging equation (5.4.13) as follows:

$$a_j f_{i,j-1} + b_j f_{i,j} + c_j f_{i,j+1} = R_{i+1,j}, \quad (5.4.14)$$

where the right-hand side, $R_{i+1,j}$, is

$$R_{i+1,j} = \bar{a}_j f_{i+1,j-1} + \bar{b}_j f_{i+1,j} + \bar{c}_j f_{i+1,j+1}. \quad (5.4.15)$$

The six coefficients are the following:

$$a_j = (1 - \Theta_m)\frac{\Delta t}{2}\left\{(r-q)j - \sigma^2 j^2\right\}, \quad (5.4.16)$$

$$b_j = 1 + (1 - \Theta_m)\Delta t \left\{r + \sigma^2 j^2\right\}, \quad (5.4.17)$$

$$c_j = -(1 - \Theta_m)\frac{\Delta t}{2}\left\{(r-q)j + \sigma^2 j^2\right\}, \quad (5.4.18)$$

$$\bar{a}_j = -\Theta_m \frac{\Delta t}{2}\left\{(r-q)j - \sigma^2 j^2\right\}, \quad (5.4.19)$$

$$\bar{b}_j = 1 - \Theta_m \Delta t \left\{r + \sigma^2 j^2\right\}, \quad (5.4.20)$$

$$\bar{c}_j = \Theta_m \frac{\Delta t}{2}\left\{(r-q)j + \sigma^2 j^2\right\}. \quad (5.4.21)$$

For each value of j, equation (5.4.14) gives us a relationship between three option values, $f_{i+1,j-1}$, $f_{i+1,j}$, and $f_{i+1,j+1}$, at time index $i + 1$ and three option values $f_{i,j-1}$, $f_{i,j}$, and $f_{i,j+1}$ at time index i.

This situation is shown in Fig. 5.5 where we have labelled the grid nodes that contribute to the option value $f_{5,5}$ at grid node E. These are the known option values:

node A: $f_{6,6}$, node B: $f_{6,5}$, and node C: $f_{6,4}$
and the unknown option values:
node D: $f_{5,6}$, node E: $f_{5,5}$, and node F: $f_{5,4}$.

Before we solve equation (5.4.14) we will briefly consider its characteristics for different values of the weight parameter Θ_m.

When $\Theta_m = 1$, the values of the coefficients in equation (5.4.14) are $a_j = c_j = 0$ and $b_j = 1$. This means that equation (5.4.14) reduces to

$$f_{i,j} = \bar{a}_j f_{i+1,j-1} + \bar{b}_j f_{i+1,j} + \bar{c}_j f_{i+1,j+1}.$$

This is termed the *explicit method*, and it can be seen that the unknown option value $f_{i,j}$ at the grid node (i, j) is just a weighted sum of the (known) option values $f_{i+1,j-1}$, $f_{i+1,j}$, and $f_{i+1,j+1}$. This is the simplest situation to deal with and actually corresponds to a trinomial lattice. However, it has poor numerical properties and usually requires a very small step size to obtain accurate results, see Smith (1985).

When $\Theta_m \neq 1$, the unknown option value $f_{i,j}$ depends not only on the known option values $f_{i+1,j-1}$, $f_{i+1,j}$, and $f_{i+1,j+1}$ (as in the explicit method above) but also on the neighbouring *unknown* option values $f_{i,j-1}$ and $f_{i,j+1}$. It is now necessary to solve a set of simultaneous in order to compute the value $f_{i,j}$. This is therefore called an *implicit method*, see Smith (1985).

The implicit method $\Theta_m = 0$ is also called the *fully implicit method*, since now the unknown value $f_{i,j}$ only depends on the neighbouring values $f_{i,j-1}$, $f_{i,j+1}$, and its *previous* value, $f_{i+1,j}$, at time step $i + 1$. This can be shown by substituting $\Theta_m = 0$ in equation (5.4.16) to equation (5.4.21). We then obtain $\bar{a}_j = \bar{c}_j = 0$ and $\bar{b}_j = 1$, which means that equation (5.4.14) reduces to

$$a_j f_{i,j-1} + b_j f_{i,j} + c_j f_{i,j+1} = f_{i+1,j}.$$

The implicit method $\Theta_m = 0.5$ is also termed the *Crank–Nicolson method*. This method, first used by John Crank and Phyllis Nicolson in 1946 (see Crank and Nicolson (1947)), computes $f_{i,j}$ by giving equal weight to the contributions from time step $i + 1$ and time step i. Substituting $\Theta_m = 0.5$ in equation (5.4.16) to equation (5.4.21), we obtain the following Crank–Nicolson coefficients:

$$a_j = -\bar{a}_j = \frac{\Delta t}{4} \left\{ (r - q)j - \sigma^2 j^2 \right\},$$

$$b_j = 1 + \frac{\Delta t}{2} \left\{ r + \sigma^2 j^2 \right\},$$

$$\bar{b}_j = 1 - \frac{\Delta t}{2} \left\{ r + \sigma^2 j^2 \right\},$$

$$c_j = -\bar{c}_j = -\frac{\Delta t}{4}\left\{(r-q)j + \sigma^2 j^2\right\}.$$

We notice that since we are solving backwards in time, but index time in the forward direction, our values of Θ_m corresponding to implicit and explicit are different from those normally used. For example, in Smith (1985), $\Theta_m = 0$ is the explicit method and $\Theta_m = 1$ is the implicit method; the Crank–Nicolson method is still $\Theta_m = 0.5$.

The Boundary Conditions

In order to solve equation (5.4.14) at time instant $i\Delta t$, we need to obtain the option values at the upper asset boundary, the lower asset boundary, and the *initial* values that are specified at option maturity.

Here, we calculate the boundary values by using the time independent payoff, p_j, at the jth asset index within the grid. If E is the strike price, then vanilla call options have payoffs

$$p_j = \max(j\Delta S - E, 0), \quad j = 0, \ldots, n_{s-1},$$

and vanilla put options have payoffs

$$p_j = \max(E - j\Delta S, 0), \quad j = 0, \ldots, n_{s-1}.$$

Upper asset boundary values

At the upper boundary, $j = n_s - 1$ and $(n_s - 1)\Delta S = S_{\max}$, where we note that for the grid to be *useful*, we require $S_{\max} > E$.

Here, we assume that $S_{\max} > E$ and so for call options

$$p_{n_{s-1}} = S_{\max} - E,$$

and for put options

$$p_{n_{s-1}} = 0.$$

The option value at the upper boundary, denoted by f_{BU}, is set to $p_{n_{s-1}}$, and we have $f_{i,n_{s-1}} = f_{BU}, i = 0, \ldots, n_t$.

Lower asset boundary values

At the lower boundary, $j = 0$ and the value of $j\Delta S$ is zero.

So for call options

$$p_0 = 0,$$

and for put options

$$p_0 = E.$$

The option value at the lower boundary, denoted by f_{BL}, is set to p_0, and we have $f_{i,0} = f_{BL}, i = 0, \ldots, n_t$.

Boundary values at option maturity

At option maturity ($i = n_t$), the initial option (boundary) values are the previously mentioned payouts. If E is the strike price, then for vanilla call options,

$$f_{n_t,j} = \max(j\Delta S - E, 0), \quad j = 0, \ldots, n_{s-1},$$

and for vanilla put options,

$$f_{n_t,j} = \max(E - j\Delta S, 0), \quad j = 0, \ldots, n_{s-1}.$$

This is illustrated in Fig. 5.5 for a vanilla put option with current asset value $S_0 = 20$, strike, $E = 25$, and maturity $\tau = 2$. The grid asset price spacing is $\Delta S = 5$, and the time increment is $\Delta t = 0.2$. At option maturity, corresponding to time index $i = 10$, the value of the put option is zero for all asset indices $j \geq 5$.

Computation of the Option Values at a Given Time Instant

Having found the option boundary values, we are now in a position to solve equation (5.4.14) at time instant $t_i = i\Delta t$.

First we note that since $f_{i,0} = f_{BL}$ and $f_{i,n_{s-1}} = f_{BU}$, equation (5.4.14) only needs to be solved for values of the asset index j in the range $j = 1$ to $j = n_{s-2}$.

We now deal with the following situations:

- *Case 1:* $j = 1$, the asset grid line just above the lower boundary.
- *Case 2:* $j = n_{s-2}$, the asset grid line just below the upper boundary.
- *Case 3:* all other asset grid lines not included in *Case 1* or *Case 2*

and consider the form that equation (5.4.14) takes under each condition.
Case 1: $j = 1$

Substituting $j = 1$ into equation (5.4.14), we obtain

$$a_1 f_{i,0} + b_1 f_{i,1} + c_1 f_{i,2} = \bar{a}_1 f_{i+1,0} + \bar{b}_1 f_{i+1,1} + \bar{c}_1 f_{i+1,2}.$$

Now, since $f_{i,0} = f_{BL}$, this becomes

$$b_1 f_{i,1} + c_1 f_{i,2} = (\bar{a}_1 - a_1) f_{BL} + \bar{b}_1 f_{i+1,1} + \bar{c}_1 f_{i+1,2},$$

or equivalently

$$b_1 f_{i,1} + c_1 f_{i,2} = R_{i+1,1}, \tag{5.4.22}$$

where

$$R_{i+1,1} = (\bar{a}_1 - a_1) f_{BL} + \bar{b}_1 f_{i+1,1} + \bar{c}_1 f_{i+1,2}. \tag{5.4.23}$$

Case 2: $j = n_{s-2}$

Substituting $j = n_{s-2}$ into equation (5.4.14), we obtain

$$a_{n_{s-2}} f_{i,n_{s-3}} + b_{n_{s-2}} f_{i,n_{s-2}} + c_{n_{s-2}} f_{i,n_{s-1}}$$
$$= \bar{a}_{n_{s-2}} f_{i+1,n_{s-3}} + \bar{b}_{n_{s-2}} f_{i+1,n_{s-2}} + \bar{c}_{n_{s-2}} f_{i+1,n_{s-1}}.$$

Since $f_{i,n_{s-1}} = f_{BU}$, this gives

$$a_{n_{s-2}} f_{i,n_{s-3}} + b_{n_{s-2}} f_{i,n_{s-2}} = \bar{a}_{n_{s-2}} f_{i+1,n_{s-3}} + \bar{b}_{n_{s-2}} f_{i+1,n_{s-2}} + (\bar{c}_{n_{s-2}} - c_{n_{s-2}}) f_{BU},$$

or equivalently

$$a_{n_{s-2}} f_{i,n_{s-3}} + b_{n_{s-2}} f_{i,n_{s-2}} = R_{i+1,n_{s-2}}, \tag{5.4.24}$$

where

$$R_{i+1,n_s-2} = \bar{a}_{n_s-2} f_{i+1,n_s-3} + \bar{b}_{n_s-2} f_{i+1,n_s-2} + (\bar{c}_{n_s-2} - c_{n_s-2}) f_{BU}. \qquad (5.4.25)$$

Case 3

In this case, the boundary values do not enter into the expressions and we simply restate equation (5.4.14) as

$$a_j f_{i,j-1} + b_j f_{i,j} + c_j f_{i,j+1} = R_{i+1,j}, \quad j = 3,\ldots,n_s-3, \qquad (5.4.26)$$

where as before the right-hand side, $R_{i+1,j}$, is

$$R_{i+1,j} = \bar{a}_j f_{i+1,j-1} + \bar{b}_j f_{i+1,j} + \bar{c}_j f_{i+1,j+1}. \qquad (5.4.27)$$

We can now gather all the information in equation (5.4.23) to equation (5.4.27) and represent it by the following tridiagonal system:

$$\begin{pmatrix} b_1 & c_1 & 0 & 0 & 0 & 0 \\ a_2 & b_2 & c_2 & 0 & 0 & 0 \\ 0 & 0 & . & . & 0 & 0 \\ 0 & 0 & 0 & . & . & 0 \\ 0 & 0 & 0 & a_{n_s-3} & b_{n_s-3} & c_{n_s-3} \\ 0 & 0 & 0 & 0 & a_{n_s-2} & b_{n_s-2} \end{pmatrix} \begin{pmatrix} f_{i,1} \\ f_{i,2} \\ . \\ . \\ f_{i,n_s-3} \\ f_{i,n_s-2} \end{pmatrix} = \begin{pmatrix} R_{i+1,1} \\ R_{i+1,2} \\ . \\ . \\ R_{i+1,n_s-3} \\ R_{i+1,n_s-2} \end{pmatrix}. \qquad (5.4.28)$$

In matrix notation, equation (5.4.28) can be written as

$$Ax = R, \qquad (5.4.29)$$

where A is the $n_s-2 \times n_s-2$ tridiagonal matrix containing the known coefficients $a_j, j = 2,\ldots,n_s-2$, $b_j, j = 1,\ldots,n_s-2$, and $c_j, j = 1,\ldots,n_s-3$. The vector R denotes the known right-hand side, $R_{i+1,j}, j = 1,\ldots,n_s-2$, and the vector x contains the unknown option values that we wish to compute, $f_{i,j}, j = 1,\ldots,n_s-2$.

It is well-known that, if matrix A is "non-singular", equation (5.4.29) can be solved using an LU decomposition. Here, we factorize the $n \times n$ matrix A as

$$A = LU,$$

where L is an $n \times n$ lower triangular matrix with 1s on the diagonal and U is an $n \times n$ upper triangular matrix. We illustrate the LU decomposition for a full 4×4 matrix below

$$\begin{pmatrix} a_{1,1} & a_{1,2} & a_{1,3} & a_{1,4} \\ a_{2,1} & a_{2,2} & a_{2,3} & a_{2,4} \\ a_{3,1} & a_{3,2} & a_{3,3} & a_{3,4} \\ a_{4,1} & a_{4,2} & a_{4,3} & a_{4,4} \end{pmatrix} = \begin{pmatrix} 1 & 0 & 0 & 0 \\ l_{2,1} & 1 & 0 & 0 \\ l_{3,1} & l_{3,2} & 1 & 0 \\ l_{4,1} & l_{4,2} & l_{4,3} & 1 \end{pmatrix} \begin{pmatrix} u_{1,1} & u_{1,2} & u_{1,3} & u_{1,4} \\ 0 & u_{2,2} & u_{2,3} & u_{2,4} \\ 0 & 0 & u_{3,3} & u_{3,4} \\ 0 & 0 & 0 & u_{4,4} \end{pmatrix}. \qquad (5.4.30)$$

If A is a tridiagonal matrix, then the LU decomposition takes the simpler form

$$
\begin{pmatrix}
a_{1,1} & a_{1,2} & 0 & 0 \\
a_{2,1} & a_{2,2} & a_{2,3} & 0 \\
0 & a_{3,2} & a_{3,3} & a_{3,4} \\
0 & 0 & a_{4,3} & a_{4,4}
\end{pmatrix}
=
\begin{pmatrix}
1 & 0 & 0 & 0 \\
l_{2,1} & 1 & 0 & 0 \\
0 & l_{3,2} & 1 & 0 \\
0 & 0 & l_{4,3} & 1
\end{pmatrix}
\begin{pmatrix}
u_{1,1} & u_{1,2} & 0 & 0 \\
0 & u_{2,2} & u_{2,3} & 0 \\
0 & 0 & u_{3,3} & u_{3,4} \\
0 & 0 & 0 & u_{4,4}
\end{pmatrix},
\qquad (5.4.31)
$$

where it can be seen that now both L and U are bidiagonal.

Once the LU decomposition of A has been found, it is possible to solve for x in equation (5.4.29) by using a two-stage method (see, for example, Golub and Van Loan (1989)). Here, forward elimination is used to solve $Ly = \mathcal{R}$, and then back-substitution is applied to $Ux = y$. We can thus write the procedure as

$$Ax = (LU)x = L(Ux) = Ly = \mathcal{R}.$$

We will now provide code excerpts which show how to solve the $n_{s-2} \times n_{s-2}$ tridiagonal system represented by equation (5.4.29). These excerpts are in fact contained within the larger Code excerpt 5.18, which displays the complete C code for the option pricing function `opt_gfd`. If the reader requires more detail concerning the precise code used for option pricing, then this code should be consulted. (It should be noted that in Code excerpt 5.18, time is indexed using j and asset price using index i. We have modified the indices for the smaller code excerpts given below so that, as might be expected, time is indexed using i and asset price using j. The author apologizes for any inconvenience this may cause.) Here, for brevity, we will assume that all the required arrays have already been allocated and loaded with the relevant information.

First we need to compute the LU decomposition of the tridiagonal matrix A. The code to achieve this is given in Code excerpt 5.14 below. Here, we use the following three arrays to store the elements of the tridiagonal matrix A: array **b** contains the diagonal elements, array **c** contains the upper diagonal elements, and array **a** holds the lower diagonal elements.

```
u[1] = b[1];
if (u[1] == 0.0) printf ("ERROR in array u \n");
for(j=2; j <=ns-2; ++j) {
  u[j] = b[j] - a[j]*c[j-1]/u[j-1];
  if (u[j] == 0.0) printf ("ERROR in array u \n");
}
```

Code excerpt 5.14 Computer code which calculates the diagonal elements of the matrix U, in an LU decomposition of a tridiagonal matrix, A. The elements of matrix A are stored in the following arrays: array b contains the diagonal elements, array c contains the upper diagonal elements, and array a holds the lower diagonal elements. The diagonal elements of U are stored in the array u for later use, in Code excerpts 5.15 and 5.16.

It should be noted that we do not explicitly compute the elements of the matrix L. This is because all the diagonal elements of L are known to be 1, and the sub-diagonal elements of L can be computed from the diagonal elements of U by using `l[j] = a[j]/u[j-1]`. Also we do not need to compute the upper diagonal elements of U since they are known to be the same as the upper diagonal elements of the original matrix A and are contained in the array **c**, see, for example, Hager (1988).

Having computed the LU decomposition, we can now solve the lower triangular system $Ly = \mathcal{R}$ using forward elimination; this is shown in Code excerpt 5.15.

```
work[1] = rhs[1];
for(j=2; j<=ns-2; ++j) {
    work[j] = rhs[j] - a[j]*work[j-1]/u[j-1];
}
```

Code excerpt 5.15 Computer code which uses forward elimination to solve the lower triangular system $Ly = \mathcal{R}$, where y is stored in the array work.

In Code excerpt 5.15, we make use of the following two arrays: the array **rhs** which is used to store the elements of the right-hand side $\mathcal{R}$, and the array **work** which is both used as workspace and to store the computed solution vector y. As previously mentioned, the sub-diagonal elements of L are given by l[j] = a[j]/u[j-1]. This means that in Code excerpt 5.15, the line

```
work[j] = rhs[j] - a[j]*work[j-1]/u[j-1];
```

is in fact be equivalent to

```
work[j] = rhs[j] - l[j]*work[j-1];
```

where l[j], j=2,..,ns-2 contains the sub-diagonal elements of L, if we had (needlessly) decided to allocate space for an extra array called 1.

We are now in a position to solve the triangular system $Ux = y$ by using back-substitution. The code to achieve this is given in Code excerpt 5.16. Here, the array **work** contains the previously computed values of y, the diagonal elements of U are contained in the array **u**, and (as previously mentioned) the upper diagonal elements of U are stored in the array **a**.

```
opt_vals[ns-2] = work[ns-2]/u[ns-2];
for(j = ns-2; j >= 1; --j)
    opt_vals[j] = (work[j] - c[j]*opt_vals[j+1])/u[j];
```

Code excerpt 5.16 Computer code which uses back-substitution to solve the upper triangular system $Ux = y$. At time instant $t_i = i\Delta t$, the elements of x are the calculated option values $f_{i,j}, i = 1, \ldots, n_{s-2}$.

In Code excerpt 5.16, the array **opt_vals** contains the solution vector x. As its name suggests the contents of the array **opt_vals** are in fact the computed option values, $f_{i,j}, j = 1, \ldots, n_{s-2}$, in equation (5.4.28) and represent the solution of the Black–Scholes partial differential equation at time instant $t_i = i\Delta t$, based on the previously computed option values $f_{i+1,j}, j = 1, \ldots, n_{s-2}$.

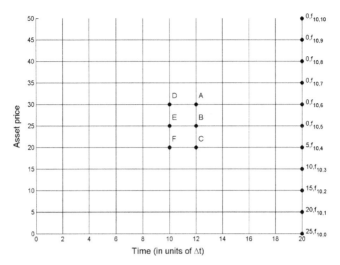

FIGURE 5.5 An example uniform grid, which could be used to estimate the value of a vanilla option which matures in two-year time. The grid parameters are $n_s = n_t = 10$, $\Delta t = 0.2$, $\Delta S = 5$, and $S_{max} = 50$. The option parameters are $E = 25$, $S_O = 20$, and $\tau = 2.0$. As usual we denote the grid node option values by $f_{i,j}$, where i is the time index and j is the asset index. The option values of the grid nodes at maturity for a vanilla put are thus labelled as val, $f_{10,j}$, $j = 0, \ldots, 10$, where val is the value of the option at the node; these are shown on the right-hand grid boundary. Since $E = 25$, only those nodes with $j < 5$ have nonzero option values.

Backwards Iteration and Early Exercise

The Black–Scholes equation can be solved over the time interval t to $t + \tau$ by iteratively solving equation (5.4.28). We iterate backwards in time by solving equation (5.4.28) at the ith time step and then using the computed values to solve equation (5.4.28) for the $(i - 1)$th time step. The option values at current time t are obtained when time index $i = 0$ is reached. It can be seen that the grid method yields n_{s-2} option values, $f_{0,j}, j = 1, \ldots, n_{s-2}$, which correspond to the current asset prices

$$S_0^j = j\Delta S, \quad j = 1, \ldots, n_{s-2}.$$

As previously mentioned, the asset price S_0 coincides with grid index $j = n_1$. Therefore, $S_0 = S_0^{n_1}$, and the option value for the current asset price S_0 is given by f_{0,n_1}.

This is in contrast to the lattice methods discussed in Chapter 4 which yield a single option value corresponding to the root node.

The option values obtained using the grid methods we have just described are for vanilla European options. However, vanilla European options can be more accurately valued by using the Black–Scholes option pricing formula discussed in Chapter 4. The importance of finite-difference grids is that, by slightly modify our backward iterative method, we can take into account the possibility of *early exercise* and thus price American options.

This can be achieved by using Code excerpt 5.17 to modify the option prices contained in the array **opt_vals** as follows:

```
if (put) {  /* a put */
    for(j=1; j<=ns-2; ++j)
        opt_vals[j] = MAX(opt_vals[j],E-s[j]);
    }
    else {  /* a call */
    for(j=1; j<=ns-2; ++j)
        opt_vals[j] = MAX(opt_vals[j],s[j]-E);
    }
```

Code excerpt 5.17 Computer code which modifies the computed option values contained in array opt_vals to include the possibility of *early exercise*; this is required if we are to determine the value of American options. Here, $s[j]$ contains the asset value at asset index j, opt_vals[j] contains the option value (computed by Code excerpt 5.16) at asset index j, and E is the strike price.

Now we know how to solve the Black–Scholes equation, and it is possible to include, without much difficulty, more *exotic features* such as lock out periods, barriers, rebates, etc.

The routine **opt_gfd** solves the Black–Scholes equation using a uniform grid. The asset price is set to one of the grid lines, which means that interpolation is not required.

```
void opt_gfd(double theta_m, double asset_price, double sigma, double r, double T,
             double strike, long is_american, long put, double *option_value,
             double greeks[], double q, long pns, long nt, double smax, long *iflag)
{
/* Input parameters:
   =================
   theta_m         - the value of theta used for the finite difference method,
   asset_price     - the current price of the underlying asset,
   sigma           - the volatility,
   r               - the interest rate,
   T               - the time to maturity,
   strike          - the strike price,
   is_american     - if is_american is 0 then a European option, otherwise an American option,
   put             - if put is 0 then a call option, otherwise a put option,
   q               - the continuous dividend yield,
   pns             - the maximum asset index on the grid, corresponding to the upper boundary,
   nt              - the number of time intervals,
   smax            - the maximum asset price.
   Output parameters:
   option_value    - the value of the option,
   greeks[]        - the hedge statistics output as follows: greeks[0] is gamma, greeks[1] is delta, and greeks[2]
                     is theta,
   iflag           - an error indicator.
*/
    double *a,*b,*c,*a1,*b1,*c1,*opt_vals,*vals,*rhs,*s,*work,*u;
    double ds,dt;
    long i,j;
    double tmp,t2,time_2mat;
    long n1,n2,ind=0;
    double sig2,temp[4];

    if (asset_price >= smax) printf ("ERROR asset price >= smax");
    n1 = floor((asset_price/smax)*(double)pns);
    n2 = pns - n1;
    ds = asset_price/(double)n1;
    dt = T/(double)nt;      /* time interval size */
    ns = n1+n2+1;
/* Note: Now nps = ns-1. Since we define asset grid lines 0...ns-1, this is the maximum grid line; corresponding
   to the upper boundary. The lower boundary is at the asset grid line 0, and we solve for option values between
   the asset grid line 1 and the asset grid line ns-2 */

/* Allocate (all size ns+1) the arrays: a, b, c, a1, b1, c1, opt_vals, vals, rhs, s, work  and u */
        . . .
```

Code excerpt 5.18 Function to compute the value of a vanilla option using a uniform grid.

```
          s[0] = 0.0;
          s[n1] = asset_price;
          for(i=1; i<=n1-1; ++i )  /* set prices below asset_price */
             s[i] = (double)i * ds;
          for(i=1; i<= n2+1; ++i )  /* set prices above asset_price */
             s[n1+i] = asset_price + (double)i * ds;

/* Set up the RHS and LHS coefficients a[], b[] and c[] are the LHS coefficients
   for the unknown option values (time step j) a1[], b1[] and c1[] are the values of the
   RHS coefficients for the known option prices (time step j+1).
   Note: a1, b1 and c1 are used to form the RHS vector rhs[] of the tridiagonal system.  */
          sig2 = sigma*sigma;
          t2 = dt/2.0;
          tmp = 1.0-theta_m;  /* 1 - theta (for theta method) */
          for( i=1; i<=ns-2; ++i) { /* Assign elements of the (ns-2)*(ns-2) tridiagonal matrix */
             a[i] = -i*(i*sig2-(r-q))*t2*tmp;
             a1[i] = i*(i*sig2-(r-q))*t2*theta_m;;
             c[i] = -i*(i*sig2+(r-q))*t2*tmp;
             c1[i] = i*(i*sig2+(r-q))*t2*theta_m;;
             b[i] = 1.0+r*dt*tmp+(i*i*sig2)*dt*tmp;
             b1[i]= 1.0-(i*i*sig2+r)*dt*theta_m;
          }
/* Perform LU decomposition of the tridiagonal matrix with:
   diagonal elements contained in the array b[],  upper diagonal elements contained in the array c[]
   and lower diagonal elements in the array a[]. Store the elements of U but not those of L
   (they will be computed from U)
   Matrix U: The diagonal elements of U are stored in the array u[] and the upper diagonal elements of U
   are just c[].
   Matrix L: For the lower triangular matrix L, the diagonal elements are 1 and the lower diagonal elements
   are l[i] = a[i]/u[i-1], where u[] is the upper diagonal of U. */

          u[1] = b[1];
          if (u[1] == 0.0) printf ("ERROR in array u \n");
          for(i=2; i <=ns-2; ++i) {
             u[i] = b[i] - a[i]*c[i-1]/u[i-1];
             if (u[i] == 0.0) printf ("ERROR in array u \n");
          }
/*  Set option values at maturity.  Note : opt_vals[0] and opt_vals[ns-1] are the lower and upper
   (put/call) option price boundary values. */
          if (!put) { /* a call */
             for( i=0; i<ns; ++i )
                opt_vals[i] = MAX(s[i]-strike, 0.0 );
          }
          else { /* a put */
             for( i=0; i<ns; ++i)
                opt_vals[i] = MAX(strike - s[i], 0.0);
          }
/* From the option values at maturity (t = nt*dt) calculate values at earlier times (nt-1)*dt etc..   */
          for( j=nt-1; j>=-2; --j) { /* Go two steps past current time (0) so that can evaluate theta */
             time_2mat = T-j*dt;
             for(i=2; i<=ns-3; ++i) /* set up the rhs of equation for Crank-Nicolson method */
                rhs[i] = a1[i]*opt_vals[i-1]+b1[i]*opt_vals[i]+c1[i]*opt_vals[i+1];

/* Incorporate the boundary conditions at the upper/lower asset value boundaries */
             rhs[1] = (a1[1]-a[1])*opt_vals[0]+ b1[1]*opt_vals[1]+c1[1]*opt_vals[2];
             rhs[ns-2] = a1[ns-2]*opt_vals[ns-3]+b1[ns-2]*opt_vals[ns-2]+(c1[ns-2]-c[ns-2])*opt_vals[ns-1];

/* Solve the lower triangular system Ly = b, where y is stored in array work[].
             Compute the elements of L from those of U, l[i] = a[i]/u[i-1].  */
             work[1] = rhs[1];
             for( i=2; i<=ns-2; ++i ) {
                work[i] = rhs[i] - a[i]*work[i-1]/u[i-1];
             }
/* Solve the upper (ns-2)*(ns-2) triangular system Ux = y (where x = opt_vals) */
             opt_vals[ns-2] = work[ns-2]/u[ns-2];
             for( i = ns-2; i >= 1; --i )
                opt_vals[i] = (work[i] - c[i]*opt_vals[i+1])/u[i];
             if (is_american) {  /* take into account early exercise for american options */
                if (put) {  /* a put */
                   for(i=1; i<=ns-2; ++i)
                      opt_vals[i] = MAX(opt_vals[i],strike-s[i]);
                }
                else { /* a call */
                   for(i=1; i<=ns-2; ++i)
                      opt_vals[i] = MAX(opt_vals[i],s[i]-strike);
                }
             }
             if (j==0) {
                for (i=0; i < ns; ++i)
                   vals[i] = opt_vals[i];
             }
             if ((j==1)||(j==2)||(j==-1)||(j==-2)) { /* Store option values so that can compute theta */
                temp[ind] = opt_vals[n1];
                ++ind;
             }
```

Code excerpt 5.18 (*Continued*).

```
    }
    if (greeks) {
/* Compute gamma (4th order accuracy) */
        greeks[0] = (-vals[n1+2]+16.0*vals[n1+1]-30.0*vals[n1]+16.0*vals[n1-1]-vals[n1-2])/(12.0*ds*ds);
/* Compute delta (4th order accuracy) */
        greeks[1] = (-vals[n1+2]+8.0*vals[n1+1]-8.0*vals[n1-1]+vals[n1-2])/(12.0*ds);
/* Compute theta (4th order accuracy) */
        greeks[2] = (-temp[0]+8.0*temp[1]-8.0*temp[2]+temp[3])/(12.0*dt);
/* Note: could also compute theta as greeks[2] = (-temp[0]+4.0*temp[1]-3.0*vals[n1])/(2.0*dt); */
    }
    *option_value = vals[n1]; /* Return option value */
}
```

Code excerpt 5.18 (*Continued*).

5.4.3 Nonuniform Grids

In the previous section, we showed how to solve the Black–Scholes equation using a uniform grid. Although this approach will provide satisfactory solutions to many option pricing problems, there are situations in which it is important to be able to place grid lines at locations which do not correspond to those available in a uniform grid. Increasing the density of grid lines in regions of interest can lead to improved accuracy in both the estimated option values and also the estimates of the hedge statistics (the Greeks).

Here, we provide an example which illustrates the benefits of using a nonuniform grids in the evaluation of down and out call barrier options. Later on in Section 5.4.6, we give a further example which shows the use of nonuniform grids to evaluate double barrier options.

The purpose of this section is to show how to discretize the Black–Scholes equation using a nonuniform grid and to derive an expression, see equation (5.4.39), that is equivalent to equation (5.4.14). Although the tridiagonal system of equations we have to solve in this section will be different from that in Section 5.4, the solution method is exactly the same. This means that once we have derived equation (5.4.39) all the other information which we require to evaluate both European and American options is available in Section 5.4 under the headings:

- The boundary conditions.
- Computation of the option values at a given time instant.
- Backwards iteration and early exercise.

We will now consider the finite-difference approximation for a nonuniform grid and then show how to value the down and out call barrier option.

The Finite-Difference Approximation

Here, we consider how to discretize the Black–Scholes equation using a nonuniform grid, in which both the asset price interval ΔS and the time step Δt are not constant but can vary throughout the grid.

Allowing for a nonconstant time step is quite simple. The time step occurs in both the first derivative $f_{i,j}$, see equation (5.4.4), and in the option value equations, see equation (5.4.14) to equation (5.4.21), as the constant Δt. To incorporate a varying time step, $\Delta t_i, i = 0, n_t$, thus only requires setting $\Delta t = \Delta t_i$, at the ith time step and then continuing with the solution method outlined in Section 5.4.

The incorporation of nonconstant asset price intervals requires more work. This is because the finite-difference approximations to the first and second derivatives $f'_{i,j}$ and $f''_{i,j}$, in equation (5.4.10) and equation (5.4.11), are based on a Taylor expansion about the point $f_{i,j}$.

We will now derive expressions for these derivatives.

If we let $\Delta X_j^- = S_j - S_{j-1}$ and $\Delta X_j^+ = S_{j+1} - S_j$ and then using a Taylor expansion about the $f_{i+1,j}$, we have

$$f_{i+1,j+1} = f_{i+1,j} + f'_{i+1,j}\Delta X_j^+ + \frac{1}{2}f''_{i+1,j}\left(\Delta X_j^+\right)^2 \tag{5.4.32}$$

and also

$$f_{i+1,j-1} = f_{i+1,j} - f'_{i+1,j}\Delta X_j^- + \frac{1}{2}f''_{i+1,j}\left(\Delta X_j^-\right)^2. \tag{5.4.33}$$

Multiplying equation (5.4.32) by ΔX_j^- and adding it to ΔX_j^+ times equation (5.4.33) give

$$\Delta X_j^+ f_{i+1,j-1} + \Delta X_j^- f_{i+1,j+1}$$
$$= \Delta X_j^- f_{i+1,j} + \Delta X_j^+ f_{i+1,j} + \frac{1}{2}f''_{i+1,j}\left\{(\Delta X_j^+)^2\Delta X_j^- + (\Delta X_j^-)^2\Delta X_j^+\right\}.$$

Therefore,

$$\frac{1}{2}f''_{i+1,j} = \frac{\Delta X_j^+ f_{i+1,j-1} + \Delta X_j^- f_{i+1,j+1} - \Delta X_j^- f_{i+1,j} - \Delta X_j^+ f_{i+1,j}}{(\Delta X_j^+)^2\Delta X_j^- + (\Delta X_j^-)^2\Delta X_j^+}.$$

So

$$f''_{i+1,j} = \frac{2\left\{\Delta X_j^+ f_{i+1,j-1} + \Delta X_j^- f_{i+1,j+1} - f_{i+1,j}(\Delta X_j^- + \Delta X_j^+)\right\}}{(\Delta X_j^+)^2\Delta X_j^- + (\Delta X_j^-)^2\Delta X_j^+}. \tag{5.4.34}$$

To calculate $f'_{i+1,j}$, we rearrange equation (5.4.33) to obtain

$$-f'_{i+1,j}\Delta X_j^- = f_{i+1,j-1} - f_{i+1,j} - \frac{1}{2}f''_{i+1,j}(\Delta X_j^-)^2$$

and

$$f'_{i+1,j} = \frac{f_{i+1,j} - f_{i+1,j-1}}{\Delta X_j^-} + \frac{1}{2}f''_{i+1,j}\Delta X_j^-. \tag{5.4.35}$$

If we now substitute for $f''_{i+1,j}$, from equation (5.4.34) into equation (5.4.35), we have

$$f'_{i+1,j} = \frac{f_{i+1,j} - f_{i+1,j-1}}{\Delta X_j^-}$$
$$+ \frac{\left\{\Delta X_j^+ f_{i+1,j-1} - (\Delta X_j^- + \Delta X_j^+)f_{i+1,j} + \Delta X_j^- f_{i+1,j+1}\right\}\Delta X_j^-}{(\Delta X_j^+)^2\Delta X_j^- + (\Delta X_j^-)^2\Delta X_j^+},$$

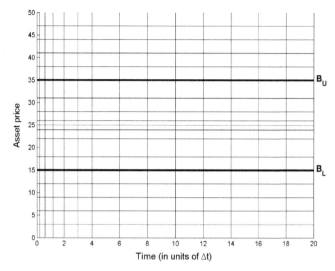

FIGURE 5.6 A nonuniform grid in which the grid spacing is reduced near current time t and also in the neighbourhood of the asset price 25; this can lead to greater accuracy in the computed option values and the associated *Greeks*. Grid lines are also placed at asset prices of B_U and B_L, and this enables the accurate evaluation of options which have barriers at these asset prices.

which simplifies to give

$$f'_{i+1,j} = \frac{(\Delta X_j^+)^2(f_{i+1,j} - f_{i+1,j-1}) - (\Delta X_j^-)^2 f_{i+1,j} + (\Delta X_j^-)^2 f_{i+1,j+1}}{(\Delta X_j^+)^2 \Delta X_j^- + (\Delta X_j^-)^2 \Delta X_j^+}$$

so that we finally have

$$f'_{i+1,j} = \frac{(\Delta X_j^-)^2 f_{i+1,j+1} + ((\Delta X_j^+)^2 - (\Delta X_j^-)^2) f_{i+1,j} - (\Delta X_j^+)^2 f_{i+1,j-1}}{(\Delta X_j^+)^2 \Delta X_j^- + (\Delta X_j^-)^2 \Delta X_j^+}. \quad (5.4.36)$$

As in Section 5.4, we can now substitute the expressions for $f'_{i+1,j}$ and $f''_{i+1,j}$ given in equation (5.4.36) and equation (5.4.34) into the equation (5.4.7), the discretized Black–Scholes equation. If we let $D = (\Delta X_j^+)^2 \Delta X_j^- + (\Delta X_j^-)^2 \Delta X_j^+$, we then obtain

$$r\Delta t(\Theta_m f_{i+1,j} + \Theta_m^* f_{i,j}) = f_{i+1,j} - f_{i,j} + \frac{(r-q)S_j \Delta t \mathcal{A}_1}{D} + \frac{\sigma^2 S_j^2 \Delta t \mathcal{A}_2}{D}, \quad (5.4.37)$$

where $\Theta_m^* = 1 - \Theta_m$, and

$$\mathcal{A}_1 = \Theta_m \left[f_{i+1,j+1}(\Delta X_j^-)^2 - f_{i+1,j-1}(\Delta X_j^+)^2 - f_{i+1,j}\left\{ (\Delta X_j^-)^2 - (\Delta X_j^+)^2 \right\} \right]$$
$$+ \Theta_m^* \left[f_{i,j+1}(\Delta X_j^-)^2 - f_{i,j-1}(\Delta X_j^+)^2 - f_{i,j}\left\{ (\Delta X_j^-)^2 - (\Delta X_j^+)^2 \right\} \right]$$

and

$$\mathcal{A}_2 = \Theta_m \left[f_{i+1,j+1}\Delta X_j^- + f_{i+1,j-1}\Delta X_j^+ - f_{i+1,j}\left\{\Delta X_j^- + \Delta X_j^+\right\} \right]$$
$$+ \Theta_m^* \left[f_{i,j+1}\Delta X_j^- + f_{i,j-1}\Delta X_j^+ - f_{i,j}\left\{\Delta X_j^- + \Delta X_j^+\right\} \right].$$

Collecting like terms, we obtain

$$\mathcal{B}_1 f_{i,j-1} + \mathcal{B}_2 f_{i,j} + \mathcal{B}_3 f_{i,j+1} + \mathcal{C}_1 f_{i+1,j-1} + \mathcal{C}_2 f_{i+1,j} + \mathcal{C}_3 f_{i+1,j+1} = 0, \quad (5.4.38)$$

where

$$\mathcal{B}_1 = \frac{-\Theta_m^*(r-q)S_j\Delta t(\Delta X_j^+)^2}{D} + \frac{(1-\theta)\sigma^2 S_j^2 \Delta t \Delta X_j^+}{D},$$

$$\mathcal{B}_2 = -1 - r\Delta t \Theta_m^* - \frac{\Theta_m^* \sigma^2 S_j^2 \Delta t(\Delta X_j^- + \Delta X_j^+)}{D}$$
$$- \frac{\Theta_m^*(r-q)S_j\Delta t\left\{(\Delta X_j^-)^2 - (\Delta X_j^+)^2\right\}}{D},$$

$$\mathcal{B}_3 = \frac{\Theta_m^*(r-q)S_j\Delta t(\Delta X_j^-)^2}{D} + \frac{\Theta_m^* \sigma^2 S_j^2 \Delta t \Delta X_j^-}{D},$$

$$\mathcal{C}_1 = \frac{\Theta_m \sigma^2 S_j^2 \Delta t \Delta X_j^+}{D} - \frac{\Theta_m(r-q)S_j\Delta t(\Delta X_j^+)^2}{D},$$

$$\mathcal{C}_2 = 1 - r\Delta t \Theta_m - \frac{\Theta_m(r-q)S_j\Delta t\left\{(\Delta X_j^-)^2 - (\Delta X_j^+)^2\right\}}{D} - \frac{\Theta_m \sigma^2 S_j^2 \Delta t\left\{\Delta X_j^- + \Delta X_j^+\right\}}{D},$$

$$\mathcal{C}_3 = \frac{\Theta_m(r-q)S_j\Delta t(\Delta X_j^-)^2}{D} + \frac{\Theta_m \sigma^2 S_j^2 \Delta t \Delta X_j^-}{D}.$$

Since we are solving the Black–Scholes equation backwards in time, we will rearrange equation (5.4.38) as

$$a_j f_{i,j-1} + b_j f_{i,j} + c_j = R_{i+1,j}, \quad (5.4.39)$$

where the right-hand side $R_{i+1,j}$ is

$$R_{i+1,j} = \bar{a}_j f_{i+1,j-1} + \bar{b}_j f_{i+1,j} + \bar{c}_j f_{i+1,j+1} \quad (5.4.40)$$

and the coefficients are

$$a_j = \Theta_m^* \Delta t \left\{ \frac{(r-q)S_j(\Delta X_j^+)^2}{D} - \frac{\sigma^2 S_j^2 \Delta X_j^+}{D} \right\}, \quad (5.4.41)$$

$$b_j = 1 + \Delta t \Theta_m^* \left\{ r + \frac{\sigma^2 S_j^2(\Delta X_j^- + \Delta X_j^+)}{D} + \frac{(r-q)S_j\left\{(\Delta X_j^-)^2 - (\Delta X_j^+)^2\right\}}{D} \right\},$$
$$(5.4.42)$$

$$c_j = \Theta_m^* \Delta t \left\{ \frac{-(r-q)S_j(\Delta X_j^-)^2}{D} - \frac{\sigma^2 S_j^2 \Delta X_j^-}{D} \right\}, \quad (5.4.43)$$

$$\bar{a}_j = \Theta_m \Delta t \left\{ \frac{\sigma^2 S_j^2 \Delta X_j^+}{D} - \frac{(r-q)S_j(\Delta X_j^+)^2}{D} \right\}, \tag{5.4.44}$$

$$\bar{b}_j = 1 - \Theta_m r \Delta t$$

$$- \Theta_m \Delta t \left\{ \frac{(r-q)S_j\left\{(\Delta X_j^-)^2 - (\Delta X_j^+)^2\right\}}{D} + \frac{\sigma^2 S_j^2 \left\{\Delta X_j^- + \Delta X_j^+\right\}}{D} \right\}, \tag{5.4.45}$$

$$\bar{c}_j = \Theta_m \Delta t \left\{ \frac{(r-q)S_j(\Delta X_j^-)^2}{D} + \frac{\sigma^2 S_j^2 \Delta X_j^-}{D} \right\}. \tag{5.4.46}$$

Here, equation (5.4.39), as is the case for equation (5.4.14) in Section 5.4, provides the relationship between the three option values $f_{i+1,j-1}$, $f_{i+1,j}$, and $f_{i+1,j+1}$ at time index $i + 1$, and the three option values $f_{i,j-1}$, $f_{i,j}$, and $f_{i,j+1}$ at time index i. It can also be seen that equation (5.4.39) is the nonuniform grid equivalent of equation (5.4.14) given in Section 5.4. We will now show that equation (5.4.39) and equation (5.4.14) are identical when a uniform grid is used, that is, $\Delta X_j^+ = \Delta X_j^-$. We proceed as follows:

Let $\Delta X_j^+ = \Delta X_j^- = \Delta S$ and $S_j = j\Delta S$.

So

$$D = (\Delta X_j^+)^2 \Delta X_j^- + (\Delta X_j^-)^2 \Delta X_j^+ = 2(\Delta S)^3,$$

$$\frac{(\Delta X_j^+)^2}{D} = \frac{(\Delta X_j^-)^2}{D} = \frac{(\Delta S)^2}{2(\Delta S)^3} = \frac{1}{2\Delta S},$$

$$\frac{\Delta X_j^+}{D} = \frac{\Delta X_j^-}{D} = \frac{1}{2\Delta S^2},$$

$$\frac{(\Delta X_j^+)^2 - (\Delta X_j^-)^2}{D} = 0.$$

If we substitute the above values into equation (5.4.41) to equation (5.4.46), we obtain the following expressions for the coefficients in equation (5.4.39):

$$a_j = (1 - \Theta_m)\Delta t \left\{ \frac{(r-q)S_j}{2\Delta S} - \frac{\sigma^2 S_j^2}{2\Delta S^2} \right\} = (1 - \Theta_m)\frac{\Delta t}{2} \left\{ (r-q)j - \sigma^2 j^2 \right\},$$

$$b_j = 1 + \Delta t(1 - \Theta_m) \left\{ r + \frac{\sigma^2 S_j^2}{\Delta S^2} \right\} = 1 + (1 - \Theta_m)\Delta t \left\{ r + \sigma^2 j^2 \right\},$$

$$c_j = (1 - \Theta_m)\Delta t \left\{ \frac{-(r-q)S_j}{2\Delta S} - \frac{\sigma^2 S_j^2}{2\Delta S^2} \right\} = -(1 - \Theta_m)\frac{\Delta t}{2} \left\{ (r-q)j + \sigma^2 j^2 \right\},$$

$$\bar{a}_j = \Theta_m \Delta t \left\{ \frac{\sigma^2 S_j^2}{2\Delta S^2} - \frac{(r-q)S_j}{2\Delta S} \right\} = -\Theta_m \frac{\Delta t}{2} \left\{ (r-q)j - \sigma^2 j^2 \right\},$$

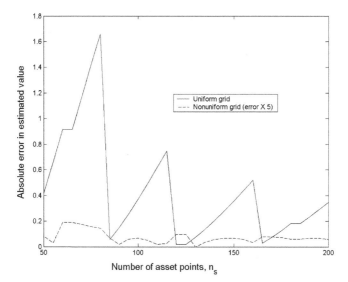

FIGURE 5.7 The absolute error in the estimated values for a European down and out call barrier option ($B < E$) as the number of asset grid points, n_s, is varied. Here, we show a comparison of the results obtained using both uniform and nonuniform grids; logarithmic transformations were not employed. The algorithm for the uniform grid is described in Section 5.4.2, and that for the nonuniform grid is outlined in Section 5.4.3. The Crank–Nicolson method ($\Theta_m = 0.5$) was used and the other parameters were $E = 50.0$, $B = 47.5$, $S_0 = 55.0$, $S_{max} = 300.0$, $T = 0.5$, $\sigma = 0.2$, $r = \log(1.1)$, $q = 0.0$, and $n_t = 100$. The correct option value was 7.6512 which was obtained using the analytic formulae given in Code excerpt 4.7.

$$\bar{b}_j = 1 - \Theta_m r\Delta t - \frac{\Theta_m \sigma^2 S_j^2 \Delta t}{\Delta S^2} = 1 - \Theta_m \Delta t \left\{ r + \sigma^2 j^2 \right\},$$

$$\bar{c}_j = \Theta_m \Delta t \left\{ \frac{(r-q)S_j}{2\Delta S} + \frac{\sigma^2 S_j^2}{\Delta S^2} \right\} = \Theta_m \frac{\Delta t}{2} \left\{ (r-q)j + \sigma^2 j^2 \right\}.$$

It can be seen that these coefficients are identical to those given in Section 5.4.2 equation (5.4.16) to equation (5.4.21).

We now provide examples of using nonuniform grids to evaluate European down and out call options.

Valuation of a Down and Out Call Option

Here, the improved accuracy that can be achieved by using nonuniform grids instead of uniform grids is illustrated in Figs 5.7 and 5.8. The uniform grids are constructed using the method outlined in Section 5.4 and Code excerpt 5.18. That is an asset grid line is set to coincide with the current asset price S_0, and the other grid lines are positioned above and below S_0 with a uniform spacing of ΔS. The disadvantage of this approach is that there will be an unspecified pricing error that depends on the distance, d_s, of the barrier level, B, to the

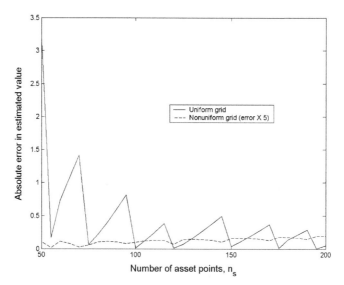

FIGURE 5.8 The absolute error in the estimated values for a European down and out call barrier option ($E < B$) as the number of asset grid points, n_s, is varied. Here, we show a comparison of the results obtained using both uniform and nonuniform grids; logarithmic transformations are not employed. The algorithm for the uniform grid is described in Section 5.4.2, and that for the nonuniform grid is outlined in Section 5.4.3. The Crank–Nicolson method ($\Theta_m = 0.5$) was used and the other parameters were $E = 50.0$, $B = 52.5$, $S_0 = 65.0$, $S_{max} = 300.0$, $T = 0.5$, $\sigma = 0.2$, $r = \log(1.1)$, $q = 0.0$, and $xn_t = 100$. The correct option value was 17.0386 which was obtained using the analytic formulae given in Code excerpt 4.7.

nearest asset grid line. Furthermore, as the number of asset points, n_s, increases, the magnitude of d_s will oscillate within the range 0 to $\Delta S/2$.

When $d_s \sim 0$ the grid will be accurate, but when $|d_s| \sim \Delta S/2$ there will be a large pricing error. This gives rise to the oscillating pricing errors shown in Figs 5.7 and 5.8.

The nonuniform grids are constructed using the techniques mentioned earlier in this section and also Code excerpt 5.19. We now, irrespective of n_s, arrange for one asset grid line to coincide with the current asset value, S_0, and another asset grid line to coincide with B, the barrier asset price. In Fig. 5.6, this corresponds to setting B_L to B and not using B_U.

It can be seen in Figs 5.7 and 5.8 that in this case the pricing error is very much less and also does not exhibit the pronounced oscillations that are produced by a uniform grid. In Code excerpt 5.19 below, we give the computer program which was used to obtained the nonuniform grid values for the down and out call options presented in Figs 5.7 and 5.8. Although this program only deals with European options, it can easily be altered, using the same techniques as in Code excerpt 5.18, to deal with American style options; this is left as an exercise for the reader.

```
void barrier_downout(double barrier_level, double theta_m, double asset_price, double sigma, double r, double T,
      double strike, long put, double *option_value, double greeks[], double q, long ns, long nt, double smax, long *ifail)
{
  /* ns - the number of asset intervals
     nt - the number of time intervals
  */
      double *a,*b,*c,*a1,*b1,*c1,*opt_vals,*vals,*rhs,*s,*work,*u;
      double ds,time_step;
      long i,j,barrier_index;
      double tmp,t2,time_2mat,zero = 0.0;
      long n1,n2,ind=0,ns1;
      double sig2,temp[4],ds_plus,ds_minus,temp1,temp2,temp3;
      double D;

      n1 = floor((asset_price/smax)*(double)ns);
      if (n1 < 3) {
         printf ("increase the number of asset points \n");
      }
      n2 = ns - n1;
      ds = asset_price/(double)n1;
      time_step = T/(double)nt;      /* time interval size  */
      ns1 = n1+n2+2; /* number of nodes - including extra grid line*/
      /* allocate the required arrays (all of size ns1+1): a, b, c, a1, b1, c1, opt_vals, vals, rhs, s, work, u */
               .       .       .
      /* set prices below asset_price */
      s[0] = zero;
      s[n1] = asset_price;
      for(i=1; i < n1; ++i )
         s[i] = (double)i * ds;
      /* set prices above asset_price */
      for(i=1; i<= n2+2; ++i ) {
         s[n1+i] = asset_price + (double)i * ds;
      }
/* find out the index corresponding to barrier_level */
      barrier_index = 0;
      while(barrier_level > s[barrier_index]) {
         ++barrier_index;
      }
      if (barrier_level != s[barrier_index]) { /* decrement barrier index */
         --barrier_index;
      }
      if (s[barrier_index] != barrier_level) { /* then barrier does not correspond
                                   to an existing grid line  so create another one*/
         for (i=1; i < ns1-barrier_index; ++i) {
            s[barrier_index+1+i] = s[barrier_index] + (double)i*ds;
         }
         ++barrier_index;
         s[barrier_index] = barrier_level;
         if (n1>barrier_index) {
            ++n1;
         }
      }
      /* set up the RHS and LHS coefficients a[], b[] and c[] are the LHS coefficients
         for the unknown option values (time step j) a1[], b1[] and c1[] are the values of the
         RHS coefficients for the known option prices (time step j+1).
         Note: a1, b1 and c1 are used to form the RHS vector rhs[] of the tridiagonal system. */
      sig2 = sigma*sigma;
      t2 = time_step/2.0;
      tmp = 1.0-theta_m;  /* 1 - theta (for theta method) */
      /* assign elements of the (ns1-2)*(ns1-2) tridiagonal matrix */
      for( i=1; i<=ns1-2; ++i) {
         ds_plus  = s[i+1]-s[i];
         ds_minus = s[i] - s[i-1];
         D = ((ds_plus*ds_plus*ds_minus) + (ds_minus*ds_minus*ds_plus));
         temp1 = time_step/D;
         a[i] = temp1*((r-q)*s[i]*ds_plus*ds_plus) -temp1*ds_plus*(s[i]*s[i]*sig2);
         temp1 = theta_m*time_step/D;
         a1[i] = -(temp1*((r-q)*s[i]*ds_plus*ds_plus) -temp1*ds_plus*(s[i]*s[i]*sig2));
         temp1 = (ds_minus*ds_minus)/D;
         temp2 = ds_minus/D;
         c[i] = -time_step*tmp*(temp1*s[i]*(r-q)+(sig2*s[i]*s[i]*temp2));
         c1[i] = time_step*theta_m*(temp1*s[i]*(r-q)+(sig2*s[i]*s[i]*temp2));
         temp1 = ((ds_minus*ds_minus) - (ds_plus*ds_plus))/D;
         temp2 = (ds_minus+ds_plus)/D;
         b[i] = 1.0+time_step*tmp*(r+((r-q)*s[i]*temp1)+(s[i]*s[i]*sig2)*temp2);
         b1[i] = 1.0-time_step*theta_m*(r+((r-q)*s[i]*temp1)+(s[i]*s[i]*sig2)*temp2);
      }
      /* Perform LU decomposition of the tridiagonal matrix with: diagonal elements contained in the array b[],
         upper diagonal elements contained in the array c[]  and lower diagonal elements in the array a[].
         Store the elements of U but not those of L (they will be computed from U)
         Matrix U: The diagonal elements of U are stored in the array u[] and the upper
         diagonal elements of U are just c[]. */
```

Code excerpt 5.19 Function to compute the value of a European down and out barrier option using a nonuniform grid.

```
         Matrix L: For the lower triangular matrix L, the diagonal elements are 1 and the lower diagonal
         elements are l[i] = a[i]/u[i-1], where u[] is the upper diagonal of U. */
    u[1] = b[1];
    if (u[1] == zero) printf ("error in array u \n");
    for( i=2; i <=ns1-2; ++i) {
        u[i] = b[i] - a[i]*c[i-1]/u[i-1];
        if (u[i] == zero) printf ("error in array u \n");
    }
/* Set option values at maturity. Note : opt_vals[0] and opt_vals[ns1-1] are the lower and upper
   (put/call) option price boundary values. */
    if (!put) { /* a call */
        for( i=0; i<ns1; ++i )
            opt_vals[i] = MAX(s[i]-strike, zero );
        /* now modify option values to include the barrier */
        for( i=0; i <= barrier_index; ++i )
            opt_vals[i] = zero;
    }
    else { /* a put */
        for( i=0; i<ns1; ++i)
            opt_vals[i] = MAX(strike - s[i], zero);
    }
    /* From the option values at maturity, t = nt*time_step, compute
       the values at times (nt-1)*time_step to 0 (current time)
     */
    for( j=nt-1; j>=-2; --j) { /* go two steps past current time so that can evaluate theta */
        time_2mat = T-j*time_step;
        /* set up the rhs of equation for the Theta method */
        for(i=2; i<=ns1-3; ++i)
            rhs[i] = a1[i]*opt_vals[i-1]+b1[i]*opt_vals[i]+c1[i]*opt_vals[i+1];
        /* incorporate the boundary conditions1 at the upper/lower asset value boundaries */
        rhs[1] = (a1[1]-a[1])*opt_vals[0]+ b1[1]*opt_vals[1]+c1[1]*opt_vals[2];
        rhs[ns1-2] = a1[ns1-2]*opt_vals[ns1-3]+b1[ns1-2]*opt_vals[ns1-2]+(c1[ns1-2]-c[ns1-2])*opt_vals[ns1-1];
        /* Solve the lower triangular system Ly = b, where y is stored in array work[].
           Compute the elements of L from those of U, l[i] = a[i]/u[i-1]. */
        work[1] = rhs[1];
        for( i=2; i<=ns1-2; ++i ) {
            work[i] = rhs[i] - a[i]*work[i-1]/u[i-1];
        }
        /* Solve the upper (ns1-2)*(ns1-2) triangular system Ux = y (where x = opt_vals) */
        opt_vals[ns1-2] = work[ns1-2]/u[ns1-2];
        for( i = ns1-2; i >= 1; --i )
            opt_vals[i] = (work[i] - c[i]*opt_vals[i+1])/u[i];
        if (j==0) {
            for (i=0; i < ns1; ++i)
                vals[i] = opt_vals[i];
        }
        /* store option values so that can compute theta */
        if ((j==1)||(j==2)||(j==-1)||(j==-2)) {
            temp[ind] = opt_vals[n1];
            ++ind;
        }
        /* now modify for barrier */
        for( i=0; i <= barrier_index; ++i )
            opt_vals[i] = zero;
    }
    if (greeks) { /* assume an irregular grid */
        ds_minus = s[n1]-s[n1-1];
        ds_plus = s[n1+1]-s[n1];
        D = (ds_minus*ds_minus*ds_plus) + (ds_plus*ds_plus*ds_minus);
        temp1 = ds_minus*ds_minus;
        temp2 = ds_plus*ds_plus;
        temp3 = temp1-temp2;
        /* GAMMA */
        greeks[0] = (ds_minus*vals[n1+1]+ds_plus*vals[n1-1]-vals[n1]*(ds_plus+ds_minus))/(0.5*D);
        /* DELTA */
        greeks[1] = (temp1*vals[n1+1] - temp2*vals[n1-1] - vals[n1]*temp3)/D;
        /*  THETA */
        greeks[2] = (-temp[0]+8.0*temp[1]-8.0*temp[2]+temp[3])/(12.0*time_step);
    /* could also compute theta like this:
        greeks[2] = (-temp[0]+4.0*temp[1]-3.0*vals[n1])/(2.0*time_step); */
    }
    *option_value = vals[n1]; /* Return option value */
    /* deallocate the arrays that were previously allocated */
         .    .    .
}
```

Code excerpt 5.19 (*Continued*).

5.4.4 The Log Transformation and Uniform Grids

Up to this point, we have been dealing with the standard Black–Scholes equation, which is

$$\frac{\partial f}{\partial t} + (r - q)S\frac{\partial f}{\partial S} + \frac{\sigma^2 S^2}{2}\frac{\partial^2 f}{\partial S^2} = rf. \tag{5.4.47}$$

However, if we introduce the change of variable $Z = \log S$, we obtain the following equation:

$$\frac{\partial f}{\partial t} + b\frac{\partial f}{\partial Z} + \frac{\sigma^2}{2}\frac{\partial^2 f}{\partial Z^2} = rf, \tag{5.4.48}$$

where $b = r - q - (\sigma^2/2)$. This has beneficial numerical properties since it does not contain the original Black–Scholes terms in S and S^2.

Derivation of Equation (5.4.48)

We will now derive an expression for the logarithmic Black–Scholes equation and show that it agrees with equation (5.4.48).

Since $Z = \log S$, we have $\partial Z/\partial S = 1/S$. This gives

$$\frac{\partial f}{\partial S} = \frac{\partial f}{\partial Z}\frac{\partial Z}{\partial S} = \frac{1}{S}\frac{\partial f}{\partial Z}$$

and

$$\frac{\partial^2 f}{\partial S^2} = \frac{\partial}{\partial S}\left(\frac{\partial f}{\partial S}\right) = \frac{1}{S^2}\frac{\partial f}{\partial Z} + \frac{1}{S}\frac{\partial}{\partial S}\left(\frac{\partial f}{\partial Z}\right) = -\frac{1}{S^2}\frac{\partial f}{\partial Z} + \frac{1}{S}\frac{\partial Z}{\partial S}\frac{\partial}{\partial Z}\left(\frac{\partial f}{\partial Z}\right),$$

$$\frac{\partial^2 f}{\partial S^2} = -\frac{1}{S^2}\frac{\partial f}{\partial Z} + \frac{1}{S^2}\frac{\partial^2 f}{\partial Z^2}.$$

So equation (5.4.47) becomes

$$\frac{\partial f}{\partial t} + \frac{(r - q)S}{S}\frac{\partial f}{\partial Z} - \frac{\sigma^2 S^2}{2S^2}\frac{\partial f}{\partial Z} + \frac{\sigma^2 S^2}{2S^2}\frac{\partial^2 f}{\partial Z^2} = rf;$$

thus, setting $b = r - q - (\sigma^2/2)$, we obtain

$$\frac{\partial f}{\partial t} + b\frac{\partial f}{\partial Z} + \frac{\sigma^2}{2}\frac{\partial^2 f}{\partial Z^2} = rf. \qquad QED$$

We will now consider the finite-difference discretization of equation (5.4.48).

The Finite-Difference Method

Application of the finite-difference method to the log transformed Black–Scholes equation is very similar to that already outlined in Sections 5.4.2 and 5.4.3.

Use of the Θ_m method on equation (5.4.48) results in

$$\frac{f_{i+1,j} - f_{i,j}}{\Delta t} + b\left\{\Theta_m f'_{i+1,j} + \Theta^*_m f'_{i,j}\right\} + \frac{1}{2}\sigma^2\left\{\Theta_m f''_{i+1,j} + \Theta^*_m f''_{i,j}\right\}$$
$$= r\left\{\Theta_m f_{i+1,j} + \Theta^*_m f_{i,j}\right\},$$

where $\Theta^*_m = 1 - \Theta_m$. Applying a uniform discretization at node (i, j), we obtain

$$f_{i+1,j} - f_{i,j} + \frac{b\Delta t \mathcal{A}_1}{2\Delta Z} + \frac{\sigma^2 \Delta t \mathcal{A}_2}{2\Delta Z^2} = r\Delta t\left\{\Theta_m f_{i+1,j} + \Theta^*_m f_{i,j}\right\}, \tag{5.4.49}$$

where

$$\mathcal{A}_1 = \Theta_m \{f_{i+1,j+1} - f_{i+1,j-1}\} + \Theta_m^* \{f_{i,j+1} - f_{i,j-1}\},$$
$$\mathcal{A}_2 = \Theta_m \{f_{i+1,j+1} - 2f_{i+1,j} + f_{i+1,j-1}\} + \Theta_m^* \{f_{i,j+1} - 2f_{i,j} + f_{i,j-1}\}.$$

Collecting like terms, we obtain

$$\mathcal{B}_1 f_{i,j-1} + \mathcal{B}_2 f_{i,j} + \mathcal{B}_3 f_{i,j+1} + C_1 f_{i+1,j-1} + C_2 f_{i+1,j} + C_3 f_{i+1,j+1} = 0,$$

where

$$\mathcal{B}_1 = \frac{-\Theta_m^* b\Delta t}{2\Delta Z} + \frac{\Theta_m^* \sigma^2 \Delta t}{2\Delta Z^2},$$

$$\mathcal{B}_2 = -1 - r\Delta t\Theta_m^* - \frac{\Theta_m^* \sigma^2 \Delta t}{\Delta Z^2},$$

$$\mathcal{B}_3 = \frac{\Theta_m^* b\Delta t}{2\Delta Z} + \frac{\Theta_m^* \sigma^2 \Delta t}{2\Delta Z^2},$$

$$C_1 = \frac{\Theta_m \sigma^2 \Delta t}{2\Delta Z^2} - \frac{\Theta_m b\Delta t}{2\Delta Z},$$

$$C_2 = 1 - r\Delta t\Theta_m - \frac{\Theta_m \sigma^2 \Delta t}{\Delta Z^2},$$

$$C_3 = \frac{\Theta_m b\Delta t}{2\Delta Z} + \frac{\Theta_m \sigma^2 \Delta t}{2\Delta Z^2}.$$

If we rearrange, we have the following equation:

$$a_j f_{i,j-1} + b_j f_{i,j} + c_j f_{i,j+1} = \bar{a}_j f_{i+1,j-1} + \bar{b}_j f_{i+1,j} + \bar{c}_j f_{i+1,j+1},$$

where

$$a_j = \frac{(1 - \Theta_m)\Delta t}{2\Delta Z^2} \left\{b\Delta Z - \sigma^2\right\}, \tag{5.4.50}$$

$$b_j = 1 + (1 - \Theta_m)\Delta t \left\{r + \frac{\sigma^2}{\Delta Z^2}\right\}, \tag{5.4.51}$$

$$c_j = -\frac{(1 - \Theta_m)\Delta t}{2\Delta Z^2} \left\{b\Delta Z + \sigma^2\right\}, \tag{5.4.52}$$

$$\bar{a}_j = -\frac{\Theta_m \Delta t}{2\Delta Z^2} \left\{b\Delta Z - \sigma^2\right\}, \tag{5.4.53}$$

$$\bar{b}_j = 1 - \Theta_m \Delta t \left\{r + \frac{\sigma^2}{\Delta Z^2}\right\}, \tag{5.4.54}$$

$$\bar{c}_j = \frac{\Theta_m \Delta t}{2\Delta Z^2} \left\{b\Delta Z + \sigma^2\right\}. \tag{5.4.55}$$

It can be seen that, unlike in Section 5.4.2, the coefficients in equation (5.4.50) to equation (5.4.55) are independent of the asset price index j.

When $\Theta_m = 0.5$ (the Crank–Nicolson method), we have the following coefficients:

TABLE 5.7 Valuation Results and Pricing Errors for a Vanilla American Put Option using a Uniform Grid with and without a Logarithmic Transformation; the Implicit Method and Crank–Nicolson Method are used. The Accurate Values (Obtained using a Logarithmic Transformed Grid with n_s = 1000 and n_t = 1000) are Presented in the Column Labelled "Value". The Absolute Pricing Errors $ABS(accurate\ value - estimated\ value)$ are Presented in the Column Labelled BS were Obtained using a Standard Uniform Grid (as Outlined in Section 5.4.2), and those in the Column Labelled Log BS use a Uniform Grid and Logarithmic Transformation as Explained in this Section. The Maturity of the Option was Varied from 0.1 Years to 1.5 Years, the Other Parameters were S = 9.0, X = 9.7, r = 0.1, q = 0.0, σ = 0.30, S_{max} = 100.0, n_s = 50, and n_t = 50

| | | $\Theta_m = 0.0$ | | $\Theta_m = 0.5$ | |
Time	Value	BS	Log BS	BS	Log BS
0.1	0.7599	1.4733×10^{-2}	7.7803×10^{-3}	1.4719×10^{-2}	7.6716×10^{-3}
0.2	0.8335	4.5838×10^{-2}	1.2924×10^{-2}	4.5682×10^{-2}	1.1997×10^{-2}
0.3	0.8921	6.4218×10^{-2}	1.4125×10^{-2}	6.3800×10^{-2}	1.2567×10^{-2}
0.4	0.9403	7.4699×10^{-2}	1.6559×10^{-2}	7.3924×10^{-2}	1.4655×10^{-2}
0.5	0.9812	8.0297×10^{-2}	1.8471×10^{-2}	7.9101×10^{-2}	1.6041×10^{-2}
0.6	1.0167	8.2796×10^{-2}	1.9125×10^{-2}	8.1135×10^{-2}	1.6067×10^{-2}
0.7	1.0479	8.3285×10^{-2}	1.8959×10^{-2}	8.1131×10^{-2}	1.5273×10^{-2}
0.8	1.0758	8.2470×10^{-2}	1.8408×10^{-2}	7.9803×10^{-2}	1.4159×10^{-2}
0.9	1.1009	8.0829×10^{-2}	1.7756×10^{-2}	7.7647×10^{-2}	1.3020×10^{-2}
1.0	1.1237	7.8646×10^{-2}	1.7138×10^{-2}	7.4947×10^{-2}	1.1997×10^{-2}
1.1	1.1445	7.6164×10^{-2}	1.6643×10^{-2}	7.1961×10^{-2}	1.1174×10^{-2}
1.2	1.1637	7.3514×10^{-2}	1.6290×10^{-2}	6.8803×10^{-2}	1.0552×10^{-2}
1.3	1.1813	7.0785×10^{-2}	1.6092×10^{-2}	6.5594×10^{-2}	1.0143×10^{-2}
1.4	1.1977	6.8080×10^{-2}	1.6042×10^{-2}	6.2419×10^{-2}	9.9309×10^{-3}
1.5	1.2129	6.5424×10^{-2}	1.6128×10^{-2}	5.9295×10^{-2}	9.8909×10^{-3}

$$a_j = -\bar{a}_j = \frac{\Delta t}{4 \Delta Z^2} \left\{ b \Delta Z - \sigma^2 \right\}$$

$$b_j = 1 + \frac{\Delta t}{2} \left\{ r + \frac{\sigma^2}{\Delta Z^2} \right\},$$

$$c_j = -\bar{c}_j = -\frac{\Delta t}{4 \Delta Z^2} \left\{ b \Delta Z + \sigma^2 \right\},$$

$$\bar{b}_j = 1 - \frac{\Delta t}{2} \left\{ r + \frac{\sigma^2}{\Delta Z^2} \right\}.$$

The method of using the finite-difference grid to compute option prices is identical to that already outlined Section 5.4.2, which solves the standard (non-logarithmic) Black–Scholes equation. Table 5.7 compares the results obtained with and without a logarithmic transformation.

5.4.5 The Log Transformation and Nonuniform Grids

In the previous section, we considered the use of a uniform grid to discretize the logarithmically transformed Black–Scholes equation,

$$\frac{\partial f}{\partial t} + b\frac{\partial f}{\partial Z} + \frac{\sigma^2}{2}\frac{\partial^2 f}{\partial Z^2} = rf, \qquad (5.4.56)$$

where

$$b = r - q - \frac{\sigma^2}{2} \quad \text{and} \quad Z = \log S.$$

Here, we will generalize these results and use a nonuniform grid to solve equation (5.4.56).

Our description will be very brief since most of the details have already been discussed in previous sections. Here, we are only concerned with the finite-difference approximation and derive the equations that need to be solved at each time step. Later, in Section 5.4.6, we will apply our results to solving a European double knockout barrier option.

The Finite-Difference Approximation

At the grid node (i, j), we have

$$\Delta Z_j^- = Z_j - Z_{j-1} \quad \text{and} \quad \Delta Z_j^+ = Z_j + 1 - Z_j.$$

Following Section 5.4.2, the first and second derivatives of f with respect to Z are

$$f''_{i+1,j} = \frac{2\left\{\Delta Z_j^+ f_{i+1,j-1} + \Delta Z_j^- f_{i+1,j+1} - \Delta Z_j^- f_{i+1,j} - \Delta Z_j^+ f_{i+1,j}\right\}}{(\Delta Z_j^+)^2 \Delta Z_j^- + (\Delta Z_j^-)^2 \Delta Z_j^+}$$

and

$$f'_{i+1,j} = \frac{(\Delta Z_j^-)^2 f_{i+1,j+1} + ((\Delta Z^+)^2 - (\Delta Z_j^-)^2) f_{i+1,j} - (\Delta Z_j^+)^2 f_{i+1,j-1}}{(\Delta Z_j^+)^2 \Delta Z_j^- + (\Delta Z_j^-)^2 \Delta Z^+}.$$

Then discretizing equation 3.186 in the *usual manner*, we obtain

$$\frac{f_{i+1,j} - f_{i,j}}{\Delta t} + b\left\{\Theta_m f'_{i+1,j} + \Theta_m^* f'_{i,j}\right\} + \frac{\sigma^2}{2}\left\{\Theta_m f''_{i+1,j} + \Theta_m^* f''_{i,j}\right\}$$
$$= r\left\{\Theta_m f_{i+1,j} + \Theta_m^* f_{i,j}\right\},$$

where $\Theta_m^* = 1 - \Theta_m$. Letting $D = (\Delta Z_j^+)^2 \Delta Z_j^- + (\Delta Z_j^-)^2 \Delta Z_j^+$, we obtain

$$r\Delta t (\Theta_m f_{i+1,j} + \Theta_m^* f_{i,j}) = f_{i+1,j} - f_{i,j} + \frac{b\Delta t \mathcal{A}_1}{D} + \frac{\sigma^2 \Delta t \mathcal{A}_2}{D}, \qquad (5.4.57)$$

where

$$\begin{aligned}
\mathcal{A}_1 &= \Theta_m \left[f_{i+1,j+1}(\Delta Z_j^-)^2 - f_{i+1,j-1}(\Delta Z_j^+)^2 - f_{i+1,j}\left\{(\Delta Z_j^-)^2 - (\Delta Z_j^+)^2\right\}\right] \\
&\quad + \Theta_m^* \left[f_{i,j+1}(\Delta Z_j^-)^2 - f_{i,j-1}(\Delta Z_j^+)^2 - f_{i,j}\left\{(\Delta Z_j^-)^2 - (\Delta Z_j^+)^2\right\}\right], \\
\mathcal{A}_2 &= \Theta_m \left[f_{i+1,j+1}\Delta Z_j^- + f_{i+1,j-1}\Delta Z_j^+ - f_{i+1,j}\left\{\Delta Z_j^- + \Delta Z_j^+\right\}\right] \\
&\quad + \Theta_m^* \left[f_{i,j+1}\Delta Z_j^- + f_{i,j-1}\Delta Z_j^+ - f_{i,j}\left\{\Delta Z_j^- + \Delta Z_j^+\right\}\right].
\end{aligned}$$

Collecting like terms, we obtain

$$\mathcal{B}_1 f_{i,j-1} + \mathcal{B}_2 f_{i,j} + \mathcal{B}_3 f_{i,j+1} + \mathcal{C}_1 f_{i+1,j-1} + \mathcal{C}_2 f_{i+1,j} + \mathcal{C}_3 f_{i+1,j+1} = 0,$$

where

$$\mathcal{B}_1 = \frac{-\Theta_m^* b\Delta t (\Delta Z_j^+)^2}{D} + \frac{\Theta_m^* \sigma^2 \Delta t \Delta Z_j^+}{D},$$

$$\mathcal{B}_2 = -1 - r\Delta t \Theta_m^* - \frac{\Theta_m^* \sigma^2 \Delta t (\Delta Z_j^- + \Delta Z_j^+)}{D} - \frac{\Theta_m^* b\Delta t \left\{(\Delta Z_j^-)^2 - (\Delta Z_j^+)^2\right\}}{D},$$

$$\mathcal{B}_3 = \frac{\Theta_m^* b\Delta t (\Delta Z_j^-)^2}{D} + \frac{\Theta_m^* \sigma^2 \Delta t \Delta Z_j^-}{D},$$

$$\mathcal{C}_1 = \frac{\Theta_m \sigma^2 \Delta t \Delta Z_j^+}{D} - \frac{\Theta_m b\Delta t (\Delta Z_j^+)^2}{D},$$

$$\mathcal{C}_2 = 1 - r\Delta t \Theta_m - \frac{\Theta_m b\Delta t \left\{(\Delta Z_j^-)^2 - (\Delta Z_j^+)^2\right\}}{D} - \frac{\Theta_m \sigma^2 \Delta t \left\{\Delta Z_j^- + \Delta Z_j^+\right\}}{D},$$

$$\mathcal{C}_3 = \frac{\Theta_m b\Delta t (\Delta Z_j^-)^2}{D} + \frac{\Theta_m \sigma^2 \Delta t \Delta Z_j^-}{D}.$$

If we rearrange, we have the following equation:

$$a_j f_{i,j-1} + b_j f_{i,j} + c_j f_{i,j+1} = \bar{a}_j f_{i+1,j-1} + \bar{b}_j f_{i+1,j} + \bar{c}_j f_{i+1,j+1}, \qquad (5.4.58)$$

where

$$a_j = (1 - \Theta_m)\Delta t \left\{ \frac{b(\Delta Z_j^+)^2}{D} - \frac{\sigma^2 \Delta Z_j^+}{D} \right\}, \qquad (5.4.59)$$

$$b_j = 1 + \Delta t(1 - \Theta_m)\left\{ r - \frac{\sigma^2(\Delta Z_j^- + \Delta Z_j^+)}{D} - \frac{b\left\{(\Delta Z_j^-)^2 - (\Delta Z_j^+)^2\right\}}{D} \right\}, \qquad (5.4.60)$$

$$c_j = (1 - \Theta_m)\Delta t \left\{ \frac{-b(\Delta Z_j^-)^2}{D} - \frac{\sigma^2 \Delta Z_j^-}{D} \right\}, \qquad (5.4.61)$$

$$\bar{a}_j = \Theta_m \Delta t \left\{ \frac{\sigma^2 \Delta Z_j^+}{D} - \frac{b(\Delta Z_j^+)^2}{D} \right\}, \tag{5.4.62}$$

$$\bar{b}_j = 1 - \Theta_m r \Delta t - \Theta_m \Delta t \left\{ \frac{b\left\{ (\Delta Z_j^-)^2 - (\Delta Z_j^+)^2 \right\}}{D} + \frac{\sigma^2 \left\{ \Delta Z_j^- + \Delta Z_j^+ \right\}}{D} \right\}, \tag{5.4.63}$$

$$\bar{c}_j = \Theta_m \Delta t \left\{ \frac{b(\Delta Z_j^-)^2}{D} + \frac{\sigma^2 \Delta Z_j^-}{D} \right\}. \tag{5.4.64}$$

The incorporation of boundary conditions and the solution of equation (5.4.58) is similar manner to that already discussed in Section 5.4.2. If further details are required, Code excerpt 5.19, which uses a nonuniform grid to solve the log transformed Black–Scholes equation, can be consulted.

When a uniform grid is used, $\Delta Z_j^+ = \Delta Z_j^- = \Delta Z$, and therefore,

$$D = (\Delta Z_j^+)^2 \Delta Z_j^- + (\Delta Z_j^-)^2 \Delta Z_j^+ = 2(\Delta Z)^3,$$

$$\frac{(\Delta Z_j^+)^2}{D} = \frac{(\Delta Z_j^-)^2}{D} = \frac{(\Delta Z)^2}{2(\Delta Z)^3} = \frac{1}{2 \Delta Z},$$

$$\frac{\Delta Z_j^+}{D} = \frac{\Delta Z_j^-}{D} = \frac{1}{2 \Delta Z^2}, \quad \text{and} \quad \frac{(\Delta Z_j^+)^2 - (\Delta Z_j^-)^2}{D} = 0.$$

In these circumstances,

$$a_j = \frac{(1 - \Theta_m) \Delta t}{2 \Delta Z^2} \left\{ b \Delta Z - \sigma^2 \right\},$$

$$b_j = 1 + \Delta t (1 - \Theta_m) \left\{ r - \frac{\sigma^2}{\Delta Z^2} \right\},$$

$$c_j = (1 - \Theta_m) \Delta t \left\{ \frac{-b}{2 \Delta Z} - \frac{\sigma^2}{2 \Delta Z^2} \right\},$$

$$\bar{a}_j = -\frac{\Theta_m \Delta t}{2 \Delta Z^2} \left\{ b \Delta Z - \sigma^2 \right\},$$

$$\bar{b}_j = 1 - \Theta_m \Delta t \left\{ r + \frac{\sigma^2}{\Delta Z^2} \right\},$$

$$\bar{c}_j = \frac{\Theta_m \Delta t}{2 \Delta Z^2} \left\{ b \Delta Z + \sigma^2 \right\},$$

which are the same as equations (5.4.50)–(5.4.55) in Section 5.4.4.

5.4.6 The Double Knockout Call Option

The purpose of this section is to provide an example which illustrates the benefits to be gained from using both the log transformed Black–Scholes equation and also a nonuniform grid.

The problem we will consider is the European double knockout call option with strike price E and expiry date T. This is a barrier option with both an upper barrier at B_U and a lower barrier at B_L. If, during the life of the option, the asset price either goes above the upper barrier or below the lower barrier, then the option becomes worthless. If, on the other hand, the asset price stays between the barriers, then the option is has value $\max(S_T - E, 0)$, where S_T is the asset price at time T.

This problem has been previously investigated by Boyle and Tian (1998), henceforth referred to as BT, who used an explicit finite-difference method

TABLE 5.8 Estimated Value of a European Double Knock Out Call Option. The Values in Column two were Computed by the Function dko_call, and those in Column Three are the Results Reported in Table 2 of Boyle and Tian (1998). The Model Parameters were Current Asset Price $S = 95.0$, Exercise Price $E = 100.0$, Volatility $\sigma = 0.25$, Maturity $\tau = 1.0$, Interest Rate $r = 0.1$, and Dividend Yield $q = 0.0$. The Upper Barrier Level is Set at 140.0 and the Lower Barrier is Set at 90.0. The Other Parameters used by the Function dko_call were nt = n, ns_below_S0 = $n/2$, ns_above_S0 = $n/2$, and $\Theta_m = 0.5$ (i.e., the Crank–Nicolson Method)

Time steps (n)	Estimated value	Boyle and Tian (1998)
50	1.4569	1.4238
100	1.4578	1.4437
200	1.4583	1.4495
300	1.4583	1.4524
400	1.4584	1.4542
500	1.4584	1.4553
600	1.4584	1.4557
700	1.4584	1.4559
800	1.4584	1.4563
900	1.4584	1.4565
1000	1.4584	1.4566
2000	1.4584	1.4576
3000	1.4584	1.4578
4000	1.4584	1.4580
5000	1.4584	1.4581

based on a modified trinomial lattice. The method we use here is based on the finite-difference equations given in Section 5.4.5, and all the results in Tables 5.8–5.12 were obtained by using the function `dko_call` which is provided in Code excerpt 5.20.

```
void dko_call(double lower_barrier, double upper_barrier, double theta_m,
        double S0, double sigma_array[], double sigma_times[], long n_sigma, double r,
        double opt_mat, double X, double *option_value, double greeks[], double q,
        long ns_below_S0, long ns_above_S0, long nt, long *iflag)
{
/* Input parameters:
   ==================
   lower_barrier          - the asset price corresponding to the lower barrier,
   upper_barrier          - the asset price corresponding to the upper barrier,
   theta_m                - the value of theta used for the finite difference method,
   S0                     - the current price of the underlying asset,
   sigma_array[]          - an array containing values of the volatility: sigma_array[0] is the
                            first value of the volatility,
                            sigma_array[1] is the second value of the volatility, etc..,
   sigma_times[]          - an array containing the times for different volatilities:
                            sigma_times[0] is the time corresponding to
                            the first volatility, sigma_times[1] is the time corresponding to
                            the second volatility, etc..,
   n_sigma                - the number of elements in sigma_array[], and sigma_times[],
   r                      - the interest rate,
   opt_mat                - the time to maturity,
   X                      - the strike price,
   q                      - the continuous dividend yield,
   ns_below_S0            - the number of asset intervals below the current price S0,
   ns_above_S0            - the number of asset intervals above the current price S0,
   nt                     - the number of time intervals.
   Output parameters:
   ==================
   option_value           - the value of the option,
   greeks[]               - the hedge statistics output as follows: greeks[0] is gamma,
                            greeks[1] is delta, and greeks[2] is theta,
   iflag                  - an error indicator.
*/
    double *a,*b,*c,*vals,*a1,*b1,*c1,*opt_vals,*rhs,*z,*delta,*gamma,*work,*u;
    double dt,dz,dz1,dz2,zmax,zmin;
    long i,j;
    double tmp,t2,t4,dt2;
    long ind=0,n1,n2,ns1;
    double ds,log_asset,sig2,alpha,v2,b_fac,temp[4];
    double zero = 0.0;
    long barrier_index,ind2;
    double dz_shift,time_step,log_barrier_level1,log_barrier_level2;
    double temp1, temp2, ds_plus, ds_minus, bb, D;
    double curr_time;

    if (S0 >= upper_barrier) printf ("ERROR current asset price is greater than upper_barrier \n");
    if (lower_barrier >= S0) printf("ERROR lower barrier is greater than current asset price \n");
    if (S0 <= zero) printf ("ERROR asset price is not > 0 \n");
    if (upper_barrier <= lower_barrier) printf("ERROR upper_barrier must be > lower_barrier \n");
    log_asset = log(S0);
    log_barrier_level1 = log(lower_barrier);
    log_barrier_level2 = log(upper_barrier);
    dz1 = (log_asset-log_barrier_level1)/(double)ns_below_S0;
    n1 = ns_below_S0;
/* Include 5 extra points above the asset price so that don't get discontinuity in grid spacing
   which may adversely affect the computation of the greeks */
    n2 = ns_above_S0 + 5;
    dz_shift = dz1*5.0; /* shift caused by extra 5 grid points */
    dz2 = (log_barrier_level2-log_asset-dz_shift)/(double)ns_above_S0;
    dt = opt_mat/(double)nt;     /* time interval size */
    time_step = dt;
    --n2;
    ns1 = n1+n2+2;
/* Set up the RHS and LHS coefficients a[], b[] and c[] are the LHS coefficients for the unknown option
   values (time step j) a1[], b1[] and c1[] are the values of the RHS coefficients for the known option prices
   (time step j+1). Note: a1, b1 and c1 are used to form the RHS vector rhs[] of the tridiagonal system. */

/* Allocate the required arrays (all of size (ns1+2): a,b,c,a1,b1,c1,opt_vals,vals, rhs,z,delta,gamma,work,u */

/* Set up the RHS and LHS coefficients a[], b[] and c[] are the LHS coefficients
   for the unknown option values (time step j) a1[], b1[] and c1[] are the values of the
```

Code excerpt 5.20 Function to compute the value and Greeks of a European double knock out call option using a nonuniform grid and a logarithmic transformation.

```
                RHS coefficients for the known option prices (time step j+1). Note: a1, b1 and c1 are used to form the RHS
                vector rhs[] of the tridiagonal system. */
   /* Set grid line asset values, set one grid spacing to align with the asset price, then won't have to
      interpolate to get the option value */
                z[n1] = log_asset;
                for (i = 1; i <=n1; ++i) /* This should be the fine mesh */
                    z[n1-i] = log_asset - (double)i*dz1;
                for (i = 1; i <= 5; ++i) /* Include 5 extra fine mesh points here */
                    z[n1+i] = log_asset + (double)i*dz1;
                for (i = 6; i <= n2+2; ++i) { /* The coarse mesh */
                    j = i - 5;
                    z[n1+i] = z[n1+5] + (double)j*dz2;
                }
   /* Set option values at maturity (for a call). Note : opt_vals[0] and opt_vals[ns1-1] are the lower and upper
      (put/call) option price boundary values. */
                for( i=1; i<ns1; ++i ) {
                    opt_vals[i] = MAX(exp(z[i])-X, zero);
                }
                opt_vals[0] = zero;
                opt_vals[ns1-1] = zero;
                tmp = 1.0-theta_m;  /* 1 - theta (for theta method) */
                curr_time = -1.0;
                ind2 = n_sigma - 1;
                for( j=nt-1; j>=-2; --j) { /* Iterate from maturity to current time  */
                    if ((ind2 >= 0) && (curr_time <= sigma_times[ind2])) {
                        sig2 = sigma_array[ind2]*sigma_array[ind2];
                        t2 = time_step/2.0;
                        bb = r - q - (sig2/2.0);
                        --ind2;
                        for( i=1; i<=ns1-2; ++i) { /* Assign elements of the (ns1-2)*(ns1-2) tridiagonal matrix */
                            ds_plus = z[i+1]-z[i];
                            ds_minus = z[i] - z[i-1];
                            D = ((ds_plus*ds_plus*ds_minus) + (ds_minus*ds_minus*ds_plus));
                            temp1 = tmp*time_step/D;
                            a[i] = temp1*(bb*ds_plus*ds_plus) -temp1*ds_plus*(sig2);
                            temp1 = theta_m*time_step/D;
                            a1[i] = temp1*ds_plus*(sig2)-temp1*(bb*ds_plus*ds_plus);
                            temp1 = (ds_minus*ds_minus)/D;
                            temp2 = ds_minus/D;
                            c[i]  = -time_step*tmp*(temp1*bb+(sig2*temp2));
                            c1[i] = time_step*theta_m*(temp1*bb+(sig2*temp2));
                            temp1 = ((ds_minus*ds_minus) - (ds_plus*ds_plus))/D;
                            temp2 = (ds_minus+ds_plus)/D;
                            b[i] = 1.0+time_step*tmp*(r+(bb*temp1)+(sig2)*temp2);
                            b1[i] = 1.0-time_step*theta_m*(r+(bb*temp1)+(sig2)*temp2);
                        }
                        u[1] = b[1];
                        if (u[1] == zero) printf ("ERROR in array u \n");
                          for( i=2; i <=ns1-2; ++i) {
                            u[i] = b[i] - a[i]*c[i-1]/u[i-1];
                            if (u[i] == zero) printf ("ERROR in array u \n");
                        }
                    }
                    curr_time = j*dt;
   /* Set up the rhs of equation for the theta method */
                    for(i=2; i<=ns1-3; ++i)
                        rhs[i] = a1[i]*opt_vals[i-1]+b1[i]*opt_vals[i]+c1[i]*opt_vals[i+1];
   /* Incorporate the boundary conditions1 at the upper/lower asset value boundaries */
                    rhs[1] = (a1[1]-a1[1])*opt_vals[0]+ b1[1]*opt_vals[1]+c1[1]*opt_vals[2];
                    rhs[ns1-2] = a1[ns1-2]*opt_vals[ns1-3]+b1[ns1-2]*opt_vals[ns1-2]+(c1[ns1-2]-c[ns1-2])*opt_vals[ns1-1];
   /* Solve the lower triangular system Ly = b, where y is stored in array work[]. Compute the elements
      of L from those of U, l[i] = a[i]/u[i-1]. */
                    work[1] = rhs[1];
                    for( i=2; i<=ns1-2; ++i ) {
                      work[i] = rhs[i] - a[i]*work[i-1]/u[i-1];
                    }
   /* Solve the upper (ns1-2)*(ns1-2) triangular system Ux = y (where x = vold) */
                    opt_vals[ns1-2] = work[ns1-2]/u[ns1-2];
                    for( i = ns1-2; i >= 1; --i )
                        opt_vals[i] = (work[i] - c[i]*opt_vals[i+1])/u[i];
                    if (j==0) {
                        for (i=0; i < ns1; ++i)
                            vals[i] = opt_vals[i];
                    }
   /* Store option values so that can compute theta */
                    if ((j==1)||(j==2)||(j==-1)||(j==-2)) {
                        temp[ind] = opt_vals[n1];
                        ++ind;
                    }
                }
                if (greeks) {
   /* Compute gamma and delta (4th order accuracy) */
                    greeks[1] = (-vals[n1+2]+8.0*vals[n1+1]-8.0*vals[n1-1]+vals[n1-2])/(12.0*dz1);
   /* Compute gamma (4th order accuracy) - use chain rule to obtain derivative wrt S */
                    greeks[0] = (-vals[n1+2]+16.0*vals[n1+1]-30.0*vals[n1]+16.0*vals[n1-1]-vals[n1-2])/(12.0*dz1*dz1);
```

Code excerpt 5.20 (*Continued*).

```
        greeks[0] = greeks[0]-greeks[1];
        greeks[0] = greeks[0]/(S0*S0);
        greeks[1] = greeks[1]/S0;
/* Compute theta (4th order accuracy) */
        greeks[2] = (-temp[0]+8.0*temp[1]-8.0*temp[2]+temp[3])/(12.0*dt);
        /* could also compute theta as: greeks[2] = (-temp[0]+4.0*temp[1]-3.0*vals[n1])/(2.0*dt); */
        }
        *option_value = vals[n1];
}
```

Code excerpt 5.20 (*Continued*).

Inspection of the results shows that the finite-difference grid method has both greater accuracy and faster convergence than the method proposed by BT. The key to the accuracy achieved by dko_call is a combination of the following:

TABLE 5.9 The Estimated Values of European Down and Out Call Options Calculated by the Function dko_call. The Fixed Model Parameters were Exercise Price E = 100.0, Volatility σ = 0.25, Maturity τ = 1.0, Interest Rate r = 0.1, Dividend Yield q = 0.0, and the Lower Barrier is Set at 90.0. The Other Parameters used by the Function dko_call were nt = n, ns_below_S0 = $n/2$, ns_above_S0 = $n/2$, upper_barrier = 1000.0, lower_barrier = 90.0, and Θ_m = 0.5 (i.e., the Crank–Nicolson Method)

	Stock price					
Time steps	92	91	90.5	90.4	90.3	90.2
50	2.5652	1.3046	0.6588	0.5282	0.3971	0.2653
100	2.5221	1.2816	0.6466	0.5182	0.3894	0.2601
200	2.5104	1.2758	0.6435	0.5157	0.3875	0.2588
300	2.5080	1.2747	0.6429	0.5152	0.3871	0.2585
400	2.5072	1.2743	0.6427	0.5150	0.3869	0.2584
500	2.5069	1.2742	0.6426	0.5149	0.3869	0.2584
600	2.5067	1.2741	0.6425	0.5149	0.3868	0.2583
700	2.5066	1.2740	0.6425	0.5149	0.3868	0.2583
800	2.5065	1.2740	0.6424	0.5148	0.3868	0.2583
900	2.5065	1.2739	0.6424	0.5148	0.3868	0.2583
1000	2.5064	1.2739	0.6424	0.5148	0.3868	0.2583
2000	2.5063	1.2738	0.6424	0.5148	0.3868	0.2583
Closed form	2.5063	1.2738	0.6424	0.5148	0.3868	0.2583

TABLE 5.10 The Estimated Values of European Down and Out Call Options as Calculated by the Function dko_call. The Fixed Parameters used were Exercise Price $E = 100.0$, Volatility $\sigma = 0.25$, Maturity $\tau = 1.0$, Interest Rate $r = 0.1$, Dividend Yield $q = 0.0$, and the Lower Barrier is Set at 90.0. The Other Parameters used by the Function dko_call were nt $= n$, ns_below_S0 $= n/2$, ns_above_S0 $= n/2$, upper_barrier $= 1000.0$, Lower_barrier $= 90.0$, and $\Theta_m = 0.0$ (i.e., the Implicit Method)

			Stock price			
Time steps	92	91	90.5	90.4	90.3	90.2
50	2.5572	1.3005	0.6567	0.5266	0.3958	0.2645
100	2.5181	1.2796	0.6455	0.5174	0.3888	0.2597
200	2.5084	1.2748	0.6429	0.5153	0.3872	0.2586
300	2.5067	1.2741	0.6425	0.5149	0.3869	0.2584
400	2.5062	1.2738	0.6424	0.5148	0.3868	0.2583
500	2.5061	1.2738	0.6424	0.5148	0.3868	0.2583
600	2.5061	1.2737	0.6423	0.5148	0.3867	0.2583
700	2.5060	1.2737	0.6423	0.5147	0.3867	0.2583
800	2.5060	1.2747	0.6423	0.5147	0.3867	0.2583
900	2.5060	1.2737	0.6423	0.5147	0.3867	0.2583
1000	2.5060	1.2737	0.6423	0.5147	0.3867	0.2583
2000	2.5061	1.2737	0.6423	0.5147	0.3867	0.2583
Closed form	2.5063	1.2738	0.6424	0.5148	0.3868	0.2583

- The logarithmic transformation of the Black–Scholes equation.
- The ability to place a grid line at both the upper barrier B_U and also at the lower boundary B_L.
- The use of a weighted Θ_m finite-difference scheme, $0 \leq \Theta_m \leq 1$, instead of the numerically unstable explicit finite-difference method used by a trinomial lattice, which in *our notation* (see Section 5.4.2) is equivalent to $\Theta_m = 1$.

It should be mentioned that the function dko_call could, without much difficulty, be modified to deal with the following:

- American double knockout call options,
- European double knockout put options,
- American double knockout put options,

TABLE 5.11 The Estimated Values of European Double Knock Out Call Options Computed by the Function dko_call. In Column 2 and Column 3 the Values Given in Boyle and Tian (1998), Table 5, are Shown for Comparison. The Fixed Model Parameters were Exercise Price E = 100.0, Volatility σ = 0.25, Dividend Yield q = 0.0, Maturity τ = 1.0, Interest Rate r = 0.1, the Lower Barrier is Set at 90.0, and the Upper Barrier is Set at 140.0. The Other Parameters used by the Function dko_call were nt = n, ns_below_S0 = $n/2$, ns_above_S0 = $n/2$, and Θ_m = 0.5 (i.e., the Crank–Nicolson Method)

	Stock price					
Time steps	92	91	90.5	90.4	90.3	90.2
50	0.6251 (0.6184)	0.3189 (0.3177)	0.1610	0.1290	0.0969	0.0647
100	0.6260 (0.6212)	0.3194 (0.3184)	0.1613	0.1292	0.0971	0.0649
200	0.6263 (0.6228)	0.3196 (0.3186)	0.1613	0.1293	0.0972	0.0649
300	0.6263 (0.6236)	0.3196 (0.3187)	0.1613	0.1293	0.0972	0.0649
400	0.6263 (0.6242)	0.3196 (0.3189)	0.1613	0.1293	0.0972	0.0649
500	0.6263 (0.6252)	0.3196 (0.3190)	0.1613	0.1293	0.0972	0.0649
600	0.6263 (0.6253)	0.3196 (0.3191)	0.1613	0.1293	0.0972	0.0649
700	0.6263 (0.6253)	0.3196 (0.3191)	0.1613	0.1293	0.0972	0.0649
800	0.6263 (0.6255)	0.3196 (0.3192)	0.1613	0.1293	0.0972	0.0649
900	0.6263 (0.6256)	0.3196 (0.3192)	0.1613	0.1293	0.0972	0.0649
1000	0.6263 (0.6255)	0.3196 (0.3192)	0.1613	0.1293	0.0972	0.0649
2000	0.6263 (0.6260)	0.3196 (0.3195)	0.1613	0.1293	0.0972	0.0649

and also a range of other variations which may include lockout periods, rebates, etc. In particular, options with time varying barrier levels can be dealt with by using grid lines to locate the barrier position at each time instant.

TABLE 5.12 The Estimated Greeks for European Double Knock Out Call Options Computed by the Function dko_call. The Fixed Model Parameters: the Exercise Price $E = 100.0$, Volatility $\sigma = 0.25$, Dividend Yield $q = 0.0$, Maturity $\tau = 1.0$, Interest Rate $r = 0.1$, the Lower Barrier is Set at 90.0, and the Upper Barrier is Set at 140.0. The Other Parameters used by the Function dko_call were nt = 200, ns_below_S0 = 100, ns_above_S0 = 100, and $\Theta_m = 0.5$ (i.e., the Crank–Nicolson Method). The Results for $\Theta_m = 0.0$ (i.e., the Implicit Method) are Shown in Brackets, see Table 6, Boyle and Tian (1998)

Asset price	Gamma	Delta	Theta
95.0	-0.0165 (-0.0166)	0.2536 (0.2551)	2.3982 (2.3928)
92.0	-0.0141 (-0.0141)	0.2998 (0.3016)	1.0268 (1.0242)
91.0	-0.0129 (-0.0130)	0.3133 (0.3151)	0.5237 (0.5224)
90.5	-0.0123 (-0.0123)	0.3196 (0.3215)	0.2643 (0.2636)
90.4	-0.0121 (-0.0122)	0.3208 (0.3227)	0.2119 (0.2113)
90.3	-0.0120 (-0.0121)	0.3221 (0.3239)	0.1592 (0.1588)
90.2	-0.0119 (-0.0119)	0.3233 (0.3251)	0.1063 (0.1060)

5.5 PRICING AMERICAN OPTIONS USING A STOCHASTIC LATTICE

In this section, we consider the use of Monte Carlo simulation and stochastic lattices to price American options. Information on the use of Monte Carlo simulation to value both single asset and multi-asset European options is provided in Chapters 4 and 6. The main difficulty in using simulation to value American options is the need to incorporate optimal early exercise policies. The standard simulation algorithms for valuing European contracts are *forward in time*. That is each price path, which contributes to the value of the option, is generated by stepping forward from current time, t, to option maturity, $t + \tau$, where τ is the duration of the option. For instance if there are n equispaced time steps of size Δt and only one underlying asset, then we use the asset values $S_i, i = 0, \ldots, n$, where S_i corresponds to the asset value at time the ith time instant, t_i, and $t_0 = t$. Here, S_{i+1} is generated from the previous asset value S_i as follows:

$$\frac{S_{i+1}}{S_i} = dS_i, \quad \text{for } i = 0, \ldots, n - 1, \tag{5.5.1}$$

where dS_i is a random variate taken from a *given* distribution. When S_i follows GBM, we have from equation (2.3.11) that

$$\frac{S_{i+1}}{S_i} = \exp\left\{\left(r - \sigma_i^2/2\right)\Delta t + \sigma_i dX_i\right\}, \quad i = 0,\ldots,n-1, \qquad (5.5.2)$$

where $dX_i \sim N(0,\Delta t)$ and the usual definitions are used for σ_i and r.

For European exotic options (such as time dependent barrier options), the value of a particular price path will depend on the asset values $S_i, i = 0,\ldots,n$. This is not true of European vanilla options whose value only depends on S_n, the underlying asset price at option maturity. The Monte Carlo approximation to the value of a European option is thus

$$f = \frac{\sum_{j=1}^{nsim} p_j(n_j)}{nsim},$$

where $nsim$ is the number of simulations used, n_j is the number of time steps associated with the jth price path, and $p_j(n_j)$ is the value of the jth price path. In the case of European vanilla options, we can use $n_j = 1, j = 1,\ldots,nsim$; the accuracy obviously improves with increasing $nsim$.

The valuation of American style options, which include the possibility of early exercise, is more complicated. In Chapter 5, we described the use of binomial lattices to price American options when the underlying asset price process is GBM. Dynamic programming was used and the option prices were computed by working backwards in time through the lattice. The application of Monte Carlo methods for pricing American options is described in Tilley (1993), Barraquand and Martineau (1995), and also Boyle et al. (1997). Here, we will outline the stochastic lattice approach discussed in Broadie and Glasserman (1997), where both a high estimator and a low estimator of the American option value are calculated. Since both of these biased estimators converge (with increasing number of simulations and lattice nodes) to the true option value, we will only consider how to compute the high estimator, θ_H. We summarize the approach as follows:

- Set the parameters.
- Generate the lattice asset prices.
- Compute the lattice option prices.
- Compute the Monte Carlo estimate.

We will now consider each of these steps in more detail.

Set the Parameters

First we set the simulation parameters, that is, $nsim$ is the number of lattice simulations, b is the number of branches per lattice node, and d is the number of time instants in the lattice. Note: This definition of d here is different from that used in the original paper by Broadie and Glasserman (1997), where d is defined as the number of time steps in the lattice.

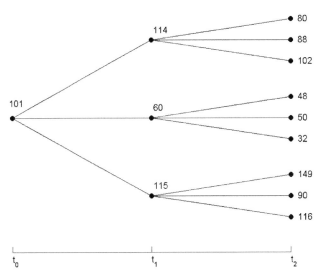

FIGURE 5.9 An example showing the asset prices generated for a stochastic lattice with three branches per node and two time steps, that is, $b = 3$ and $d = 3$. The current asset value, 101, is at time t_0, and the asset values at option maturity are at time t_2.

Generate the Lattice Asset Prices

Next we generate the asset prices for the pth stochastic lattice. Since the lattice is non-recombining at the i lattice time instant, there are b^i nodes/asset prices. This contrasts with the binomial lattice of Chapter 5 where the asset prices at a given time step are arranged in ascending order, that is, S_i^j increases with increasing j. We will denote the jth value at the ith time step by S_i^j. For example, in Fig. 5.9, where $b = 3$ and $d = 3$, we have for the first time step

$$S_1^1 = 115, S_1^2 = 60, \text{ and } S_1^3 = 114$$

and for the second time step

$$S_2^1 = 116, S_2^2 = 90, S_2^3 = 149, \dots, S_2^7 = 102, S_2^8 = 88, S_2^9 = 80.$$

The kth asset price at the ith time step, S_i^k then generates the following asset prices at the $(i + 1)$th time step,

$$\frac{S_{i+1}^{(k-1)b+j}}{S_i^k} = dS^j, \quad j = 1, \dots, b, \ k = 1, \dots, b^i,$$

where dS^j is, as before, a random variate from a *given* distribution. When S_i follows GBM, we therefore have

$$\frac{S_{i+1}^{(k-1)b+j}}{S_i^k} = \exp\left\{\left(r - \sigma_i^2/2\right) \Delta t + \sigma_i dX_i\right\}, \quad j = 1, \dots, b, \ k = 1, \dots, b^i.$$

Compute the Lattice Option Prices

The method used to compute the option values is *similar* to that used by the binomial lattice. The main difference is that there are now b branches per node instead of two. The option values are computed by starting at the lattice terminal nodes and then iterating backwards. Here, we denote the kth option value at the ith time step by f_i^k.

The option values at the terminal nodes, time instant t_{d-1}, are computed in the usual manner. For a put, we have

$$f_{d-1}^k = \text{MAX}(E - S_{d-1}^k, 0), \quad k = 1, \ldots, b^{d-1},$$

where E is the exercise price.

The option values at the $(i-1)$th time step are computed from those at the ith time step as follows:

$$f_{i-1}^k = \text{MAX}(g_{i-1}^k, h_{i-1}^k),$$

where

$$h_{i-1}^k = \frac{\exp(-r\Delta t)}{b} \sum_{j=1}^{b} f_i^{(k-1)b+j}$$

and

$$g_{i-1}^k = \text{MAX}(E - S_{i-1}^k, 0).$$

The option value for the pth stochastic lattice is therefore

$$\theta_H^p = f_0^1 = \frac{\exp(-r\Delta t)}{b} \sum_{j=1}^{b} f_1^j.$$

Figure 5.10 shows the option values for an American call with strike price $E = 100$ and interest rate $r = 0$, when the lattice asset prices in Fig. 5.9 are been used. To make things as clear as possible, we will show how the value of each node is computed.

Terminal nodes

The option values at the terminal nodes are the following:

$f_2^1 = \max(116 - 100, 0) = 16$, $f_2^2 = \max(90 - 100, 0) = 0$, $f_2^3 = \max(149 - 100, 0) = 49$,

$f_2^4 = \max(32 - 100, 0) = 0$, $f_2^5 = \max(50 - 100, 0) = 0$, $f_2^6 = \max(48 - 100, 0) = 0$,

$f_2^7 = \max(102 - 100, 0) = 2$, $f_2^8 = \max(88 - 100, 0) = 0$, $f_2^9 = \max(80 - 100, 0) = 0$.

Time step 1

Here, we have

$g_1^1 = \max(115 - 100, 0) = 15$, $g_1^2 = \max(60 - 100, 0) = 0$, $g_1^3 = \max(114 - 100, 0) = 14$.

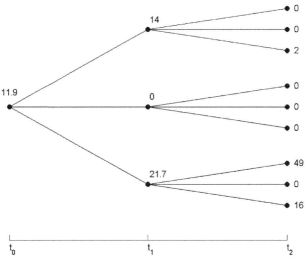

FIGURE 5.10 The option prices for the $b = 3$ and $d = 3$ lattice in Fig. 5.9 corresponding to an American put with strike $E = 100$ and interest rate $r = 0$. The option values at the lattice nodes are computed backwards in time from the payoffs at maturity, t_2 to the current time t_0; the value of the option is 11.9.

Since $r = 0$, we have $\exp(-r\Delta t) = 1$ which gives

$$h_1^1 = \frac{1}{3}\left\{f_2^1 + f_2^2 + f_2^3\right\} = \frac{1}{3}\{16 + 0 + 49\} = 21.7,$$

$$h_1^2 = \frac{1}{3}\left\{f_2^4 + f_2^5 + f_2^6\right\} = \frac{1}{3}\{0 + 0 + 0\} = 0,$$

$$h_1^3 = \frac{1}{3}\left\{f_2^7 + f_2^8 + f_2^9\right\} = \frac{1}{3}\{2 + 0 + 0\} = 0.66.$$

The option values are then computed as follows:

$$f_1^1 = \max(h_1^1, g_1^1) = \max(21.7, 15) = 21.7,$$

$$f_1^2 = \max(h_1^2, g_1^2) = \max(0, 0) = 0,$$

$$f_1^3 = \max(h_1^3, g_1^3) = \max(0.66, 14.0) = 14.0.$$

Time step 0

Here,

$$g_0^1 = \max(101 - 100, 0) = 1, \quad \text{and}$$

$$h_0^1 = \frac{1}{3}\left\{f_1^1 + f_1^2 + f_1^3\right\} = \frac{1}{3}\{21.7 + 0 + 0.66\} = 11.9.$$

The final value of the option is for this particular lattice is therefore

$$f_1^1 = \max(h_0^1, g_0^1) = \max(11.9, 1) = 11.9.$$

Compute the Monte Carlo Estimate

The Monte Carlo estimate, θ_H, is computed as the average of $\theta_H^p, p = 1, \ldots, nsim$, where $nsim$ is the number of simulations,

$$\theta_H = \frac{\sum_{i=1}^{nsim} \theta_H^i}{nsim}.$$

Below, in Code excerpt 5.21, we provide a computer program which prices single asset American put and call options using a stochastic lattice. The method used by the program is the *depth first* procedure outlined in Broadie and Glasserman (1997), which has the advantage that the memory requirements are only of order $b \times d$; as before, b is the number of branches per node and d is the number of time intervals.

Here, it is assumed the underlying asset follows GBM and the function normal(M, S) is used to generate a normal distribution with mean M and standard deviation S. We can therefore check the accuracy of the simulation with that obtained by a closed form solution which assumes a lognormal asset distribution, in this case the formula in Geske and Johnson (1984).

However, the real power of this method is when the underlying asset follows a more realistic process which is non-Gaussian and time varying. The only modification to the code is to replace the call to normal with that of another probability distribution and supply the time varying parameters to it.

```
// Stochastic lattice for computing the value of American and European options via Monte Carlo simulation.
// Here we assume that the asset prices have a lognormal distribution, and so generate
// normal variates; this assumption can easily be removed.
 void __cdecl main()
 {
   long i,j,jj,is_put,is_american,w[200],num_simulations,b,d,seed;
   double T,time_step,sqrt_time_step,opt_value,pay_off,log_fac,asset_price;
   double temp,opt_val,hold,sum_opt_val,disc;
   double tot_opt_vals, X, drift_term, std_term, S0, q, r, sigma, zero = 0.0;
   double v[200][60], opt_v[200][60];

   printf("Stochastic lattice for pricing European and American options \n");
   is_put = 1;       // If is_put == 0 then a call option, otherwise a put option
   T = 1.0;          // The time to maturity of the option
   is_american = 1;  // If is_american  == 0 then an European option, otherwise an American option
   sigma = 0.2;      // The volatility of the underlying asset
   X = 110.0;        // The strike price
   S0 = 100.0;       // The current price of the underlying asset
   r = 0.1;          // The risk free interest rate
   q = 0.05;         // The continuous dividend yield
   d = 4;            // The number of time steps, the number time intervals = d - 1
   b = 50;           // The number of branches per node in the lattice
   time_step = T/(double)(d-1); // time step = T/(number of time intervals)
   sqrt_time_step = sqrt(time_step);
   disc = exp(-r*time_step); // The discount factor between time steps
   std_term = sigma*sqrt(time_step); // The standard deviation of each normal variate generated
   drift_term = (r - q - sigma*sigma*0.5)*time_step; // The mean value of each normal variate generated
   seed = 111;       // The seed for the random number generator
   srand(seed);
   tot_opt_vals = zero;
   num_simulations = 100;
   for (jj = 1; jj <= num_simulations; ++jj) {
     v[1][1] = S0;
     w[1] = 1;
     asset_price = S0;
     for (j = 2; j <= d; ++j) {
       w[j] = 1;
       log_fac = normal(drift_term,std_term); // A normal variate:mean==drift_term, standard deviation==std_term
```

Code excerpt 5.21 A computer program which uses a stochastic lattice to value American and European options.

```
        asset_price = asset_price*exp(log_fac); // Compute the new asset price: assuming a lognormal distribution
        v[1][j] = asset_price;
    }
    j = d;
    while (j > 0) {
        if ((j == d) && (w[j] < b)) { // CASE 1::Terminal node, set asset prices
        for b branches, and option values for b-1 branches
            if (is_put ) {
                pay_off = MAX (X - v[w[j]][j],zero);
            }
            else {
                pay_off = MAX (v[w[j]][j]-X,zero);
            }
            opt_v[w[j]][j] = pay_off;
            asset_price = v[w[j-1]][j-1];
            log_fac = normal(drift_term,std_term);
            v[w[j]+1][j] = asset_price*exp(log_fac);
            w[j] = w[j] + 1;
        }
        else if ((j == d) && (w[j] == b)) { // CASE 2::Terminal node, set option value for last branch
            if (is_put) {
                pay_off = MAX (X - v[w[j]][j],zero);
            }
            else {
                pay_off = MAX (v[w[j]][j]-X,zero);
            }
            opt_v[w[j]][j] = pay_off;
            w[j] = 0;
            j = j - 1;
        }
        else if ((j < d) && (w[j] < b)) { // CASE 3::Internal node, calculate option value for node
        (parent wrt to cases 1 & 2)
            sum_opt_val = zero;              // Also generate a new terminal node and set asset values.
            for (i = 1; i <= b; ++i) {
                sum_opt_val += opt_v[i][j+1];
            }
            temp = sum_opt_val/(double)b;
            hold = temp*disc;
            if (is_american) { // An American option
                if (is_put) {
                    pay_off = MAX(X-v[w[j]][j],zero); // pay off for a put option
                }
                else {
                    pay_off = MAX(v[w[j]][j]-X,zero);  // pay off for a call option
                }
                opt_val = MAX(pay_off,hold);
            }
            else { // A European option
                opt_val = hold;
            }
            opt_v[w[j]][j] = opt_val;
            if (j > 1) {
                asset_price = v[w[j-1]][j-1];
                log_fac = normal(drift_term,std_term);
                v[w[j]+1][j] = asset_price*exp(log_fac);
                w[j] = w[j] + 1;
                for (i = j + 1; i <= d; ++i) { // Generate a new terminal node
                    log_fac = normal(drift_term,std_term);
                    asset_price = asset_price*exp(log_fac);
                    v[1][i] = asset_price;
                    w[i] = 1;
                }
                j = d;
            }
            else {
                j = 0;
            }
        }
        else if ((j < d) && (w[j] == b)) { // CASE 4::Internal node, calculate the option value for the last branch
            sum_opt_val = zero;
            for (i = 1; i <= b; ++i) {
                sum_opt_val += opt_v[i][j+1];
            }
            temp = sum_opt_val/(double)b;
            hold = temp*disc;
            if (is_american) { // An American option
                if (is_put) {
                    pay_off = MAX(X - v[w[j]][j],zero); // pay off for a put option
                }
                else {
                    pay_off = MAX(v[w[j]][j]-X,zero); // pay off for a call option
                }
                opt_val = MAX(pay_off,hold);
            }
            else { // A European option
```

Code excerpt 5.21 (*Continued*).

```
      opt_val = hold;
    }
    opt_v[w[j]][j] = opt_val;
    w[j] = 0;
    j = j - 1;
    }
  }
  tot_opt_vals = tot_opt_vals + opt_v[1][1]; // Sum the option values for each simulation
  }
  opt_value = tot_opt_vals/(double)num_simulations; // Compute the average option value
  printf ("The estimated option value = %12.4f\n", opt_value);
}
```

Code excerpt 5.21 (*Continued*).

In Table 5.13, we present computed values of an American put option with maturity τ that can only be exercised at the following four times: $t, t + \tau/3, t + 2\tau/3$, and $t + \tau$, where t is the current time.

The column labelled MC_{50}^{100} are the results obtained using 100 simulations of a stochastic lattice with 50 branches per node, and the column labelled MC_{250}^{1}

TABLE 5.13 American Put Options Values, Computed using the Stochastic Lattice Given in Code excerpt 5.21, with Four the Exercise Times $t, t+\tau/3, t+2\tau/3$, and $t + \tau$. The Option Parameters used were $r = 0.1, q = 0.05, \tau = 1.0, \sigma = 0.2$, and $S = 100.0$. The Column Labelled MC_{50}^{100} Refers to the Results Obtained using $d = 4, b = 50, num\_simulations = 100$, and the Column Labelled MC_{250}^{1} Refers to the Results Obtained using $d = 4, b = 50, num\_simulations = 1$. The *true* Values are those Given in Broadie *et. al* (1997) and were Computed with the Formula in Geske and Johnson (1984). The Absolute Error, $ABS(stochastic\_lattice\_value - true\_value)$, is Given in Brackets. The Last Column Gives the Values Computed using an Accurate (6000 time step) Binomial Lattice

X	MC_{50}^{100}	MC_{250}^{1}	True	Binomial lattice
70	0.118 (0.003)	0.123 (0.002)	0.121	0.126
80	0.663 (0.007)	0.672 (0.002)	0.670	0.696
90	2.317 (0.014)	2.307 (0.004)	2.303	2.389
100	5.830 (0.099)	5.720 (0.011)	5.731	5.928
110	11.564 (0.223)	11.361 (0.020)	11.341	11.770
120	20.205 (0.205)	20.000 (0.000)	20.000	20.052
130	30.054 (0.054)	30.000 (0.000)	30.000	30.000

are the values computed using a single stochastic lattice with 250 branches per node. These values demonstrate that one high accuracy stochastic lattice can give better results than using the average of 100 lower accuracy lattices. In the last column, we present the results obtained using a 6000-step binomial lattice in which it is possible to exercise the option at every time step. It can be seen that the binomial option values are higher than the *true* values, which only permit the option to be exercised at four distinct times. This is in agreement with the extra flexibility present in the binomial lattice.

5.6 SELECTED EXERCISES

1. Write a program to price a Bermudan option – in contrast to American options these can only be exercised at specific times.
2. Price an option with time varying barriers – place grid lines at the barrier positions.
3. Show that a binomial lattice with equal jump probability ($p = 1/2$) has

$$d = \exp(rdt) \left\{ 1 - \sqrt{\exp(\sigma^2 dt) - 1} \right\}$$

and

$$u = \exp(rdt) \left\{ 1 + \sqrt{\exp(\sigma^2 dt) - 1} \right\}.$$

4. Show that the lattice for $Z_t = \log(S_t)$ is characterized by

$$\Delta Z = \sqrt{\sigma^2 \Delta t + \left(r - \frac{\sigma^2}{2} \right)^2 \Delta t^2}$$

and

$$p = \frac{1}{2} \left\{ 1 + \left(r - \frac{\sigma^2}{2} \right) \left(\frac{\Delta t}{\Delta Z} \right) \right\}.$$

5. Price an option with a strike that depends on whether the asset price is above or below a given barrier level.

Chapter 6

Multi-asset Options

6.1 INTRODUCTION

In this section we consider the valuation of multi-asset, *basket*, options within the Black–Scholes pricing framework. These options will be priced using the following techniques:

- Analytic methods.
- Monte Carlo methods.
- Multidimensional lattices.

Analytic methods can be useful for pricing multi-asset European options which have a known *closed form* solution. They are particularly appropriate for low-dimensional European options, when the closed form expressions are not too difficult to evaluate.

Monte Carlo methods have the advantage that they can easily compute the value of multi-asset European options but have difficultly including the possibility of early exercise; this is required for American style options.

On the other hand, multidimensional lattice techniques allow American options to be evaluated with ease. However, lattices become increasingly difficult to program as the number of dimensions increases, and the constraints of computer storage limits their use to problems involving (about) four or less assets.

6.2 THE MULTI-ASSET BLACK–SCHOLES EQUATION

In Chapter 2, we mentioned that when the price, S, of a single asset follows GBM the change in price, dS, over a time interval, dt, is given by

$$dS = rSdt + \sigma SdW,$$

where r is the risk-free interest rate, σ is the volatility of asset S, and $dW \sim N(0, dt)$.

We also proved using Ito's lemma that the process followed by $Y = \log(S)$ is

$$dY = (r - \sigma^2/2)dt + \sigma dW,$$

where dY is the change in the value of $\log(S)$ over the time interval dt. Later on we derived the (Black–Scholes) partial differential equation that is satisfied by the value, V, of an option written on a single underlying asset. The equation is

$$\frac{\partial V}{\partial t} + \frac{\sigma^2 S^2}{2}\frac{\partial^2 V}{\partial S^2} + rS\frac{\partial V}{\partial S} - rV = 0.$$

The above result can be generalized to deal with multi-asset options. Suppose that m assets follow the following processes:

$$dY_i = (r - \sigma_i^2/2)dt + \sigma_i dW_i, \quad i = 1,\ldots,m, \tag{6.2.1}$$

where the subscript i refers to the value associated with the ith asset. The m element random vector dW is distributed according to $dW \sim N(0,C)$. The diagonal elements of C are $C_{ii} = Var[dW_i] = dt$, $i = 1,\ldots,m$ and off-diagonal elements are

$$C_{ij} = E[dW_i\,dW_j] = \rho_{i,j}\,dt, \quad i = 1,\ldots,m, \quad j = 1,\ldots,m, \quad i \neq j,$$

We can also write the above equation in vector form by introducing the m element vector dY which is normally distributed as

$$dY \sim N(v,\bar{C}), \tag{6.2.2}$$

where v is the mean vector and $\bar{C}$ is the covariance matrix. The elements of the covariance matrix are

$$\bar{C}_{ii} = \sigma_i^2 dt, \quad i = 1,\ldots,m, \quad \bar{C}_{ij} = \sigma_i\sigma_j\rho_{ij}\,dt, \quad i \neq j, i = 1,\ldots,m, j = 1,\ldots,m, \tag{6.2.3}$$

where ρ_{ij} is the correlation coefficient between asset i and asset j, that is, the correlation between dW_i and dW_j. The elements of the mean vector v are

$$v_i = r - \sigma_i^2/2, \quad i = 1,\ldots,m. \tag{6.2.4}$$

The value V of an option written on n assets satisfies the following partial differential equation:

$$\frac{\partial V}{\partial t} + \frac{1}{2}\sum_{i=1}^{m}\sum_{j=1}^{m}\sigma_i\sigma_j\rho_{ij}S_iS_j\frac{\partial^2 V}{\partial S_i\partial S_j} + r\sum_{i=1}^{m}S_i\frac{\partial V}{\partial S_i} - rV = 0.$$

For a European call on the maximum of m assets, the payoff $\mathcal{P}_c^{MAX}$ at maturity (time τ) is given by $\mathcal{P}_c^{MAX} = \max(\max(S_1^\tau,S_2^\tau,\ldots,S_m^\tau) - E,0)$, where $S_i^\tau, i = 1,\ldots,m$ denotes the value of the ith asset at maturity, and E represents the strike price. Similarly, a European put option on the minimum of m assets has a payoff, $\mathcal{P}_p^{MIN}$, at time τ, given by $\mathcal{P}_p^{MIN} = \max(E - \min(S_1^\tau,S_2^\tau,\ldots,S_m^\tau),0)$.

6.3 MULTIDIMENSIONAL MONTE CARLO METHODS

We have already mentioned that Monte Carlo simulation can easily price European multi-asset options (also sometimes referred to as basket options or rainbow options) involving a large number of assets (say 20 or more).

In addition, Monte Carlo simulation can also include the following features into a option without much difficulty:

TABLE 6.1 The Computed Values and Absolute Errors, in Brackets, for European Options on the Maximum of Three Assets. Monte Carlo Simulation was used with both Quasirandom (Sobol) Sequences and Pseudorandom Sequences. The Number of Paths used Varied from 500 to 3000. The Parameters were $E = 100.0$, $S1 = S2 = S3 = 100.0$, $r = 0.1$, $\tau = 1.0$, $\sigma_1 = \sigma_2 = \sigma_3 = 0.2$, $\rho_{12} = \rho_{13} = \rho_{23} = 0.5$, and $q1 = q2 = q3 = 0.0$. The *Accurate* Values were 0.936 for a Put and 22.672 for a Call, See Table 6.7 and Table 2 of Boyle Evnine and Gibbs (1989)

	Put		Call	
nsim	Quasi	Pseudo	Quasi	Pseudo
500	0.890 (4.5948×10^{-2})	1.1044 (1.6839×10^{-1})	22.629 (4.3231×10^{-2})	22.4089 (2.6312×10^{-1})
1000	0.924 (1.1534×10^{-2})	1.0193 (8.3297×10^{-2})	22.683 (1.1306×10^{-2})	22.3520 (3.1998×10^{-1})
1500	0.919 (1.6807×10^{-2})	0.8957 (4.0344×10^{-2})	22.670 (2.2954×10^{-3})	22.6346 (3.7430×10^{-2})
2000	0.932 (4.3221×10^{-3})	0.8995 (3.6488×10^{-2})	22.685 (1.3299×10^{-2})	22.7675 (9.5491×10^{-2})
2500	0.932 (3.5698×10^{-3})	0.8886 (4.7352×10^{-2})	22.670 (1.6619×10^{-3})	22.9326 (2.6058×10^{-1})
3000	0.937 (1.1376×10^{-3})	0.9025 (3.3548×10^{-2})	22.679 (7.2766×10^{-3})	22.8050 (1.3301×10^{-1})

- Non-Gaussian distribution of stock returns; distributions with *heavy tails* are usually of interest because they more accurately represent what is observed in the financial markets.
- Options with path dependency (such as barrier options, etc.), these are known as *exotic options*.
- Complex time dependency (e.g., ARMA, GARCH, or Levy processes) of model parameters such as interest rates, asset prices, etc.

The main drawbacks with Monte Carlo simulation are the following:

- It is difficult compute the value of American style options.
- It is difficult (or impossible) to achieve the same accuracy that can be obtained using finite difference methods.

In a different section of this book, we will show how Monte Carlo simulation can be used to price American options by using a hybrid *Monte Carlo lattice* approach originally developed by Boyle Evnine and Gibbs (1989).

In Chapter 3, we show that when pseudorandom numbers are used, the standard errors of integrals computed via Monte Carlo simulation decrease at the rate $N^{1/2}$, where N is the number of simulations. This means that it can

TABLE 6.2 The Computed Values and Absolute Errors, in Brackets, for European Options on the Minimum of Three Assets. Monte Carlo Simulation was used with both Quasirandom (Sobol) Sequences and Pseudorandom Sequences. The Number of Paths used Varied from 500 to 3000. The Parameters were $E = 100.0$, $S_1 = S_2 = S_3 = 100.0$, $r = 0.1$, $\tau = 1.0$, $\sigma_1 = \sigma_2 = \sigma_3 = 0.2$, $\rho_{12} = \rho_{13} = \rho_{23} = 0.5$, and $q_1 = q_2 = q_3 = 0.0$. The *Accurate* Values were 7.403 for a Put and 5.249 for a Call, See Table 6.8 and Table 2 of Boyle Evnine and Gibbs (1989)

	Put		Call	
nsim	Quasi	Pseudo	Quasi	Pseudo
500	7.365 (3.8122×10^{-2})	7.6760 (2.7298×10^{-1})	5.312 (6.3431×10^{-2})	5.3086 (5.9591×10^{-2})
1000	7.425 (2.1554×10^{-2})	7.7607 (3.5772×10^{-1})	5.293 (4.3958×10^{-2})	5.4376 (1.8857×10^{-1})
1500	7.408 (5.1232×10^{-3})	7.5654 (1.6240×10^{-1})	5.253 (4.0761×10^{-3})	5.4121 (1.6307×10^{-1})
2000	7.399 (3.6364×10^{-3})	7.4820 (7.8995×10^{-2})	5.266 (1.7236×10^{-2})	5.4029 (1.5390×10^{-1})
2500	7.407 (4.1463×10^{-3})	7.3592 (4.3754×10^{-2})	5.267 (1.7707×10^{-2})	5.4690 (2.2005×10^{-1})
3000	7.400 (2.7166×10^{-3})	7.3997 (3.3236×10^{-3})	5.245 (3.5024×10^{-3})	5.4331 (1.8407×10^{-1})

require hundreds of thousands of simulations just to achieve an accuracy of 10^{-1} or 10^{-2} in the estimated option price. It is because of this that various Monte Carlo variance reduction techniques are used to increase the accuracy of the computed integral.

In this section, we show how to price a three-asset basket option using Monte Carlo simulation; the accuracy of the results obtained with quasirandom numbers and pseudorandom numbers is compared.

The options we consider are European put and call options on the maximum and minimum of three assets. All the options have a maturity of one year, and the other model parameters used are given in Tables 6.1 and 6.2.

In Code excerpt 6.1, most of the work is done by the routine `multivariate_normal`. This generates a vector of multivariate pseudorandom numbers with a particular covariance matrix. In the program the values of the assets at current time, t are $S_1 = S_2 = S_3 = 100$, and the option matures in one year.

The asset process evolve according to

$$dY_i = \log(S_{i,t+dt}) - \log(S_{i,t}) = \left(r - \sigma_i^2/2\right) dt + \sigma_i dW_i, \quad i = 1, \ldots, m,$$

where we have used the notation $S_{i,t}$ to denote the value of the ith asset at current time t, and $S_{i,t+dt}$ to denote the value of the asset at the future time $t+dt$. Simple rearrangement of the above equation gives

$$\log\left(\frac{S_{i,t+dt}}{S_{i,t}}\right) = \left(r - \sigma_i^2/2\right)dt + \sigma_i dW_i, \quad i = 1,\ldots,m.$$

Taking exponentials of both sides, we obtain

$$\frac{S_{i,t+dt}}{S_{i,t}} = \exp\left\{\left(r - \sigma_i^2/2\right)dt + \sigma_i dW_i\right\}, \quad i = 1,\ldots,m,$$

which is equivalent to

$$S_{i,t+dt} = S_{i,t}\exp\left\{\left(r - \sigma_i^2/2\right)dt + \sigma_i dW_i\right\}. \tag{6.3.1}$$

```
/* Monte Carlo simulation: 3 dimensional Black Scholes, The results are compared with those of Boyle et. al.,1989
   George Levy: 2007
*/
  long seed,i,num_simulations,iflag;
  double time_step,sqrt_time_step,rho, zero = 0.0, half = 0.5;
  double r,opt_val, opt_val1, tol;
  double the_max, the_min, X, ST1, ST2, ST3, ST4, S1, S2, S3, S4;
  double disc, sumit_max_put, sumit_max_call;
  double sumit_min_put, sumit_min_call;
  double *rvec = (double *)0;
  double rho_12, rho_13, rho_23;
  double  *c3, *c4, *z, *std, *means;
  double tmp1, tmp2, tmp3, tmp4, sigma1, sigma2, sigma3, sigma4;
  long is_fcall;

#define MEANS(I) means[(I)-1]
#define XBAR(I) xbar[(I)-1]
#define Z(I) z[(I)-1]
#define STD(I) std[(I)-1]
#define C3(I,J) c3[((I)-1) * 3 + ((J)-1)]

      seed = 111;
      r = 0.1;

      sigma1 = 0.2;
      sigma2 = 0.2;
      sigma3 = 0.2;
      S1 = 100.0;
      S2 = 100.0;
      S3 = 100.0;
      X = 100.0;

      rho_12 = 0.5;
      rho_13 = 0.5;
      rho_23 = 0.5;

      time_step = 1.0;
      sqrt_time_step = sqrt(time_step);
      disc = exp(-r*time_step);

      c3 = ALLOCATE(3*3, double);
      means = ALLOCATE(3, double);
      z = ALLOCATE(3, double);
      std = ALLOCATE(3, double);

      if ((!means) || (!std) || (!z) ) {
        printf("Allocation error \n");
      }

      tmp1 = sigma1*sigma1*time_step;
      tmp2 = sigma2*sigma2*time_step;
      tmp3 = sigma3*sigma3*time_step;

      C3(1,1) = tmp1;
```

Code excerpt 6.1 A Monte Carlo simulation computer program, using pseudorandom numbers, for estimating the value of European put and call options on the maximum and minimum of three underlying assets. The results are presented in Tables 6.1 and 6.2.

```
        C3(2,2) = tmp2;
        C3(3,3) = tmp3;
        C3(1,2) = sigma1*sigma2*time_step*rho_12;
        C3(2,3) = sigma2*sigma3*time_step*rho_23;
        C3(1,3) = sigma1*sigma3*time_step*rho_13;
        C3(2,1) = C3(1,2);
        C3(3,1) = C3(1,3);
        C3(3,2) = C3(2,3);

        tmp1 = (r - sigma1*sigma1*half)*time_step;
        tmp2 = (r - sigma2*sigma2*half)*time_step;
        tmp3 = (r - sigma3*sigma3*half)*time_step;

        MEANS(1) = tmp1;
        MEANS(2) = tmp2;
        MEANS(3) = tmp3;

        sumit_max_put = zero;
        sumit_max_call = zero;
        sumit_min_put = zero;
        sumit_min_call = zero;

        tol = 1.0e-8;

        srand(seed);
        is_fcall = 1;  /* initialisation call to the random number generator */
        multivariate_normal(is_fcall,&MEANS(1),3,&C3(1,1),3,tol,&rvec,&Z(1),&iflag);

        num_simulations = 6000;
        is_fcall = 0;
        for (i = 1; i <= num_simulations ; ++i) {

                /* continuation calls to the random number generator */
                multivariate_normal(is_fcall,&MEANS(1),3,&C3(1,1),3,tol,&rvec,&Z(1),&iflag);

                ST1 = S1*exp(Z(1));
                ST2 = S2*exp(Z(2));
                ST3 = S3*exp(Z(3));

// options on the maximum
                tmp2 = MAX(ST1,ST2);
                the_max = MAX(tmp2,ST3);
                tmp1 = the_max-X;
                opt_val1 = MAX(tmp1, zero);
                sumit_max_call += opt_val1*disc;

                tmp1 = X-the_max;
                opt_val1 = MAX(tmp1, zero);
                sumit_max_put += opt_val1*disc;

// options on the minimum
                tmp2 = MIN(ST1,ST2);
                the_min = MIN(tmp2,ST3);

                tmp1 = the_min-X;
                opt_val1 = MAX(tmp1, zero);
                sumit_min_call += opt_val1*disc;

                tmp1 = X-the_min;
                opt_val1 = MAX(tmp1, zero);
                sumit_min_put += opt_val1*disc;
        }

        opt_val = sumit_max_put/(double)num_simulations;  /* put option value on the maximum of three assets */
        opt_val = sumit_max_call/(double)num_simulations; /* call option value on the maximum of three assets */

        opt_val = sumit_min_put/(double)num_simulations; /* put option value on the minimum of three assets */
        opt_val = sumit_min_call/(double)num_simulations; /* call option value on the maximum of three assets */
}
```

Code excerpt 6.1 (*Continued*).

6.4 INTRODUCTION TO MULTIDIMENSIONAL LATTICE METHODS

Finite difference lattices can be used to value options on up to about four assets before they require impossibly large amounts of computer memory. The main advantage of finite difference method is that they are able to easily cater for

American style early exercise facilities within the option. This is not true of Monte Carlo methods. They can easily model complex European options but have difficulty modelling American style options.

In this section, we use the approach of Kamrad and Ritchken (1991), and Boyle Evnine and Gibbs (1989), which we will call the BEGKR method, to price multi-asset options. We first derive expressions for the jump size and jump probabilities for a single asset and show that these are equivalent to those of the CRR binomial lattice discussed in Chapter 5. We will then give a expressions for the jump sizes and jump probabilities of a general multi-asset option.

To derive the BEGKR equations for one asset, we first assume that the asset follows a lognormal processes with drift $\mu = r - \sigma^2/2$, where r is the riskless interest rate and σ is the instantaneous volatility.

Therefore, if S_t is the price of the asset at time t, and $S_{t+\Delta t}$ is the price at time instant $t + \Delta t$, we then have the following equations:

$$\log(S_{t+\Delta t}) = \log(S_t) + \epsilon_t, \quad \epsilon_t \sim N(\mu\Delta t, \sigma^2\Delta t)$$

or equivalently

$$\log\left(\frac{S_{t+\Delta t}}{S_t}\right) \sim N(\mu\Delta t, \sigma^2\Delta t),$$

where ϵ_t represents a random variable and as usual $N(\mu\Delta t, \sigma^2\Delta t)$ denotes a Gaussian with mean $\mu\Delta t$ and variance $\sigma^2\Delta t$.

We will now consider the situation when ϵ_t either jumps up or down by an amount $\nu = \sigma \sqrt{\Delta t}$. For an up-jump,

$$\log\left(\frac{S_{t+\Delta t}}{S_t}\right) = \sigma \sqrt{\Delta t},$$

and therefore, $S_{t+\Delta t} = S_t \exp(\sigma \sqrt{\Delta t})$.

While for a down-jump, we have

$$\log\left(\frac{S_{t+\Delta t}}{S_t}\right) = -\sigma \sqrt{\Delta t},$$

and therefore, $S_{t+\Delta t} = S_t \exp(-\sigma \sqrt{\Delta t})$.

The reader will notice that these expressions are the same as those for the CRR lattice of Chapter 5. That is for an up-jump, $S_{t+\Delta t} = S_t u$, and for a down-jump, $S_{t+\Delta t} = S_t d$ and $u = 1/d = \exp(\sigma \sqrt{\Delta t})$.

The probability undergoing either an up- or down-jump occurring can be found by matching the mean and variance of ϵ_t.

From the mean,

$$E[\epsilon_t] = \nu(p_u - p_d) = \mu\Delta t, \tag{6.4.1}$$

and from the variance,

$$Var[\epsilon_t] = \nu^2(p_u + p_d) = \sigma^2\Delta t. \tag{6.4.2}$$

So combining equation (6.4.1) and equation (6.4.2), we obtain

$$v\mu\Delta t + \sigma^2\Delta t = 2v^2 p_u,$$

so

$$p_u = \frac{1}{2}\left\{\frac{\sigma^2\Delta t}{v^2} + \frac{\mu\Delta t}{v}\right\};$$

substituting $v = \sigma\sqrt{\Delta t}$, we obtain

$$p_u = \frac{1}{2}\left\{1 + \frac{\mu\sqrt{\Delta t}}{\sigma}\right\} \qquad (6.4.3)$$

and using the fact that $p_d = 1 - p_u$ gives

$$p_d = \frac{1}{2}\left\{1 - \frac{\mu\sqrt{\Delta t}}{\sigma}\right\}, \qquad (6.4.4)$$

we shall now show that is equivalent to the **CRR** binomial model.

For the CRR model (Chapter 5, equation (5.3.19)), we have

$$p_u = \frac{\exp(r\Delta t) - d}{u - d};$$

expanding $\exp(r\Delta t)$, u, and d to order Δt, we obtain

$$\exp(r\Delta t) \sim 1 + r\Delta t,$$

$$u = \exp(\sigma\sqrt{\Delta t}) \sim 1 + \sigma\sqrt{\Delta t} + \frac{\sigma^2}{2}\Delta t,$$

$$d = \exp(\sigma\sqrt{\Delta t}) \sim 1 - \sigma\sqrt{\Delta t} + \frac{\sigma^2}{2}\Delta t,$$

so

$$\exp(r\Delta t) - d \sim r\Delta t + \sigma\sqrt{\Delta t} - \frac{\sigma^2\Delta t}{2}$$

and

$$u - d \sim 2\sigma\sqrt{\Delta t}.$$

So

$$p_u = \frac{\exp(r\Delta t) - d}{u - d} \sim \frac{r\Delta t + \sigma - \sigma^2/2\Delta t}{2\sigma\sqrt{\Delta t}},$$

which simplifies to

$$p_u = \frac{1}{2}\left\{1 + \frac{\mu\sqrt{\Delta t}}{\sigma}\right\}$$

and therefore

$$p_d = 1 - p_u = \frac{1}{2}\left\{1 - \frac{\mu\sqrt{\Delta t}}{\sigma}\right\},$$

which are the expressions for p_u and p_d given in equation (6.4.1) and equation (6.4.2) respectively. So we have shown that, to first order in Δt, both the size of the jump and the probability of the jump are the same as the CRR binomial model.

The attractive feature of the BEGKR binomial lattice model is that it can easily be generalized to describe a model consisting of k assets. Here, we will merely quote the results in Kamrad and Ritchken (1991). As before it is assumed that the asset prices follow a multivariate lognormal distribution. Let $\mu_i = r - \sigma_i^2/2$, and σ_i be the instantaneous mean and variance respectively $(i = 1, 2, \ldots, k)$ and let ρ_{ij} be the correlation between assets i and j. The binomial model now requires 2^k possible jumps in the time interval Δt. Let m denote the state of the process after time Δt with p_m representing the probability of state m $(m = 1, \ldots, 2^k)$. The probabilities of these jumps are now given by

$$p_m = \left\{ 1 + \sqrt{\Delta t} \sum_{i=1}^{k} x_{im} \left(\frac{\mu_i}{\sigma_i} \right) + \sum_{i=1}^{k-1} \sum_{j=i+1}^{k} (x_{ij}^m \rho_{ij}) \right\}, \quad m = 1, 2, \ldots, 2^k, k \geq 2,$$

where $x_{im} = 1$ if asset i has an up-jump in state m, and $x_{im} = -1$ if asset i has a down-jump in state m. In addition, $x_{ij}^m = 1$ if asset i and asset j have jumps in the same direction in state m, and $x_{ij}^m = -1$ if asset i and asset j have jumps in the opposite direction in state m.

6.5 TWO-ASSET OPTIONS

In this section, we consider options based on the underlying prices of two assets, S_1 and S_2. We give analytic formulae to price European exchange options and also those based on the maximum or minimum of two assets. In addition, we show how to construct binomial lattices for the valuation of two-asset American style options.

6.5.1 European Exchange Options

A European exchange option gives the holder the right to exchange one asset for another asset at maturity, see Margrabe (1978). Let the real world processes of assets S^A and S^B be

$$dS_t^A = S_t^A \mu_A dt + S_t^A \sigma_A dW_A^P,$$

$$dS_t^B = S_t^B \mu_B dt + S_t^B \sigma_B dW_B^P,$$

where S_t^A denotes the value of asset A at time t and S_t^B denotes the value of asset B at time t – the other symbols have their *obvious* meanings.

We will now find the value, at current time t_0, of an option which gives the holder the right to exchange asset A for asset B at maturity T. The payoff at maturity is $H_T = \max\left(S_T^B - S_T^A, 0\right)$.

If we use the value of asset A as the numeraire then, from equation (4.2.1), the value of the exchange option at time t_0 is

$$V(t_0) = S_t^A E^{\mathbb{Q}} \left[\frac{\max\left(S_T^B - S_T^B, 0\right)}{S_T^A} \right],$$

which can be written as

$$V(t_0) = S_t^A E^Q \left[\max \left(\left(\frac{S_T^B}{S_T^A} \right) - 1, 0 \right) \right], \tag{6.5.1}$$

where Q is the probability measure under which the relative price (S_t^B / S_t^A) is a martingale.

The process followed by (S_t^B / S_t^A) can be found by substituting $X_1 = S_t^B$ and $X_2 = S_t^A$ into equation (2.6.7). This yields

$$d \left(\frac{S_t^B}{S_t^A} \right) = \left(\frac{S_t^B}{S_t^A} \right) \left\{ \mu_B - \mu_A + \sigma_A^2 - \sigma_A \sigma_B \rho_{AB} \right\} dt + \left(\frac{S_t^B}{S_t^A} \right) \left\{ \sigma_B dW_B^P - \sigma_A dW_A^P \right\}.$$

Let $\hat{X} = \sigma_B dW_B^P - \sigma_A dW_A^P$, so $E[\hat{X}] = \sigma_B E\left[dW_B^P\right] - \sigma_A E\left[dW_A^P\right] = 0$ and $Var[\hat{X}] = \sigma_B^2 dt + \sigma_A^2 dt - 2\sigma_B \sigma_A \rho_{AB} dt$ where we have used (see Appendix C.3)

$$Var[a\, dW_1 + b\, dW_2] = a^2 Var[dW_1] + b^2 Var[dW_2] + 2ab Cov[dW_1, dW_2],$$

$Var[dW_B^P] = Var[dW_A^P] = dt$ and $Cov\left[dW_B^P, dW_A^P\right] = \sigma_B \sigma_A \rho_{AB} dt$,

which means that $\hat{X} \sim N\left(0, \sigma_B^2 dt + \sigma_A^2 dt - 2\sigma_B \sigma_A \rho_{AB} dt\right)$ and the variate $\left(\sigma_B^2 + \sigma_A^2 - 2\sigma_B \sigma_A \rho_{AB}\right) dW^P$ is from the same distribution as $\hat{X}$.

Therefore, we can write

$$d \left(\frac{S_t^B}{S_t^A} \right) = \left(\frac{S_t^B}{S_t^A} \right) \overline{\mu} dt + \left(\frac{S_t^B}{S_t^A} \right) \overline{\sigma} dW^P, \tag{6.5.2}$$

where

$$\overline{\sigma} = \sqrt{\sigma_B^2 + \sigma_A^2 - 2\sigma_B \sigma_A}$$

and

$$\overline{\mu} = \mu_B - \mu_A + \sigma_A^2 - \sigma_B \sigma_A \rho_{AB}.$$

Following Section 4.4.3 we choose the probability measure Q so that the drift term in equation (6.5.2) is zero. We have

$$dW^P = dW^Q - \left(\frac{\overline{\mu}}{\overline{\sigma}} \right) dt.$$

Substituting this into equation (6.5.2) gives

$$d \left(\frac{S_t^B}{S_t^A} \right) = \left(\frac{S_t^B}{S_t^A} \right) \overline{\sigma} dW^Q. \tag{6.5.3}$$

It can be seen that equation (6.5.3) is identical to equation (4.4.31) but with the mapping

$$S \to \left(\frac{S_t^B}{S_t^A} \right), \quad \sigma \to \overline{\sigma}, \quad r \to 0. \tag{6.5.4}$$

Now combining equations (4.4.35) and equation (4.4.47), we have

$$\exp(-r\tau) E^Q \left[\max(S_T - E, 0)\right] = S N_1(d_1) - E \exp(-r\tau) N_1(d_2),$$

where d_1 and d_2 have been defined in Chapter 4.

Therefore,
$$E^Q[\max(S_T - 1, 0)] = \exp(r\tau)SN_1(d_1) - N_1(d_2).$$
Using the mapping defined in equation (6.5.4), we have
$$E^Q\left[\left(\left(\frac{S_T^B}{S_T^A}\right) - 1, 0\right)\right] = \left(\frac{S_t^B}{S_t^A}\right)N_1(d_1) - N_1(d_2)$$

and so from equation (6.5.1)
$$V(t_0) = S_{t_0}^A\left\{\left(\frac{S_t^B}{S_t^A}\right)N_1(d_1) - N_1(d_2)\right\},$$

which means that the value of the exchange option at time t_0 is
$$V(t_0) = S_{t_0}^B N_1(d_1) - S_{t_0}^A N_1(d_2),$$

where
$$d_1 = \frac{\log\left(\frac{S_{t_0}^A}{S_{t_0}^B}\right) + \frac{1}{2}(T - t_0)\bar{\sigma}^2}{\bar{\sigma}\sqrt{(T - t_0)}},$$

$$d_2 = \frac{\log\left(\frac{S_{t_0}^A}{S_{t_0}^B}\right) - \frac{1}{2}(T - t_0)\bar{\sigma}^2}{\bar{\sigma}\sqrt{(T - t_0)}}.$$

6.5.2 European Options on the Maximum or Minimum

Here, we present the results from Stulz (1982) and Johnson (1987) concerning the value of European call option on the maximum and minimum of two assets, see Code excerpts 6.2 and 6.3 and results in Tables 6.3 and 6.4.

Call Options on the Maximum and Minimum of Two Assets

Let the value of a European call option on the minimum of two assets, S_1 and S_2, with strike price E, maturity τ, and correlation coefficient ρ be denoted by c_{min}. The value of the corresponding call option on the maximum of these assets be will represented by c_{max}.

Then, following Stulz (1982) and Johnson (1987), we have
$$\begin{aligned}
c_{max} = {} & S_1 N_2(d_1(S_1, E, \sigma_1^2), d_1'(S_1, S_2, \sigma_*^2), \rho_1) \\
& + S_2 N_2(d_1(S_2, E, \sigma_2^2), d_1'(S_2, S_1, \sigma_*^2), \rho_2) \\
& - E\exp(-r\tau)\left\{1 - N_2(-d_2(S_1, E, \sigma_1^2), -d_2(S_2, E, \sigma_2^2), \rho)\right\}
\end{aligned} \quad (6.5.5)$$

and
$$\begin{aligned}
c_{min} = {} & S_1 N_2(d_1(S_1, E, \sigma_1^2), -d_1'(S_1, S_2, \sigma_*^2), -\rho_1) \\
& + S_2 N_2(d_1(S_2, E, \sigma_2^2), -d_1'(S_2, S_1, \sigma_*^2), -\rho_2) \\
& - E\exp(-r\tau)N_2(d_2(S_1, E, \sigma_1^2), d_2(S_2, E, \sigma_2^2), \rho),
\end{aligned} \quad (6.5.6)$$

where $N_2(a, b, \rho)$ is the bivariate cumulative normal. It gives the cumulative probability, in a standardized bivariate normal distribution, that the variables x_1

and x_2 satisfy $x_1 \le a$ and $x_2 \le b$ when with correlation coefficient between x_1 and x_2 is ρ – the value is computed using the routine cum_norm2. The other symbols are defined as follows:

$$\sigma_*^2 = \sigma_1^2 - 2\rho\sigma_1\sigma_2 + \sigma_2^2,$$

$$d_1(S_i, E, \sigma_i^2) = \frac{\log(S_i/E) + (r + \sigma_i^2/2)\tau}{\sigma_i \sqrt{\tau}}, \quad i = 1, 2,$$

$$d_2(S_i, E, \sigma_i^2) = \frac{\log(S_i/E) + (r - \sigma_i^2/2)\tau}{\sigma_i \sqrt{\tau}}, \quad i = 1, 2,$$

$$d_1'(S_i, S_j, \sigma_*^2) = \frac{\log(S_i/S_j) + (\sigma_*^2/2)\tau}{\sigma_* \sqrt{\tau}}, \quad \text{for } i = 1, j = 2, \text{ or } i = 2, j = 1,$$

and

$$\rho_1 = \frac{\sigma_1 - \rho\sigma_2}{\sigma_*}, \qquad \rho_2 = \frac{\sigma_2 - \rho\sigma_1}{\sigma_*}.$$

It can also be shown that

$$c_{\max}(S_1, S_2, E, \tau) + c_{\min}(S_1, S_2, E, \tau) = c(S_1, E, \tau) + c(S_2, E, \tau), \tag{6.5.7}$$

where $c(S, E, \tau)$ is the value of a vanilla European call.

We will now derive expression for the value of the corresponding European put options.

Put Options on the Minimum of Two Assets

It will now be shown that the price of a European put option on the minimum of two assets, $p_{\min}(S_1, S_2, E, \tau)$ is

$$p_{\min}(S_1, S_2, E, \tau) = E \exp(-r\tau) - c_{\min}(S_1, S_2, 0, \tau) + c_{\min}(S_1, S_2, E, \tau), \tag{6.5.8}$$

where the meaning of the symbols has been previously defined.

This result can be proved by considering the following two investments:

Portfolio A:
Purchase one put option on the minimum of S_1 and S_2 with exercise price E.

Portfolio B:
Purchase one discount bond which pays E at maturity. Write (that is sell) one option on the minimum of S_1 and S_2 with an exercise price of zero. Purchase one option on the minimum of S_1 and S_2 with exercise price E.

We now consider the values of these portfolios at option maturity, time τ.

If $\min(S_1, S_2) \ge E$
    Portfolio A: pays zero
    Portfolio B: Pays $E - \min(S_1, S_2) + \min(S_1, S_2) - E = 0$.

If $\min(S - 1, S_2) = S_1 < E$
    Portfolio A: Pays $E - S_1$
    Portfolio B: Pays $E - S_1 + 0 = E - S_1$.

If $\min(S_1, S_2) = S_2 < E$

Portfolio A: Pays $E - S_2$

Portfolio B: Pays $E - S_2 + 0 = E - S_2$.

We have therefore shown that, under all possible circumstances, Portfolio A has the same value as Portfolio B. This means that equation (6.5.8) is true.

Put Options on the Maximum of Two Assets

It will now be shown that the price of a European put option on the maximum of two assets, $p_{max}(S_1, S_2, E, \tau)$ is

$$p_{max}(S_1, S_2, E, \tau) = E \exp(-r\tau) - c_{max}(S_1, S_2, 0, \tau) + c_{max}(S_1, S_2, E, \tau), \quad (6.5.9)$$

where, as before, the meaning of the symbols has been previously defined.

This result can be proved by considering the following two investments:

Portfolio A:

Purchase one put option on the maximum of S_1 and S_2 with exercise price E.

Portfolio B:

Purchase one discount bond which pays E at maturity. Write (that is sell) one option on the maximum of S_1 and S_2 with an exercise price of zero. Purchase one option on the maximum of S_1 and S_2 with exercise price E.

As before we now consider the values of these portfolios at option maturity, time τ.

If $\max(S_1, S_2) \geq E$

Portfolio A: Pays zero

Portfolio B: Pays $E - \max(S_1, S_2) + \max(S_1, S_2) - E = 0$.

If $\max(S_1, S_2) = S_1 < E$

Portfolio A: Pays $E - S_1$

Portfolio B: Pays $E - S_1 + 0 = E - S_1$.

If $\max(S_1, S_2) = S_2 < E$

Portfolio A: Pays $E - S_2$

Portfolio B: Pays $E - S_2 + 0 = E - S_2$.

It therefore follows that, under all possible circumstances, Portfolio A has the same value as Portfolio B, and this means that equation (6.5.9) is true.

```
void rainbow_bs_2d(double *opt_value, double S1, double S2, double X, double sigma1,
                   double sigma2, double rho, double opt_mat, double r, long is_max, long *iflag)
{
/* Input parameters:
   ==================
   S1              - the current price of the underlying asset 1,
   S2              - the current price of the underlying asset 2,
   X               - the strike price,
   sigma1          - the volatility of asset 1,
   sigma2          - the volatility of asset 2,
   rho             - the correlation coefficient between asset 1 and asset 2,
   opt_mat         - the time to maturity,
   r               - the interest rate,
```

Code excerpt 6.2 Function to calculate the value of a European call on the maximum or minimum of two assets using the analytic result of Johnson (1987) and Stulz (1982).

```
    is_max          - if is_max is 1 then the option is a call on the maximum of two assets, otherwise the option is a
                      call on the minimum of two assets.
    Output parameters:
    ==================
    opt_value       - the value of the option,
    iflag           - an error indicator.
*/

double one=1.0,two=2.0,zero=0.0;
double eps,d1,d2_1,d2_2,temp,temp1,temp2,pi,np;
double rho_112, rho_212, d1_prime;
double sigma, term1, term2, term3;
long ifailx = 0;

    if(X < EPS) {    /*  ERROR the strike price is too small */
        *iflag = 2;
        return;
    }
    if (sigma1 < EPS) {    /*  ERROR the volatility (sigma1) is too small */
        *iflag = 3;
        return;
    }
    if (sigma2 < EPS) {    /*  ERROR the volatility (sigma2) is too small */
        *flag = 3;
        return;
    }
    if (opt_mat < EPS) {  /*  ERROR the time to maturity (opt_mat) is too small */
        *iflag = 3;
        return;
    }
    sigma = sqrt((sigma1*sigma1 + sigma2*sigma2) - two*sigma1*sigma2*rho);
    if (is_max == 1) { /* then the maximum of two assets */
        /* calculate term1 */
        temp = log(S1/X);
        d1 = temp+(r+(sigma1*sigma1/two))*opt_mat;
        d1 = d1/(sigma1*sqrt(opt_mat));
        temp = log(S1/S2);
        d1_prime = temp+(sigma*sigma/two)*opt_mat;
        d1_prime = d1_prime/(sigma*sqrt(opt_mat));
        rho_112 = (sigma1 - rho*sigma2) / sigma;
        term1 =  cum_norm2(d1,d1_prime,rho_112,&ifailx);
        term1 = term1*S1;
        /* calculate term2 */
        temp = log(S2/X);
        d1 = temp+(r+(sigma2*sigma2/two))*opt_mat;
        d1 = d1/(sigma2*sqrt(opt_mat));
        temp = log(S2/S1);
        d1_prime = temp+(sigma*sigma/two)*opt_mat;
        d1_prime = d1_prime/(sigma*sqrt(opt_mat));
        rho_212 = (sigma2 - rho*sigma1) / sigma;
        term2 =  S2*cum_norm2(d1,d1_prime,rho_212,&ifailx);
        /* calculate term3 */
        temp = log(S1/X);
        d2_1 = temp+(r-(sigma1*sigma1/two))*opt_mat;
        d2_1 = d2_1/(sigma1*sqrt(opt_mat));
        temp = log(S2/X);
        d2_2 = temp+(r-(sigma2*sigma2/two))*opt_mat;
        d2_2 = d2_2/(sigma2*sqrt(opt_mat));
        term3 =  one-cum_norm2(-d2_1,-d2_2,rho,&ifailx);
        *opt_value = term1+term2-X*exp(-r*opt_mat)*term3;
    }
    else {  /* the minimum of two assets */
        /* calculate term1 */
        temp = log(S1/X);
        d1 = temp+(r+(sigma1*sigma1/two))*opt_mat;
        d1 = d1/(sigma1*sqrt(opt_mat));
        temp = log(S1/S2);
        d1_prime = temp+(sigma*sigma/two)*opt_mat;
        d1_prime = d1_prime/(sigma*sqrt(opt_mat));
        rho_112 = (sigma1 - rho*sigma2) / sigma;
        term1 =  cum_norm2(d1,-d1_prime,-rho_112,&ifailx);
        term1 = term1*S1;
        /* calculate term2 */
        temp = log(S2/X);
        d1 = temp+(r+(sigma2*sigma2/two))*opt_mat;
        d1 = d1/(sigma2*sqrt(opt_mat));
        temp = log(S2/S1);
        d1_prime = temp+(sigma*sigma/two)*opt_mat;
        d1_prime = d1_prime/(sigma*sqrt(opt_mat));
        rho_212 = (sigma2 - rho*sigma1) / sigma;
        term2 =  S2*cum_norm2(d1,-d1_prime,-rho_212,&ifailx);
        /* calculate term3 */
        temp = log(S1/X);
        d2_1 = temp+(r-(sigma1*sigma1/two))*opt_mat;
        d2_1 = d2_1/(sigma1*sqrt(opt_mat));
```

Code excerpt 6.2 (*Continued*).

```
        temp = log(S2/X);
        d2_2 = temp+(r-(sigma2*sigma2/two))*opt_mat;
        d2_2 = d2_2/(sigma2*sqrt(opt_mat));
        term3 =  cum_norm2(d2_1,d2_2,rho,&ifailx);
        *opt_value = term1+term2-X*exp(-r*opt_mat)*term3;
    }
    return;
}
```

Code excerpt 6.2 (*Continued*).

```
void opt_rainbow_bs_2d(double *opt_value, double S1, double S2, double X, double sigma1,
              double sigma2, double rho, double opt_mat, double r, long is_max, long putcall, long *flag)
{
/* Input parameters:
   ==================
   S1                - the current price of the underlying asset 1,
   S2                - the current price of the underlying asset 2,
   X                 - the strike price,
   sigma1            - the volatility of asset 1,
   sigma2            - the volatility of asset 2,
   rho               - the correlation coefficient between asset 1 and asset 2,
   opt_mat           - the time to maturity,
   r                 - the interest rate,
   is_max            - if is_max is 1 then the option is on the maximum of two assets, otherwise the option is on
                       the minimum of two assets,
   putcall           - if putcall is 0 then the option is a call, otherwise the option is a put.
   Output parameters:
   ==================
   opt_value         - the value of the option,
   iflag             - an error indicator.
*/

    double temp1;
    double temp2;
    double fac;
    double a_zero = 1.0e-6; /* approximate zero number to prevent overflow in rainbow_bs_2d */
    if (putcall) { /* a put option */
        fac = X*exp(-r*opt_mat);
        rainbow_bs_2d(&temp1, S1, S2, a_zero, sigma1, sigma2, rho, opt_mat, r, is_max, flag);
        rainbow_bs_2d(&temp2, S1, S2, X, sigma1, sigma2, rho, opt_mat, r, is_max, flag);
        *opt_value = fac - temp1 + temp2;
    } else { /* a call option */
        rainbow_bs_2d(opt_value, S1, S2, X, sigma1, sigma2, rho, opt_mat, r, is_max, flag);
    }
}
```

Code excerpt 6.3 Function to calculate the value of a European put or call on the maximum or minimum of two assets using the analytic result of Johnson (1987) and Stulz (1982).

6.5.3 American Options

We assume that the prices of asset 1 and asset 2 follow a lognormal process with drifts terms of $\mu_1 = r - \sigma_1^2/2$ and $\mu_2 = r - \sigma_2^2/2$ respectively. As before r is the riskless interest rate and σ_1 and σ_2 are the instantaneous volatilities of asset 1 and asset 2.

If we let $S_{1,t}$ and $S_{2,t}$ denote the respective prices of asset 1 and asset 2 at time t, then we can write

$$\log(S_{1,t+\Delta t}) = \log(S_{1,t}) + \epsilon_{1,t} \tag{6.5.10}$$

and

$$\log(S_{2,t+\Delta t}) = \log(S_{2,t}) + \epsilon_{2,t}, \tag{6.5.11}$$

where $\epsilon_{1,t}$ is a random normal variable with mean $\mu_1 \Delta t$ and variance $\sigma_1^2 \Delta t$, and $\epsilon_{2,t}$ is a random normal variable with mean $\mu_2 \Delta t$ and variance $\sigma_2^2 \Delta t$.

TABLE 6.3 The Computed Values and Absolute Errors for European Put and Call Options on the Maximum of Two Assets. The Results were Obtained using a Binomial Lattice and the Analytic Formula (Johnson (1987) and Stulz (1982)). The Time to Maturity of the Option is Varied from 0.1 Years to 0.8 Years. The Parameters are $E = 44.0$, $S_1 = 40.0$, $S_2 = 50.0$, $r = 0.1$, $\sigma_1 = 0.2$, $\sigma_2 = 0.2$, $q_1 = q_2 = 0.0$, $\rho = 0.5$, and $n\_steps = 50$

	Call			Put		
Time	Analytic	Lattice	Error	Analytic	Lattice	Error
0.1	6.45320	6.45245	7.4972×10^{-4}	0.01524	0.01451	7.3344×10^{-4}
0.2	6.96192	6.95953	2.3845×10^{-3}	0.08252	0.08001	2.5106×10^{-3}
0.3	7.49587	7.49376	2.1084×10^{-3}	0.15787	0.15580	2.0675×10^{-3}
0.4	8.03710	8.04022	3.1260×10^{-3}	0.22362	0.22680	3.1768×10^{-3}
0.5	8.57808	8.57916	1.0757×10^{-3}	0.27762	0.27683	7.8867×10^{-4}
0.6	9.11529	9.10809	7.2006×10^{-3}	0.32115	0.31872	2.4328×10^{-3}
0.7	9.64700	9.64838	1.3826×10^{-3}	0.35598	0.35714	1.1548×10^{-3}
0.8	10.17238	10.17663	4.2571×10^{-3}	0.38372	0.38711	3.3891×10^{-3}

In the binomial lattice model, over the time interval Δt, the variate $\log(S_{1,t})$ is only allowed to jump up or down by an amount $v_1 = \sigma_1 \sqrt{\Delta t}$, and similarly the variate $\log(S_{2,t})$ is only permitted to jump up and down by the amount $v_2 = \sigma_2 \sqrt{\Delta t}$. We will denote the probability of both $\log(S_{1,t})$ and $\log(S_{2,t})$ having an up-jump over Δt by p_{uu}, and the probability of $\log(S_{1,t})$ having an up-jump and $\log(S_{2,t})$ having a down-jump by p_{ud}, etc.

The mean values in equation (6.5.10) and equation (6.5.11) then give

$$E[\epsilon_{1,t}] = v_1(p_{uu} + p_{ud} - p_{dd} - p_{du}) = \mu_1 \Delta t, \qquad (6.5.12)$$

$$E[\epsilon_{2,t}] = v_2(p_{uu} + p_{ud} - p_{dd} - p_{du}) = \mu_2 \Delta t, \qquad (6.5.13)$$

and the variance/covariance terms yields

$$Var[\epsilon_{1,t}] = v_1^2(p_{uu} + p_{ud} + p_{dd} + p_{du}) = \sigma_1^2 \Delta t, \qquad (6.5.14)$$

$$Var[\epsilon_{2,t}] = v_2^2(p_{uu} + p_{ud} + p_{dd} + p_{du}) = \sigma_2^2 \Delta t, \qquad (6.5.15)$$

$$E[\epsilon_{1,t}\epsilon_{2,t}] = v_1 v_2(p_{uu} - p_{ud} + p_{dd} - p_{du}) = \rho\, \sigma_1\, \sigma_2\, \Delta t, \qquad (6.5.16)$$

where ρ is the correlation coefficient between $\epsilon_{1,t}$ and $\epsilon_{2,t}$.

We therefore obtain

$$p_{uu} + p_{ud} - p_{dd} + p_{du} = \frac{\mu_1 \sqrt{\Delta t}}{\sigma_1},$$

TABLE 6.4 The Computed Values and Absolute Errors for European Put and Call Options on the Minimum of Two Assets. The Results were Obtained using a Binomial Lattice and the Analytic Formula (Johnson (1987) and Stulz (1982)). The Time to Maturity of the Option is Varied from 0.1 Years to 0.8 Years. The Parameters are $E = 44.0$, $S_1 = 40.0$, $S_2 = 50.0$, $r = 0.1$, $\sigma_1 = 0.2$, $\sigma_2 = 0.2$, $q_1 = q_2 = 0.0$, $\rho = 0.5$, and $n\_steps = 50$

	Call			Put		
Time	Analytic	Lattice	Error	Analytic	Lattice	Error
0.1	0.10810	0.10753	5.7048×10^{-4}	3.67044	3.66993	5.0955×10^{-4}
0.2	0.40862	0.40781	8.1047×10^{-4}	3.54551	3.54514	3.6961×10^{-4}
0.3	0.74162	0.73418	7.4339×10^{-3}	3.47882	3.47206	6.7642×10^{-3}
0.4	1.06989	1.07299	3.1076×10^{-3}	3.43283	3.43715	4.3214×10^{-3}
0.5	1.38675	1.38909	2.3414×10^{-3}	3.39540	3.40159	6.1826×10^{-3}
0.6	1.69203	1.69025	1.7757×10^{-3}	3.36145	3.35775	3.6964×10^{-3}
0.7	1.98691	1.96939	1.7520×10^{-2}	3.32859	3.31517	1.3417×10^{-2}
0.8	2.27276	2.26274	1.0018×10^{-2}	3.29566	3.29157	4.0885×10^{-3}

$$p_{uu} - p_{ud} - p_{dd} + p_{du} = \frac{\mu_2 \sqrt{\Delta t}}{\sigma_2},$$

$$p_{uu} + p_{ud} + p_{dd} + p_{du} = 1,$$

$$p_{uu} - p_{ud} + p_{dd} - p_{du} = \rho.$$

These lead to the following jump probabilities:

$$p_{uu} = \frac{1}{4}\left\{1 + \sqrt{\Delta t}\left(\frac{\mu_1}{\sigma_1} + \frac{\mu_2}{\sigma_2}\right) + \rho\right\},$$

$$p_{ud} = \frac{1}{4}\left\{1 + \sqrt{\Delta t}\left(\frac{\mu_1}{\sigma_1} - \frac{\mu_2}{\sigma_2}\right) - \rho\right\},$$

$$p_{dd} = \frac{1}{4}\left\{1 + \sqrt{\Delta t}\left(-\frac{\mu_1}{\sigma_1} - \frac{\mu_2}{\sigma_2}\right) + \rho\right\},$$

$$p_{du} = \frac{1}{4}\left\{1 + \sqrt{\Delta t}\left(-\frac{\mu_1}{\sigma_1} + \frac{\mu_2}{\sigma_2}\right) - \rho\right\}.$$

In Code excerpt 6.4, we provide the computer code for a standard binomial lattice which prices options on the maximum and minimum of two assets.

The parameter M is the number of time steps used, and the lattice is constructed under the assumption that M is even.

```
void standard_2D_binomial(double *value, double S1, double S2, double X,
                          double sigma1, double sigma2, double rho, double T,
                          double r, double q1, double q2, long put,
                          long M, long opt_type, long is_american, long *iflag)
{
/* Input parameters:
   ==================
   S1                - the current price of the underlying asset 1
   S2                - the current price of the underlying asset 2
   X                 - the strike price
   sigma1            - the volatility of asset 1
   sigma2            - the volatility of asset 2
   rho               - the correlation coefficient between asset 1 and asset 2
   T                 - the time to maturity
   r                 - the interest rate
   q1                - the continuous dividend yield for asset 1
   q2                - the continuous dividend yield for asset 2
   put               - if put is 0 then a call option, otherwise a put option
   M                 - the number of time steps, the zeroth time step is the root node of the lattice
   opt_type          - if opt_type is 0 then an option on the maximum of two asset
                       otherwise an option on the minimum of two assets
   is_american       - if is_american is 0 then a European option, otherwise an American option
   Output parameters:
   ==================
   value             - the value of the option,
   iflag             - an error indicator.
*/
    double discount,t1,dt,d1,d2,u1,u2;
    long i,j,m1,n,iflagx,jj,ind;
    double zero=0.0,hold;
    double temp,ds1,ds2,dv1,dv2,h,tmp;
    double *s1, *s2, *v;
    double p[4];
    long P1,P2,tdv;
    double sqrt_dt, t, mu1, mu2, jp1, jp2;
    double one = 1.0, half = 0.5, quarter = 0.25;
    long v1;

    if (!((M+1)/2) == (M/2)) printf ("ERROR THE NUMBER OF TIME STEPS IS NOT EVEN \n");
    tdv = M + 1;
#define V(I,J) v[(I) * tdv + (J)]
#define UU  0
#define UD  1
#define DD  2
#define DU  3
    dt = T/(double)M;
    sqrt_dt = sqrt(dt);
    jp1 = sigma1*sqrt_dt;
    jp2 = sigma2*sqrt_dt;
    mu1 = r - q1 - sigma1*sigma1*half;
    mu2 = r - q2 - sigma2*sigma2*half;
    u1 = exp(jp1); /* assign the jump sizes */
    u2 = exp(jp2);
    d1 = exp(-jp1);
    d2 = exp(-jp2);
    p[UU] = quarter*(one + sqrt_dt * ((mu1/sigma1) + (mu2/sigma2)) + rho); /* set up the jump probabilities */
    p[UD] = quarter*(one + sqrt_dt * ((mu1/sigma1) - (mu2/sigma2)) - rho);
    p[DD] = quarter*(one + sqrt_dt * (-(mu1/sigma1) - (mu2/sigma2)) + rho);
    p[DU] = quarter*(one + sqrt_dt * (-(mu1/sigma1) + (mu2/sigma2)) - rho);
    for (i = 0; i < 4; ++i) {
        if ((p[i] < zero) || (p[i] > 1.0)) printf ("ERROR p out of range\n");
    }
    discount = exp(-r*dt);
    for (i = 0; i < 4; ++i) {
        p[i] = p[i]*discount;
    }
/* Allocate the arrays v[(M+1)*(M+1)], s1[2*M+1] and s2[2*M+1] */

    s1[M] = S1; /* assign the 2*M+1 asset values for s1 */
    for (i = 1; i <= M; ++i) {
        s1[M+i] = u1*s1[M+i-1];
        s1[M-i] = d1*s1[M-i+1];
    }
    s2[M] = S2; /* assign the 2*M+1 asset values for s2 */
    for (i = 1; i <= M; ++i) {
        s2[M+i] = u2*s2[M+i-1];
        s2[M-i] = d2*s2[M-i+1];
    }
    P1 = 0;
    for (i = 0; i <= M; ++i) { /* Calculate the option values at maturity */
        P2 = 0;
        for (j = 0; j <= M; ++j) {
```

Code excerpt 6.4 Function to calculate the value of a European put or call on the maximum or minimum of two assets using a standard binomial lattice.

```
    if (opt_type == 0) { /* Maximum of two assets */
        if (put) {
            V(i,j)  = MAX(X - MAX(s1[P1],s2[P2]),zero);
        }
        else {
            V(i,j)  = MAX(MAX(s1[P1],s2[P2])-X,zero);
        }
    }
    else {
        if (put) { /* Minimum of two assets */
            V(i,j)  = MAX(X - MIN(s1[P1],s2[P2]),zero);
        }
        else {
            V(i,j)  = MAX(MIN(s1[P1],s2[P2])-X,zero);
        }
    }
    P2 = P2 + 2;
    }
    P1 = P1 + 2;
}
for (m1 = M-1; m1 >= 0; --m1) { /* work backwards through the lattice to calculate option value */
    P1 = M-m1;
    for (i = 0; i <= m1; ++i) {
        P2 = M-m1;
        for (j = 0; j <= m1; ++j) {
            hold = p[UD]*V(i+1,j) + p[UU]*V(i+1,j+1) + p[DU]*V(i,j+1) + p[DD]*V(i,j);
            if (is_american) {        /* An American option */
                if (opt_type == 0) {  /* Maximum of two assets */
                    if (put)
                        V(i,j) = MAX(hold,X-MAX(s1[P1],s2[P2]));
                    else
                        V(i,j) = MAX(hold,MAX(s1[P1],s2[P2])-X);
                }
                else {                   /* Minimum of two assets */
                    if (put)
                        V(i,j) = MAX(hold,X-MIN(s1[P1],s2[P2]));
                    else
                        V(i,j) = MAX(hold,MIN(s1[P1],s2[P2])-X);
                }
            }
            else {
                V(i,j) = hold;
            }
            P2 = P2 + 2;
        }
        P1 = P1 + 2;
    }
}
*value = V(0,0);
}
```

Code excerpt 6.4 (*Continued*).

6.6 THREE-ASSET OPTIONS

For three asset options (see Code excerpt 6.5 and results in Tables 6.5–6.8), we have the following jump probabilities:

$$p_{uuu} = \frac{1}{8}\left\{ 1 + \sqrt{\Delta t}\left(\frac{\mu_1}{\sigma_1} + \frac{\mu_2}{\sigma_2} + \frac{\mu_3}{\sigma_3}\right) + \rho_{12} + \rho_{13} + \rho_{23} \right\},$$

$$p_{uud} = \frac{1}{8}\left\{ 1 + \sqrt{\Delta t}\left(\frac{\mu_1}{\sigma_1} + \frac{\mu_2}{\sigma_2} - \frac{\mu_3}{\sigma_3}\right) + \rho_{12} - \rho_{13} - \rho_{23} \right\},$$

$$p_{udu} = \frac{1}{8}\left\{ 1 + \sqrt{\Delta t}\left(\frac{\mu_1}{\sigma_1} - \frac{\mu_2}{\sigma_2} + \frac{\mu_3}{\sigma_3}\right) - \rho_{12} + \rho_{13} - \rho_{23} \right\},$$

$$p_{udd} = \frac{1}{8}\left\{ 1 + \sqrt{\Delta t}\left(\frac{\mu_1}{\sigma_1} - \frac{\mu_2}{\sigma_2} - \frac{\mu_3}{\sigma_3}\right) - \rho_{12} - \rho_{13} + \rho_{23} \right\},$$

$$p_{duu} = \frac{1}{8}\left\{ 1 + \sqrt{\Delta t}\left(-\frac{\mu_1}{\sigma_1} + \frac{\mu_2}{\sigma_2} + \frac{\mu_3}{\sigma_3}\right) - \rho_{12} - \rho_{13} + \rho_{23} \right\},$$

$$p_{dud} = \frac{1}{8}\left\{1 + \sqrt{\Delta t}\left(-\frac{\mu_1}{\sigma_1} + \frac{\mu_2}{\sigma_2} + \frac{\mu_3}{\sigma_3}\right) - \rho_{12} + \rho_{13} - \rho_{23}\right\},$$

$$p_{ddu} = \frac{1}{8}\left\{1 + \sqrt{\Delta t}\left(-\frac{\mu_1}{\sigma_1} - \frac{\mu_2}{\sigma_2} + \frac{\mu_3}{\sigma_3}\right) + \rho_{12} - \rho_{13} - \rho_{23}\right\},$$

$$p_{ddd} = \frac{1}{8}\left\{1 + \sqrt{\Delta t}\left(-\frac{\mu_1}{\sigma_1} - \frac{\mu_2}{\sigma_2} - \frac{\mu_3}{\sigma_3}\right) + \rho_{12} + \rho_{13} + \rho_{23}\right\}.$$

```
void standard_3D_binomial(double *value, double S1, double S2, double S3, double X,
    double sigma1, double sigma2, double sigma3, double rho_12, double rho_13, double rho_23,
    double T, double r, long put, long M, long opt_type, long is_american, long *iflag)
{
/* Input parameters:
   =================
   S1                - the current price of the underlying asset 1
   S2                - the current price of the underlying asset 2
   S3                - the current price of the underlying asset 3
   X                 - the strike price
   sigma1            - the volatility of asset 1
   sigma2            - the volatility of asset 2
   sigma3            - the volatility of asset 3
   rho_12            - the correlation coefficient between asset 1 and asset 2
   rho_13            - the correlation coefficient between asset 1 and asset 3
   rho_23            - the correlation coefficient between asset 2 and asset 3
   T                 - the time to maturity
   r                 - the interest rate
   put               - if put is 0 then a call option, otherwise a put option
   M                 - the number of time steps, the zeroth time step is the root node of the lattice
   opt_type          - if opt_type is 0 then an option on the maximum of two asset
                       otherwise an option on the minimum of two assets
   is_american       - if is_american is 0 then a European option, otherwise an American option.
   Output parameters:
   ==================
   value             - the value of the option,
   iflag             - an error indicator.
*/
   double discount,t1,dt,d1,d2,d3,u1,u2,u3;
   long i,j,k,m1,n,iflagx,jj,ind;
   double zero=0.0,hold;
   double temp,ds1,ds2,dv1,dv2,h,tmp,tmp1,tmp2;
   double *s1, *s2, *s3, *v;
   double p[9];
   long P1,P2,P3,tdv, tdv2;
   double sqrt_dt, t, mu1, mu2, mu3, jp1, jp2, jp3;
   double one = 1.0, half = 0.5, eighth = 0.125;
   long v1;

   if (!((M+1)/2) == (M/2)) printf ("ERROR THE NUMBER OF TIME STEPS IS NOT EVEN \n");
   tdv = M + 1;
   tdv2 = tdv*tdv;
#define V(I,J, K) v[(I) * tdv2 + (J)*tdv + (K)]
#define UUU  0
#define UUD  1
#define UDU  2
#define UDD  3
#define DUU  4
#define DUD  5
#define DDU  6
#define DDD  7
   dt = T/(double)M;
   sqrt_dt = sqrt(dt);
   jp1 = sigma1*sqrt_dt;
   jp2 = sigma2*sqrt_dt;
   jp3 = sigma3*sqrt_dt;
   mu1 = r - sigma1*sigma1*half;
   mu2 = r - sigma2*sigma2*half;
   mu3 = r - sigma3*sigma3*half;
   u1 = exp(jp1); /* assign the jump sizes */
   u2 = exp(jp2);
   u3 = exp(jp3);
   d1 = exp(-jp1);
   d2 = exp(-jp2);
   d3 = exp(-jp3);
/* set up the jump probabilities  */
   p[UUU] = eighth*(one + sqrt_dt * ((mu1/sigma1) + (mu2/sigma2) + (mu3/sigma3)) + rho_12 + rho_13 + rho_23);
   p[UUD] = eighth*(one + sqrt_dt * ((mu1/sigma1) + (mu2/sigma2) - (mu3/sigma3)) + rho_12 - rho_13 - rho_23);
   p[UDU] = eighth*(one + sqrt_dt * ((mu1/sigma1) - (mu2/sigma2) + (mu3/sigma3)) - rho_12 + rho_13 - rho_23);
   p[UDD] = eighth*(one + sqrt_dt * ((mu1/sigma1) - (mu2/sigma2) - (mu3/sigma3)) - rho_12 - rho_13 + rho_23);
```

Code excerpt 6.5 Standard 3-dimensional binomial lattice.

```
   p[DUU] = eighth*(one + sqrt_dt * (-(mu1/sigma1) + (mu2/sigma2) + (mu3/sigma3))) - rho_12 - rho_13 + rho_23);
   p[DUD] = eighth*(one + sqrt_dt * (-(mu1/sigma1) + (mu2/sigma2) - (mu3/sigma3))) - rho_12 + rho_13 - rho_23);
   p[DDU] = eighth*(one + sqrt_dt * (-(mu1/sigma1) - (mu2/sigma2) + (mu3/sigma3))) + rho_12 - rho_13 - rho_23);
   p[DDD] = eighth*(one + sqrt_dt * (-(mu1/sigma1) - (mu2/sigma2) - (mu3/sigma3))) + rho_12 + rho_13 + rho_23);
   for (i = 0; i < 8; ++i) {
     if ((p[i] < zero) || (p[i] > 1.0)) printf ("ERROR p[%ld] = %12.4f out of range\n",i, p[i]);
   }
   discount = exp(-r*dt);
   for (i = 0; i < 8; ++i) {
     p[i] = p[i]*discount;
   }
/* Allocate the arrays v[(M+1)*(M+1)*(M+1)], s1[2*M+1], s2[2*M+1], and s3[2*M+1] */
       .     .      .
   s1[M] = S1;
   for (i = 1; i <= M; ++i) { /* assign the 2*M+1 asset values for s1 */
     s1[M+i] = u1*s1[M+i-1];
     s1[M-i] = d1*s1[M-i+1];
   }
   s2[M] = S2;
   for (i = 1; i <= M; ++i) { /* assign the 2*M+1 asset values for s2 */
     s2[M+i] = u2*s2[M+i-1];
     s2[M-i] = d2*s2[M-i+1];
   }
   s3[M] = S3;
   for (i = 1; i <= M; ++i) { /* assign the 2*M+1 asset values for s2 */
     s3[M+i] = u3*s3[M+i-1];
     s3[M-i] = d3*s3[M-i+1];
   }
   /* Calculate the option values at maturity  */
   P1 = 0;
   for (i = 0; i <= M; ++i) {
     P2 = 0;
     for (j = 0; j <= M; ++j) {
       P3 = 0;
       for (k = 0; k <= M; ++k) {
         if (put) { /* put */
           if (opt_type == 0) { /* Maximum of 3 assets */
             tmp = MAX(s1[P1],s2[P2]);
             V(i,j,k)  = MAX(X - MAX(tmp,s3[P3]),zero);
           }
           else if (opt_type == 1) { /* Minimum of 3 assets */
             tmp = MIN(s1[P1],s2[P2]);
             V(i,j,k)  = MAX(X - MIN(tmp,s3[P3]),zero);
           }
         }
         else { /* call */
           ** Insert call option code using the supplied put option code as a template **
         }
         P3 = P3 + 2;
       }
       P2 = P2 + 2;
     }
     P1 = P1 + 2;
   }
   for (m1 = M-1; m1 >= 0; --m1) {  /* work backwards through the lattice to calculate the option value */
     P1 = M-m1;
     for (i = 0; i <= m1; ++i) {
       P2 = M-m1;
       for (j = 0; j <= m1; ++j) {
         P3 = M-m1;
         for (k = 0; k <= m1; ++k) {
           hold = p[UUU]*V(i+1,j+1,k+1) + p[UUD]*V(i+1,j+1,k) + p[UDU]*V(i+1,j,k+1) + p[UDD]*V(i+1,j,k) +
                  p[DUU]*V(i,j+1,k+1) + p[DUD]*V(i,j+1,k) + p[DDU]*V(i,j,k+1) + p[DDD]*V(i,j,k);
           if (is_american) {
             if (put) {
               if (opt_type == 0) { /* Maximum of 3 assets */
                 tmp = MAX(s1[P1],s2[P2]);
                 tmp1  = MAX(tmp,s3[P3]);
                 tmp2 = MAX(X-tmp1,hold);
                 V(i,j,k) = MAX(tmp2,zero);
               }
               else if (opt_type == 1) { /* Minimum of 3 assets */
                 tmp = MIN(s1[P1],s2[P2]);
                 tmp1 = MIN(tmp,s3[P3]);
                 tmp2 = MAX(X-tmp1,hold);
                 V(i,j,k)  = MAX(tmp2,zero);
               }
             }
             else { /* call option */
               ** Insert call option code using the supplied put option code as a template **
             }
           }
           else { /* European option */
             V(i,j,k) = hold;
           }
```

Code excerpt 6.5 (*Continued*).

```
        P3 = P3 + 2;
      }
      P2 = P2 + 2;
    }
    P1 = P1 + 2;
  }
}
*value = V(0,0,0);
}
```

Code excerpt 6.5 (*Continued*).

6.7 FOUR-ASSET OPTIONS

The results for four assets are presented in Tables 6.9 and 6.10. We have the following jump probabilities:

$$
p_{uuuu} = \frac{1}{16} \left\{ 1 + \sqrt{\Delta t} \left(\frac{\mu_1}{\sigma_1} + \frac{\mu_2}{\sigma_2} + \frac{\mu_3}{\sigma_3} + \frac{\mu_4}{\sigma_4} \right) \right.
$$
$$
\left. + \rho_{12} + \rho_{13} + \rho_{14} + \rho_{23} + \rho_{24} + \rho_{34} \right\},
$$

$$
p_{uuud} = \frac{1}{16} \left\{ 1 + \sqrt{\Delta t} \left(\frac{\mu_1}{\sigma_1} + \frac{\mu_2}{\sigma_2} + \frac{\mu_3}{\sigma_3} - \frac{\mu_4}{\sigma_4} \right) \right.
$$
$$
\left. + \rho_{12} + \rho_{13} - \rho_{14} + \rho_{23} - \rho_{24} + \rho_{34} \right\},
$$

$$
p_{uudu} = \frac{1}{16} \left\{ 1 + \sqrt{\Delta t} \left(\frac{\mu_1}{\sigma_1} + \frac{\mu_2}{\sigma_2} - \frac{\mu_3}{\sigma_3} + \frac{\mu_4}{\sigma_4} \right) \right.
$$
$$
\left. + \rho_{12} - \rho_{13} + \rho_{14} - \rho_{23} + \rho_{24} - \rho_{34} \right\},
$$

TABLE 6.5 The Computed Values and Absolute Errors for European Options on the Maximum of Three Assets. A Binomial Lattice was used and We Show How the Accuracy of the Results Depends on the Number of Time Steps. The Parameters are $E = 100.0$, $S_1 = S_2 = S_3 = 100.0$, $r = 0.1$, $\tau = 1.0$, $\sigma_1 = \sigma_2 = \sigma_3 = 0.2$, $\rho_{12} = \rho_{13} = \rho_{23} = 0.5$, and $q_1 = q_2 = q_3 = 0.0$. The *Accurate* Values are 0.936 for a Put and 22.672 for a Call, See Table 2 (Boyle Evnine and Gibbs, 1989)

	Put			Call	
nsteps	Computed value	Error		Computed value	Error
10	0.9112	2.485×10^{-2}		21.8601	8.119×10^{-1}
20	0.9192	1.678×10^{-2}		22.2807	3.913×10^{-1}
30	0.9232	1.276×10^{-2}		22.4137	2.583×10^{-1}
40	0.9254	1.056×10^{-2}		22.4792	1.928×10^{-1}
50	0.9268	9.180×10^{-3}		22.5182	1.538×10^{-1}
60	0.9278	8.236×10^{-3}		22.5441	1.279×10^{-1}

TABLE 6.6 The Computed Values and Absolute Errors for European Options on the Minimum of Three Assets. A Binomial Lattice was used and We Show How the Accuracy of the Results Depends on the Number of Time Steps. The Parameters are $E = 100.0$, $S_1 = S_2 = S_3 = 100.0$, $r = 0.1$, $\tau = 1.0$, $\sigma_1 = \sigma_2 = \sigma_3 = 0.2$, $\rho_{12} = \rho_{13} = \rho_{23} = 0.5$, and $q_1 = q_2 = q_3 = 0.0$. The *Accurate* Values are 7.403 for a Put and 5.249 for a Call, See Table 2 (Boyle Evnine and Gibbs, 1989)

	Put		Call	
nsteps	Computed value	Error	Computed value	Error
10	7.0759	3.271×10^{-1}	5.2072	4.176×10^{-2}
20	7.2402	1.628×10^{-1}	5.2263	2.269×10^{-2}
30	7.2953	1.077×10^{-1}	5.2334	1.560×10^{-2}
40	7.3229	8.015×10^{-2}	5.2371	1.192×10^{-2}
50	7.3394	6.357×10^{-2}	5.2393	9.665×10^{-2}
60	7.3505	5.251×10^{-2}	5.2409	8.143×10^{-3}

$$P_{uudd} = \frac{1}{16}\left\{ 1 + \sqrt{\Delta t}\left(\frac{\mu_1}{\sigma_1} + \frac{\mu_2}{\sigma_2} - \frac{\mu_3}{\sigma_3} - \frac{\mu_4}{\sigma_4} \right) \right.$$
$$\left. + \rho_{12} - \rho_{13} - \rho_{14} - \rho_{23} - \rho_{24} + \rho_{34} \right\},$$

$$P_{uduu} = \frac{1}{16}\left\{ 1 + \sqrt{\Delta t}\left(\frac{\mu_1}{\sigma_1} - \frac{\mu_2}{\sigma_2} + \frac{\mu_3}{\sigma_3} + \frac{\mu_4}{\sigma_4} \right) \right.$$
$$\left. - \rho_{12} + \rho_{13} + \rho_{14} - \rho_{23} - \rho_{24} + \rho_{34} \right\},$$

$$P_{udud} = \frac{1}{16}\left\{ 1 + \sqrt{\Delta t}\left(\frac{\mu_1}{\sigma_1} - \frac{\mu_2}{\sigma_2} + \frac{\mu_3}{\sigma_3} - \frac{\mu_4}{\sigma_4} \right) \right.$$
$$\left. - \rho_{12} + \rho_{13} - \rho_{14} - \rho_{23} + \rho_{24} - \rho_{34} \right\},$$

$$P_{uddu} = \frac{1}{16}\left\{ 1 + \sqrt{\Delta t}\left(\frac{\mu_1}{\sigma_1} - \frac{\mu_2}{\sigma_2} - \frac{\mu_3}{\sigma_3} + \frac{\mu_4}{\sigma_4} \right) \right.$$
$$\left. - \rho_{12} - \rho_{13} + \rho_{14} + \rho_{23} - \rho_{24} - \rho_{34} \right\},$$

$$P_{uddd} = \frac{1}{16}\left\{ 1 + \sqrt{\Delta t}\left(\frac{\mu_1}{\sigma_1} - \frac{\mu_2}{\sigma_2} - \frac{\mu_3}{\sigma_3} - \frac{\mu_4}{\sigma_4} \right) \right.$$
$$\left. - \rho_{12} - \rho_{13} - \rho_{14} + \rho_{23} + \rho_{24} + \rho_{34} \right\},$$

$$p_{duuu} = \frac{1}{16}\left\{1 + \sqrt{\Delta t}\left(-\frac{\mu_1}{\sigma_1} + \frac{\mu_2}{\sigma_2} + \frac{\mu_3}{\sigma_3} + \frac{\mu_4}{\sigma_4}\right)\right.$$
$$\left. - \rho_{12} - \rho_{13} - \rho_{14} + \rho_{23} + \rho_{24} + \rho_{34}\right\},$$

$$p_{duud} = \frac{1}{16}\left\{1 + \sqrt{\Delta t}\left(-\frac{\mu_1}{\sigma_1} + \frac{\mu_2}{\sigma_2} + \frac{\mu_3}{\sigma_3} - \frac{\mu_4}{\sigma_4}\right)\right.$$
$$\left. - \rho_{12} - \rho_{13} + \rho_{14} + \rho_{23} - \rho_{24} - \rho_{34}\right\},$$

$$p_{dudu} = \frac{1}{16}\left\{1 + \sqrt{\Delta t}\left(-\frac{\mu_1}{\sigma_1} + \frac{\mu_2}{\sigma_2} - \frac{\mu_3}{\sigma_3} + \frac{\mu_4}{\sigma_4}\right)\right.$$
$$\left. - \rho_{12} + \rho_{13} - \rho_{14} - \rho_{23} + \rho_{24} - \rho_{34}\right\},$$

$$p_{dudd} = \frac{1}{16}\left\{1 + \sqrt{\Delta t}\left(-\frac{\mu_1}{\sigma_1} + \frac{\mu_2}{\sigma_2} - \frac{\mu_3}{\sigma_3} - \frac{\mu_4}{\sigma_4}\right)\right.$$
$$\left. - \rho_{12} + \rho_{13} + \rho_{14} - \rho_{23} - \rho_{24} + \rho_{34}\right\},$$

$$p_{dduu} = \frac{1}{16}\left\{1 + \sqrt{\Delta t}\left(-\frac{\mu_1}{\sigma_1} - \frac{\mu_2}{\sigma_2} + \frac{\mu_3}{\sigma_3} + \frac{\mu_4}{\sigma_4}\right)\right.$$
$$\left. + \rho_{12} - \rho_{13} - \rho_{14} - \rho_{23} - \rho_{24} + \rho_{34}\right\},$$

$$p_{ddud} = \frac{1}{16}\left\{1 + \sqrt{\Delta t}\left(-\frac{\mu_1}{\sigma_1} - \frac{\mu_2}{\sigma_2} + \frac{\mu_3}{\sigma_3} - \frac{\mu_4}{\sigma_4}\right)\right.$$
$$\left. + \rho_{12} - \rho_{13} + \rho_{14} - \rho_{23} + \rho_{24} - \rho_{34}\right\},$$

$$p_{dddu} = \frac{1}{16}\left\{1 + \sqrt{\Delta t}\left(-\frac{\mu_1}{\sigma_1} - \frac{\mu_2}{\sigma_2} - \frac{\mu_3}{\sigma_3} + \frac{\mu_4}{\sigma_4}\right)\right.$$
$$\left. + \rho_{12} + \rho_{13} - \rho_{14} + \rho_{23} - \rho_{24} - \rho_{34}\right\},$$

$$p_{dddd} = \frac{1}{16}\left\{1 + \sqrt{\Delta t}\left(-\frac{\mu_1}{\sigma_1} - \frac{\mu_2}{\sigma_2} - \frac{\mu_3}{\sigma_3} - \frac{\mu_4}{\sigma_4}\right)\right.$$
$$\left. + \rho_{12} + \rho_{13} - \rho_{14} + \rho_{23} + \rho_{24} + \rho_{34}\right\}.$$

6.8 SELECTED EXERCISES

1. Write a program that computes the value of European and American options on the sum and difference of two-asset prices following correlated GBM.
2. Check your result for problem 1 by using Monte Carlo simulation to compute the value for a European option. You can generate correlated variates by using the method given in exercise 4 Chapter 4.

TABLE 6.7 The Computed Values and Absolute Errors for European Options on the Maximum of Three Assets. A Binomial Lattice was used and We Show How the Accuracy Depend on the Number of Time Steps. The Parameters are $E = 100.0$, $S_1 = S_2 = S_3 = 100.0$, $r = 0.1$, $\tau = 1.0$, $\sigma_1 = \sigma_2 = \sigma_3 = 0.2$, $\rho_{12} = -0.5$, $\rho_{13} = -0.5$, $\rho_{23} = 0.5$, and $q_1 = q_2 = q_3 = 0.0$. The *Accurate* Values are 0.0526 for a Put and 27.8271 for a Call and were Computed using Monte Carlo Simulation with 10^7 Paths

	Put		Call	
nsteps	Computed value	Error	Computed value	Error
10	0.0122	4.041×10^{-2}	27.3180	5.091×10^{-1}
20	0.0295	2.314×10^{-2}	27.5743	2.528×10^{-1}
30	0.0366	1.600×10^{-2}	27.6589	1.682×10^{-1}
40	0.0404	1.221×10^{-2}	27.7010	1.261×10^{-1}
50	0.0427	9.868×10^{-3}	27.7263	1.008×10^{-1}
60	0.0443	8.280×10^{-3}	27.7431	8.396×10^{-2}

TABLE 6.8 The Computed Values and Absolute Errors for European Options on the Minimum of Three Assets. A Binomial Lattice was used and We Show How the Accuracy Depend on the Number of Time Steps. The Parameters are $E = 100.0$, $S_1 = S_2 = S_3 = 100.0$, $r = 0.1$, $\tau = 1.0$, $\sigma_1 = \sigma_2 = \sigma_3 = 0.2$, $\rho_{12} = -0.5$, $\rho_{13} = -0.5$, $\rho_{23} = 0.5$, and $q_1 = q_2 = q_3 = 0.0$. The *Accurate* Values are 9.2776 for a Put and 1.5847 for a Call and were Computed using Monte Carlo Simulation with 10^7 Paths

	Put		Call	
nsteps	Computed value	Error	Computed value	Error
10	8.9646	3.130×10^{-1}	1.4047	1.800×10^{-1}
20	9.1231	1.545×10^{-1}	1.4963	8.836×10^{-2}
30	9.1749	1.027×10^{-1}	1.5261	5.857×10^{-2}
40	9.2007	7.694×10^{-2}	1.5409	4.381×10^{-2}
50	9.2161	6.151×10^{-2}	1.5497	3.499×10^{-2}
60	9.2264	5.123×10^{-2}	1.5556	2.913×10^{-2}

TABLE 6.9 The Computed Values and Absolute Errors for European Options on the Maximum of Four Assets. A Binomial Lattice was used and We Show How the Accuracy Depend on the Number of Time Steps. The Parameters are $E = 100.0$, $S_1 = S_2 = S_3 = S_4 = 100.0$, $r = 0.1$, $\tau = 1.0$, $\sigma_1 = \sigma_2 = \sigma_3 = \sigma_4 = 0.2$, $\rho_{12} = 0.5$, $\rho_{13} = 0.5$, $\rho_{23} = 0.5$, and $q_1 = q_2 = q_3 = q_4 = 0.0$. The *Accurate* Values are 0.6309 for a Put and 25.2363 for a Call and were Computed using Monte Carlo Simulation with 10^7 Paths

	Put		Call	
nsteps	Computed value	Error	Computed value	Error
4	0.6548	2.386×10^{-2}	22.1403	3.096
8	0.6268	4.129×10^{-3}	23.8640	1.372
12	0.6246	6.275×10^{-3}	24.3630	8.733×10^{-1}
16	0.6251	5.836×10^{-3}	24.5934	6.429×10^{-1}
20	0.6257	5.167×10^{-3}	24.7270	5.093×10^{-1}
24	0.6263	4.570×10^{-3}	24.8144	4.219×10^{-1}
28	0.6268	4.074×10^{-3}	24.8762	3.601×10^{-1}
32	0.6272	3.665×10^{-3}	24.9222	3.141×10^{-1}

3. Use Monte Carlo simulation to value European options on the sum and difference of three-asset prices following correlated GBM. You can generate correlated variates by using the Cholesky factorization in exercise 5 Chapter 4.

4. Use Monte Carlo simulation to value an option on the sum and difference of the average values two correlated assets, X and Y, following GBM. That is if the price is observed at times t_i, $i = 1, \ldots, n$ and the values are X_i and Y_i, then the payoff of a call option on the sum is

$$C = \max\left(\frac{1}{n}\sum_{i=1}^{n} X_i + \frac{1}{n}\sum_{i=1}^{n} Y_i - K, 0\right)$$

and on the difference is

$$C = \max\left(\frac{1}{n}\sum_{i=1}^{n} X_i - \frac{1}{n}\sum_{i=1}^{n} Y_i - K, 0\right),$$

where K is the strike.

5. Use Monte Carlo simulation to value an option on the sum and difference of two-asset prices X and Y following correlated Ornstein–Uhlenbeck

TABLE 6.10 The Computed Values and Absolute Errors for European Options on the Minimum of Four Assets. A Binomial Lattice was used and We Show How the Accuracy Depend on the Number of Time Steps. The Parameters are $E = 100.0$, $S_1 = S_2 = S_3 = S_4 = 100.0$, $r = 0.1$, $\tau = 1.0$, $\sigma_1 = \sigma_2\sigma_3 = \sigma_4 = 0.2$, $\rho_{12} = 0.5$, $\rho_{13} = 0.5$, $\rho_{23} = 0.5$, and $q_1 = q_2 = q_3 = q_4 = 0.0$. The *Accurate* Values are 8.5394 for a Put and 4.0662 for a Call and were Computed using Monte Carlo Simulation with 10^7 Paths

	Put		Call	
nsteps	Computed value	Error	Computed value	Error
4	7.8274	7.120×10^{-1}	3.5676	4.986×10^{-1}
8	8.1571	3.823×10^{-1}	3.8528	2.134×10^{-1}
12	8.2794	2.600×10^{-1}	3.9300	1.362×10^{-1}
16	8.3429	1.965×10^{-1}	3.9659	1.003×10^{-1}
20	8.3815	1.579×10^{-1}	3.9868	7.944×10^{-2}
24	8.4075	1.319×10^{-1}	4.0004	6.577×10^{-2}
28	8.4262	1.132×10^{-1}	4.0101	5.612×10^{-2}
32	8.4402	9.920×10^{-2}	4.0173	4.894×10^{-2}

processes. That is, using notation of Section 2.10,

$$dX = \alpha_X(\mu_X - X)dt + \sigma_X dW_X,$$

$$dY = \alpha_Y(\mu_Y - Y)dt + \sigma_Y dW_Y,$$

and

$$\rho = < dW_X, dW_Y > .$$

Chapter 7

Other Financial Derivatives

7.1 INTRODUCTION

In the preceding sections of the book, we have only dealt with the valuation of equity derivatives. We are now going to consider some of the other types of trades such as the following:

- Interest rate derivatives.
- Foreign exchange derivatives.
- Credit derivatives.

A selection of these trades will be used by the C# portfolio pricing example in Chapter 8.

7.2 INTEREST RATE DERIVATIVES

It is not possible to make *real* profit without risk. For example, if we (*without risk*) invest £1 in a bank account, then allowing for interest, the total number of pounds at future time T will be $1 + \Delta I(t,T)$, where $\Delta I(t,T)$ is the amount of interest accrued from t to time T. Since our investment grew by the riskless interest rate, the *real* value which allows for inflation must still be £1, so

$$DF(t,T)\{1 + \Delta I(t,T)\} = 1,$$

where $DF(t,T)$ is the discount factor from t to T.

Continuously Compounded Spot Rate

When continuous compounding is used $1 + \Delta I(t,T) = \exp\{R(t,T)(T-t)\}$, where $R(t,T)$ is the *annual* continuously compounded spot rate between times t *years* and T *years*. We thus have

$$DF(t,T)\exp\{R(t,T)(T-t)\} = 1, \tag{7.2.1}$$

so the discount factor is given by

$$DF(t,T) = \exp\{-R(t,T)(T-t)\} \tag{7.2.2}$$

and the continuously compounded rate is

$$R(t,T) = -\frac{\log(DF(t,T))}{(T-t)}. \tag{7.2.3}$$

Computational Finance Using C and C#: Derivatives and Valuation.
Copyright © 2016 Elsevier Ltd. All rights reserved.

Simply Compounded Spot Rate

When simple compounding is used $\Delta I(t,T) = L(t,T)(T - t)$, where $L(t,T)$ is the simply compounded spot rate between time t and T. Thus,

$$DF(t,T) \{1 + L(t,T)(T - t)\} = 1$$

and so the simply compounded rate is

$$L(t,T) = \frac{1}{(T - t)} \left\{ \frac{1}{DF(t,T)} - 1 \right\}. \tag{7.2.4}$$

7.2.1 Forward Rate Agreement

A forward rate agreement (FRA) is a contract between two counterparties (referred to here as A and B), in which one counterparty (say A) agrees to pay interest at the (variable) spot rate, while the other agrees to pay at a fixed interest rate. Let the agreement start at time T_s and end at the maturity T_m, at which time the counterparties settle the amount that is owed. If P is the principal then, at time T_m, the contract has the following value to A:

$$V(T_m) = P \{(T_m - T_s)K - L(T_s,T_m)(T_m - T_s)\}, \tag{7.2.5}$$

where K is the agreed fixed rate, and $L(T_s,T_m)$ is the simply compounded rate between times T_s and T_m. From equation (7.2.4), we have

$$L(T_s,T_m) = \frac{1}{(T_m - T_s)} \left\{ \frac{1}{DF(T_s,T_m)} - 1 \right\}$$

so

$$V(T_m) = P \left\{ (T_m - T_s)K - \left(\frac{1}{DF(T_s,T_m)} - 1 \right) \right\}. \tag{7.2.6}$$

The value of the FRA to A at time $t \leq T_m$ is therefore $FRA(t) = DF(t,T_m) V(T_m)$ which means that

$$FRA(t) = DF(t,T_m)P \left\{ (T_m - T_s)K - \left(\frac{1}{DF(T_s,T_m)} - 1 \right) \right\}. \tag{7.2.7}$$

Using $DF(t,T_m) = DF(t,T_s)DF(T_s,T_m)$, we can rewrite equation (7.2.7) as

$$FRA(t) = DF(t,T_m)P \left\{ (T_m - T_s)K - \left(\frac{DF(t,T_s)}{DF(t,T_m)} - 1 \right) \right\}. \tag{7.2.8}$$

The value of K which sets $FRA(t)$ to zero is termed the time t forward rate between times T_s and T_m, and is here denoted by $F(t,T_s,T_m)$. From equation (7.2.8),

$$F(t,T_s,T_m) = \frac{1}{(T_m - T_s)} \left\{ \frac{DF(t,T_s)}{DF(t,T_m)} - 1 \right\}, \tag{7.2.9}$$

Combining equation (7.2.8) and equation (7.2.10), we can express the value of the FRA as

$$FRA(t) = DF(t,T_m)P \tau \{K - F(t,T_s,T_s + \tau)\}, \tag{7.2.10}$$

where $\tau = T_m - T_s$ is known as the *tenor* of the FRA, and T_s is the *reset time* for forward rate $F(t,T_s,T_s + \tau)$.

7.2.2 Interest Rate Swap

Interest rate swaps (IRS's) are very common financial instruments – it is not unusual for 80% of the trades in a portfolio to be IRS deals. Here, we will provide a description of some of the characteristics of IRS's, more detail can be found in Hull (2003).

A *vanilla* IRS consists of a strip of FRA trades, each FRA starting when the previous FRA finishes. The maturity date of the IRS thus corresponds to the maturity date of the last FRA.

Let the start times of the FRAs be $t_i, i = 0, \ldots, n-1$, and the maturity times of the FRAs be $t_i, i = 1, \ldots, n$; note that the FRA start times correspond to the forward rate reset times, and the maturity times correspond to the FRA payment times. We will now adopt the (common) convention of calling the FRA trades *swaplets*, so an IRS is made up of a number of swaplets.

When the counterparty A pays the fixed rate and receives the floating rate, the trade (from A perspective) is termed a *payer* IRS. Alternatively, if A receives the fixed rate and pays the floating rate, then the trade is termed a *receiver* IRS.

The value of an IRS at time t, where $t_{k-1} < t < t_k$, will now be considered.

We will assume that discount factors used to compute the forward rates and those used to discount the coupon payments are associated with the same yield curve. Using equation (7.2.10), we have

$$IRS(t) = C\,DF(t,t_k) + \sum_{i=k+1}^{n} DF(t,t_i)P\,\tau_i\,\{K - F(t,t_{i-1},t_{i-1}+\tau_i)\}, \quad (7.2.11)$$

where C is the *next coupon payment* after current time t (this occurs at time t_k), and τ_i is the tenor of the ith swaplet which starts at time t_{i-1} and ends at time t_i.

Note that the next coupon payment C for the swaplet starting at time t_{k-1} and maturing at time t_k is already known with certainty at time t because the forward rate $F(t,t_{k-1},t_k)$ was reset in the past, $t_{k-1} < t$

We will now rewrite (7.2.11) as

$$IRS(t) = C\,DF(t,t_k) + FXD(t) - FLT(t), \quad (7.2.12)$$

where $FXD(t)$, the time t value of the *fixed leg*, is

$$FXD(t) = P\,K \sum_{i=k+1}^{n} DF(t,t_i)\,\tau_i \quad (7.2.13)$$

and $FLT(t)$, the time t value of the *floating leg*, is

$$FLT(t) = P \sum_{i=k+1}^{n} DF(t,t_i)\,\tau_i\,F(t,t_{i-1},t_{i-1}+\tau_i). \quad (7.2.14)$$

The Floating Leg

We will now evaluate equation (7.2.14). The floating leg coupon payment at time t_i will be denoted by C_i and has value

$$C_i = P\,F(t,t_{i-1},t_{i-1}+\tau_i)\,\tau_i,$$

where

$$F(t,t_{i-1},t_{i-1}+\tau_i) = \left\{ \frac{DF(t,t_{i-1})}{DF(t,t_{i-1}+\tau_i)} - 1 \right\} \frac{1}{\tau_i}.$$

From equation (7.2.14), we thus have

$$FLT(t) = \sum_{i=k+1}^{i=n} C_i DF(t,t_i)$$

$$= P \sum_{i=k+1}^{i=n} DF(t,t_i)\tau_i \left\{ \frac{DF(t,t_{i-1})}{DF(t,t_i)} - 1 \right\} \frac{1}{\tau_i}$$

$$= P \sum_{i=k+1}^{i=n} \{DF(t,t_{i-1}) - DF(t,t_i)\}$$

$$= P \{DF(t,t_k) - DF(t,t_{k+1}) + DF(t,t_{k+1}) \dots$$
$$-DF(t,t_i) + DF(t,t_i) \dots - DF(t,t_n)\}$$

$$= P \{DF(t,t_k) - DF(t,t_n)\},$$

and so the value of the floating leg is

$$FLT(t) = P \{DF(t,t_k) - DF(t,t_n)\}. \tag{7.2.15}$$

The Swap Rate

The time t swap rate SR_t is the value of the fixed rate K which makes the $IRS(t)$ zero. Thus, from equations (7.2.12)–(7.2.14),

$$P \{DF(t,t_k) - DF(t,t_n)\} - C DF(t,t_k) = P SR_t \sum_{i=k+1}^{n} DF(t,t_i)\,\tau_i, \tag{7.2.16}$$

so

$$SR_t = \frac{\{DF(t,t_k) - DF(t,t_n)\} - \frac{C}{P} DF(t,t_k)}{\sum_{i=k+1}^{n} DF(t,t_i)\,\tau_i}. \tag{7.2.17}$$

Amortisation

So far we have assumed that the principal is fixed and set to the value P. We will now deal with the situation were the principal varies with time according to the following *amortization* schedule:

$$AM_i = P_{i-1} - P_i, \quad i = 0,\dots,n-1, \tag{7.2.18}$$

where P_i is the value of the principal at time t_i and $P_0 = P$.

The value of the floating leg is now computed as

$$FLT(t) = \sum_{i=k+1}^{i=n} P_{i-1} DF(t,t_i)\tau_i \left\{ \frac{DF(t,t_{i-1})}{DF(t,t_i)} - 1 \right\} \frac{1}{\tau_i}$$

$$= \sum_{i=k+1}^{i=n} P_{i-1} \{DF(t,t_{i-1}) - DF(t,t_i)\}$$

$$= P_k DF(t,t_k) - P_k DF(t,t_{k+1}) + P_{k+1} DF(t,t_{k+1}) - P_{k+1} DF(t,t_{k+2})$$
$$+ \ldots + P_{n-2} DF(t,t_{n-1}) - P_{n-1} DF(t,t_{n-1}) - P_{n-1} DF(t,t_n)$$

$$= P_k DF(t,t_k) - DF(t,t_{k+1}) \{P_k - P_{k+1}\} - P_{k+1}$$
$$- \ldots - DF(t,t_{n-2}) \{P_{n-2} - P_{n-1}\} - P_{n-1} DF(t,t_n)$$

$$= P_k DF(t,t_k) - P_{n-1} DF(t,t_n) + \sum_{i=k+1}^{n-1} AM_i DF(t,t_i), \qquad (7.2.19)$$

and so the value of the floating leg is

$$FLT(t) = P_k DF(t,t_k) - P_{n-1} DF(t,t_n) + \sum_{i=k+1}^{n-1} AM_i DF(t,t_i). \qquad (7.2.20)$$

When there is no amortization ($P_k = P_{n-1}$ and $AM_i = 0, i = 0, \ldots, n-1$), then equation (7.2.20) reduces to equation (7.2.15).

Basis Swap

This is very similar to an IRS, but now there are two floating legs each with their associated principal amount.

For example, floating leg 1 could be associated with the 1-month LIBOR (London Inter-Bank Offer Rate) and have a schedule of monthly payments, while floating leg 2 could use the 3-month LIBORs and have quarterly payments. In this case, the forward rates and discount factors for leg 1 would be computed using the 1-month LIBOR yield curve, and the forward rates and discount factors for leg 2 will be computed using the 3-month LIBOR yield curve.

We will use the subscripts 1 and 2 to denote quantities associated with legs 1 and 2 respectively. The payment times associated with leg 1 are $t_1^i, i = 1, \ldots, n_1$. While those for leg 2 are $t_2^i, i = 1, \ldots, n_2$, and (for this example) $n_1 = 3n_2$.

If counterparty A makes the quarterly payments (that is receives the payments made on leg 1), then the time t value of the basis swap is

$$BS(t) = C_1 DF_1(t,t_{k_1}) + FLT_1(t) - C_2 DF_2(t,t_{k_2}) - FLT_2(t), \qquad (7.2.21)$$

where we have used similar notation to that used in equation (7.2.12), with

$$FLT_1(t) = P_1 \left(DF_1(t,t_{k_1}) - DF_1(t,t_n)\right) \qquad (7.2.22)$$

and

$$FLT_2(t) = P_2 \left(DF_2(t,t_{k_2}) - DF_2(t,t_n)\right) \qquad (7.2.23)$$

In equations (7.2.22) and (7.2.23), P_1 is the principal for leg 1 and P_2 is the principal for leg 2. The time of the next coupon payment for leg 1 is t_{k_1}, while that for leg 2 is t_{k_2}: in addition, we have used the fact that $t_{n_1} = t_{n_2} = t_n$

We will now consider the case in which the basis swap has been traded at time t and shall also assume that $C_1 = C_2 = 0$ and $t = t_{k_1} = t_{k_2}$. In addition, we will specify that *principal exchange* occurs at the start (time t) and end (time t_n) of the swap.

The cash flows associated with principal exchange at the start of the swap leg are in the *opposite* direction to those for the remainder of the swap leg, see Hull (2003). We have

$$FLT_1(t) = P_1 - P_1 \, DF_1(t,t_n) + \{-P_1 + P_1 \, DF(t,t_n)\} \qquad (7.2.24)$$

and

$$FLT_2(t) = P_2 - P_2 \, DF_2(t,t_n) + \{-P_2 + P_2 \, DF(t,t_n)\}, \qquad (7.2.25)$$

where the principal exchange terms are in the curly brackets and use discount factors $DF(t,T)$ derived from the *main currency* yield curve (in this case GBP) rather than $DF_1(t,T)$ or $DF_2(t,T)$.

It can be seen from equation (7.2.21) that principal exchange at the start of the swap causes leg 2 to contribute the *positive* amount P_2 to the value of the swap, while leg 1 contributes the *negative* amount P_2 to the value of the swap. In contrast, principal exchange at the end of the swap results in leg 2 contributing the *negative* amount $-P_2 DF(t,t_n)$ to the swap value while leg 1 contributes the *positive* amount $P_1 DF(t,t_n)$. If $P_1 = P_2 = P$, then principal exchange does not affect the value of the basis swap. It can also be seen from equation (7.2.24) that if leg 1 used the *main* GBP yield curve instead of the 1-month LIBOR curve then $DF_1(t,t_n) = DF(t,t_n)$, which would result in $FLT_1(t) = 0$. Similarly, $DF_2(t,t_n) = DF(t,t_n)$ would mean that $FLT_2(t) = 0$.

If the valuation time t is after the trade has started, then equation (7.2.21) can be used to price the basis swap, but equations (7.2.24) and (7.2.25) need to be modified as follows:

$$FLT_1(t) = P_1 \, DF_1(t,t_{k_1}) - P_1 \, DF_1(t,t_n) + \{P_1 \, DF(t,t_n)\} \qquad (7.2.26)$$

and

$$FLT_2(t) = P_2 \, DF_2(t,t_{k_2}) - P_2 \, DF_2(t,t_n) + \{P_2 \, DF(t,t_n)\}. \qquad (7.2.27)$$

We will now consider how the timing of the coupon payment in relation to its associated forward rate affects the *present value*, V_{t_0}, of the coupon.

Coupon Payment on Time

In this section, we will justify the approach we have adopted in obtaining the present value of future cash flows generated from *vanilla* forward rates.

From equation (4.2.1), we know that the value at time t_0 of a coupon payment at time t_k is

$$V_{t_0} = DF(t_0,t_k) \, E^{Q^k} \left[\frac{F(t_{k-1},t_{k-1},t_k)}{DF(t_k,t_k)} \right] \tau P,$$

where the symbols have their usual meaning, and we have chosen the numeraire to be the zero coupon bond which matures at time t_k. Since $DF(t_k,t_k) = 1$, we can write

$$V_{t_0} = DF(t_0,t_k) \, E^{Q^k} \left[F(t_{k-1},t_{k-1},t_k) \right] \tau P. \qquad (7.2.28)$$

In Section 7.2.3, we show that $F(t, t_{k-1}, t_k)$ follows the process

$$d\left(F(t, t_{k-1}, t_k)\right) = \sigma_k F(t, t_{k-1}, t_k) \, dW^k. \tag{7.2.29}$$

If we assume that σ_k is constant, then equation (7.2.29) is GBM and (see Chapter 2) has the solution

$$F(t, t_{k-1}, t_k) = F(t_0, t_{k-1}, t_k) \exp\left(-\frac{(t - t_0)\sigma_k^2}{2} + \sigma_k W_t^k\right), \tag{7.2.30}$$

where we have taken $W_{t_0}^k = 0$.

Substituting $t = t_{k-1}$ into equation (7.2.30) gives

$$F(t_{k-1}, t_{k-1}, t_k) = F(t_0, t_{k-1}, t_k) \exp\left(-\frac{(t_{k-1} - t_0)\sigma_k^2}{2} + \sigma_k W_{t_{k-1}}^k\right), \tag{7.2.31}$$

which means that

$$E^{Q^k}\left[F(t_{k-1}, t_{k-1}, t_k)\right]$$

$$= E^{Q^k}\left[F(t_0, t_{k-1}, t_k) \exp\left(-\frac{(t_{k-1} - t_0)\sigma_k^2}{2} + \sigma_k W_{t_{k-1}}^k\right)\right]$$

$$= F(t_0, t_{k-1}, t_k) E^{Q^k}\left[\exp\left(-\frac{(t_{k-1} - t_0)\sigma_k^2}{2} + \sigma_k W_{t_{k-1}}^k\right)\right]$$

$$= F(t_0, t_{k-1}, t_k) E^{Q^k}\left[\exp\left(-\frac{(t_{k-1} - t_0)\sigma_k^2}{2} + \sigma_k \sqrt{(t_{k-1} - t_0)}N(0, 1)\right)\right]$$

$$= F(t_0, t_{k-1}, t_k),$$

where we have used the fact (see Appendix D.2) that

$$E^{Q^k}\left[\exp\left(-\frac{(t_{k-1} - t_0)\sigma_k^2}{2} + \sigma_k \sqrt{(t_{k-1} - t_0)}N(0, 1)\right)\right]$$

$$= \exp\left(-\frac{(t_{k-1} - t_0)\sigma_k^2}{2} + \frac{(t_{k-1} - t_0)\sigma_k^2}{2}\right) = 1.$$

Substituting for $E^{Q^k}\left[F(t_{k-1}, t_{k-1}, t_k)\right]$ in equation (7.2.28)

$$V_{t_0} = P\tau F(t_0, t_{k-1}, t_k) = DF(t_0, t_k)\frac{1}{\tau}\left(\frac{DF(t_0, t_{k-1})}{DF(t_0, t_k)} - 1\right)P\tau.$$

This yields

$$V_{t_0} = P\left\{DF(t_0, t_{k-1}) - DF(t_0, t_k)\right\}, \tag{7.2.32}$$

which is our current method of valuing the future coupons generated by forward rates.

General Payment Timing

For the general case, in which the coupon payment date does not correspond to the end of its associated forward rate, we use the result from equation (7.2.43) that

$$dW^k = \left(\frac{\mu_k}{\sigma_k}\right) dt + dW^i, \quad i \neq k. \tag{7.2.33}$$

Equation (7.2.33) states that Brownian motion W^i under numeraire $DF\,(t,t_i)$ can be transformed into Brownian motion W^k under numeraire $DF\,(t,t_k)$ by the addition of a drift term, more detail can be found in Section 7.2.3. If we assume constant drift μ_k, $W^k_{t_0} = W^i_{t_0} = 0$, we obtain

$$W^k_t = (t - t_0)\left(\frac{\mu_k}{\sigma_k}\right) + W^i_t \tag{7.2.34}$$

and in equation (7.2.30)

$$\sigma_k W^k_t = (t - t_0)\,\mu_k + \sigma_k W^i_t.$$

A constant μ_k can be achieved by *freezing* the forward rates that make up μ_k, for example, $F\,(t,t_{k-1},t_k) \rightarrow F\,(t_0,t_{k-1},t_k)$, see Section 7.2.3 for more details concerning μ_k.

This means that $F\,(t,t_{k-1},t_k)$ follows the process

$$d\,(F\,(t,t_{k-1},t_k)) = F\,(t,t_{k-1},t_k)\,\mu_k\,dt + F\,(t,t_{k-1},t_k)\,\sigma_k\,dW^i.$$

The above equation is GBM with drift and can be solved by modifying equation (7.2.30) to

$$F\,(t,t_{k-1},t_k) = F\,(t_0,t_{k-1},t_k)\exp\left((t - t_0)\,\mu_k - \frac{(t - t_0)\,\sigma_k^2}{2} + \sigma_k W^i_t\right). \tag{7.2.35}$$

As before, the time t_0 value of the coupon payment at time t_i is

$$V_{t_0} = DF\,(t_0,t_i)\,E^{\mathbb{Q}^i}\left[\frac{F\,(t_{k-1},t_{k-1},t_k)}{DF\,(t_i,t_i)}\right]\tau P,$$

which since $DF\,(t_i,t_i) = 1$ becomes

$$V_{t_0} = DF\,(t_0,t_i)\,E^{\mathbb{Q}^i}\,[F\,(t_{k-1},t_{k-1},t_k)]\,\tau P. \tag{7.2.36}$$

Now from equation (7.2.35), we have

$$E^{\mathbb{Q}^i}\,[F\,(t_{k-1},t_{k-1},t_k)]$$

$$= E^{\mathbb{Q}^i}\left[F\,(t_0,t_{k-1},t_k)\exp\left((t - t_0)\,\mu_k - \frac{(t_{k-1} - t_0)\,\sigma_k^2}{2} + \sigma_k W^i_{t_{k-1}}\right)\right]$$

$$= F\,(t_0,t_{k-1},t_k)\exp\,((t_{k-1} - t_0)\,\mu_k)\,E^{\mathbb{Q}^i}\left[\exp\left(-\frac{(t_{k-1} - t_0)\,\sigma_k^2}{2} + \sigma_k W^i_{t_{k-1}}\right)\right]$$

$$= F\,(t_0,t_{k-1},t_k)\exp\,((t_{k-1} - t_0)\,\mu_k), \tag{7.2.37}$$

where, as before, we have used the expectation given in Appendix D.2.

By expanding equation (7.2.37) to first order, we obtain

$$E^{Q^i} \left[F(t_{k-1}, t_{k-1}, t_k) \right] = F(t_0, t_{k-1}, t_k) + F(t_0, t_{k-1}, t_k)(t_{k-1} - t_0) \mu_k. \quad (7.2.38)$$

Substituting equation (7.2.38) into equation (7.2.36), we obtain a general expression for the value of the coupon payment,

$$V_{t_0} = DF(t_0, t_i) \tau \left\{ F(t_0, t_{k-1}, t_k) + F(t_0, t_{k-1}, t_k)(t_{k-1} - t_0) \mu_k \right\}. \quad (7.2.39)$$

We will now consider the cases of early and late coupon payments.

Early Coupon Payment

Let us consider the case when $i = k - 1$. From equation (7.2.50),

$$\mu_k = \frac{\tau \sigma_k^2 F(t, t_{k-1}, t_k)}{(1 + \tau F(t, t_{k-1}, t_k))}.$$

First, we freeze the forward rates in μ_k so we use the following:

$$\mu_k = \frac{\tau \sigma_k^2 F(t_0, t_{k-1}, t_k)}{(1 + \tau F(t_0, t_{k-1}, t_k))}.$$

Substituting for μ_k is equation (7.2.39), we obtain

$$V_{t_0} = DF(t_0, t_{k-1}) \tau P \left\{ F(t_0, t_{k-1}, t_k) + (t_{k-1} - t_0) \frac{\sigma_k^2 \tau_k F^2(t_0, t_{k-1}, t_k)}{1 + \tau F(t_0, t_{k-1}, t_k)} \right\},$$

see Brigo and Mercurio (2001), p 387, and Hull (2003).

Late Coupon Payment

We consider the case when $i = k + 1$. From equation (7.2.66),

$$\mu_k = - \frac{\tau \rho_{k,k+1} \sigma_k \sigma_{k+1} F(t, t_k, t_{k+1})}{(1 + \tau F(t, t_k, t_{k+1}))}.$$

Freezing the forward rates, we obtain

$$\mu_k = - \frac{\tau \rho_{k,k+1} \sigma_k \sigma_{k+1} F(t_0, t_k, t_{k+1})}{(1 + \tau F(t_0, t_k, t_{k+1}))}.$$

Substituting for μ_k is equation (7.2.39), we obtain

$$V_{t_0} = DF(t_0, t_{k+1}) \tau P$$
$$\times \left\{ F(t_0, t_{k-1}, t_k) - (t_k - t_0) \frac{\tau \rho_{k,k+1} \sigma_k \sigma_{k+1} F(t_0, t_{k-1}, t_k) F(t_0, t_k, t_{k+1})}{(1 + \tau F(t_0, t_k, t_{k+1}))} \right\}.$$

7.2.3 Timing Adjustment

In this section, we derive expressions for the drift of the forward rate $F(t, t_{k-1}, t_k)$ under various probability measures. We will denote the time t value of a zero coupon bond which pays 1 unit of currency at maturity t_i by $DF(t, t_i)$. For convenience, we will also use the shortened notation $F_k = F(t, t_{k-1}, t_k)$ and $DF_i = DF(t, t_i)$.

The probability measure under which all tradable assets are priced relative to the zero coupon bond price DF_i (that is DF_i is the numeraire) will be denoted by $\mathbb{Q}^i$; under this probability measure, the relative prices will be martingales. We will also denote Brownian motion under probability measure $\mathbb{Q}^i$ by W^i

Case i = k

Here, the maturity of the numeraire DF_k is at the expiry of the forward rate F_k.

Since $DF_k (1 + \tau F_k)$ is a tradable its relative price, $(1 + \tau F_k)/DF_k$ is a martingale under $\mathbb{Q}^k$ and thus has zero drift.

Also $DF_k (1 + \tau F_k)/DF_k = 1 + \tau F_k$ and, since both τ and 1 are constants, F_k must be martingale under $\mathbb{Q}^k$. Thus, the process for F_k has zero drift and is

$$dF_k = F_k \sigma_k dW^k. \tag{7.2.40}$$

For the general case in which $i \neq k$, the process followed by F_k is

$$dF_k = F_k \mu_k dt + F_k \sigma_k dW^i, \tag{7.2.41}$$

where μ_k is a drift that needs to be determined. Equation (7.2.41) can be rewritten as

$$dF_k = F_k \sigma_k \left(\left(\frac{\mu_k}{\sigma_k} \right) dt + dW^i \right). \tag{7.2.42}$$

Comparing equations (7.2.41) and (7.2.42), we have

$$dW^k = \left(\frac{\mu_k}{\sigma_k} \right) dt + dW^i. \tag{7.2.43}$$

This equation gives the relation between Brownian motions under probability measures $\mathbb{Q}^k$ and $\mathbb{Q}^i$. We will now show how to compute the value of μ_k.

Case i < k

Here, we consider situations in which the maturity of the numeraire DF_i is before the expiry of the forward rate F_k.

$\underline{i = k - 1}$

In this case, DF_{k-1} is the numeraire, the forward rate is $F_k = F(t, t_{k-1}, t_k)$, and the numeraire matures at time t_{k-1}, while the forward rate has expiry t_k.

Since DF_k is a tradable the relative price, $\phi = DF_k/DF_{k-1}$ is a martingale under $\mathbb{Q}^{k-1}$ and thus has zero drift.

Now

$$\phi = \frac{DF_k}{DF_{k-1}} = \frac{1}{1 + \tau F_k}, \tag{7.2.44}$$

where we have used

$$DF_{k-1} = DF_k (1 + \tau F_k). \tag{7.2.45}$$

Let the stochastic process followed by F_k under $\mathbb{Q}^{k-1}$ be

$$dF_k = F_k \mu_k dt + F_k \sigma_k dW^{k-1} \tag{7.2.46}$$

and the drift, μ_k, is to be determined.

Using Ito, we have

$$d\phi = \frac{\partial \phi}{\partial F_k} dF_k + \frac{1}{2} \frac{\partial^2 \phi}{\partial F_k^2} E\left[(dF_k)^2\right], \quad \text{where } E\left[(dF_k)^2\right] = \sigma_k^2 F_k^2 dt, \quad (7.2.47)$$

where from equation (7.2.44)

$$\frac{\partial \phi}{\partial F_k} = -\frac{\tau}{(1 + \tau F_k)^2}, \qquad \frac{\partial^2 \phi}{\partial F_k^2} = \frac{2\tau^2}{(1 + \tau F_k)^3}. \qquad (7.2.48)$$

Substituting the values in equation (7.2.48) into equation (7.2.47), we obtain

$$d\phi = -\frac{\tau\phi}{(1 + \tau F_k)}\left\{F_k\mu_k dt + F_k\sigma_k dW^{k-1}\right\} + \frac{1}{2}\frac{\tau^2 2\phi\sigma^2 F_k^2 dt}{(1 + \tau F_k)^2},$$

which can be re-arranged as

$$d\phi = \left\{-\frac{\tau F_k\mu_k\phi}{1 + \tau F_k} + \frac{\phi\tau^2\sigma_k^2 F_k^2}{(1 + \tau F_k)^2}\right\}dt - \frac{\tau\phi F_k\sigma_k}{1 + \tau F_k}dW^{k-1}. \qquad (7.2.49)$$

Now since equation (7.2.49) is driftless,

$$\left\{-\frac{\tau F_k\mu_k\phi}{1 + \tau F_k} + \frac{\phi\tau^2\sigma_k^2 F_k^2}{(1 + \tau F_k)^2}\right\}dt = 0$$

and

$$\mu_k = \frac{\tau\sigma_k^2 F_k}{(1 + \tau F_k)}. \qquad (7.2.50)$$

Substituting equation (7.2.50) into equation (7.2.46),

$$dF_k = \frac{\tau\sigma_k^2 F_k^2}{1 + F_k\tau}dt + F_k\sigma_k dW^{k-1}$$

or

$$dF_k = F_k\sigma_k\left\{\frac{\tau\sigma_k^2 F_k}{1 + F_k\tau}dt + dW^{k-1}\right\}. \qquad (7.2.51)$$

Comparing equations (7.2.51) and (7.2.40) thus yields

$$dW^k = \frac{\tau\sigma_k F_k}{1 + F_k\tau}dt + dW^{k-1}, \qquad (7.2.52)$$

which is the relationship between the Brownian motions dW^{k-1} and dW^k under the respective probability measures $\mathbb{Q}^{k-1}$ and $\mathbb{Q}^k$.

$i \leq k - 2$

Let the stochastic process followed by F_k under $\mathbb{Q}^{k-2}$ be

$$dF_k = F_k\mu_k dt + F_k\sigma_k dW^{k-2}, \qquad (7.2.53)$$

where W^{k-2} is Brownian motion under probability measure $\mathbb{Q}^{k-2}$, and the drift, μ_k, is unknown.

Replacing k with $k - 1$ in equation (7.2.52) gives

$$dW^{k-1} = \frac{\tau\sigma_{k-1}F_{k-1}}{1 + F_{k-1}\tau}dt + dW^{k-2}, \qquad (7.2.54)$$

and using equation (7.2.54) to substitute for dW^{k-1} in equation (7.2.52), we obtain

$$dW^k = \frac{\tau\sigma_k F_k}{1 + F_k\tau}dt + \frac{\tau\sigma_{k-1}F_{k-1}}{1 + F_{k-1}\tau}dt + dW^{k-2}. \qquad (7.2.55)$$

Replacing dW^k in equation (7.2.40) with that given in equation (7.2.55),

$$dF_k = F_k\sigma_k \left\{ \frac{\tau\sigma_k F_k}{1 + F_k\tau}dt + \frac{\tau\sigma_{k-1}F_{k-1}}{1 + F_{k-1}\tau}dt \right\} + F_k\sigma_k dW^{k-2}, \qquad (7.2.56)$$

so the drift is

$$\mu_k = \frac{\tau\sigma_k^2 F_k}{(1 + \tau F_k)} + \frac{\tau F_{k-1}\sigma_k\sigma_{k-1}\rho_{k,k-1}}{(1 + \tau F_{k-1})}. \qquad (7.2.57)$$

The following general expression can be derived in a similar manner:

$$dF_k = \sigma_k F_k \sum_{j=i+1}^{k} \frac{\rho_{k,j}\tau\sigma_j F_j}{1 + \tau F_j}dt + \sigma_k F_k dW^i, \qquad (7.2.58)$$

where all the symbols have the same meanings as before, but now i can take any integer value less than k.

Case $i > k$

We now consider the case when the maturity of the numeraire DF_i is after the expiry of the forward rate F_k.

Case $i = k + 1$

Here, DF_{k+1} is the numeraire and F_k is the forward rate which starts at time t_{k-1} and ends at time t_k.

Since DF_{k-1} is a tradable, its relative price, $\phi = DF_{k-1}/DF_{k+1}$, is a martingale under $\mathbb{Q}^{k+1}$ and thus has zero drift.

Now

$$\phi = \frac{DF_{k-1}}{DF_{k+1}} = (1 + \tau F_k)(1 + \tau F_{k+1}), \qquad (7.2.59)$$

where the processes for F_k and F_{k+1} are

$$dF_{k+1} = F_{k+1}\sigma_{k+1}dW^{k+1}, \qquad (7.2.60)$$

$$dF_k = F_k\mu_k dt + F_k\sigma_k dW^{k+1}, \qquad (7.2.61)$$

and the drift, μ_k, is to be determined.

Using Ito, we have

$$d\phi = \frac{\partial\phi}{\partial F_k}dF_k + \frac{\partial\phi}{\partial F_{k+1}}dF_{k+1} + \frac{1}{2}\sum_{i=k}^{k+1}\sum_{j=k}^{k+1}\frac{\partial^2\phi}{\partial F_i\partial F_j}E[dF_i, dF_j], \qquad (7.2.62)$$

where

$$\frac{\partial \phi}{\partial F_k} = \tau \left(1 + \tau F_{k+1}\right), \qquad \frac{\partial \phi}{\partial F_{k+1}} = \tau \left(1 + \tau F_k\right),$$

$$\frac{\partial^2 \phi}{\partial F_k^2} = \frac{\partial^2 \phi}{\partial F_{k+1}^2} = 0, \qquad \frac{\partial^2 \phi}{\partial F_{k+1} \partial F_k} = \frac{\partial^2 \phi}{\partial F_k \partial F_{k+1}} = \tau^2.$$

$$E\left[dF_k, dF_{k+1}\right] = \left[dF_{k+1}, dF_k\right] = \rho_{k,k+1} \sigma_k \sigma_{k+1} F_k F_{k+1} dt \qquad (7.2.63)$$

Substituting the values in (7.2.63) into equation (7.2.62), we obtain

$$d\phi = \tau \left(1 + \tau F_{k+1}\right) dF_k + \tau \left(1 + \tau F_k\right) dF_{k+1} + \tau^2 \rho_{k,k+1} \sigma_k \sigma_{k+1} F_k F_{k+1} dt.$$

After expanding the terms in dF_k and dF_{k+1}, we have

$$d\phi = \tau \left(1 + \tau F_{k+1}\right) \left\{ F_k \mu_k dt + F_k \sigma_k dW^{k+1} \right\} + \tau \left(1 + \tau F_k\right) F_{k+1} \sigma_{k+1} dW^{k+1}$$
$$+ \tau^2 \rho_{k,k+1} \sigma_k \sigma_{k+1} F_k F_{k+1} dt,$$

and this can re-expressed as

$$d\phi = D + \tau \left(1 + \tau F_{k+1}\right) F_k \sigma_k dW^{k+1} + \tau \left(1 + \tau F_k\right) F_{k+1} \sigma_{k+1} dW^{k+1}, \qquad (7.2.64)$$

where the drift term D in equation (7.2.64) is given by

$$D = \tau \left(1 + \tau F_{k+1}\right) F_k \mu_k dt + \tau^2 \rho_{k,k+1} \sigma_k \sigma_{k+1} F_k F_{k+1} dt. \qquad (7.2.65)$$

Now since ϕ is a martingale under $\mathbb{Q}^{k+1}$, we know that $D = 0$, and therefore equation (7.2.65) results in

$$\left(1 + \tau F_{k+1}\right) F_k \mu_k dt = -\rho_{k,k+1} \sigma_k \sigma_{k+1} F_k F_{k+1} dt.$$

This means that the drift is

$$\mu_k = -\frac{\tau \rho_{k,k+1} \sigma_k \sigma_{k+1} F_{k+1}}{\left(1 + \tau F_{k+1}\right)}. \qquad (7.2.66)$$

Substituting for μ_k in equation (7.2.61) gives

$$dF_k = F_k \sigma_k \left\{ -\frac{\tau \rho_{k,k+1} \sigma_{k+1} F_{k+1}}{\left(1 + \tau F_{k+1}\right)} dt + dW^{k+1} \right\}. \qquad (7.2.67)$$

Comparing equation (7.2.67) with equation (7.2.40), we have

$$dW^k = -\frac{\tau \rho_{k,k+1} \sigma_{k+1} F_{k+1}}{\left(1 + \tau F_{k+1}\right)} dt + dW^{k+1}, \qquad (7.2.68)$$

which is the relationship between Brownian motions dW^k and dW^{k+1}.

$i \geq k + 2$

Let the stochastic process followed by F_k under $\mathbb{Q}^{k+2}$ be

$$dF_k = F_k \mu_k dt + F_k \sigma_k dW^{k+2}, \qquad (7.2.69)$$

where W^{k+2} is Brownian motion under probability measure $\mathbb{Q}^{k+2}$, and drift term μ_k is to be found.

Replacing k with $k+1$ in equation (7.2.68) gives

$$dW^{k+1} = -\frac{\tau \rho_{k+1,k+2}\sigma_{k+2}F_{k+2}}{(1+\tau F_{k+2})}dt + dW^{k+2}, \qquad (7.2.70)$$

and using equation (7.2.70) to substitute for dW^{k+1} in equation (7.2.68) gives

$$dW^k = -\frac{\tau \rho_{k,k+1}\sigma_{k+1}F_{k+1}}{(1+\tau F_{k+1})}dt - \frac{\tau \rho_{k+1,k+2}\sigma_{k+2}F_{k+2}}{(1+\tau F_{k+2})}dt + dW^{k+2}.$$

Substituting for dW^k in equation (7.2.40) gives

$$dW^k = -F_k\sigma_k\left\{\frac{\tau \rho_{k,k+1}\sigma_{k+1}F_{k+1}}{(1+\tau F_{k+1})}dt + \frac{\tau \rho_{k+1,k+2}\sigma_{k+2}F_{k+2}}{(1+\tau F_{k+2})}dt\right\} + F_k\sigma_k dW^{k+2}, \qquad (7.2.71)$$

and thus, the drift is

$$\mu_k = -\frac{\tau \rho_{k,k+1}\sigma_{k+1}F_{k+1}}{(1+\tau F_{k+1})} - \frac{\tau \rho_{k+1,k+2}\sigma_{k+2}F_{k+2}}{(1+\tau F_{k+2})}. \qquad (7.2.72)$$

The following general expression can be derived in a similar manner:

$$dF_k = -\sigma_k F_k \sum_{j=k+1}^{i} \frac{\rho_{k,j}\tau \sigma_j F_j}{1+\tau F_j}dt + \sigma_k F_k dW^i, \qquad (7.2.73)$$

where all the symbols have the same meanings as before, but now i can take any integer value greater than k.

7.2.4 Interest Rate Quantos

This section considers derivatives whose value depends on the foreign interest rate yield curve but have a payoff in domestic currency. We use the same notation as in Section 7.3, which deals with foreign exchange derivatives.

For example, a standard interest rate caplet has a payoff in domestic currency and also depends on the domestic currency forward rates. The value at time t_0 of a caplet which pays at time t_k and extends from time t_{k-1} to time t_k is

$$Caplet(t_0) = P\tau DF^d(t_0,t_k)E^{Q^k}\left[\max\left(F_k^d - K,0\right)\right], \qquad (7.2.74)$$

where P is the principal, K is the strike, $\tau = t_{k-1}-t_k$, F_k is the domestic forward rate $F(t_0,t_{k-1},t_k)$. Equation (7.2.74) can be evaluated using the Black Scholes formula as follows:

$$Caplet(t_0) = P\tau DF^d(t_0,t_k)\left\{F^d(t_0,t_{k-1},t_k)N_1(d_1) - KN_1(d_2)\right\}, \qquad (7.2.75)$$

σ_k is the where σ_d is the volatility of F_k, and

$$d_1 = \frac{\log\left(\left(\frac{F^d(t_0,t_{k-1},t_k)}{K}\right)\right) + \frac{\sigma_d^2}{2}(t_{k-1}-t_0)}{\sigma_d\sqrt{t_{k-1}-t_0}},$$

$$d_2 = \frac{\log\left(\left(\frac{F^d(t_0,t_{k-1},t_k)}{K}\right)\right) - \frac{\sigma_d^2}{2}(t_{k-1}-t_0)}{\sigma_d\sqrt{t_{k-1}-t_0}}. \qquad (7.2.76)$$

In Section 7.2.3, we showed that the process $\left[F^d(t,t_{k-1},t_k)/DF^d(t,t_k)\right]$ is a martingale, that is, has zero drift when $DF^d(t,t_k)$ is used as a numeraire,

$$d\left(F^d(t,t_{k-1},t_k)\right) = \sigma_d\, F^d(t,t_{k-1},t_k)\, dW_k^Q.$$

Quanto Caplet

In a quanto caplet instead of using the domestic forward rate $F^d(t_0,t_{k-1},t_k)$, we use the foreign forward rate $F^f(t_0,t_{k-1},t_k)$. Under the probability measure $\mathbb{F}$ associated with a foreign zero coupon bond $DF^f(t,k_k)$, the foreign forward rate is a martingale and is described by the following equation:

$$d\left(F^f(t,t_{k-1},t_k)\right) = \sigma_f\, F^f(t,t_{k-1},t_k)\, dW_f^{\mathbb{F}}. \tag{7.2.77}$$

However, when we use $DF^d(t,t_k)$ as a numeraire, the process $\left[F^f(t,t_{k-1},t_k)/DF^d(t,t_k)\right]$ has a drift and follows the process,

$$d\left(F^f(t,t_{k-1},t_k)\right) = F^f(t,t_{k-1},t_k)\alpha dt + \sigma_f F^f(t,t_{k-1},T_k)dW_f^Q. \tag{7.2.78}$$

Our aim is to find the value of α and then price the quanto caplet using

$$QCaplet(t_0) = P\tau DF^d(t_0,t_k)\left\{F^f(t_0,t_{k-1},t_k)\exp\left(\alpha\,(t_{k-1}-t_0)\right)N_1(d_1) - KN_1(d_2)\right\}, \tag{7.2.79}$$

where P is the principal, K is the strike, $\tau = t_{k-1} - t_k$, $F^f(t_0,t_{k-1},t_k)$ is the foreign currency forward rate, σ_f is the volatility of $F^f(t_0,t_{k-1},t_k)$ and

$$d_1 = \frac{\log\left(\left(\frac{F^f(t_0,t_{k-1},t_k)}{K}\right)\right) + \left(\alpha + \frac{\sigma_f^2}{2}\right)(t_{k-1}-t_0)}{\sigma_f\,\sqrt{t_{k-1}-t_0}},$$

$$d_2 = \frac{\log\left(\left(\frac{F^f(t_0,t_{k-1},t_k)}{K}\right)\right) + \left(\alpha - \frac{\sigma_f^2}{2}\right)(t_{k-1}-t_0)}{\sigma_f\,\sqrt{t_{k-1}-t_0}}.$$

We will now derive the value of α.

First we define two processes $X_1(t)$ and $X_2(t)$ such that

$$X_1(t) = \left(\frac{DF^f(t,t_{k-1}) - DF^f(t,t_k)}{DF^d(t,t_k)}\right)X_d^f(t) \tag{7.2.80}$$

and

$$X_2(t) = \tau X_d^f(t)\frac{DF^f(t,t_k)}{DF^d(t,t_k)} = \tau X_d^f(t,t_k), \tag{7.2.81}$$

where $X_d^f(t,t_k)$ is the forward foreign exchange rate, see Section 7.3. Therefore,

$$\left(\frac{X_1(t)}{X_2(t)}\right) = \frac{DF^f(t,t_{k-1}) - DF^f(t,t_k)}{\tau DF^f(t,t_k)} = F^f(t,t_{k-1},t_k). \tag{7.2.82}$$

Now X_1 and X_2 are martingales under $\mathbb{Q}$ so we have

$$dX_1 = \sigma_1 X_1 dW_1^{\mathbb{Q}} \tag{7.2.83}$$

and

$$dX_2 = \sigma_2 X_2 dW_2^{\mathbb{Q}}. \tag{7.2.84}$$

Equation (7.2.84) can also be expressed as

$$\frac{d\left(\tau X_d^f(t,t_k)\right)}{\tau X_d^f(t,t_k)} = \sigma_x dW_x^{\mathbb{Q}}. \tag{7.2.85}$$

Using Ito we obtain

$$d\left(\frac{X_1}{X_2}\right) = \left(\frac{X_1}{X_2}\right)\left\{\sigma_1 dW_1^{\mathbb{Q}} - \sigma_2 dW_2^{\mathbb{Q}}\right\}$$
$$+ \left(\frac{X_1}{X_2}\right)\left\{E\left[\left(\sigma_2 dW_2^{\mathbb{Q}}\right)^2\right] - E\left[\left(\sigma_1 dW_1^{\mathbb{Q}}\right)\left(\sigma_2 dW_2^{\mathbb{Q}}\right)\right]\right\} \tag{7.2.86}$$

and the following processes for $\log(X_1)$ and $\log(X_2)$:

$$d(\log(X_1)) = -\frac{\sigma_1^2}{2}dt + \sigma_1 dW_1^{\mathbb{Q}},$$
$$d(\log(X_2)) = -\frac{\sigma_2^2}{2}dt + \sigma_2 dW_2^{\mathbb{Q}}. \tag{7.2.87}$$

Using equation (7.2.85) we can write equation (7.2.87) as

$$d\left(\log\left(\tau X_d^f(t,t_k)\right)\right) = -\frac{\sigma_x^2}{2}dt + \sigma_x dW_x^{\mathbb{Q}} \tag{7.2.88}$$

Now

$$E\left[d(\log(X_2))\left\{d(\log(X_2)) - d(\log(X_1))\right\}\right]$$
$$= E\left[(d(\log(X_2)))^2\right] - E\left[d(\log(X_1))d(\log(X_2))\right]$$
$$= E\left[\left(\sigma_2 dW_2^{\mathbb{Q}}\right)^2\right] - E\left[\left(\sigma_1 dW_1^{\mathbb{Q}}\right)\left(\sigma_2 dW_2^{\mathbb{Q}}\right)\right],$$

where we have ignored terms in dt with order greater than 1.
In addition,

$$E\left[d(\log(X_2))\left\{d(\log(X_2)) - d(\log(X_1))\right\}\right]$$
$$= -E\left[d(\log(X_2))d\left(\log\left(\frac{X_1}{X_2}\right)\right)\right]$$
$$= -E\left[d(\log(X_2))d\left(\log\left(F^f(t,t_{k-1},t_k)\right)\right)\right]$$
$$= -E\left[d\left(\log(\tau X_d^f(t,t_k))\right)d\left(\log\left(F^f(t,t_{k-1},t_k)\right)\right)\right]$$
$$= -E\left[d\left(\log(X_d^f(t,t_k))\right)d\left(\log\left(F^f(t,t_{k-1},t_k)\right)\right)\right]$$
$$= -\sigma_x \sigma_f \rho_{x,f}\, dt,$$

where σ_x is the volatility of the forward foreign exchange rate $X_d^f(t,t_k)$, σ_f is the volatility of the foreign forward rate $F^f(t,t_{k-1},k)$, and $\rho_{x,f}$ is the correlation between dW_x^Q and dW_f^F.

Therefore, equation (7.2.86) can be written as

$$d\left(\frac{X_1}{X_2}\right) = -\left(\frac{X_1}{X_2}\right)\{\sigma_x\,\sigma_f\,\rho_{x,f}\}\,dt + \left(\frac{X_1}{X_2}\right)\{\sigma_1 dW_1^Q - \sigma_2 dW_2^Q\},$$

which means that

$$d\left(F^f(t,t_{k-1},t_k)\right)$$
$$= -F^f(t,t_{k-1},t_k)\{\sigma_x\sigma_f\,\rho_{x,f}\}\,dt + F^f(t,t_{k-1},t_k)\{\sigma_1 dW_1^Q - \sigma_2 dW_2^Q\}$$

comparing the above equation with equation (7.2.78)

$$d\left(F^f(t,t_{k-1},t_k)\right) = -F^f(t,t_{k-1},t_k)\{\sigma_x\,\sigma_f\,\rho_{x,F}\}\,dt + \sigma_f F^f(t,t_{k-1},t_k)dW^Q \tag{7.2.89}$$

and so $\alpha = -\sigma_x\,\sigma_f\,\rho_{x,f}$.

Quanto Floorlet

The formula to value a quanto floorlet can be obtained in similar manner to that used for the quanto caplet.

The value at time t_0 of a standard floorlet which pays at time t_k and extends from time t_{k-1} to time t_k is

$$Floorlet(t_0) = P\tau DF^d(t_0,t_k)E^{Q^k}\left[\max\left(K - F_k^d,0\right)\right], \tag{7.2.90}$$

where P is the principal, K is the strike, $\tau = t_{k-1} - t_k$, F_k is the domestic forward rate $F(t_0,t_{k-1},t_k)$. Equation (7.2.90) can be evaluated using the Black Scholes formula as follows:

$$Floorlet(t_0) = P\tau DF^d(t_0,t_k)\left\{-F^d(t_0,t_{k-1},t_k)N_1(-d_1) + KN_1(-d_2)\right\}, \tag{7.2.91}$$

where the symbols have the same meaning as for the corresponding quanto caplet,

$$d_1 = \frac{\log\left(\left(\frac{F^d(t_0,t_{k-1},t_k)}{K}\right)\right) + \frac{\sigma_d^2}{2}(t_{k-1} - t_0)}{\sigma_d\sqrt{t_{k-1} - t_0}},$$

$$d_2 = \frac{\log\left(\left(\frac{F^d(t_0,t_{k-1},t_k)}{K}\right)\right) - \frac{\sigma_d^2}{2}(t_{k-1} - t_0)}{\sigma_d\sqrt{t_{k-1} - t_0}}. \tag{7.2.92}$$

In a quanto floorlet instead of using the domestic forward rate $F^d(t_0,t_{k-1}, t_k)$, we use the foreign forward rate $F^f(t_0,t_{k-1},t_k)$,

$$QFloorlet(t_0) = P\tau DF^d(t_0,t_k)$$
$$\times \left\{-F^f(t_0,t_{k-1},t_k)\exp\left(\alpha\,(t_{k-1} - t_0)\right)N_1(-d_1) + KN_1(-d_2)\right\}, \tag{7.2.93}$$

where P is the principal, K is the strike, $\tau = t_{k-1} - t_k$, $F^f(t_0, t_{k-1}, t_k)$ is the foreign currency forward rate, σ_f is the volatility of $F^f(t_0, t_{k-1}, t_k)$ and

$$d_1 = \frac{\log\left(\left(\frac{F^f(t_0, t_{k-1}, t_k)}{K}\right)\right) + \left(\alpha + \frac{\sigma_f^2}{2}\right)(t_{k-1} - t_0)}{\sigma_f \sqrt{t_{k-1} - t_0}},$$

$$d_2 = \frac{\log\left(\left(\frac{F^f(t_0, t_{k-1}, t_k)}{K}\right)\right) + \left(\alpha - \frac{\sigma_f^2}{2}\right)(t_{k-1} - t_0)}{\sigma_f \sqrt{t_{k-1} - t_0}}$$

and as before $\alpha = -\sigma_x \sigma_f \rho_{x,f}$

Quanto Swaplet

A quanto (also known as diff or differential) swaplet is an agreement in which one party makes floating rate payments based on the foreign forward rate while the other makes fixed or floating payments based on the domestic interest rates.

Here, we consider quanto swaplets in which the received floating leg coupons (in domestic currency) are computed using foreign forward rates.

The value of a standard swaplet (in which all the currencies are domestic) can be found by using equation (7.2.90) and (7.2.74) to write

$$\begin{aligned}
Caplet(t_0) - Floorlet(t_0) &= P\tau DF^d(t_0, t_k)E^{Q^k}\left[\max\left(F_k^d - K, 0\right) - \max\left(K - F_k^d, 0\right)\right] \\
&= P\tau DF^d(t_0, t_k)E^{Q^k}\left[F_k^d - K\right] \\
&= P\tau DF^d(t_0, t_k)\left\{E^{Q^k}\left[F_k^d\right] - K\right\} \\
&= P\tau DF^d(t_0, t_k)\left\{F_k^d(t_0, t_{k-1}, t_k) - K\right\}. \tag{7.2.94}
\end{aligned}$$

From equation (7.2.94), we can see that $Caplet(t_0) - Floorlet(t_0)$ is the value of a swaplet in which the owner pays the fixed rate K and receives the floating rate $F_k^d(t_0, t_{k-1}, t_k)$.

The value of the floating leg payment can be found by setting $K = 0$ in equation (7.2.94) and is $P\tau DF^d(t_0, t_k)F_k^d(t_0, t_{k-1}, t_k)$.

The value of the floating leg payments in a quanto swap can be found in a similar manner,

$$\begin{aligned}
&QCaplet(t_0) - QFloorlet(t_0) \\
&= P\tau DF^d(t_0, t_k)E^{Q^k}\left[\max\left(F_k^f - K, 0\right) - \max\left(K - F_k^f, 0\right)\right].
\end{aligned}$$

Substituting from equations (7.2.79) and (7.2.93),

$$\begin{aligned}
&QCaplet(t_0) - QFloorlet(t_0) \\
&= P\tau DF^d(t_0, t_k)\left\{F^f(t_0, t_{k-1}, t_k)\exp\left(\alpha\left(t_{k-1} - t_0\right)\right)N_1(d_1) - KN_1(d_2)\right. \\
&\quad \left. - F^f(t_0, t_{k-1}, t_k)N_1(-d_1) + KN_1(-d_2)\right\}.
\end{aligned}$$

When $K = 0$ we have $d_1 = \infty$, $N_1(d_1) = 1$, and $N_1(-d_1) = 0$, which means that the value of the floating leg payment is

$$FloatLeg(t_0) = P\tau DF^d(t_0,t_k) F^f(t_0,t_{k-1},t_k) \exp\left(\alpha\left(t_{k-1} - t_0\right)\right), \qquad (7.2.95)$$

where as before $\alpha = -\sigma_x \sigma_f \rho_{x,f}$.

Using equation (7.2.95), the value of a quanto swaplet with (pay) fixed domestic rate and (receive) foreign floating rate is

$$QSwaplet(t_0) = P\tau DF^d(t_0,t_k) \left\{ F^f(t_0,t_{k-1},t_k) \exp\left(\alpha\left(t_{k-1} - t_0\right)\right) - K \right\}.$$

7.3 FOREIGN EXCHANGE DERIVATIVES

Here, we consider derivatives based on the exchange rate between a *domestic* currency and a *foreign* currency. We will use the convention that quantities relating to the domestic currency will have the superscript d, while those for the foreign currency will have the superscript f. The notation for the various exchange rates is as follows:

$X_d^f(t)$ is the spot value of one unit of foreign currency in domestic currency at time t,

$X_b^f(t)$ is the spot value of one unit of foreign currency in base currency at time t,

$X_b^d(t)$ is the spot value of one unit of domestic currency in base currency at time t,

$X_d^f(t,T)$ is the (time t) forward value of one unit of foreign currency in domestic currency at time T.

Covered Interest Arbitrage

If the current spot exchange rate, $X_d^f(t)$, is known then using *Covered Interest Arbitrage*, it is possible to obtain a value for future spot exchange rate – we denote this forward exchange rate by $X_d^f(t,T)$, where $T > t$.

Let us consider the following two scenarios:

Scenario A

At time t an investor deposits one unit of foreign currency which grows at the (constant) foreign risk-free interest rate r^f. By time T the initial amount will have increased to $1/DF^f(t,T)$ units of foreign currency, where $DF^f(t,T) = \exp\left(-r^f(T-t)\right)$. The foreign currency is then converted into domestic currency at the time T forward exchange rate $X_d^f(t,T)$ and thus yields $X_d^f(t,T)/DF^f(t,T)$ units of domestic currency.

Scenario B

At time t an investor deposits $X_d^f(t)$ units of domestic currency (the sum is *equivalent* to one unit of foreign currency), and this grows at the (constant) domestic risk-free interest rate r^d. At time T the initial sum will have increased to $X_d^f(t)/DF^d(t,T)$ units of domestic currency, where $DF^d(t,T) = \exp\left(-r^d(T-t)\right)$.

For no arbitrage to occur the final amount of domestic currency in both scenarios must be the same – we have assumed that there is no charge in converting one currency into another.

We thus have

$$\frac{X_d^f(t,T)}{DF^f(t,T)} = \frac{X_d^f(t)}{DF^d(t,T)},$$

which means that the forward exchange rate, at time T, is

$$X_d^f(t,T) = X_d^f(t)\frac{DF^f(t,T)}{DF^d(t,T)}. \tag{7.3.1}$$

7.3.1 FX Forward

A foreign exchange (FX) forward is a contract to exchange a given amount of domestic currency for an agreed amount of foreign currency at a future time T. If P^f is the amount (number of units) of foreign currency, and P^d is the amount (number of units) of domestic currency, then the value (in domestic currency) of the FX contract at time T is

$$FX_d(T) = P^f\ X_d^f(T) - P^d.$$

The value of the contract at time t is thus

$$FX_d(t) = \left\{ P^f\ X_d^f(t,T) - P^d \right\} DF^d(t,T),$$

where $t < T$. Substituting for $X_d^f(t,T)$ from equation (7.3.1) then gives

$$FX_d(t) = \left\{ P^f\ X_d^f(t)\frac{DF^f(t,T)}{DF^d(t,T)} - P^d \right\} DF^d(t,T),$$

which can be re-expressed as

$$FX_d(t) = P^f\ X_d^f(t)\ DF^f(t,T) - P^d\ DF^d(t,T). \tag{7.3.2}$$

The value of this FX Forward contract in base currency is thus

$$FX_b(t) = \left\{ P^f\ X_d^f(t)\ DF^f(t,T) - P^d\ DF^d(t,T) \right\} X_b^d,$$

that is,

$$FX_b(t) = P^f\ X_b^f(t)\ DF^f(t,T) - P^d\ DF^d(t,T)\ X_b^d(t), \tag{7.3.3}$$

where we have used the fact that $X_d^f(t)\ X_b^d(t) = X_b^f(t)$.

An alternative way of expressing equation (7.3.3) is as

$$FX_b(t) = P^f\ \left\{ X_b^f(t)\ DF^f(t,T) - K\ DF^d(t,T)\ X_b^d(t) \right\}, \tag{7.3.4}$$

where $K = P^d/P^f$. In the next section, we will see that K, the agreed rate to be paid for one unit of foreign currency in units of domestic currency, corresponds to the *strike* of an FX call option.

7.3.2 European FX Option

Foreign exchange option can be priced using the Black Scholes formula, (Garman and Kohlhagen, 1983). There are three processes involved in foreign exchange options and, under the real world probability measure $\mathbb{P}$, they are

$$dB^f = r^f B^f \, dt,$$
$$dX_d^f = X_d^f \mu dt + X_d^f \sigma dW^P, \quad dW^P \sim N(0, dt),$$
$$dB^d = r^d B^d \, dt, \tag{7.3.5}$$

where X_d^f is the value of one unit of foreign currency in units of domestic currency, B^d is the domestic money account where money grows at the (constant) risk-free rate r^d, B^f is the foreign money account where money grows at the (constant) risk-free rate r^f, and σ is the volatility of X_d^f. From a domestic point of view, there are only two assets – the money market account B^d and the value of the foreign money market account in domestic currency, $B^f X_d^f$.

From Ito's product rule in Chapter 2 and using equation (2.6.3) with $X_1 = X_d^f$ and $X_2 = B^d$, we have

$$d\left(X_d^f B^f\right) = \left(X_d^f B^f\right)\left\{r^f + \mu\right\} dt + \left(X_d^f B^f\right)\sigma dW^P.$$

We will now choose B^d as the numeraire and obtain the process for $B^f X_d^f / B^d$ and using the Ito quotient rule given in Chapter 2. Substituting $X_1 = B^f X_d^f$ and $X_2 = B^d$ in equation (2.6.8), we obtain

$$d\left(\frac{B^f X_d^f}{B^d}\right) = \left(\frac{B^f X_d^f}{B^d}\right)\left\{\left(r^f - r^d + \mu\right) dt\right\} + \left(\frac{B^f X_d^f}{B^d}\right)\sigma dW^P.$$

If we choose the probability measure $\mathbb{Q}$ such that

$$dW^P = dW^Q - \frac{\left(r^f - r^d + \mu\right)}{\sigma} dt, \tag{7.3.6}$$

then $\left(B^f X_d^f / B^d\right)$ is a martingale since

$$d\left(\frac{B^f X_d^f}{B^d}\right) = \left(\frac{B^f X_d^f}{B^d}\sigma\right) dW^Q.$$

Substituting for dW^P in equation (7.3.5) yields

$$dX_d^f = X_d^f \mu dt + X_d^f \sigma \left\{dW^Q - \frac{\left(r^f - r^d + \mu\right) dt}{\sigma}\right\}$$
$$= X_d^f \mu dt - X_d^f \left(r^f - r^d + \mu\right) dt + X_d^f \sigma dW^Q,$$

so

$$dX_d^f = X_d^f \left(r^d - r^f \right) dt + X_d^f \sigma dW^Q. \tag{7.3.7}$$

It can be seen that equation (7.3.7) is identical to equation (4.4.53) if the following mapping is used,

$$S \to X_d^f, \qquad r \to r^d, \qquad q \to r^f. \tag{7.3.8}$$

This means that the above mapping allows us to price European FX puts and calls with the Black Scholes formulae given in equations (4.4.55) and (4.4.56)

FX Call

The time t value (in domestic currency) of an FX call to buy *one unit of foreign currency* can be found from equation (4.4.55) and the substitutions given in (7.3.8). We have

$$C_d(t) = X_d^f(t) \exp\left(-r^f(T-t)\right) N(d_1) - K \exp\left(-r^d(T-t)\right) N(d_2), \tag{7.3.9}$$

$$d_1 = \frac{1}{\sigma \sqrt{T-t}} \left\{ \log\left(\frac{X_d^f(t)}{K}\right) + (r^d - r^f)(T-t) + \frac{1}{2}(\sigma)^2 (T-t) \right\}, \tag{7.3.10}$$

$$d_2 = d_1 - \sigma \sqrt{T-t}, \tag{7.3.11}$$

where K is the strike, the rate that has been agreed to pay for one unit of foreign currency in units of domestic currency, and σ is the implied foreign/domestic currency exchange rate FX option volatility, which may depend on effects such as time to maturity, volatility smile, etc.

In practice, the following, modified version of equation (7.3.9) is usually used

$$C_d(t) = P^f \{X_d^f(t) \exp\left(-r^f(T-t)\right) N(d_1) - K \exp\left(-r^d(T-t)\right) N(d_2)\}, \tag{7.3.12}$$

where P^f is the number of units of foreign currency and all the other symbols have their previous meanings.

The value $C_b(t)$ of the call option in base currency can be found by using $C_b(t) = X_b^d C_d(t)$. From equation (7.3.12), we have

$$C_b(t) = P^f \{X_b^f(t) N(d_1) DF^f(t,T) - K X_b^d(t) N(d_2) DF^d(t,T)\}, \tag{7.3.13}$$

where we have used the fact that $X_b^d(t) X_d^f(t) = X_b^f(t)$, $DF^f(t,T) = \exp(-r^f(T-t))$, and $DF^d(t,T) = \exp(-r^d(T-t))$. We can also re-express the values for d_1 given in equation (7.3.10) as

$$d_1 = \frac{1}{\sigma \sqrt{T-t}} \left\{ \log\left(\frac{X_b^f(t)}{K X_b^d(t)}\right) + \log\left(\frac{DF^f(t,T)}{DF^d(t,T)}\right) + \frac{1}{2}\sigma^2(T-t) \right\}, \tag{7.3.14}$$

where we have used the fact that

$$\log\left(DF^f(t,T)\right) = -r^f(T-t), \qquad \log\left(DF^d(t,T)\right) = -r^d(T-t)$$

and

$$\log\left(\frac{X_d^f(t)}{K}\right) = \log\left(\frac{X_b^f(t)\, X_b^d(t)}{K\, X_b^d(t)}\right) = \log\left(\frac{X_b^f(t)}{K\, X_b^d(t)}\right).$$

We note that the term $K\, X_b^d$ is the strike in units of base currency, that is, the amount that has been agreed to pay for one unit of foreign currency in units of *base currency*.

In the case when $N(d_1) = N(d_2) = 1$ (i.e., there is no uncertainty), equation (7.3.13) becomes

$$C_b(t) = P^f\,\{X_b^f(t)\, DF^f(t,T) - K\, X_b^d(t)\, DF^d(t,T)\},$$

which is the same as that already given in equation (7.3.4) for the FX Forward.

FX Put

The time t value of the corresponding put in units of base currency is

$$P_b(t) = P^f\,\{-X_b^f(t)\, DF^f(t,T)\, N(-d_1) + K\, X_b^d(t)\, DF^d(t,T)\, N(-d_2)\}, \qquad (7.3.15)$$

where the symbols have the same meanings as for the FX call.

7.4 CREDIT DERIVATIVES

Credit derivatives take into account the fact that a counterparty may and not honour (for reasons of bankruptcy, etc.) the obligations set out in a given financial contract. In order to obtain the time t value of these derivatives, it is necessary to determine the probability that the counterparty (and thus the contract) will survive until some future time $T > t$. Here, we will denote the survival probability between times t and T by $S(t,T)$, and we compute its value from the hazard rate.

The Hazard Rate

As previously mentioned, the survival probability between times t and T, where $T > t$, is denoted by $S(t,T)$. This means that the probability of default between times t and T is

$$P_{\text{def}}(t,T) = 1 - S(t,T),$$

and the probability of default, as seen from time t, between times T_1 and T_2 is

$$P_{\text{def}}(t,T_1,T_2) = S(t,T_1) - S(t,T_2), \quad T_2 > T_1. \qquad (7.4.1)$$

The time t *discrete hazard rate* between times T and $T + \Delta T$, denoted by $H(t,T,T + \Delta T)$, is defined by

$$H(t,T,T + \Delta T) = \frac{1}{\Delta T}\left\{\frac{P_{\text{def}}(t,T,T + \Delta T)}{S(t,T + \Delta T)}\right\}$$

$$= \frac{1}{\Delta T}\left\{\frac{S(t,T) - S(t,T + \Delta T)}{S(t,T + \Delta T)}\right\},$$

which means that

$$H(t,T,T+\Delta T) = -\left\{\frac{S(t,T+\Delta T) - S(t,T)}{\Delta T}\right\}\left\{\frac{1}{S(t,T+\Delta T)}\right\}. \qquad (7.4.2)$$

As $\Delta T \rightarrow 0, H(t,T,T+\Delta T) \rightarrow h(t,T)$, where $h(t,T)$ is termed the *continuous hazard rate* between times t and T.

We observe that as $\Delta T \rightarrow 0$ equation (7.4.2) becomes

$$h(t,T) = -\left\{\frac{\partial S(t,T)}{\partial T}\right\}\frac{1}{S(t,T)}. \qquad (7.4.3)$$

Now equation (7.4.3) can be re-expressed as

$$h(t,s) = -\frac{\partial S(t,s)}{\partial s}\frac{\partial\{\ln(S(t,s))\}}{\partial S(t,s)} = -\frac{\partial\{\ln(S(t,s))\}}{\partial s}, \qquad (7.4.4)$$

where $s > t$, and we have used

$$\frac{1}{S(t,T)} = -\frac{\partial\{\ln(S(t,T))\}}{\partial S(t,T)}.$$

Integrating equation (7.4.4) yields

$$\int_{s=t}^{T} h(t,s)\,ds = -\int_{s=t}^{T} d\{\ln(S(t,s))\}$$
$$= -\{\ln(S(t,T)) - \ln(S(t,t))\}$$
$$= -\ln(S(t,T)), \qquad (7.4.5)$$

where we have used $S(t,t) = 1$ and $\ln(S(t,t)) = 0$.

So using equation (7.4.5), the survival probability can be expressed as

$$S(t,T) = \exp\left\{-\int_{s=t}^{T} h(t,s)\,ds\right\} \qquad (7.4.6)$$

or

$$S(t,T) = \exp\{I(t,T)\}, \qquad (7.4.7)$$

where $I(t,T)$ is the cumulative hazard rate from time t to time T.

It is usual to approximate $I(t,T)$ as follows:

$$I(t,T) \sim I(t,t_k) = \sum_{i=1}^{k} h(t_{i-1},t)(t_i - t_{i-1}), \qquad (7.4.8)$$

where $t_0 = t$, $t_k = T$, and the following section gives details on how to estimate $h(t_{i-1},t)$ from market *observables*.

One way on representing the hazard rates is to use a *hazard rate curve* which is defined as

$$\{t_0, I(t_0,t_i)\}, \quad i = 0,,\ldots,n. \qquad (7.4.9)$$

If we further define $t_0 = t = 0$ and $t_n = T$, then equation (7.4.9) becomes

$$\{0,0\}, \{t_1, I(0,t_1)\}, \{t_2, I(0,t_2)\}, \ldots, \{t_n, I(0,t_n)\}, \qquad (7.4.10)$$

where we have used the fact that $I(t_0,t_0) = I(0,0) = 0$.

Estimating the Hazard Rate from Market Observables

From equation (7.2.10), we know that the time t forward rate between times T_1 and T_2 is given by

$$F(t,T_1,T_2) = \frac{1}{(T_2 - T_1)} \left\{ \frac{DF(t,T_1)}{DF(t,T_2)} - 1 \right\}, \qquad (7.4.11)$$

where $DF(t,T_1)$ and $DF(t,T_2)$ are the prices of the non-defaultable zero coupon bonds with maturities T_1 and T_2 respectively.

Letting $T_1 = T$ and $T_2 = T + \Delta T$, we obtain

$$F(t,T,T + \Delta T) = \frac{1}{\Delta T} \left\{ \frac{DF(t,T)}{DF(t,T + \Delta T)} - 1 \right\}, \qquad (7.4.12)$$

which can be re-expressed as

$$F(t,T,T + \Delta T) = - \left\{ \frac{DF(t,T + \Delta T) - DF(t,T)}{\Delta T} \right\} \frac{1}{DF(t,T + \Delta T)}. \qquad (7.4.13)$$

If $\Delta T \to 0$, then $F(t,T,T + \Delta T) \to f(t,T)$, and from equation (7.4.13), we obtain

$$\begin{aligned} f(t,T) &= -\frac{\partial DF(t,T)}{\partial T} \frac{1}{DF(t,T)} \\ &= -\frac{\partial DF(t,T)}{\partial T} \frac{\ln(DF(t,T))}{\partial DF(t,T)}. \end{aligned} \qquad (7.4.14)$$

Using equation (7.4.14), the instantaneous forward rate computed using non-defaultable zero coupon bond prices is

$$f(t,T) = -\frac{\ln(DF(t,T))}{\partial T}, \qquad (7.4.15)$$

and the corresponding instantaneous forward rate computed from defaultable zero coupon bond prices is

$$\bar{f}(t,T) = -\frac{\ln\left(\overline{DF}(t,T)\right)}{\partial T}. \qquad (7.4.16)$$

Taking the survival probability $S(t,T)$ to be the ratio of the prices of defaultable and non-defaultable zero coupon bonds,

$$S(t,T) = \frac{\overline{DF}(t,T)}{DF(t,T)}. \qquad (7.4.17)$$

Now from equations (7.4.15) and (7.4.16), we have

$$\begin{aligned} \bar{f}(t,T) - f(t,T) &= -\frac{\ln\left(\overline{DF}(t,T) - DF(t,T)\right)}{\partial T} \\ &= -\frac{\partial}{\partial T} \ln \left\{ \frac{\overline{DF}(t,T)}{DF(t,T)} \right\}, \end{aligned} \qquad (7.4.18)$$

so from equation (7.4.18) and equation (7.4.17),

$$\bar{f}(t,T) - f(t,T) = -\frac{\partial}{\partial T} \ln(S(t,T)). \tag{7.4.19}$$

Combining equation (7.4.19) and equation (7.4.4), we have

$$h(t,T) = \bar{f}(t,T) - f(t,T). \tag{7.4.20}$$

This means that we can compute the hazard rate $h(t,T)$ by taking the difference between the instantaneous forward rates computed using defaultable and non-defaultable zero coupon bonds.

7.4.1 Defaultable Bond

For a defaultable bond, we need to take into account the fact that the bond issuer may default, that is, cease to make the bond coupon payments.

The time t value of a defaultable bond is

$$\bar{B}(t) = P\,\overline{DF}(t,t_m) \qquad\qquad\qquad \text{principal}$$

$$+ \sum_{j=1}^{m} C_j \overline{DF}(t,t_j) \qquad\qquad\qquad \text{coupons}$$

$$+ P\,R \sum_{j=1}^{m} DF(t,t_j)\{S(t,t_{j-1}) - S(t,t_j)\} \quad \text{recovery value,}$$

where t_m is the maturity of the bond, P is the principal, C_j is the value of jth coupon, R is the recovery rate, $S(t,t_j)$ probability that the bond will survive until time t_j, and the zero coupon defaultable bond prices are defined by $\overline{DF}(t,t_m) = S(t,t_m)DF(t,t_m)$ and $\overline{DF}(t,t_j) = DF(t,t_j)S(t,t_j)$. The term $\{S(t,t_{j-1}) - S(t,t_j)\}$ is the probability that the bond will default between times t_{j-1} and t_j.

7.4.2 Credit Default Swap

A Credit Default Swap (CDS) is a contract between two counterparties in which one (say A) makes periodic fixed payments to the other (say B) in order to obtain protection on the default of a reference credit. In the event of default B pays A, the default payment of $1 - R$, where R is the recovery rate, and contract ceases.

The time t value of the CDS to A, the purchaser of the insurance, is

$$CDS(t) = -\sum_{j=1}^{m} C_j \overline{DF}(t,t_j) \qquad\qquad\qquad \text{coupons}$$

$$+ P(1-R) \sum_{j=1}^{m} DF(t,t_j)\{S(t,t_{j-1}) - S(t,t_j)\} \quad \text{recovery value,}$$

where the symbols have the same meanings as for the defaultable bond.

7.4.3 Total Return Swap

A total return swap (TRS) is a synthetic replication of the return of a reference asset (bond) B. The *receiver* of the TRS receives the coupon payments of the reference asset during the life of the swap in return for making periodic coupon payments at the risk-free floating rate plus an agreed margin. In the event of default, the receiver makes a default payment to the payer equal to the agreed initial price of the reference asset less the price at default, and the transaction terminates. If there is no default, then the difference between the initial asset (bond) price B_0 and the price at maturity $B(t_m)$ is settled between the payer and the receiver, with the receiver paying (receiving) if the asset (bond) is worth less (more) at maturity. The maturity of the reference asset (bond) may be longer than the maturity t_m of the swap.

To the receiver of the reference asset coupons, a TRS has value TRS_r, which is given by

TRS_r = **total bond return – total floating coupon payments of the swap**

where **total bond return** is given by

total bond return = total bond fixed coupons over the duration of the TRS + increase in the bond value at maturity of the TRS – default payment, if the bond defaults over the duration of the TRS.

The value of TRS_r at time t is

$TRS_r(t)$

$$
= \bar{C} \sum_{t_j=t_1}^{t_m} \overline{DF}(t,t_j) \qquad \text{fixed reference bond payments}
$$

$$
+ P \left\{ \frac{B(t_m) - B_0}{B_0} \right\} \overline{DF}(t,t_m) \qquad \text{increase in value of reference bond}
$$

$$
- \sum_{t_j=t_1}^{t_m} C_j \overline{DF}(t,t_j) \qquad \text{floating payments of swap at LIBOR + margin}
$$

$$
- P(1-R) \sum_{t_j=t_1}^{t_m} DF(t,t_j) \left\{ S(t,t_{j-1}) - S(t,t_j) \right\} \quad \text{bond default payments,}
$$

and the reference bond satisfies

$$
B(t_R) = 1
$$

$$
B(t_m) = \overline{DF}(t_m,t_R)|t + \bar{C} \sum_{t_j=t_m}^{t_R} \overline{DF}(t_m,t_j)|t
$$

$$
+ R \sum_{t_j=t_m}^{t_R} DF(t_m,t_j)|t \left\{ S(t,t_{j-1}) - S(t_m,t_j) \right\}.
$$

All symbols already defined in this chapter have their previous meanings. In addition,

P – the swap principal.

$\bar{C}$ – the fixed coupon of the reference bond.

t_m – the swap maturity.

t_R – the maturity of the reference bond B.

B_0 – the initial price of the reference bond.

$B(t_m)$ – the final price of the reference bond (at swap maturity).

C_j – the floating coupon payment at time t_j. It is computed as
$C_j = P\{F(t, t_{j-1}, t_j) + margin^{TRS}\}\{t_j - t_{j-1}\}$.

$DF(t_1, t_2)|t$ – the discount factor between times t_1 and t_2 (as seen from time t) is

$$DF(t_1, t_2)|t = \frac{D(t, t_2)}{D(t, t_1)}.$$

$\overline{DF}(t_1, t_2)|t$ – the defaultable discount factor between times t_1 and t_2 (as seen from time t) is

$$\overline{DF}(t_1, t_2)|t = \frac{\overline{DF}(t, t_2)}{\overline{DF}(t, t_1)} = \frac{DF(t, t_2)}{DF(t, t_1)} \frac{S(t, t_2)}{S(t, t_1)}.$$

$\overline{DF}(t, t_1)$ – the defaultable discount factor between times t and t_1 is

$$\overline{DF}(t, t_1) = DF(t, t_1) S(t, t_1).$$

7.5 EQUITY DERIVATIVES

7.5.1 TRS

An equity TRS consists of an equity leg (whose coupons are determined by the change in value of the equity) and a floating leg which pays according to the forwards of the floating interest rate.

Here, we ignore the effect of equity dividends and also assume that the currencies for both the floating and equity legs of the swap are the same.

Equity Leg

Let the equity leg be specified by coupon payments at times $t_k, k = 1, \ldots, N_e$, where $\tau_e = t_k - t_{k-1}$. If at time t the next coupon payment occurs at t_i, then the value of the equity leg is

$$V_e(t) = \left\{ \frac{S(t)}{DF(t, t_i)} - L(t_{i-1}) \right\} DF(t, t_i) + \sum_{k=i+1}^{N_e} \left\{ \frac{S(t)}{DF(t, t_k)} - \frac{S(t)}{DF(t, t_{k-1})} \right\} DF(t, t_k),$$

(7.5.1)

where $S(t)$ is the equity value at current time t, $L(t_{i-1})$ is the *reset* value of the equity at time t_{i-1}, and $DF(t, t_k)$ is the discount factor between times t and t_k, $t_k > t$. It can be seen that the value of the equity $S(t_1)$ at time $t_1 > t$ is obtained by inflating the current value, and $S(t)$ by the reciprocal of the discount factor, $DF(t, t_1)$, that is, $S(t_1) = S(t)/DF(t, t_1)$

Floating Leg

Let the floating leg have coupon payments at times $t_m, m = 1, \ldots, N_f$, where $\tau_f = t_m - t_{m-1}$. If the next coupon is at time t_j, then the value of the floating leg is

$$V_f(t) = L(t_{j-1}) \{R(t_{j-1}) + \Phi\} \, \tau_f \, DF(t, t_j)$$

$$+ \sum_{m=j+1}^{N_f} \frac{S(t)}{DF(t, t_{m-1})} \{F(t, t_{m-1}, t_m) + \Phi\} \, \tau_f \, DF(t, t_m), \qquad (7.5.2)$$

where Φ is the *margin* added to the forward rate used to compute coupons, $F(t, t_{m-1}, t_m)$ is the time t forward rate between times t_{m-1} and t_m, and $R(t_{j-1})$ is the reset rate that is used between times t_{j-1} and t_j to compute the coupon payment at time t_j.

Payer Equity TRS

The owner of a payer equity TRS pays the equity leg coupons, and thus at time t the swap has value

$$ETRS_p(t) = V_f(t) - V_e(t). \qquad (7.5.3)$$

The owner of a receiver equity TRS receives the equity leg coupons, and the value of the swap is

$$ETRS_r(t) = -V_f(t) + V_e(t). \qquad (7.5.4)$$

We will now compute an expression for the value of a payer equity swap. Since

$$F(t, t_{m-1}, t_m) = \frac{1}{(t_m - t_{m-1})} \left(\frac{DF(t, t_{m-1})}{DF(t, t_m)} - 1 \right),$$

we have

$$\tau_f \, F(t, t_{m-1}, t_m) = \left(\frac{DF(t, t_{m-1})}{DF(t, t_m)} - 1 \right). \qquad (7.5.5)$$

Substituting equation (7.5.5) into equation (7.5.2) and using equation (7.5.3), we obtain

$$ETRS_p(t) = \sum_{m=j+1}^{N_f} \frac{S(t) DF(t, t_m)}{DF(t, t_{m-1})} \left\{ \frac{DF(t, t_{m-1})}{DF(t, t_m)} - 1 \right\}$$

$$+ \sum_{m=j+1}^{N_f} \frac{S(t)}{DF(t, t_{m-1})} \Phi \, \tau_f \, DF(t, t_m)$$

$$+ L(t_{j-1}) \left(R(t_{j-1}) + \Phi \right) \tau_f \, DF(t, t_j)$$

$$- \sum_{k=i+1}^{N_e} S(t) \left\{ 1 - \frac{DF(t, t_k)}{DF(t, t_{k-1})} \right\} - \left\{ \frac{S(t)}{DF(t, t_i)} - L(t_{i-1}) \right\} DF(t, t_i). \qquad (7.5.6)$$

If $N_e = N_f = N$, and $\tau_e = \tau_f = \tau$, then and all the equity and float leg payments coincide and equation (7.5.6) simplifies to

$$
ETRS_p(t) = S(t) \sum_{k=j+1}^{N} \frac{DF(t,t_k)}{DF(t,t_{k-1})} \Phi \tau DF(t,t_k)
$$

$$
+ L(R + \Phi) \tau DF(t,t_j) - \left\{ \frac{S(t)}{DF(t,t_j)} - L \right\} DF(t,t_j). \qquad (7.5.7)
$$

Thus if the spread Φ is zero, the value of the payer equity TRS is

$$
ETRS_p(t) = L(t_{j-1}) R(t_{j-1}) \tau DF(t,t_j) - \left\{ \frac{S(t)}{DF(t,t_j)} - L(t_{j-1}) \right\} DF(t,t_j). \quad (7.5.8)
$$

In these circumstances, the value of the equity TRS at time t only depends on the current swaplet, which is extended from t_{j-1} to t_j, where $t_{j-1} < t < t_j$.

Equity Swap

A special case of an equity TRS is an equity swap. Here, one party (say A) pays the total returns on a given equity one and receives (from party B) the returns on another equity, together with the interest on the net difference of the last reset notional of the two equity assets. An equity swap, $ESWP$, can be constructed from a *structured deal* consisting of a long position in one equity TRS and a short position in the another equity TRS, with the same coupon payment dates and currency. If the individual equity TRS deals are denoted by $ETRS_p^1$ and $ETRS_p^2$, then the value of the equity swap at time t is

$$
ESWP(t) = ETRS_p^1(t) - ETRS_p^2(t). \qquad (7.5.9)
$$

Substituting equation (7.5.8) into equation (7.5.9), we have

$$
ESWP(t) = L^1(t_{j-1}) R(t_{j-1}) \tau DF(t,t_j) - \left\{ \frac{S^1(t)}{DF(t,t_j)} - L^1(t_{j-1}) \right\} DF(t,t_j)
$$

$$
- \left\{ L^2(t_{j-1}) R(t_{j-1}) \tau DF(t,t_j) - \left\{ \frac{S^2(t)}{DF(t,t_j)} - L^2(t_{j-1}) \right\} DF(t,t_j) \right\},
$$

so the value of the equity swap to party A is

$$
ESWP(t) = - \left\{ \frac{S^1(t)}{DF(t,t_j)} - L^1(t_{j-1}) \right\} DF(t,t_j) \qquad \text{equity 1 returns paid by } A
$$

$$
+ \left(L^1(t_{j-1}) - L^2(t_{j-1}) \right) R(t_{j-1}) \tau DF(t,t_j)
$$

$$
\text{interest on difference of reset notionals paid by } B
$$

$$
+ \left\{ \frac{S^2(t)}{DF(t,t_j)} - L^2(t_{j-1}) \right\} DF(t,t_j) \qquad \text{equity 2 returns paid by } B.
$$

7.5.2 Equity Quantos

The Black Scholes equation can also be used to price Equity quanto options, (Reiner, 1992). We have the following processes:

$$dS^f = \mu_s S^f dt + \sigma_s S^f dW_s^P,$$
$$dX_d^f = \mu_x X_d^f dt + \sigma_x X_d^f dW_x^P,$$
$$dB^f = r^f B^f dt,$$
$$dB^d = r^d B^d dt. \tag{7.5.10}$$

Here, S^f is the price (in foreign currency units) of the foreign stock, B^d the domestic money market account where money grows at the (constant) risk-free interest rate r^d, B^f the foreign money market account where money grows at the (constant) risk-free interest rate r^f, and X_d^f the foreign exchange rate, that is, the value of one unit of foreign currency in units of domestic currency.

The tradables for the domestic investor are the foreign money market account priced in domestic currency units (that is, $X_d^f B^f$) and the foreign stock priced in domestic currency units, $X_d^f S^f$.

We know from equation (4.4.30) that there is a probability measure (the risk neutral measure) $\mathbb{Q}$ under which the relative price of domestic tradables such as equities is martingales. Also we established that under $\mathbb{Q}$ the process followed by these tradables is GBM with constant drift r^d. So the process for the domestic equity S^d is

$$dS^d = S^d r^d dt + \sigma S^d dW^{\mathbb{Q}}. \tag{7.5.11}$$

Similarly, the process followed by the price of a foreign equity S^f under the foreign risk neutral measure $\mathbb{F}$ is

$$dS^f = S^f r^f dt + \sigma_s S^f dW_s^{\mathbb{F}}. \tag{7.5.12}$$

However, the process followed by the price of a foreign equity S^f under the domestic risk neutral measure $\mathbb{Q}$ is

$$dS^f = S^f \left(r^f + \alpha \right) dt + \sigma_s S^f dW_s^{\mathbb{Q}}, \tag{7.5.13}$$

where α (the *quanto adjustment*) is to be determined.

We will now derive the value for α and then use this to price both quanto forwards and quanto options.

Determining the Quanto Adjustment, α

Since $X_d^f B^f$ and $X_d^f S^f$ are domestic tradables, it means that the relative prices $\left(X_d^f B^f / B^d \right)$ and $\left(X_d^f S^f / B^d \right)$ are also martingales under the probability measure $\mathbb{Q}$.

Now since $\left(X_d^f B^f / B^d \right)$ is a martingale,

$$d\left(\frac{X_d^f B^f}{B^d} \right) = \sigma_x \left(\frac{X_d^f B^f}{B^d} \right) dW_x^{\mathbb{Q}}. \tag{7.5.14}$$

We will start by writing $\left(X_d^f B^f / B^d \right)$ as $\left(S^f / B^f \right) \left(X_d^f B^f / B^d \right)$.
Using the Ito product rule, we have

$$
d\left\{ \left(\frac{S^f}{B^f} \right) \left(\frac{X_d^f B^f}{B^d} \right) \right\} = \left(\frac{X_d^f B^f}{B^d} \right) d\left(\frac{S^f}{B^f} \right) + \left(\frac{S^f}{B^f} \right) d\left(\frac{X_d^f B^f}{B^d} \right)
$$

$$
+ E\left[d\left(\frac{S^f}{B^f} \right) d\left(\frac{X_d^f B^f}{B^d} \right) \right]. \tag{7.5.15}
$$

Substituting for $d\left(X_d^f B^f / B^d \right)$ from equation (7.5.14) into equation (7.5.15) gives

$$
d\left\{ \left(\frac{S^f}{B^f} \right) \left(\frac{X_d^f B^f}{B^d} \right) \right\} = \left(\frac{X_d^f B^f}{B^d} \right) d\left(\frac{S^f}{B^f} \right) + \sigma_x \left(\frac{S^f}{B^f} \right) \left(\frac{X_d^f B^f}{B^d} \right) dW_x^Q
$$

$$
+ E\left[d\left(\frac{S^f}{B^f} \right) d\left(\frac{X_d^f B^d}{B^f} \right) \right]. \tag{7.5.16}
$$

Using the Ito quotient rule (see Section 2.6.2) with one source of randomness, equation (7.5.13) and equation (7.5.10) yield

$$
d\left(\frac{S^f}{B^f} \right) = \left(\frac{S^f}{B^f} \right) \alpha \, dt + \left(\frac{S^f}{B^f} \right) \sigma_s \, dW_s^Q. \tag{7.5.17}
$$

We now consider the term $E\left[d\left(S^f / B^f \right) d\left(X_d^f B^f / B^d \right) \right]$ in equation (7.5.16)

$$
E\left[d\left(\frac{S^f}{B^f} \right) d\left(\frac{X_d^f B^f}{B^d} \right) \right] = E\left[\frac{S^f}{B^f} \left\{ \alpha \, dt + \frac{S^f}{B^f} \sigma_s dW_s^Q \right\} \sigma_x \left(\frac{X_d^f B^f}{B^d} \right) dW_x^Q \right]
$$

$$
= \left(\frac{X_d^f B^f}{B^d} \right) \frac{S^f}{B^f} \left\{ \alpha \, dt \sigma_x E\left[dW_x^Q \right] \right\} + \frac{S^f}{B^f} \frac{X_d^f B^f}{B^d} \sigma_s \sigma_x E\left[dW_x^Q dW_s^Q \right].
$$

Since $E\left[dW_x^Q \right] = 0$ and $E\left[dW_x^Q dW_s^Q \right] = \rho_{xs} dt$, we have

$$
E\left[d\left(\frac{S^f}{B^f} \right) d\left(\frac{X_d^f B^d}{B^f} \right) \right] = \left(\frac{S^f}{B^f} \right) \left(\frac{X_d^f B^f}{B^d} \right) \sigma_s \sigma_x \rho_{xs} dt. \tag{7.5.18}
$$

Using the values of $d\left(S^f / B^f \right)$ and $E\left[d\left(S^f / B^f \right) d\left(X_d^f B^d / B^f \right) \right]$ from equations (7.5.17) and (7.5.18) in equation (7.5.16) results in

$$
d\left\{ \left(\frac{S^f}{B^f} \right) \left(\frac{X_d^f B^f}{B^d} \right) \right\} = \left(\frac{X_d^f B^f}{B^d} \right) \left(\frac{S^f}{B^f} \right) \alpha \, dt + \left(\frac{X_d^f B^f}{B^d} \right) \left(\frac{S^f}{B^f} \right) \sigma_s \sigma_x dW_s^Q
$$

$$
+ \sigma_x \left(\frac{X_d^f S^f}{B^d} \right) dW_x^Q + \left(\frac{S^f}{B^f} \right) \left(\frac{X_d^f B^f}{B^d} \right) \sigma_s \sigma_x \rho_{xs} dt.
$$

Re-arranging we obtain

$$d\left\{\left(\frac{X_d^f S^f}{B^d}\right)\right\} = \left(\frac{X_d^f S^f}{B^d}\right)\{\alpha + \sigma_s\sigma_x\rho_{xs}\}\,dt + \left(\frac{X_d^f S^f}{B^d}\right)\left(\sigma_s\,dW_s^Q + \sigma_x\,dW_x^Q\right).$$

$$(7.5.19)$$

We already mentioned that $\left(X_d^f B^f / B^d\right)$ is a martingale under probability measure $\mathbb{Q}$ so the drift term in equation (7.5.19) must be zero. This means that

$$\alpha = -\sigma_s\sigma_x\rho_{xs},$$

where σ_s is volatility of the foreign equity, σ_x is volatility of the foreign exchange rate, and ρ_{xs} is the correlation between dW_s and dW_x.

Equation (7.5.13) can then be written as

$$dS^f = \{r^f - \sigma_s\sigma_x\rho_{xs}\}\,S^f\,dt + \sigma_s S^f\,dW_s^Q.$$

$$(7.5.20)$$

Equity Quanto Forward

The (time t) value of a domestic equity forward contract with maturity T,

$$F(t) = DF^d(t,T)\left\{S^d(t,T) - K^d\right\},$$

where K^d is the strike in domestic currency and $S^d(t,T)$ is the domestic forward price.

To value an equity quanto forward contract, we need to know the forward price of the foreign equity S^f.

It can be seen from equations (4.4.31), (4.4.32) and (7.5.20) that this forward price is

$$S^f(t,T) = S^f(t)\exp\left(\left(r^f - \sigma_x\sigma_s\rho_{xs}\right)(T-t)\right),$$

$$(7.5.21)$$

where $S^f(t)$ is the current price of the foreign equity and T is the maturity of the forward.

In an equity quanto forward, the payoff is in foreign currency but it is converted to domestic currency at a predetermined exchange rate (which we denote here by X). The value equity quanto forward is thus

$$pQF(t) = DF^d(t,T)\left\{S^f(t,T) - K^f\right\}X,$$

where X is the prespecified exchange rate, K^f is the strike in units of foreign currency, and $S^f(t,T)$ is the foreign forward equity price.

Equity Quanto Option

In Chapter 4, equations (4.4.58) and (4.4.59) expressed the value of vanilla European put and call options as

$$Call(t) = \exp(-r^d(T-t))\left\{S^d(t,T)N_1(d_1) - EN_1(d_2)\right\},$$

$$Put(t) = \exp(-r^d(T-t))\left\{-S^d(t,T)N_1(-d_1) + EN_1(-d_2)\right\},$$

$$d_1 = \frac{\log(S^d(t,T)/E^d) + \sigma^2/2)\tau}{\sigma\sqrt{(T-t)}}, \qquad d_2 = \frac{\log(S^d(t,T)/E^d) - \sigma^2/2)(T-t)}{\sigma\sqrt{(T-t)}},$$

where we have used superscripts to denote the domestic currency, and the current equity forward price with maturity T is

$$S^d(t,T) = S^d(t)\exp\left(r^d\,(T-t)\right), \quad t \le T.$$

The value of an equity quanto option can be found by substituting S^f for S^d in the above expression. We obtain

$$QCall(t) = \exp(-r^d\,(T-t))\left\{S^f(t,T)N_1(d_1) - E^f\,N_1(d_2)\right\}X,$$

$$QPut(t) = \exp(-r^d\,(T-t))\left\{-S^f(t,T)N_1(-d_1) + E^f\,N_1(-d_2)\right\}X,$$

$$d_1 = \frac{\log(S^f(t,T)/E^f) + (\sigma_s^2/2)\tau}{\sigma_s\sqrt{(T-t)}}, \qquad d_2 = \frac{\log(S^f(t,T)/E^f) - (\sigma_s^2/2)(T-t)}{\sigma_s\sqrt{(T-t)}},$$

where E^f is the strike in foreign currency units, $S^f(t,T)$ is the foreign equity forward price (obtained from equation (7.5.21)), and X is the prespecified exchange rate (number of units of domestic currency per foreign currency unit).

7.6 SELECTED EXERCISES

1. Let $F(0,t_i), i = 1,\ldots,n$ be the current forward curve, with contracts maturing at times $t_i, i = 1,\ldots,n$, and let $F(t,T)$ be the value at time $t > 0$ of a forward contract that matures at time T, with $S(t) = F(t,t)$ the spot price at time t. If the evolution of the forward curve is governed by the equation,

$$\frac{dF(t,T)}{F(t,T)} = \sigma\exp\left\{-\alpha(T-t)\right\}dW$$

show that

$$F(t,T) = F(0,T)\left(\frac{S(t)}{F(0,t)}\right)^{\exp(-\alpha(t-T))}$$

$$\times \exp\left\{\frac{\sigma^2}{4\alpha}\exp(-\alpha T)(\exp(2\alpha t) - 1)(\exp(-\alpha T) - \exp(-\alpha t))\right\}.$$

2. If, in exercise 1, the evolution of the forward curve is now governed by

$$\frac{dF(t,T)}{F(t,T)} = (\sigma\exp\left\{-\alpha(T-t)\right\} + d)\,dW,$$

where d is a constant, show that

$$F(t,T) = F(0,T)\left(\frac{S(t)}{F(0,t)}\right)^{\exp(-\alpha(t-T))}$$

$$\times \exp\left\{d_T + \frac{\sigma^2}{4\alpha}\exp(-\alpha T)(\exp(2\alpha t) - 1)(\exp(-\alpha T) - \exp(-\alpha t))\right\},$$

where $d_I = (1 - \exp(-\alpha(T-t)))\int_{u=0}^{t}dW_u$.

3. Consider the following GBM process with jumps:

$$\frac{dS_t}{S_t} = (\mu - \lambda k) + \sigma dW_t + (Y_t - 1) dq_t,$$

where q_t is a Poisson process with intensity λ, $Y_t - 1$ is the magnitude of the jumps in price returns ($Y_t \geq 0$), and k is the expected jump magnitude of $E(Y_t - 1)$. The other symbols have their usual definitions. If $\log(Y_t) \sim N(\gamma, \delta)$ show that the value of European put and call options are the same as those in Section 4.4.3 but with r replaced by $r - \lambda k + n\lambda/\tau$ and σ replaced by $\sqrt{\sigma^2 + n\delta^2/\tau}$

4. The Hull and White stochastic differential equation for the short rate is

$$dr_t = (\Theta_t - ar_t) dt + \sigma dW_t, \qquad dB_t = B_t r_t dt,$$

where B is the money account, $\alpha > 0$ is the rate of mean reversion, and β is the long run mean. Show that the price of a discount bond at time T, $P(t,T)$ is given by

$$P(t,T) = \exp\left(A(t,T) - r_t B(t,T)\right),$$

where

$$B(t,T) = \frac{1}{a}\left\{1 - \exp\left(-a(T-t)\right)\right\}$$

and

$$A(t,T) = \log\left(\frac{P(0,T)}{P(0,t)}\right) - \frac{\partial \log(P(0,t))}{\partial t} B(t,T) - \frac{\sigma^2}{4a} B^2(t,T)\left(1 - \exp\left(-2at\right)\right).$$

5. The Vasicek SDE for the short rate r is defined by where

$$dr_t = \alpha(\beta - r_t) dt + \sigma dW_t, \qquad dB_t = B_t r_t dt,$$

where B is the money account, $\alpha > 0$ is the rate of mean reversion, and Θ_t is a time dependent mean. Show that the price of a discount bond at time T, $P(t,T)$ is given by

$$P(t,T) = C(t,T) \exp\left(-r_t A(t,T)\right),$$

$$A(t,T) = \frac{1}{\alpha}\left\{1 - \exp\left(-\alpha(T-t)\right)\right\},$$

and

$$C(t,T) = \exp\left\{\frac{\left(\alpha^2\beta - \frac{\sigma^2}{2}\right)(A(t,T) - T + t)}{\alpha^2} - \frac{\sigma^2}{4\alpha} A(t,T)^2\right\}.$$

Chapter 8

C# Portfolio Pricing Application

8.1 INTRODUCTION

This section provides details concerning a C# portfolio valuing application. It has been included to illustrate how the pricing functions discussed in the previous sections of the book can be incorporated into the kind of software which may be found in a bank, financial institution, or educational establishment.

Here, we provide code excerpts from the application; however, additional source is available from the publisher's website.

The main features of this application are as follows:

- User-defined portfolios of deals can be valued without the need to compile either C++ or C# programs. This means that the application is easy to use and is accessible to those who may possess business or financial knowledge but do not have the technical skills required to write computer code.
- This application only deals with equity, foreign exchange derivatives — the exception is the inclusion of an interest rate forward rate trade. However, the software can be easily extended to include new deal types.
- All input/output to the application is by means of text files which can be easily edited.
- The software is modular and consists of a main C# program which calls both a compiled C# `DealLibrary` and also a compiled utility library `GeorgeLevy_ComputationalFinance_UtilsLibrary`. The reader also has the choice of using a simpler C# project called *Deal-Valuer*; this does not use text file input and also is independent of `GeorgeLevy_ComputationalFinance_UtilsLibrary`.

We will now provide a brief overview of each component part of the application, more detail will be given later when specific deal class is described.

The C# Code

The application is defined by the C# solution `PortfolioValuer.sln`, which contains the projects `DealLibrary.csproj` and `PortfolioValuer.csproj`.

The project `PortfolioValuer.csproj` is the driver for the application, see Code excerpt 8.2. The user interface is simply a windows form with a button to start the application, and if required this could easily be customized by the reader. Once the application has been started, it first loads a market data file and then reads a portfolio configuration file to determine which portfolios are to be valued. Valuation then proceeds for all the deals contained in the portfolio files and the results are written to the appropriate portfolio results' file.

The project `DealLibrary.csproj` is concerned with the valuation of the available trades in the application. A separate C# *deal class*, derived from a single abstract base class `BaseDeal`, is provided for each trade type. The `BaseDeal` class provides abstract methods such as `Price()` and `Validate()`, which need to be implemented in deal classes. We will be primarily concerned with the method `Price()`, which is used to return the current value of a trade.

```
public abstract class BaseDeal     // The declaration for BaseDeal
{
    public abstract string Name();

    public abstract double Price();
    protected abstract void Validate();
    public string Reference { get { return Reference_; } set { Reference_ = value; } }

    protected string Reference_;

    public string BaseCurrency {get { return MarketDataDictionaries.GetBaseCurrency(); }}
}

public class EquityOptionDeal: BaseDeal      // The declaration for EquityOptionDeal
{
    public string Equity { get { return EquityName_; } set { EquityName_ = value; } }
    public int NumberOfUnits { get { return NumberOfUnits_; } set { NumberOfUnits_ = value; } }
    public double Time_To_Expiry { get { return Time_To_Expiry_; } set { Time_To_Expiry_ = value; } }



    public override string Name()   // implement method Name()
    {
      return "Equity Option";
    }

    public override double Price()   // implement method Price()
    {
      Validate();

      double val=0.0;
      double[] greeks = new double[6];
      double s0 = 0.0;
      double fx_spot = 0.0;
      try
      {
          s0 = MarketDataDictionaries.EquityTable[EquityName_].Spot;  // get current equity price
          Currency_ = MarketDataDictionaries.EquityTable[EquityName_].Currency; // get equity volatility (assumed constant)
          DividendYield_ = MarketDataDictionaries.EquityTable[EquityName_].DivYield; // get equity dividend yield
      }
      catch
      {
          throw new Exception(Pre_string_ + "--- No Market Data supplied for " + EquityName_);
      }


      val *= fx_spot * NumberOfUnits_; // return value in base currency
      return val;
    }

    protected override void Validate()    // implement method Validate()
    {
      Pre_string_ = Name() + "  (" + Reference_ +")";
      if (Time_To_Expiry_ < 0.0)
      {
         throw new Exception(Pre_string_ + "--- Time to expiry cannot be less than zero years");
      }
      if (Strike_ < 0.0)
      {
         throw new Exception(Pre_string_ + "--- The strike cannot be less than zero");
      }


    }
```

Code excerpt 8.1   C# code showing the declaration of class BaseDeal and illustrating the implementation of methods Price(), Validate(), and Name().

Code excerpt 8.1 provides the declaration of `BaseDeal` and illustrates how the deal class `EquityOptionDeal` implements the necessary methods; the complete C# code for a range of deals is provided later.

It can be seen that the deal class also needs to specify the attributes which it will present to the user and in addition access market such as equity price.

```
namespace PortfolioValuer
{
    public partial class Form1 : Form
    {
        public Form1()
        {
            InitializeComponent();
        }
        private void button1_Click(object sender, EventArgs e)
        {
            StreamReader sr_config;
            StreamReader sr_tests;
            StreamWriter sw;

            MessageBox.Show("Computing value of portfolios");
            string AppDir = Path.GetDirectoryName(Application.ExecutablePath);
            string config_filename = AppDir + "\\Portfolios.txt";
            string MD_filename = AppDir + "\\MarketData.txt";
            try {
                BaseDeal.LoadMarketData(MD_filename);
             // Load and execute the specified tests
                sr_config = new StreamReader(config_filename);
                string assembly_name = AppDir + "\\DealLibrary.dll";
                Assembly Assm = Assembly.LoadFrom(assembly_name);
                Type[] LoadedTypes = Assm.GetTypes();
                string test_file;
                int block_comment_depth = 0;
                double port_val = 0.0;
                string BaseCurrency = BaseDeal.GetBaseCurrency();
                while ((test_file = sr_config.ReadLine()) != null)
                {
                    sr_tests = new StreamReader(test_file + ".txt");
                    string current_test;
                    string sdate = DateTime.Now.ToString();
                    string results_filename = AppDir + "\\" + test_file + "results.txt";
                    bool append = false;
                    sw = new StreamWriter(results_filename, append, Encoding.ASCII);
                    sw.WriteLine("============================");
                    sw.WriteLine(test_file + " in units of " + BaseCurrency);
                    sw.WriteLine(test_file +"    :" +sdate);
                    sw.WriteLine("============================");
                    port_val = 0.0;
                    block_comment_depth = 0;
                    while ((current_test = sr_tests.ReadLine()) != null) {

                        block_comment_depth += ((current_test.Length > 1) &&
                          (current_test.Substring(0,2) == "/*")) ? 1:0;
                        block_comment_depth -= ((current_test.Length > 1) &&
                          (current_test.Substring(0, 2) == "*/")) ? 1 : 0;
                                        .  .  .
                        try
                        {
                            deal_value = ac1.Price(); // return the value of the deal
                        }
                        catch (Exception ex)
                        {
                            sr_config.Close();
                            sw.Close();
                            sr_tests.Close();
                            throw new Exception(ex.Message);
                        }
                        port_val += deal_value; // add to the value to the portfolio
                        string str_deal_val = deal_value.ToString(" 0.0000;-0.0000; 0.0000");
                        sw.WriteLine(str_deal_val + "=" + ac1.Reference+","+ac1.Name());
                    }

                } // end of tests for a given portfolio

                // write the portfolio value
                sw.WriteLine("========================");
                string str_port_val = port_val.ToString(" 0.00;-0.00; 0.00");
```

Code excerpt 8.2 The main driver for the C# portfolio valuer application. After reading the market data file, it prices the trades contained in the portfolio definition files. The total value of each portfolio is also computed.

```
        sw.WriteLine("TOTAL VALUE = " + str_port_val + " " + BaseCurrency + "  ");
        sw.WriteLine("=========================");
        sw.Close();
        sr_tests.Close();
    }
    MessageBox.Show("Have completed computing portfolio values");
    sr_config.Close();
    // Clear the dictionaries
    BaseDeal.CurrencyTable.Clear();
    BaseDeal.EquityTable.Clear();
    BaseDeal.BondTable.Clear();
    BaseDeal.CorrelationTable.Clear();
    }
}
catch (Exception ex)
{
    MessageBox.Show("Computation aborted : exception : " + ex.Message);
}
}
}
```

Code excerpt 8.2 *(Continued).*

The Text Files

The application is driven by a *portfolio configuration* file and also a number of *portfolio definition* files, each of which is plain text format and thus can easily be edited by the user. The portfolio configuration file specifies the names of the portfolio files which are to be valued, and each portfolio definition file provides the details of the trades contained in a given portfolio. In addition, there is also a *market data* file (also in text format) which provides the market data required to value the trades.

A portfolio configuration file and also two portfolio definition files are given in Exhibit 8.1. It can be seen that comments can be included in the portfolio definition files, which is useful to document the deals contained in the portfolio. It is also possible to ignore a single trade by using a // at the beginning of a line. Complete sections of portfolio definition file can also be ignored by using the C style comment syntax /* */.

The syntax of each deal entry in the portfolio definition file is as follows:

```
Trade=<DealClass>,Reference=<Descriptive Text>,DealClassParam1=<Value1>, . . . ,DealClassParamN=<ValueN>
```

Each deal line must begin with an assignment to the **Trade** *attribute* using the syntax **Trade=<DealClass>**, where **<DealClass>** is the name of the C# class used to represent the given deal, i.e., **EquityOptionDeal** for an Equity Option. The other deal attributes are the public properties of **DealClass** and can be in any order. Deal valuation proceeds by first constructing an empty class object of type **DealClass**. The application then converts the string representation of the deal attribute values to the types expected by the **DealClass** and assignment to the deal object occurs. Once the deal object has been populated with the required trade data, the deal's **Price()** method is run. This retrieves the required market data, computes the deal value, and returns this to the application for output to the portfolio results file. All deals have the reference attribute which is used for the purposes of identification. It is a description (or alpha-numeric code) assigned to the trade, for instance **Reference=EQ:LaserComm-1001** or

`Reference=Tech-10008_Generic`. The portfolio results files contain both the value and reference for each deal which has been valued.

The Portfolio Driver File

```
EQ-Investments
Broad-Investments
```

Portfolio Definition File: EQ-Investments

```
// EQ-Investments : Only contains equities
//============================================
Trade=EquityOptionDeal,Reference=EQ:LaserComm-1001,Equity=LaserComm,Volatility=0.1,Strike=95.0,Time_To_Expiry=1.5,_
OptionType=Put,ExerciseStyle=European

Trade=EquityOptionDeal,Reference=EQ:WebComm-1004A,Equity=WebComm,Volatility=0.1,Strike=95.0,Time_To_Expiry=1.0,_
OptionType=Call,ExerciseStyle=European

Trade=EquityOptionDeal,Reference=EQ:LaserComm-1004,Equity=LaserComm,Volatility=0.1,Strike=95.0,Time_To_Expiry=1.0,_
OptionType=Call,ExerciseStyle=American

Trade=TwoEquityOptionDeal,Reference=EQ:CompuKalc-1005,Equity1=Mobile-Tech,Equity2=CompuKalc,Volatility1=0.2,_
Volatility2=0.2,RiskFreeRate=0.1,Strike=44.0,Time_To_Expiry=0.8,OptionType=Call,MinMax=Minimum,ExerciseStyle=European

Trade=TwoEquityOptionDeal,Reference=EQ:MobileTech|CompuKalc-1006,Equity1=Mobile-Tech,Equity2=CompuKalc,Volatility1=0.2,_
Volatility2=0.2,RiskFreeRate=0.1,Strike=94.0,Time_To_Expiry=0.8,OptionType=Call,_
MinMax=Maximum,ExerciseStyle=European

Trade=ThreeEquityOptionDeal,Reference=Tech-10001,Equity1=LaserComm,Equity2=TelComm,Equity3=SmartWeb,Volatility1=0.2,_
Volatility2=0.2,Volatility3=0.2,NumberOfUnits=100,Strike=100.0,Time_To_Expiry=1.0,OptionType=Put,_
MinMax=Maximum,MonteCarlo=No

Trade=GenericEquityBasketOptionDeal,Reference=Tech-10008_Generic,Volatilities=0.2%0.2%0.2,_
Equities=LaserComm%TelComm%SmartWeb,NumberOfUnits=100,_
Strike=100.0,Time_To_Expiry=1.0,OptionType=Call,MinMax=Maximum,MonteCarlo=Yes

Trade=FourEquityOptionDeal,Reference=Drinks-20001,Equity1=Drinks-4U,Equity2=Beverage-Ltd,Equity3=H2O-Ltd,_
Equity4=Fine-Wines-Ltd,Volatility1=0.2,_
Volatility2=0.2,Volatility3=0.2,Volatility4=0.2,NumberOfUnits=100,Strike=100.0,Time_To_Expiry=1.0,OptionType=Call,_
MinMax=Maximum,MonteCarlo=No

Trade=DownOutEquityOptionDeal,Reference=JPCA_111,Equity=H2O-Ltd,Volatility=0.2,Strike=100.0,_
Time_To_Expiry=1.0,Barrier_Level=90.0,OptionType=Call

Trade=DoubleKnockOutCallEquityOptionDeal,Reference=JPCAPP_115,Equity=LaserComm,Volatility=0.2,Strike=100.0,_
Time_To_Expiry=1.0,Lower_Barrier_Level=90.0,Upper_Barrier_Level=340.0
```

Portfolio Definition File: Broad-Investments

```
// Broad-Investments : Contains equity, FX and IR products
//============================================================
// Example FX deal Foreign currency = GBP Domestic Currency = USD, Strike = 1.5, Settlement = 4.0 years
// Note: The Strike is the number of units of domestic currency that have been agreed to be paid for one unit
// of foreign currency.

Trade=FXForwardDeal,Reference=FX-5001,ForeignAmount=100,Strike=1.5,ForeignCurrency=GBP,DomesticCurrency=USD,_
Settlement=4.0,BuySell=Buy

Trade=ForwardRateAgreementDeal,Reference=IR-6001,Principal=100.0,Strike=3.0,Currency=GBP,Maturity=4.5,_
Start=4.0,BuySell=Buy

//Trade=FXOptionDeal,Reference=FXOption_Call,NumberOfUnits=123,Strike=0.5,Volatility=0.1375,_
ForeignCurrency=USD,DomesticCurrency=GBP,_
Time_To_Expiry=5.0,ExerciseStyle=European,OptionType=Call,BuySell=Buy

Trade=DownOutEquityOptionDeal,Reference=Tech-7001,Equity=Real-Computers,Volatility=0.2,,Strike=100.0,_
Time_To_Expiry=1.0,Barrier_Level=90.0,OptionType=Call,CalcMethod=Analytic
/*
Trade=DownOutEquityOptionDeal,Reference=Tech-7002,Equity=Real-Computers,Volatility=0.2,Strike=100.0,Time_To_Expiry=1.0,_
Barrier_Level=90.0,CalcMethod=MonteCarlo,OptionType=Call,NumberScenarios=10000,UseBrownianBridge=true

Trade=DownOutEquityOptionDeal,Reference=Tech-7005,Equity=Real-Computers,Volatility=0.2,Strike=100.0,Time_To_Expiry=1.0,_
```

Exhibit 8.1   Here, we show an example portfolio driver file and the individual portfolio definition files `EQ-Investments.txt` and `Broad-Investments.txt`. The symbol _ is used to indicate a line continuation, and it should be noted the C# application requires each deal to be specified on a single line.

```
Barrier_Level=90.0,CalcMethod=Analytic,OptionType=Call
*/
Trade=DownOutEquityOptionDeal,Reference=Tech-7006,Equity=Real-Computers,Volatility=0.2,Strike=100.0,Time_To_Expiry=1.0,_
Barrier_Level=90.0,CalcMethod=Numeric,OptionType=Call

Trade=DownOutEquityOptionDeal,Reference=Tech-7007,Equity=Real-Computers,Volatility=0.2,Strike=100.0,Time_To_Expiry=1.0,_
Barrier_Level=90.0,CalcMethod=Numeric,OptionType=Call,ExerciseStyle=American

//Trade=DownOutEquityOptionDeal,Reference=JPCA_BB_False,Equity=Real-Computers,Strike=100.0,Time_To_Expiry=1.0,_
Barrier_Level=90.0,CalcMethod=MonteCarlo,OptionType=Call,NumberScenarios=10000,UseBrownianBridge=false

Trade=DownOutFXOptionDeal,Reference=FX-5004,NumberOfUnits=123,Strike=0.5,Volatility=0.1375,_
ForeignCurrency=USD,DomesticCurrency=GBP,
Time_To_Expiry=5.0,ExerciseStyle=European,OptionType=Call,BuySell=Buy,CalcMethod=Analytic,Barrier_Level=0.01

Trade=DownOutFXOptionDeal,Reference=FX-5006,NumberOfUnits=123,Strike=0.5,Volatility=0.1375,ForeignCurrency=USD,_
DomesticCurrency=GBP,Time_To_Expiry=5.0,ExerciseStyle=European,OptionType=Call,BuySell=Buy,CalcMethod=MonteCarlo,_
UseBrownianBridge=true,Barrier_Level=0.01

// American FX Barrier Call
Trade=DownOutFXOptionDeal,Reference=FX-5007,NumberOfUnits=123,Strike=0.5,Volatility=0.1375,ForeignCurrency=USD,_
DomesticCurrency=GBP,Time_To_Expiry=5.0,OptionType=Call,BuySell=Buy,CalcMethod=Numeric,_
Barrier_Level=0.01,ExerciseStyle=American

// European Put
Trade=FXOptionDeal,Reference=FX-5008,NumberOfUnits=123,Strike=0.5,Volatility=0.1375,ForeignCurrency=USD,_
DomesticCurrency=GBP,Time_To_Expiry=5.0,ExerciseStyle=European,OptionType=Put,BuySell=Buy

Trade=DownOutFXOptionDeal,Reference=FX-5009,NumberOfUnits=123,Strike=0.5,Volatility=0.1375,ForeignCurrency=USD,_
DomesticCurrency=GBP,Time_To_Expiry=5.0,OptionType=Put,BuySell=Buy,CalcMethod=MonteCarlo,_
Barrier_Level=0.01,ExerciseStyle=European
```

Exhibit 8.1 (*Continued*).

In the C++ derivative pricing functions developed in the earlier part of this book, all the deal information such as asset price, risk-free interest rate, etc., was passed explicitly to the pricing function.

For instance, let us consider the pricing of the simple `EquityOption`, `Reference=EQ:WebComm-1004A`, which is specified in Exhibit 8.1. The entry (which we will refer to as *E1* in the portfolio definition file EQ-investments) is

```
Trade=EquityOptionDeal,Reference=EQ:WebComm-1004A,Equity=WebComm,Volatility=0.1,_
Strike=95.0,Time_To_Expiry=1.0,OptionType=Call,ExerciseStyle=European
```

The reason for the inclusion of the `Volatility` attribute will be discussed later.

If we explicitly passed all the information required by the underlying C++ function `black_scholes`, then the form of the required entry (referred to here as E2) would be

```
Trade=EquityOptionDeal,Reference=EQ:WebComm-1004A,Equity=WebComm,Volatility=0.1,_
Strike=95.0,Time_To_Expiry=1.5,OptionType=Put,ExerciseStyle=European,EquitySpot=100,_
FXEquityCurrency=0.5565,RiskFreeRate=0.1,DividendYield=0.05
```

The reason that *E1* does not require the extra four deal attributes `EquitySpot` `=100`, `FXEquityCurrency=0.5565,RiskFreeRate=0.1,DividendYield=0.05`, is that these are stored in *market data dictionaries* and accessed by the C# class `EquityOptionDeal` before the C++ function `black_scholes` is called.

The market data dictionaries are populated as soon as the application starts. Exhibit 8.2 shows an example market data file. This is a plain text file and provides a common repository for market parameters that are required by the deal classes. For instance, all foreign exchange derivatives will need access to the current FX rates, and all equity derivatives will require the current equity price. The contents of the market data file can be updated as frequently as required (i.e., daily, hourly, etc.) but will always maintain a set of market values that can be used consistently across all deal valuations.

It should be mentioned that the main advantage of type *E1* deal entries is not just that the portfolio definition file is smaller, it also ensures that consistent market data values are used to price all the trades in the portfolio. When type *E2* deal entries are used, it is necessary to ensure that all the extra deal attributes are updated as new market data becomes available. This would be a time-consuming task, and if only a partial update occurs could give rise to invalid deal valuations caused by inconsistent deal attribute values such as FXEquityCurrency and DividendYield.

```
// Currency market data. This is used for pricing interest rate swaps, FX options, etc...

Currency.USD,FXSpot=0.5565,YieldCurve=[(0.0027,0.0184),...,(40.58,0.0533)],
VolCurve=[(0.0,0.10),(1.0,0.12),(3.0,0.13),(6.0,0.14),(20,0.15)]
Currency.GBP<<--Base,FXSpot=1.0,YieldCurve=[(0.0027,0.047),...,(50.03,0.042)],
VolCurve=[(0.0,0.10),(1.0,0.12),(3.0,0.13),(6.0,0.14),(20,0.15)]
Currency.EUR,FXSpot=0.689024,YieldCurve=[(0.0,0.04),...,(20,0.056)],
VolCurve=[(0.0,0.10),(1.0,0.12),(3.0,0.13),(6.0,0.14),(20,0.15)]
Currency.CAD,FXSpot=1.5,YieldCurve=[(0.0,0.04),...,(20,0.056)],
VolCurve=[(0.0,0.10),(1.0,0.12),(3.0,0.13),(6.0,0.14),(20,0.15)]

// Equity market data. This is used for pricing equity options, etc...

Equity.Imperial-Art,Currency=GBP,Spot=9.0,DivYield=0.03
Equity.Real-Computers,Currency=USD,Spot=200.0,DivYield=0.04
Equity.TelComm,Currency=GBP,Spot=120.0,DivYield=0.09
Equity.WebComm,Currency=USD,Spot=100.0,DivYield=0.07
Equity.Hackers,Currency=GBP,Spot=40.0,DivYield=0.02
Equity.LaserComm,Currency=GBP,Spot=95.0,DivYield=0.05
Equity.SmartWeb,Currency=GBP,Spot=100.0,DivYield=0.01
Equity.Web-Comm,Currency=GBP,Spot=100.0,DivYield=0.04
Equity.Mobile-Tech,Currency=GBP,Spot=92.0,DivYield=0.02
Equity.CompuKalc,Currency=GBP,Spot=95.0,DivYield=0.11
Equity.The-Bookshop,Currency=GBP,Spot=100.0,DivYield=0.02
Equity.Everyman-Books,Currency=GBP,Spot=100.0,DivYield=0.03
Equity.The-RealBook-Company,Currency=GBP,Spot=100.0,DivYield=0.04
Equity.Drinks-4U,Currency=GBP,Spot=100.0,DivYield=0.05
Equity.Beverage-Ltd,Currency=GBP,Spot=100.0,DivYield=0.06
Equity.H2O-Ltd,Currency=GBP,Spot=100.0,DivYield=0.05
Equity.Fine-Wines-Ltd,Currency=GBP,Spot=100.0,DivYield=0.03
Equity.French-Wines-Ltd,Currency=EUR,Spot=100.0,DivYield=0.2
Equity.The-English-Beer-Company,Currency=GBP,Spot=100.0,DivYield=0.03
Equity.Water-Works-Ltd,Currency=GBP,Spot=100.0,DivYield=0.012
Equity.Welsh-Spring,Currency=GBP,Spot=100.0,DivYield=0.06
Equity.ThamesBeer,Currency=GBP,Spot=100.0,DivYield=0.05
Equity.Edingburgh-Whiskey,Currency=GBP,Spot=100.0,DivYield=0.04
Equity.The-Wine-Box,Currency=GBP,Spot=100.0,DivYield=0.085

// Bond market data. This is used for pricing bonds, and credit derivatives such as CDS, and TRS

Bond.Fine-Wines-Ltd-Bond-2020,Currency=GBP,Spot=150.0,SurvivalProb=[(0.0,1.0),(1.0,0.9),(3.0,0.96),(6.0,0.9),(20,0.5)]
Bond.Hackers-Bond-2018,Currency=GBP,Spot=200.0,SurvivalProb=[(0.0,1.0),(2.0,0.91),(5.0,0.9),(8.0,0.8),(30,0.6)]
Bond.Hackers-Bond-2060,Currency=GBP,Spot=260.0,SurvivalProb=[(0.0,1.0),(1.0,0.92),(20.0,0.8),(20,0.65),(60,0.7)]
Bond.Real-Computers-Bond-2020,Currency=USD,Spot=100.0,SurvivalProb=[(0.0,1.0),(1.0,0.94),(4.0,0.9),(8.0,0.6),(30,0.5)]

// Market data correlation. These are used for multi-asset options

Correlation.Imperial-Art,Real-Computers=0.5

Correlation.Real-Computers,WebComm=0.4
Correlation.Real-Computers,Hackers=0.5
Correlation.Real-Computers,LaserComm=0.3
Correlation.Real-Computers,SmartWeb=0.4

Correlation.TelComm,Hackers=0.5
Correlation.TelComm,LaserComm=0.5
Correlation.TelComm,SmartWeb=0.5
Correlation.TelComm,Web-Comm=0.5
Correlation.LaserComm,SmartWeb=0.5

Correlation.Hackers,Mobile-Tech=0.4
Correlation.LaserComm,Mobile-Tech=0.4
Correlation.SmartWeb,Mobile-Tech=0.5
Correlation.Web-Comm,Mobile-Tech=0.5

Correlation.Mobile-Tech,The-Bookshop=0.1
```

```
Correlation.CompuKalc,LaserComm=0.3

Correlation.ThamesBeer,French-Wines-Ltd=0.3
Correlation.ThamesBeer,Fine-Wines-Ltd=0.5
Correlation.ThamesBeer,H2O-Ltd=0.5
Correlation.ThamesBeer,Beverage-Ltd=0.6
Correlation.ThamesBeer,Drinks-4U=0.6
Correlation.ThamesBeer,The-RealBook-Company=0.8
Correlation.ThamesBeer,People-Books=0.1


          .   .   .

Correlation.Edingburgh-Whiskey,French-Wines-Ltd=0.5
Correlation.Edingburgh-Whiskey,Water-Works-Ltd=0.5
Correlation.Edingburgh-Whiskey,The-English-Beer-Company=0.6
```

Exhibit 8.2   An example market data file, which is used to specify the current market values such as equity spot, FX spot, interest rate yield curves, etc. The third line in the file provides currency information for GBP, and the entry currency. GBP<< −−Base specifies that the base currency will be GBP, and thus, all portfolio and deal values will be computed in GBP.

The format of the result files is shown in Exhibit 8.3 below. The output syntax is simply

<deal value>=<deal reference>,<deal type>

It can be seen that each deal is valued in base currency (which here is specified in the market data file as **GBP**) and the total value for the portfolio is also reported.

Results File for Portfolio EQ-Investments

```
==============================
EQ-Investments in units of GBP
EQ-Investments   :14/07/2007 00:00:00
==============================
  4.3501=EQ:LaserComm-1001,Equity Option
  2.9278=EQ:LaserComm-1002,Equity Option
  3.5716=EQ:LaserComm-1003,Equity Option
  2.0245=EQ:LaserComm-1004,Equity Option
  2.2171=EQ:WebComm-1004A,Equity Option
 41.7119=EQ:CompuKalc-1005,Rainbow option(two equities)
 14.0274=EQ:MobileTech|CompuKalc-1006,Rainbow option(two equities)
  8.8511=EQ:MobileTech|CompuKalc-1007,Rainbow option(two equities)
 70.3151=EQ:MobileTech|TelComm-1008,Rainbow option(two equities)
 13.3263=JPCAM11,Rainbow option(two equities)
  6.5840=JPCAM111,Rainbow option(two equities)
 72.7866=Tech-10001,Three Equity Option
 70.1046=Tech-10002,Three Equity Option
 69.7412=Tech-10003,Three Equity Option
1010.6123=Tech-10004,Three Equity Option
1030.3894=Tech-10005,Three Equity Option
2850.8918=Tech-10006,Three Equity Option
2838.9643=Tech-10007,Three Equity Option
2838.9643=Tech-10008_Generic,Generic Equity Option
399.4981=Tech-10009,Three Equity Option
409.1153=Tech-10010,Three Equity Option
2646.6473=Drinks-20001,Four Equity Option
2644.3642=Drinks-20002,Four Equity Option
 15.3381=Drinks-20003,Four Equity Option
 21.8691=Drinks-20004,Four Equity Option
 53.8106=Drinks-20005,Four Equity Option
 63.2889=Drinks-20006,Four Equity Option
1511.6543=Drinks-20007,Four Equity Option
1524.5000=Drinks-20008,Four Equity Option
1510.7045=Drinks-20009,Four Equity Option
1518.8670=Drinks-20010,Four Equity Option
1513.7578=Drinks-20011,Four Equity Option
1524.5000=Drinks-20012,Generic Equity Option
1513.7578=Drinks-20013,Four Equity Option
2030.2451=Drinks-20013,Generic Equity Option
  6.1238=JPCA_111,Down Out Equity Option
```

```
6.1240=JPCA_111A,Down Out Equity Option
3.0006=JPCA_112,Down Out Equity Option
3.0006=JPCA_113,Down Out Equity Option
3.0006=JPCA_114,Down Out Equity Option
3.0036=JPCAPP_115,Double Knock Out Call Equity Option
=========================
TOTAL VALUE =  29878.53 GBP
=========================
```

Results File for Portfolio Broad-Investments

```
==============================
Broad-Investments in units of GBP
Broad-Investments   :14/07/2007 00:00:00
==============================
 9.4359=FX-5001,FX Forward
-9.4359=FX-5002,FX Forward
 0.8661=IR-6001,Forward Rate Agreement
 1.1755=IR-6002,Forward Rate Agreement
52.6353=Tech-7001,Down Out Equity Option
52.6757=Tech-7002,Down Out Equity Option
52.6757=Tech-7003,Down Out Equity Option
52.6583=Tech-7004,Down Out Equity Option
52.6353=Tech-7005,Down Out Equity Option
52.6358=Tech-7006,Down Out Equity Option
55.6500=Tech-7007,Down Out Equity Option
11.6849=FX-5003,FX Option
11.6849=FX-5004,Down Out FX Option
11.6813=FX-5005,Down Out FX Option
11.5356=FX-5006,Down Out FX Option
11.9998=FX-5007,Down Out FX Option
 2.9173=FX-5008,FX Option
 2.9827=FX-5009,Down Out FX Option
=========================
TOTAL VALUE =  438.09 GBP
=========================
```

Exhibit 8.3 Portfolio results' files. The reporting currency is set in the market data file; in this example, all values are given in pounds sterling.

8.2 STORING AND RETRIEVING THE MARKET DATA

As mentioned before, the market data required to price derivatives is stored in market data dictionaries. The `MarketDataDictionaries` class, shown in Code excerpt 8.4, contains a set of C# dictionary member items which hold all the market data required by the deal classes. Below, we give the declaration of the `CurrencyTable`, `EquityTable`, and `CorrelationTable` dictionaries,

```
public static Dictionary<string, Currency> CurrencyTable = new Dictionary<string, Currency>();
public static Dictionary<string, Equity> EquityTable = new Dictionary<string, Equity>();
public static Dictionary<string, Correlation> CorrelationTable = new Dictionary<string, Correlation>();
```

Each dictionary entry is made up of a `{<unique-key>, <value-object>}` pair, where `unique-key` is a unique string, and `value-object` is a class containing the corresponding market data. We will now consider each of the above dictionaries and the information they hold in more detail.

CurrencyTable

In a `CurrencyTable` dictionary, `value-object` is a class of type `Currency` and is used to store currency information. The class declaration is provided below.

```csharp
public class TPair : IComparable
{
    public double t;
    public double val;

    public TPair(double t1, double val1)
    {
        t = t1;
        val = val1;
    }

    int IComparable.CompareTo(object obj)
    {
        TPair temp = (TPair)obj;
        if (this.t > temp.t)
            return (1);
        if (this.t < temp.t)
            return (-1);
        else
            return (0);
    }
}

// ICurve - a curve for storing interest rates
public class ICurve: List<TPair>
{
    private double t_pt;  // internal value used for matching
    private string name_ = "";

    public ICurve (string name) {
        name_ = name;
    }

    public double this[double t_0, double t]
    { get { // return the discount factor between t and t1

        double eps = 1.0e-6;
        double val;

        t_pt = t;
        // find the bounding indicies corresponding to a given t value
        int indx1 = this.FindIndex(TPairFind);

        if (indx1 == -1)
        throw new Exception("Invalid market data interest rate yield curve for currency " + name_);

        double v2 = this[indx1].val;
        double v1 = this[indx1 - 1].val;
        double t2 = this[indx1].t;
        double t1 = this[indx1 - 1].t;

        if (Math.Abs(t2 - t) < eps)
        {
            val = v2;
        }
        else
        { // use linear interpolation to compute the value of DF
            val = v1 + ((v2 - v1) / (t2 - t1)) * (t - t1);
        }

        val = Math.Exp(-val * t);

        return val;
        }
    }

    public double this[double t, double t1, double t2] {
    get {
        // return the forward rate between t1 and t2
        // t2 >= t1
        double DF1 = this[t, t1];
        double DF2 = this[t, t2];
        double fwd = (DF1 / DF2 - 1.0) / (t2 - t1);

        return fwd;
        }
    }

    private bool TPairFind(TPair v)
    {
        if ((v.t >= t_pt))
        {
```

Code excerpt 8.3   Showing the class Currency and also the classes ICurve and TPair which all enable the interest rate yield curve to be stored.

```
                return true;
        }
        else
        {
            return false;
        }
    }
}

public class Currency
{
    public string name;            // the name of the currency (e.g GBP, or USD)
    public double spot;            // the FX spot of the currency with respect to base currency
    public ICurve YieldCurve;      // the currency yield curve
    public VCurve VolCurve;        // the volatility of the yield curve (not currently used by the C# application)

    public Currency(string name1, double spot1) // two parameter constructor
    {
        name = name1;
        spot = spot1;
        YieldCurve = new ICurve(name1);
    }

    public Currency(string name1) // single parameter constructor
    {
        YieldCurve = new ICurve(name1);
        VolCurve = new VCurve(name1);
    }
}
```

Code excerpt 8.3 (*Continued*).

It is straightforward to add currency data to `CurrencyTable`. The following C# code fragment illustrates the addition of USD information.

```
string CcyCode = "USD"; // set the unique currency code to USD

// create a new (empty) entry in the CurrencyTable for USD
CurrencyTable.Add(CcyCode, new Currency(CcyCode));

double FXSpot = 0.5565; // set the USD to base currency FX spot

// assign to public data member spot, in class Currency
CurrencyTable[CcyCode].spot = FXSpot;
// assign to public data member name, in class Currency
CurrencyTable[CcyCode].name = CcyCode;

double t;
double rt;

t= 0.0027;      // time - for point 1
rt = 0.0184;    // rate - for point 1
 // add the first point to the public data member YieldCurve, in class Currency
CurrencyTable[CcyCode].YieldCurve.Add(new TPair(t, rt));
          .    .    .
t = 40.58;
rt = 0.0533;
CurrencyTable[CcyCode].YieldCurve.Add(new TPair(t, rt));
```

Code excerpt 8.4   Showing the addition of USD currency market data to the CurrencyTable dictionary.

The information in the `CurrencyTable` is accessed by the deal classes and used to compute discount factors, forward rates, and FX spots. In the market data file, see Exhibit 8.2, the YieldCurve consists of a set of time/value pairs and is defined using the following syntax:

YieldCurve $= [(t_1, r_1), ..., (t_i, r_i), ..., (t_n, r_n)]$, where t_i is the time in years, and r_i is the corresponding zero coupon rate with tenor t_i.

The value, at $t = 0$, of a zero coupon bond with unit cash-flow at maturity, t_i, is $\exp(-r_i t_i)$ and is known as the discount factor $DF(0, t_i)$. Code excerpt 8.4 shows the addition of two data items to the USD yield curve, while Code excerpt 8.5 illustrates the retrieval from $DF(0, t_i)$ of r_i. The code fragment

```
double discount_fac = DF[0, Time_To_Expiry_];
RiskFreeRate = -Math.Log(discount_fac) / Time_To_Expiry_;
```

computes the zero coupon rate `RiskFreeRate`. It should be mentioned that it would have been more efficient to have written code to directly obtain the interpolated risk-free rate from the USD yield curve (without first computing the associated discount factor). However, the required code can easily be supplied by the reader.

```
try
{
    string Currency_ = "USD";
    // DF will be used to access discount factors
    ICurve DF = MarketDataDictionaries.CurrencyTable[Currency_].YieldCurve;

    // FWD will be used to access forward rates
    ICurve FWD = MarketDataDictionaries.CurrencyTable[BaseCurrency].YieldCurve;

    // obtain the discount factor DF(0,1) using methods in class ICurve
    double discount_fac = DF[0, Time_To_Expiry_];

    RiskFreeRate = -Math.Log(discount_fac) / Time_To_Expiry_;
    double Time_To_Expiry_ = 1.0;
    double FXspot =

    // obtain the FX spot with respect the base currency (GBP)
    MarketDataDictionaries.CurrencyTable[Currency_].spot;

    double t1 = 1.0;;
    double t2 = 1.5;

    // obtain the forward rate F(0,1,1.5) using methods in class ICurve
    double forward_rate = FWD[0, t1, t2];
}
catch
{
    throw new Exception(Pre_string_ + "--- No Market Data supplied for " + Currency_);
}
```

Code excerpt 8.5   Showing the retrieval of USD currency market data from the CurrencyTable dictionary.

Discount factors and forward rates are accessed by from an `ICurve` object. The discount factor is obtained as follows:

```
ICurve DF = MarketDataDictionaries.
            CurrencyTable[Currency_].YieldCurve;
```

declares the `ICurve` object `DF`. Then the discount factor, between `0` and `Time_To_Expiry_`, is computed with the statement

```
double discount_fac = DF[0, Time_To_Expiry_];
```

where `DF[0, Time_To_Expiry_]` calls the `ICurve` accessor (declared as `public double this[double t_0, double t]`) with `t_0 = 0` and `t = Time_To_Expiry`. It can be seen from Code excerpt 8.3 that linear interpolation is performed by the accessor if required.

The forward rate is accessed in a similar manner:

```
ICurve FWD = MarketDataDictionaries.
             CurrencyTable[Currency_].YieldCurve;
```

declares the `ICurve` object `FWD`. Then the forward rate $F(0,t_1,t_2)$ is returned with the statement

```
double forward_rate = FWD[0, 0.5, 1.5];
```

where `FWD[0, t1, t2]` calls the `ICurve` accessor (declared as `public double this[double t, double t1, double t2]`) with `t = 0`, `t1=0.5`, and `t2 = 1.5`. It can be seen from Code excerpt 8.3 that the accessor computes the forward rate as

```
FWD[0,t1,t2] = (DF[0,t1] / DF[0,t2] - 1.0) / (t2 - t1);
```

EquityTable and CorrelationTable
Code excerpt 8.6 shows how equities and correlations are stored.

```
public class Equity
{
    public string Name;
    public double Spot;
    public string Currency;
    public double DivYield;

    public Equity(string Name1, double Spot1, string Currency1, double DivYield1)
    {
        Name = Name1;
        Spot = Spot1;
        Currency = Currency1;
        DivYield = DivYield1;
    }

    public Equity()
    {
    }
}

public class Correlation
{
    public string Name1;
    public string Name2;
    public double Correl;

    public Correlation(string Name11, string Name12, double Correl1)
    {
        Name1 = Name11;
        Name2 = Name12;
        Correl = Correl1;
    }
    public Correlation()
    {
    }
}
```

Code excerpt 8.6   The equity and correlation classes.

```
public class MarketDataDictionaries
{
    public static Dictionary<string, Currency> CurrencyTable = new Dictionary<string, Currency>();
    public static Dictionary<string, Equity> EquityTable = new Dictionary<string, Equity>();
    public static Dictionary<string, Correlation> CorrelationTable = new Dictionary<string, Correlation>();
    protected static string BaseCurrency_ = "";

    public static string GetBaseCurrency()
    {
        return BaseCurrency_;
    }

    public static void LoadMarketData(string marketdata_file)
    {
        // Load the market data file and assign values to dictionaries
        StreamReader MDFILE = new StreamReader(marketdata_file);
        string cur_line = "";

        while ((cur_line = MDFILE.ReadLine()) != null)  // loop through the market data file
        {
            if ((cur_line.Length > 1) && ((cur_line.Substring(0, 2) != "//")))
            {
                char[] seps = new char[] { '=', ',' };
                string[] v = cur_line.Split(seps, StringSplitOptions.None);

                int num_elems = v.GetUpperBound(0);
                int k = 0;
                double t_, val_;
                bool stop;
                double FXSpot = 0.0;

                if (v[0].Substring(0, 8) == "Currency") // currency data
                {
                    string CcyCode = v[0].Substring(9, 3);
```

Code excerpt 8.7   The MarketDataDictionaries class, illustrating how market data is added to the internal dictionaries.

```
            if (v[0].IndexOf("<<--Base") != -1) BaseCurrency_ = CcyCode;

            k += 2;

            if (!CurrencyTable.ContainsKey(CcyCode))
            {
                CurrencyTable.Add(CcyCode, new Currency(CcyCode));
            }
            else
            {
                throw new Exception("Spot & interest rate market data already supplied for " + CcyCode);
            }

            FXSpot = (double)Convert.ChangeType(v[k], typeof(double));
            CurrencyTable[CcyCode].spot = FXSpot;
            CurrencyTable[CcyCode].name = CcyCode;

            k += 2;
            t_ = (double)Convert.ChangeType(v[k].Substring(2, v[k].Length - 2), typeof(double));
            k += 1;
            val_ = (double)Convert.ChangeType(v[k].Substring(0, v[k].Length - 1), typeof(double));

            CurrencyTable[CcyCode].YieldCurve.Add(new TPair(t_, val_));
            k += 1;
            int vv = v[k].IndexOf(")]");
            stop = false;
            while (!stop) // Add the yield curve data
            {
                t_ = (double)Convert.ChangeType(v[k].Substring(1, v[k].Length - 1), typeof(double));
                k += 1;
                if (v[k].IndexOf(")]") == -1)
                {
                    val_ = (double)Convert.ChangeType(v[k].Substring(0, v[k].Length - 1), typeof(double));
                }
                else
                {
                    val_ = (double)Convert.ChangeType(v[k].Substring(0, v[k].Length - 2), typeof(double));
                    stop = true;
                }
                k += 1;
                CurrencyTable[CcyCode].YieldCurve.Add(new TPair(t_, val_));
            }
            CurrencyTable[CcyCode].YieldCurve.Sort();

                        .        .        .

        }
        else if (v[0].Substring(0, 6) == "Equity") // equity data
        {
            int idx = v[k].IndexOf(".");
            string EquityName = v[0].Substring(idx + 1, v[0].Length - idx - 1);
            k += 2;
            string CcyCode = v[k];
            k += +2;
            double spot = (double)Convert.ChangeType(v[k], typeof(double));
            k += +2;
            double div = (double)Convert.ChangeType(v[k], typeof(double));

            if (!EquityTable.ContainsKey(EquityName))
            {
                EquityTable.Add(EquityName, new Equity());
                EquityTable[EquityName].Currency = CcyCode;
                EquityTable[EquityName].Name = EquityName;
                EquityTable[EquityName].Spot = spot;
                EquityTable[EquityName].DivYield = div;
            }
            else
            {
                throw new Exception("Spot & currency market data already supplied for " + EquityName);
            }
        }

                        .        .        .

        else if (v[0].Length >= 12 && v[0].Substring(0, 11) == "Correlation") // correlation data
        {
            int idx = v[0].IndexOf(".");
            string AssetName1 = v[0].Substring(idx + 1, v[0].Length - idx - 1);
            k += 1;
            string AssetName2 = v[k];
            k += 1;
            double corr = (double)Convert.ChangeType(v[k], typeof(double));
            string CorrelationKey = AssetName1 + "%" + AssetName2;

            if(!CorrelationTable.ContainsKey(CorrelationKey))
            {
```

Code excerpt 8.7 (*Continued*).

```
                    // ie The-Wine-Box%Water-Works-Ltd and The-Wine-Box%Water-Works-Ltd

                    CorrelationTable.Add(CorrelationKey, new Correlation());
                    CorrelationTable[CorrelationKey].Correl = corr;
                    CorrelationTable[CorrelationKey].Name1 = AssetName1;
                    CorrelationTable[CorrelationKey].Name2 = AssetName2;

                    CorrelationKey = AssetName2 + "%" + AssetName1;
                    CorrelationTable.Add(CorrelationKey, new Correlation());
                    CorrelationTable[CorrelationKey].Correl = corr;
                    CorrelationTable[CorrelationKey].Name1 = AssetName2;
                    CorrelationTable[CorrelationKey].Name2 = AssetName1;
                }
                else
                {
                    throw new Exception("market data already supplied for " + CorrelationKey);
                }
            }
        }
    }
    MDFILE.Close();
    }
}
```

Code excerpt 8.7 (*Continued*).

Code excerpt 8.7 shows how market data is added to the internal dictionaries of the `MarketDataDictionaries` class. For instance to add a correlation entry, it is first necessary to construct the dictionary key and then determine whether or not the entry already exists in the dictionary. This is shown in the code fragment below

```
// first construct the unique key string from AssetName1 and AssetName2

  string CorrelationKey = AssetName1 + "%" + AssetName2;

  // Now check whether this key already exists in the dictionary CorrelationTable.
  // If it doesn't then add a new entry, if it does then raise an exception

  if(!CorrelationTable.ContainsKey(CorrelationKey))
  {
        // Create a new empty dictionary entry for the unique key
        CorrelationTable.Add(CorrelationKey, new Correlation());

        // Now fill out the entry by assigning the correlation and the asset names
        CorrelationTable[CorrelationKey].Correl = corr;
        CorrelationTable[CorrelationKey].Name1 = AssetName1;
        CorrelationTable[CorrelationKey].Name2 = AssetName2;

        // Create another empty dictionary entry with the asset names in reverse order
        // (because correlation(a,b) = correlation(b,a)

        CorrelationKey = AssetName2 + "%" + AssetName1;

        // Now fill out the entry by assigning the correlation and the asset names
         CorrelationTable.Add(CorrelationKey, new Correlation());
         CorrelationTable[CorrelationKey].Correl = corr;
         CorrelationTable[CorrelationKey].Name1 = AssetName2;
         CorrelationTable[CorrelationKey].Name2 = AssetName1;
  }
  else
  {
     throw new Exception("market data already supplied for " + CorrelationKey);
  }
```

8.3 EQUITY DEAL CLASSES

In this section, we provide the C# code for both single and multi-asset equity options. The trade attributes correspond to the public properties of the deal class, and attribute default values can be readily found by reading the C# code.

The enumerations used by the deal attributes are declared below.

```
public enum BuySell { Buy, Sell };
public enum PutCall { Put, Call };
public enum EuropeanAmerican { European, American };
public enum MinimumMaximum { Minimum, Maximum };
public enum UseMonteCarlo { Yes, No };
public enum CalculationMethod { Analytic, Numeric, MonteCarlo };
```

and it can be seen that the enumerator names have *obvious* names.

It has already been noted that the volatility used by the application to price options is supplied as a deal attribute, rather than being stored as market data. The reason for this is simplicity. In Chapter 4, we mentioned that a volatility surface is required to represent the implied volatility used to price options. Storing the implied volatility would thus require a set of volatility surfaces in the market data file and also multidimensional interpolation to retrieve the volatility applicable to a given option. It was thus decided to supply the volatility as a trade attribute and update its value appropriately.

8.3.1 Single Equity Option

Code excerpt 8.8 shows the class which computes the value of a single equity option.

```
using System;

namespace Computational_Lib
{
    public class EquityOptionDeal: BaseDeal
    {
        public string Equity { get { return EquityName_; } set { EquityName_ = value; } }
        public int NumberOfUnits { get { return NumberOfUnits_; } set { NumberOfUnits_ = value; } }
        public double Time_To_Expiry { get { return Time_To_Expiry_; } set { Time_To_Expiry_ = value; } }
        public PutCall OptionType{ get {return OptionType_;} set { OptionType_= value;}}
        public EuropeanAmerican ExerciseStyle { get { return ExerciseStyle_; } set { ExerciseStyle_ = value; } }
        public double Strike { get { return Strike_; } set { Strike_ = value; } }
        public BuySell BuySell { get { return BuySell_; } set { BuySell_ = value; } }
        public double Volatility { get { return Sigma_; } set { Sigma_ = value; } }

        protected PutCall  OptionType_ = PutCall.Put;
        protected EuropeanAmerican ExerciseStyle_ = EuropeanAmerican.European;
        protected double    Strike_ = 0;
        protected string    EquityName_ = "";
        protected double    Time_To_Expiry_ = 0.0;
        protected string    Currency_ = "";
        protected double    DividendYield_ = 0.0;
        protected string    Pre_string_ = "";
        protected BuySell   BuySell_ = BuySell.Buy;
        protected int NumberOfUnits_ = 1;
        protected double Sigma_ = 0.0;

        public override string Name()
        {
            return "Equity Option";
        }

        public override double Price()
        {
            Validate();

            double val=0.0;
            double[] greeks = new double[6];
            double s0 = 0.0;
            double fx_spot = 0.0;
            try
            {
                s0 = MarketDataDictionaries.EquityTable[EquityName_].Spot; // get current equity price
```

Code excerpt 8.8   The complete C# code for class EquityOptionDeal, which computes the value of a single equity option.

```
            Currency_ = MarketDataDictionaries.EquityTable[EquityName_].Currency;
              // get equity volatility (assumed constant)
            DividendYield_ = MarketDataDictionaries.EquityTable[EquityName_].DivYield; // get equity dividend yield
        }
        catch
        {
            throw new Exception(Pre_string_ + "--- No Market Data supplied for " + EquityName_);
        }
        // get the risk free rate to use
        double discount_fac = 0.0;
        double RiskFreeRate = 0.0;
        try
        {
            ICurve DF = MarketDataDictionaries.CurrencyTable[Currency_].YieldCurve;  // obtain the discount factor
            discount_fac = DF[0, Time_To_Expiry_];
            RiskFreeRate = -Math.Log(discount_fac) / Time_To_Expiry_;
            fx_spot = MarketDataDictionaries.CurrencyTable[Currency_].spot;
        }
        catch
        {
            throw new Exception(Pre_string_ + "--- No Market Data supplied for " + Currency_);
        }

        int iflag, put;

        iflag = 0;
        put = OptionType_ == PutCall.Put ? 1 : 0;

        if (ExerciseStyle_ == EuropeanAmerican.European)  // use BlackScholes
        {
            // call C++ routine.
            // Note: A null pointer is supplied so that the greeks are not computed
            PricingUtils.black_scholes(ref val, IntPtr.Zero, s0, Strike_, Sigma_, Time_To_Expiry_,
                        RiskFreeRate, DividendYield_, put, ref iflag);
        }
        else
        {
            // Use Crank Nicolson
            double theta = 0.5;
            int is_american = 1;
            // fix the geometry of the grid (these values should give "reasonable" results)
            int ns = 50;  // 50 divisions on asset axis
            int nt = 50;  // 50 divisions on time axis
            double smax = 10.0 * s0;

            PricingUtils.opt_gfd(theta, s0, Sigma_,RiskFreeRate, Time_To_Expiry_, Strike_,
                is_american, put, ref val, IntPtr.Zero, DividendYield_, ns,
                nt, smax, ref iflag);
        }

        if (iflag != 0)
            throw new Exception(Pre_string_ + "--- An error occurred in a call to the pricing library");

        val *= fx_spot * NumberOfUnits_; // return value in base currency

        return val;
    }

    protected override void Validate()
    {
        Pre_string_ = Name() + "  (" + Reference_ +")";
        if (Time_To_Expiry_ < 0.0)
        {
            throw new Exception(Pre_string_ + "--- Time to expiry cannot be less than zero years");
        }
        if (Strike_ < 0.0)
        {
            throw new Exception(Pre_string_ + "--- The strike cannot be less than zero");
        }
        if (NumberOfUnits_ < 0)
        {
            throw new Exception(Pre_string_ + "--- The number of units cannot be less than zero");
        }
        if (Sigma_ < 0.0)
        {
            throw new Exception(Pre_string_ + "--- Volatility cannot be less than zero");
        }
    }
  }
 }
}
```

Code excerpt 8.8 (*Continued*).

8.3.2 Option on Two Equities

Computer code to value options on two equities is provided below in Code excerpt 8.9.

```csharp
using System;

namespace Computational_Lib
{
    public class TwoEquityOptionDeal : BaseDeal
    {
        public string Equity1 { get { return EquityName1_; } set { EquityName1_ = value; } }
        public string Equity2 { get { return EquityName2_; } set { EquityName2_ = value; } }
        public double Time_To_Expiry { get { return Time_To_Expiry_; } set { Time_To_Expiry_ = value; } }
        public int NumberOfUnits { get { return NumberOfUnits_; } set { NumberOfUnits_ = value; } }
        public PutCall OptionType { get { return OptionType_; } set { OptionType_ = value; } }
        public MinimumMaximum  MinMax{ get { return MinMax_; } set { MinMax_ = value; } }
        public EuropeanAmerican ExerciseStyle { get { return ExerciseStyle_; } set { ExerciseStyle_ = value; } }
        public double Strike { get { return Strike_; } set { Strike_ = value; } }
        public BuySell BuySell { get { return BuySell_; } set { BuySell_ = value; } }
        public double Volatility1 { get { return Sigma1_; } set { Sigma1_ = value; } }
        public double Volatility2 { get { return Sigma2_; } set { Sigma2_ = value; } }

        protected PutCall OptionType_ = PutCall.Put;
        protected MinimumMaximum MinMax_ = MinimumMaximum.Maximum;
        protected EuropeanAmerican ExerciseStyle_ = EuropeanAmerican.European;
        protected double Strike_ = 0;
        protected string EquityName1_ = "";
        protected string EquityName2_ = "";
        protected string Currency_ = "";
        protected int NumberOfUnits_ = 1;
        protected double Time_To_Expiry_ = 0.0;
        protected string Pre_string_ = "";
        protected double S1_ = 0.0;
        protected double S2_ = 0.0;
        protected double Sigma1_ = 0.0;
        protected double Sigma2_ = 0.0;
        protected BuySell BuySell_ = BuySell.Buy;

        public override string Name()
        {
            return "Rainbow option(two equities)";
        }

        public override double Price()
        {
            Validate();

            double val = 0.0;
            double rho = 0.0; // default correlation set to zero
            double RiskFreeRate = 0.0;
            double fx_spot = 0.0;

            try
            {
                S1_ = MarketDataDictionaries.EquityTable[EquityName1_].Spot;
            }
            catch
            {
                throw new Exception(Pre_string_ + "--- No Market Data supplied for " + EquityName1_);
            }

            try
            {
                S2_ = MarketDataDictionaries.EquityTable[EquityName2_].Spot;
                S1_ = MarketDataDictionaries.EquityTable[EquityName1_].Spot;
            }
            catch
            {
                throw new Exception(Pre_string_ + "--- No Market Data supplied for " + EquityName2_);
            }

            if(string.Compare(MarketDataDictionaries.EquityTable[EquityName1_].Currency,
                    MarketDataDictionaries.EquityTable[EquityName2_].Currency) != 0){

                throw new Exception(Pre_string_ + "--- Currencies for both equities are not the same");
            }

            Currency_ = MarketDataDictionaries.EquityTable[EquityName1_].Currency;

            try
```

Code excerpt 8.9   C# code to compute the value of an option on two equities.

```
    {
        ICurve DF = MarketDataDictionaries.CurrencyTable[Currency_].YieldCurve;  // obtain the discount factor
        double discount_fac = DF[0, Time_To_Expiry_];
        RiskFreeRate = -Math.Log(discount_fac) / Time_To_Expiry_;
        fx_spot = MarketDataDictionaries.CurrencyTable[Currency_].spot;
    }
    catch
    {
        throw new Exception(Pre_string_ + "--- No Market Data supplied for " + Currency_);
    }

    string corr_key = EquityName1_ + "%" + EquityName2_;

    if (MarketDataDictionaries.CorrelationTable.ContainsKey(corr_key))
        rho = MarketDataDictionaries.CorrelationTable[corr_key].Correl;
    else
        rho = 0.0;

    int iflag, put, is_max;

    iflag = 0;
    put = OptionType_ == PutCall.Put ? 1 : 0;
    is_max = MinMax_ == MinimumMaximum.Maximum ? 1 : 0;

    if (ExerciseStyle_ == EuropeanAmerican.European)  // use analytic method
    {
        PricingUtils.opt_rainbow_bs_2d(ref val, S1_, S2_, Strike_, Sigma1_, Sigma2_,
                        rho, Time_To_Expiry_, RiskFreeRate, is_max,
                        put, ref iflag);
    }
    else { // use numeric method

        double q1 = 0.0;
        double q2 = 0.0;
        int num_steps = 200; // need to use an even number of time steps for the lattice
        int is_american = 1;
        PricingUtils.standard_2D_binomial(ref val, S1_, S2_, Strike_, Sigma1_, Sigma2_,
                        rho, Time_To_Expiry_, RiskFreeRate,
                        q1, q2, put, num_steps, is_max, is_american, ref iflag);
    }
    if (iflag != 0)
        throw new Exception(Pre_string_ + "--- An error occurred in a call to the pricing library");
    val *= fx_spot * NumberOfUnits_; // return value in base currency
    return val;
}

protected override void Validate()
{
    Pre_string_ = Name() + "  (" + Reference_ + ")";

    if (Time_To_Expiry_ < 0.0)
    {
        throw new Exception(Pre_string_ + "--- Time to expiry cannot be less than zero years");
    }
    if (NumberOfUnits_ < 0)
    {
        throw new Exception(Pre_string_ + "--- Number of units cannot be less than zero");
    }
    if (Strike_ < 0.0)
    {
        throw new Exception(Pre_string_ + "--- The strike cannot be less than zero");
    }
    if (Sigma1_ < 0.0)
    {
        throw new Exception(Pre_string_ + "--- Volatility1 cannot be less than zero");
    }
    if (Sigma2_ < 0.0)
    {
        throw new Exception(Pre_string_ + "--- Volatility2 cannot be less than zero");
    }
    }
    }
}
```

Code excerpt 8.9 (*Continued*).

8.3.3 Generic Equity Basket Option

Here, we consider the abstract deal class `GenericEquityBasketOptionDeal`
which enables its derived classes to value an option on an arbitrary number of

underlying assets – the derived class also must implement the abstract method Payoff. In the earlier sections of this book, we have considered options with standard payoffs such as vanilla put, vanilla call, and call/put on the min/max of a number of assets. However, the class GenericEquityBasketOptionDeal now opens the possibility of supplying a user-defined Payoff function so that options with nonstandard payoffs can be valued, see Code excerpt 8.10.

```
using System;

namespace Computational_Lib
{
    public abstract class GenericEquityBasketOptionDeal : BaseDeal
    {
        public string Equities { set { Equities_ = value; } }
        public string Volatilities { set { Volatilities_ = value; } }
        public double Time_To_Expiry { get { return Time_To_Expiry_; } set { Time_To_Expiry_ = value; } }
        public int NumberScenarios { get { return NumberScenarios_; } set { NumberScenarios_ = value; } }
        public BuySell BuySell { get { return BuySell_; } set { BuySell_ = value; } }
        public int NumberOfUnits { get { return NumberOfUnits_; } set { NumberOfUnits_ = value; } }
        public string Currency { get { return Currency_; } set { Currency_ = value; } }
        public double Strike { get { return Strike_; } set { Strike_ = value; } }

        protected string Equities_ = "";
        protected string Volatilities_ = "";
        protected double Time_To_Expiry_ = 0.0;
        protected double RiskFreeRate_ = 0.0;
        protected string Pre_string_ = "";
        protected double[] S_;
        protected double[] Sigma_;
        protected int NumberScenarios_ = 3000;
        protected double[,] Correlations_;
        protected int n_ = 0;
        protected int NumberOfUnits_ = 1;
        protected string Currency_ = "";
        protected BuySell BuySell_ = BuySell.Buy;
        protected double[] ST_;
        protected double Strike_ = 0.0;

        public override string Name()
        {
            return "Generic Equity Option";
        }

        public abstract double Payoff();

        public override double Price()
        {
            Validate();
            double val = 0.0;
            double fx_spot = 0.0;

            char[] seps = new char[] { '%' };
            string[] EquityNames = Equities_.Split(seps, StringSplitOptions.None);

            n_ = EquityNames.Length;

            ST_ = new double[n_];

            S_ = new double[n_];
            Sigma_ = new double[n_];
            for (int k = 0; k < n_; ++k)
            {
                try
                {
                    S_[k] = MarketDataDictionaries.EquityTable[EquityNames[k]].Spot;
                }
                catch
                {
                    throw new Exception(Pre_string_ + "--- No Market Data supplied for " + EquityNames[k]);
                }
            }

            for (int k = 1; k < n_; ++k)
            {
                if (string.Compare(MarketDataDictionaries.EquityTable[EquityNames[k - 1]].Currency,
                    MarketDataDictionaries.EquityTable[EquityNames[k]].Currency) != 0)
```

Code excerpt 8.10 C# code for the abstract class GenericEquityBasketOptionDeal. It contains the abstract method Payoff().

```
                    throw new Exception(Pre_string_ + "--- Not all the currencies are the same");
        }

        Currency_ = MarketDataDictionaries.EquityTable[EquityNames[1]].Currency;

        try
        {
            ICurve DF = MarketDataDictionaries.CurrencyTable[Currency_].YieldCurve;  // obtain the discount factor
            double discount_fac = DF[0, Time_To_Expiry_];
            RiskFreeRate_ = -Math.Log(discount_fac) / Time_To_Expiry_;
            fx_spot = MarketDataDictionaries.CurrencyTable[Currency_].spot;
        }
        catch
        {
            throw new Exception(Pre_string_ + "--- No Market Data supplied for " + Currency_);
        }

        string[] Vols = Volatilities_.Split(seps, StringSplitOptions.None);
        int n_v;
        n_v = Vols.Length;

        if (n_v != n_)
            throw new Exception(Pre_string_ + "--- Number of volatilities is not the same
              as the number of equities ");

        Sigma_ = new double[n_];
        for (int k = 0; k < n_; ++k)
        {
            try
            {
                Sigma_[k] = double.Parse(Vols[k]);
            }
            catch
            {
                throw new Exception(Pre_string_ + "--- Invalid volatility supplied for  " + EquityNames[k]);
            }
        }

        Correlations_ = new double[n_, n_];

        for (int i = 0; i < n_; ++i)
        {
            for (int j = 0; j < n_; ++j)
            {
                if (i != j)
                {
                    string corr_key = EquityNames[i] + "%" + EquityNames[j];
                    if (MarketDataDictionaries.CorrelationTable.ContainsKey(corr_key))
                        Correlations_[i, j] = MarketDataDictionaries.CorrelationTable[corr_key].Correl;
                    else
                        Correlations_[i, j] = 0.0; // default correlation is zero
                }
                else
                {
                    Correlations_[i, j] = 1.0;
                }
            }
        }

        int iflag=0;

        val = MonteCarloSim(ref iflag);

        if (iflag != 0)
            throw new Exception(Pre_string_ + "--- An error occurred in a call to the pricing library");

        val *= fx_spot * NumberOfUnits_;

        return val;
    }

    protected override void Validate()
    {

        Pre_string_ = Name() + "  (" + Reference_ + ")";

        if (Time_To_Expiry_ < 0.0)
        {
            throw new Exception(Pre_string_ + "--- Time to expiry cannot be less than zero years");
        }

        if (NumberOfUnits_ < 0)
        {
            throw new Exception(Pre_string_ + "--- Number of units cannot be less than zero");
        }
```

Code excerpt 8.10 (*Continued*).

```
        if (Strike_ < 0.0)
        {
            throw new Exception(Pre_string_ + "--- The strike cannot be less than zero");
        }

    }
    private double MonteCarloSim(ref int iflag)
    {

        double[] C = new double[n_ * n_];
        double half = 0.5;
        double zero = 0.0;
        double sumit_val = zero;
        double tol = 1.0e-8;
        double opt_val = 0.0;

        // set the covariance matrix
        for (int i = 0; i < n_; ++i)
        {
            for (int j = 0; j < n_; ++j) {
                C[i * n_ + j] = Sigma_[i] * Sigma_[j] * Correlations_[i, j] * Time_To_Expiry_;
            }
        }

        double[] MEANS = new double[n_];
        // set the means
        for (int i = 0; i < n_; ++i) {
            MEANS[i] = (RiskFreeRate_ - Sigma_[i] * Sigma_[i] * half) * Time_To_Expiry_;
        }

        int seed = 111;

        PricingUtils.set_seed(seed);

        int len_rvec = ((n_ + 1) * (n_ + 2)) / 2 + 1;
        double[] rvec = new double[len_rvec];
        double[] Z = new double[n_];

        double disc = Math.Exp(-RiskFreeRate_ * Time_To_Expiry_);

        int is_fcall = 1;
        PricingUtils.multivariate_normal(is_fcall, ref MEANS[0], n_, ref C[0], n_, tol, ref rvec[0],
            ref Z[0], ref iflag);
        is_fcall = 0;
        for (int i = 1; i <= NumberScenarios_; ++i)
        {
            PricingUtils.multivariate_normal(is_fcall, ref MEANS[0], n_, ref C[0], n_, tol, ref rvec[0],
                ref Z[0], ref iflag);
            for (int jj=0; jj < n_; ++jj) {
                ST_[jj] = S_[jj] * Math.Exp(Z[jj]);
            }
            sumit_val += Payoff();
        }
        opt_val = sumit_val * disc / (double)NumberScenarios_;

        return opt_val;
    }

  }
}
```

Code excerpt 8.10 (*Continued*).

Below, we provide some example results for options on four and ten assets. The assets were Drinks-4U, Beverage-Ltd, H2O-Ltd, and Fine-Wines-Ltd. The trade attributes are a time to expiry of one year, all volatilities are 0.2, and the number of units is 100. Other information required to price the option, such as the correlations between the equities and the risk-free interest rate, is taken from the market data dictionaries.

The syntax for using the deal class GenericEquityBasketOptionDeal with the portfolio definition file is

```
Trade=GenericEquityBasketOptionDeal:Payoff_MaxPut,Reference=1A,Strike=100.0,Volatilities=0.2%0.2%0.2%0.2,_
Equities=Drinks-4U%Beverage-Ltd%H2O-Ltd%Fine-Wines-Ltd,NumberOfUnits=100,Time_To_Expiry=1.0,NumberScenarios=1000
```

while that for calling the deal class `FourEquityOptionDeal` is

```
Trade=FourEquityOptionDeal,Reference=1B,Volatility1=0.2,Volatility2=0.2,Volatility3=0.2,Volatility4=0.2,_
Equity1=Drinks-4U,Equity2=Beverage-Ltd,Equity3=H2O-Ltd,Equity4=Fine-Wines-Ltd,NumberOfUnits=100,Strike=100.0,_
Time_To_Expiry=1.0,OptionType=Put,MinMax=Maximum,MonteCarlo=Yes,NumberScenarios=1000
```

The crucial difference is that entry for `GenericEquityBasketOptionDeal` contains the extra directive `Trade=GenericEquityBasketOptionDeal: Payoff_MaxPut`, whereas `FourEquityOptionDeal` is the usual `Trade=Four EquityOptionDeal`. The directive `GenericEquityBasketOptionDeal: Payoff_MaxPut` means that the contents of the file `Payoff_MaxPut.txt` will be compiled at runtime and thereby create the (sub)class `GenericEquity BasketOptionDeal_MaxPut`, which is derived from the abstract base class `GenericEquityBasketOptionDeal`. The .NET assembly containing the class `GenericEquityBasketOptionDeal_MaxPut` is stored in memory and its `Price()` method is called to value the option.

The file `Payoff_MaxPut.txt` contains the following C# code:

```csharp
using System;
namespace Computational_Lib
{
    public class GenericEquityBasketOptionDeal_MaxPut : GenericEquityBasketOptionDeal
    {
        public override string Name()
        {
            string temp_string = "";
            temp_string = "Generic option: Put on the maximum of " + n_.ToString() + " assets";
            return temp_string;
        }

        public override double Payoff() { // implement max, put
            double the_max = 0.0;
            double pay_val = 0.0;
            double zero = 0.0;

            the_max = ST_[0];
            for (int jj = 1; jj < n_; ++jj)
            {
                if (ST_[jj] > the_max) the_max = ST_[jj];
            }
            pay_val = Math.Max(Strike_ - the_max, zero);

            return pay_val;
        }
    }
}
```

In the above code, the `ST_`, `Strike_`, and `n_` are data members of the base class `GenericEquityBasketOptionDeal`. We now present some other entries in the portfolio definition file which illustrate the versatility of the deal class `GenericEquityBasketOptionDeal`.

```
// Call on average of 4 assets
Trade=GenericEquityBasketOptionDeal:Payoff_AvgCall,Reference=5,Strike=100.0,Volatilities=0.2%0.2%0.2%0.2,_
Equities=Drinks-4U%Beverage-Ltd%H2O-Ltd%Fine-Wines-Ltd,NumberOfUnits=100,Time_To_Expiry=1.0,NumberScenarios=1000

// Put on the average of 10 assets (Strike=100)
Trade=GenericEquityBasketOptionDeal:Payoff_AvgPut,Reference=8,Strike=100.0,_
Volatilities=0.2%0.2%0.2%0.2%0.2%0.2%0.2%0.2%0.2%0.2,_
Equities=Drinks-4U%Beverage-Ltd%H2O-Ltd%Fine-Wines-Ltd%The-English-Beer-Company%Water-Works-Ltd%Welsh-Spring%ThamesBeer_
%Edinburgh-Whiskey%The-Wine-Box,NumberOfUnits=100,Time_To_Expiry=1.0,NumberScenarios=10000

// Put on the average of 10 assets (Strike=99)
Trade=GenericEquityBasketOptionDeal:Payoff_AvgPut,Reference=9,Strike=99.0,_
Volatilities=0.2%0.2%0.2%0.2%0.2%0.2%0.2%0.2%0.2%0.2,_
Equities=Drinks-4U%Beverage-Ltd%H2O-Ltd%Fine-Wines-Ltd%The-English-Beer-Company%Water-Works-Ltd%Welsh-Spring%ThamesBeer%_
Edinburgh-Whiskey%The-Wine-Box,NumberOfUnits=100,Time_To_Expiry=1.0,NumberScenarios=10000
```

where the file `Payoff_AvgCall.txt` contains the C# code

```
using System;

namespace Computational_Lib
{
    public class GenericEquityBasketOptionDealAverageCall : GenericEquityBasketOptionDeal
    {
        public override string Name()
            string temp_string = "";
            temp_string = "Generic option: Call on the average of " + n_.ToString() + " assets";
            return temp_string;
        }

        public override double Payoff() {  // implement Call on average of n_ assets
            double the_average = 0.0;
            double pay_val = 0.0;
            double zero = 0.0;
            the_average = ST_[0];
            for (int jj = 1; jj < n_; ++jj)
            {
                the_average += ST_[jj];
            }
            the_average = the_average/n_;

            pay_val = Math.Max(the_average - Strike_, zero);

            return pay_val;
        }
    }
}
```

The contents of the file `Payoff_AvgPut` can be deduced from `Payoff_AvgCall` in the obvious manner.

The output from the application is given below.

```
=================================================================
TestGenericEQ in units of GBP
TestGenericEQ   :31/07/2007 19:05:10
=================================
 23.0100=1A,Generic option: Put on the maximum of 4 assets
 23.0100=1B,Four Equity Option

681.4034=5,Generic option: Call on the average of 4 assets

338.3212=8,Generic option: Put on the average of 10 assets
302.6056=9,Generic option: Put on the average of 10 assets
=================================
TOTAL VALUE =  10936.18 GBP
=================================
```

It can be seen that result 1A, obtained using the deal class `GenericEquityBasketOptionDeal`, is exactly the same as result 1B, which was computed with the deal class `FourEquityOptionDeal`. This is because in both cases Monte Carlo simulation is used, and the same initial random seed is used for all Monte Carlo simulations.

8.3.4 Equity Barrier Option

Code excerpt 8.11 computes the value of an equity barrier option.

```
using System;

namespace Computational_Lib
{
    public class DownOutEquityOptionDeal : BaseDeal
    {
        public string Equity { get { return EquityName_; } set { EquityName_ = value; } }
        public double Barrier_Level { get { return BarrierLevel_; } set { BarrierLevel_ = value; } }
        public double Time_To_Expiry { get { return Time_To_Expiry_; } set { Time_To_Expiry_ = value; } }
```

Code excerpt 8.11   C# code to compute the value of an equity barrier option.

```
public PutCall OptionType { get { return OptionType_; } set { OptionType_ = value; } }
public double Strike { get { return Strike_; } set { Strike_ = value; } }
public CalculationMethod CalcMethod { get { return CalcMethod_; } set { CalcMethod_ = value; } }
public EuropeanAmerican ExerciseStyle { get { return ExerciseStyle_; } set { ExerciseStyle_ = value; } }
public int TimeSteps { get { return TimeSteps_; } set { TimeSteps_ = value; } }
public int NumberScenarios { get { return NumberScenarios_; } set { NumberScenarios_ = value; } }
public bool UseBrownianBridge{ get { return UseBrownianBridge_; } set { UseBrownianBridge_ = value; } }
public BuySell BuySell { get { return BuySell_; } set { BuySell_ = value; } }
public double Volatility { get { return Sigma1_; } set { Sigma1_ = value; } }
public int NumberOfUnits { get { return NumberOfUnits_; } set { NumberOfUnits_ = value; } }

protected PutCall OptionType_ = PutCall.Call;
protected double Strike_ = 0;
protected double BarrierLevel_ = 0.0;
protected string EquityName_ = "";
protected double Time_To_Expiry_ = 0.0;
protected double RiskFreeRate_ = 0.0;
protected double DividendYield_ = 0.0;
protected string Pre_string_ = "";
protected CalculationMethod CalcMethod_ = CalculationMethod.Analytic;
protected int TimeSteps_ = 300;
protected int NumberScenarios_ = 3000;
protected bool UseBrownianBridge_ = true;
protected double S1_ = 0.0;
protected double Sigma1_ = 0.0;
protected int NumberOfUnits_ = 1;
protected BuySell BuySell_ = BuySell.Buy;
protected EuropeanAmerican ExerciseStyle_ = EuropeanAmerican.European;
protected string Currency_ = "";

public override string Name()
{
    return "Down Out Equity Option";
}

public override double Price()
{
    Validate();
    double val = 0.0;
    double fx_spot = 0.0;
    try
    {
        S1_ = MarketDataDictionaries.EquityTable[EquityName_].Spot;
        Currency_ = MarketDataDictionaries.EquityTable[EquityName_].Currency;
          // get equity volatility (assumed constant)
        DividendYield_ = MarketDataDictionaries.EquityTable[EquityName_].DivYield; // get equity dividend yield
    }
    catch
    {
        throw new Exception(Pre_string_ + "--- No Market Data supplied for " + EquityName_);
    }

    double discount_fac = 0.0;
    try
    {
        ICurve DF = MarketDataDictionaries.CurrencyTable[Currency_].YieldCurve;  // obtain the discount factor
        discount_fac = DF[0, Time_To_Expiry_];
        RiskFreeRate_ = -Math.Log(discount_fac) / Time_To_Expiry_;
        fx_spot = MarketDataDictionaries.CurrencyTable[Currency_].spot;
    }
    catch
    {
        throw new Exception(Pre_string_ + "--- No Market Data supplied for " + Currency_);
    }

    int iflag, put, is_american;

    iflag = 0;
    put = OptionType_ == PutCall.Put ? 1 : 0;
    is_american = ExerciseStyle_ == EuropeanAmerican.American ? 1 : 0;
    BarrierLevel_ = Math.Max(BarrierLevel_, PricingUtils.EPS);

    if (CalcMethod_ == CalculationMethod.Analytic)
    {
        if (put == 1) throw new Exception(Pre_string_ + "--- Can't price a put uisng this calculation method");
        if (is_american == 1) throw new Exception(Pre_string_ + "--- Can't price an American option
          uisng this calculation method");

        PricingUtils.bs_opt_barrier_downout_call(ref val, BarrierLevel_,
                            S1_, Strike_, Sigma1_,
                            Time_To_Expiry_, RiskFreeRate_, DividendYield_, ref iflag);
        if (iflag != 0)
            throw new Exception(Pre_string_ + "--- An error occurred in a call to the pricing library");
    }
    else if (CalcMethod_ == CalculationMethod.Numeric)
```

Code excerpt 8.11 (*Continued*).

```
        {
            if (put == 1) throw new Exception(Pre_string_ + "--- Can't price a put uisng this calculation method");

            int n_sigma = 2;

            // set up the parameters so that have "reasonable accuracy"
            double[] sigma_array = new double[n_sigma];
            double[] sigma_times = new double[n_sigma];

            sigma_array[0] = Sigma1_;
            sigma_array[1] = Sigma1_;

            sigma_times[0] = 0.0;
            sigma_times[1] = Time_To_Expiry_;

            int nt = 100;
            int ns_below_S0 = nt / 2;
            int ns_above_S0 = nt / 2;
            double theta_m = 0.5;
            double UpperBarrierLevel = S1_ * 5.0;

            iflag = 0;

            PricingUtils.dko_call(BarrierLevel_, UpperBarrierLevel,
                        theta_m, S1_, ref sigma_array[0], ref sigma_times[0],
                        n_sigma, RiskFreeRate_, Time_To_Expiry_,
                        Strike_, is_american, ref val,
                        IntPtr.Zero, DividendYield_, ns_below_S0, ns_above_S0,
                        nt, ref iflag);

            if (iflag != 0)
                throw new Exception(Pre_string_ + "--- An error occurred in a call to the pricing library");
        }
        else
        {
            bool is_put = (put == 1);
            if (is_american == 1) throw new Exception(Pre_string_ + "--- Can't price an American option uisng
              this calculation method");

            if (S1_ < BarrierLevel_)  // the option is already knocked out
                val = 0.0;
            else
                val = MonteCarloSim(is_put);
        }

        val *= fx_spot * NumberOfUnits_;

        return val;
    }

    protected override void Validate()
    {
        Pre_string_ = Name() + "  (" + Reference_ + ")";

        if (NumberOfUnits_ < 0)
        {
            throw new Exception(Pre_string_ + "--- Number of units cannot be less than zero");
        }
        if (Time_To_Expiry_ < 0.0)
        {
            throw new Exception(Pre_string_ + "--- Time to expiry cannot be less than zero years");
        }
        if (RiskFreeRate_ < 0.0)
        {
            throw new Exception(Pre_string_ + "--- Risk free rate cannot be less than zero");
        }
        if (Strike_ < 0.0)
        {
            throw new Exception(Pre_string_ + "--- The strike cannot be less than zero");
        }
        if (BarrierLevel_ < 0.0)
        {
            throw new Exception(Pre_string_ + "--- BarrierLevel cannot be less than zero");
        }
        if (Sigma1_ < 0.0)
        {
            throw new Exception(Pre_string_ + "--- Volatility cannot be less than zero");
        }
    }

    private double MonteCarloSim(bool is_put)
    {
        // Use the Brownian Bridge to compute the value of a down and out call option

        int seed = 111;
```

Code excerpt 8.11 (*Continued*).

```
double[] asset_path = new double[TimeSteps_];
double time_step = Time_To_Expiry_ / TimeSteps_;
double sqrt_time_step = System.Math.Sqrt(time_step);
double disc = System.Math.Exp(-RiskFreeRate_ * Time_To_Expiry_);

PricingUtils.set_seed(seed);

double opt_val = 0.0;
bool not_out = true;
int k = 0;
double STN = 0.0;
double mean = (RiskFreeRate_ - DividendYield_ - Sigma1_ * Sigma1_ * 0.5) * time_step;
double std = System.Math.Sqrt(Sigma1_ * Sigma1_ * time_step);
double z;
double sum_opt_vals = 0.0;

for (int i = 0; i < NumberScenarios_; ++i)
{
    // generate the asset path
    double ST1 = S1_;
    not_out = true;
    k = 0;

    while (not_out && k < TimeSteps_)
    {
        z = PricingUtils.RndNorm(mean, std);
        STN = ST1 * System.Math.Exp(z);
        if (STN < BarrierLevel_) not_out = false;
        ST1 = STN;
        asset_path[k] = STN;
        ++k;
    }
    if (is_put)
    {
        opt_val = System.Math.Max(Strike_ - STN, 0.0);
    }
    else
    {
        opt_val = System.Math.Max(STN - Strike_, 0.0);
    }

    if (not_out)
    { // only has value if asset value is above the barrier_level
      // compute the probability that the asset remained above the barrier
        if (UseBrownianBridge)
        {
            double total_probability_above = 1.0, pr;
            double sigma_2 = Sigma1_ * Sigma1_;
            double log_barrier_level = System.Math.Log(BarrierLevel_);
            double fac;
            for (int jj = 0; jj < TimeSteps_ - 1; ++jj)
            {
                double log_S_i = System.Math.Log(asset_path[jj]);
                double log_S_i1 = System.Math.Log(asset_path[jj + 1]);
                fac = 2.0 * (log_barrier_level - log_S_i) * (log_barrier_level - log_S_i1) /
                  (sigma_2 * time_step);
                pr = (1.0 - System.Math.Exp(-fac)); // probability of staying above the
                  barrier between i and i+1
                total_probability_above *= pr;
            }
            sum_opt_vals += total_probability_above * opt_val * disc;
        }
        else
        { // don't use the Brownian Bridge
            sum_opt_vals += opt_val * disc;
        }
    }
}
double temp = sum_opt_vals / (double)NumberScenarios_;

return temp;
            }
        }
    }
}
```

Code excerpt 8.11 (*Continued*).

Below, we show the results of using the deal class DownOutEquityOption Deal to value Down and Out call options on LaserComm which is a GBP equity with current (spot) price of £95 and a dividend yield of 5 percent (i.e., 0.05). All the options priced had a barrier level of £90, a strike of £90, a time to expiry of one year, and a volatility of 20 percent (i.e., 0.2). The first value 3.8347 was computed by a call to `bs_opt_barrier_downout_call`, which uses the closed form analytic expression provided in Code excerpt 4.7.

The second price 3.8269, which is in close agreement with the first, was obtained from `dko_call` and uses a finite difference grid. The third valuation was also computed using `dko_call` and illustrates the early exercise premium for an American call option (with a nonzero dividend). The other values were estimated using Monte Carlo simulation as the number of scenarios varied from 1000 to 64,000; the default of 300 time steps was used throughout.

It can be seen that when the Brownian bridge is used much closer agreement is obtained with both the analytic and numeric estimates.

```
DownOutTests in units of GBP
DownOutTests    :26/07/2007 13:11:28
=========================
 3.8347=Analytic,Down Out Equity Option
 3.8269=Numeric,Down Out Equity Option
 3.8860=Numeric (American style),Down Out Equity Option
 4.1871=MonteCarlo(1000 Scenarios: not using BrownianBridge),Down Out Equity Option
 3.8908=MonteCarlo(2000 Scenarios: not using BrownianBridge),Down Out Equity Option
 4.1968=MonteCarlo(4000 Scenarios: not using BrownianBridge),Down Out Equity Option
 4.1176=MonteCarlo(8000 Scenarios: not using BrownianBridge),Down Out Equity Option
 4.1790=MonteCarlo(16000 Scenarios: not using BrownianBridge),Down Out Equity Option
 4.1961=MonteCarlo(32000 Scenarios: not using BrownianBridge),Down Out Equity Option
 4.1833=MonteCarlo(64000 Scenarios: not using BrownianBridge),Down Out Equity Option
 3.8375=MonteCarlo(1000 Scenarios: using BrownianBridge),Down Out Equity Option
 3.5469=MonteCarlo(2000 Scenarios: using BrownianBridge),Down Out Equity Option
 3.8737=MonteCarlo(4000 Scenarios: using BrownianBridge),Down Out Equity Option
 3.7356=MonteCarlo(8000 Scenarios: using BrownianBridge),Down Out Equity Option
 3.8089=MonteCarlo(16000 Scenarios: using BrownianBridge),Down Out Equity Option
 3.8506=MonteCarlo(32000 Scenarios: using BrownianBridge),Down Out Equity Option
 3.8482=MonteCarlo(64000 Scenarios: using BrownianBridge),Down Out Equity Option
=========================
TOTAL VALUE =  70.83 GBP
=========================
```

8.4 FX DEAL CLASSES

Here, we provide code for valuing FX derivatives. The FX option routines are very similar to the equity option routines we have already considered. The fundamental difference being that for FX routines there is both a domestic and a foreign currency. The FX routine calls the Black–Scholes routine with the dividend yield set to the foreign currency risk-free interest rate, and the supplied volatility is that of the foreign/domestic exchange rate. In the market data file, the currency FX spot rates are with respect to the base currency.

8.4.1 FX Forward

Code excerpt 8.12 provides C# code to compute the value of FX Forwards.

```
using System;

namespace Computational_Lib
{
    public class FXForwardDeal : BaseDeal
    {
        public double ForeignAmount { get { return fForeignAmount; } set { fForeignAmount = value; } }

        // Note: Strike is the number of units of domestic currency required to
```

Code excerpt 8.12 C# code to compute the value of FX forwards.

```
//      obtain one unit of foreign currency.
public double Strike { get { return fStrike; } set { fStrike = value; } }
public string ForeignCurrency { get { return fForeignCurrency; } set { fForeignCurrency = value; } }
public string DomesticCurrency { get { return fDomesticCurrency; } set { fDomesticCurrency = value; } }
public BuySell BuySell { get { return fBuySell; } set { fBuySell = value; } }
public double Settlement { get { return fSettlement; } set { fSettlement = value; } }

protected double fStrike    = 0;
protected string fForeignCurrency = "";
protected string fDomesticCurrency = "";
protected double fForeignAmount = 0;
protected BuySell fBuySell = BuySell.Buy;
protected double fSettlement = 0;

protected string pre_string = "";

public override string  Name()
{
    return "FX Forward";
}

public override double Price()
{
    double val=0.0;
    Validate();
    double sign = fBuySell == BuySell.Buy ? 1.0 : -1.0;

    try
    {
        ICurve DF_F = CurrencyTable[fForeignCurrency].YieldCurve;  // obtain the discount factor
        ICurve DF_D = CurrencyTable[fDomesticCurrency].YieldCurve;  // obtain the discount factor
        double X_fb = CurrencyTable[fForeignCurrency].spot;
        double X_db = CurrencyTable[fDomesticCurrency].spot;
        double DF_f = DF_F[0,fSettlement];
        double DF_d = DF_D[0,fSettlement];

        val = fForeignAmount *( DF_f * X_fb - X_db * DF_d * fStrike);

        val = val * sign;
    }
    catch(Exception ex)
    {
        throw new Exception(pre_string + " : " + ex.Message);
    }

    return val;
}

protected override void Validate()
{
    pre_string = Name() + "  (" + fReference + ")";
}
    }
  }
}
```

Code excerpt 8.12 (*Continued*).

8.4.2 Single FX Option

The code for the single FX option (see Code excerpt 8.13) is very similar to that
for the single equity option. For example, European equity options are priced
using the call

```
PricingUtils.black_scholes(ref val, IntPtr.Zero, s0, Strike_, Sigma_,
  Time_To_Expiry_, RiskFreeRate, DividendYield_, put, ref iflag);
```

while European FX options use

```
PricingUtils.black_scholes(ref val, IntPtr.Zero, S0, Strike_b, Sigma_f_d_,
  Time_To_Expiry_, DomesticRiskFreeRate_, ForeignRiskFreeRate_, put, ref iflag);
```

It can be seen that when pricing FX options, the foreign risk-free rate is
used instead of the dividend yield, and the supplied volatility is that of the
foreign/domestic exchange rate. Another difference is that the equity option
value val returned by the call to black_scholes is in domestic currency units

and is then converted to base currency units, while in the case of FX options, the value `val` is already in base currency units and requires no conversion.

```csharp
using System;

namespace Computational_Lib
{
    public class FXOptionDeal: BaseDeal
    {

        public int NumberOfUnits { get { return NumberOfUnits_; } set { NumberOfUnits_ = value; } }
        // Note: Strike is the number of units of domestic currency required to
        //       obtain one unit of foreign currency.
        public double Strike { get { return Strike_f_d_; } set { Strike_f_d_ = value; } }

// Volatility is that of the Foreign/Domestic exchange rate.
        public double Volatility { get { return Sigma_f_d_; } set { Sigma_f_d_ = value; } }

        public string ForeignCurrency { get { return ForeignCurrency_; } set { ForeignCurrency_ = value; } }
        public string DomesticCurrency { get { return DomesticCurrency_; } set { DomesticCurrency_ = value; } }
        public BuySell BuySell { get { return BuySell_; } set { BuySell_ = value; } }
        public double Time_To_Expiry { get { return Time_To_Expiry_; } set { Time_To_Expiry_ = value; } }
        public PutCall OptionType { get { return OptionType_; } set { OptionType_ = value; } }
        public EuropeanAmerican ExerciseStyle { get { return ExerciseStyle_; } set { ExerciseStyle_ = value; } }

        protected double Strike_f_d_ = 0.0;
        protected string ForeignCurrency_ = "";
        protected string DomesticCurrency_ = "";
        protected BuySell BuySell_ = BuySell.Buy;
        protected int NumberOfUnits_ = 1;
        protected PutCall OptionType_ = PutCall.Put;
        protected EuropeanAmerican ExerciseStyle_ = EuropeanAmerican.European;
        protected double Time_To_Expiry_ = 0.0;
        protected double ForeignRiskFreeRate_ = 0.0;
        protected double DomesticRiskFreeRate_ = 0.0;
        protected double Sigma_f_d_ = 0.0;
        protected string Pre_string_ = "";

        public override string Name()
        {
            return "FX Option";
        }

        public override double Price()
        {

            Validate();

            double val = 0.0;
            double[] greeks = new double[6];

            int iflag, put;
            double discount_fac = 0.0;
            double X_f_b = 0.0, X_d_b = 0.0;
            double S0=0.0,Strike_b;

            // Get domestic currency information
            try
            {
                ICurve DF = MarketDataDictionaries.CurrencyTable[DomesticCurrency_].YieldCurve;
                // obtain the domestic discount factor
                discount_fac = DF[0, Time_To_Expiry_];
                DomesticRiskFreeRate_ = -Math.Log(discount_fac) / Time_To_Expiry_;
                X_d_b = MarketDataDictionaries.CurrencyTable[DomesticCurrency_].spot;
                Strike_b = X_d_b * Strike_f_d_;  // Strike_b is the Strike in base currency units
            }
            catch
            {
                throw new Exception(Pre_string_ + "--- No Market Data supplied for " + DomesticCurrency_);
            }

            // Get foreign currency information
            try
            {
                ICurve DF = MarketDataDictionaries.CurrencyTable[ForeignCurrency_].YieldCurve;
                // obtain the domestic discount factor
                discount_fac = DF[0, Time_To_Expiry_];
                ForeignRiskFreeRate_ = -Math.Log(discount_fac) / Time_To_Expiry_;
                X_f_b = MarketDataDictionaries.CurrencyTable[ForeignCurrency_].spot;
                S0 = X_f_b;  // Foreign exchange wrt base currency
            }
            catch
            {
```

Code excerpt 8.13   C# code to compute the value of FX options.

```
            throw new Exception(Pre_string_ + "--- No Market Data supplied for " + ForeignCurrency_);
        }

        iflag = 0;
        put = OptionType_ == PutCall.Put ? 1 : 0;

        if (ExerciseStyle_ == EuropeanAmerican.European)  // use BlackScholes
        {
            // Note: A null pointer is supplied so that the greeks are not computed
            // Dividend yield is set to foreign risk free rate
            // Risk free interest rate is set to the domestic rate
            // S0 the value of the "asset" in base currency units
            // val is  the value of the FX option in base currency units
            PricingUtils.black_scholes(ref val, IntPtr.Zero, S0, Strike_b, Sigma_f_d_, Time_To_Expiry_,
                            DomesticRiskFreeRate_, ForeignRiskFreeRate_, put, ref iflag);

        }
        else
        {  // Use Finite Difference Grid - Crank Nicolson
            double theta = 0.5;
            int is_american = 1;

            // fix the geometry of the grid (these avluse should give "reasonable" results)
            int ns = 50;  // 50 divisions on asset axis
            int nt = 50;  // 50 divisions on time axis
            double smax = 10.0 * S0;

            PricingUtils.opt_gfd(theta, S0, Sigma_f_d_, DomesticRiskFreeRate_, Time_To_Expiry_, Strike,
                    is_american, put, ref val, IntPtr.Zero, ForeignRiskFreeRate_, ns,
                    nt, smax, ref iflag);

            // val is  the value of the FX option in base currency units
        }

        if (iflag != 0)
            throw new Exception(Pre_string_ + "--- An error occurred in a call to the pricing library");

        val *= NumberOfUnits_;

        return val;
    }

    protected override void Validate()
    {
        Pre_string_ = Name() + "  (" + Reference_ + ")";
        if (Time_To_Expiry_ < 0.0)
        {
            throw new Exception(Pre_string_ + "--- Time to expiry cannot be less than zero years");
        }
        if (NumberOfUnits_ < 0)
        {
            throw new Exception(Pre_string_ + "--- Number of units cannot be less than zero");
        }
        if (Strike_f_d_ < 0.0)
        {
            throw new Exception(Pre_string_ + "--- The strike cannot be less than zero");
        }
    }
  }
}
```

Code excerpt 8.13 (*Continued*).

Code excerpt 8.14 provides C# code to compute the value of FX Barrier Options.

8.4.3 FX Barrier Option

```
using System;

namespace Computational_Lib
{
    public class DownOutFXOptionDeal: BaseDeal
    {
        public int NumberOfUnits { get { return NumberOfUnits_; } set { NumberOfUnits_ = value; } }
        // Note: Strike is the number of units of domestic currency required to obtain one unit of foreign currency.
        public double Strike { get { return Strike_f_d_; } set { Strike_f_d_ = value; } }
```

Code excerpt 8.14 C# code to compute the value of FX barrier options.

```
       // Barrier is in the same units a the strike
       public double Barrier_Level { get { return Barrier_f_d_; } set { Barrier_f_d_ = value; } }
// Volatility is that of the Foreign/Domestic exchange rate.
       public double Volatility { get { return Sigma_f_d_; } set { Sigma_f_d_ = value; } }
       public string ForeignCurrency { get { return ForeignCurrency_; } set { ForeignCurrency_ = value; } }
       public string DomesticCurrency { get { return DomesticCurrency_; } set { DomesticCurrency_ = value; } }
       public BuySell BuySell { get { return BuySell_; } set { BuySell_ = value; } }

       public CalculationMethod CalcMethod { get { return CalcMethod_; } set { CalcMethod_ = value; } }
       public EuropeanAmerican ExerciseStyle { get { return ExerciseStyle_; } set { ExerciseStyle_ = value; } }
       public int NumberScenarios { get { return NumberScenarios_; } set { NumberScenarios_ = value; } }
       public bool UseBrownianBridge { get { return UseBrownianBridge_; } set { UseBrownianBridge_ = value; } }

       protected double Strike_f_d_ = 0.0;
       protected double Barrier_f_d_ = 0.0;
       protected string ForeignCurrency_ = "";
       protected string DomesticCurrency_ = "";
       protected BuySell BuySell_ = BuySell.Buy;
       protected int NumberOfUnits_ = 1;
       public double Time_To_Expiry { get { return Time_To_Expiry_; } set { Time_To_Expiry_ = value; } }
       public PutCall OptionType { get { return OptionType; } set { OptionType_ = value; } }
       protected PutCall OptionType_ = PutCall.Call;
       protected double Time_To_Expiry_ = 0.0;
       protected double ForeignRiskFreeRate_ = 0.0;
       protected double DomesticRiskFreeRate_ = 0.0;
       protected double Sigma_f_d_ = 0.0;
       protected EuropeanAmerican ExerciseStyle_ = EuropeanAmerican.European;
       protected CalculationMethod CalcMethod_ = CalculationMethod.Analytic;
       protected int TimeSteps_ = 300;
       protected int NumberScenarios_ = 3000;
       protected double S0_,Strike_b_,BarrierLevel_b_;
       protected bool UseBrownianBridge_ = true;

       protected string Pre_string_ = "";

       public override string Name()
       {
           return "Down Out FX Option";
       }

       public override double Price()
       {
           Validate();

           double val = 0.0;
           int iflag, put, is_american;
           double discount_fac = 0.0;
           double X_f_b = 0.0, X_d_b = 0.0;

           // Get domestic currency information
           try
           {
               ICurve DF = MarketDataDictionaries.CurrencyTable[DomesticCurrency_].YieldCurve;
                 // obtain the domestic discount factor
               discount_fac = DF[0, Time_To_Expiry_];
               DomesticRiskFreeRate_ = -Math.Log(discount_fac) / Time_To_Expiry_;
               X_d_b = MarketDataDictionaries.CurrencyTable[DomesticCurrency_].spot;
               Strike_b_ = X_d_b * Strike_f_d_;  // Strike is the Strike in base currency units
               BarrierLevel_b_ = X_d_b * Barrier_f_d_;
               BarrierLevel_b_ = Math.Max(BarrierLevel_b_, PricingUtils.EPS);
           }
           catch
           {
               throw new Exception(Pre_string_ + "--- No Market Data supplied for " + DomesticCurrency_);
           }

           // Get foreign currency information
           try
           {
               ICurve DF = MarketDataDictionaries.CurrencyTable[ForeignCurrency_].YieldCurve;
                 // obtain the domestic discount factor
               discount_fac = DF[0, Time_To_Expiry_];
               ForeignRiskFreeRate_ = -Math.Log(discount_fac) / Time_To_Expiry_;
               X_f_b = MarketDataDictionaries.CurrencyTable[ForeignCurrency_].spot;
               S0_ = X_f_b;  // Foreign exchange wrt base currency
           }
           catch
           {
               throw new Exception(Pre_string_ + "--- No Market Data supplied for " + ForeignCurrency_);
           }

           iflag = 0;
           put = OptionType_ == PutCall.Put ? 1 : 0;
           is_american = ExerciseStyle_ == EuropeanAmerican.American ? 1 : 0;
```

Code excerpt 8.14 (*Continued*).

```
if (CalcMethod_ == CalculationMethod.Analytic)
{
    if (put == 1) throw new Exception(Pre_string_ + "--- Can't price a put uisng this calculation method");
    if (is_american == 1) throw new Exception(Pre_string_ + "--- Can't price an
        American option uisng this calculation method");

    // call C++ routine.
    // Note: A null pointer is supplied so that the greeks are not computed
    // Dividend yield is set to foreign risk free rate
    // Risk free interest rate is set to the domestic rate
    // val is  the value of the FX option in base currency units
    PricingUtils.bs_opt_barrier_downout_call(ref val, BarrierLevel_b_,
                        S0_, Strike_b_, Sigma_f_d_,
                        Time_To_Expiry_, DomesticRiskFreeRate_, ForeignRiskFreeRate_, ref iflag);

    if (iflag != 0)
        throw new Exception(Pre_string_ + "--- An error occurred in a call to the pricing library");
}
else if (CalcMethod_ == CalculationMethod.Numeric)
{
    if (put == 1) throw new Exception(Pre_string_ + "--- Can't price a put uisng this calculation method");

    int n_sigma = 2;

    // set up the parameters so that have "reasonable accuracy"
    double[] sigma_array = new double[n_sigma];
    double[] sigma_times = new double[n_sigma];

    sigma_array[0] = Sigma_f_d_;
    sigma_array[1] = Sigma_f_d_;

    sigma_times[0] = 0.0;
    sigma_times[1] = Time_To_Expiry_;

    int nt = 100;
    int ns_below_S0 = nt / 2;
    int ns_above_S0 = nt / 2;
    double theta_m = 0.5;
    double UpperBarrierLevel = S0_ * 5.0;

    iflag = 0;
    // val is  the value of the FX option in base currency units
    PricingUtils.dko_call(BarrierLevel_b_, UpperBarrierLevel,
            theta_m, S0_, ref sigma_array[0], ref sigma_times[0],
            n_sigma, DomesticRiskFreeRate_, Time_To_Expiry_,
            Strike_b_, is_american, ref val,
            IntPtr.Zero, ForeignRiskFreeRate_, ns_below_S0, ns_above_S0,
            nt, ref iflag);

    if (iflag != 0)
        throw new Exception(Pre_string_ + "--- An error occurred in a call to the pricing library");
}
else
{
    bool is_put = (put == 1);
    if (is_american == 1) throw new Exception(Pre_string_ + "--- Can't price an
        American option uisng this calculation method");

    if (S0_ < BarrierLevel_b) // the option has already been knocked out
        val = 0.0;
    else
        val = MonteCarloSim(is_put);

}

 val *= NumberOfUnits_;

return val;
}

protected override void Validate()
{

    Pre_string_ = Name() + "  (" + Reference_ + ")";
    if (Time_To_Expiry_ < 0.0)
    {
        throw new Exception(Pre_string_ + "--- Time to expiry cannot be less than zero years");
    }
    if (NumberOfUnits_ < 0)
    {
        throw new Exception(Pre_string_ + "--- Number of units cannot be less than zero");
    }
    if (Strike_f_d_ < 0.0)
    {
        throw new Exception(Pre_string_ + "--- The strike cannot be less than zero");
```

Code excerpt 8.14 (*Continued*).

```
    }
    if (Barrier_f_d_ < 0.0)
    {
        throw new Exception(Pre_string_ + "--- BarrierLevel cannot be less than zero");
    }
    if (Sigma_f_d_ < 0.0)
    {
        throw new Exception(Pre_string_ + "--- Volatility cannot be less than zero");
    }
}

private double MonteCarloSim(bool is_put)
{
    // Use the Brownian Bridge to compute the value of a down and out call option

    int seed = 111;
    double[] asset_path = new double[TimeSteps_];
    double time_step = Time_To_Expiry_ / TimeSteps_;
    double sqrt_time_step = System.Math.Sqrt(time_step);
    double disc = System.Math.Exp(-DomesticRiskFreeRate_ * Time_To_Expiry_);

    PricingUtils.set_seed(seed);

    double opt_val = 0.0;
    bool not_out = true;
    int k = 0;
    double STN = 0.0;
    double mean = (DomesticRiskFreeRate_ - ForeignRiskFreeRate_ - Sigma_f_d_ * Sigma_f_d_ * 0.5) * time_step;
    double std = System.Math.Sqrt(Sigma_f_d_ * Sigma_f_d_ * time_step);
    double z;
    double sum_opt_vals = 0.0;

    for (int i = 0; i < NumberScenarios_; ++i)
    {
        // generate the asset path
        double ST1 = S0_;
        not_out = true;
        k = 0;

        while (not_out && k < TimeSteps_)
        {
            z = PricingUtils.RndNorm(mean, std);
            STN = ST1 * System.Math.Exp(z);
            if (STN < BarrierLevel_b_) not_out = false;
            ST1 = STN;
            asset_path[k] = STN;
            ++k;
        }
        if (is_put)
        {
            opt_val = System.Math.Max(Strike_b_ - STN, 0.0);
        }
        else
        {
            opt_val = System.Math.Max(STN - Strike_b_, 0.0);
        }

        if (not_out)
        { // only has value if asset value is above the barrier_level
            // compute the probability that the asset remained above the barrier
            if (UseBrownianBridge)
            {
                double total_probability_above = 1.0, pr;
                double sigma_2 = Sigma_f_d_ * Sigma_f_d_;
                double log_barrier_level = System.Math.Log(BarrierLevel_b_);
                double fac;
                for (int jj = 0; jj < TimeSteps_ - 1; ++jj)
                {
                    double log_S_i = System.Math.Log(asset_path[jj]);
                    double log_S_i1 = System.Math.Log(asset_path[jj + 1]);
                    fac = 2.0 * (log_barrier_level - log_S_i) *
                        (log_barrier_level - log_S_i1) / (sigma_2 * time_step);
                    pr = (1.0 - System.Math.Exp(-fac)); // probability of staying
                        above the barrier between i and i+1
                    total_probability_above *= pr;
                }
                sum_opt_vals += total_probability_above * opt_val * disc;
            }
            else
            { // don't use the Brownian Bridge
                sum_opt_vals += opt_val * disc;
            }
        }
    }
    double temp = sum_opt_vals / (double)NumberScenarios_;
```

Code excerpt 8.14   (*Continued*).

```
        return temp;
      }
   }
}
```

Code excerpt 8.14 (*Continued*).

8.5 SELECTED EXERCISES

1. Create a deal class in C# to price an up and out option, see Section 4.5.3. Check your result using equation (4.5.17) in Chapter 4.
2. Create a deal class in C# to price a European exchange option.
3. Modify the EquityOptionDeal so that it returns the delta of the option.
4. Create a deal class which values an equity quanto option.
5. Create a deal class that values a strip of European put and call options.
6. Create a deal class that values an IRS with timing adjustment.

Chapter 9

A Brief History of Finance

9.1 INTRODUCTION

Today it would be difficult to survive a few days without money. Trade between different groups has always existed, and there is evidence that in both the stone age and bronze age there was significant trade in various implements. Before the industrial revolution, most people had live stock and grew the food that they consumed. They also generally lived in family housing that was passed down through the generations. As towns grew in size the majority of people were paid money that was used to buy essential food and accommodation. In today's capitalist society, consumers are offered the possibility of obtaining a bewildering choice of both essential and non-essential goods. Methods of payment include physical cash, electronic money or legally binding contracts (such as a mortgages). Formerly, it was only the rich who were concerned with investing money, but now money is used like a commodity (rather like sheep and goats were in agrarian societies several hundred years ago) and it is important for all citizens to understand it.

The aim of this chapter is to provide a brief, non-technical, historical perspective on the role of money and financial transactions in society. We will start with the Sumerians and finish with the Credit Crisis of 2008. Much of the content concerning the Credit Crisis is taken from the extensive summary provided by THE FINANCIAL CRISIS INQUIRY COMMISSION (2011). It should be mentioned this will be a lightning tour and will of necessity leave out a great deal of detail.

9.2 EARLY HISTORY

9.2.1 The Sumerians

In ancient Sumer (3000BC–1900BC), although the standard method of payment was grain, ingots of copper and silver were also used. Silver was mainly used in the town economies that developed in Mesopotamia, while grain was used in the country – coined money was not introduced until the first millennium BC, see Homer and Sylla (1996). The financial transactions of the early Sumerians were codified in the Babylonian Code of Hammurabi (c. 1800 BC). This code, which endured for the next 1200 years, regulated ownership of land, employment of agricultural labour, civil obligations, land rental and credit. For example, creditors had to wait until after the harvest before demanding

FIGURE 9.1 Interest-free loan (inner tablet), from Sippar, reign of Sabium (Old Babylonian period, c.1780 BC); BM 082512. (© *Trustees of the British Museum*)

FIGURE 9.2 The outer clay envelope of BM 082512. (Old Babylonian period, c.1780 BC); BM 082513. (© *Trustees of the British Museum*)

repayment from a farmer, and crop failure caused by storm damage would cancel the interest due on a loan for that year. It also set a higher maximum interest rate for loans of grain than those of silver: 33.33% per annum for loans of grain and 20% per annum for loans of silver. All loan contracts had to be drawn up in the presence of an official witness. To protect the creditor, pledges and sureties were allowed. Any property, real or personal, could be pledged – wife, concubine, children, slaves, land and utensils. However, servitude for debt was limited to three years. The temples were also active in finance and they granted loans of silver and grain, sometimes making loans to the poor without interest.

Figures 9.1 and 9.2 show a financial loan from the second millennium BC. It was excavated at Sippar and is now in the British Museum. The contract is written in cuneiform on clay tablets and consists of both inner and outer sections. The outer envelope bears a duplicate text of the inner tablet as well as the impressions of the cylinder seals of the debtor and three of the witnesses. These clay tablets record a charitable loan of silver, issued by the temple of the sun-god Šamaš of Sippar, the so-called Ebabbar. The temple provides a man called Kišušu with the means to satisfy his creditor Ilum-abi, without charging any interest. Kišušu is to pay back the loan to the temple after he has brought in his harvest. This was the commonest time of year for paying off debts, as Mesopotamian landowners were usually solvent then. The witnesses include high temple functionaries. The first one, Lipit-Ištar, impressed his father's seal on the upper edge of the envelope.

9.2.2 Biblical Times

The Old Testament contains various directives and references relating to loans, the purchase of property and debts. Many of these are concerned with protecting the poor and preventing a skewed distribution of wealth.

Leviticus 25:8-17 states that every fifty years (the year of the Jubilee) all property was to be restored to its original owners, and in Leviticus 25:35-43 we are told to help the poor but not charge interest on loans. Deuteronomy 24:10-13 gives the following description of a collateralised loan:

10 When you make a loan of any kind to your neighbour, do not go into his house to get what he is offering as a pledge. 11 Stay outside and let the man to whom you are making the loan bring the pledge out to you. 12 If the man is poor, do not go to sleep with his pledge in your possession. 13 Return his cloak to him by sunset so that he may sleep in it. Then he will thank you, and it will be regarded as a righteous act in the sight of the LORD your God (New International Version)

Money also played an important part in the marriage contract. Usually it was the fathers who arranged the match, and had to give a dowry to the prospective father-in-law. Genesis relates the story of Abraham's servant, Eliezer, who was sent to find a bride for Isaac, see Fig. 9.3:

22 When the camels had finished drinking, the man took out a gold nose ring weighing a beka and two gold bracelets weighing ten shekels. Genesis 24:2 (New International Version)

FIGURE 9.3 Eliezer and Rebecca at the Well, Nicolas Poussin, 1648. Musée du Louvre, Paris. *(Eliezer and Rebecca. Oil on canvas, 118 × 199 cm, Nicolas Poussin (1594–1665), © RMN-Grand Palais / Art Resource, NY)*

9.2.3 The Greeks

The first official coinage was made from a mixture of gold and silver and was minted in Lydia during the seventh century BC. In Greece, from the sixth century BC to the first century AD, there were the following six types of loans:

1. Loans for personal or productive use; similar to bank loan for a small business.
2. Loans secured on real estate.
3. Loans to cities.
4. Endowments invested and paying a specified rate of return.
5. Loans to industry and commerce – these were probably speculative short-term loans.
6. Personal and miscellaneous loans – these could be as high as 48% per month.

There is also mention of the first option contract dating back to 624 BC–546 BC. According to Aristotle, Thales predicted, through studying the stars during the winter, that there would be a great harvest of olives in the following year. He then bought the rights to use all the olive presses in Chios and Miletus; he did this at a low price because no one bid against him. Thales' forecast turned out to be correct. The ensuing abundant harvest meant that there was a great demand for olive presses, and Thales was able to sell the rights to use the presses at a great profit, see Aristotle's Politics, Book I, Chapter 11.

9.2.4 Medieval Europe

Around the time of the first crusade (1095–1099), Genoa emerged as a major sea power and trading centre and its fairs attracted traders from around the Mediterranean. To deal with the issue of different currencies, a forum was established for arbitrating the exchange rates to use. On the third day of each fair, a representative body composed of recognised merchant bankers would assemble and determine the exchange rates that would prevail. The process involved each banker suggesting a rate and, after some discussion, a vote would determine the currency exchange rates. Similar practices were later adopted at other medieval fairs. For example, at Lyon, Florentine, Genoa and Lucca, bankers would meet to determine exchange rates. Fairs at different locations would typically have different exchange rates, and these provided an opportunity to profit from the variation. Bills of exchange were developed during the Middle Ages as a means of transferring funds and making payments over long distances without physically moving large quantities of precious metals. Thirteenth-century Italian merchants, bankers and foreign exchange dealers developed the bill of exchange into a powerful financial tool, enabling short-term credit transactions as well as foreign exchange transactions, for more detail see Smith (1776). The following example shows the usefulness of bills of exchange: Assume that a merchant in Flanders sold goods to a Venetian merchant and accepted in payment a bill of exchange drawn on the Venetian merchant promising to pay an agent of the Flemish merchant in Venice at a certain date in the future, and in a certain currency. The bill of exchange allowed the Venetian merchant to accept delivery of the goods from Flanders, sell them and take the proceeds to redeem the bill of exchange in Venice, probably in Venetian currency. Bills of exchange were also instruments for foreign exchange transactions. Merchants in Italy and major trading centres in Europe bought bills of exchange payable at future dates, in other places, and in different currencies. In the example above, the Flemish merchant could sell the bill of exchange to an exchange dealer for currency of his own choosing. In turn, the exchange dealer could sell the bill of exchange to a Flemish merchant engaged in buying goods in Venice. When the bill came due for payment in Venice, the Flemish merchant would use it to buy goods in Venice where the bill of exchange was paid. While this process seems complicated, it substantially reduced the transportation of precious metals. In our example, a Venetian merchant bought goods from Flanders, and a Flemish merchant bought goods from Venice without any foreign currency leaving Venice or Flanders. Bills of exchange also allowed bankers to evade usury laws by hiding interest charges in exchange rate adjustments that governed foreign exchange transactions.

9.3 EARLY STOCK EXCHANGES

Much of the early history of commodity and financial exchanges is linked to the movement of Jews across Europe. Jewish communities had tight knit family and religious ties with others throughout Europe, and this formed a powerful network through which trade and commerce could be conducted. For example, the brothers Francis and Diego Mendez were such merchants, the former residing in Lisbon and the latter at Antwerp, see Wegg (1916). The mass movement of Jews from Spain and Portugal during the 15th and 16th centuries is linked with the eventual establishment of commodity and financial exchanges in Antwerp, Amsterdam, London, Paris, and many other major cities throughout the world.

9.3.1 The Anwterp Exchange

Many Jews left Spain and Portugal because of the massacres and conversions of 1391 and 1497. By the early sixteenth century, a large number had settled in Antwerp and were engaged in international and domestic trade, banking and finance.

The Antwerp exchange was created in 1460 for commodities trading and settlement purposes. The exchange has a *pagadder* tower which is a look-out tower that wealthy merchants built onto their houses overlooking the river Schelde in Antwerp. From these towers, they could look out over the river and see when their ships arrived – knowing this information before others could be used to advantage when making deals concerning the safe arrival of goods, see Fig. 9.4.

FIGURE 9.4 Padagger tower Antwerpen Old Exchange building at Hofstraat 15 Antwerpen (Mark Ahsmann). *(Available under a CC BY-SA 3.0 license at* `https://commons.wikimedia.org/wiki/File:Padagger_tower_Antwerpen_Old_Exchange_building_at_Hofstraat_15_Antwerpen.JPG?uselang=en-gb)`

FIGURE 9.5 The New Exchange, Antwerp, first built in 1531. It burnt down in 1858 and was rebuilt in the gothic style. *(Available at* https://commons.wikimedia.org/wiki/Category: Handelsbeurs_%28Antwerpen%29?uselang=engb#/media/File:Maxime_Lalanne_B%C3% B6rse_von_Antwerpen.jpg)

In 1531, the world's first purpose built exchange was constructed, see Fig. 9.5. It has the following statement emblazoned across the façade. *The practice of merchants from all countries and languages.* Antwerp soon became the international financial capital of Europe, especially as a secondary market in bonds. However, no stocks were listed in this exchange.

The Antwerp Exchange encouraged speculative trading, and bets were often made on such things as the safe return of ships, on the possibility of Philip II visiting the Netherlands, the sex of children as yet unborn, etc. Lotteries, both private and public, were also extremely popular. With the Antwerp Exchange providing a systematic and organised environment for speculation, trading in 'to arrive' contracts evolved into trade in 'futures' contracts where the forward contracts involved standardised transactions in fictitious goods for a future delivery and payment that was settled by the payment of 'differences.'

9.3.2 Amsterdam Stock Exchange

When Antwerp declined in importance the Jews moved to Amsterdam which, during the seventeenth century, even became known as *the Dutch Jerusalem.* They played an important role in large trading companies, such as the Dutch East Indies and West Indies Companies, where they worked in trading commodities such as coral, sugar, tobacco and precious stones.

During the sixteenth century, the Amsterdam Bourse (Fig. 9.6) only traded wheat, herring, and species. However, in 1602, the world's first public company, the VOC (the Vereenigde Oost-Indische Compagnie or United East India Company) was created, and people began to trade the company's shares, see Figs 9.7 and 9.8. The Amsterdam Exchange was established for this purpose and thus became the first Stock Exchange in the world, see Fleuriet (2008).

The VOC had over 150 trading vessels, 40 warships, 20,000 seamen and 10,000 soldiers and employed nearly 50,000 civilians. It managed to pay out a dividend of 40% and was the envy of its rivals. Its trading routes connected

FIGURE 9.6 The Courtyard of the Old Exchange in Amsterdam, Emanuel de Witte (1617–1692). *(Available at* https://commons.wikimedia.org/wiki/File:Emanuel_de_Witte_-_The_ Courtyard_of_the_Old_Exchange_in_Amsterdam_-_WGA25798.jpg?uselang=en-gb)

Japan, China, India, the Persian Gulf, Africa and Europe to Amsterdam. In the Persian Gulf, it traded spices for salt, in Zanzibar salt for cloves, in India cloves for gold, in China gold for tea and silk, in Japan silk for copper and in the islands of south-east Asia copper for spices. The whole inner-Asian trade was nearly as profitable as the main trade between the Orient and Europe. In 27 September 1602, the Dutch East India Company issued shares at a nominal value of 3000 Guilders, see Fig. 9.9. By 1622, the share price was 300% higher; and, in 1720, at the height of speculation its price had increased by 1200%. The dividend was on average 18% per year and the highest dividend was paid in 1606 at 75%. Shareholders did not receive their dividends regularly and were not always paid out in cash but sometimes also in spices, company bonds or state bonds.

A firsthand account of the activity in the Amsterdam Stock Exchange is given by Josseph de la Vega, a Spanish/Portuguese Jew, who worked there. We will now give some excerpts from his book Confusion of Confusions (de la Vega, 2006). On the United East India Company, he writes the following:

The Company has since become world famous. Every year, fresh shiploads of treasure and wealth come sailing home. Their profit is paid out to the

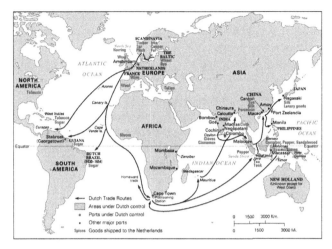

FIGURE 9.7 Map of the Cape of Good Hope up to and including Japan (Isaac de Graaff), between 1690 and 1743. *(From the Atlas of Mutual Heritage and the Nationaal Archief, the Dutch National Archives, metadata available under a CC-ZERO license. Available at* `https://commons.wikimedia.org/wiki/File:AMH-5191-NA_Map_of_the_Cape_of_Good_Hope_up_to_and_including_Japan.jpg`*)*

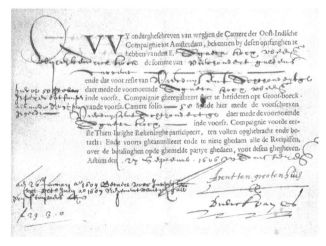

FIGURE 9.8 A share certificate issued by the Dutch East India Company. (© `www.oldest-share.com/Private collection`)

shareholders or, as the Directors may decide, is reinvested so that the company grows even further. Profits are sometimes paid in cloves, or in the form of company credits, and sometimes in cash, as the Directors think best. The dividends paid out since the establishment of the Company now amount to

1482% of the initial investment, and the company capital has increased five-fold. In short it is a goldmine, and it has been compared to a tree, because it bears fruit almost every year. . . There are also people who call the Company the tree of knowledge of good and evil, like that in paradise, because it provides everything for those who take care of its branches.

concerning the frustrations of shareholders:

If you have bought a few shares and you see them go down, you become mad, but if you see them rise you also go mad out of regret that you did not buy more. If you buy, and the shares rise, and you sell at a profit, and then they rise even higher, you are maddened by the low price you have accepted . . . .Thus, there is nothing but agitation, repentance and anger.

on the manipulation of share prices for gain:

Ten or twelve people join together to form a league which, as I have previously explained, we call a cabal. When they think that the time is ripe to sell shares, they think of a way to achieve their purpose to the greatest advantage.

and the use of options:

Suppose that the price of shares is at present 580, and I think that they will continue to rise considerably. . . . I ask people who want to write options how much they are asking for the obligation to sell me the shares at 600 per share on a particular date. When we have agreed the premium, I immediately have it transferred to them at the bank. Now I know that I can lose no more than the amount that I have deposited at the bank. If the shares rise above 600, the amount above 600 is my profit. And if they are worth less than that, my peace of mind, sanity and honour is not in danger.

9.3.3 Other Early Financial Centres

London

In 1565, Gresham made a proposal to build a Royal Exchange, modelled on the Antwerp Exchange – the building was opened in 1570 by Queen Elizabeth I, see Fig. 9.9.

The overthrow of King James II by William in 1688 (known as the Glorious Revolution) meant that many of the speculative practices carried out in Amsterdam were also adopted in England. Dutch investors and speculators also conducted a considerable amount of their British securities trading outside the Amsterdam Bourse at various locations in London, such as on the Royal Exchange and in Exchange Alley where coffee-house trading was conducted.

New York

The name Wall Street derives from the seventeenth century when Wall Street formed the northern boundary of the New Amsterdam settlement, see Fig. 9.10. It was constructed as a protection from neighbouring English colonists. In the 1640s, only picket and plank fences denoted plots and residences in the colony. However, later the Dutch West India Company strengthened the stockade with

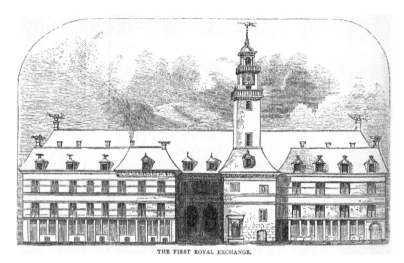

THE FIRST ROYAL EXCHANGE.

FIGURE 9.9 The Royal Exchange, London. (© *Old and New London by Walter Thornbury (1878) and British History Online)*

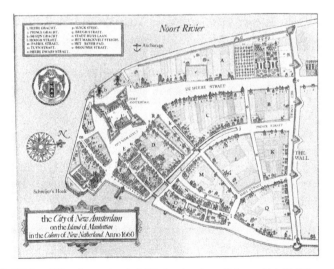

FIGURE 9.10 Map of New Amsterdam in 1600 showing the wall from which Wall Street is named. *(From the New York Public Library)*

the help of African slave labour. A 12-foot wall was constructed to prevent attack from various Native American tribes, and in 1685 surveyors laid out Wall Street along the lines of the original stockade. The wall was dismantled by the British colonial government in 1699. In the late eighteenth century, there was a buttonwood tree at the foot of Wall Street under which traders and speculators would gather to trade informally. The Buttonwood Agreement of

1792 formalised the traders' association and marked the beginning of the New York Stock Exchange.

9.4 TULIP MANIA

The tulip was introduced to Europe in the middle of the sixteenth century from the Ottoman Empire and became very popular in the Netherlands, where the price of the rare tulips reached very high prices. The most sought-after tulips had vivid colours, lines and flames on the petals, which were as a result of being infected with a virus known as *Tulip Breaking potyvirus*, see Figs 9.11 and 9.12.

People who had no connection with bulb growing, such as weavers, spinners, cobblers and bakers, bought tulips. By the end of 1634, a thriving tulip market had emerged.

Speculators were attracted by the specific characteristics of the tulip market: the significant separation in time of the purchase agreement from the delivery and payment provided a commodity where speculative buyers of bulbs, not intending to take delivery, could trade with sellers that did not possess the bulb on the purchase agreement date. By 1635, a sale of 40 bulbs for 100,000 florins was recorded. By way of comparison, a ton of butter cost around 100 florins, a skilled labourer might earn 150 florins a year, and *eight fat swine* cost 240 florins. Charles Mackay, in Memoirs of Extraordinary Popular Delusions and the Madness of Crowds, see Mackay (1841), recounts the following:

tulip of the species called Admiral Liefken, weighing 400 perits, was worth 4400 florins; an Admiral Van der Eyck, weighing 446 perits, was worth 1260 florins; a Childer of 106 perits was worth 1615 florins; a Viceroy of 400 perits, 3000 florins and, most precious of all, a Semper Augustus, weighing 200 perits, was thought to be very cheap at 5500 florins. The latter was much sought after, and even an inferior bulb might command a price of 2000 florins. . . . So anxious were the speculators to obtain them that one person offered the fee-simple of twelve acres of building ground for the Harlaem tulip. That (tulip) of Amsterdam was bought for 4600 florins, a new carriage, two grey horses and a complete suit of harness. . . . A wealthy merchant, who prided himself not a little on his rare tulips, received upon one occasion a very valuable consignment of merchandise from the Levant. Intelligence of its arrival was brought him by a sailor, who presented himself for that purpose at the counting-house, among bales of goods of every description. The merchant, to reward him for his news, munificently made him a present of a fine red herring for his breakfast. The sailor had, it appears, a great partiality for onions, and seeing a bulb very like an onion lying upon the counter of this liberal trader, and thinking it, no doubt, very much out of its place among silks and velvets, he slily seized an opportunity and slipped it into his pocket, as a relish for his herring. He got clear off with his prize, and proceeded to the quay to eat his breakfast. Hardly was his back turned when the merchant missed his valuable Semper Augustus, worth three thousand florins, or about 280l. sterling.

FIGURE 9.11 Pamphlet from the Dutch tulipomania, printed in 1637. *(Available at* https: //commons.wikimedia.org/wiki/File:Pamphlet_dutch_tulipomania_1637.jpg*)*

Many individuals grew rich, and everyone imagined that the passion for tulips would last forever, and that the wealthy would pay whatever prices were asked. People purchased bulbs at higher and higher prices, intending to re-sell them for a profit. However, such a scheme could not last unless someone was ultimately willing to pay such high prices and take possession of the bulbs. In February 1637, tulip traders could no longer find new buyers willing to pay increasingly inflated prices for their bulbs. As this realisation set in, the demand for tulips collapsed, and prices plummeted – the speculative bubble burst. Some were left holding contracts to purchase tulips at prices now ten times greater than those on the open market, while others found themselves in possession of bulbs now worth a fraction of the price they had paid. The panicked tulip speculators sought help from the Dutch government, which responded by declaring that anyone who had bought contracts to purchase bulbs in the future could void their contract by payment of a 10% fee. Attempts were made to resolve the situation to the satisfaction of all parties, but these were unsuccessful. The mania finally

FIGURE 9.12 Semper Augustus tulip, 17th century. *(Available at* `https://commons.wikimedia.org/wiki/File:Semper_Augustus_Tulip_17th_century.jpg`*)*

ended, Mackay says, with individuals stuck with the bulbs they held at the end of the crash – no court would enforce payment of a contract, since judges regarded the debts as contracted through gambling, and thus not enforceable by law. The self-regulating guild of Dutch florists, in a decision that was later ratified by the Dutch Parliament, announced that all futures contracts written after November 30, 1636 and before the re-opening of the cash market in the early Spring, were to be interpreted as option contracts. They did this by simply relieving the futures' buyers of the obligation to buy the future tulips, forcing them merely to compensate the sellers with a small fixed percentage of the contract price (Thompson, 2007). Before this parliamentary decree, the purchaser of a tulip (futures) contract was legally obliged to buy the bulbs. The decree changed the nature of these contracts, so that if the current market price fell, the purchaser could opt to pay a penalty and forgo receipt of the bulb, rather than pay the full contracted price. This change in law meant that the futures contracts had been transformed into options contracts. This decree allowed someone who purchased a contract to void the contract with a payment of only 3.5% of the contract price. Thus, investors bought increasingly expensive contracts. A speculator could sign a contract to purchase a tulip for 100 guilders. If the price rose above 100 guilders, the speculator would pocket the difference as profit. If the price remained low, the speculator could void the contract for only 3.5 guilders. Thus, a contract nominally for 100 guilders would actually cost an investor no more than 3.5 guilders. In early February, as contract prices reached a peak, Dutch authorities stepped in and halted the trading of these contracts. When the Dutch economy entered a recession in 1638 the tulip craze came to an end. Tulip bulbs experienced a staggering drop, and many speculators who had sold put options could not pay for the bulbs they were obligated to pay for. The Dutch government intervened and attempted to force the sellers of the contracts to make good on their obligations, but lack of prior regulation made enforcement impossible. These broken contracts further fuelled the recession and, as a result, options developed a terrible reputation throughout Holland and all of Europe.

9.5 EARLY USE OF DERIVATIVES IN THE USA

In the United States trading in stock options started after the opening of the New York Stock Exchange. The trading of puts and calls took place in an over-the-counter market and was facilitated by broker dealers who tried to match option buyers with option sellers – this was a cumbersome process. There could be protracted negotiations over price, since every new option contract had its own set of terms and conditions such as length of time, number of shares and strike price. As a result of every option contract being unique, the buyer and writer were essentially linked for the term of the option contract. In the cases where an agreement to close an existing contract could not be reached between the two involved parties, a broker might advertise the contract in a financial journal under the heading of 'Special Options.' In addition, because no standard existed to determine the fair price of an option, buyers and sellers might argue for days before agreement was reached. However, despite these short comings, the traded volume increased (Bookbinder, 1976).

John Hinkling, a nineteenth century broker on Wall Street, provides the following description of puts, calls and spreads (Hinkling, 1875):

A Put – A person holding a Put contract on Pacific Mail at 35 is entitled to any decline below that price, and can close the privilege any time during the thirty days, but in order to realise the profit it is necessary to take the market price of the stock at the time you close the contract.

A Call – The holder of a call contract makes a profit in proportion as the stock advances at the time the contract is closed. If you had a call on Union Pacific at 30, and the stock advanced to 40, you could present the Call to us and we should pay you 10.

Therefore, recommend buying Spread to having a Put and Call. In one contract, you are prepared to take advantage of the market whichever way it may go. If it advances so as to make a good profit you can Call the stock. Should it decline you can Put it. It is a matter of indifference to you whether it goes up or down.

In addition he also discusses market manipulation, for example, the following.

The 'Milking' Process – This is putting down the prices a little to get people to sell out, when the clique step in and take the stock. They then raise it by bulling the market and unload at high figures. This operation being repeated is called 'milking the street.'

Filer (1959) also contains a short historical section. Another abusive practice that gained notoriety was the granting of call options to stockbrokers by speculators with large holdings of the underlying stock. In return, the brokers would recommend the stock to their clients. The resulting demand for the stock would benefit both the brokers and the speculators, who would then sell into the rising price. After the brokers and speculators positions were liquidated, it was the unsuspecting public who were left holding the bag. This unethical practice was employed on a larger scale by 'option pools' which acquired options directly from major stockholders of a company including directors, banks and the company itself. In some instances, pools owned call options on 20% of the outstanding shares of the companies, see Filer (1959). With control over such a high percentage of the outstanding stock, it was easy to manipulate the price of the stock by trading in large numbers of shares and simultaneously spreading false rumours. When the prices of stocks traded by the pools began to change, option dealers began following the moves of the pools. As a result, trading in many options was based solely on rumours of whether pools were buying or selling that stock. In October 1929, the Wall Street Crash occurred and the Securities Exchange Commission (SEC) was formed to regulate the financial markets. The SEC's initial recommendation was to totally outlaw all options trading, but Congress offered the put–call brokers a chance to respond. Here is the account in Filer (1959):

The almost universal lack of understanding of options and the heightened public awareness of option pools led many in Congress to conclude that all options trading was manipulative. In his response to a Congressional committee, Filer explained the difference between 'the options in which [put–call dealers] deal which are primarily offered openly and sold for a consideration, and the manipulative options secretly given, for no fee, but for manipulative purposes'. With that explanation, members of the committee then expressed concern about the number of options that expire worthless. Filer was asked 'If only 12.5% are exercised, then the other 87.5% of the people who bought options have thrown money away?' Filer replied, 'No Sir. If you insure your house against fire and it did not burn down you would not say that you had thrown away you insurance premium.'

This argument convinced the SEC that not all option trading is manipulative, but could also be used as an investment tool.

9.6 SECURITISATION AND STRUCTURED PRODUCTS

In the United States Government Sponsored Enterprises (GSEs), Ginnie Mae, Fannie Mae and Freddie Mac were set up to buy residential mortgages and so guarantee the supply of mortgage credit that banks could extend to homebuyers. Initially the GSE either held the mortgages in its portfolio or resold them to insurance companies, or other investors. It profited from the difference (the spread) between the cost of funds and the interest paid on these mortgages.

By 1970 these GSEs could also securitise the mortgages. A lender would assemble a pool of mortgages and issue securities backed by the mortgage pool. Those securities would be sold to investors, with the GSE guaranteeing timely payment of principal and interest. The GSE charged a fee to issuers for this guarantee. In 1971, Freddie got into the business of buying mortgages, pooling them and then selling mortgage-backed securities. Freddie collected fees from lenders for guaranteeing timely payment of principal and interest.

While GSEs had a near-monopoly on securitising fixed-rate mortgages that were within their permitted loan limits, in the 1980s the markets began to securitise many other types of loans, including adjustable-rate mortgages and other mortgages that the GSEs were not eligible or willing to buy. The same mechanism was used: an investment bank, such as Lehman Brothers or Morgan Stanley, bundled loans from a bank or other lender into securities and sold them to investors, who received investment returns funded by the principal and interest payments from the loans. Investors held or traded these securities, which were often more complicated than the GSEs basic mortgage-backed securities; the assets were not just mortgages but equipment leases, credit card debt, car loans and housing loans. Over time, banks and securities' firms used securitisation to mimic banking activities outside the regulatory framework for banks. For example, where banks traditionally took money from deposits to make loans and held them until maturity, banks now used money from the capital markets – often from money market mutual funds to make loans, packaging them into securities to sell to investors.

Private securitisations, or structured finance securities, had two key benefits to investors: pooling and tranching. If many loans were pooled into one security, a few defaults would have minimal impact. Structured finance securities could also be sliced up and sold in portions – known as tranches – which let buyers customise their payments. Risk-averse investors would buy tranches that paid off first in the event of default, but had lower yields. Return-oriented investors bought riskier tranches with higher yields. Bankers often compared it to a waterfall; the holders of the senior tranches – at the top of the waterfall – were paid before the more junior tranches. If payments came in below expectations, those at the bottom would be the first to be left high and dry. Securitisation was designed to benefit lenders, investment bankers and investors. Lenders earned fees for originating and selling loans. Investment banks earned fees for issuing mortgage-backed securities. These securities fetched a higher price than if the underlying loans were sold individually, because the securities were customised to investors' needs, were more diversified, and could be easily traded. Purchasers of the safer tranches got a higher rate of return than ultra-safe Treasury notes without much extra risk – at least in theory. However, the financial engineering behind these investments made them harder to understand and to price than individual loans.

This complexity transformed the three leading credit rating agencies Moody's, Standard & Poor's (S & P) and Fitch into key players in the process, positioned between the issuers and the investors of securities. Before securitisation became common, the credit rating agencies had mainly helped investors evaluate the safety of municipal and corporate bonds and commercial paper.

Participants in the securitisation industry realised that they needed to secure favourable credit ratings in order to sell structured products to investors. Investment banks therefore paid handsome fees to the rating agencies to obtain the desired ratings, and thus convince investors that is was *safe* to buy these bonds.

By 1990, when the market was 16 years old, about $900 billion worth of securitisations, beyond those done by the GSEs, were outstanding. That included $114 billion of automobile loans and over $250 billion of credit card debt; nearly $150 billion worth of securities were mortgages ineligible for securitisation by GSEs. Many were subprime. Securitisation was not just good business for commercial banks; it was also a lucrative business for Wall Street investment banks, with which the commercial banks worked to create the new securities. Wall Street firms such as Salomon Brothers and Morgan Stanley became major players in these complex markets and relied increasingly on quantitative analysts. As early as the 1970s, Wall Street executives had hired quantitative analysts to develop mathematical computer models that predicted how markets or securities might change. Securitisation increased the importance of this expertise. However, many of these models relied on assumptions based on limited historical data, and for mortgage-backed securities, see Fig. 9.13, were inadequate.

9.7 COLLATERALISED DEBT OBLIGATIONS

One problem with mortgage-backed securities was that, despite their relatively high returns, tranches rated other than triple-A could be hard to sell. If borrowers were delinquent or defaulted, investors in these tranches would receive no payments because of where they were in the payments waterfall. The solution to this was the financial product called the collateralised debt obligation, or CDO. Bankers would take low investment-grade tranches, largely rated BBB or A, from many mortgage-backed securities and repackage them into the CDOs. Approximately 80% of these CDO tranches would be rated triple-A despite the fact that they generally comprised the lower-rated tranches of mortgage-backed securities. CDO securities would be sold with their own waterfalls, with the risk-averse investors, again, paid first and the risk-seeking investors paid last. As in the case of mortgage-backed securities, rating agencies gave their highest, triple-A ratings to the securities at the top, see Fig. 9.14.

The securities firms and rating agencies reasoned that by pooling many BBB-rated mortgage-backed securities, they would create additional diversifi-

Residential Mortgage-Backed Securities

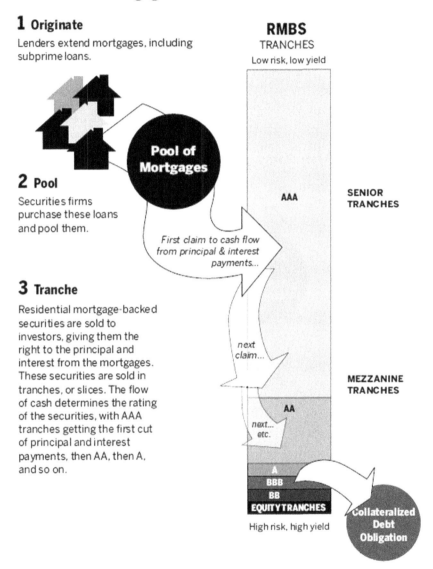

1 Originate

Lenders extend mortgages, including subprime loans.

2 Pool

Securities firms purchase these loans and pool them.

3 Tranche

Residential mortgage-backed securities are sold to investors, giving them the right to the principal and interest from the mortgages. These securities are sold in tranches, or slices. The flow of cash determines the rating of the securities, with AAA tranches getting the first cut of principal and interest payments, then AA, then A, and so on.

RMBS
TRANCHES
Low risk, low yield

Pool of Mortgages

First claim to cash flow from principal & interest payments...

AAA

SENIOR TRANCHES

next claim...

next... etc.

AA

MEZZANINE TRANCHES

A
BBB
BB
EQUITY TRANCHES
High risk, high yield

Collateralized Debt Obligation

FIGURE 9.13 Typical mortgage-backed security flow chart. *(Based on a chart from The Financial Crisis Inquiry Report, 2011)*

cation benefits. That is if one security did not pay, then the probability of another security not paying at the same time would be very small. As long as losses were limited, only those investors at the bottom of the waterfall would lose money;

Collateralized Debt Obligations

Collateralized debt obligations (CDOs) are structured financial instruments that purchase and pool financial assets such as the riskier tranches of various mortgage-backed securities.

3. CDO tranches

Similar to mortgage-backed securities, the CDO issues securities in tranches that vary based on their place in the cash flow waterfall.

1. Purchase

The CDO manager and securities firm select and purchase assets, such as some of the lower-rated tranches of mortgage-backed securities.

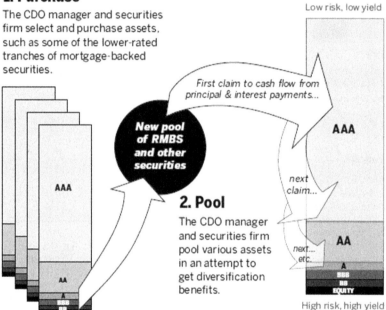

Low risk, low yield

First claim to cash flow from principal & interest payments...

New pool of RMBS and other securities

AAA

AAA

next claim...

2. Pool

The CDO manager and securities firm pool various assets in an attempt to get diversification benefits.

next... etc.

AA

A
BBB
BB
EQUITY

AA

A
BBB
BB

High risk, high yield

FIGURE 9.14 Typical collateralised debt obligation flow chart. *(Based on a chart from The Financial Crisis Inquiry Report, 2011)*

they would absorb the shock, and the other investors would continue to get paid.

Using that logic CDOs began gobbling up the BBB and other lower-rated tranches of mortgage-backed securities. Between 2003 and 2007, $4 trillion in mortgage-backed securities were created, and Wall Street issued nearly $700 billion in CDOs that included mortgage-backed securities as collateral.

With ready buyers for their product, mortgage securitisers continued to demand loans for their pools, and hundreds of billions of dollars flooded the mortgage market.

Many people were involved in feeding the CDO machine: the CDO managers and underwriters who packaged and sold the securities, the rating

Synthetic CDO

1. Short investors

Short investors enter into credit default swaps with the CDO, referencing assets such as mortgage-backed securities. The CDO receives swap premiums. If the reference securities do not perform, the CDO pays out to the short investors.

CDO

2. Unfunded investors

Unfunded investors, who typically buy the super senior tranche, are effectively in a swap with the CDO and receive premiums. If the reference securities do not perform and there are not enough funds within the CDO, the investors pay.

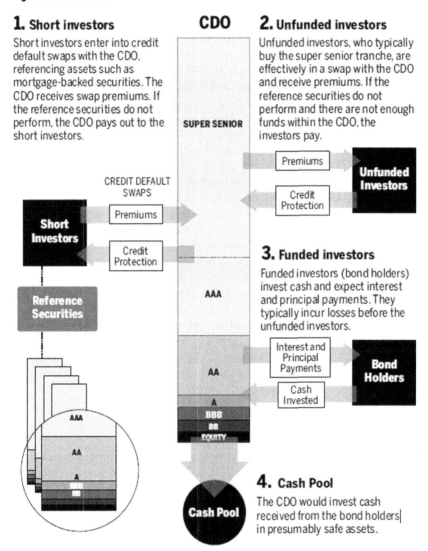

3. Funded investors

Funded investors (bond holders) invest cash and expect interest and principal payments. They typically incur losses before the unfunded investors.

4. Cash Pool

The CDO would invest cash received from the bond holders| in presumably safe assets.

FIGURE 9.15 Typical synthetic collateralised debt obligation flow chart. *(Based on a chart from The Financial Crisis Inquiry Report, 2011)*

agencies that gave most of them good ratings and the guarantors who sold protection against their defaulting and collected fees based on the dollar volume of securities sold.

The bankers and company executives who created these deals could receive bonuses worth millions of dollars.

Unlike the traditional cash CDO, synthetic CDOs contained no actual tranches of mortgage-backed securities, or even tranches of other CDOs. Instead, they simply referenced these mortgage securities and thus were bets on whether borrowers would pay their mortgages. In the place of real mortgage assets, these CDOs contained credit default swaps (CDSs) and did not finance a single home purchase. Investors in these CDOs included funded long investors, who paid cash to purchase actual securities issued by the CDO; unfunded long investors, who entered into swaps with the CDO, making money if the reference securities performed well; and short investors, who bought CDSs on the reference securities, making money if the securities defaulted. While funded investors received interest if the reference securities performed well, they could lose all of their investment if the reference securities defaulted. Unfunded investors, which were highest in the payment waterfall, received premium-like payments from the CDO as long as the reference securities performed but would have to pay if the reference securities deteriorated beyond a certain point and if the CDO did not have sufficient funds to pay the short investors. Short investors, often hedge funds, bought the CDSs from the CDOs and paid those premiums. Hybrid CDOs were a combination of traditional and synthetic CDOs. Firms like Goldman Sachs found synthetic CDOs cheaper and easier to create than traditional CDOs at the same time as the supply of mortgages was beginning to dry up. Also, because there were no mortgage assets to collect and finance, creating synthetic CDOs took a fraction of the time. In addition they were easier to customise, because CDO managers and underwriters could reference any mortgage-backed security – they were not limited to the universe of securities available for them to buy. Figure 9.15 provides an example of how such a deal worked.

9.8 THE 2008 FINANCIAL CRISIS

As 2007 went on, increasing mortgage delinquencies and defaults compelled the ratings agencies to first downgrade mortgage-backed securities, and then CDOs. Alarmed investors sent prices plummeting.

In October 2008, The International Monetary Fund (IMF) estimated how severe the losses would be. It calculated that roughly $10 trillion in mortgage assets were held throughout the financial system. Of these, $3.8 trillion were GSE mortgage-backed securities; the IMF expected losses of $80 billion, but investors holding these securities would lose no money, because of US Government guarantees. Another $4.8 trillion in mortgage assets were estimated to be prime and non-prime mortgages held largely by the banks and the Government Agencies. These were expected to suffer as much as $170 billion in write-downs due to declines in market value. The remaining $1.5 trillion in assets were estimated to be mortgage-backed securities and CDOs. Losses on those assets were expected to be $500 billion, and over half of this was expected to be borne by the investment and commercial banks. The rest of the losses from non-agency mortgage-backed securities were shared among institutions such as insurance companies, pension funds, the Government and hedge funds. The October report also expected another $655 billion loss on commercial mortgage-backed securities with commercial banks and investment banks bearing much of the brunt.

We end with two quotes from Vince Cable, see Cable (2009):

At the end of 2007, the value of all derivative contracts was $ 600 trillion (from $ 15 trillion a decade earlier), over ten times world output. CDSs account for $ 60 trillion.

The mortgage debt in America was $ 200 billion, but resulted in world debt of $ 100 trillion. How did this happen? In hind sight it would have been better to pay off the American mortgage debt.

9.8.1 The Collapse of AIG

To illustrate the Credit Crisis we will consider the events that led to the collapse of American International Group, Inc. (AIG), see Sjostrom Jr (2009).

In February 28, 2008, AIG had $1 trillion in assets and $95.8 billion in shareholders' equity and its stock closed at $50.15 per share, but by the end of the year it was on the verge of bankruptcy, and has since received at least $180 billion in government aid.

From January 2007 to September 2008, the company suffered $32.4 billion in losses, caused mainly by its $526 billion CDS portfolio. AIG's CDS business consisted mostly of selling protection on the super-senior risk tranches of CDOs.

Approximately $379 billion of AIG's CDSs were written to provide various European financial institutions *regulatory capital relief*. By owning CDSs, banks could make it appear as if they had off-loaded most of the risk of a loan to AIG or another firm, thereby reducing their capital needs. This perfectly legal ploy allowed banks across the Continent to free up money to make more loans. An institution would buy a CDS only if its expected return from the resulting regulatory capital relief exceeded the cost of the CDS.

Since almost all of AIG's CDSs were written on super-senior tranches substantial defaults would occur before these tranches were affected. If lower-rated tranches absorbed all the losses, there would be no credit event with respect to the super-senior tranche and, therefore, no payment obligation under the CDS AIG wrote on the tranche. AIG's historical models supported the conclusion that these credit events would never occur.

It was because of this that a former AIG senior executive characterised writing CDSs as *gold* and *free money*; since the CDSs would expire un-triggered, and AIG would pocket the premiums. Basically, AIG speculated against a drop in credit quality with respect to innumerable asset-backed securities. However, this *logical* strategy omitted to include the effects of collateral responsibilities.

AIG wrote protection on super-senior tranches of these CDOs as well as high grade and mezzanine tranches. In addition $61.4 billion of AIG's CDS portfolio was written on multi-sector CDOs with underlying residential mortgage-backed securities whose asset pools included subprime mortgage loans.

As AIG noted in its 2007 annual report, in mid-2007, the US residential mortgage market began to experience serious disruption due to credit quality deterioration in a significant portion of loans originated, particularly to non-prime and subprime borrowers. Defaults by these borrowers rippled through the chain, ultimately leading to massive losses in the CDS portfolio totalling $11.2 billion in 2007 and $19.9 billion for the first nine months of 2008.

While these losses certainly contributed to AIG's cash problems, they were not the main cause of its eventual bankruptcy. The principal cause of this was its obligation to make regular collateral postings. The large majority of these were on the difference between the notional amount of the particular CDS and the market value of the underlying CDO security. Therefore, as CDO values decreased, AIG was obligated to post (that is pay) more and more cash collateral. For example, from July 1, 2008 to August 31, 2008, declines in the CDO securities on which AIG wrote protection, together with rating downgrades on these securities, resulted in AIG posting or agreeing to post $6.0 billion in collateral, representing approximately 34% of the $17.6 billion in cash and cash equivalents AIG had available on July 1, 2008, to meet the cash needs of its operations.

Adding to AIG's cash struggles was its securities lending programme, a programme managed by AIG Investments, AIG's institutional asset management unit. Under the programme, AIG investments loaned securities from the investment portfolios of AIG's insurance companies to various financial institutions (the typical reason an institution borrows securities is to sell them short) in exchange for cash collateral posted by the borrower. AIG Investments would then invest the collateral in debt securities to earn a return which would serve as compensation for lending securities. At one point, AIG Investment had loaned $76 billion in securities to US companies. As borrowers received news about AIG's massive write-downs and collateral posting obligations, they became concerned about the safety of the cash collateral they had posted with AIG Investments. Thus, many of them decided to return lent securities and get their collateral back. Unfortunately, AIG Investments had invested a significant portion of the cash in residential mortgage-backed securities which had plummeted in value and liquidity. As a result, the programme lacked sufficient funds to satisfy collateral-return obligations. Accordingly, AIG was forced to transfer billions in cash to the programme, cash which was immediately paid out to these borrowers. Through August 31, 2008, AIG had transferred $3.3 billion in cash to the programme.

In September 2008, S&P downgraded AIG's long-term debt by three notches and Moody's and Fitch by two notches. These downgrades triggered over $20 billion in additional collateral calls because the collateral posting provisions contained in many of AIG's CDSs also took into account the credit rating of AIG, with a credit downgrade triggering additional posting obligations.

The day after the downgrade, AIG made a last ditch effort to raise additional financing. The management met with representatives of Goldman, Sachs & Co., J.P. Morgan, and the Federal Reserve Bank of New York (NY Fed) to discuss putting together a $75 billion secured lending facility syndicated among various financial institutions. However, no private sector lending was forthcoming and the US government decided to step in.

In September 16, 2008 it was announced that NY Fed would bail out AIG with a $85 billion credit facility.

In March 2009 the New York Times published an article based on a confidential 21-page document prepared for regulators by AIG entitled "A.I.G.: Is the Risk Systemic?" It noted that AIG's insurance subsidiaries had issued 375 million policies in the US with a face value of $19 trillion.

Nobody knew for certain the scope of the damage that would result from an AIG bankruptcy. Its size and interconnectedness, and the fact that financial markets were already under serious distress, created the fear that AIG's failure would lead to the collapse of the entire financial system. The federal government was unwilling to take this risk and, therefore, bailed out AIG with a rescue package of over $182.5 billion.

Appendix A

The Greeks for Vanilla European Options

A.1 INTRODUCTION

In this section, we will present some useful results which will be used later on to derive expressions for the Greeks.

A fundamental result of calculus is that

$$\frac{\partial}{\partial x} \int f(x)dx = f(x). \tag{A.1.1}$$

Also the indefinite integral, $\int f(x)dx$, can be expressed as a definite integral with variable upper bound as follows:

$$\int f(x)dx = \int_a^x f(x)dx + c,$$

so

$$\frac{\partial}{\partial x} \int_{y=a}^{y=x} f(y)dy = f(x). \tag{A.1.2}$$

We can now use this result for obtain the derivative of the cumulative distribution function

$$N_1(x) = \frac{1}{\sqrt{2\pi}} \int_{y=-\infty}^{y=x} \exp(-y^2/2)dy,$$

which gives

$$\frac{\partial N_1(x)}{\partial x} = n(x), \tag{A.1.3}$$

where

$$n(x) = \frac{1}{\sqrt{2\pi}} \exp(-x^2/2).$$

We now derive various results for the parameters d_1 and d_2 which appear in the Black–Scholes equation

$$d_1 = \frac{\log(S/E) + (r - q + \sigma^2/2)(T - t)}{\sigma\sqrt{T - t}} \tag{A.1.4}$$

and

$$d_2 = \frac{\log(S/E) + (r - q - \sigma^2/2)(T - t)}{\sigma\sqrt{T - t}} = d_1 - \sigma\sqrt{(T - t)}. \tag{A.1.5}$$

We have

$$\frac{\partial d_2}{\partial S} = \frac{\partial d_1}{\partial S} = \frac{1}{S\sigma\sqrt{T-t}}, \tag{A.1.6}$$

$$\frac{\partial d_2}{\partial \sigma} = \frac{\partial d_1}{\partial \sigma} - \sqrt{T-t}, \tag{A.1.7}$$

$$\frac{\partial d_1}{\partial r} = \frac{\partial d_2}{\partial r} = \frac{\sqrt{T-t}}{\sigma}, \tag{A.1.8}$$

$$\frac{\partial d_2}{\partial t} = \frac{\partial d_1}{\partial t} + \frac{\sigma}{2(T-t)}. \tag{A.1.9}$$

Also

$$n(d_2) = \frac{1}{\sqrt{2\pi}} \exp(-d_2{}^2/2)$$

$$= \frac{1}{\sqrt{2\pi}} \exp(-d_1{}^2/2) \exp\left\{\sigma d_1 \sqrt{T-t} - \sigma^2(T-t)/2\right\}$$

$$= n(d_1) \exp\left\{\log(S/E) + (r-q+\sigma^2/2)(T-t) - \sigma^2(T-t)/2\right\},$$

so

$$n(d_2) = \frac{S}{E} n(d_1) \exp(r(T-t)) \exp(-q(T-t)). \tag{A.1.10}$$

We note that

$$\frac{\partial N_1(d_1)}{\partial S} = \frac{\partial N_1(d_1)}{\partial d_1}\frac{\partial d_1}{\partial S} = n(d_1)\frac{1}{S\sigma\sqrt{T-t}}.$$

This technique will be used for computing *The Greeks*.

A.2 GAMMA

Gamma is defined as the second derivative of the option value with respect to the underlying stock price. This means (see Appendix A.3) it is the rate of change of delta with the underlying stock price.

For a European call, the value of gamma is

$$\Gamma_c = \frac{\partial^2 c}{\partial S^2} = \frac{\partial \Delta_c}{\partial S} = \frac{\partial}{\partial S}\left\{N_1(d_1)\exp(-q(T-t))\right\},$$

where the value of Δ_c is given in Appendix A.3. So

$$\Gamma_c = \exp(-q(T-t))\frac{\partial N_1(d_1)}{\partial S} = \exp(-q(T-t))n(d_1)\frac{\partial d_1}{\partial S}.$$

Therefore,

$$\Gamma_c = \frac{n(d_1)}{S\sigma\sqrt{T-t}}\exp(-q(T-t)). \tag{A.2.1}$$

The value of gamma for a European put can be calculated similarly

$$\Gamma_p = \frac{\partial^2 p}{\partial S^2} = \frac{\partial \Delta_p}{\partial S} = \frac{\partial}{\partial S}\left\{(N_1(d_1)-1)\exp(-q(T-t))\right\},$$

where we have used the value of Δ_p, derived in Appendix A.3. Therefore,

$$\Gamma_p = \exp(-q(T-t))\frac{\partial(N_1(d_1)-1)}{\partial S} = \exp(-q(T-t))n(d_1)\frac{\partial d_1}{\partial S}.$$

So

$$\Gamma_p = \Gamma_c = \frac{n(d_1)}{S\sigma\sqrt{T-t}}\exp(-q(T-t)). \qquad (A.2.2)$$

So the value of gamma for both a put and a call is the same.

A.3 DELTA

Delta is defined as the rate of change of option value with the underlying stock price.

For a European call, we have

$$\Delta_c = \frac{\partial c}{\partial S} = \frac{\partial}{\partial S}\left\{S\exp(-q(T-t))N_1(d_1) - E\exp(-r(T-t))N_1(d_2)\right\}.$$

So

$$\Delta_c = \exp(-q(T-t))\left\{N_1(d_1) + Sn(d_1)\frac{\partial d_1}{\partial S}\right\} - E\exp(-r(T-t))n(d_2)\frac{\partial d_2}{\partial S}. \quad (A.3.1)$$

Substituting for $n(d_2)$ and $\partial d_2/\partial S$, we obtain

$$\Delta_c = \exp(-q(T-t))N_1(d_1). \qquad (A.3.2)$$

In similar manner, we have for a European put

$$\Delta_p = \frac{\partial p}{\partial S} = \frac{\partial}{\partial S}\left\{E\exp(-r(T-t))(1 - N_1(d_2)) - S\exp(-q(T-t))(1 - N_1(d_1))\right\}.$$

So

$$\Delta_p = -E\exp(-r(T-t))n(d_2)\frac{\partial d_2}{\partial S} - \exp(-q(T-t))\left\{(1 - N_1(d_1)) + Sn(d_1)\frac{\partial d_1}{\partial S}\right\}.$$
$$\qquad (A.3.3)$$

Substituting for $n(d_2)$ and $\partial d_2/\partial S$, we obtain

$$\Delta_p = \exp(-q(T-t))\left\{N_1(d_1) - 1\right\}. \qquad (A.3.4)$$

A.4 THETA

Theta is defined as the rate of change of the option value with time.

For a European call option, we have

$$\Theta_c = \frac{\partial c}{\partial t} = \frac{\partial}{\partial t}\left\{S\exp(-q(T-t))N_1(d_1) - E\exp(-r(T-t))N_1(d_2)\right\}$$
$$= q\exp(-q(T-t))SN_1(d_1) + \exp(-q(T-t))Sn(d_1)\frac{\partial d_1}{\partial t}$$
$$- rE\exp(-r(T-t))N_1(d_2) - E\exp(-r(T-t))n(d_2)\frac{\partial d_2}{\partial t};$$

substituting for $n(d_2)$ and $\partial d_2/\partial t$, we obtain

$$\Theta_c = q\exp(-q(T-t))SN_1(d_1) - rE\exp(-r(T-t))N_1(d_2) + \exp(-q(T-t))Sn(d_1)\frac{\partial d_1}{\partial t}$$

$$- E\exp(-r(T-t))n(d_1)\frac{S}{E}\exp(r(T-t))\exp(-q(T-t))\left\{\frac{\partial d_1}{\partial t} + \frac{\sigma}{2(T-t)}\right\}$$

$$= q\exp(-q(T-t))SN_1(d_1) - rE\exp(-r(T-t))N_1(d_2) - \frac{Sn(d_1)\sigma\exp(-q(T-t))}{2\sqrt{T-t}}.$$

Therefore, the value of theta is

$$\Theta_c = \exp(-q(T-t))\left\{q - SN_1(d_1)\frac{Sn(d_1)\sigma}{2\sqrt{T-t}}\right\} - rE\exp(-r(T-t))N_1(d_2). \quad \text{(A.4.1)}$$

For a put, we can similarly show that

$$\Theta_p = \frac{\partial p}{\partial t} = \frac{\partial}{\partial t}\{E\exp(-r(T-t))(1-N_1(d_2)) - S\exp(-q(T-t))(1-N_1(d_1))\},$$

$$\Theta_p = rE\exp(-r(T-t))(1-N_1(d_2)) - E\exp(-r(T-t))n(d_2)\frac{\partial d_2}{\partial t}$$

$$- qS\exp(-q(T-t))(1-N_1(d_1)) + S\exp(-q(T-t))n(d_1)\frac{\partial d_1}{\partial t};$$

substituting for $n(d_2)$ and $\partial d_2/\partial t$, we obtain

$$\Theta_p = rE\exp(-r(T-t))N_1(-d_2) - qS\exp(-q(T-t))N_1(-d_1)$$

$$- E\exp(-r(T-t))\exp(r(T-t))\exp(-q(T-t))n(d_1)\frac{S}{E}\left\{\frac{\partial d_1}{\partial t} + \frac{\partial \sigma}{2(T-t)}\right\}$$

$$+ S\exp(-q(T-t))n(d_1)\frac{\partial d_1}{\partial t}.$$

So we have

$$\Theta_p = -\exp(-q(T-t))\left\{qSN_1(-d_1) + \frac{Sn(d_1)\sigma}{2\sqrt{T-t}}\right\} + rE\exp(-r(T-t))N_1(-d_2). \quad \text{(A.4.2)}$$

A.5 RHO

Rho is the rate of change of the option value with interest rate.
    For a call, we have

$$\rho_c = \frac{\partial c}{\partial r} = \frac{\partial}{\partial r}\{S\exp(-q(T-t))N_1(d_1) - E\exp(-r(T-t))N_1(d_2)\}$$

$$= S\exp(-q(T-t))n(d_1)\frac{\partial d_1}{\partial r} + E(T-t)N_1(d_2) - E\exp(-r(T-t))n(d_2)\frac{\partial d_2}{\partial r};$$

substituting for $n(d_2)$ and $\partial d_2/\partial r$, we obtain

$$\rho_c = E(T-t)N_1(d_2). \quad \text{(A.5.1)}$$

For a European put, we have

$$
\rho_p = \frac{\partial p}{\partial r} = \frac{\partial}{\partial r} \{ E \exp(-r(T-t))(1-N_1(d_2)) - S \exp(-q(T-t))(1-N_1(d_2)) \}
$$

$$
= -E(T-t)(1-N_1(d_2)) - E \exp(-r(T-t))n(d_2)\frac{\partial d_2}{\partial r}
$$

$$
+ S \exp(-q(T-t))n(d_1)\frac{\partial d_1}{\partial r}
$$

$$
= -E(T-t)N_1(-d_2) - E \exp(-r(T-t))n(d_2)\frac{\partial d_2}{\partial r}
$$

$$
+ S \exp(-q(T-t))n(d_1)\frac{\partial d_1}{\partial r};
$$

substituting for $n(d_2)$ and $\partial d_2/\partial r$, we obtain

$$
\rho_p = -E(T-t)N_1(-d_2). \tag{A.5.2}
$$

A.6 VEGA

Vega is the rate of change of option value with volatility. For a call, we have

$$
\mathcal{V}_c = \frac{\partial c}{\partial \sigma} \tag{A.6.1}
$$

$$
= \frac{\partial}{\partial \sigma} \{ S \exp(-q(T-t))N_1(d_1) - E \exp(-r(T-t))N_1(d_2) \}
$$

$$
= S \exp(-q(T-t))n(d_1)\frac{\partial d_1}{\partial \sigma} - E \exp(-r(T-t))n(d_2)\frac{\partial d_2}{\partial r};
$$

substituting for $n(d_2)$ and $\partial d_2/\partial \sigma$, we obtain

$$
\mathcal{V}_c = S \exp(-q(T-t))n(d_1)\frac{\partial d_1}{\partial \sigma} - Sn(d_1)\exp(-q(T-t))\left\{ \frac{\partial d_1}{\partial \sigma} - \sqrt{T-t} \right\}.
$$

Therefore,

$$
\mathcal{V}_c = S \exp(-q(T-t))n(d_1)\sqrt{T-t}. \tag{A.6.2}
$$

For a European put, we have

$$
\mathcal{V}_p = \frac{\partial c}{\partial \sigma} \tag{A.6.3}
$$

$$
= \frac{\partial}{\partial \sigma} \{ E \exp(-r(T-t))(1-N_1(d_2)) - S \exp(-q(T-t))(1-N_1(d_1)) \}
$$

$$
= -E \exp(-r(T-t))n(d_2)\frac{\partial d_2}{\partial \sigma} + S \exp(-q(T-t))n(d_1)\frac{\partial d_1}{\partial \sigma};
$$

substituting for $n(d_2)$ and $\partial d_2/\partial \sigma$, we obtain

$$
\mathcal{V}_p = S \exp(-q(T-t))n(d_1)\sqrt{T-t}, \tag{A.6.4}
$$

which is the same as for a call.

Appendix B

Barrier Option Integrals

B.1 THE DOWN AND OUT CALL

We will now derive the formula for the value, c_{do} of a European down and out call option with dividend yield q when the strike, E, satisfies $E > B$,

$$c_{do} = \frac{\exp(-r\tau)}{\sigma \sqrt{\tau} \sqrt{2\pi}} \int_{X=\log(E/S)}^{\infty} \{S \exp(X) - E\} f(X > B) dX. \qquad (B.1.1)$$

Substituting for $f(X > B)$, we have $c_{do} = I_A + I_B$, where

$$I_A = \frac{\exp(-r\tau)}{\sigma \sqrt{\tau} \sqrt{2\pi}} \int_{X=\log(E/S)}^{\infty} \{S \exp(X) - E\} \exp\left(-\frac{\left\{X - (r - q - \sigma^2/2)\tau\right\}^2}{2\sigma^2\tau}\right) dX$$

and

$$I_B = -\frac{\exp(-r\tau)}{\sigma \sqrt{\tau} \sqrt{2\pi}} \int_{X=\log(E/S)}^{\infty} \{S \exp(X) - E\} \exp\left(-\frac{\left\{X - (r - q - \sigma^2/2)\tau\right\}^2}{2\sigma^2\tau}\right)$$
$$\times \exp\left(\frac{2\log(B/S)(X - \log(B/S))}{\sigma^2\tau}\right) dX.$$

Now comparing I_A with equation (4.4.54), we can identify I_A as c, the price of a European call. That is,

$$I_A = S \exp(-q\tau)N_1(d_1) - E \exp(-r\tau)N_1(d_2), \qquad (B.1.2)$$

where

$$d_1 = \frac{\log(S/E) + (r - q + \sigma^2/2)\tau}{\sigma \sqrt{\tau}},$$

$$d_2 = \frac{\log(S/E) + (r - q - \sigma^2/2)\tau}{\sigma \sqrt{\tau}}.$$

We now consider the term I_B, and let $I_B = I_C + I_D$, where

$$I_C = -\frac{S \exp(-r\tau)}{\sigma \sqrt{\tau} \sqrt{2\pi}} \int_{X=\log(E/S)}^{\infty} \exp(X) \exp\left(-\frac{\left\{X - (r - q - \sigma^2/2)\tau\right\}^2}{2\sigma^2\tau}\right)$$
$$\times \exp\left(\frac{2\log(B/S)(X - \log(B/S))}{\sigma^2\tau}\right) dX$$

and

$$I_D = \frac{E \exp(-r\tau)}{\sigma \sqrt{\tau} \sqrt{2\pi}} \int_{X=\log(E/S)}^{\infty} \exp\left(-\frac{\{X - (r - q - \sigma^2/2)\tau\}^2}{2\sigma^2\tau}\right)$$
$$\times \exp\left(\frac{2\log(B/S)(X - \log(B/S))}{\sigma^2\tau}\right) dX.$$

We will first consider I_D and factor the integrand as follows:

$$-\exp\left(-\frac{\{X - (r - q - \sigma^2/2)\tau\}^2}{2\sigma^2\tau}\right)\exp\left(\frac{2\log(B/S)(X - \log(B/S))}{\sigma^2\tau}\right)$$

$$= \exp\left(-\frac{\{X - (r - q - \sigma^2/2)\tau\}^2 - 4\log(B/S)(X - \log(B/S))}{2\sigma^2\tau}\right)$$

$$= \exp\left(-\frac{\{X - (r - q - \sigma^2/2)\tau - 2\log(B/S)\}^2}{2\sigma^2\tau}\right)\exp\left(\frac{4(r - q - \sigma^2/2)\tau\log(B/S)}{2\sigma^2\tau}\right).$$

$$(B.1.3)$$

This means that I_D can be expressed as

$$\therefore I_D = \left(\frac{B}{S}\right)^{\frac{2((r-q)\sigma^2/2)}{\sigma^2}} \frac{E \exp(-r\tau)}{\sigma \sqrt{\tau} \sqrt{2\pi}}$$
$$\times \int_{X=\log(E/S)}^{\infty} \exp\left(-\frac{\{X - (r - q\sigma^2/2)\tau - 2\log(B/S)\}^2}{2\sigma^2\tau}\right) dX.$$

Letting $u = [X - (r - q - \sigma^2/2)\tau - 2\log(B/S)]/\sigma \sqrt{\tau}$, we have $dX = \sigma \sqrt{(\tau)} du$ and

$$I_D = \left(\frac{B}{S}\right)^{2(r-q-\sigma^2/2)/\sigma^2} \frac{E \exp(-r\tau)}{\sigma \sqrt{\tau} \sqrt{2\pi}} \int_{u=k3}^{\infty} \exp\left(-\frac{u^2}{2}\right) du,$$

where

$$k_3 = \frac{\log(E/S) - (r - q - \sigma^2/2)\tau - 2\log(B/S)}{\sigma \sqrt{\tau}}$$
$$= \frac{\log(ES/B^2) - (r - q - \sigma^2/2)\tau}{\sigma \sqrt{\tau}}.$$

So

$$I_D = \left(\frac{B}{S}\right)^{2r/\sigma^2-1} E \exp(-r\tau)N_1(-k_3). \tag{B.1.4}$$

Letting $d_3 = -k_3$, we have $d_3 = [\log(B^2/SE) + (r - q - \sigma^2/2)\tau]/\sigma \sqrt{\tau}$ and

$$I_D = \left(\frac{B}{S}\right)^{2r/\sigma^2 - 1} E \exp(-r\tau) N_1(d_3). \tag{B.1.5}$$

Now consider the term

$$I_C = \frac{S \exp(-r\tau)}{\sigma \sqrt{\tau} \sqrt{2\pi}} \int_{X = \log(E/S)}^{\infty} \exp(X) \exp\left(-\frac{\left\{X - (r - \sigma^2/2)\tau\right\}^2}{2\sigma^2\tau}\right)$$

$$\exp\left(\frac{2\log(B/S)(X - \log(B/S))}{\sigma^2\tau}\right) dX.$$

Now we have

$$\exp(X) \exp\left(-\frac{(X - (r - q - \sigma^2/2)\tau)^2}{2\sigma^2\tau}\right) \exp\left(\frac{2\log(B/S)(X - \log(B/S))}{\sigma^2\tau}\right)$$

$$= \exp\left(\frac{-\left\{(X - (-qr - \sigma^2/2)\tau)^2 - 2\sigma^2\tau X - 4\log(B/S)X + 4(\log(B/S))^2\right\}}{2\sigma^2\tau}\right)$$

$$= \exp\left(\frac{(\sigma^2\tau)^2 + 2(r - q - \sigma^2/2)\tau^2\sigma^2 + 4(r - q - \sigma^2/2)\tau \log(B/S) + 4\sigma^2\tau \log(B/S)}{2\sigma^2\tau}\right)$$

$$\times \exp\left(\frac{-\left\{X - (r - q - \sigma^2/2)\tau - \sigma^2\tau - 2\log(B/S)\right\}^2}{2\sigma^2\tau}\right)$$

$$= \exp((r - q)\tau) \exp\left(\left\{\frac{2(r - q)}{\sigma^2} + 1\right\} \log(B/S)\right)$$

$$\times \exp\left(\frac{-\left\{X - (r - q - \sigma^2/2)\tau - \sigma^2\tau - 2\log(B/S)\right\}^2}{2\sigma^2\tau}\right)$$

$$= \exp((r - q)\tau) \left(\frac{B}{S}\right)^{\frac{2(r-q)}{\sigma^2} + 1} \exp\left(\frac{-\left\{X - (r - q - \sigma^2/2)\tau - \sigma^2\tau - 2\log(B/S)\right\}^2}{2\sigma^2\tau}\right).$$

So we have

$$I_C = -\left(\frac{B}{S}\right)^{\frac{2(r-q)}{\sigma^2} + 1} \frac{S \exp(-q\tau)}{\sigma \sqrt{\tau} \sqrt{2\pi}}$$

$$\times \int_{X = \log(E/S)}^{\infty} \exp\left(-\frac{\left\{X - (r - q - \sigma^2/2)\tau - \sigma^2\tau - 2\log(B/S)\right\}^2}{2\sigma^2\tau}\right) dX.$$

Letting $u = [X - (r - q - \sigma^2/2)\tau - \sigma^2\tau - 2\log(B/S)]/\sigma \sqrt{\tau}$, we have $dX = \sigma \sqrt{\tau} du$ and

$$I_C = -S \exp(-q\tau) \left(\frac{B}{S}\right)^{\frac{2(r-q)}{\sigma^2} + 1} N_1(-k_4), \tag{B.1.6}$$

where

$$k_4 = \frac{\log(E/S) - (r - q - \sigma^2/2)\tau - \sigma^2\tau - 2\log(B/S)}{\sigma\sqrt{\tau}}$$

$$= \frac{\log(ES/B^2) - (r - q + \sigma^2/2)\tau}{\sigma\sqrt{\tau}}.$$

$$\therefore I_C = -S\exp(-q\tau)\left(\frac{B}{S}\right)^{\frac{2(r-q)}{\sigma^2}+1} N_1(-k_4),$$

or letting $d_4 = -k_4$, we have

$$d_4 = \frac{\log(B^2/ES) + (r - q + \sigma^2/2)\tau}{\sigma\sqrt{\tau}},$$

$$I_C = -S\exp(-q\tau)\left(\frac{B}{S}\right)^{\frac{2(r-q)}{\sigma^2}+1} N_1(d_4). \tag{B.1.7}$$

Therefore, the value for the down and out call option is

$$c_{do} = I_A + I_C + I_D = I_A - (-I_C - I_D).$$

Since $c_{do} + c_{di} = c$, where c is the value of vanilla call and c_{di} is the value of down and in call, we can write

$$c_{do} = c - c_{di},$$

where

$$c_{di} = S\exp(-q\tau)N_1(d_4)\left(\frac{B}{S}\right)^{\frac{2(r-q)}{\sigma^2}+1} - E\exp(-r\tau)N_1(d_3)\left(\frac{B}{S}\right)^{\frac{2(r-q)}{\sigma^2}-1}.$$

B.2 THE UP AND OUT CALL

We will now derive the formula for a European up and out call option with dividend yield q when the strike, E, satisfies $B > E$,

$$c_{uo} = \frac{\exp(-r\tau)}{\sigma\sqrt{\tau}\sqrt{2\pi}} \int_{X=\log(E/S)}^{\log(B/S)} \{S\exp(X) - E\}f(X < B)dX. \tag{B.2.1}$$

Substituting for $f(X < B)$, we have $c_{uo} = I_A + I_B$, where

$$I_A = \frac{\exp(-r\tau)}{\sigma\sqrt{\tau}\sqrt{2\pi}} \int_{X=\log(E/S)}^{\log(B/S)} \{S\exp(X) - E\}\exp\left(-\frac{\{X - (r - q - \sigma^2/2)\tau\}^2}{2\sigma^2\tau}\right)dX$$

and

$$I_B = -\frac{\exp(-r\tau)}{\sigma\sqrt{\tau}\sqrt{2\pi}} \int_{X=\log(E/S)}^{\log(B/S)} \{S\exp(X) - E\}\exp\left(-\frac{\{X - (r - q - \sigma^2/2)\tau\}^2}{2\sigma^2\tau}\right)$$

$$\times \exp\left(\frac{2\log(B/S)(X - \log(B/S))}{\sigma^2\tau}\right)dX.$$

Letting $I_A = I_1 + I_2$, where

$$I_1 = \frac{S \exp(-r\tau)}{\sigma \sqrt{\tau} \sqrt{2\pi}} \int_{X=\log(E/S)}^{\log(B/S)} \exp(X) \exp\left(-\frac{\{X - (r - q - \sigma^2/2)\tau\}^2}{2\sigma^2\tau}\right) dX$$

and

$$I_2 = \frac{-E \exp(-r\tau)}{\sigma \sqrt{\tau} \sqrt{2\pi}} \int_{X=\log(E/S)}^{\log(B/S)} \exp\left(-\frac{\{X - (r - q - \sigma^2/2)\tau\}^2}{2\sigma^2\tau}\right) dX.$$

From our previous derivation of the Black–Scholes formula in Chapter 4, we have

$$I_1 = \frac{S \exp(-q\tau)}{\sigma \sqrt{\tau} \sqrt{2\pi}} \int_{u=k_1}^{k_2} \exp\left(-\frac{u^2}{2}\right) du = S \exp(-q\tau) \{N_1(k_2) - N_1(k_1)\},$$

where

$$k_1 = \frac{\log(E/S) - (r - q + \sigma^2/2)\tau)}{\sigma \sqrt{\tau}}$$

and

$$k_2 = \frac{\log(B/S) - (r - q + \sigma^2/2)\tau}{\sqrt{\tau}},$$

$$I_2 = \frac{-E \exp(-r\tau)}{\sigma \sqrt{\tau} \sqrt{2\pi}} \int_{u=k_3}^{k_4} \exp\left(-\frac{u^2}{2}\right) du = -E \exp(-r\tau) \{N_1(k_4) - N_1(k_3)\},$$

where

$$k_3 = \frac{\log(E/S) - (r - q - \sigma^2/2)\tau}{\sigma \sqrt{\tau}}$$

and

$$k_4 = \frac{\log(B/S) - (r - q - \sigma^2/2)\tau}{\sigma \sqrt{\tau}}.$$

Therefore,

$$I_A = S \exp(-q\tau) \{N_1(k_2) - N_1(k_1)\} - E \exp(-r\tau) \{N_1(k_4) - N_1(k_3)\}.$$

Since $N_1(-x) = 1 - N_1(x)$, we have

$$N_1(k_2) - N_1(k_1) = N_1(-k_1) - N_1(-k_2)$$

so

$$I_A = S \exp(-q\tau) \{N_1(d_1) - N_1(d_2)\} - E \exp(-r\tau) \{N_1(d_3) - N_1(d_4)\}$$
$$= S \exp(-q\tau)N_1(d_1) - E \exp(-r\tau)N_1(d_3) - S \exp(-q\tau)N_1(d_2) + E \exp(-r\tau)N_1(d_4),$$

which gives

$$I_A = c - S \exp(-q\tau)N_1(d_2) + E \exp(-r\tau)N_1(d_4), \tag{B.2.2}$$

where c is the value of a vanilla call and

$$d_1 = \frac{\log(S/E) + (r - q + \sigma^2/2)\tau}{\sigma\sqrt{\tau}}, \qquad d_2 = \frac{\log(S/B) + (r - q + \sigma^2/2)\tau}{\sqrt{\tau}},$$

$$d_3 = \frac{\log(S/E) + (r - q - \sigma^2/2)\tau}{\sigma\sqrt{\tau}}, \qquad d_4 = \frac{\log(S/B) + (r - q - \sigma^2/2)\tau}{\sigma\sqrt{\tau}}.$$

Letting $I_B = I_C + I_D$, where

$$I_C = -\frac{S\exp(-r\tau)}{\sigma\sqrt{\tau}\sqrt{2\pi}} \int_{X=\log(E/S)}^{\log(B/S)} \exp(X)\exp\left(-\frac{\{X - (r - q - \sigma^2/2)\tau\}^2}{2\sigma^2\tau}\right)$$
$$\times \exp\left(\frac{2\log(B/S)(X - \log(B/S))}{\sigma^2\tau}\right) dX$$

and

$$I_D = \frac{E\exp(-r\tau)}{\sigma\sqrt{\tau}\sqrt{2\pi}} \int_{X=\log(E/S)}^{\log(B/S)} \exp\left(-\frac{\{X - (r - q - \sigma^2/2)\tau\}^2}{2\sigma^2\tau}\right)$$
$$\times \exp\left(\frac{2\log(B/S)(X - \log(B/S))}{\sigma^2\tau}\right) dX.$$

In a similar manner to that in Appendix B.1, we have

$$I_D = \left(\frac{B}{S}\right)^{2(r-q-\sigma^2/2)/\sigma^2} \frac{E\exp(-r\tau)}{\sigma\sqrt{\tau}\sqrt{2\pi}}$$
$$\times \int_{X=\log(E/S)}^{\log(B/S)} \exp\left(-\frac{\{X - (r - q - \sigma^2/2)\tau - 2\log(B/S)\}^2}{2\sigma^2\tau}\right) dX.$$

Letting $u = [X - (r - q - \sigma^2/2)\tau - 2\log(B/S)]/\sigma\sqrt{\tau}$ gives

$$I_D = \left(\frac{B}{S}\right)^{2(r-q-\sigma^2/2)/\sigma^2} \frac{E\exp(-r\tau)}{\sigma\sqrt{\tau}\sqrt{2\pi}} \int_{u=k_5}^{k_6} \exp\left(-\frac{u^2}{2}\right) du, \tag{B.2.3}$$

where

$$k_5 = \frac{\log(E/S) - (r - q - \sigma^2/2)\tau - 2\log(B/S)}{\sigma\sqrt{\tau}}$$
$$= \frac{\log(ES/B^2) - (r - q - \sigma^2/2)\tau}{\sigma\sqrt{\tau}}$$

and

$$k_6 = \frac{\log(B/S) - (r - q - \sigma^2/2)\tau - 2\log(B/S)}{\sigma\sqrt{\tau}}$$
$$= \frac{\log(S/B) - (r - q - \sigma^2/2)\tau}{\sigma\sqrt{\tau}}$$

and so

$$I_D = \left(\frac{B}{S}\right)^{\frac{2(r-q)}{\sigma^2}-1} E \exp(-r\tau)\{N_1(k_6) - N_1(k_5)\}.$$

This can be re-expressed as

$$I_D = \left(\frac{B}{S}\right)^{\frac{2(r-q)}{\sigma^2}-1} E \exp(-r\tau)\{N_1(d_5) - N_1(d_6)\},\tag{B.2.4}$$

where

$$d_5 = \frac{\log(B^2/ES) - (r - q - \sigma^2/2)\tau}{\sigma\sqrt{\tau}}, \qquad d_6 = \frac{\log(B/S) + (r - q - \sigma^2/2)\tau}{\sigma\sqrt{\tau}}.$$

We now consider the term

$$I_C = -\frac{S\exp(-r\tau)}{\sigma\sqrt{\tau}\sqrt{2\pi}} \int_{X=\log(E/S)}^{\log(B/S)} \exp(X) \exp\left(-\frac{\{X - (r - q - \sigma^2/2)\tau\}^2}{2\sigma^2\tau}\right)$$

$$\times \exp\left(\frac{2\log(B/S)(X - \log(B/S))}{\sigma^2\tau}\right) dX.$$

In a similar manner to Appendix B.1, we let $u = [X - (r - q - \sigma^2/2)\tau - \sigma^2\tau - 2\log(B/S)]/\sigma\sqrt{\tau}$ which gives

$$I_C = -S\exp(-r\tau)\left(\frac{B}{S}\right)^{\frac{2(r-q)}{\sigma^2}+1}\{N_1(k_8) - N_1(k_7)\},$$

where

$$k_7 = \frac{\log(E/S) - (r - q - \sigma^2/2)\tau - \sigma^2\tau - 2\log(B/S)}{\sigma\sqrt{\tau}}$$

$$= \frac{\log(ES/B^2) - (r - q + \sigma^2/2)\tau}{\sigma\sqrt{\tau}}$$

and

$$k_8 = \frac{\log(B/S) - (r - q - \sigma^2/2)\tau - \sigma^2\tau - 2\log(B/S)}{\sigma\sqrt{\tau}}$$

$$= \frac{\log(S/B) - (r - q + \sigma^2/2)\tau}{\sigma\sqrt{\tau}}.$$

This can be re-expressed as

$$I_C = -S\exp(-r\tau)\left(\frac{B}{S}\right)^{\frac{2(r-q)}{\sigma^2}+1}\{N_1(d_7) - N_1(d_8)\},$$

where

$$d_7 = \frac{\log(B^2/ES) + (r - q + \sigma^2/2)\tau}{\sigma\sqrt{\tau}}, \qquad d_8 = \frac{\log(B/S) + (r - q + \sigma^2/2)\tau}{\sigma\sqrt{\tau}}.$$

So we have

$$c_{uo} = I_A + I_C + I_D,$$

which can be written as

$$c_{uo} = c - c_{ui},$$

where c is the value of a vanilla call and c_{ui}, the value of an up and in call is given by

$$c_{ui} = S \exp(-q\tau) N_1(d_2) - E \exp(-r\tau) N_1(d_4)$$

$$- E \exp(-r\tau) \{ N_1(d_5) - N_1(d_6) \} \left(\frac{B}{S} \right)^{\frac{2(r-q)}{\sigma^2} - 1}$$

$$+ S \exp(-r\tau) \{ N_1(d_7) - N_1(d_8) \} \left(\frac{B}{S} \right)^{\frac{2(r-q)}{\sigma^2} + 1}. \qquad \text{(B.2.5)}$$

Appendix C

Standard Statistical Results

C.1 THE LAW OF LARGE NUMBERS

Let $x_1, x_2, \ldots$ be a sequence of independent, identically distributed random variables (IID), each with expected value μ and variance σ^2. Define the sequence of averages

$$y_n = \frac{\sum_{i=1}^{n} x_i}{n} = \frac{x_1 + x_2 + \ldots + x_n}{n}, \quad n = 1, 2, \ldots.$$

Then the law of large numbers states that y_n converges to μ as $n \to \infty$, that is, $Var[y_n] \to 0$.

The mean of y_n is

$$E[y_n] = \frac{1}{n} (E[x_1] + E[x_2] + + \ldots + E[x_n]) = \frac{1}{n} n\mu = \mu.$$

For the variance of y_n, we have

$$Var[y_n] = Var\left[\frac{\sum_{i=1}^{n} x_i}{n}\right] = \frac{1}{n^2} Var\left[\sum_{i=1}^{n} x_i\right] = \frac{1}{n^2} \sum_{i=1}^{n} Var[x_i] = \frac{1}{n^2} n\sigma^2 = \frac{\sigma^2}{n},$$

where we have used the fact that the variance of the sum of independent random variables is the sum of their variances, see Appendix C.2.

We have therefore shown that as $n \to \infty$, $Var[y_n] \to 0$.

C.2 THE CENTRAL LIMIT THEOREM

Let $x_1, x_2, \ldots$ be a sequence of IID random variables, each with expected value μ and variance σ^2. If we define $u_i = x_i - \mu$, then

$$E[u_i] = E[u] = 0, \qquad Var[u_i] = E\left[u^2\right] = \sigma^2.$$

Let

$$s_n = \sum_{i=1}^{n} u_i + n\mu.$$

So

$$s_n = \sum_{i=1}^{n} x_i.$$

We now introduce the normalized value z_n, as follows:

$$z_n = \frac{S_n - n\mu}{\sigma \sqrt{n}} = \frac{1}{\sigma \sqrt{n}} \sum_{i=1}^{n} u_i.$$

The central limit theorem states that as n tends to infinity the probability distribution of z_n tends to a normal distribution with zero mean and unit variance, mathematically $z_n \to N(0,1)$ as $n \to \infty$.

Proof. From Appendix C.5 equation (C.5.3),

$$M_{z_n} = E[\exp(tz_n)] = E\left[\exp\left\{\frac{t}{\sigma \sqrt{n}} \sum_{i=1}^{n} u_i\right\}\right],$$

and using (C.5.5)

$$M_{z_n} = \left\{M_u\left(\frac{t}{\sigma \sqrt{n}}\right)\right\}^n.$$

Equation (C.5.1) then yields

$$M_u\left(\frac{t}{\sigma \sqrt{n}}\right) \approx 1 + \frac{t}{\sigma \sqrt{n}} E[u] + \frac{1}{2}\left(\frac{t}{\sigma \sqrt{n}}\right)^2 E[u^2] + +.$$

As $n \to \infty \; t/(\sigma \sqrt{n}) \to 0$, an

$$M_u\left(\frac{t}{\sigma \sqrt{n}}\right) \to 1 + \frac{t}{\sigma \sqrt{n}} E[u] + \frac{1}{2}\left(\frac{t}{\sigma \sqrt{n}}\right)^2 E[u^2] = 1 + \frac{t^2}{2n}.$$

Thus,

$$\left\{M_u\left(\frac{t}{\sigma \sqrt{n}}\right)\right\}^n = \left(1 + \frac{t^2}{2n}\right)^n \to 1 + \frac{t^2}{2} \quad \text{as } n \to \infty,$$

where we have use the fact that $t \ll 1$ see Grimmett and Welsh (1986).
    We have therefore shown that as $n \to \infty$

$$M_{z_n}(t) \to 1 + \frac{t^2}{2} \to e^{\frac{t^2}{2}}.$$

However from Appendix D.1, the moment generating function $M_z(t)$ for a standard normal distribution ($\mu = 0, \sigma^2 = 1$) is

$$M_z(t) = e^{\frac{t^2}{2}}, \quad \text{where } z \sim N(0,1).$$

Thus, we have proved that $z_n \to N(0,1)$ as $n \to \infty$.

C.3 THE VARIANCE AND COVARIANCE OF RANDOM VARIABLES

C.3.1 Variance

One Variable

Let X be a variate from a given distribution, and Z be the following linear function of this variate:

$$Z = a + bX,$$

where a and b are constants. Then

$$E[Z] = E[a] + E[bX] = a + bE[X]$$

and

$$\begin{aligned} Var[Z] &= E[(Z - E[Z])^2] \\ &= E[(a + bX - a - bE[X])^2] \\ &= E[(bX - bE[X])^2] \\ &= E[b^2(X - E[X])^2] \\ &= b^2 E[(X - E[X])^2]. \end{aligned}$$

Therefore, the mean is $a + bE[X]$, and the variance is $b^2 Var[X]$.

Two Variables

Let $Z = a + b_1 X_1 + b_2 X_2$, where a, b_1, and b_2 are constants.
    Then mean is $E[Z] = E[a] + E[b_1 X_1] + E[b_2 X_2] = a + b_1 E[X_1] + b_2 E[X_2]$.
The variance $Var[Z]$ is computed as follows:

$$\begin{aligned} Var[Z] &= E\left[\{a + b_1 X_1 + b_2 X_2 - a - b_1 E[X_1] - b_2 E[X_2]\}^2\right] \\ &= E\left[\{b_1(X_1 - E[X_1]) + b_2(X_2 - E[X_2])\}^2\right] \\ &= b_1^2 E\left[(X_1 - E[X_1])^2\right] + b_2^2 E\left[(X_2 - E[X_2])^2\right] \\ &\quad + 2b_1 b_2 E\left[(X_1 - E[X_1])\right] E\left[(X_2 - E[X_2])\right] \\ &= b_1^2 Var[X_1] + b_2^2 Var[X_2] + 2b_1 b_2 Cov[X_1, X_2], \end{aligned}$$

where $Cov[X_1, X_2]$ is the covariance between X_1 and X_2. If X_1 and X_2 are *IID* random variables, then $Cov[X_1, X_2] = 0$, and we thus have

$$Var[Z] = b_1^2 Var[X_1] + b_2^2 Var[X_2].$$

Three Variables

Let $Z = a + b_1 X_1 + b_2 X_2 = b_3 X_3$, where a, b_1, b_2, and b_3 are constants.

Then mean is $E[Z] = E[a] + E[b_1 X_1] + E[b_2 X_2] + E[b_3 X_3] = a + b_1 E[X_1] + b_2 E[X_2] + b_3 E[X_3]$.

The variance $Var[Z]$ is computed as follows:

$$
\begin{aligned}
Var[Z] &= E\left[\{a + b_1 X_1 + b_2 X_2 + b_3 X_3 - a - b_1 E[X_1] - b_2 E[X_2] - b_3 E[X_3]\}^2\right] \\
&= E\left[\{b_1(X_1 - E[X_1]) + b_2(X_2 - E[X_2]) + b_3(X_3 - E[X_3])\}^2\right] \\
&= b_1^2 E\left[(X_1 - E[X_1])^2\right] + b_2^2 E\left[(X_2 - E[X_2])^2\right] + b_3^2 E\left[(X_3 - E[X_3])^2\right] \\
&\quad + 2b_1 b_2 E\left[(X_1 - E[X_1])\right] E\left[(X_2 - E[X_2])\right] \\
&\quad + 2b_2 b_3 E\left[(X_2 - E[X_2])\right] E\left[(X_3 - E[X_3])\right] \\
&\quad + 2b_1 b_3 E\left[(X_1 - E[X_1])\right] E\left[(X_3 - E[X_3])\right] \\
&= b_1^2 Var[X_1] + b_2^2 Var[X_2] + b_3^2 Var[X_2] + 2b_2 b_3 Cov[X_2, X_3] \\
&\quad + 2b_1 b_2 Cov[X_2, X_3] + 2b_1 b_3 Cov[X_1, X_3].
\end{aligned}
$$

If X_1, X_2, and X_3 are IID, all the covariance terms are zero and the variance is

$$
Var[Z] = b_1^2 Var[X_1] + b_2^2 Var[X_2] + b_3^2 Var[X_3].
$$

Variance of n Variables

We will now derive an expression for the sum of n IID random variables.

Let $Z = a + \sum_{i=1}^{n} b_i X_i$, where a and $b_i, i = 1, \ldots, n$ are constants.

Then we have $E[Z] = E[a] + E\left[\sum_{i=1}^{n} b_i X_i\right] = a + \sum_{i=1}^{n} b_i E[X_i]$ and

$$
\begin{aligned}
Var[Z] &= E\left[\left\{a + \sum_{i=1}^{n} b_i X_i - a - \sum_{i=1}^{n} b_i E[X_i]\right\}^2\right] \\
&= E\left[\left\{\sum_{i=1}^{n} b_i X_i - \sum_{i=1}^{n} b_i E[X_i]\right\}^2\right] \\
&= E\left[\left\{\sum_{i=1}^{n} b_i (X_i - E[X_i])\right\}^2\right] \\
&= \sum_{i=1}^{n} b_i^2 E\left[(X_i - E[X_i])^2\right] + \sum_{i=1}^{n} \sum_{j=1(j\neq i)}^{n} b_i b_j E\left[(X_i - E[X_i])(X_j - E[X_j])\right] \\
&= \sum_{i=1}^{n} b_i^2 Var[X_i] + \sum_{i=1}^{n} \sum_{j=1(j\neq i)}^{n} b_i b_j Cov[X_i, X_j].
\end{aligned}
$$

As before if all the X variables are IID, then the covariance terms are zero and we have

$$Var[Z] = \sum_{i=1}^{n} b_i^2 Var[x_i].$$

If in addition all the b_i terms are one and all the X variable have variance σ^2, we obtain

$$Var[Z] = \sum_{i=1}^{n} Var[x_i] = n\sigma^2.$$

C.3.2 Covariance

The covariance between two variables X and Y is defined by

$$Cov[X,Y] = E\Big[(X - E[X])(Y - E[Y])\Big] = E\Big[XY - YE[X] - XE[Y] + E[X]E[Y]\Big]$$
$$= E[XY] - E[Y]E[X] - E[X]E[Y] + E[X]E[Y]$$
$$= E[XY] - E[X]E[Y].$$

By symmetry, it can be seen that $Cov[X,Y] = Cov[Y,X]$.

Two Variables

Let $Z_1 = a + bX$ and $Z_2 = c + dY$, where a, b, c, and d are constants.
  We have

$$Cov[Z_1,Z_2] = Cov[a + bX, c + dY]$$
$$= E[(a + bX)(c + dY)] - E[(a + bX)]E[(c + dY)]$$
$$= E[ac + bcX + adY + bdXY] - \Big\{(a + bE[X])(c + dE[Y])\Big\}$$
$$= ac + bcE[X] + adE[Y] + bdE[XY] - ac$$
$$\quad + bcE[X] - adE[Y] - bdE[X]E[Y]$$
$$= bd\Big\{E[XY] - E[X]E[Y]\Big\},$$
$$\therefore Cov[Z_1,Z_2] = bdCov[X,Y].$$

Three Variables

Let $Z_1 = a + b_1 X_1 + b_2 X_2$ and $Z_2 = c + dY$, where a, b_1, b_2, c, and d are constants.
  We have

$$Cov[Z_1,Z_2] = Cov[a + b_1 X_1 + b_2 X_2, c + dY]$$
$$= E[(a + b_1 X_1 + b_2 X_2)(c + dY)] - E[(a + b_1 X_1 + b_2 X_2)]E[(c + dY)]$$
$$= E[(a + b_1 X_1)(c + dY) + b_2 X_2(c + dY)]$$
$$\quad - \Big\{E[(a + b_1 X_1)] + E[b_2 X_2]E[c + dY]\Big\}$$

$$= E[(a + b_1 X_1)(c + dY)] + E[b_2 X_2(c + dY)]$$
$$- E[(a + b_1 X_1)]E[c + dY] - E[b_2 X_2]E[c + dY]$$
$$= \left\{ E[(a + b_1 X_1)(c + dY)] - E[(a + b_1 X_1)]E[c + dY] \right\}$$
$$- \left\{ E[(b_2 X_2)(c + dY)] - E[b_2 X_2]E[c + dY] \right\},$$
$$\therefore Cov[Z_1, Z_2] = b_1 d Cov[X_1, Y] + b_2 d Cov[X_2, Y].$$

Four Variables

Let $Z_1 = a + b_1 X_1 + b_2 X_2 + b_3 X_3$ and $Z_2 = c + dY$, where a, b_1, b_2, b_3, c, and d are constants.

We have

$$Cov[Z_1, Z_2] = Cov[a + b_1 X_1 + b_2 X_2 + b_3 X_3, c + dY]$$
$$= E[(a + b_1 X_1 + b_2 X_2 + b_3 X_3)(c + dY)]$$
$$- E[(a + b_1 X_1 + b_2 X_2 + b_3 X_3)]E[(c + dY)]$$
$$= E[(a + b_1 X_1 + b_2 X_2)(c + dY) + b_3 X_3(c + dY)]$$
$$- \left\{ E[(a + b_1 X_1 + b_2 X_2)] + E[b_3 X_3]E[c + dY] \right\}$$
$$= E[(a + b_1 X_1 + b_2 X_2)(c + dY)] + E[b_3 X_3(c + dY)]$$
$$- E[(a + b_1 X_1 + b_2 X_2)]E[c + dY] - E[b_3 X_3]E[c + dY]$$
$$= \left\{ E[(a + b_1 X_1 + b_2 X_2)(c + dY)] - E[(a + b_1 X_1 + b_2 X_2)]E[c + dY] \right\}$$
$$- \left\{ E[(b_3 X_3)(c + dY)] - E[b_3 X_3]E[c + dY] \right\}$$
$$= Cov[(a + b_1 X_1 + b_2 X_2), c + dY] + Cov[b_3 X_3, c + dY],$$
$$\therefore Cov[Z_1, Z_2] = b_1 d Cov[X_1, Y] + b_2 d Cov[X_2, Y] + b_3 d Cov[X_3, Y].$$

Covariance of n Variables

In a similar manner to that outlined above,

$$Cov\left[a + \sum_{i=1}^{n} b_i X_i, c + dY \right] = d \sum_{i=1}^{n} b_i Cov[X_i, Y].$$

For the most general case, let $Z_1 = a + \sum_{i=1}^{n} b_i X_i$ and $Z_2 = c + \sum_{j=1}^{M} d_j Y_j$.

So

$$Cov[Z_1, Z_2] = Cov\left[a + \sum_{i=1}^{n} b_i X_i, c + \sum_{j=1}^{M} d_j Y_j \right] = Cov\left[a + \sum_{i=1}^{n} b_i X_i, c + \sum_{j=1}^{M} d_j Y_j \right].$$

So

$$Cov\left[a + \sum_{i=1}^{n} b_i X_i, c + \sum_{j=1}^{M} d_j Y_j \right] = \sum_{i=1}^{n} Cov\left[b_i X_i, \sum_{j=1}^{M} d_j Y_j \right]$$

$$= \sum_{i=1}^{n} b_i Cov\left[X_i, \sum_{j=1}^{M} d_j Y_j\right]$$

$$= \sum_{i=1}^{n} b_i Cov\left[\sum_{j=1}^{M} d_j Y_j, X_i\right],$$

$$\therefore Cov[Z_1, Z_2] = \sum_{i=1}^{n} \left\{b_i \sum_{j=1}^{M} d_j Cov[Y_j, X_i]\right\}.$$

C.3.3 Covariance Matrix

Let X denote the n element vector containing the random variates $X_i, i = 1, \ldots, n$. The mean and variance of the ith variate are then $E[X_i]$ and $E\left[(X_i - E[X_i])^2\right]$ respectively. The covariance $Cov[X]_{ij}$ between the ith and jth variates is $E[(X_i - E[X_i])(X_j - E[X_j])]$. The elements of n by n covariance matrix $Cov[X]$ are then

$$Cov[X]_{ij} = E[(X_i - E[X_i])(X_j - E[X_j])], \quad i = 1, \ldots, n, j = 1, \ldots, n. \tag{C.3.1}$$

We will now show that $Cov[X + A] = Cov[X]$ where A is an n element vector containing the constants $A_i, i = 1, \ldots, n$. Since $E[X_i + A_i] = E[X_i] + A_i$, we obtain

$$Var[(X + A)_i] = Var[X_i + A_i]$$

$$= E\left[(X_i + A_i - E[X_i + A_i])^2\right] = E\left[(X_i - E[X_i])^2\right]$$

and

$$Cov[X + A]_{ij} = E[(X_i + A_i - E[X_i + A_i])(X_j + A_j - E[X_j + A_j])]$$

$$= E\left[(X_i - E[X_i])(X_j - E[X_j])\right]$$

$$= Cov[X]_{ij}. \tag{C.3.2}$$

C.4 CONDITIONAL MEAN AND COVARIANCE OF NORMAL DISTRIBUTIONS

Let $X = [X_1/X_2]$ be distributed as $N_p(\mu, \Sigma)$ with $\mu = [\mu_1/\mu_2]$, and $\Sigma = [(\Sigma_{11}|\Sigma_{12})/(\Sigma_{21}|\Sigma_{22})]$, and $|\Sigma_{22}| > 0$.

We will prove that the conditional distribution of X_1, given that $X_2 = x_2$, is normal and has

Mean $= \mu_1 + \Sigma_{12}\Sigma_{22}^{-1}(x_2 - \mu_2)$, and covariance $= \Sigma_{11} - \Sigma_{12}\Sigma_{22}^{-1}\Sigma_{21}$.

Let the inverse of Σ be Σ^{-1}, where

$$\Sigma^{-1} = \begin{pmatrix} \Sigma^{11} & \Sigma^{12} \\ \Sigma^{21} & \Sigma^{22} \end{pmatrix}. \tag{C.4.1}$$

So $\Sigma^{-1}\Sigma = I_p$, where I_p represents the $p \times p$ unit matrix, and

$$\begin{pmatrix} \Sigma^{11} & \Sigma^{12} \\ \Sigma^{21} & \Sigma^{22} \end{pmatrix} \begin{pmatrix} \Sigma_{11} & \Sigma_{12} \\ \Sigma_{21} & \Sigma_{22} \end{pmatrix} = \begin{pmatrix} I_q & 0 \\ 0 & I_{p-q} \end{pmatrix}. \tag{C.4.2}$$

Multiplying out these matrices yields the following equations:

$$\Sigma^{11}\Sigma_{11} + \Sigma^{21}\Sigma_{21} = I_q, \tag{C.4.3}$$

$$\Sigma^{21}\Sigma_{11} + \Sigma^{22}\Sigma_{22} = 0, \tag{C.4.4}$$

$$\Sigma^{11}\Sigma_{12} + \Sigma^{12}\Sigma_{22} = 0, \tag{C.4.5}$$

$$\Sigma^{21}\Sigma_{12} + \Sigma^{22}\Sigma_{22} = I_{p-q}. \tag{C.4.6}$$

Multiplying equation (C.4.5) on the left by $(\Sigma^{11})^{-1}$ and on the right by Σ_{22}^{-1} gives

$$(\Sigma^{11})^{-1}\Sigma^{12} = -\Sigma_{12}\Sigma_{22}^{-1}. \tag{C.4.7}$$

Multiplying equation (C.4.3) on the left by $(\Sigma^{11})^{-1}$ yields

$$\Sigma_{11} + (\Sigma^{11})^{-1}\Sigma^{12}\Sigma_{21} = (\Sigma_{11})^{-1}, \tag{C.4.8}$$

and substituting for $(\Sigma^{11})^{-1}\Sigma^{12}$ from equation (C.4.7) into equation (C.4.8) gives

$$(\Sigma_{11})^{-1} = \Sigma_{11} - \Sigma_{12}\Sigma_{22}^{-1}\Sigma_{21}. \tag{C.4.9}$$

The joint probability density function of x is

$$f(x) = (2\pi)^{-p/2}|\Sigma|^{-1/2}\exp\left\{-\frac{1}{2}(x-\mu)^T\Sigma^{-1}(x-\mu)\right\},$$

writing x, μ, and Σ^{-1} in their partitioned form and expanding gives

$$f(x) = (2\pi)^{-p/2}|\Sigma|^{-1/2}\exp\left[-\frac{1}{2}\left\{(x_1-\mu_1)^T\Sigma^{11}(x_1-\mu_1)\right.\right.$$

$$\left.\left. +2(x_1-\mu_1)^T\Sigma^{12}(x_2-\mu_2) + (x_2-\mu_2)^T\Sigma^{22}(x_2-\mu_2)\right\}\right]. \tag{C.4.10}$$

The conditional distribution of x_1 given the value of x_2 is thus obtained by dividing this density by the marginal density of x_2 and treating x_2 as constant in the resulting expression. The only portion of the resultant that is not constant is the portion involving terms in x_1. It can easily be shown that

$$f(x_1|x_2) \propto \exp\left[-\frac{1}{2}\left\{(x_1-\mu_1)^T\Sigma^{11}(x_1-\mu_1) + 2(x_1-\mu_1)^T\Sigma^{12}(x_2-\mu_2)\right\}\right],$$

where the constant of proportionality is obtained using $\int f(x_1|x_2)dx_1 = 1$.

If we let $G = (x_1 - \mu_1)^T \Sigma^{11}(x_1 - \mu_1) + 2(x_1 - \mu_1)^T \Sigma^{12}(x_2 - \mu_2)$, we then obtain

$$G = (x_1 - \mu_1)^T \Sigma^{11}(x_1 - \mu_1) + (x_1 - \mu_1)^T \Sigma^{12}(x_2 - \mu_2)$$
$$+ (x_2 - \mu_2)^T \Sigma^{21}(x_1 - \mu_1),$$

$$G = \left\{x_1 - \mu_1 + (\Sigma^{11})^{-1}\Sigma^{12}(x_2 - \mu_2)\right\}^T \Sigma^{11} \left\{x_1 - \mu_1 + (\Sigma^{11})^{-1}\Sigma^{12}(x_2 - \mu_2)\right\}$$
$$- (x_2 - \mu_2)^T \Sigma^{21}(\Sigma^{12})^{-1}(x_2 - \mu_2), \tag{C.4.11}$$

where for instance we have used the fact that the scalar quantity

$$\left\{(x_1 - \mu_1)^T \Sigma^{12}(x_2 - \mu_2)\right\} = (x_2 - \mu_2)^T \Sigma^{21}(x_1 - \mu_1).$$

Since the last term in equation (C.4.11) only involves constants (as far as $f(x_1|x_2)$ is concerned), it follows that

$$f(x_1|x_2) \propto \exp\left[-\frac{1}{2}\left\{x_1 - \mu_1 + (\Sigma^{11})^{-1}\Sigma^{12}(x_2 - \mu_2)\right\}^T\right.$$
$$\left. \times \Sigma^{11}\left\{x_1 - \mu_1 + (\Sigma^{11})^{-1}\Sigma^{12}(x_2 - \mu_2)\right\}\right],$$

which is the density of a multivariate normal distribution that has a mean of $\mu_1 - (\Sigma^{11})^{-1}\Sigma^{12}(x_2 - \mu_2)$, which from equation (C.4.7) can be expressed as $\mu_1 + \Sigma_{12}\Sigma_{22}^{-1}(x_2 - \mu_2)$. The covariance matrix is $(\Sigma^{11})^{-1}$, which from equation (C.4.9) can be written as $\Sigma_{11} - \Sigma_{12}\Sigma_{22}^{-1}\Sigma_{21}$.

C.5 MOMENT GENERATING FUNCTIONS

If x is a random variable with probability distribution $f_x(x)$, then the moment generating function $M_x(t)$ is defined by

$$M_x(t) = E\left[e^{tx}\right] = \int_{-\infty}^{\infty} e^{tx} f_x(x)dx.$$

We can expand the above expression as follows:

$$E\left[e^{tx}\right] = E\left[1 + tx + \frac{1}{2}(tx)^2 + +\right],$$

$$M_x(t) = 1 + tE\left[x\right] + \frac{1}{2}t^2 E\left[x^2\right] + +. \tag{C.5.1}$$

Now

$$\frac{d^k (M_x(t))}{dt^k} = \frac{d^k}{dt^k}\{E\left[e^{tx}\right]\} = E\left[\frac{d^k e^{tx}}{dt^k}\right] = E\left[x^k e^{tx}\right].$$

For $t = 0$, we thus have

$$\left.\frac{d^k (M_x(t))}{dt^k}\right|_{t=0} = \frac{d^k (M_x(0))}{dt^k} = E\left[x^k e^0\right] = E\left[x^k\right]. \tag{C.5.2}$$

Moment generating function of a linear function of a random variable x

If the random variable y is defined as $y = ax+b$, then the moment generating function of y, $M_y(t)$ is obtained as follows:

$$M_y(t) = M_{ax+b}(t) = E\left[e^{ty}\right] = E\left[e^{atx+bt}\right] = e^{bt} E\left[e^{tx}\right].$$

Therefore,

$$M_y(t) = e^{bt} M_x(at). \tag{C.5.3}$$

Moment generating function of a linear combination of random variables

Let $z = x + y$ where x and y are independent random variables then

$$M_z(t) = E\left[e^{tz}\right] = E\left[e^{x+y}\right] = E\left[e^{tx} e^{ty}\right].$$

Since x and y are independent,

$$E\left[e^{tx} e^{ty}\right] = E\left[e^{tx}\right] E\left[e^{ty}\right] = M_x(t) M_y(t).$$

More generally, if $s_n = \sum_{i=1}^n x_i$ where $x_i, i = 1,\ldots,n$ are independent variables, then

$$M_{s_n}(t) = \prod_{i=1}^n M_{x_i}(t). \tag{C.5.4}$$

If $x_i, i = 1,\ldots,n$ are *IID*, then we have

$$M_{s_n}(t) = E\left[\exp\left(t \sum_{i=1}^n x_i\right)\right] = \left(E\left[e^{tx}\right]\right)^n = \left(M_x(t)\right)^n. \tag{C.5.5}$$

Appendix D

Statistical Distribution Functions

D.1 THE NORMAL (GAUSSIAN) DISTRIBUTION

Here, we describe some properties of the normal distribution. If x comes from a normal distribution, then the associated moment generating function, $M_x(t)$ is given by

$$M_x(t) = E\left[e^{tx}\right]$$

$$= \frac{1}{\sigma\sqrt{2\pi}} \int_{-\infty}^{\infty} \exp(tx) \exp\left(-\frac{(x-\mu)^2}{2\sigma^2}\right) dx$$

$$= \frac{1}{\sigma\sqrt{2\pi}} \int_{-\infty}^{\infty} \exp\left(-\frac{(x-\mu)^2 - 2\sigma^2 tx}{2\sigma^2}\right) dx.$$

Now completing the square we have

$$-\frac{1}{2\sigma^2}\left\{(x-\mu)^2 - 2t\sigma^2 x\right\} = -\frac{1}{2\sigma^2}\left\{x^2 + \mu^2 - 2\mu x - 2t\sigma^2\right\}$$

$$= -\frac{1}{2\sigma^2}\left\{\left(x - \sigma^2 t - \mu\right)^2 - 2\mu t\sigma^2 - \sigma^4 t^2\right\}$$

$$= \mu t + \frac{\sigma^2 t^2}{2} - \frac{1}{2\sigma^2}\left\{\left(x - \sigma^2 t - \mu\right)^2\right\}. \quad \text{(D.1.1)}$$

We thus have

$$E\left[e^{tx}\right] = \frac{1}{\sigma\sqrt{2\pi}} \exp\left(\mu t + \frac{\sigma^2 t^2}{2}\right) \int_{x=-\infty}^{x=\infty} \exp\left(-\frac{(x - \sigma^2 t - \mu)^2}{2\sigma^2}\right) dx.$$

Now letting $y = x - \sigma^2 t - \mu$, $dx = dy$, and

$$E\left[e^{tx}\right] = \frac{1}{\sigma\sqrt{2\pi}} \exp\left(\mu t + \frac{\sigma^2 t^2}{2}\right) \int_{y=-\infty}^{y=\infty} \exp\left(-\frac{y^2}{2\sigma^2}\right) dy$$

$$= \frac{1}{\sigma\sqrt{2\pi}} \sigma\sqrt{2\pi} \exp\left(\mu t + \frac{\sigma^2 t^2}{2}\right)$$

$$= \exp\left(\mu t + \frac{\sigma^2 t^2}{2}\right),$$

where we have used (see Appendix E.1) the fact that

$$\int_{-\infty}^{\infty} \exp\left(-ay^2\right) dy = \sqrt{\frac{\pi}{a}}.$$

Thus, the moment generating function $M_x(t)$ for a normal distribution with mean μ and variance σ^2 is

$$M_x(t) = \exp\left(\mu t + \frac{\sigma^2 t^2}{2}\right).$$

Some Elementary Results Involving the Mean and Variance of a Normal Distribution

From first principles, we have the following:

The mean:

$$E[x] = \frac{1}{\sigma\sqrt{2\pi}} \int_{x=-\infty}^{x=\infty} x \exp\left(-\frac{(x-\mu)^2}{2\sigma^2}\right) dx.$$

Letting $y = x - \mu$ we have $dx = dy$ and $x = y + \mu$; therefore,

$$E[x] = \frac{1}{\sigma\sqrt{2\pi}} \int_{y=-\infty}^{y=\infty} (y + \mu) \exp\left(-\frac{y^2}{2\sigma^2}\right) dy,$$

$$E[x] = \mu\frac{1}{\sigma\sqrt{2\pi}} \int_{y=-\infty}^{y=\infty} \exp\left(-\frac{y^2}{2\sigma^2}\right) dy + \frac{1}{\sigma\sqrt{2\pi}} \int_{y=-\infty}^{y=\infty} y \exp\left(-\frac{y^2}{2\sigma^2}\right) dy.$$

Since

$$\int_{-\infty}^{\infty} y \exp\left(-\frac{y^2}{2\sigma^2}\right) dy = 0,$$

we have using the integral result (i) in Appendix E.1 with $a = 1/2\sigma^2$,

$$E[x] = \mu\frac{1}{\sigma\sqrt{2\pi}} \int_{-\infty}^{\infty} \exp\left(-\frac{y^2}{2\sigma^2}\right) dy = \mu.$$

The variance:

$$E\left[x^2\right] = \frac{1}{\sigma\sqrt{2\pi}} \int_{x=-\infty}^{x=\infty} x^2 \exp\left(-\frac{(x-\mu)^2}{2\sigma^2}\right) dx.$$

Letting $y = x - \mu$ we have $dx = dy$ and $x^2 = y^2 + 2\mu y + \mu^2$; therefore,

$$E\left[x^2\right] = \frac{1}{\sigma\sqrt{2\pi}} \int_{y=-\infty}^{y=\infty} \left(y^2 + 2\mu y + \mu^2\right) \exp\left(-\frac{y^2}{2\sigma^2}\right) dy,$$

$$E\left[x^2\right] = \mu^2\frac{1}{\sigma\sqrt{2\pi}} \int_{-\infty}^{\infty} \exp\left(-\frac{y^2}{2\sigma^2}\right) dy + \frac{1}{\sigma\sqrt{2\pi}} \int_{-\infty}^{\infty} y^2 \exp\left(-\frac{y^2}{2\sigma^2}\right) dy.$$

So

$$E\left[x^2\right] = \mu^2 + \sigma^2,$$

where we have used (see Appendix E.1 result(ii) with $a = 1/2\sigma^2$) that

$$\frac{1}{\sigma \sqrt{2\pi}} \int_{-\infty}^{\infty} y^2 \exp\left(-\frac{y^2}{2\sigma^2}\right) dy = \sigma^2.$$

Therefore,

$$Var\,[x] = E\left[x^2\right] - (E\,[x])^2 = \mu^2 + \sigma^2 - \mu^2 = \sigma^2.$$

The mean and variance can also be obtained by using the moment generating function, $M_x(t)$.

From Appendix C.5,

$$E\,[x] = \left.\frac{dM_x(t)}{dt}\right|_{t=0} = \left.\frac{d}{dt}\left\{\exp\left(\mu t + \frac{\sigma^2 t^2}{2}\right)\right\}\right|_{t=0}$$

$$= \left.\left(\mu + \sigma^2 t\right)\exp\left(\mu t + \frac{\sigma^2 t^2}{2}\right)\right|_{t=0} = \mu$$

also

$$E\left[x^2\right] = \left.\frac{d^2 M_x(t)}{dt^2}\right|_{t=0} = \left.\frac{d}{dt}\left\{\left(\mu + \sigma^2 t\right)\exp\left(\mu t + \frac{\sigma^2 t^2}{2}\right)\right\}\right|_{t=0},$$

$$E\left[x^2\right] = \left.\left\{\exp\left(\mu t + \frac{\sigma^2 t^2}{2}\right)\left(\left(\mu + \sigma^2 t\right)^2 + \sigma^2\right)\right\}\right|_{t=0}$$

$$= \mu^2 + \sigma^2.$$

These results are the same as those we previously derived from first principles,

$$E\,[x] = \mu \quad \text{and} \quad E\left[x^2\right] = \mu^2 + \sigma^2.$$

D.2 THE LOGNORMAL DISTRIBUTION

If the variable x follows a lognormal distribution, then the probability density function $f(x)$ is given by

$$\frac{1}{x\sigma \sqrt{2\pi}} \exp\left(-\frac{(\log(x) - \mu)^2}{2\sigma^2}\right), \tag{D.2.1}$$

where $x > 0$. Here, we denote the lognormal distribution for x as $x \sim \Lambda\left(\mu, \sigma^2\right)$. Setting $y = \log(x)$, it can be seen that $y \sim N\left(\mu, \sigma^2\right)$. Thus, if x is a lognormal distribution $\Lambda\left(\mu, \sigma^2\right)$, then $\log(x)$ is a normal distribution with mean μ and variance σ^2. Conversely, if $y \sim N\left(\mu, \sigma^2\right)$, then the distribution for $x = e^y$ is $x \sim \Lambda\left(\mu, \sigma^2\right)$.

The expectation of the tth moment (where t is a positive integer) of x is thus

$$E\left[x^t\right] = \frac{1}{\sigma\sqrt{2\pi}} \int_{x=-\infty}^{x=\infty} x^t \frac{1}{x} \exp\left(-\frac{(\log(x) - \mu)^2}{2\sigma^2}\right) dx.$$

Using $y = \log(x)$, we have

$$\frac{dy}{dx} = \frac{d\log(x)}{dx} = \frac{1}{x}, \quad dx = x\,dy \text{ and } x^t = (e^y)^t = e^{ty}.$$

Thus,

$$E\left[x^t\right] = E\left[e^{ty}\right] = M_y(t) = \frac{1}{\sigma\sqrt{2\pi}} \int_{y=-\infty}^{y=\infty} e^{ty} \exp\left(-\frac{(y - \mu)^2}{2\sigma^2}\right) dy,$$

where $M_y(t)$ is the moment generating function of a normal distribution with mean μ and variance σ^2.

From Appendix D.1,

$$E\left[x^t\right] = M_y(t) = \exp\left(\mu t + \frac{\sigma^2 t^2}{2}\right).$$

Therefore, if $x \sim \Lambda\left(\mu, \sigma^2\right)$, then
for $t = 1$,

$$E[x] = \exp\left(\mu + \frac{\sigma^2}{2}\right), \tag{D.2.2}$$

for $t = 2$,

$$E\left[x^2\right] = \exp\left(2\mu + 2\sigma^2\right), \tag{D.2.3}$$

and the variance is obtained using

$$Var[x] = E\left[x^2\right] - (E[x])^2 = \exp\left(2\mu + 2\sigma^2\right) - \exp\left(2\mu + \sigma^2\right).$$

So

$$Var[x] = \exp\left(2\mu + \sigma^2\right)\left(\exp\left(\sigma^2\right) - 1\right)$$

or

$$Var[x] = (E[x])^2 \left(\exp\left(\sigma^2\right) - 1\right). \tag{D.2.4}$$

Note: If $x_1 = \exp(\mu + \sigma Z)$, where $Z \sim N(0, 1)$, then $x_1 \sim \Lambda\left(\mu, \sigma^2\right)$. So $E[x_1]$ and $Var[x_1]$ are given by equations (D.2.2) and (D.2.4).

D.3 THE STUDENT'S t DISTRIBUTION

This section derives an expression for the kurtosis of the Student's t distribution.
Since the Student's t distribution density function is

$$f(\epsilon_i) = \mathcal{K}\left[1 + \frac{\epsilon_i^2}{h_i(\nu - 2)}\right]^{-\frac{(\nu+1)}{2}},$$

where

$$\mathcal{K} = \frac{\Gamma((v + 1)/2)(v - 2)^{-\frac{1}{2}} h_i^{-\frac{1}{2}}}{\pi^{\frac{1}{2}} \Gamma(v/2)},$$

we have

$$E[\epsilon_i^2] = 2\mathcal{K} \int_0^\infty \frac{\epsilon_i^2 d\epsilon_i}{\left(1 + \epsilon_i^2/(h_i(v - 2))\right)^{(v+1)/2}}$$

$$= 2\mathcal{K}(h_i(v - 2))^{\frac{(v+1)}{2}} \int_0^\infty \frac{\epsilon_i^2 d\epsilon_i}{(h_i(v - 2) + \epsilon_i^2)^{(v+1)/2}}.$$

Using the standard integrals in Appendix E.1 with $a = 2$, $b = 2$, $c = (v + 1)/2$, and $m = (v - 2)h_i$ gives

$$\frac{m^{\frac{a+1-bc}{b}}}{b} = \frac{(h_i(v - 2))^{\frac{2-v}{2}}}{2}, \qquad \Gamma\left(\frac{a + 1}{b}\right) = \Gamma(3/2),$$

$$\Gamma\left(c - \frac{a + 1}{b}\right) = \Gamma\left(\frac{v - 2}{2}\right), \qquad \Gamma(c) = \Gamma\left(\frac{v + 1}{2}\right).$$

This gives

$$E[\epsilon_i^2] = 2\mathcal{K} (h_i(v - 2))^{\frac{v+1}{2}} \left\{ \frac{(h_i(v - 2))^{\frac{2-v}{2}} \sqrt{\pi} \Gamma((v - 2)/2)}{4\Gamma((v + 1)/2)} \right\}.$$

Substituting for $\mathcal{K}$ and simplifying, we obtain

$$E[\epsilon_i^2] = \frac{h_i(v - 2)\Gamma((v - 1)/2)}{\Gamma(v/2)}.$$

But

$$\left(\frac{v - 2}{2}\right) \Gamma\left(\frac{v - 2}{2}\right) = \Gamma\left(\frac{v - 1}{2} + 1\right) = \Gamma\left(\frac{v}{2}\right).$$

So

$$E[\epsilon_i^2] = \frac{h_i(v - 2)\Gamma(v/2)}{2(v - 2)\Gamma(v/2)} = h_i.$$

Similarly, we have

$$E[\epsilon_i^4] = 2\mathcal{K} \int_0^\infty \frac{\epsilon_i^4 d\epsilon_i}{\left(1 + \epsilon_i^2/(h_i(v - 2))\right)^{(v+1)/2}}$$

$$= 2\mathcal{K}(h_i(v - 2))^{\frac{(v+1)}{2}} \int_0^\infty \frac{\epsilon_i^4 d\epsilon_i}{(h_i(v - 2) + \epsilon_i^2)^{(v+1)/2}}.$$

Using the standard integrals in Appendix E.1 with $a = 4$, $b = 2$, $c = (v + 1)/2$, and $m = (v - 2)h_i$ gives

$$\frac{m^{\frac{a+1-bc}{b}}}{b} = \frac{(h_i(v - 2))^{\frac{4-v}{2}}}{2}, \qquad \Gamma\left(\frac{a + 1}{b}\right) = \Gamma(5/2),$$

$$\Gamma\left(c - \frac{a + 1}{b}\right) = \Gamma\left(\frac{v - 4}{2}\right), \qquad \Gamma(c) = \Gamma\left(\frac{v + 1}{2}\right)$$

and

$$E[\epsilon_i^4] = 2\mathcal{K} \, (h_i(\nu - 2))^{\frac{\nu+1}{2}} \left\{ \frac{(h_i(\nu - 2))^{\frac{4-\nu}{2}} 3 \sqrt{\pi} \, \Gamma((\nu - 4)/2)}{8\Gamma((\nu + 1)/2)} \right\}.$$

Substituting for $\mathcal{K}$ and simplifying, we obtain

$$E[\epsilon_i^4] = \frac{3h_i(\nu - 2)^2 \Gamma((\nu - 4)/2) h_i^2}{4\Gamma(\nu/2)}.$$

But

$$\left(\frac{\nu - 4}{2}\right) \Gamma\left(\frac{\nu - 4}{2}\right) = \Gamma\left(\frac{\nu - 2}{2}\right)$$

and

$$\left(\frac{\nu - 2}{2}\right) \Gamma\left(\frac{\nu - 2}{2}\right) = \Gamma\left(\frac{\nu}{2}\right).$$

Therefore,

$$\Gamma\left(\frac{\nu - 4}{2}\right) = \frac{4\Gamma(\nu/2)}{(\nu - 4)(\nu - 2)}.$$

So

$$E[\epsilon_i^4] = \frac{3(\nu - 2)^2 4\Gamma(\nu/2) h_i^2}{4\Gamma(\nu/2)(\nu - 4)(\nu - 2)}$$

$$= \frac{3(\nu - 2) h_i^2}{(\nu - 4)}.$$

The kurtosis is then

$$\aleph = \frac{E[e_i^4]}{(E[e_i^2])^2} = \frac{3(\nu - 2) h_i^2}{(\nu - 4) h_i^2} = \frac{3(\nu - 2)}{(\nu - 4)}. \tag{D.3.1}$$

D.4 THE GENERAL ERROR DISTRIBUTION

This section proves various relations for the generalized error distribution.

The density function for the generalized error distribution is

$$f(\epsilon_i) = \mathcal{K} \exp\left(-\frac{1}{2} \left|\frac{\epsilon_i}{\lambda}\right|^a\right), \quad \text{where} \quad \mathcal{K} = \frac{a}{\lambda \, 2^{(1+1/a)} \, \Gamma(1/a)}. \tag{D.4.1}$$

D.4.1 Value of λ for Variance h_i

Calculation of the scale factor λ required for a generalized error distribution with mean 0 and variance h_i.

The variance of the distribution, $E(\epsilon_i^2)$, is given by

$$E(\epsilon_i^2) = \mathcal{K} \int_{-\infty}^{\infty} \epsilon_i^2 \exp\left(-\frac{1}{2} \left|\frac{\epsilon_i}{\lambda}\right|^a\right) d\epsilon_i = 2\mathcal{K} \int_{0}^{\infty} \epsilon_i^2 \exp\left(-\frac{1}{2} \left(\frac{\epsilon_i}{\lambda}\right)^a\right) d\epsilon_i.$$

Using the standard integrals in Appendix E.1 with $n = 2$, $p = a$, and $b = (1/2)(1/\lambda)^a$ gives

$$h_i = \frac{2\mathcal{K}}{a}\Gamma\left(\frac{3}{a}\right)\left\{\frac{1}{2}\left(\frac{1}{\lambda}\right)^a\right\}^{-3/a},$$

which after some simplification yields

$$h_i = \frac{2\,\mathcal{K}\,2^{3/a}\,\lambda^3}{a}\Gamma\left(\frac{3}{a}\right).$$

Substituting for $\mathcal{K}$ and simplifying then gives

$$h_i = \lambda^2\,2^{2/a}\,\frac{\Gamma(3/a)}{\Gamma(1/a)}.$$

The required value of λ is therefore

$$\lambda = \left\{h_i\,2^{-2/a}\,\frac{\Gamma(1/a)}{\Gamma(3/a)}\right\}^{1/2}.$$

D.4.2 The Kurtosis

$$E(\epsilon_i^4) = \mathcal{K}\int_{-\infty}^{\infty}\epsilon_i^4\exp\left(-\frac{1}{2}\left|\frac{\epsilon_i}{\lambda}\right|^a\right)d\epsilon_i$$

$$= 2\mathcal{K}\int_0^{\infty}\epsilon_i^4\exp\left(-\frac{1}{2}\left(\frac{\epsilon_i}{\lambda}\right)^a\right)d\epsilon_i.$$

However from standard mathematical tables

$$\int_0^{\infty}\epsilon_i^4\exp\left(-b\,\epsilon_i^p\right) = \frac{\Gamma(k)}{p\,b^k},$$

where $p = a$, $b = \frac{1}{2}\left(\frac{1}{\lambda}\right)^a$ and $k = \frac{5}{a}$ which gives

$$E[\epsilon_i^4] = \frac{2\,\mathcal{K}\,2^{5/a}\,\lambda^5}{a}\Gamma\left(\frac{5}{a}\right)$$

$$= 2^{2/a}\,\lambda^2\,h_i\,\frac{\Gamma(5/a)}{\Gamma(3/a)}.$$

From Appendix E.1, we have

$$E[\epsilon_i^2] = h_i = \frac{2\,\mathcal{K}\,2^{3/a}\,\lambda^3}{a}\Gamma\left(\frac{3}{a}\right)\quad\text{and}\quad\lambda^2 = \frac{h_i\,2^{-2/a}\,\Gamma(1/a)}{\Gamma(3/a)}.$$

Therefore,

$$E[\epsilon_i^4] = h_i^2\,\frac{\Gamma(5/a)\,\Gamma(1/a)}{\Gamma(3/a)\,\Gamma(3/a)},$$

which gives the kurtosis as

$$\aleph = \frac{E[\epsilon_i^4]}{(E[\epsilon_i^2])^2} = \frac{h_i^2\,\Gamma(5/a)\,\Gamma(1/a)}{h_i^2\,\Gamma(3/a)\,\Gamma(3/a)} = \frac{\Gamma(5/a)\,\Gamma(1/a)}{\Gamma(3/a)\,\Gamma(3/a)}.$$

D.4.3 The Distribution for Shape Parameter, a

If the distribution has variance h_i, then from Appendix D.4.1

$$\lambda = \left(\frac{2^{-2/a}\, \Gamma(1/a)\, h_i}{\Gamma(3/a)} \right)^{1/2}.$$

Now for $0 < x < 1$ we have $\Gamma(1 + x) = 1 + a_1 x + a_2 x^2 + a_3 x^3 + +$, where the coefficients are $|a_i| < 1$, see Abramowitz and Stegun (1968). Since $x\Gamma(x) = \Gamma(1 + x)$, to third order in x, we have:
$x\Gamma(x) = 1 + a_1 x + a_2 x^2 + a_3 x^3$.
This gives $\Gamma(x) = \dfrac{1}{x} + a_1 + a_2 x + a_3 x^2$ and $\Gamma(x) \approx \dfrac{1}{x}$ as $x \longrightarrow 0$.
So as $a \longrightarrow \infty$, we have the following:

$$2^{(1+1/a)} \approx 2, \quad 2^{-2/a} \approx 1, \quad \frac{1}{\Gamma(1/a)} \approx \frac{1}{a},$$

$$\frac{\Gamma(1/a)}{\Gamma(3/a)} \approx \frac{3a}{a} = 3, \quad \text{and} \quad \frac{\Gamma(5/a)}{\Gamma(3/a)} \approx \frac{3a}{5a} = \frac{3}{5}.$$

The kurtosis is then

$$\aleph = \frac{\Gamma(5/a)\,\Gamma(1/a)}{\Gamma(3/a)\,\Gamma(3/a)} = \frac{9}{5}.$$

Also as $a \to \infty$ $\lambda \approx (3h_i)^{1/2}$ and for the range $-(3h_i)^{1/2} < \epsilon_i < (3h_i)^{1/2}$, we have

$$\left| \frac{\epsilon_i}{\lambda} \right|^a \approx \left| \frac{\epsilon_i}{(3h_i)^{1/2}} \right| \approx 0, \quad \text{and therefore } \exp\left(-\frac{1}{2}\left| \frac{\epsilon_i}{\lambda} \right|^a \right) \approx 1.$$

Substituting the above results into equation (D.4.1), the probability density function reduces to

$$f(\epsilon_i) \approx \frac{1}{2(3h_i)^{1/2}},$$

which is a uniform distribution $\mathcal{U}(-(3h_i)^{1/2}, (3h_i)^{1/2})$, with lower limit $-(3h_i)^{1/2}$ and upper limit $-(3h_i)^{1/2}$.

Appendix E

Mathematical Reference

E.1 STANDARD INTEGRALS

$$\int_0^\infty \exp\left(-ay^2\right) dy = \frac{1}{2}\sqrt{\frac{\pi}{a}}, \quad (i)$$

$$\int_0^\infty y \exp\left(-ay^2\right) dy = \frac{1}{2}, \quad (ii)$$

$$\int_0^\infty y^2 \exp\left(-ay^2\right) dy = \frac{1}{4a}\sqrt{\frac{\pi}{a}}, \quad (iii)$$

$$\int_0^\infty y^4 \exp\left(-ay^2\right) dy = \frac{3}{8a^2}\sqrt{\frac{\pi}{a}}, \quad (iv)$$

$$\int_0^\infty y^{2n} \exp\left(-ay^2\right) dy = \frac{1 \times 3 \times 5 \ldots (2n-1)}{2^{n+1} a^n}\sqrt{\frac{\pi}{a}}, \quad (v)$$

$$\int_0^\infty \epsilon_i^n \exp\left(-b\,\epsilon_i^p\right) = \frac{\Gamma(k)}{p\,b^k}, \quad \text{where } n > -1, p > 0, b > 0, \text{ and } k = \frac{(n+1)}{p}, \quad (vi)$$

$$\int_0^\infty \frac{\epsilon_i^a\, d\epsilon_i}{(m + \epsilon_i^b)^c} = m^{\frac{a+1-bc}{b}} \frac{\Gamma\left((a+1)/b\right)\Gamma\left(c - (a+1)/b\right)}{b\,\Gamma(c)}, \quad (vii)$$

where $a > -1, b > 0, m > 0$, and $c > (a+1)/b$.

E.2 GAMMA FUNCTION

For more detail, see Abramowitz and Stegun (1968)

$$\Gamma(1+x) = x!,$$
$$x\Gamma(x) = \Gamma(x+1),$$
$$\Gamma\left(\frac{1}{2}\right) = \sqrt{\pi},$$
$$\Gamma\left(\frac{3}{2}\right) = \frac{\sqrt{\pi}}{2},$$
$$\Gamma\left(\frac{5}{2}\right) = \frac{3\sqrt{\pi}}{4},$$
$$\frac{\partial \log(\Gamma(x))}{\partial x} = \psi(x).$$

For $0 \le x \le 1$, we have

$$\Gamma(1+x) = 1 + a_1 x + a_2 x^2 + a_3 x^3 + a_4 x^4 + a_5 x^5,$$

where $a_1 = -0.5748, a_2 = 0.9512, a_3 = -0.6998, a_4 = 0.4245$, and $a_5 = -0.1010$.

E.3 THE CUMULATIVE NORMAL DISTRIBUTION FUNCTION

In this section, we show that the cumulative normal distribution function, $N_1(x)$, is related to the complementary error function, erfc(x), by the following equation:

$$N_1(x) = \frac{1}{2}\text{erfc}(-x/\sqrt{2}). \tag{E.3.1}$$

If we let the error function be represented by erf(x), then we have

$$\text{erf}(x) = \frac{2}{\sqrt{\pi}} \int_0^\infty \exp(-t^2)dt.$$

Now we have the following:

$$\text{erfc}(x) = 1 - \text{erf}(x), \quad \text{erf}(-x) = -\text{erf}(x), \quad \text{erf}(\infty) = 1, \quad \text{and } \text{erfc}(-x) = 2 - \text{erfc}(x).$$

We will consider the integral

$$I(x) = \frac{2}{\sqrt{\pi}} \int_{-\infty}^x \exp(-t^2)dt = \frac{2}{\sqrt{\pi}} \int_{-\infty}^0 \exp(-t^2)dt + \frac{2}{\sqrt{\pi}} \int_0^x \exp(-t^2)dt.$$

Since

$$\frac{2}{\sqrt{\pi}} \int_{-\infty}^0 \exp(-t^2)dt = 1.$$

We therefore have

$$I(x) = 1 + \text{erf}(x) = 1 + \{1 - \text{erfc}(x)\} = 2 - \text{erfc}(x).$$

Substituting for erfc(x), we obtain

$$I(x) = 2 - \{2 - \text{erfc}(-x)\} = \text{erfc}(-x).$$

So we have

$$\text{erfc}(-x) = \frac{2}{\sqrt{\pi}} \int_{-\infty}^x \exp(-t^2)dt. \tag{E.3.2}$$

Now the cumulative normal distribution is defined as

$$N_1(x) = \frac{1}{\sqrt{2\pi}} \int_{-\infty}^x \exp(-t^2)\, dt.$$

Letting $u = t\sqrt{2}$, we have $du = \sqrt{2}\, dt$, and for the upper limit, we have $x = t\sqrt{2}$ or $t = x/\sqrt{2}$.
This integral becomes

$$N_1(x) = \frac{1}{\sqrt{2\pi}} \int_\infty^{t=x/\sqrt{2}} \exp(-t^2)\sqrt{2}\, dt. \tag{E.3.3}$$

So from equation (E.3.2), we have

$$N_1(x) = \frac{1}{2}\text{erfc}(-x/\sqrt{2}). \quad \text{QED}$$

We also note that

$$N_1(-x) = 1 - N_1(x).$$

E.4 ARITHMETIC AND GEOMETRIC PROGRESSIONS

Arithmetic progression

The sum of the first n terms of an arithmetic progression is

$$s_n = \frac{n}{2}\{2a_1 + (n-1)d\}, \tag{E.4.1}$$

where a_1 is the first term, and d is the common difference, that is, the terms in the sequence are $a_1,\ a_1 + d,\ a_1 + 2d, a_1 + 3d,\ \ldots$.

Geometric progression

The sum of the first n terms of an arithmetic progression is

$$s_n = \frac{a_1(1 - r^n)}{1 - r}, \tag{E.4.2}$$

where a_1 is the first term, and r is the common ratio, that is, the terms in sequence are $a_1,\ a_1 r,\ a_1 r^2,\ a_1 r^3,\ \ldots$.

Appendix F

Black–Scholes Finite-Difference Schemes

F.1 THE GENERAL CASE

In this section, we consider the stability of the finite-differences schemes described in Chapter 5. It is assumed that the grid contains n_s asset points, and we will denote the time dependent option values at the ith and $(i + 1)$th time instants by the n_{s-2} element vectors X^i and X^{i+1} respectively. We can therefore write

$$T_1 X^i = T_2 X^{i+1}, \tag{F.1.1}$$

where T_1 and T_2 are $n_{s-2} \times n_{s-2}$ tridiagonal matrices, and $x_k^i, k = 1, \ldots, n_{s-2}$ will be used to denote the elements of the vector X^i.

The option values at the ith time instant are computed from those at the $(i + 1)$th time instant by using

$$X^i = T_1^{-1} T_2 X^{i+1}. \tag{F.1.2}$$

However, equation (F.1.2) is only *stable* if the eigenvalues of the $n_{s-2} \times n_{s-2}$ matrix $T_1^{-1} T_2$ all have modulus less than one, see Smith (1985).

F.2 THE LOG TRANSFORMATION AND A UNIFORM GRID

We will now prove that the *implicit* finite-difference method, $\theta_m = 0$, when used on the log transformed Black–Scholes equation with a uniform grid is *unconditionally stable*, which means that the stability does not depend on the values of $\sigma, \Delta t, \Delta Z$, etc.

From Chapter 5, the finite-difference scheme is described by the following tridiagonal system:

$$
\begin{pmatrix}
B & C & 0 & 0 & 0 & 0 \\
A & B & C & 0 & 0 & 0 \\
0 & 0 & . & . & 0 & 0 \\
0 & 0 & 0 & . & . & 0 \\
0 & 0 & 0 & A & B & C \\
0 & 0 & 0 & 0 & A & B
\end{pmatrix}
\begin{pmatrix}
x_1^i \\
x_2^i \\
. \\
. \\
x_{s-1}^i \\
x_{s-2}^i
\end{pmatrix}
=
\begin{pmatrix}
\bar{B} & \bar{C} & 0 & 0 & 0 & 0 \\
\bar{A} & \bar{B} & \bar{C} & 0 & 0 & 0 \\
0 & 0 & . & . & 0 & 0 \\
0 & 0 & 0 & . & . & 0 \\
0 & 0 & 0 & \bar{A} & \bar{B} & \bar{C} \\
0 & 0 & 0 & 0 & \bar{A} & \bar{B}
\end{pmatrix}
\begin{pmatrix}
x_1^{i+1} \\
x_2^{i+1} \\
. \\
. \\
x_{s-3}^{i+1} \\
x_{s-2}^{i+1}
\end{pmatrix},
$$

where

$$A = \frac{(1 - \Theta_m)\Delta t}{2\Delta Z^2}\left\{b\Delta Z - \sigma^2\right\}, \tag{F.2.1}$$

$$B = 1 + (1 - \Theta_m)\Delta t\left\{r + \frac{\sigma^2}{\Delta Z^2}\right\}, \tag{F.2.2}$$

$$C = -\frac{(1 - \Theta_m)\Delta t}{2\Delta Z^2}\left\{b\Delta Z + \sigma^2\right\}, \tag{F.2.3}$$

$$\bar{A} = -\frac{\Theta_m\Delta t}{2\Delta Z^2}\left\{b\Delta Z - \sigma^2\right\}, \tag{F.2.4}$$

$$\bar{B} = 1 - \Theta_m\Delta t\left\{r + \frac{\sigma^2}{\Delta Z^2}\right\}, \tag{F.2.5}$$

$$\bar{C} = \frac{\Theta_m\Delta t}{2\Delta Z^2}\left\{b\Delta Z + \sigma^2\right\}. \tag{F.2.6}$$

As in Chapter 5, $b = r - q - (\sigma^2/2)$, and $r > 0$.

Substituting $\theta_m = 0$ into equations (F.2.1)–(F.2.6), we have $\bar{A} = \bar{C} = 0, \bar{B} = 1$, and

$$A = \frac{\Delta t}{2\Delta Z^2}\left\{b\Delta Z - \sigma^2\right\}, \quad B = 1 + \Delta t\left\{r + \frac{\sigma^2}{\Delta Z^2}\right\}, \quad C = -\frac{\Delta t}{2\Delta Z^2}\left\{b\Delta Z + \sigma^2\right\}.$$

The finite-difference scheme is thus represented by the equations

$$
\begin{pmatrix}
B & C & 0 & 0 & 0 & 0 \\
A & B & C & 0 & 0 & 0 \\
0 & 0 & . & . & 0 & 0 \\
0 & 0 & 0 & . & . & 0 \\
0 & 0 & 0 & A & B & C \\
0 & 0 & 0 & 0 & A & B
\end{pmatrix}
\begin{pmatrix}
x_1^i \\
x_2^i \\
. \\
. \\
x_{s-1}^i \\
x_{s-2}^i
\end{pmatrix}
=
\begin{pmatrix}
1 & & 0 & 0 & 0 & 0 \\
0 & 1 & & 0 & 0 & 0 \\
0 & 0 & . & . & 0 & 0 \\
0 & 0 & 0 & . & . & 0 \\
0 & 0 & 0 & 0 & 1 & 0 \\
0 & 0 & 0 & 0 & 0 & 1
\end{pmatrix}
\begin{pmatrix}
x_1^{i+1} \\
x_2^{i+1} \\
. \\
. \\
x_{s-3}^{i+1} \\
x_{s-2}^{i+1}
\end{pmatrix}
$$

or in matrix notation

$$X^i = T_1^{-1}X^{i+1}, \tag{F.2.7}$$

where $T_2 = I$ in equation (F.1.1).

As mentioned in Appendix F.1, equation (F.2.7) is stable if the moduli of all the eigenvalues of T_1^{-1} are less than one. We will now show that this is in fact the case.

If the eigenvalues of T_1 are $\lambda_k, k = 1, \ldots, n_{s-2}$, then the eigenvalues of T_1^{-1} are $\lambda_k^{-1}, k = 1, \ldots, n_{s-2}$. This means that the system is stable if all the eigenvalues of T_1 have a modulus *greater* than one. This result can be proved by considering the eigenvalue with the smallest modulus, $\lambda_{\min}$. If $|\lambda_{\min}| > 1$, then the result is proved.

Now the eigenvalues of T_1, see Smith (1985), are given by

$$\lambda_k = 1 + \Delta t \left(r + \frac{\sigma^2}{\Delta Z^2} \right) + 2\sqrt{AC}\cos\left(\frac{k\pi}{n_{s-2}+1} \right), \quad k = 1,\ldots,n_{s-2}, \quad \text{(F.2.8)}$$

where the term

$$2\sqrt{AC} = \sqrt{\frac{\Delta t^2 \left(\sigma^4 - b^2 \Delta Z^2 \right)}{\Delta Z^4}}. \quad \text{(F.2.9)}$$

It can be seen that if $b^2 \Delta Z^2 > \sigma^4$, then the eigenvalues are complex, and if $\sigma^4 \geq b^2 \Delta Z^2$, then eigenvalues are real. We will consider each of these cases in turn.

Complex eigenvalues: $b^2 \Delta Z^2 > \sigma^4$

We will represent the kth complex eigenvalue as

$$\lambda_k = R + iY,$$

where the real part is

$$R = 1 + \Delta t \left(r + \frac{\sigma^2}{\Delta Z^2} \right)$$

and the imaginary part is

$$Y = 2\sqrt{AC}\cos\left(\frac{k\pi}{n_{s-2}+1} \right).$$

Since

$$|\lambda_k| > |R| + |Y| \quad \text{and} \quad |R| > 1,$$

we conclude that

$$|\lambda_{\min}| > 1.$$

Real eigenvalues: $\sigma^4 \geq b^2 \Delta Z^2$

In this case, the kth eigenvalue is real, and from equation (F.2.8), we have

$$\lambda_k > 1 + \Delta t \left(r + \frac{\sigma^2}{\Delta Z^2} \right) - 2\sqrt{AC}.$$

Since $b^2 \Delta^2 > 0$ from equation (F.2.9) we have

$$2\sqrt{AC} < \sqrt{\frac{\sigma^4 \Delta t^2}{\Delta Z^4}}$$

or

$$\left| 2\sqrt{AC} \right| < \frac{\sigma^2 \Delta t}{\Delta Z^2}.$$

So

$$\lambda_{\min} > 1 + \Delta t \left(r + \frac{\sigma^2}{\Delta Z^2} \right)' - \frac{\sigma^2 \Delta t}{\Delta Z^2}.$$

Therefore, we have

$$|\lambda_{\min}| > 1 + r \Delta t,$$

and since $r > 0$, we have

$$|\lambda_{\min}| > 1.$$

Appendix G

The Brownian Bridge: Alternative Derivation

Here, we provide an alternative derivation of the Brownian bridge equation given in Chapter 2.

Let a Brownian process have values W_{t_0} at time t_0 and W_{t_1} at time t_1. We want to find the conditional distribution of W_t, where $t_0 < t < t_1$. This distribution will be denoted by $P\left(W_t \mid \{W_{t_0}, W_{t_1}\}\right)$, to indicate that W_t is conditional on the end values W_{t_0} and W_{t_1}.

We have

$$P\left(W_t \mid W_{t_0}\right) = \frac{1}{\sqrt{2\pi(t - t_0)}} \exp\left\{-\frac{(W_t - W_{t_0})^2}{2(t - t_0)}\right\}.$$

The joint distribution of W_t and W_{t_1} given W_{t_0} is

$$P\left(\{W_t, W_{t_1}\} \mid W_{t_0}\right) = P\left(W_{t_1} \mid W_t\right) P\left(W_t \mid W_{t_0}\right)$$

$$= \frac{1}{\sqrt{2\pi(t - t_0)(t_1 - t)}} \exp\left\{-\frac{(W_t - W_{t_0})^2}{2(t - t_0)} - \frac{(W_{t_1} - W_t)^2}{2(t_1 - t)}\right\}$$

$$= \frac{1}{\sqrt{2\pi(t - t_0)(t_1 - t)}} \exp\left\{-\frac{1}{2}\left(\frac{(W_t - W_{t_0})^2}{2(t - t_0)} + \frac{(W_{t_1} - W_t)^2}{2(t_1 - t)}\right)\right\}.$$

Similarly,

$$P\left(W_{t_1} \mid W_{t_0}\right) = \frac{1}{\sqrt{2\pi(t_1 - t_0)}} \exp\left\{-\frac{(W_{t_1} - W_{t_0})^2}{2(t_1 - t_0)}\right\}.$$

Now we have

$$P\left(W_t \mid \{W_{t_0}, W_{t_1}\}\right) = \frac{P\left(W_t, W_{t_1} \mid W_{t_0}\right)}{P\left(W_{t_1} \mid W_{t_0}\right)}$$

$$= \frac{1}{\sqrt{2\pi}} \sqrt{\frac{(t_1 - t_0)}{(t - t_0)(t_1 - t)}}$$

$$\times \exp\left\{-\frac{1}{2}\left(\frac{(W_t - W_{t_0})^2}{2(t - t_0)} + \frac{(W_{t_1} - W_t)^2}{2(t_1 - t)} - \frac{(W_{t_1} - W_{t_0})^2}{2(t_1 - t_0)}\right)\right\}.$$

For ease of reference we will write the above equation as

$$P\left(W_t \mid \{W_{t_0}, W_{t_1}\}\right) = \frac{1}{\sqrt{2\pi}} \sqrt{\frac{(t_1 - t_0)}{(t - t_0)(t_1 - t)}} \exp\{A\}.$$

Computational Finance Using C and C#: Derivatives and Valuation.

We now consider the terms in the exponent A,

$$A = -\frac{1}{2}\left\{ \frac{(X - X_{t_0})^2(t_1 - t)(t_1 - t_0)}{(t - t_0)(t_1 - t)(t_1 - t_0)} + \frac{(X_1 - X)^2(t - t_0)(t_1 - t_0)}{(t - t_0)(t_1 - t)(t_1 - t_0)} \right.$$
$$\left. -\frac{(X_1 - X_{t_0})^2(t - t_0)(t_1 - t)}{(t - t_0)(t_1 - t)(t_1 - t_0)} \right\}.$$

Dividing top and bottom of the above expression for A by $(t_1 - t_0)^2$, we then obtain

$$A = -\frac{1}{2V}\left\{ (W_t^2 + W_{t_0}^2 - 2W_t W_{t_0})\frac{(t_1 - t)}{(t_1 - t_0)} + (W_{t_1}^2 + W_t^2 - 2W_t W_{t_1})\frac{(t - t_0)}{(t_1 - t_0)} \right.$$
$$\left. - (W_{t_1}^2 + W_{t_0}^2 - 2W_{t_1} W_{t_0})\frac{(t - t_0)(t_1 - t)}{(t_1 - t_0)^2} \right\},$$

where

$$V = \frac{(t - t_0)(t_1 - t)}{(t_1 - t_0)}.$$

So

$$A = -\frac{1}{2V}\left(W_t^2\left\{ \frac{(t_1 - t)}{(t_1 - t_0)} + \frac{(t - t_0)}{(t_1 - t_0)} \right\} + W_{t_1}^2\left\{ \frac{(t - t_0)}{(t_1 - t_0)} - \frac{(t - t_0)(t_1 - t)}{(t_1 - t_0)^2} \right\} \right.$$
$$+ W_{t_0}^2\left\{ \frac{(t - t_0)}{(t_1 - t_0)} - \frac{(t - t_0)(t_1 - t)}{(t_1 - t_0)^2} \right\} - 2W_t W_{t_0}\left\{ \frac{(t_1 - t)}{(t_1 - t_0)} \right\}$$
$$\left. - 2W_t W_{t_1}\left\{ \frac{(t - t_0)}{(t_1 - t_0)} \right\} + 2W_{t_1} W_{t_0}\left\{ \frac{(t - t_0)(t_1 - t)}{(t_1 - t_0)^2} \right\} \right).$$

We now show that A can be expressed as quadratic form

$$B = -\frac{1}{2V}(W_t - \mu)^2 = -\frac{1}{2V}(W_t^2 + \mu^2 - 2\mu W_t),$$

where

$$V = \frac{(t - t_0)(t_1 - t)}{(t_1 - t_0)} \quad \text{and} \quad \mu = W_{t_0}\frac{(t_1 - t)}{(t_1 - t_0)} + W_{t_1}\frac{(t - t_0)}{(t_1 - t_0)}.$$

Therefore, we have

$$B = -\frac{1}{2V}\left(W_t^2 + \left\{ W_{t_0}\frac{(t_1 - t)}{(t_1 - t_0)} + W_{t_1}\frac{(t - t_0)}{(t_1 - t_0)} \right\}^2 \right.$$
$$\left. -2W_t\left\{ W_{t_0}\frac{(t_1 - t)}{(t_1 - t_0)} + W_{t_1}\frac{(t - t_0)}{(t_1 - t_0)} \right\} \right).$$

Expanding and gathering terms, we obtain

$$B = -\frac{1}{2V}\left(W_t^2 + W_{t_0}^2\frac{(t_1 - t)^2}{(t_1 - t_0)^2} + W_{t_1}^2\frac{(t - t_0)^2}{(t_1 - t_0)^2} + 2W_{t_0} W_{t_1}\frac{(t_1 - t)(t - t_0)}{(t_1 - t_0)^2} \right.$$
$$\left. - 2W_t W_{t_0}\frac{(t_1 - t)}{(t_1 - t_0)} - 2W_t W_{t_1}\frac{(t - t_0)}{(t_1 - t_0)} \right).$$

Comparing coefficients of A and B, we have the following:

Coefficients for W_t^2:

$$A : -\frac{1}{2V} \left\{ \frac{(t_1 - t)}{(t_1 - t_0)} + \frac{(t - t_0)}{(t_1 - t_0)} \right\} = -\frac{1}{2V} \left\{ \frac{t_1 - t + t - t_0}{t_1 - t_0} \right\} = -\frac{1}{2V},$$

$$B : -\frac{1}{2V}.$$

Coefficients for $W_{t_0}^2$:

$$A : -\frac{1}{2V} \left\{ \frac{(t_1 - t)}{(t_1 - t_0)} - \frac{(t - t_0)(t_1 - t)}{(t_1 - t_0)^2} \right\} = -\frac{1}{2V} \left\{ \frac{(t_1 - t)(t_1 - t_0) - (t - t_0)(t_1 - t)}{(t_1 - t_0)^2} \right\},$$

$$A : -\frac{1}{2V} \left\{ \frac{(t_1 - t)(t_1 - t_0 - t + t_0)}{(t_1 - t_0)^2} \right\} = -\frac{1}{2V} \left\{ \frac{(t_1 - t)^2}{(t_1 - t_0)^2} \right\},$$

$$B : -\frac{1}{2V} \left\{ \frac{(t_1 - t)^2}{(t_1 - t_0)^2} \right\}.$$

Coefficients for $W_{t_1}^2$:

$$A : -\frac{1}{2V} \left\{ \frac{(t - t_0)(t_1 - t_0) - (t - t_0)(t_1 - t)}{(t_1 - t_0)^2} \right\} = -\frac{1}{2V} \left\{ \frac{(t - t_0)(t_1 - t_0 - t_1 + t)}{(t_1 - t_0)^2} \right\},$$

$$A : -\frac{1}{2V} \left\{ \frac{(t_1 - t)^2}{(t_1 - t_0)^2} \right\},$$

$$B : -\frac{1}{2V} \left\{ \frac{(t - t_0)^2}{(t_1 - t_0)^2} \right\}.$$

The remaining coefficients in A and B for $W_{t_0} W_{t_1}$, $W_t W_{t_1}$, and $W_{t_0} W_t$ are identical.

We have thus shown that

$$P\left(W_t | \{W_{t_0}, W_{t_1}\}\right) = \frac{1}{\sqrt{2\pi}} \sqrt{\frac{(t_1 - t_0)}{(t - t_0)(t_1 - t)}} \exp\left\{ -\left(\frac{(W_t - \mu)^2}{2V} \right) \right\}$$

$$= \frac{1}{\sqrt{2\pi V}} \exp\left\{ -\left(\frac{(W_t - \mu)^2}{2V} \right) \right\}.$$

Thus, the conditional distribution of W_t is a Gaussian with mean

$$\mu = W_{t_0} \frac{(t_1 - t)}{(t_1 - t_0)} + W_{t_1} \frac{(t - t_0)}{(t_1 - t_0)}$$

and variance

$$V = \frac{(t - t_0)(t_1 - t)}{(t_1 - t_0)},$$

and we can obtain a variate $\hat{W}_t$ from this distribution by using

$$\hat{W}_t = W_{t_0} \frac{(t_1 - t)}{(t_1 - t_0)} + W_{t_1} \frac{(t - t_0)}{(t_1 - t_0)} + \sqrt{\frac{(t - t_0)(t_1 - t)}{(t_1 - t_0)}} Z, \quad \text{where } Z \sim N(0, 1).$$

Appendix H

Brownian Motion: More Results

H.1 SOME RESULTS CONCERNING BROWNIAN MOTION

Here, we will prove some facts concerning Brownian motion.
If the Brownian motion has zero drift, then

$$dX_t = \sigma \sqrt{dt}\, dZ_t, \quad dZ_t \sim N(0,1), \tag{H.1.1}$$

and

$$P\left(m_t^X \le b, X_t \ge x\right) = N_1\left(\frac{2b - x}{\sigma \sqrt{t}}\right), \tag{H.1.2}$$

where m_t^X denotes the minimum value of X_t over the time interval $[0,t]$, $b \le 0$, and $x \ge 0$.

When the Brownian motion has nonzero drift

$$d\bar{X}_t = v dt + \sigma \sqrt{dt}\, dZ_t, \quad dZ_t \sim N(0,1) \tag{H.1.3}$$

and the following equations are satisfied by $m_t^{\bar{X}}$ and $\bar{X}_t$,

$$P\left(\bar{X}_t \le K\right) = N_1\left(\frac{K - vt}{\sigma \sqrt{t}}\right), \tag{H.1.4}$$

$$P\left(\bar{X}_t \ge K\right) = N_1\left(\frac{vt - K}{\sigma \sqrt{t}}\right), \tag{H.1.5}$$

$$P\left(m_t^{\bar{X}} \le b, \bar{X}_t \ge x\right) = \exp\left(\frac{2vb}{\sigma^2}\right) N_1\left(\frac{2b - x + vt}{\sigma \sqrt{t}}\right), \tag{H.1.6}$$

$$P\left(m_t^{\bar{X}} \ge b, \bar{X}_t \ge x\right) = N_1\left(\frac{vt - x}{\sigma \sqrt{t}}\right) - \exp\left(\frac{2vb}{\sigma^2}\right) N_1\left(\frac{2b - x + vt}{\sigma \sqrt{t}}\right), \tag{H.1.7}$$

$$P\left(m_t^{\bar{X}} \le b\right) = N_1\left(\frac{b - vt}{\sigma \sqrt{t}}\right) + \exp\left(\frac{2vb}{\sigma^2}\right) N_1\left(\frac{b + vt}{\sigma \sqrt{t}}\right), \tag{H.1.8}$$

$$P\left(m_t^{\bar{X}} \ge b\right) = N_1\left(\frac{vt - b}{\sigma \sqrt{t}}\right) - \exp\left(\frac{2vb}{\sigma^2}\right) N_1\left(\frac{b + vt}{\sigma \sqrt{t}}\right), \tag{H.1.9}$$

where K is a constant, $\bar{X} \ge 0$, $b \le 0$, and $P(\text{condition})$ denotes the probability associated with the appropriate condition, i.e., $\bar{X}_t \ge K$, $m_t^{\bar{X}} \ge b, \bar{X}_t \ge x$, etc.

The conditional probability density function associated with $P\left(m_t^{\bar{X}} \le b, \bar{X}_t \ge x\right)$ is

$$p\left(\left\{m_{t_1,t_2}^{\bar{X}} \le b, \bar{X}_{t_2}\right\} | \bar{X}_{t_1}\right) = \frac{1}{\sigma \sqrt{2\pi \Delta t}} \exp\left(\frac{2v(b - \bar{X}_{t_1})}{\sigma^2}\right)$$

Computational Finance Using C and C#: Derivatives and Valuation.

$$\times \exp\left(-\frac{(\bar{X}_{t_1} + \bar{X}_{t_2} - 2b + \nu\Delta t)^2}{2\sigma^2 \Delta t}\right), \quad \text{(H.1.10)}$$

where $t_2 \geq t_1$ and $\Delta t = t_2 - t_1$.

H.2 PROOF OF EQUATION (H.1.2)

From equation (H.1.1),

$$X_t = \sigma \sqrt{t} \, Z_t, \quad Z_t \sim N(0,1),$$

where $X_0 = 0$. We will derive the probability of events $m_t^X \leq b$ and $X_t \geq x$ occurring. For event m_t^X to occur, there must be a time τ at which $X_\tau \leq b$, where $0 < \tau \leq t$. At time τ instead of continuing with the original Brownian motion, X_t we will consider the *reflected* motion X_t^R defined by

$$X_s^R = X_s, \quad s < \tau$$
$$X_s^R = 2b - X_s, \quad s \geq \tau.$$

Therefore, before time τ, the motion X_s is identical to X_s^R. For $s \geq \tau$, the *coordinates* of X_s^R are obtained by reflecting those of X_s about the level b. The event $X_t \geq x$ is thus equivalent to the event $X_t^R \leq 2b - x$ (remember $b \leq 0$ and $x \geq 0$). However, the event $X_t^R \leq 2b - x$ only occurs if $m_t^X \leq b$ also occurs, giving

$$P\left(X_t^R \leq 2b - x\right) = P\left(m_t^X \leq b, X_t \leq x\right).$$

At time τ, we have

$$X_\tau^R = 2b - X_\tau, \quad \text{(H.2.1)}$$

and after time τ,

$$X_{\tau+\gamma}^R = 2b - X_{\tau+\gamma}, \quad \gamma > 0. \quad \text{(H.2.2)}$$

Thus, subtracting equation (H.2.1) from equation (H.2.2) gives

$$X_{\tau+\gamma}^R - X_\tau^R = X_\tau - X_{\tau+\gamma},$$
$$X_{\tau+\gamma}^R - X_\tau^R = -\left(X_{\tau+\gamma} - X_\tau\right). \quad \text{(H.2.3)}$$

However, we know that

$$\left(X_{\tau+\gamma} - X_\tau\right) \sim N(0, \sigma^2 \gamma). \quad \text{(H.2.4)}$$

So

$$\left(X_{\tau+\gamma}^R - X_\tau^R\right) \sim -N(0, \sigma^2 \gamma),$$

which means that

$$\left(X_{\tau+\gamma}^R - X_\tau^R\right) \sim N(0, \sigma^2 \gamma). \quad \text{(H.2.5)}$$

Since the left-hand sides of equation (H.2.4) and equation (H.2.5) have the same distribution, and X_t satisfies the three Brownian properties given in Section 2.1, we can write

$$P\left(X_t^R \leq 2b - x\right) = P\left(X_t \leq 2b - x\right)$$
$$= N_1\left(\frac{2b - x}{\sigma \sqrt{t}}\right).$$

Therefore,

$$P\left(m_t^X \le b, X_t \ge x\right) = N_1\left(\frac{2b - x}{\sigma\sqrt{t}}\right).$$

H.3 PROOF OF EQUATION (H.1.4)

From equation (H.1.3), $\bar{X}_t = vt + \sigma\sqrt{t}\,Z_t$, $Z_t \sim N(0,1)$.
So we can write

$$P\left(\bar{X}_t \le K\right) = P\left(vt + \sigma\sqrt{t}\,Z_t \le K\right), \quad Z_t \sim N(0,1)$$

$$= P\left(Z_t \le \frac{K - vt}{\sigma\sqrt{t}}\right)$$

$$= N_1\left(\frac{K - vt}{\sigma\sqrt{t}}\right).$$

H.4 PROOF OF EQUATION (H.1.5)

We know that $P\left(\bar{X}_t \ge K\right) = 1 - P\left(\bar{X}_t \le K\right)$.
 Substituting from equation (H.1.4) gives

$$P\left(\bar{X}_t \ge K\right) = 1 - N_1\left(\frac{K - vt}{\sigma\sqrt{t}}\right).$$

Since $1 - N_1(x) = N_1(-x)$, we obtain

$$P\left(\bar{X}_t \ge K\right) = N_1\left(\frac{vt - K}{\sigma\sqrt{t}}\right).$$

H.5 PROOF OF EQUATION (H.1.6)

From equation (H.1.1),

$$dX_t = \sigma\sqrt{dt}\,dZ_t, \quad dZ_t \sim N(0,1).$$

This can be expressed zero drift Brownian motion under probability measure $\mathbb{P}$,

$$dX_t = \sigma dW^{\mathbb{P}}, \qquad dW^{\mathbb{P}} \sim N(0, dt) \tag{H.5.1}$$

or

$$X_t = \sigma W_t^{\mathbb{P}}, \qquad W_t^{\mathbb{P}} \sim N(0, t).$$

Now we can choose another probability measure $\mathbb{Q}$ so that

$$dW^{\mathbb{P}} = dW^{\mathbb{Q}} + \frac{v}{\sigma}dt, \tag{H.5.2}$$

where v is a constant.
 Under probability measure $\mathbb{Q}$, the motion in equation (H.5.1) is

$$d\bar{X}_t = \sigma\left(dW^{\mathbb{Q}} + \frac{v}{\sigma}dt\right) \tag{H.5.3}$$

so

$$d\bar{X}_t = vdt + \sigma dW^{\mathbb{Q}}. \tag{H.5.4}$$

It can be seen from Section 2.4 that the transformation between measures $\mathbb{P}$ and $\mathbb{Q}$ can be accomplished using $k = v/\sigma$, and that the associated Radon–Nikodym derivative is

$$\frac{d\mathbb{Q}}{d\mathbb{P}} = \exp\left(kW_t^{\mathbb{P}} - \frac{1}{2}k^2 t\right)$$

$$= \exp\left(\frac{v}{\sigma}W_t^{\mathbb{P}} - \frac{1}{2}\frac{v^2 t}{\sigma}\right)$$

$$= \exp\left(\frac{v}{\sigma^2}X_t - \frac{1}{2}\frac{v^2 t}{\sigma}\right), \tag{H.5.5}$$

where we have use that fact that under measure probability measure $\mathbb{P}$, we can write $W_t^{\mathbb{P}} = X_t/\sigma$.

Now

$$P\left(m_t^{\bar{X}} \leq b, \bar{X}_t \geq x\right) = E^{\mathbb{Q}}\left[\mathbb{I}_{\{m_t^{\bar{X}} \leq b\}}\mathbb{I}_{\{\bar{X}_t \geq x\}}\right], \tag{H.5.6}$$

where $\mathbb{I}_{\{condition\}}$ is an indicator function which takes unit value when condition is satisfied and zero otherwise – for example, $\mathbb{I}_{\{m_t^{\bar{X}} \leq b\}}$ is one when $m_t^{\bar{X}} \leq b$ and zero when $m_t^{\bar{X}} > b$.

However, see for example Baxter and Rennie (1996), we have

$$E^{\mathbb{Q}}\left[\mathbb{I}_{\{m_t^{\bar{X}} \leq b\}}\mathbb{I}_{\{\bar{X}_t \geq x\}}\right] = E^{\mathbb{P}}\left[\mathbb{I}_{\{m_t^{X} \leq b\}}\mathbb{I}_{\{X_t \geq x\}}\frac{d\mathbb{Q}}{d\mathbb{P}}\right]. \tag{H.5.7}$$

So substituting for $\dfrac{d\mathbb{Q}}{d\mathbb{P}}$ from equation (H.5.5) gives

$$E^{\mathbb{Q}}\left[\mathbb{I}_{\{m_t^{\bar{X}} \leq b\}}\mathbb{I}_{\{\bar{X}_t \geq x\}}\right] = E^{\mathbb{P}}\left[\mathbb{I}_{\{m_t^{X} \leq b\}}\mathbb{I}_{\{X_t \geq x\}}\exp\left(\frac{vX_t}{\sigma^2} - \frac{v^2 t}{2\sigma^2}\right)\right]. \tag{H.5.8}$$

Expressed in terms of the *reflected Brownian motion*, $X_t^R = 2b - X_t$, equation (H.5.8) can be written

$$P\left(m_t^{\bar{X}} \leq b, \bar{X}_t \geq x\right) = E^{\mathbb{P}}\left[\mathbb{I}_{\{2b-X_t^R \geq x\}}\exp\left(\frac{v(2b - X_t^R)}{\sigma^2} - \frac{v^2 t}{2\sigma^2}\right)\right]$$

$$= \exp\left(\frac{2vb}{\sigma^2}\right)E^{\mathbb{P}}\left[\mathbb{I}_{\{2b-X_t \geq x\}}\exp\left(-\frac{vX_t^R}{\sigma^2} - \frac{v^2 t}{2\sigma^2}\right)\right]. \tag{H.5.9}$$

Since

$$\mathbb{I}_{\{2b-X_t^R > x\}} = \mathbb{I}_{\{-2b+X_t^R < -x\}} = \mathbb{I}_{\{X_t^R < 2b-x\}},$$

equation (H.5.9) becomes

$$P\left(m_t^{\bar{X}} \leq b, \bar{X}_t \geq x\right) = \exp\left(\frac{2vb}{\sigma^2}\right)E^{\mathbb{P}}\left[\mathbb{I}_{\{X_t < 2b-x\}}\exp\left(-\frac{vX_t}{\sigma^2} - \frac{v^2 t}{2\sigma^2}\right)\right], \tag{H.5.10}$$

where, for ease of notation, we now denote X_t^R by X_t on the right-hand side of equation (H.5.10).

Therefore,

$$P\left(m_t^{\bar{X}} \le b, \bar{X}_t \ge x\right)$$

$$= \exp\left(\frac{2vb}{\sigma^2}\right) \int_{X_t=-\infty}^{X_t=2b-x} \frac{1}{\sigma\sqrt{2\pi t}} \exp\left(-\frac{X_t^2}{2\sigma^2 t}\right) \exp\left(\frac{vX_t}{\sigma^2} - \frac{v^2 t}{\sigma^2}\right) dX_t$$

$$= \frac{1}{\sigma\sqrt{2\pi t}} \exp\left(\frac{2vb}{\sigma^2}\right) \int_{X_t=-\infty}^{X_t=2b-x} \exp\left(-\frac{(X_t^2 + 2vX_t t + v^2 t^2)}{2\sigma^2 t}\right) dX_t$$

$$= \frac{1}{\sigma\sqrt{2\pi t}} \exp\left(\frac{2vb}{\sigma^2}\right) \int_{X_t=-\infty}^{X_t=2b-x} \exp\left(-\frac{(X_t + vt)^2}{2\sigma^2 t}\right) dX_t.$$

If $V = (X_t + vt)/(\sigma\sqrt{t})$, then $dX_t = \sigma\sqrt{t}\, dV$, $X_t = 2b - x$ corresponds to $V = (2b - x + vt)/(\sigma\sqrt{t})$, and $X_t = -\infty$ corresponds to $V = -\infty$,

$$\frac{1}{\sigma\sqrt{2\pi t}} \int_{X_t=-\infty}^{X_t=2b-x} \exp\left(-\frac{(X_t + vt)^2}{2\sigma^2 t}\right) dX_t = \frac{1}{\sigma\sqrt{2\pi t}} \int_{V=-\infty}^{V=\frac{2b-x+vt}{\sigma\sqrt{t}}} \exp\left(-\frac{V^2}{2}\right) dV$$

$$= N_1\left(\frac{2b - x + vt}{\sigma\sqrt{t}}\right).$$

We thus obtain

$$P\left(m_t^{\bar{X}} \le b, \bar{X}_t \ge x\right) = \exp\left(\frac{2vb}{\sigma^2}\right) N_1\left(\frac{2b - x + vt}{\sigma\sqrt{t}}\right).$$

H.6 PROOF OF EQUATION (H.1.7)

Since $P\left(\bar{X}_t \ge x\right) = P\left(m_t^{\bar{X}} \ge b, \bar{X}_t \ge x\right) + P\left(m_t^{\bar{X}} \ge b, \bar{X}_t \le x\right)$, we have

$$P\left(m_t^{\bar{X}} \ge b, \bar{X}_t \ge x\right) = P(\bar{X}_t \ge x) - P\left(m_t^{\bar{X}} \ge b, \bar{X}_t \le x\right). \tag{H.6.1}$$

Substituting the results of equation (H.1.4) and equation (H.1.6) into equation (H.6.1) yields

$$P\left(m_t^{\bar{X}} \ge b, \bar{X}_t \ge x\right) = N_1\left(\frac{vt - x}{\sigma\sqrt{t}}\right) - \exp\left(\frac{2vb}{\sigma^2}\right) N_1\left(\frac{2b - x + vt}{\sigma\sqrt{t}}\right).$$

H.7 PROOF OF EQUATION (H.1.8)

We start by writing

$$P\left(m_t^{\bar{X}} \le b\right) = P\left(m_t^{\bar{X}} \le b, \bar{X}_t \le b\right) + P\left(m_t^{\bar{X}} \le b, \bar{X}_t \ge b\right).$$

However, $P\left(m_t^{\bar{X}} \le b, \bar{X}_t \le b\right) = P(\bar{X}_t \le b)$ since the probability that the minimum is less than b and the final value, $\bar{X}_t$ is less than b is the same as the probability that the final value, $\bar{X}_t$, is less than b. Therefore,

$$P\left(m_t^{\bar{X}} \le b\right) = P(\bar{X}_t \le b) + P\left(m_t^{\bar{X}} \le b, \bar{X}_t \ge b\right).$$

Substituting for $P\left(\bar{X}_t \leq b\right)$ from equation (H.1.4) gives

$$P\left(m_t^{\bar{X}} \leq b\right) = N_1\left(\frac{b - vt}{\sigma \sqrt{t}}\right) + P\left(m_t^{\bar{X}} \leq b, \bar{X}_t \geq b\right). \qquad (\text{H.7.1})$$

From equation (H.1.6),

$$P\left(m_t^{\bar{X}} \leq b, \bar{X}_t \geq b\right) = \exp\left(\frac{2vb}{\sigma^2}\right) N_1\left(\frac{2b - b + vt}{\sigma \sqrt{t}}\right)$$

$$= \exp\left(\frac{2vb}{\sigma^2}\right) N_1\left(\frac{b + vt}{\sigma \sqrt{t}}\right). \qquad (\text{H.7.2})$$

Combining equation (H.7.2) and equation (H.7.1) yields

$$P\left(m_t^{\bar{X}} \leq b\right) = N_1\left(\frac{b - vt}{\sigma \sqrt{t}}\right) + \exp\left(\frac{2vb}{\sigma^2}\right) N_1\left(\frac{b + vt}{\sigma \sqrt{t}}\right).$$

H.8 PROOF OF EQUATION (H.1.9)

We start with

$$P\left(m_t^{\bar{X}} \geq b\right) = 1 - P\left(m_t^{\bar{X}} \leq b\right).$$

Substituting from (H.1.8),

$$P\left(m_t^{\bar{X}} \geq b\right) = 1 - N_1\left(\frac{b - vt}{\sigma \sqrt{t}}\right) + \exp\left(\frac{2vb}{\sigma^2}\right) N_1\left(\frac{b + vt}{\sigma \sqrt{t}}\right). \qquad (\text{H.8.1})$$

But since $1 - N_1(x) = N_1(-x)$, equation (H.8.1) can be expressed as

$$P\left(m_t^{\bar{X}} \geq b\right) = N_1\left(\frac{vt - b}{\sigma \sqrt{t}}\right) + \exp\left(\frac{2vb}{\sigma^2}\right) N_1\left(\frac{b + vt}{\sigma \sqrt{t}}\right).$$

H.9 PROOF OF EQUATION (H.1.10)

We will use equation (H.1.6) to compute $\partial P / \partial x$, where $P\left(m_t^{\bar{X}} \leq b, \bar{X}_t \geq x\right)$ is denoted by P.

Letting $\Theta = (2b - x + vt)/(\sigma \sqrt{t})$, we obtain

$$\frac{\partial P}{\partial x} = \exp\left(\frac{2vb}{\sigma^2}\right) \frac{\partial}{\partial x}\{N_1(\Theta)\}$$

$$= \exp\left(\frac{2vb}{\sigma^2}\right) \frac{\partial}{\partial \Theta}\{N_1(\Theta)\} \frac{\partial \Theta}{\partial x}$$

$$= -\exp\left(\frac{2vb}{\sigma^2}\right) \frac{1}{\sigma \sqrt{t}} n(\Theta)$$

$$= -\frac{1}{\sigma \sqrt{2\pi t}} \exp\left(\frac{2vb}{\sigma^2}\right) \exp\left(-\frac{(2b - x + vt)^2}{2\sigma^2 t}\right). \qquad (\text{H.9.1})$$

Now since the probability $P\left(m_t^{\bar{X}} \le b, \bar{X}_t \ge x\right)$ decreases as x increases, we have

$$P\left(m_t^{\bar{X}} \le b, \bar{X}_t \ge x\right) - P\left(m_t^{\bar{X}} \le b, \bar{X}_t \ge x + \Delta x\right) = -\frac{\partial P}{\partial x}\Delta x \qquad \text{(H.9.2)}$$

and also

$$P\left(m_t^{\bar{X}} \le b, \bar{X}_t \ge x\right) - P\left(m_t^{\bar{X}} \le b, \bar{X}_t \ge x + \Delta x\right) \sim p\left(m_t^{\bar{X}} \le b, \bar{X}_t = x\right)\Delta x, \quad \text{(H.9.3)}$$

where $p\left(m_t^{\bar{X}} \le b, \bar{X}_t = x\right)$ is the probability density function of $P\left(m_t^{\bar{X}} \le b, \bar{X}_t \ge x\right)$ and $\Delta x \to 0$.

Combining equations (H.9.2) and (H.9.3), we thus obtain

$$p\left(m_t^{\bar{X}} \le b, \bar{X}_t = x\right) = -\frac{\partial P}{\partial x}\Delta x.$$

So

$$p\left(m_t^{\bar{X}} \le b, \bar{X}_t = x\right) = \frac{1}{\sigma \sqrt{2\pi t}} \exp\left(\frac{2vb}{\sigma^2}\right) \exp\left(-\frac{(2b - x + vt)^2}{2\sigma^2 t}\right),$$

which means that

$$p\left(\left\{m_t^{\bar{X}} \le b, \bar{X}_t\right\} | \bar{X}_0\right) = \frac{1}{\sigma \sqrt{2\pi t}} \exp\left(\frac{2vb}{\sigma^2}\right) \exp\left(-\frac{(2b - \bar{X}_t + vt)^2}{2\sigma^2 t}\right), \qquad \text{(H.9.4)}$$

where as usual we take $\bar{X}_0 = 0$. So equation (H.9.4) gives the probability density for the Brownian motion which goes through the points $\bar{X}_0$ and $\bar{X}_t$ and has a minimum value which is less or equal to b

If instead of considering the complete path of $\bar{X}_t$ from $\bar{X}_0$, we can move the origin to the point $\bar{X}_{t_1}$, where $t_1 \le t$. Substituting into equation (H.9.4), we then obtain

$$p\left(\left\{m_{t_1,t}^{\bar{X}} \le b, \bar{X}_t\right\} | \bar{X}_{t_1}\right)$$

$$= \frac{1}{\sigma \sqrt{2\pi(t - t_1)}} \exp\left(\frac{2v(b - \bar{X}_{t_1})}{\sigma^2}\right) \exp\left(-\frac{(2(b - \bar{X}_{t_1}) - (\bar{X}_t - \bar{X}_{t_1}) + v(t - t_1))^2}{2\sigma^2(t - t_1)}\right)$$

$$= \frac{1}{\sigma \sqrt{2\pi(t - t_1)}} \exp\left(\frac{2v(b - \bar{X}_{t_1})}{\sigma^2}\right) \exp\left(-\frac{(2b - \bar{X}_{t_1} - \bar{X}_t + v(t - t_1))^2}{2\sigma^2(t - t_1)}\right),$$

which can be re-expressed as

$$p\left(\left\{m_{t_1,t_2}^{\bar{X}} \le b, \bar{X}_{t_2}\right\} | \bar{X}_{t_1}\right)$$

$$= \frac{1}{\sigma \sqrt{2\pi\Delta t}} \exp\left(\frac{2v(b - \bar{X}_{t_1})}{\sigma^2}\right) \exp\left(-\frac{(\bar{X}_{t_1} + \bar{X}_{t_2} - 2b - v\Delta t)^2}{2\sigma^2\Delta t}\right),$$

where $t_2 \ge t_1$ and $\Delta t = t_2 - t_1$.

Appendix I

Feynman–Kac Formula

I.1 SOME RESULTS

The Feynman–Kac formula provides a link between stochastic processes and partial differential equations, which we will now illustrate.

In the risk-neutral measure, the equation followed by the asset price is

$$dS = rSdt + \sigma SdW \tag{I.1.1}$$

and that of the money account

$$dB = Brdt. \tag{I.1.2}$$

If $f(S,t)$ is the value of a derivative, then using Ito's lemma we have

$$df = \left\{ \frac{\partial f}{\partial t} + rS\frac{\partial f}{\partial S} + \frac{\sigma^2 S^2}{2}\frac{\partial^2 f}{\partial S^2} \right\} dt + \frac{\partial f}{\partial S}\sigma dW. \tag{I.1.3}$$

Since f is a tradable, we know that the process (f/B) must be a martingale in the risk-neutral measure and therefore have zero drift.

We will now evaluate $d(f/B)$ using the Ito quotient rule (see equation (2.6.4))

$$d\left(\frac{X_1}{X_2}\right) = \left(\frac{X_1}{X_2}\right)\left\{\frac{dX_1}{X_1} - \frac{dX_2}{X_2}\right\} + E\left[\left(\frac{dX_2}{X_2}\right)\left(\frac{dX_2}{X_2}\right)\right] - E\left[\left(\frac{dX_2}{X_2}\right)\left(\frac{dX_1}{X_1}\right)\right] \tag{I.1.4}$$

and rewrite equation (I.1.2) and equation (I.1.3) as

$$dX_1 = \bar{\mu}_1 dt + \bar{\sigma}_1 dW,$$
$$dX_2 = X_2\bar{\mu}_2 dt,$$

where

$$d\left(\frac{X_1}{X_2}\right) = d\left(\frac{f}{B}\right), \quad \bar{\mu}_1 = \left\{\frac{\partial f}{\partial t} + rS\frac{\partial f}{\partial S} + \frac{\sigma^2 S^2}{2}\frac{\partial^2 f}{\partial S^2}\right\},$$

$$\bar{\sigma}_1 = \sigma\frac{\partial f}{\partial S}, \quad \bar{\sigma}_2 = r, \quad X_1 = f, \quad X_2 = B, \quad \bar{\mu}_2 = r.$$

Evaluating equation (I.1.4), we obtain

$$E\left[\left(\frac{dX_2}{X_2}\right)\left(\frac{dX_2}{X_2}\right)\right] = E\left[\bar{\mu}_2^2 dt^2\right] \to 0,$$

$$E\left[\left(\frac{dX_1}{X_1}\right)\left(\frac{dX_2}{X_2}\right)\right] = E\left[\left(\frac{\bar{\mu}_1 dt + \sigma_1 dW}{X_1}\right)\left(\frac{X_2\bar{\mu}_2 dt}{X_2}\right)\right] \to 0,$$

and therefore,

$$d\left(\frac{X_1}{X_2}\right) = \left(\frac{X_1}{X_2}\right)\left\{\frac{\bar{\mu}_1 dt + \bar{\sigma}_1 dW}{X_1} - \frac{X_2\bar{\mu}_2 dt}{X_2}\right\}$$

$$= \left\{\frac{\bar{\mu}_1}{X_2} - \left(\frac{X_1}{X_2}\right)\bar{\mu}_2\right\} dt + \left(\frac{\bar{\sigma}_1}{X_2}\right) dW$$

$$= \frac{1}{X_2}\left\{\bar{\mu}_1 - X_1\bar{\mu}_2\right\} dt + \left(\frac{\bar{\sigma}_1}{X_2}\right) dW. \tag{I.1.5}$$

Since (X_1/X_2) is a martingale, the drift term in equation (I.1.5) is zero so

$$\bar{\mu}_1 - X_1\bar{\mu}_2 = 0. \tag{I.1.6}$$

Therefore, substituting for $\bar{\mu}_1, X_1$ and $\bar{\mu}_2$ in equation (I.1.6), we obtain

$$\frac{\partial f}{\partial t} + rS\frac{\partial f}{\partial S} + \frac{\sigma^2 S^2}{2}\frac{\partial^2 f}{\partial S^2} - rf = 0 \tag{I.1.7}$$

or

$$\frac{\partial f}{\partial t} + rS\frac{\partial f}{\partial S} + \frac{\sigma^2 S^2}{2}\frac{\partial^2 f}{\partial S^2} = rf, \tag{I.1.8}$$

which is the Black–Scholes partial differential equation, which we derived in Chapter 4.

In general, if an asset follows the process

$$dS = \bar{\mu}dt + \bar{\sigma}dW, \tag{I.1.9}$$

then the price of a derivative $f(S,t)$ obeys the partial differential equation

$$\frac{\partial f}{\partial t} + \bar{\mu}\frac{\partial f}{\partial S} + \frac{\bar{\mu}^2}{2}\frac{\partial^2 f}{\partial S^2} = rf \tag{I.1.10}$$

or

$$\left(\frac{\partial}{\partial t} + \bar{\mu}\frac{\partial}{\partial S} + \frac{\bar{\mu}^2}{2}\frac{\partial^2}{\partial S^2}\right) f = rf. \tag{I.1.11}$$

Glossary

The notation used is as follows:

GBM Geometric Brownian motion.

BM Brownian motion.

W_t Brownian motion at time t - the term may be non-zero.

ρ The correlation coefficient.

$E[x]$ The expectation value of X.

$Var[X]$ The variance of X.

$Cov[X,Y]$ The covariance between X and Y.

$Cov[X]$ The covariance between the variates contained in the vector X.

σ The volatility. Since assets are assumed to follow GBM it is computed as the *annualised* standard deviation of the n continuously compounded returns.

$N_1(a)$ The univariate cumulative normal distribution function. It gives the cumulative probability, in a standardized univariate normal distribution, that the variable x_1 satisfied $x_1 \leq a$.

$N_2(a,b,\rho)$ The bivariate cumulative normal distribution. It gives the cumulative probability, in a standardized bivariate normal distribution, that the variables x_1 and x_2 satisfy $x_1 \leq a$ and $x_2 \leq b$ when with correlation coefficient between x_1 and x_2 is ρ.

r The risk free interest rate.

q The continuously compounded dividend yield.

S_{it} The ith asset price at time t.

I_{nn} The n by n unit matrix.

$\Lambda(\mu,\sigma^2)$ A lognormal distribution with paramters μ and σ^2. If $y = \log(x)$ and $y \sim N\left(\mu,\sigma^2\right)$ then the distribution for $x = e^y$ is $x \sim \Lambda(\mu,\sigma^2)$. We have $E[x] = \exp\left(\mu + \frac{\sigma^2}{2}\right)$ and $Var[x] = \exp\left(2\mu + \sigma^2\right)\left(\exp\left(\sigma^2\right) - 1\right)$.

$DF(t,T)$ The discount factor between times t and T, where $T \geq t$. The price of a non-defaultable zero coupon bond which matures at time T is the expected value of $DF(t,T)$. In this book we assume that interest rates are deterministic and thus $DF(t,T)$ is the value of a non-defaultable zero coupon bond maturing at T.

$\overline{DF}(t,T)$ The discount factor (including the possibility of default) between times t and T, where $T \geq t$: $\overline{DF}(t,T) = S(t,T)DF(t,T)$. The price of a defaultable zero coupon bond which matures at time T is the expected value of $\overline{DF}(t,T)$. In this book we assume that interest rates are deterministic and thus $\overline{DF}(t,T)$ is the value of a defaultable zero coupon bond maturing at T.

$F(t,T_1,T_2)$ The forward rate at time t between times T_1 and T_2 where $T_2 \geq T_1$ and $T_1 \geq t$.

$L(T_1,T_2)$ is the simply compounded spot rate between times T_1 and T_2, where $T_2 \geq T_1$.

$\log(x)$ The natural logarithm of x.

$N(a,b)$ Normal distribution, with mean a and variance b.

dW_t A Brownian increment, this is simulated as normal variate (sampled at time t) from the distribution $N(0,dt)$, where dt a specified time interval e.g. $dx = \mu dt + dW_t$.

dZ_t A Normal variate (sampled at time t) from the distribution $N(0,1)$. Note: The variate $d\psi = \sqrt{dt}\, dZ_t$ has the same distribution as dW_t.

IID Independently and Identically Distributed.

$\mathcal{U}(a,b)$ The uniform distribution, with lower limit a and upper limit b.

$|x|$ The absolute value of the variable x.

PDF The probability density function of a given distribution.

$x \wedge y$ The minimum of x and y, that is $\min(x,y)$.

$S(t,T)$ The survival probability between time t and T, $T > t$.

$\|A - B\|$ The distance between two matrices with the same dimensions. If A and B are both have n rows and m columns then this distance is

$$\sqrt{\sum_{i=1}^{n}\sum_{j=1}^{m}\left\{A_{i,j} - B_{i,j}\right\}^2}$$

where $A_{i,j}$, and $B_{i,j}$ refer to the element in the ith row and jth column.

Bibliography

REFERENCES

Abramowitz M., Stegun I.A., 1968. Handbook of Mathematical Functions. Dover Publications.

Bachelier L., 1900. Theory de la speculation. Annales Scientifiques de l'École Normale Supérieure 17, 21–86.

Barone-Adesi G., Whaley R.E., 1987. Efficient analytic approximation of American option values. The Journal of Finance 42 (2), 301–320.

Barraquand J., Martineau D., 1995. Numerical valuation of high dimensional multivariate American securties. Journal of Finance and Quantitative Analysis 30, 383–405.

Baxter M., Rennie A., 1996. Financial Calculus, An Introduction to Derivative Pricing. Cambridge University Press.

Black F., 1973. Fact and fantasy in the use of options and corporate liabilities. Financial Analysts Journal 31, 36–41xlpagesep, 61–72. Journal of Political Economy 81, 637–657.

Bookbinder A., 1976. Security Options Strategy. Programmed Press f.

Boyle P.P., Tian Y., 1998. An explicit finite difference approach to the pricing of barrier options. Applied Mathematical Finance 5, 17–43.

Boyle P.P., Broadie M., Glasserman P., 1997. Monte Carlo methods for security pricing. Journal of Economic Dynamics and Control 21, 1267–1321.

Boyle P.P., Evnine J., Gibbs S., 1989. Numerical evaluation of multivariate contingent claims. The Review of Management Studies 2 (2), 241–250.

Box G.E.P., Muller M.E., 1958. A note on the generation of random normal deviates. Annals of Mathematical Statistics 29, 610–611.

Brigo D., Mercurio F., 2001. Interest Rate Models: Theory and Practice. Springer.

Broadie M., Detemple J., 1996. American option valuation: new bounds, approximations, and a comparison of existings methods. The Review of Financial Studies 9 (4), 1211–1250.

Broadie M., Glasserman P., 1997. Pricing American-style securities simulation. Journal of Economic Dynamics and Control 21, 1323–1352.

Brotherton-Ratcliffe R., 1994. Monte Carlo motoring. Risk 7 (12), 53–58.

Cable V., 2009. The Storm: The World Economic Crisis and What it Means. Atlantic Books.

Caflisch R.E., Morokoff W., Owen A., 1997. Valuation of mortgage-backed securities using Brownian bridges to reduce effective dimension. The Journal of Computational Finance 1 (1), 27–46.

Cox D.R., Miller H.D., 1965. The Theory of Stochastic Processes. Methuen & Co Ltd.

Cox J.C., Ross S.A., Rubinstein M., 1979. Option pricing: a simplified approach. Journal of Financial Economics 7, 229–263.

Crank J., Nicolson P., 1947. A practical method for numerical evaluation of solutions of partial differential equations of the heat conduction type. Proceedings of the Cambridge Philosophical Society 43, 50–67.

de la Vega J., 2006. Confusion of Confusions: An Adaptation of Confusion de Confusiones. Sonsbeek Publishers.

Einstein A., 1905. On the movement of small particles suspended in a stationary liquid demanded by the molecular-kinetic theory of heat. Annalen der Physik 17.

Evans M., Hastings N., Peacock B., 2000. Statistical Distributions, third ed. John Wiley.

Filer H., 1959. Understanding Put and Call Options. Popular Library, New York.

Fleuriet M., 2008. Investment Banking Explained: An Insider's Guide to the Industry. McGraw Hill.

Freedman D., 1983. Brownian Motion and Diffusion. Springer-Verlag, New York.

Garman M.B., Kohlhagen S.W., 1983. Foreign currency option values. Journal of International Money and Finance 2, 231–237.

Geske R., 1979. A note on an analytic valuation formula for unprotected American options on stocks with known dividends. Journal of Econometrics 7, 375–380.

Geske R., Johnson H.E., 1984. The American put options valued analytically. Journal of Finance 39, 1511–1524.

Golub G.H., 1989. Matrix Computation. The John Hopkins University Press.

Grimmett G., Welsh D., 1986. Probability An Introduction. Oxford Science Publications.

Hager W., 1988. Applied Numerical Linear Algebra. Prentice Hall.

Harrison J.M., Kreps D., 1979. Martingales and arbitrage in multiperiod securities markets. Journal of Economic Theory 20, 381–408.

Harrison J.M., Pliska D., 1981. Martingales and stochastic integrals in the theory of continuous trading. Stochastic Processes and their Applications 11, 215–260.

Higham N.J., 2002. Computing the nearest correlation matrix - A problem from finance. IMA Journal of Numerical Analysis 22 (3), 329–343.

Hinkling J., 1875. Men and Idioms of Wall Street: Explaining the Daily Operations in Stocks, Bonds and Gold. John Hinkling & Co, New York.

Homer S., Sylla R A, 1996. History of Interest Rates. Rutgers University Press.

Hull J.C., 1997. Options Futures and Other Derivatives, third ed. Prentice Hall.

Hull J.C., 2003. Options Futures and Other Derivatives, fifth ed. Prentice Hall.

Johnson H., 1987. Options on the maximum or the minimum of several assets. Journal of Financial and Quantitative Analysis 22 (3), 277–283.

Kamrad B., Ritchken P., 1991. Multinomial approximating models for options with k state variables. Management Science 37 (12), 1640–1652.

Karatzas I., Shreve S., 2000. Brownian Motion and Stochastic Calculus, second ed. Springer-Verlag, New York.

Levy P., 1939. Sur certain processus stochastiques homogenes. Compositio Mathematica 7, 283–339.

Levy P., 1948. Processus Stochastiques et Mouvement Brownian. Gauthier-Villar, Paris.

Mackay C., 1841. Memoirs of Extraordinary Popular Delusions and the Madness of Crowds.

Macmillan L.W., 1986. Analytic approximation for the American put option. Advances in Futures and Options Research 1, 119–139.

Marchuk G.I., Shaidurov V.V., 1983. Difference Methods and their Extrapolations. Springer-Verlag.

Margrabe W., 1978. The value of an option to exchange one asset for another. Journal of Finance 33 (1), 177–186.

Musiela M., Rutkowski M., 1998. Martingale Methods in Financial Modelling. Springer-Verlag.

Øksendal B., 2003. Stochastic Differential Equations: An Introduction with Applications. Springer.

Perrin J.B., 1910. Brownian Movement and Molecular Reality (F. Soddy, Trans.). Taylor and Francis, London (Annales de Chimie et de Physique, 8me series, September 1909).

Press W.H., Teukolsky S.A., Vetterling W.T., Flannery B.P., 1992. Numerical Recipes in C: The Art of Scientific Computing, second ed. Cambridge University Press.

Qi. H.D., Sun D., 2006. A quadratically convergent newton method for computing the nearest correlation matrix. SIAM Journal of Matrix Analysis and Applications 28 (2), 360–385.

Ramsbottom J., 1932. Centenary of Robert Brown's Discovery of the Nucleus - Exhibit at natural history museum. The Journal of Botany British and Foreign (January), 13–16.

Rebonato R., Jäckel P., 1999. The most general methodology for creating a valid correlation matrix for risk management and option pricing purposes. Journal of Risk 2 (2).

Reiner E., 1992. Quanto mechanics. Risk 5 (3), 59–63.

Roll R., 1977. An analytic valuation formula for unprotected American call options on stocks with known dividends. Journal of Econometrics 5, 251–258.

Shreve S., Chalasani P., Jha S., 1997. Stochastic Calculus and Finance.

Sjostrom Jr., W.K., 2009. Washington and Lee Law Review 66, 943–991.

Smith A., 1776. An Inquiry into the Nature and Causes of the Wealth of Nations.

Smith G.D., 1985. Numerical Solution of Partial Differential Equations: Finite Difference Methods. Oxford University Press.

Stulz R.M., 1982. Options on the minimum or maximum of two risky assets. Journal of Financial Economics 10, 161–185.

The Financial Crisis Inquiry Commission, 2011. Financial Crisis Inquiry Report. U.S. Government Printing Office.

Thompson E., 2007. The tulipmania: Fact or artifact?. Public Choice 130 (1V2), 99–114.

Tilley J.A., 1993. Valuing American options in a path simulation model. Transactions of the Society of Actuaries 45, 83–104.

Wegg J., 1916. Antwerp 1477-1559 From the Battle of Nancy to the Treatu of Gateau Gambresis. Methuen, London.

Whaley R.E., 1981. On the valuation of American call options on stocks with known dividends. Journal of Financial Economics 9, 207–211.

Wiener N., 1923. Differential spaces. Journal of Mathematical Physics 2, 131–174.

Wiener N., 1924. Un problem de probabilies denombrables. Bulletin de la Société Mathématique de France 52, 569–578.

FURTHER READING

Aitchison J., Brown J.A.C., 1966. The Lognormal Distribution. Cambridge University Press.

Andersen L.B.G., Brotherton-Ratcliffe R., 1998. The equity option volatility smile: an implicit finite-difference approach. Journal of Computational Finance 1 (2), 5–37.

Anderson T.W., 1984. An Introduction to Multivariate Statistical Analysis, second ed. Wiley, New York.

Berndt E.K., Hall B.H., Hall R.E., Hausman J.A., 1974. Estimation and inference in nonlinear structural models. Annal of Economic and Social Measurement 3/4, 653–665.

Beyer W.H., 1982. CRC Standard Mathematical Tables. CRC Press, Florida.

Black F., Scholes M., 1973. The pricing of corporate liabilities. Journal of Political Economy 81, 637–657.

Bratley P., 1986. Algorithm 647: Implementation and relative efficiency of quasirandom sequence generators. ACM Transactions on Mathematical Software 12 (4), 362–376.

Bratley P., Fox B.L., 1988. Algorithm 659: Implementing Sobol's quasirandom sequence generator. ACM Transactions on Mathematical Software 14 (1), 88–100.

Bratley P., Fox B.L., Niederreiter H., 1992. Implementation and tests of low-discrepancy sequences. ACM Transactions on Modeling and Computer Simulation 2 (3), 195–213.

Brennan M.J., Schwartz E.S., 1978. Finite difference methods and jump processes arising in the pricing of contingent claims: a synthesis. Journal of Financial and Quantitative Analysis 13, 462–474.

Chan T.F., Golub G.H., Leveque R.J., 1982. Updating Formulae and a Pairwise Algorithm for Computing Sample Variances Compstat 1982. Physica-Verlag.

Cotton I.W., 1975. Remark on stably updating mean and standard deviation of data. Communications of the ACM 18 (8), 458.

Cox D.R., Hinkley D.V., 1979. Theoretical Statistics. Chapman and Hall.

Craig I.J.D., Sneyd A.D., 1988. An alternating direction implicit scheme for parabolic equations with mixed derivatives. Computers & Mathematics with Applications 16 (4), 341–350.

Davidoff Solomon S.M., Morrison A.D., Wilhelm Jr., W.J., 2012. The SEC v. Goldman Sachs: Reputation, Trust, and Fiduciary Duties in Investment Banking. 37 J. Corp. L. 529.

Dickey J.M., 1967. Multivariate generalizations of the multivariate t distribution and the inverted multivariate t distribution. Annals of Mathematical Statistics 38 (2), 551–518.

Duffie D., 1996. Dynamic Asset Pricing Theory, second ed. Princeton University Press.

Engle R.F., 1995. ARCH Selected Readings. In: Advanced Texts in Econometrics. Oxford University Press.

Faure H., 1982. Discrepance de suites associees a un systeme de numeration (en dimension s). Acta Arithmetica 41, 337–351.

Feller W., 1971. An Introduction to Probability Theory and Its Applications. Vol. II John Wiley and Sons.

Glasserman P., 2004. Monte Carlo Methods in Financial Engineering. Springer-Verlag, New York.

Glasserman P., Heidelberger P., 2000. Variance reduction techniques for value-at-risk with heavy-tailed risk factors. In: Joines J.A., Barton R.R., Kang K., Fishwick P.A., (Eds.), Proceedings of the 2000 Winter Simulation Conference.

Goldberger A.S., 1997. A course in Econometrics. Havard University Press.

Good I.J., 1979. Computer generation of the exponential power distribution. Journal of Statistical Computation and Simulation 9 (3), 239–240.

Hamilton J., 1994. Time Series Analysis. Princeton University Press.

Hanson R.J., 1975. Stably updating mean and standard deviation of data. Communications of the ACM 18 (1), 57–58.

Haug E.G., 1998. Option Pricing Formulas. Mc Graw Hill.

Hunt P.J., Kennedy J.E., 2004. Financial Derivatives in Theory and Practice. Wiley.

Jäckel P., 2002. Monte Carlo Methods in Finance. Wiley.

Johnson N.L., Kotz S., 1992. Distributions in Statistics: Continuous Multivariate Distributions. Wiley.

Johnson N.L., Kotz S., Kemp A., 1992. Univariate Discrete Distributions. Wiley.

Johnson N.L., Kotz S., Balakvishnam N., 1994. Continuous Univariate Distributions, second ed. Wiley.

Johnson R.A., Wichern D.W., 1999. Applied Multivariate Statistical Analysis. Prentice Hall.

Jorion P., 1997. Value at Risk. Mc Graw Hill.

Joshi M.S., 2004. The Concepts and Practice of Mathematical Finance. Cambridge University Press.

Kloeden P.E., Platen E., 1999. Numerical Solution of Stochastic Differential Equations. Springer.

Krzanowski W.J., 2000. Principles of Multivariate Analysis: A User's Perspective. Oxford University Press.

Levy G., 2004. Computational Finance: Numerical Methods for Pricing Financial Instruments. Elsevier.

Mardia K.V., Kent J.T., Bibby J., 1988. Multivariate analysis. In: Probability and Mathematical Statistics. Academic Press, London.

Markowitz H.M., 1989. Mean Variance Analysis in Portfolio Choice and Capital Markets. Basil Blackwell.

Martellini L., Priaulet P., 2001. Fixed-Income Securities, Dynamic Methods for Interest Rate Risk Pricing and Hedging. John Wiley.

McIntyre R., 1999. Black-Scholes will do. Energy & Power Risk Management (November), 26–27.

McKee S., Mitchell A.R., 1970. Alternating direction methods for parabolic equations in two space dimensions with a mixed derivative. The Computer Journal 13 (1), 81–86.

Merton R.C., 1973. The theory of rational option pricing. The Bell Journal of Economy and Management Science 4 (1), 141–181.

Mitchell A.R., Griffiths D.F., 1980. The Finite Difference Method in Partial Differential Equations. Wiley, New York.

Morokoff W., 1999. The Brownian bridge E-M algorithm for covariance estimation with missing data. Journal of Computational Finance 2 (2), 75–100.

Morgan J.P., 1996. Risk Metrics - Technical Document, fourth ed. J P Morgan, New York.

Niederreiter H., 1992. Random Number Generation and Quasi-Monte Carlo Methods. SIAM.

Pelsser A., 2000. Efficient Methods for Valuing Interest Rate Derivatives. Springer.

Poitras G., 2008. The early history of option contracts. Simon Fraser University, Vancouver, B.C.

Rebonato R., 1998. Interest-rate Option Models, second ed. John Wiley.

Richardson L., 1910. The approximate arithmetical solution by finite differences od physical problems involving differential equations, with an application to the stresses in a masonry dam. Philos. Trans. R. Soc. Lond. A 210, 307.

Richardson L.F., 1927. Philos. Trans. R. Soc. Lond. A 2226, 299.

Rogers L.C.G., Talay D., 1997. Numerical Methods in Finance. Cambridge University Press.

Schonbucher P.J., 2003. Credit Derivatives Pricing Models. Wiley.

Sobol I.M., 1967. The distribution of points in a cube and the approximate evaluation of integrals. USSR Computational Mathematics and Mathematical Physics 7 (4), 86–112.

Strang G., 1976. Linear Alegebra and Its Applications. Academic Press.

Stuart A., Ord J.K., 1987. Kendall's Advanced Theory of Statistics, fifth ed. Griffin.

The Options Institute Options, 1999. Essential Concepts & Trading Strategies. McGraw Hill.

West D.H.D., 1979. Updating mean and variance estimates: an improved method. Communications of the ACM 22 (9), 532–535.

Wilmott P., Howison S., Dewynne J., 1997. The Mathematics of Financial Derivatives. Cambridge University Press.

Index

A

Printed in the United States
By Bookmasters